D0861892

This book belongs to:

_____

_____

It was received as a gift from:

_____

_____

_____

_____

on

Day: _____

Date: _____

Month: _____

Year: _____

Editor - Ron Young
Material Co-ordinator - Sandra Young
Cover design and thumbnail sketches - Mel D'Souza
Researcher of Household Hints - Grant Young

Health and Medical Advisor - { Dr. Allan S. Ettenson, B. Sc.,
D.C., D.I. Hom

Copyright 1996 by Downhome Publishing Inc.
303 Water Street
St. John's, Newfoundland, Canada
A1C 1B9
Tel: 709-726-5113
Fax: 709-726-2135
Email: downhome@nfld.com
Home Page: www.netfx-inc.com/downhomer

ISBN: 1-895109-02-7 (Soft Cover)

ISBN: 1-895109-01-9 (Hard Cover)

Printed in Canada
First Printing - November, 1996
Second Printing - February 1997

QUICK REFERENCE INDEX
Match with grey tabs on page edges

More Detailed Index
Pages 469 t0 477

This book is dedicated to all the readers of Downhomer Magazine.

Thank you to all the people who contributed to this book, including all of those who sent household hints, home remedies and cures, folklore, stories, jokes and recipes. Thank you to Rev. John Currey, Ed Smith, Lucy Fitzpatrick-McFarlane, Dave Hagerty, Loreen Haldenby-Adams, and Rex Stirling for their contributions. Thank you to Mel D'Souza for his thumbnail sketches. Thank you to Barry and Marie Stagg, Charlene Jenkins, Mel D'Souza and Lucy McFarlane for proofreading the almost-final pages. Thank you to Doyle Roberts for the expert advise on printing books. Thank you to my wife Sandra, for the many hours spent sorting and collating the massive amount of material that went into this book, and for the second-final and final proofing of the material.

Ron Young

Life And Spice

by Mel D'Souza

Ever since I was a teenager, I have pursued many hobbies and other interests in the belief that variety is the spice of life. Among these interests, travelling across North America by road with my wife Lineth and daughters Helen and Gillian, had been a summertime preoccupation until I 'discovered' Newfoundland in 1989.

Two years ago, I took an interest in cooking and thereby added spice to the variety of my life. It was at a time when my involvement with the Downhomer Magazine was as an honorary Newfoundlander.

It was almost two years ago that Ron Young intimated to me that he was coming up with an almanac and cook book as yet another of the Downhomer Magazine's treats to its readers. My first reaction was that this would be just another of the hundreds of mundane cook books until Ron cornered me in a restaurant and outlined its format. Not only did I like the concept of the 'heirloom cookbook', but it aroused my eagerness to get involved. Ron first gave me the titles of the various sections of the book and then asked me for my comments as each section was written up. I was fascinated by the features that Ron kept on adding, many of them in moments of sheer inspiration on his part. We spent many hours over the phone discussing refinements to the book, and every conversation would end with the ubiquitous joke or wisecrack which is the hallmark of every salt-of-the-earth (I mean - water) Newfoundlander.

When the book was all ready to go, I threw Ron a curve when I said that the book lacked illustrations and suggested that I would do a few renderings to illustrate what I meant. Illustrating the words of wisdom and items of trivia that garnish the section on recipes was a labour of love. It was tough at times, because it's hard to chuckle and draw at the same time. But, eventually, the job got done.

I've had my fill; now it's time for you to savour a diet of good wholesome living. And, if you are not into food, at least you will have a bellyful of laughs.

This book definitely adds life to the variety of spice!

Facts, Figures & Fundamentals

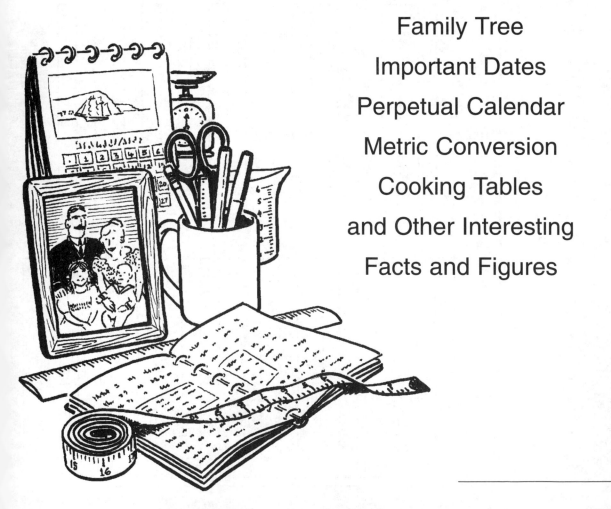

Family Tree

Important Dates

Perpetual Calendar

Metric Conversion

Cooking Tables

and Other Interesting

Facts and Figures

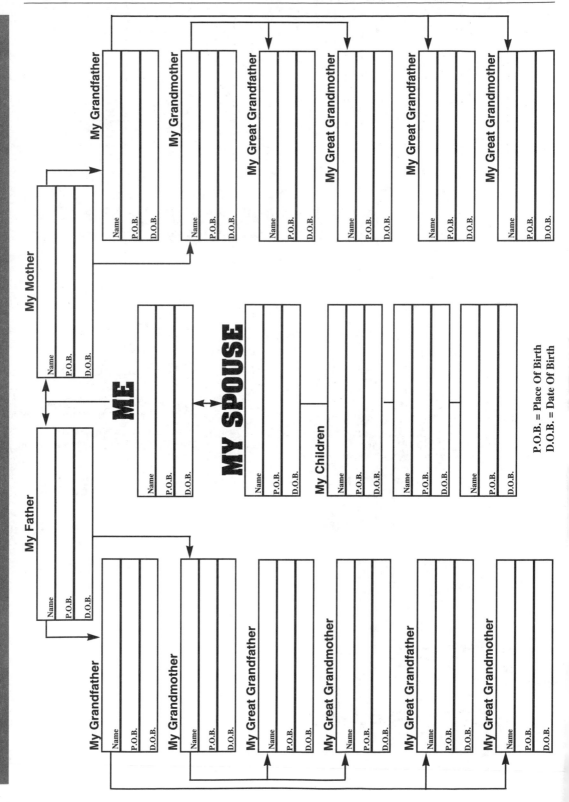

MY FAMILY TREE

P.O.B. = Place Of Birth
D.O.B. = Date Of Birth

My Children

Name					
P.O.B.					
D.O.B.					

My Step-Children

Name
P.O.B.
D.O.B.

My Brothers & Sisters

Name
P.O.B.
D.O.B.

My Spouse's Brothers & Sisters

Name
P.O.B.
D.O.B.

MY FAMILY TREE

MY FAMILY TREE

My Mother's Brothers & Sisters

Name

P.O.B.

D.O.B.

Name

P.O.B.

D.O.B.

Name

P.O.B.

D.O.B.

Name

P.O.B.

D.O.B.

Name

P.O.B.

D.O.B.

Name

P.O.B.

D.O.B.

Name

P.O.B.

D.O.B.

Name

P.O.B.

D.O.B.

My Father's Brothers & Sisters

Name

P.O.B.

D.O.B.

Name

P.O.B.

D.O.B.

Name

P.O.B.

D.O.B.

Name

P.O.B.

D.O.B.

Name

P.O.B.

D.O.B.

Name

P.O.B.

D.O.B.

Name

P.O.B.

D.O.B.

Name

P.O.B.

D.O.B.

Great Great Grandparents - Father's Side

Name

Details

Your Father's Father's Father's Father

Name

Details

Your Father's Father's Father's Mother

Name

Details

Your Father's Father's Mother's Father

Name

Details

Your Father's Father's Mother's Mother

Name

Details

Your Father's Mother's Father's Father

Name

Details

Your Father's Mother's Father's Mother

Name

Details

Your Father's Mother's Mother's Father

Name

Details

Your Father's Mother's Mother's Mother

Great Great Grandparents - Mother's Side

Name

Details

Your Mother's Father's Father's Father

Name

Details

Your Mother's Father's Father's Mother

Name

Details

Your Mother's Father's Mother's Father

Name

Details

Your Mother's Father's Mother's Mother

Name

Details

Your Mother's Mother's Father's Father

Name

Details

Your Mother's Mother's Father's Mother

Name

Details

Your Mother's Mother's Mother's Father

Name

Details

Your Mother's Mother's Mother's Mother

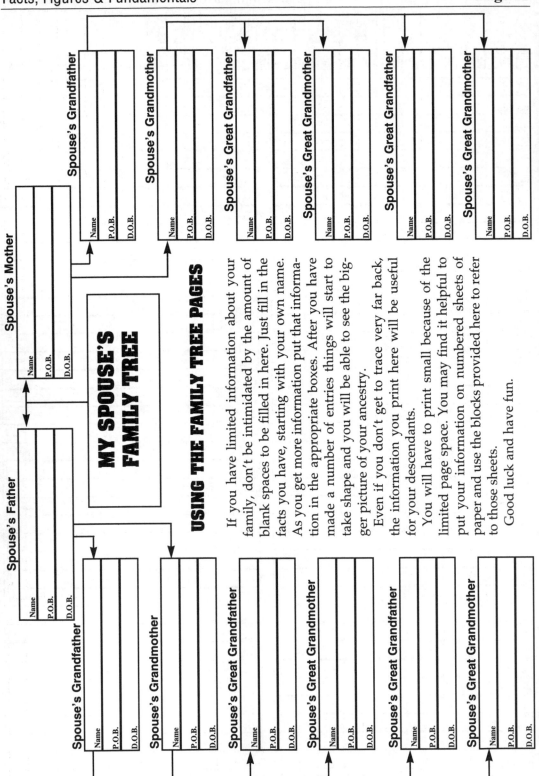

USING THE FAMILY TREE PAGES

If you have limited information about your family, don't be intimidated by the amount of blank spaces to be filled in here. Just fill in the facts you have, starting with your own name. As you get more information put that information in the appropriate boxes. After you have made a number of entries things will start to take shape and you will be able to see the bigger picture of your ancestry.

Even if you don't get to trace very far back, the information you print here will be useful for your descendants.

You will have to print small because of the limited page space. You may find it helpful to put your information on numbered sheets of paper and use the blocks provided here to refer to those sheets.

Good luck and have fun.

MY SPOUSE'S FAMILY TREE

MY FAMILY TREE

More Family Tree
Relatives not covered in other sections - including Step-Relatives and Half-Relatives

MORE FAMILY TREE

Name	Name
P.O.B.	P.O.B.
D.O.B.	D.O.B.
Relationship to me:	Relationship to me:

Name	Name
P.O.B.	P.O.B.
D.O.B.	D.O.B.
Relationship to me:	Relationship to me:

Name	Name
P.O.B.	P.O.B.
D.O.B.	D.O.B.
Relationship to me:	Relationship to me:

Name	Name
P.O.B.	P.O.B.
D.O.B.	D.O.B.
Relationship to me:	Relationship to me:

Name	Name
P.O.B.	P.O.B.
D.O.B.	D.O.B.
Relationship to me:	Relationship to me:

Name	Name
P.O.B.	P.O.B.
D.O.B.	D.O.B.
Relationship to me:	Relationship to me:

Name	Name
P.O.B.	P.O.B.
D.O.B.	D.O.B.
Relationship to me:	Relationship to me:

Name	Name
P.O.B.	P.O.B.
D.O.B.	D.O.B.
Relationship to me:	Relationship to me:

My Grandchildren - The Future Family Tree

Maybe years hence
Someone will look
At the names I have written
Down here in this book
The names of my children's children
In some small way may last
To have some future remembrance
Of their children's past

If they should look further
They'll easily see
All that I knew
Of my family tree
They'll know nothing of me
Any more than my name
But they'll know from which branch
Of life's tree that they came

MY GRANDCHILDREN

Name
P.O.B.
D.O.B.
Father
Mother

Name
P.O.B.
D.O.B.
Father
Mother

Name
P.O.B.
D.O.B.
Father
Mother

Name
P.O.B.
D.O.B.
Father
Mother

Name
P.O.B.
D.O.B.
Father
Mother

Name
P.O.B.
D.O.B.
Father
Mother

Name
P.O.B.
D.O.B.
Father
Mother

Name
P.O.B.
D.O.B.
Father
Mother

Name
P.O.B.
D.O.B.
Father
Mother

Name
P.O.B.
D.O.B.
Father
Mother

Use extra paper if necessary, and clip to this page.

Family Death Registrations

D.O.B. = Date of Birth, P.O.B. = Place of Birth, D.O.D. = Date of Death, P.O.D. = Place of Death

FAMILY DEATH REGISTRATIONS

Name	Name
D.O.B.	D.O.B.
P.O.B.	P.O.B.
D.O.D.	D.O.D.
P.O.D.	P.O.D.

Name	Name
D.O.B.	D.O.B.
P.O.B.	P.O.B.
D.O.D.	D.O.D.
P.O.D.	P.O.D.

Name	Name
D.O.B.	D.O.B.
P.O.B.	P.O.B.
D.O.D.	D.O.D.
P.O.D.	P.O.D.

Name	Name
D.O.B.	D.O.B.
P.O.B.	P.O.B.
D.O.D.	D.O.D.
P.O.D.	P.O.D.

Name	Name
D.O.B.	D.O.B.
P.O.B.	P.O.B.
D.O.D.	D.O.D.
P.O.D.	P.O.D.

Name	Name
D.O.B.	D.O.B.
P.O.B.	P.O.B.
D.O.D.	D.O.D.
P.O.D.	P.O.D.

Name	Name
D.O.B.	D.O.B.
P.O.B.	P.O.B.
D.O.D.	D.O.D.
P.O.D.	P.O.D.

My Special Friends & Neighbours Over The Years

Name

Address:

Telephone: Email: Fax:

Other Information:

Name

Address:

Telephone: Email: Fax:

Other Information:

Name

Address:

Telephone: Email: Fax:

Other Information:

Name

Address:

Telephone: Email: Fax:

Other Information:

Name

Address:

Telephone: Email: Fax:

Other Information:

Name

Address:

Telephone: Email: Fax:

Other Information:

Name

Address:

Telephone: Email: Fax:

Other Information:

Name

Address:

Telephone: Email: Fax:

Other Information:

Name

Address:

Telephone: Email: Fax:

Other Information:

Name

Address:

Telephone: Email: Fax:

Other Information:

Name

Address:

Telephone: Email: Fax:

Other Information:

Name

Address:

Telephone: Email: Fax:

Other Information:

Name

Address:

Telephone: Email: Fax:

Other Information:

Name

Address:

Telephone: Email: Fax:

Other Information:

Name

Address:

Telephone: Email: Fax:

Other Information:

Name

Address:

Telephone: Email: Fax:

Other Information:

SPECIAL FRIENDS & NEIGHBOURS

MONTHS & IMPORTANT BIRTHDAYS

About The Months Of The Year

January 1st Month	**February** 2nd Month	**March** 3rd Month
*31 days *Named for the Roman God Janus **Birthstone:** Garnet **Flower:** Carnation	*28 days (Leap Year 29) *From the Latin 'Februa' meaning 'purification' **Birthstone:** Amethyst **Flower:** Violet	*31 days *Named for Mars, the god of Spring **Birthstone:** Aquamarine **Flower:** Daffodil
April 4th Month	**May** 5th Month	**June** 6th Month
*30 days *From the Latin, 'aperire', meaning 'to open' **Birthstone:** Diamond **Flower:** Daisy	*31 days *Meaning 'prime of life' **Birthstone:** Emerald **Flower:** Lily of the Valley	*30 days *Named for the Roman God Juno **Birthstone:** Pearl **Flower:** Rose

Important Birthdays

Birth Date:			Birth Date:		
Name			Name		
Address:			Address:		
City:	Prov/State:	Postal/Zip:	City:	Prov/State:	Postal/Zip:
Tel:			Tel:		
Birth Date:			Birth Date:		
Name			Name		
Address:			Address:		
City:	Prov/State:	Postal/Zip:	City:	Prov/State:	Postal/Zip:
Tel:			Tel:		
Birth Date:			Birth Date:		
Name			Name		
Address:			Address:		
City:	Prov/State:	Postal/Zip:	City:	Prov/State:	Postal/Zip:
Tel:			Tel:		
Birth Date:			Birth Date:		
Name			Name		
Address:			Address:		
City:	Prov/State:	Postal/Zip:	City:	Prov/State:	Postal/Zip:
Tel:			Tel:		
Birth Date:			Birth Date:		
Name			Name		
Address:			Address:		
City:	Prov/State:	Postal/Zip:	City:	Prov/State:	Postal/Zip:
Tel:			Tel:		

About The Months Of The Year

July 7th Month
*31 days
*Named for Julius Caesar (it was the month he was born)
Birthstone: Ruby
Flower: Water Lily

August 8th Month
*31 days
*Named for Augustus Caesar (original name 'Sextilis')
Birthstone: Peridot
Flower: Poppy

September 9th Month
*30 days
*From the Latin 'Septem' (meaning 'seven')
Birthstone: Sapphire
Flower: Morning Glory

October 10th Month
*31 days
*From the Latin, 'octo' (meaning 'eight')
Birthstone: Opal
Flower: Cosmos

November 11th Month
*30 days
*From the Latin 'Novembris' (meaning 'ninth')
Birthstone: Topaz
Flower: Chrysanthemum

December 12th Month
*31 days
*From the Latin 'Decem' (meaning 'tenth')
Birthstone: Turquoise
Flower: Holly

Important Birthdays

Birth Date:
Name
Address:
City: Prov/State: Postal/Zip:
Tel:

Birth Date:
Name
Address:
City: Prov/State: Postal/Zip:
Tel:

Birth Date:
Name
Address:
City: Prov/State: Postal/Zip:
Tel:

Birth Date:
Name
Address:
City: Prov/State: Postal/Zip:
Tel:

Birth Date:
Name
Address:
City: Prov/State: Postal/Zip:
Tel:

Birth Date:
Name
Address:
City: Prov/State: Postal/Zip:
Tel:

Birth Date:
Name
Address:
City: Prov/State: Postal/Zip:
Tel:

Birth Date:
Name
Address:
City: Prov/State: Postal/Zip:
Tel:

Birth Date:
Name
Address:
City: Prov/State: Postal/Zip:
Tel:

Birth Date:
Name
Address:
City: Prov/State: Postal/Zip:
Tel:

MONTHS & IMPORTANT BIRTHDAYS

Anniversaries

1st - Paper	10th - Tin	35th - Coral
2nd - Cotton	11th - Steel	40th - Ruby
3rd - Leather	12th - Linen	45th - Sapphire
4th - Silk Flowers	13th - Lace	50th - Gold
5th - Wood	14th - Ivory	55th - Emerald
6th - Iron or Candy	15th - Crystal	60th - Pewter or Diamond
7th - Copper or Wool	20th - Porcelain	65th - Opal
8th - Bronze or Rubber	25th - Silver	70th - Platinum
9th - Pottery	30th - Pearl	75th - Diamond

Wedding Date: / Names: / Address: / City: / Prov/State: / Postal/Zip: / Tel:

(10 blank address entry forms with fields: Wedding Date, Names, Address, City, Prov/State, Postal/Zip, Tel)

A short biography of my life

The Date and Place of My Birth; Schooling, Jobs, Important Events and Important People in My Life

I was born

_____

_____

_____

_____

_____

_____

_____

_____

_____

_____

_____

_____

_____

_____

_____

_____

_____

_____

_____

_____

_____

_____

_____

_____

_____

_____

_____

_____

_____

_____

_____

_____

_____

_____

_____

Continued on loose page marked: _____

MY BIOGRAPHY

PHOTOS OF FAMILY & FRIENDS

Crop your special photographs
to fit. Most photographs
have wasted area anyway.
These spaces measure
2 & 3/4 inches wide
and 3 inches high.

Crop and paste a
photograph of yourself here.
Your future generations will
want to know what
you looked like.

My Picture

Use paper glue and make
sure that photographs
are securely glued.
These photographs should
remain a permanent part
of the book.

If you have more photographs
glue them to pages with leftover
space, such as page 6.
Make sure the captions
explain the photographs.

Meanings & Origins of Common First Names

Aaron - high mountain (Hebrew)
Abigail - father rejoices
Adam - redness (Hebrew)
Alan - rock, noble, saint (Celtic)
Albert - noble, bright (Germanic)
Alexander - defender of men (Greek)
Alison - of noble birth (French diminutive of Alice)
Amanda - capable of being loved (Latin)
Amy - loved (French)
Andrea - female form of Andrew (Greek)
Andrew - manly (Greek)
Angela - messenger (Greek)
Ann(e) - English form of Hannah
Anthony - Roman family name
April - from the month
Arch/Archie - from Archibald
Archibald - precious and bold (Germanic)
Arnold - powerful eagle (Germanic)
Arthur - stone (Celtic)
Ashley - dweller by the ash tree (English)
Austen/Austin - from Augustine (a saint)
Barbara - foreign (Greek)
Barney - dweller on the barley (English)
Barry - spear, rampart (Celtic)
Beatrice - messenger of happiness (Latin)
Benjamin - son of my right hand (Hebrew)
Bernard - brave, bear (Germanic)
Beth - pet form of Elizabeth
Betty - pet form of Elizabeth
Bill/Billy - pet form of William
Blake - fame (Irish)
Bob - pet form of Robert
Boyd - yellow haired (Gaelic)
Brandi - variant of Brandy
Bradley - dweller near the clearing (English)
Brandon - broom-covered hill (Germanic)
Brian - hill (Celtic)
Caitlin - from Catherine (Irish)
Carl - man (Germanic)
Carol(e) - pet form of Caroline
Carson - dweller in the marsh (Celtic)
Catherine - pure (Greek)
Charles - husbandman (Germanic)
Christine - female form or Christian (French)
Christopher - Christ bearer (Latin)

Claire - radiant (Latin)
Clark - clergyman, scholar (Celtic)
Cole - dweller on the hill (English)
Colin - form of Nicholas
Craig - rock (Celtic)
Crystal - clear-cut
Dale - blind (Irish)
Daniel - God is my judge (Hebrew)
Danielle - female form of Daniel
Darcy - dark (Irish)
Darren - Irish surname
Darryl - English and Irish surname
David - beloved friend (Hebrew)
Dawn - sunrise
Dean - dweller in the valley (English)
Deborah - bee (Hebrew)
Dennis - of Dionysus (Greek), the god of wine
Derek - ruler of the people
Diane - French form of Diana
Diana - divine (Latin)
Dick - a pet form of Richard
Dillon - destroy (Germanic)
Donald - world mighty (Gaelic)
Donna - lady (Latin)
Doreen - from Dorothy
Dora - a short form of Dorothy
Doris - woman (Greek)
Dorothy - gift of God (Greek)
Drew - lover, ghost (Germanic)
Earl - a rank of peerage (English)
Edward - guardian of land (Germanic)
Eileen - Irish form of Helen
Eli - pet form of Elias and Elijah
Elliot - elf-ruler (Celtic)
Elizabeth - perfection of God (Hebrew)
Emily - Roman family name
Emma - all-embracing (Germanic)
Eric - ruler of all (Norse)
Erica - female form of Eric
Eugene - well-born (Greek)
Eugenie - French form of Eugene
Evan - swift (Celtic)
Felix - happy (Latin)
Fletcher - maker or seller of arrows (French)
Ford - dweller by the shallows
Francis - Frenchman

Meanings & Origins of Common First Names

Frank - pet form of Francis
Frederick - peaceful ruler (Germanic)
Freeman - free born (Celtic)
Gail - pet form of Abigail
Gareth - gentle (Welsh)
Gavin - hawk of battle (Scottish-French)
Gawain - hawk (Welsh)
Gemma - gem (Italian)
Geoffrey - peace (Germanic)
George - farmer (Greek)
Glen - dweller in the valley (Celtic)
Gordon - dull, stupid, boorish (French)
Grace - attractive (English) - fat (French)
Graham - Germanic place name
Grant - big, tall, elder, senior (French)
Gregory - watchful (Greek)
Guy - forest (Germanic)
Hannah - grace, favour (Hebrew)
Hardy - bold, courageous (English)
Harold - ruler (Germanic)
Harrison - son of Harry or Henry
Harry - pet form of Henry
Harvey - battle worthy (Germanic)
Hayley - hay-meadow (English)
Hayward - keeper of the fence (English)
Hedley - dweller by the river source (English)
Heather - flower
Helen - shining one (Greek)
Henry - home ruler (Germanic)
Holly - dweller in the hollow (English)
Howard - chief warden (Germanic)
Hugh - heart and mind (French/German)
Ian - modern Scottish form of John
Irene - peace (Greek)
Jacob - one who takes by the heel (Hebrew)
Jacqueline - female form of Jacques
Jacques - French form of Jacob
James - Latin form of Jacob
Jane - female form of John
Janet - diminutive form of Jane
Jason - form of Joshua
Jean - French form of Johanna, from John
Jeffrey - peace (Germanic)
Jehovah - salvation (Hebrew)
Jennifer - fair (Celtic)
Jeremy - English from of Jeremiah

Jeremiah - Jehova exalts (Hebrew)
Jessica - he beholds (Hebrew)
Joan - contracted form of Johanna, from John
Joanne - French form of Johanna
John - Jehovah has been gracious (Hebrew)
Jonathan - Jehovah's gift (Hebrew)
Joseph - Jehovah adds (Hebrew)
Joshua - form of Jehovah
Joyce - joyful (Latin)
Julie - French female form of Latin Julius
Julius - descended from Jove (Latin)
Karen - Danish form of Katarina (Catherine)
Katherine - American spelling of Catherine
Kathleen - English form of Irish Caitlin
Kelly - warlike one - also Irish surname
Kenneth - fire-sprung (Gaelic)
Kerry - place name in Ireland
Kevin - handsome at birth (Irish)
Kimberly - South African place name
Kirk - dweller by the church (Old Norse)
Lakisha - woman (Arabic)
Latoya - form of Tonya
Laura - laurel (Latin)
Lauren - diminutive of Laura
Lawrence - bay tree (Latin)
Lee - wood clearing (Germanic)
Leonard - bold lion (Germanic)
Leroy - the king (French)
Leslie - Scottish place name
Lester - to dye (English)
Lewis - loud battle (French)
Lilian - lily (Italian)
Lily - dweller of the field (English)
Linda - serpent (symbol of wisdom) (Germ)
Lindsay - Scottish place name
Lisa - pet form of Elizabeth
Luther - flute player (French)
Margaret - pearl (Greek)
Marguerite - French form of Margaret
Marjorie - from Marguerite
Marcus - from Mars, god of war (Latin)
Mark - English form of Marcus
Martin - from Mars, god of war (Latin)
Mary - Greek form of Miriam (Hebrew)
Matthew - gift of God (Hebrew)
Melissa - bee (Greek)

Meanings & Origins of Common First Names

Michael - like God (Hebrew)
Michele - from Michael
Michelle - English spelling of French, Michele
Miles/Myles - a soldier (Latin)
Miller - flour maker (Old Norse)
Mitchell - big (English)
Morgan - bright sea (Celtic)
Morris - dark, swarthy (Latin)
Morton - the farm (Celtic)
Nancy - pet form of Ann
Natalie - birthday of the Lord (Latin)
Neil - champion (Irish)
Nelson - son of Neil (Scottish/Irish)
Newman - new comer (English)
Nicholas - victory people (Greek)
Nicola - Italian female form of Nicholas
Nicole - French female form of Nicholas
Noel - Christmas (French)
Norman - dweller of the north (English)
Owen - well born (Latin)
Pamela - honey (Greek)
Patricia - noble (Latin)
Paul - small (Latin)
Pauline - French female form of Paul
Pierce/Pearce - Peter (French)
Pearl - dealer in pearls (French)
Percy /Percey - a French town (English)
Peter - stone, rock (Greek)
Philip - horse lover (Greek)
Rachel - ewe (Hebrew)
Ralph - counsel, wolf (Germanic)
Randolf/Randolph - wolf shield (Germanic)
Randy - from Randolf
Randal/Rendell, etc. - from Randolf
Rebecca - noose (Hebrew)
Richard - strong ruler (Germanic)
Robert - famous, bright (Germanic)
Ronald - counsel and power (Germanic)
Robin - a diminutive of Robert (French)
Roger/Rodger - famous spear (Germanic)
Rose - famous and kind (German)
Ruby - a surname of England and Ireland
Russell - red (French)
Ruth - companion (Hebrew)
Ryan - surname of Ireland
Sally - pet form of Sarah

Samantha - female form of Samuel
Samuel - heard the name of God (Hebrew)
Sandra - pet form of Alexandra
Sarah - princess (Hebrew)
Scott - surname from Scotland
Sean - from John (Irish)
Sharon - the plain (Hebrew)
Shaun/Shawn - English spelling of Sean
Shirley - bright clearing (Germanic)
Silvia - dweller in the wood (Latin)
Simeon - listening attentively (Hebrew)
Simon - form of Simeon
Stephanie - French female form of Stephen
Stephen - crown (Greek)
Stewart - from Stuart
Stuart - steward (Germanic)
Susan - short form of Susannah
Susannah - lily (Hebrew)
Taylor - tailor (French)
Teresa - woman of Theresia (Greek)
Terry - ruling people (French)
Theresia - town in Greece
Thomas - twin (Hebrew)
Tiffany - manifestation of God (Greek)
Timothy - honouring God (Greek)
Tonya - form of Antonia
Trac(e)y - pet form of Teresa
Troy - a surname of England and Ireland
Vaughan - small (Welsh)
Vera - faith (Slavic)
Victoria - victory (Latin)
Vincent - conquer (Latin)
Virginia - maiden (Latin)
Wade - depart (English)
Wallace - a Welshman (Scottish)
Walter - mighty army (Germanic)
Ward - watchman (English)
Warrick - builder of scaffolds (English)
Watson - son of Watt (Celtic)
Wayne - wagon-maker
Willis - variant of William
William - will + helm (helmet) (Germanic)
Wilson - son of William
Woodrow - cottage dweller (English)
Zeke - pet form of Ezekiel
Zoe - life (Greek)

COMMON FIRST NAMES

Birth Dates of the Famous and Infamous

January 1
1449 - Lorenzo de' Medici
1735 - Paul Revere
1920 - J. D. Salinger
1901 - Xavier Cugat
1895 - J. Edgar Hoover

January 2
1727 - James Wolfe
1920 - Professor Isaac Asimov
1938 - David Bailey
1930 - Julius Larosa
1932 - Jean Little

January 3
106BC - Marcus Tullius Cicero
1888 - J. R. R. Tolkien
1909 - Victor Borge
1941 - Bobby Hull
1956 - Mel Gibson

January 4
1785 - Jakob Grimm
1914 - Jane Wyman
1809 - Louis Braille
1813 - Sir Isaac Pitman
1937 - Dyan Cannon

January 5
1779 - Stephen Decatur
1876 - Konrad Adenauer
1931 - Robert Duvall
1946 - Diane Keaton
1918 - Jean Dixon

January 6
1367 - King Richard II
1412 - St. Joan of Arc
1878 - Carl Sandburg
1880 - Tom Mix
1913 - Loretta Young

January 7
1768 - Joseph Bonaparte
1844 - Marie-Bernard Soubirous
1867 - Carl Laemmle
1925 - Gerald Durrell
1948 - Kenny Loggins

January 8
1885 - John Curtin
1899 - Solomon Bandaranaike
1912 - Jose Ferrer
1935 - Elvis Presley
1947 - David Bowie

January 9
1854 - Lady Randolph Churchill
1913 - Richard Nixon
1901 - Chic Young
1914 - Gyspy Rose Lee
1898 - Gracie Fields

January 10
1769 - Michel Ney
1904 - Ray Bolger
1945 - Rod Stewart
1935 - Ronnie Hawkins
1938 - Frank Mahovlich

January 11
1716 - Daniel Dancer
1859 - George Nathaniel Curzon

1929 - Rod Taylor
1946 - Naomi Judd
1934 - Jean Chretien

January 12
1729 - Edmund Burke
1893 - Hermann Goering
1876 - Jack London
1905 - Tex Ritter
1947 - Joe Frazier

January 13
1884 - Sophie Tucker
1918 - Lord Ted Willis
1919 - Robert Stack
1920 - Harry Worth
1931 - Charles Nelson Reilly

January 14
1741 - Benedict Arnold
1875 - Dr. Albert Schweitzer
1941 - Faye Dunaway
1938 - Jack Jones
1919 - Andy Rooney

January 15
1906 - Aristotle Onassis
1918 - General Gamal Nasser
1929 - Martin Luther King
1913 - Lloyd Bridges
1926 - Chuck Berry

January 16
1907 - Alexander Knox
1909 - Ethel Merman
1853 - Andre Michelin
1944 - Ronnie Milsap
1935 - A. J. Foyt

January 17
1706 - Benjamin Franklin
1820 - Anne Bronte
1899 - Al Capone
1942 - Muhammad Ali
1928 - Vidal Sassoon

January 18
1782 - Daniel Webster
1882 - A. A. Milne
1892 - Oliver Hardy
1904 - Cary Grant
1913 - Danny Kaye

January 19
1807 - Robert E. Lee
1809 - Edgar Allan Poe
1939 - Phil Everly
1943 - Janis Joplin
1946 - Dolly Parton

January 20
1930 - Dr. Edwin 'Buzz' Aldrin
1896 - George Burns
1920 - Frederico Fellini
1926 - Patricia Neal
1924 - Slim Whitman

January 21
1824 - Thomas 'Stonewall' Jackson
1925 - Telly Savalas
1925 - Benny Hill
1940 - Jack Nicklaus
1905 - Christian Dior

January 22
1440 - Ivan (III) the Great
1561 - Francis Bacon
1858 - Beatrice Potter Webb
1788 - Lord Byron
1959 - Linda Blair

January 23
1783 - Stendhal
1832 - Edouard Manet
1928 - Jeanne Moreau
1919 - Bob Paisley
1943 - Bill Gibb

January 24
76AD - Hadrian
1712 - Frederick the Great
1732 - Pierre Beaumarchais
1917 - Ernest Borgnine
1945 - Neil Diamond

January 25
1540 - St. Edmund Campion
1759 - Robert Burns
1874 - Wm Somerset Maugham
1882 - Virginia Woolf
1627 - Robert Boyle

January 26
1880 - Douglas MacArthur
1925 - Paul Newman
1928 - Eartha Kitt
1907 - Henry Cotton
1961 - Wayne Gretzky

January 27
1859 - Kaiser Wilhelm II
1901 - Art Rooney
1756 - Wolfgang Amadeus Mozart
1832 - Lewis Carroll
1964 - Bridget Fonda

January 28
1457 - Henry VII
1887 - Artur Rubinstein
1936 - Alan Alda
1855 - William S. Burroughs
1929 - Acker Bilk

January 29
1843 - William McKinley
1879 - W. C. Fields
1915 - Victor Mature
1941 - Tom Selleck
1954 - Oprah Winfrey

January 30
1882 - Franklin D. Roosevelt
1915 - John Profumo
1931 - Gene Hackman
1937 - Vanessa Redgrave
1938 - Boris Spassky

January 31
1797 - Franz Schubert
1872 - Zane Grey
1923 - Norman Mailer
1892 - Eddie Cantor
1921 - Mario Lanza

February 1
1895 - John Ford
1901 - Clark Gable

1895 - Stephen Potter
1937 - Don Everly
1968 - Lisa Marie Presley

February 2
1650 - Nell Gwynne
1850 - Jesse Boot
1882 - James Joyce
1946 - Farrah Fawcett
1927 - Stan Getz

February 3
1830 - Lord Robert Cecil
1874 - Gertrude Stein
1907 - James Michener
1928 - Frankie Vaughan
1962 - Clint Black

February 4
1902 - Captain Charles Lindberg
1918 - Ida Lupino
1920 - Norman Wisdom
1948 - Alice Cooper
1948 - Barbara Hershey

February 5
1788 - Sir Robert Peel
1900 - Adlai Ewing Stevenson
1919 - Andreas Papandreou
1840 - John Boyd Dunlop
1919 - Red Buttons

February 6
1665 - Queen Anne
1911 - Ronald Reagan
1912 - Eva Braun
1920 - Zsa Zsa Gabor
1895 - 'Babe' Ruth

February 7
1478 - Sir Thomas Moore
1812 - Charles Dickens
1885 - Sinclair Lewis
1870 - Alfred Adler
1962 - Garth Brooks

February 8
1820 - William Sherman
1828 - Jules Verne
1920 - Lana Turner
1925 - Jack Lemmon
1931 - James Dean

February 9
1773 - William Harrison
1854 - Edward Carson
1891 - Ronald Colman
1945 - Mia Farrow
1941 - Carole King

February 10
1894 - Harold Macmillan
1775 - Charles Lamb
1890 - Boris Pasternak
1893 - Jimmy Durante
1950 - Mark Spitz

February 11
1920 - King Farouk of Egypt
1936 - Burt Reynolds
1800 - Henry Fox Talbot
1847 - Thomas Alva Edison
1926 - Leslie Nielsen

February 12
1588 - John Winthrop
1809 - Abraham Lincoln
1870 - Marie Lloyd
1809 - Charles Darwin
1959 - Arsenio Hall

February 13
1728 - John Hunter
1933 - Kim Novak
1934 - George Segal
1938 - Oliver Reed
1944 - Stockard Channing

February 14
1766 - Thomas Robert Malthus
1944 - Carl Bernstein
1894 - Jack Benny
1944 - Alan Parker
1907 - John Longden
1951 - Kevin Keegan

February 15
1519 - Pedro Menedez de Aviles
1710 - Louis XV of France
1882 - John Barrymore
1951 - Jane Seymour
1564 - Galileo Galilei

February 16
1884 - Robert Flaherty
1926 - John Schlessinger
1935 - Sonny Bono
1959 - John McEnroe
1903 - Edgar Bergen

February 17
1929 - Yasser Arafat
1902 - Marian Anderson
1923 - Dr. John Allegro
1856 - Frederick Eugene Ives
1963 - Michael Jordan

February 18
1517 - Mary I of England
1922 - Helen Gurley Brown
1954 - John Travolta
1933 - Yoko Ono Lennon
1898 - Enzo Ferrari

February 19
1960 - Prince Andrew
1917 - Carson McCullers
1893 - Sir Cedric Hardwicke
1924 - Lee Marvin
1473 - Nicolas Copernicus

February 20
1904 - Alexei Kosygin
1694 - Voltaire
1888 - Dame Marie Rambert
1892 - Carl Mayer
1927 - Sydney Poitier

February 21
1728 - Peter III, Tsar of Russia
1794 - Antonio Lopez de Santa Anna
1801 - John Henry
1934 - Nina Simone
1866 - August von Wasserman
1946 - Tyne Daly

February 22
1857 - Sir Robert Baden-Powell
1732 - George Washington

February 22 (continued)
1932 - Senator Edward Kennedy
1907 - Robert Young
1975 - Drew Barrymore

February 23
1633 - Samuel Pepys
1685 - George Frederick Handel
1817 - Sir George Watts
1883 - Victor Fleming
1743 - Meyer Amschel Rothschild

February 24
1885 - Chester Nimitz
1786 - Wilhelm Karl Grimm
1852 - George Moore
1948 - Dennis Waterman
1942 - Paul Jones

February 25
1888 - John Foster Dulles
1841 - Pierre Auguste Renoir
1873 - Enrico Caruso
1901 - Zeppo Marx
1943 - George Harrison

February 26
1802 - Victor Hugo
1846 - 'Buffalo Bill'
1928 - 'Fats' Domino
1932 - Johnny Cash
1953 - Michael Bolton

February 27
274 - Constantine the Great
1807 - Henry Wadsworth Longfellow
1902 - John Steinbeck
1930 - Joanne Woodward
1932 - Elizabeth Taylor

February 28
1909 - Sir Stephen Spender
1824 - Charles Blondin
1913 - Vincente Minnelli
1915 - Zero Mostel
1901 - Professor Linus Pauling

February 29
1896 - Ranchhodji Morarji Desai
1792 - Gioacchino Rossini
1928 - Joss Ackland
1840 - John Philip Holland
1736 - Ann Lee

March 1
1810 - Frederic Chopin
1910 - David Niven
1917 - Dinah Shore
1927 - Harry Belafonte
1904 - Glenn Miller

March 2
1793 - Sam Houston
1931 - Mikhail Gorbachev
1919 - Jennifer Jones
1944 - Lou Reed
1950 - Karen Carpenter

March 3
1869 - Sir Henry Wood
1920 - Ronald Searle
1911 - Jean Harlow
1831 - George M. Pullman
1847 - Alexander Graham Bell

March 4
1678 - Antonio Lucio Vivaldi

March 4 (continued)
1928 - Alan Sillitoe
1928 - Patrick Moore
1936 - Jim Clark
1951 - Kenny Dalgleish

March 5
1133 - King Henry II
1751 - James Madison
1908 - Rex Harrison
1958 - Andy Gibb
1512 - Gerhardus Mercator

March 6
1937 - Valentina Tereshkova
1619 - Savinien C. Bergerac
1806 - Elizabeth Barrett Browning
1834 - George du Maurier
1959 - Tom Arnold

March 7
1905 - Jacques Caban-Dalmas
1802 - Sir Edwin H. Landseer
1875 - Maurice Ravel
1930 - Lord Snowdon
1785 - Alessandro Manzoni

March 8
1859 - Kenneth Grahame
1921 - Cyd Charisse
1943 - Lynn Redgrave
1958 - Gary Numan
1890 - Gene Fowler

March 9
1454 - Amerigo Vespucci
1763 - William Cobbett
1934 - Yuri Gagarin
1928 - Mickey Spillane
1943 - Bobby Fischer

March 10
1964 - Prince Edward
1885 - Tamara Karsavina
1892 - Arthur Honegger
1903 - Bix Beidebecke
1958 - Sharon Stone

March 11
1916 - Harold Wilson
1952 - Douglas Adams
1898 - Jessie Matthews
1885 - Sir Malcolm Campbell
1956 - Dana Delaney

March 12
1626 - John Aubrey
1917 - Googie Withers
1946 - Liza Minnelli
1838 - Sir Henry Pirkin
1932 - Andrew Young

March 13
1884 - Sir Hugh Walpole
1898 - Henry Hathaway
1918 - Tessie O'Shea
1855 - Percy Lowell
1770 - Daniel Lambert

March 14
1820 - Victor Emmanuel II
1933 - Michael Caine
1933 - Quincy Jones
1940 - Eleanor Bron
1879 - Albert Einstein

March 15
1767 - Andrew Jackson
1946 - David Wall
1941 - Mike Love
1961 - Terence Trent d'Arby
1926 - Norm Van Brocklin

March 16
1751 - James Madison
1774 - Matthew Flinders
1920 - Leo McKern
1926 - Jerry Lewis
1787 - Georg Simon Ohm

March 17
1787 - Edmund Kean
1938 - Rudolf Nureyev
1917 - Nat 'King' Cole
1902 - Bobby Jones
1964 - Rob Lowe

March 18
1609 - Frederick III
1837 - S. Grover Cleveland
1869 - A. Neville Chamberlain
1844 - Rimsky-Korsakov
1932 - John Updike

March 19
1813 - Dr. David Livingstone
1821 - Sir Richard Burton
1848 - Wyatt Earp
1906 - Adolf Eichmann
1936 - Ursula Andress

March 20
1938 - Brian Mulroney
43BC - Ovid
1890 - Beniamino Gigli
1908 - Sir Michael Redgrave
1917 - Dame Vera Lynn

March 21
1801 - Benito Pablo Juarez
1685 - Johann Sebastian Bach
1869 - Florenz Ziegfeld
1944 - Timothy Dalton
1936 - Roger Whittaker

March 22
1459 - Maximilian I
1923 - Marcel Marceau
1913 - Karl Malden
1948 - Andrew Lloyd Webber
1931 - William Shatner

March 23
1929 - Sir Roger Bannister
1908 - Joan Crawford
1920 - Jimmy Edwards
1912 - Wernher von Braun
1922 - Marty Allen

March 24
1834 - William Morris
1887 - Roscoe 'Fatty' Arbuckle
1909 - Tommy Trinder
1930 - Steve McQueen
1906 - Dwight MacDonald

March 25
1133 - Henry II
1769 - Joachim Murat
1921 - Simone Signoret
1942 - Aretha Franklin

1947 - Elton John

March 26
1874 - Robert (Lee) Frost
1914 - Tennessee Williams
1891 - Chico Marx
1931 - Leonard Nimoy
1944 - Diana Ross

March 27
1785 - Louis XVII
1898 - Gloria Swanson
1942 - Michael York
1924 - Sarah Vaughan
1863 - Sir Henry Royce

March 28
1515 - St Teresa of Avila
1660 - King George I
1921 - Dirk Bogarde
1891 - Paul Whiteman
1955 - Reba McEntire

March 29
1790 - John Tyler
1902 - Sir William Walton
1914 - Chapman Pincher
1918 - Pearl Bailey
1912 - Frederick Mackenzie

March 30
1135 - Maimonides
1853 - Vincent van Gogh
1937 - Warren Beatty
1913 - Frankie Laine
1945 - Eric Clapton

March 31
1596 - Rene Descartes
1935 - Richard Chamberlain
1934 - Shirley Jones
1693 - John Harrison
1935 - Herb Alpert

April 1
1815 - Prince Otto von Bismark
1883 - Lon Chaney
1929 - Jane Powell
1932 - Debbie Reynolds
1938 - Ali MacGraw

April 2
742 - Charlemagne
1805 - Hans Christian Andersen
1827 - William Holman Hunt
1914 - Sir Alec Guinness
1939 - Marvin Gaye

April 3
1367 - Henry IV
1783 - Washington Irving
1924 - Marlon Brando
1924 - Doris Day
1961 - Eddie Murphy

April 4
1758 - Pierre Paul Prud'hon
1896 - Robert Emmet Sherwood
1928 - Maya Angelou
1932 - Anthony Perkins
1915 - Muddy Waters
1823 - Sir William Siemens
1965 - Robert Downey

April 5
1827 - Joseph Lister

1920 - Arthur Hailey
1900 - Spencer Tracy
1908 - Bette Davis
1916 - Gregory Peck
1922 - Tom Finney

April 6
1890 - Anthony H. G. Fokker
1929 - Andre Previn
1874 - Harry Houdini
1928 - James Watson
1945 - Peter Tosh

April 7
1506 - St. Francis Xavier
1770 - William Woodsworth
1897 - Walter Winchell
1928 - James Garner
1915 - Billie Holiday

April 8
1919 - Ian Smith
1889 - Sir Adrian Boult
1893 - Mary Pickford
1818 - August W. Hofmann
1912 - Sonja Henie

April 9
1649 - James Scott
1835 - Leopold II
1909 - Sir Robert Helpmann
1926 - Hugh Heffner
1932 - Carl Perkin

April 10
1512 - King James V
1829 - William Booth
1847 - Joseph Pulitzer
1932 - Omar Sharif
1951 - Steven Seagal

April 11
1819 - Sir Charles Halle
1930 - Ronald Fraser
1932 - Joel Grey
1775 - James Parkinson
1893 - Dean Acheson

April 12
1777 - Henry Clay
1923 - Maria Callas
1949 - Alan Ayckbourn
1941 - Bobby Moore
1950 - David Cassidy

April 13
1732 - Frederick North
1743 - Thomas Jefferson
1902 - Philippe de Rothschild
1906 - Samuel Beckett
1852 - Frank W. Woolworth

April 14
1527 - Philip II of Spain
1527 - Ortelius
1925 - Rod Steiger
1940 - Julie Christie
1935 - Loretta Lynn

April 15
1800 - Sir James Clark Ross
1843 - Henry James
1940 - Jeffrey Archer
1939 - Claudia Cardinale
1793 - Friedrich G. W. Struve

April 16
1867 - Wilbur Wright
1889 - Sir Charles S. Chaplin
1921 - Peter Ustinov
1924 - Henry Mancini
1940 - Dusty Springfield

April 17
1837 - John Pierpont Morgan
1894 - Nikita Khrushchev
1897 - Thornton Wilder
1929 - James Last
1955 - Debra Winger

April 18
1480 - Lucrezia Borgia
1797 - Louis Adolphe Thiers
1882 - Leopold Antoni
Stanislaw
1946 - Hayley Mills
1958 - Malcolm Marshall
1963 - Conan O'Brien

April 19
1900 - Richard Hughes
1933 - Jayne Mansfield
1935 - Dudley Moore
1903 - Eliot Ness
1954 - Trevor Francis

April 20
1808 - Napoleon III
1889 - Adolf Hitler
1893 - Harold Lloyd
1941 - Ryan O'Neal
1951 - Luther Vandross

April 21
1926 - Queen Elizabeth II
1816 - Charlotte Bronte
1915 - Anthony Quinn
1923 - John Mortimer
1782 - Friedrich Froebel

April 22
1724 - Immanuel Kant
1707 - Henry Fielding
1904 - Robert Oppenheimer
1950 - Peter Frampton
1937 - Jack Nicholson

April 23
1897 - Lester Pearson
1564 - William Shakespeare
1928 - Shirley Temple
1942 - Lee Majors
1936 - Roy Orbison

April 24
1533 - William of Orange
1931 - Bridget Riley
1934 - Shirley MacLaine
1936 - Jill Ireland
1942 - Barbra Streisand

April 25
1284 - King Edward II
1559 - Oliver Cromwell
1873 - Walter de la Mare
1918 - Ella Fitzgerald
1874 - Guglielmo Marconi

April 26
AD121 - Marcus Aurelius
1452 - Leonardo da Vinci

1936 - Carol Burnett
1926 - David Coleman
1938 - Duane Eddy

April 27
1822 - Ulysses Grant
1737 - Edward Gibbon
1759 - Mary Wollstonecraft
1959 - Sheena Easton
1951 - Ace Frehley

April 28
1442 - King Edward IV
1889 - Antonio Salazar
1878 - Lionel Barrymore
1941 - Ann-Margret
1950 - Jay Leno

April 29
1818 - Alexander II
1863 - William Randolph Hearst
1889 - 'Duke' Ellington
1933 - Rod McKuen
1970 - Andre Agassi

April 30
1651 - Jean Baptiste
1770 - David Thompson
1944 - Jill Clayburgh
1943 - Bobby Vee
1933 - Willie Nelson

May 1
1916 - Glen Ford
1218 - Rudolf I of Hapsburb
1929 - Joseph Heller
1945 - Rita Coolidge
1960 - Steve Cauthen

May 2
1729 - Catherine II (the Great)
1892 - Baron Manfred von Richthofen
1904 - Bing Crosby
1903 - Dr. Benjamin Spock
1962 - Jon Bon Jovi

May 3
1920 - *Sugar* Ray Robinson
1898 - Golda Meir
1919 - Pete Seeger
1936 - Englebert Humperdink
1964 - Wyonna Judd

May 4
1936 - El Cordobe
1882 - Sylvia Pankhurst
1927 - Terry Scott
1929 - Audrey Hepburn
1942 - Tammy Wynette

May 5
1867 - Nellie Bly
1800 - Louis Hachette
1818 - Karl Marx
1913 - Tyrone Power
1943 - Michael Palin

May 6
1913 - Stewart Granger
1856 - Sigmund Freud
1856 - Robert Edwin Peary
1895 - Rudolph Valentino
1915 - Orson Welles

May 7
1833 - Johannes Brahms

1919 - Maria Eva Duarte Peron
1812 - Robert Browning
1840 - Piotr Ilyich Tchaikovsky
1901 - Gary Cooper

May 8
1884 - Harry S. Truman
1828 - Jean Henri Dunant
1904 - John Snagge
1926 - Sir David Attenborough
1940 - Peter Benchley
1932 - Sonny Liston

May 9
1920 - Richard Adams
1800 - John Brown
1873 - Howard Carter
1910 - Barbara Woodhouse
1946 - Candice Bergen

May 10
1938 - John Wilkes Booth
1899 - Fred Astaire
1957 - Sid Vicious
1850 - Sir Thomas Lipton
1960 - Bono

May 11
1912 - Phil Silvers
1904 - Salvador Dali
1888 - Irving Berlin
1941 - Eric Burdon
1924 - Jackie Milburn

May 12
1929 - Burt Bacharach
1765 - Lady Hamilton
1820 - Florence Nightingale
1812 - Edward Lear
1828 - Dante Gabriel Rossetti

May 13
1717 - Maria Theresa
1927 - Clive Barnes
1941 - Joe Brown
1950 - Stevie Wonder
1914 - Joe Louis

May 14
1885 - Otto Klemperer
1727 - Thomas Gainsborough
1936 - Bobby Darin
1897 - Sidney Bechet
1952 - David Byrne

May 15
1905 - Joseph Cotton
1909 - James Mason
1948 - Brian Eno
1953 - Mike Oldfield
1935 - 'Ted' Dexter

May 16
1905 - Henry Fonda
1919 - Liberace
1913 - Woody Herman
1955 - Olga Korbut
1952 - Pierce Brosnan

May 17
1911 - Maureen O'Sullivan
1900 - Ayatollah Khomeini
1936 - Dennis Hopper
1836 - Joseph Norman Lockyer
1956 - 'Sugar' Ray Leonard

May 18
1868 - Nicholas II
1920 - Pope John Paul II
1897 - Frank Capra
1912 - Perry Como
1909 - Fred Perry

May 19
1879 - William Waldorf Astor
1890 - Ho Chi Minh
1926 - Malcolm X
1945 - Pete Townsend
1941 - Nora Ephron

May 20
1944 - Joe Cocker
1818 - William George Fargo
1915 - Moshe Dayan
1908 - James Stewart
1945 - Cher

May 21
1780 - Elizabeth Fry
1930 - Malcolm Fraser
1688 - Alexander Pope
1844 - Henri Rousseau
1916 - Harold Robbins

May 22
1880 - Sir Ernest Oppenheimer
1813 - Richard Wagner
1859 - Sir Arthur Conan Doyle
1907 - Laurence Olivier
1924 - Charles Aznavour

May 23
1883 - Douglas Fairbanks
1910 - Artie Shore
1928 - Rosemary Clooney
1933 - Joan Collins
1910 - Artie Shaw

May 24
1946 - Priscilla Presley
1819 - Queen Victoria
1870 - Jan Christian Smuts
1941 - Bob Dylan
1955 - Roseanne Cash

May 25
1947 - Karen Valentine
1892 - Marshal Tito
1803 - Ralph Waldo Emerson
1927 - Robert Ludlam
1947 - Jesse Colter

May 26
1867 - Queen Mary
1907 - John Wayne
1913 - Peter Cushing
1925 - Alec McCowen
1920 - Peggy Lee

May 27
1923 - Henry Kissinger
1837 - *Wild Bill* Hickok
1915 - Herman Wouk
1911 - Vincent Price
1912 - Sam Snead

May 28
1935 - Carroll Baker
1934 - The Dionne Quintuplets
1908 - Ian Fleming
1944 - Gladys Knight

1947 - Sondra Locke

May 29
1630 - Charles II
1917 - John F. Kennedy
1874 - G. K. Chesterton
1903 - Bob Hope
1953 - Danny Elfman

May 30
1944 - Meredith MacRae
1846 - Peter Carl Faberge
1908 - Mel Blanc
1909 - Benny Goodman
1949 - Bob Willis

May 31
1941 - Johnny Paycheck
1819 - Walt Whitman
1930 - Clint Eastwood
1965 - Brooke Shields
1943 - Joe Namath

June 1
1926 - Andy Griffith
1878 - John Masefield
1934 - Pat Boone
1801 - Brigham Young
1926 - Marilyn Monroe

June 2
1840 - Thomas Hardy
1857 - Sir Edward Elgar
1903 - Johnny Weissmuller
1938 - Sally Kellerman
1941 - Stacy Keach

June 3
1808 - Jefferson Davis
1926 - Allen Ginsburg
1925 - Tony Curtis
1950 - Suzi Quatro
1954 - Dan Hill

June 4
1937 - Freddy Fender
1738 - King George III
1826 - Stephen Foster
1908 - Rosalind Russell
1925 - Dennis Weaver

June 5
1939 - Joe Clark
1723 - Adam Smith
1926 - Bill Hayes
1949 - Ken Follett
1878 - Francisco Pancho Villa

June 6
1755 - Nathan Hale
1868 - Captain Robert F. Scott
1862 - Sir Henry John Newbolt
1875 - Thomas Mann
1956 - Bjorn Borg

June 7
1952 - Liam Neeson
1896 - Imre Nagy
1899 - Elizabeth Bowen
1917 - Dean Martin
1940 - Tom Jones

June 8
1652 - William Dampier
1772 - Robert Stevenson
1869 - Frank Lloyd Wright

1934 - Millicent Martin
1937 - Joan Rivers

June 9
1672 - Peter the Great
1893 - Cole Porter
1781 - George Stephenson
1943 - Charles Saatchi
1961 - Michael J. Fox

June 10
1844 - Carl Hagenbeck
1921 - Prince Philip
1880 - Andre Derain
1901 - Frederick Loewe
1922 - Judy Garland

June 11
1864 - Richard Strauss
1572 - Ben Jonson
1935 - Gene Wilder
1910 - Jacques Yves Cousteau
1939 - Jackie Stewart

June 12
1819 - Charles Kingsley
1897 - Anthony Eden
1928 - Vic Damone
1901 - Sir Norman Hartnell
1957 - Timothy Busfield

June 13
1892 - Basil Rathbone
1910 - Mary Whitehouse
1752 - Fanny Burney
1865 - W. B. Yeats
1953 - Tim Allen

June 14
1909 - Burl Ives
1928 - Che Guevara
1811 - Harriet Beecher Stowe
1961 - Boy George
1969 - Steffi Graf

June 15
1884 - Harry Langdon
1330 - Edward the Black Prince
1843 - Edvard Grieg
1949 - Simon Callow
1923 - Erroll Garner

June 16
1892 - Lupino Lane
1922 - Enoch Powell
1890 - Stan Laurel
1927 - Tom Graveney
1943 - Joan van Ark

June 17
1239 - King Edward I
1703 - John Wesley
1818 - Charles François Gounod
1882 - Igor Stravinsky
1946 - Barry Manilow

June 18
1901 - Jeanette MacDonald
1769 - Viscount Castlereagh
1978 - Garfield
1942 - Paul McCartney
1961 - Alison Moyet

June 19
1623 - Blaise Pascal
1556 - King James I

BIRTH DATES OF THE FAMOUS & INFAMOUS

1896 - Bessie Wallis Warfield
1947 - Salman Rushdie
1954 - Kathleen Turner

June 20
1819 - Jacques Offenbach
1909 - Errol Flynn
1949 - Lionel Richie
1954 - Allan Lamb
1952 - John Goodman

June 21
1937 - John Edrich
1002 - Leo IX
1982 - Prince William
1921 - Jane Russell
1973 - Juliette Lewis

June 22
1757 - George Vancouver
1921 - Joseph Papp
1932 - Prunella Scales
1936 - Kris Kristofferson
1949 - Meryl Streep

June 23
1763 - Empress Josephine
1894 - Dr. Alfred Kinsey
1912 - Alan Turing
1927 - Bob Fosse
1916 - Sir Leonard Hutton

June 24
1850 - Horatio Herbert
1915 - Professor Fred Hoyle
1947 - Mick Fleetwood
1895 - Jack Dempsey
1825 - W. H. Smith

June 25
1903 - George Orwell
1870 - Robert Erskine Childers
1906 - Roger Livesey
1945 - Carly Simon
1924 - Sidney Lumet

June 26
1892 - Pearl S. Buck
1904 - Peter Lorre
1710 - Charles Messier
1910 - 'Colonel' Tom Parker
1914 - Babe Zaharias

June 27
1462 - King Louis XII
1550 - King Charles IX of France
1846 - Charles Stewart Parnell
1880 - Helen Adams Keller
1930 - Ross Perot

June 28
1902 - Richard Rodgers
1491 - King Henry VIII
1712 - Jean Jacques Rousseau
1948 - Kathy Bates

June 29
1798 - Conte Giacomo Leopardi
1886 - Robert Schuman
1914 - Rafael Kubelik
1901 - Nelson Eddy
1910 - Frank Loesser

June 30
1917 - Lena Horne
1893 - Harold Laski

1917 - Buddy Rich
1966 - Mike Tyson
1943 - Florence Ballard

July 1
1916 - Olivia de Havilland
1872 - Louis Bleriot
1902 - William Wyler
1931 - Leslie Caron
1952 - Dan Aykroyd

July 2
1938 - Dr. David Owen
1489 - Thomas Cranmer
1903 - King Olaf V of Norway
1903 - Sir Alec Douglas Home
1918 - Robert Sarnoff

July 3
1728 - Robert Adam
1937 - Tom Stoppard
1927 - Ken Russell
1951 - Richard Hadlee
1962 - Tom Cruise

July 4
1804 - Nathaniel Hawthorne
1826 - Stephen Collins Foster
1900 - Louis Armstrong
1927 - Gina Lollobrigida
1927 - Neil Simon

July 5
1853 - Cecil John Rhodes
1911 - Georges Pompidou
1889 - Jean Cocteau
1755 - Mrs. Sarah Siddons
1810 - P. T. Barnum

July 6
1832 - Maximilian
1935 - Dalai Lama
1921 - Nancy Reagan
1946 - Sylvester Stallone
1925 - Bill Haley

July 7
1926 - *Doc* Severinsen
1860 - Gustav Mahler
1887 - Marc Chagall
1940 - Ringo Starr
1922 - Pierre Cardin

July 8
1836 - Joseph Chamberlain
1839 - John D. Rockefeller
1851 - Sir Arthur John Evans
1781 - Tom Cribb
1958 - Kevin Bacon

July 9
1945 - Dean Koontz
1916 - Edward Heath
1819 - Elias Howe
1957 - Kelly McGillis
1976 - Fred Savage

July 10
1947 - Arlo Guthrie
1834 - James McNeill Whistler
1871 - Marcel Proust
1949 - Sunil Gavaskar
1923 - Jean Kerr

July 11
1953 - Leon Spinks

1767 - John Quincy Adams
1915 - Yul Brynner
1944 - Peter de Savary
1934 - Giorgio Armani

July 12
1854 - George Eastman
100BC - Gaius Julius Caesar
1817 - Henry David Thoreau
1908 - Milton Berle
1937 - Bill Cosby

July 13
1859 - Sidney James Webb
1527 - John Dee
1811 - Sir George Gilbert Scott
1933 - David Storey
1942 - Harrison Ford

July 14
1918 - Ingmar Bergman
1913 - Gerald Ford
1911 - Terry Thomas
1912 - Woody Guthrie
1933 - Robert Bourassa

July 15
1573 - Inigo Jones
1606 - Rembrandt
1898 - Noel Gay
1946 - Linda Rondstadt
1960 - Willie Upton

July 16
1907 - Orville Redenbacher
1872 - Roald Amundsen
1907 - Barbara Stanwyck
1911 - Ginger Rogers
1971 - Corey Feldman

July 17
1889 - Earle Stanley Gardner
1899 - James Cagney
1917 - Phyllis Diller
1935 - Donald Sutherland
1952 - David Hasselhoff

July 18
1921 - John Glenn
1887 - Vidkun Quisling
1918 - Nelson Mandela
1938 - Dudu Pukwana
1950 - Richard Branson

July 19
1814 - Samuel Colt
1860 - Lizzie Borden
1865 - Charles Horace Mayo
1834 - Edgar Degas
1896 - Dr. A. J. Cronin

July 20
1919 - Sir Edmund Hillary
1889 - Sir John Reith
1938 - Diana Rigg
1938 - Natalie Wood

July 21
1620 - Jean Piccard
1899 - Ernest Hemingway
1926 - Norman Jewison
1922 - Kay Starr
1962 - Rob Morrow

July 22
1890 - Rose Kennedy

1478 - Philip I, King of Spain
1898 - Stephen Vincent Benet
1940 - Terence Stamp
1947 - Don Henley

July 23
1888 - Raymond Chandler
1933 - Richard Rogers
1912 - Michael Wilding
1953 - Graham Gooch
1961 - Woody Harrelson

July 24
1783 - Simon Bolivar
1775 - Eugene François Vidocq
1898 - Amelia Earhart
1802 - Alexandre Dumas
1929 - Peter Yates

July 25
1848 - Arthur James Balfour
1978 - Louise Brown
1894 - Walter Brennan
1907 - Johnny 'Rabbit' Hodges
1930 - Annie Ross

July 26
1922 - Blake Edwards
1856 - George Bernard Shaw
1897 - Paul Gallico
1928 - Stanley Kubrick
1943 - Mick Jagger

July 27
1824 - Alexander Dumas
1929 - Jack Higgins
1944 - Bobbie Gentry
1955 - Allan Border
1906 - Leo Durocher

July 28
1901 - Rudy Vallee
1929 - Jacqueline Onassis
1844 - Gerard Manley Hopkins
1866 - Beatrix Potter
1909 - Malcolm Lowry

July 29
1801 - George Bradshaw
1883 - Benito Mussolini
1905 - Dag Hammarskjold
1938 - Dennis the Menace
1938 - Peter Jennings

July 30
1863 - Henry Ford
1818 - Emily Bronte
1898 - Henry Moore
1958 - Daley Thompson
1947 - Arnold Schwarzenegger

July 31
1951 - Evonne Crawley
1927 - Peter Nichols
1944 - Geraldine Chaplin
1902 - 'Gubby' Allen
1963 - Wesley Snipes

August 1
1819 - Herman Melville
10BC - Claudius I
1779 - Francis Scott Key
1921 - Jack Kramer
1936 - Yves Saint-Laurent
1939 - Robert James Waller

August 2
1924 - James Baldwin
1891 - Sir Arthur Bliss
1905 - Myrna Loy
1932 - Peter O'Toole
1954 - Sammy McIlroy

August 3
1920 - P. D. James
1924 - Leon Uris
1926 - Tony Bennett
1940 - Martin Sheen
1907 - Lawrence Brown

August 4
1900 - Queen Elizabeth II
1792 - Percy Bysshe Shelley
1908 - Sir Osbert Lancaster
1870 - Sir Harry Lauder
1870 - Oscar Ameringer

August 5
1911 - Robert Taylor
1930 - Professor Neil Armstrong
1850 - Guy de Maupassant
1951 - Bob Geldof
1882 - Hugh Johnson

August 6
1917 - Robert Mitchum
1809 - Alfred, Lord Tennyson
1911 - Lucille Ball
1881 - Alexander Fleming
1922 - Sir Freddie Laker

August 7
1948 - Greg Chappell
1876 - Mata Hari
1924 - Kenneth Kendall
1948 - Greg Chappell
1961 - Walter Swinburn

August 8
1923 - Esther Williams
1937 - Dustin Hoffman
1907 - Benny Carter
1954 - Nigel Mansell
1951 - Keith Carradine

August 9
1905 - Dame Elizabeth Lane
1757 - Thomas Telford
1593 - Izaak Walton
1922 - Philip Larkin
1957 - Melanie Griffith

August 10
1874 - Herbert Hoover
1810 - Count Cavour
1928 - Eddie Fisher
1941 - Anita Lonsborough
1896 - Louis Sobol

August 11
1935 - Anna Massey
1673 - Richard Meade
1876 - Mary Roberts Rinehart
1921 - Alex Haley
1953 - Hulk Hogan

August 12
1762 - King George IV
1924 - Mohammad Zia ul-Haq
1881 - Cecil B. De Mille
1925 - Norris & Ross McWhirter

1939 - George Hamilton

August 13
1927 - Fidel Castro
1860 - Annie Oakley
1913 - Archbishop Makarios III
1899 - Alfred Hitchcock
1912 - Ben Hogan

August 14
1910 - Pierre Schaeffer
1840 - Baron von Krafft-Ebing
1864 - John Galsworthy
1913 - Fred Davis
1968 - Halle Berry

August 15
1879 - Ethel Barrymore
1769 - Napoleon I
1950 - Princess Anne
1771 - Sir Walter Scott
1875 - Samuel Coleridge-Taylor

August 16
1913 - Menachem Begin
1958 - Madonna
1958 - Angela Bassett
1957 - Kathie Lee Gifford
1954 - James Cameron

August 17
1786 - Davy Crockett
1892 - Mae West
1920 - Maureen O'Hara
1943 - Robert de Niro
1951 - Alan Minter

August 18
1933 - Roman Polanski
1587 - Virginia Dare
1830 - Franz Joseph I
1922 - Shelly Winters
1937 - Robert Redford

August 19
1940 - Jill St. John
1902 - Ogden Nash
1871 - Orville Wright
1940 - Johnny Nash
1931 - Willy Shoemaker

August 20
1833 - Benjamin Harrison
1924 - Jim Reeves
1906 - Bunny Austin
1952 - John Emburey
1946 - Connie Chung

August 21
1938 - Kenny Rogers
1765 - King William IV
1930 - Princess Margaret
1956 - Kim Cattral
1944 - Jackie DeShannon

August 22
1956 - Paul Molitor
1893 - Dorothy Parker
1920 - Ray Bradbury
1926 - Honor Blackman
1940 - Valerie Harper

August 23
1947 - Keith Moon
1754 - Louis XVI
1869 - Edgar Lee Masters

1947 - Willy Russell
1912 - Gene Kelly

August 24
1903 - Graham Sutherland
1759 - William Wilberforce
1899 - Jorge Lius Borges
1953 - Sam Torrance
1971 - Claudia Schiffer

August 25
1924 - Monty Hall
1530 - Ivan IV ('the Terrible')
1938 - Frederick Forsyth
1930 - Sean Connery
1954 - Elvis Costello

August 26
1676 - Sir Robert Walpole
1875 - John Buchan
1980 - Macaulay Culkin
1952 - Billy Rush
1965 - Christopher Burke

August 27
1910 - Mother Teresa
551BC - Confucius
1877 - Charles Stewart Rolls
1908 - Lyndon Baines Johnson
1882 - Sam Goldwyn

August 28
1960 - Emma Samms
1828 - Count Leo Tolstoy
1899 - Charles Boyer
1925 - Donald O'Connor
1932 - Andy Bathgate

August 29
1958 - Michael Jackson
1809 - Oliver Wendell Holmes
1915 - Ingrid Bergman
1923 - Richard Attenborough
1949 - Richard Gere

August 30
1797 - Mary Wollstonecraft Shelley
1896 - Raymond Massey
1907 - Shirley Booth
1908 - Fred MacMurray
1943 - Jean Claude Killey

August 31
1918 - Ted Williams
AD12 - Caligula
1928 - James Coburn
1958 - Serge Blanco
1931 - Jean Beliveau

September 1
1854 - Englebert Humperdinck
1875 - Edgar Rice Burroughs
1866 - 'Gentleman Jim' Corbett
1923 - Rocky Marciano
1936 - Lily Tomlin

September 2
1951 - Mark Harmon
1952 - Jimmy Connors
1964 - Keanu Reeves
1948 - Terry Bradshaw
1943 - Glen Sather

September 3
1947 - Marilyn McCoo
1728 - Matthew Boulton

1913 - Alan Ladd
1965 - Charlie Sheen
1965 - Benito Santiago

September 4
1937 - Dawn Fraser
1736 - Robert Raikes
1824 - Anton Bruckner
1892 - Darius Milhaud
1929 - Mitzi Gaynor

September 5
1638 - Louis XIV
1902 - Darryl Zanuck
1929 - Bob Newhart
1940 - Raquel Welch
1950 - Cathy Guisewite

September 6
1757 - Marquis de Lafayette
1888 - Joseph Kennedy
1915 - Franz Josef Strauss
1942 - Britt Ekland
1766 - John Dalton

September 7
1533 - Queen Elizabeth I
1913 - Anthony Quayle
1923 - Peter Lawford
1936 - Buddy Holly
1951 - Chrissie Hynde

September 8
1922 - Sid Caesar
1157 - King Richard
1886 - Siegfried Sassoon
1925 - Peter Sellers
1945 - Rogie Vachon

September 9
1585 - Cardinal de Richelieu
1754 - William Bligh
1941 - Otis Redding
1946 - Billy Preston
1951 - Michael Keaton

September 10
1939 - David Hamilton
1771 - Mungo Park
1855 - Robert Koldewey
1945 - Jose Feliciano
1929 - Arnold Palmer

September 11
1917 - Ferdinand Marcos
1700 - James Thompson
1862 - O. Henry
1885 - D. H. Lawrence
1955 - Joe Jackson

September 12
1937 - George Chuvalo
1888 - Maurice Chevalier
1818 - Richard Jordan Gatling
1913 - Jesse Owens
1931 - George Jones

September 13
1944 - Jacqueline Bisset
1860 - John J. Pershing
1905 - Claudette Colbert
1944 - Jacqueline Bisset
1925 - Mel Torme

September 14
1949 - Mary Frances Crosby

BIRTH DATES OF THE FAMOUS & INFAMOUS

1909 - Sir Peter Scott
1910 - Jack Hawkins
1914 - Clayton Moore
1944 - Joey Heatherton

September 15
AD53 - Trajan
1857 - William Howard Taft
1984 - Prince Henry of Wales
1789 - James Fenimore Cooper
1890 - Agatha Christie
1907 - Fay Wray

September 16
1925 - B. B. King
1387 - King Henry V
1924 - Lauren Bacall
1927 - Peter Falk
1925 - Charlie Byrd

September 17
1901 - Sir Francis Chichester
1957 - David Bintley
1928 - Roddy McDowall
1931 - Anne Bancroft
1897 - Sir Isaac Wolfson

September 18
1933 - Bob Dylan
1895 - John George Diefenbaker
1905 - Greta Garbo
1939 - Frankie Avalon
1779 - Joseph Story

September 19
1940 - Sylvia Tyson
1911 - Sir William Golding
1949 - Twiggy
1938 - Adam West
1940 - Paul Williams

September 20
1951 - Guy LaFleur
1878 - Upton Sinclair
1869 - Sir George Robey
1934 - Sophia Loren
1924 - Gogi Grant

September 21
1866 - H. G. Wells
1931 - Larry Hagman
1934 - Leonard Cohen
1947 - Stephen King
1963 - Cecil Fielder

September 22
1515 - Anne of Cleves
1791 - Michael Faraday
1948 - Captain Mark Phillips
1954 - Shari Belafonte-Harper
1960 - Joan Jett

September 23
1932 - Ray Charles
63BC - Gaius Octavius Caesar
1920 - Mickey Rooney
1949 - Bruce Springsteen
1951 - Jeff Squire

September 24
1896 - F. Scott Fitzgerald
1952 - Joseph Kennedy III
1936 - Jim Henderson
1941 - Linda McCartney
1946 - Joe Greene

September 25
1961 - Heather Lockyear
1932 - Barbara Walters
1944 - Michael Douglas
1952 - Christopher Reeve
1952 - Mark Hamill

September 26
1897 - Pope Paul VI
1888 - T. S. Eliot
1898 - George Gershwin
1948 - Olivia Newton-John
1947 - Lynn Anderson

September 27
1722 - Samuel Adams
1862 - Louis Botha
1926 - Jayne Meadows
1943 - Randy Bachman
1958 - Shaun Cassidy

September 28
1909 - Al Capp
1916 - Peter Finch
1923 - Marcello Mastroianni
1934 - Brigitte Bardot
1905 - Max Schmeling

September 29
106BC - Pompey the Great
1725 - Robert Clive
1758 - Horatio Nelson
1907 - Gene Autry
1935 - Jerry Lee Lewis

September 30
1958 - Marty Stuart
1924 - Truman Capote
1921 - Deborah Kerr
1931 - Angie Dickinson
1935 - Johnny Mathis

October 1
1935 - Julie Andrews
1207 - King Henry III
1924 - Jimmy Carter
1920 - Walter Matthau
1933 - Richard Harris

October 2
1452 - King Richard III
1869 - Mohandas K. Gandhi
1904 - Graham Greene
1890 - *Groucho* Marx
1939 - Rex Reed

October 3
1900 - Thomas Wolfe
1925 - Gore Vidal
1938 - Eddie Cochran
1941 - Chubby Checker
1951 - Dave Winfield

October 4
1944 - Patti Labelle
1892 - Englebert Dollfuss
1814 - Jean-François Millet
1895 - Buster Keaton
1924 - Charlton Heston

October 5
1943 - Steve Miller
1923 - Glynis Johns
1924 - Barbara Kelly
1969 - Josie Bissett

1965 - Mario LeMieux

October 6
1820 - Jenny Lind
1942 - Britt Ekland
1846 - George Westinghouse
1914 - Thor Heyerdahl
1908 - Carol Lombard

October 7
1954 - Dennis Eckersley
1900 - Henrich Himmler
1923 - June Allyson
1927 - Al Martino
1951 - John 'Cougar' Melloncamp

October 8
1940 - David Carradine
1895 - Juan Peron
1941 - Reverend Jesse Jackson
1949 - Sigourney Weaver
1943 - Chevy Chase

October 9
1923 - Donald Sinden
1933 - Bill Tidy
1935 - Donald McCullin
1900 - Alistair Sim
1940 - John Lennon

October 10
1900 - Helen Brown
1825 - Paul Kruger
1738 - Benjamin West
1924 - James Clavell
1949 - Jessica Harper

October 11
1949 - Daryl Hall
1738 - Arthur Phillip
1844 - H. J. Heinz
1884 - Eleanor Roosevelt
1821 - Sir George Williams

October 12
1537 - King Edward VI
1860 - Elmer Ambrose Sperry
1866 - Ramsay MacDonald
1875 - Aleister Crowley
1935 - Luciano Pavarotti

October 13
1959 - Marie Osmond
1925 - Margaret Thatcher
1915 - Cornel Wilde
1921 - Yves Montand
1941 - Paul Simon

October 14
1633 - King James II
1644 - William Penn
1890 - Dwight D. Eisenhower
1928 - Roger Moore
1940 - Cliff Richard

October 15
70BC - Virgil
1881 - P. G. Wodehouse
1920 - Mario Puzo
1858 - John L. Sullivan
1924 - Lee Iacocco

October 16
1946 - Suzanne Somers
1758 - Noah Webster
1886 - David Ben-Gurion

1854 - Oscar Wilde
1922 - Angela Lansbury

October 17
1915 - Arthur Miller
1918 - Rita Hayworth
1920 - Montgomery Clift
1939 - Evel Knievel
1948 - Margot Kidder

October 18
1919 - Pierre Trudeau
1939 - Lee Harvey Oswald
1923 - Melina Mercouri
1927 - George C. Scott
1926 - Chuck Berry

October 19
1962 - Evander Holyfield
1931 - John Le Carre
1862 - Auguste Lumiere
1944 - Peter Tosh
1945 - Jeannie C. Riley

October 20
1942 - Mickey Mantle
1632 - Sir Christopher Wren
1946 - Joyce Brothers
1925 - Art Buchwald
1908 - Arlene Francis

October 21
1833 - Alfred Nobel
1772 - Samuel Taylor Coleridge
1956 - Carrie Fisher
1917 - Dizzy Gillespie
1940 - Manfred Mann

October 22
1942 - Annette Funicello
1811 - Franz Liszt
1844 - Sarah Bernhardt
1952 - Jeff Goldblum
1920 - Timothy Leary

October 23
1959 - 'Weird Al' Yankovic
1844 - Louis Riel
1844 - Robert Bridges
1925 - Johnny Carson
1934 - Juan Chi-Chi Rodriguez

October 24
1769 - Jacques Laffitte
1915 - Tito Gobbi
1893 - Merian C. Cooper
1924 - Jack Warner
1930 - The Big Bopper

October 25
1800 - Lord Macaulay
1888 - Richard E. Byrd
1881 - Pablo Picasso
1941 - Helen Reddy
1941 - Anne Tyler

October 26
1879 - Leon Trotsky
1916 - François Mitterand
1914 - Jackie Coogan
1942 - Bob Hoskins
1911 - Mahalia Jackson
1947 - Hillary Rodham Clinton
1948 - Jaclyn Smith

October 27
1728 - Captain James Cook
1858 - Theodore Roosevelt
1782 - Niccolo Paganini
1889 - Enid Bagnold
1914 - Dylan Thomas

October 28
1914 - Jonas Salk
1909 - Francis Bacon
1927 - Cleo Laine
1967 - Julia Roberts
1942 - Michael Crichton

October 29
1953 - Denis Potvin
1897 - Joseph Goebbels
1891 - Fanny Brice
1948 - Richard Dreyfuss
1949 - Kate Jackson

October 30
1735 - John Adams
1885 - Ezra Pound
1932 - Louis Malle
1896 - Ruth Gordon
1945 - Henry *(Fonz)* Winkler

October 31
1950 - Jane Pauley
1795 - John Keats
1926 - H. R. F. Keating
1963 - Fred McGriff
1967 - Vanilla Ice

November 1
1957 - Lyle Lovett
1935 - Gary Player
1962 - Sharon Davies
1942 - Larry Flynt
1944 - Keith Emerson

November 2
1734 - Daniel Boone
1755 - Marie Antoinette
1795 - James Polk
1865 - Warren Harding
1960 - Said Aouita

November 3
1801 - Karl Baedeker
1901 - Leopold III
1921 - Charles Bronson
1954 - Adam Ant
1949 - Larry Holmes

November 4
1879 - Will Rogers
1916 - Walter Cronkite
1918 - Art Carney
1944 - Loretta Swit
1924 - Howie Meeker

November 5
1912 - Roy Rogers
1913 - Vivien Leigh
1963 - Tatum O'Neal
1959 - Bryan Adams
1942 - Art Garfunkel

November 6
1946 - Sally Field
1638 - James Gregory
1814 - Adolphe Sax
1861 - James A. Naismith

1892 - Sir John Alcock

November 7
1918 - Billy Graham
1867 - Marie Curie
1943 - Joni Mitchell
1922 - Al Hirt
1936 - Audrey McLaughlin

November 8
1927 - Morley Safer
1656 - Edmond Halley
1847 - Bram Stoker
1883 - Sir Arnold Bax
1900 - Margaret Mitchell

November 9
1952 - Lou Ferrigno
1841 - King Edward VII
1942 - Tom Weiskopf
1936 - Bob Graham
1918 - Spiro Agnew

November 10
1959 - Mackenzie Phillips
1483 - Martin Luther
1683 - King George II
1935 - Roy Scheider
1949 - Donna Fargo

November 11
1925 - Jonathan Winters
1885 - George Smith Patton
1922 - Kurt Vonnegut
1962 - Demi Moore
1937 - Stephen Lewis

November 12
1942 - Stephanie Powers
1866 - Sun Yat-sen
1929 - Grace Kelly
1945 - Neil Young
1961 - Nadia Comaneci

November 13
1950 - Whoopi Goldberg
1312 - King Edward III
1850 - Robert Louis Stevenson
1825 - Charles Frederick Worth
1950 - Gilbert Perreault

November 14
1935 - King Hussein of Jordan
1948 - Prince Charles
1951 - Steven Bishop
1935 - King Hussein
1955 - Willie Hernandez

November 15
1929 - Ed Asner
1638 - Catherine of Braganza
1708 - William Pitt the Elder
1862 - Gerhart Hauptmann
1932 - Petula Clark

November 16
1967 - Lisa Bonet
42BC - Tiberius Claudius Nero
1908 - Burgess Meredith
1953 - Griff Rhys Jones
1905 - Eddie Condon

November 17
1925 - Rock Hudson
1755 - King Louis XVIII
1942 - Martin Scorsese

1938 - Gordon Lightfoot
1944 - Tom Seaver

November 18
1928 - Mickey Mouse
1941 - David Hemmings
1944 - Linda Evans
1939 - Margaret Atwood
1870 - Dorothy Dix

November 19
1933 - Larry King
1600 - King Charles I
1917 - Indira Gandhi
1905 - Tommy Dorsey
1963 - Jodie Foster

November 20
1932 - Richard Dawson
1925 - Robert Kennedy
1920 - Gene Tierney
1938 - Dick Smothers
1956 - Mark Gastineau

November 21
1694 - Voltaire
1888 - Harpo Marx
1922 - Telly Savalas
1945 - Goldie Hawn
1961 - Mariel Hemingway

November 22
1958 - Jamie Lee Curtis
1808 - Thomas Cook
1899 - Wiley Post
1943 - Billy Jean King
1921 - Rodney Dangerfield

November 23
1954 - Bruce Hornsby
1804 - Franklin Pierce
1859 - Billy the Kid
1869 - Valdemar Poulsen
1887 - Boris Karloff

November 24
1914 - Joe DiMaggio
1784 - Zachary Taylor
1815 - Grace Darling
1864 - Toulouse-Lautrec
1925 - William F. Buckley Jr.

November 25
1947 - John Larroquette
1835 - Andrew Carnegie
1844 - Karl Friedrich Benz
1946 - Bev Bevan
1920 - Ricardo Montalban

November 26
1938 - Rich Little
1810 - Wm George Armstrong
1731 - William Cowper
1922 - Charles Schulz
1933 - Robert Goulet

November 27
1965 - Robin Givens
1942 - Jimi Hendrix
1952 - Sheila Copps
1701 - Anders Celsius
1941 - Eddie Rabbit

November 28
1949 - Paul Shaffer
1765 - Captain George Manby

1908 - Claude Levi-Strauss
1757 - William Blake
1931 - Hope Lange

November 29
1955 - Howie Mandell
1932 - Jacques Chirac
1797 - Gaetano Donizetti
1832 - Louisa M. Alcott
1898 - C. S. Lewis

November 30
1874 - Winston Churchill
1835 - Mark Twain
1667 - Jonathan Swift
1929 - Dick Clark
1923 - Efrem Zimbalist Jr.

December 1
1939 - Lee Trevino
1761 - Madame Marie Tussaud
1935 - Woody Allen
1940 - Richard Pryor
1945 - Bette Midler

December 2
1973 - Monica Seles
1859 - Georges Seurat
1960 - Rick Savage
1955 - Dennis Christopher
1949 - Cathy Lee Crosby

December 3
1949 - Ozzie Osbourne
1857 - Joseph Conrad
1883 - Anton von Webern
1930 - Andy Williams
1932 - Jaye P. Morgan

December 4
1795 - Thomas Carlyle
1835 - Samuel Butler
1875 - Edgar Wallace
1861 - Lillian Russell
1949 - Jeff Bridges

December 5
1839 - Gen. George A. Custer
1830 - Christina Rossetti
1906 - Otto Preminger
1901 - Walt Disney
1935 - Little Richard

December 6
1778 - Joseph Louis Gay-Lussac
1732 - Warren Hastings
1896 - Ira Gershwin
1888 - Will Hay
1955 - Steven Wright

December 7
1863 - Pietro Mascagni
1888 - Joyce Cary
1915 - Eli Wallach
1932 - Ellen Burstyn
1936 - Robert Belinsky

December 8
1542 - Mary, Queen of Scots
1925 - Sammy Davis Jr.
1940 - David Carradine
1765 - Eli Whitney
1933 - Flip Wilson

December 9
1909 - Douglas Fairbanks

1886 - Clarence Birdseye
1608 - John Milton
1918 - Kirk Douglas
1957 - Donny Osmond

December 10
1819 - Count Felice Orsini
1851 - Melvil Dewey
1924 - Michael Manley
1830 - Emily Dickinson
1914 - Dorothy Lamour

December 11
1945 - Teri Garr
1929 - Sir Kenneth MacMillan
1905 - Gilbert Roland
1913 - Carlo Ponti
1944 - Brenda Lee

December 12
1923 - Bob Barker
1893 - Edward G. Robinson
1915 - Frank Sinatra
1938 - Connie Francis
1941 - Dionne Warwick

December 13
1933 - Tim Conway
1925 - Dick van Dyke
1929 - Christopher Plummer
1949 - Paula Wilcox
1948 - Ted Nugent

December 14
1946 - Patty Duke
1895 - King George VI
1920 - Clark Terry
1932 - Charlie Rich
1914 - Morey Amsterdam

December 15
1888 - George Romney
AD37 - Nero
1892 - Jean Paul Getty
1942 - Dave Clark
1949 - Don Johnson

December 16
1485 - Catherine of Aragon
1775 - Jane Austen
1899 - Sir Noel Coward
1939 - Liv Ullman
1901 - Dr. Margaret Mead

December 17
1874 - William Lyon Mackenzie Ding
1770 - Ludwig von Beethoven
1936 - Tommy Steele
1908 - Willard Frank Libby
1929 - William Safire

December 18
1950 - Janie Frickie
1707 - Charles Wesley
1913 - Willy Brandt
1916 - Betty Grable
1947 - Steven Spielberg

December 19
1947 - Robert Urich
1906 - Leonid Ilyich Brezhnev
1910 - Jean Genet
1902 - Sir Ralph Richardson
1939 - Cicely Tyson

December 20
1894 - Sir Robert Menzies
1906 - Sir Dick White
1904 - Irene Dunne
1926 - Uri Geller

1805 - Thomas Graham

December 21
1935 - Phil Donahue
1804 - Benjamin Disraeli
1937 - Jane Fonda
1954 - Chris Evert
1940 - Frank Zappa

December 22
1946 - Diane Sawyer
1639 - Jean Racine
1858 - Giacomo Puccini
1909 - Patricia Hayes
1922 - Barbara Billingsley

December 23
1805 - Joseph Smith
1918 - Helmut Schmidt
1732 - Sir Richard Arkwright
1908 - Yousuf Karsh
1947 - Bill Rodgers

December 24
1929 - Mary Higgins Clark
1491 - Ignatius Loyola
1809 - Kit Carson
1905 - Howard Hughes
1922 - Ava Gardner

December 25
1642 - Sir Isaac Newton
1887 - Conrad Hilton
1918 - Anwar Sadat
1899 - Humphrey Bogart
1946 - Jimmy Buffett

December 26
1927 - Alan King
1893 - Mao Tse-tung

1891 - Henry Miller
1914 - Richard Widmark
1921 - Steve Allen

December 27
1931 - John Charles
1571 - Johannes Kepler
1773 - Sir George Cayley
1822 - Louis Pasteur
1904 - Marlene Dietrich

December 28
1954 - Denzel Washington Jr.
1856 - Woodrow Wilson
1934 - Maggie Smith
1856 - Sam Levenson
1941 - David Peterson

December 29
1937 - Mary Tyler Moore
1938 - Jon Voight
1766 - Charles Macintosh
1800 - Charles Goodyear
1947 - Ted Danson

December 30
1930 - Jack Lord
1865 - Rudyard Kipling
1869 - Stephen Leacock
1928 - Bo Didley
1935 - Sandy Koufax

December 31
1937 - Anthony Hopkins
1491 - Jacques Cartier
1720 - Bonnie Prince Charlie
1943 - John Denver
1948 - Donna Summer

The PHOBIAS

Acrophobia - heights
Aerophobia - flying (& air)
Agoraphobia - open spaces
Alektorophobia - chickens
Algophobia - pain
Amathophobia - dust
Amaxophobia - vehicles
Androphobia - men
Anthropophobia - human beings
Apiphobia - bees
Arachnophobia - spiders
Astraphobia - lightning
Ataxiophobia - disorder
Ballistophobia - missiles
Batrachophobia - reptiles
Bibliophobia - books
Blennophobia - slime
Cancerophobia - cancer
Cardiophobia - heart disease
Chrometophobia - money
Claustrophobia - enclosed space
Clinophobia - going to bed
Cnidophobia - stings
Cynophobia - dogs

Demonophobia - demons
Dendrophobia - trees
Dipsophobia - drinking
Dysmorphophobia - deformity
Ecclesiaphobia - churches
Eisoptrophobia - mirrors
Electrophobia - electricity
Entomophobia - insects
Ereuthophobia - blushing
Ergasiophobia - surgery
Frigophobia - cold
Gamophobia - marriage
Gatophobia - cats
Genophobia - sex
Gephyrophobia - crossing a bridge
Gymnophobia - nakedness
Gynophobia - women
Haphephobia - touching
Hedonophobia - pleasure
Helminthophobia - worms
Hematophobia - blood
Hippophobia - horses
Hodophobia - travel

Homichlophobia - fog
Hydrophobia - water
Hypnophobia - sleep
Ichthyophobia - fish
Katagelophobia - ridicule
Kenophobia - empty rooms
Maieusiophobia - pregnancy
Maniaphobia - insanity
Meteorophobia - meteors
Monophobia - being alone
Musophobia - mice
Mysophobia - dirt
Mythophobia - making false statements
Necrophobia - corpse
Nosophobia - disease
Nyctophobia - night (& darkness)
Ochlophobia - crowds
Ombrophobia - rain
Ommatophobia - eyes
Oneirophobia - dreams
Ophodiophobia - snakes
Panophobia - everything
Pediophobia - children

Pharmacophobia - drugs
Phasmophobia - ghosts
Phengophobia - daylight
Phobophobia - being afraid
Phonophobia - noise
Pnigerophobia - smothering
Pnigophobia - choking
Pogonophobia - beards
Pyrophobia - fire
Rhabdophobia - being beaten
Scholionophobia - school
Scopophobia - being stared at
Sitophobia - food
Spermophobia - germs
Spheksophobia - wasps
Tachophobia - speed
Taphophobia - being buried alive
Theophobia - god
Tonitrophobia - thunder
Triskaidekaphobia - thirteen
Trypanophobia - injections
Xenophobia - strangers
Zoophobia - animals

COOKING MEASUREMENT CONVERSIONS

Dash	⇨	1/10 teaspoon, or 2-3 drops	Pint	⇨	1/8 gallon
			Quart	⇨	2 pints
Teaspoon	⇨	10 dashes	Quart	⇨	1/4 gallon
Teaspoon	⇨	1/3 tablespoon	Gallon	⇨	4 quarts
Tablespoon	⇨	3 teaspoons	Gallon	⇨	8 pints
Tablespoon	⇨	1/16 cup	Gallon	⇨	1/2 peck
Cup	⇨	16 tablespoons	Peck	⇨	8 quarts
Cup	⇨	1/2 pint	Peck	⇨	2 gallons
Cup	⇨	1/4 quart	Bushel	⇨	4 pecks
Pint	⇨	2 cups	Ounce	⇨	1/16 pound
Pint	⇨	1/2 quart	Pound	⇨	16 ounces

MEASUREMENT CONVERSIONS APPLIED TO FOODS

1 tablespoon lemon juice (squeezed)	⇨	1/3 lemon	1 cup whipping cream	⇨	2 cups whipped cream
1 tablespoon lemon peel (grated)	⇨	1 lemon	1 cup sweetened condensed milk	⇨	4/5 of a 300 ml can
1 tablespoon orange peel (grated)	⇨	1/2 orange	1 cup semisweet chocolate pieces	⇨	6 ounce package
1 tablespoon lime juice (squeezed)	⇨	1/2 lime	1 cup coconut (flaked or shredded)	⇨	3 ounces
1 tablespoon (gelatin) unflavoured	⇨	1 envelope	1 cup orange juice (squeezed)	⇨	2-3 medium oranges
1 ounce cream cheese	⇨	2 tablespoons	1 cup breadcrumbs	⇨	2 ounces, or 1/8 of a 1 pound loaf
1 ounce chocolate (unsweetened)	⇨	1 square	1 cup almonds (shelled)	⇨	12-16 oz. almonds (shelled)
1 pound all-purpose flour	⇨	3 & 1/2 cups	1 cup brazil nuts (shelled)	⇨	10-12 oz. brazil nuts (unshelled)
1 pound cake flour	⇨	4 cups	1 cup filberts (shelled)	⇨	10-12 oz. filberts (unshelled)
1 pound apples	⇨	3 medium apples	1 cup peanuts (shelled)	⇨	6-8 oz. peanuts (unshelled)
1 pound margarine	⇨	2 cups	1 cup pecans (shelled)	⇨	7 oz. pecans (unshelled)
1 pound sour cream	⇨	1 cup	1 cup walnuts (shelled)	⇨	1 cup
1 pound cheese (shredded)	⇨	4 cups	1 cup raisins	⇨	4 cups
1 pound potatoes	⇨	2 & 1/2 cups (diced)	1 cup egg whites	⇨	8-10 large eggs
1 pound cottage cheese	⇨	2 cups	1 cup egg yolks	⇨	12-14 large eggs
1 lb. sugar	⇨	2 & 1/2 cups	1 cup long-grained rice (uncooked)	⇨	3 cups (cooked)
1 lb. brown sugar	⇨	2 & 1/4 cups	1 cups salad oil	⇨	8 ounces
1 lb. tomatoes	⇨	3 medium tomatoes	1 cup corn syrup	⇨	8 ounces
1 cup sliced apples	⇨	1 medium apple	1 cup maple syrup	⇨	8 ounces
1 cup onion (chopped)	⇨	1 large onion			

METRIC CONVERSION CHART

METRIC CONVERSIONS

IMPERIAL to METRIC

If you know the length in	multiply by		to get the length in
inches	X 25.4	=	millimetres
inches	X 2.54	=	centimetres
feet	X 0.3048	=	metres
yards	X 0.9144	=	metres
miles	X 1.6093	=	kilometres
naut. miles	X 1.852	=	kilometres

If you know the area in	multiply by		to get the area in
sq. inches	X 6.4516	=	sq. centimetres
sq. feet	X 0.0929	=	sq. metres
sq. yards	X 0.8361	=	sq. metres
acres	X 0.4047	=	hectares
sq. miles	X 2.5899	=	sq. kilometres

If you know the volume in	multiply by		to get the volume in
cu. inches	X 16.3871	=	cu. centimetres
cubic feet	X 0.0283	=	cubic metres
cubic yards	X 0.7646	=	cubic metres

If you know the capacity in	multiply by		to get the capacity in
teaspoons	X 5	=	millilitres
tablespoons	X 15	=	millilitres
fluid ounces	X 28.4	=	millilitres
cubic inches	X 0.0164	=	litres
cups	X 0.284	=	litres
pints	X 0.5682	=	litres
quarts	X 1.1365	=	litres
gallons	X 4.546	=	litres
pecks	X 9.1	=	litres
bushels	X 36.4	=	litres

If you know the capacity in	multiply by		to get the capacity in
US fl. oz.	X 0.0296	=	litres
US pints	X 0.4732	=	litres
US gallons	X 3.7854	=	litres

If you know the weight in	multiply by		to get the weight in
ounces	X 28.3495	=	grams
pounds	X 0.4536	=	kilograms
tons (long)	X 1.016	=	tonnes
ounces (troy)	X 31.1035	=	grams

METRIC to IMPERIAL

If you know the length in	multiply by		to get the length in
millimetres	X 0.0394	=	inches
centimetres	X 0.3937	=	inches
metres	X 3.2806	=	feet
metres	X 1.094	=	yards
kilometres	X 0.6214	=	miles
kilometres	X 0.54	=	naut. miles

If you know the area in	multiply by		to get the area in
sq. centimetres	X 0.155	=	sq. inches
sq. metres	X 10.764	=	sq. feet
sq. metres	X 1.196	=	sq. yards
hectares	X 2.471	=	acres
sq. kilometres	X 0.386	=	sq. miles

If you know the volume in	multiply by		to get the volume in
cu. centimetres	X 0.061	=	cu. inches
cubic metres	X 35.315	=	cubic feet
cubic metres	X 1.308	=	cubic yards

If you know the capacity in	multiply by		to get the capacity in
millilitres	X .2	=	teaspoons
millilitres	X 0.6667	=	tablespoons
millilitres	X 0.0352	=	fluid ounces
litres	X 60.98	=	cubic inches
litres	X 3.52	=	cups
litres	X 1.76	=	pints
litres	X 0.88	=	quarts
litres	X 0.22	=	gallons
litres	X 0.1099	=	pecks
litres	X 0.0282	=	bushels

If you know the capacity in	multiply by		to get the capacity in
litres	X 33.8150	=	US fl. oz.
litres	X 2.1134	=	US pints
litres	X 0.2642	=	US gallons

If you know the weight in	multiply by		to get the weight in
grams	X 0.0353	=	ounces
kilograms	X 2.2046	=	pounds
tonnes	X 0.9842	=	tons (long)
grams	X 0.0322	=	ounces (troy)

Celsius - Fahrenheit Conversion

If you know the temperature in Fahrenheit, subtract 32 from that number, then multiply the answer by 5, and finally divide that answer by 9 to get the temperature in Celsius.

If you know the temperature in Celsius, multiply that number by 9, then divide the answer by 5, and finally add 32 to get the temperature in Fahrenheit.

$$°F - 32 \times 5 \div 9 = °C \qquad\qquad °C \times 9 \div 5 + 32 = °F$$

Two-Handed Finger Spelling For the Deaf

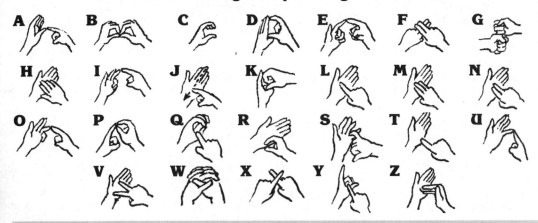

MULTIPLICATION TABLES

X	2	3	4	5	6	7	8	9	10	11	12	13	14	15	16	17	18	19	20	21	22	23	24	25
2	4	6	8	10	12	14	16	18	20	22	24	26	28	30	32	34	36	38	40	42	44	46	48	50
3	6	9	12	15	18	21	24	27	30	33	36	39	42	45	48	51	54	57	60	63	66	69	72	75
4	8	12	16	20	24	28	32	36	40	44	48	52	56	60	64	68	72	76	80	84	88	92	96	100
5	10	15	20	25	30	37	40	45	50	55	60	65	70	75	80	85	90	95	100	105	110	115	120	125
6	12	18	24	30	36	42	48	54	60	66	72	78	84	90	96	102	108	114	120	126	132	138	144	150
7	14	21	28	35	42	49	56	63	70	77	84	91	98	105	112	119	126	133	140	147	154	161	168	175
8	16	24	32	40	48	56	64	72	80	88	96	104	112	120	128	136	144	152	160	168	176	184	192	200
9	18	27	36	45	54	63	72	81	90	99	108	117	126	135	144	153	162	171	180	189	198	207	216	225
10	20	30	40	50	60	70	80	90	100	110	120	130	140	150	160	170	180	190	200	210	220	230	240	250
11	22	33	44	55	66	77	88	99	110	121	132	143	154	165	176	187	198	209	220	231	242	253	264	275
12	24	36	48	60	72	84	96	108	120	132	144	156	168	180	192	204	216	228	240	252	264	276	288	300
13	26	39	52	65	78	91	104	117	130	143	156	169	182	195	208	221	234	247	260	273	286	299	312	325
14	28	42	56	70	84	98	112	126	140	154	168	182	196	210	224	238	252	266	280	294	308	322	336	350
15	30	45	60	75	90	105	120	135	150	165	180	195	210	225	240	255	270	285	300	315	330	345	360	375
16	32	48	64	80	96	112	128	144	160	176	192	208	224	240	256	272	288	304	320	336	352	368	384	400
17	34	51	68	85	102	119	136	153	170	187	204	221	238	255	272	289	306	323	340	357	374	391	408	425
18	36	54	72	90	108	126	144	162	180	198	216	234	252	270	288	306	324	342	360	378	396	414	432	450
19	38	57	76	95	114	133	152	171	190	209	228	247	266	285	304	323	342	361	380	399	418	437	456	475
20	40	60	80	100	120	140	160	180	200	220	240	260	280	300	320	340	360	380	400	420	440	460	480	500
21	42	63	84	105	126	147	168	189	210	231	252	273	294	315	336	357	378	399	420	441	462	483	504	525
22	44	66	88	110	132	154	176	198	220	242	264	286	308	330	352	374	396	418	440	462	484	506	528	550
23	46	69	92	115	138	161	184	207	230	253	276	299	322	345	368	391	414	437	460	483	506	529	552	575
24	48	72	96	120	144	168	192	216	240	264	288	312	336	360	384	408	432	456	480	501	528	552	576	600
25	50	75	100	125	150	175	200	225	250	275	300	325	350	375	400	425	450	475	500	525	550	575	600	625

MULTIPLICATION

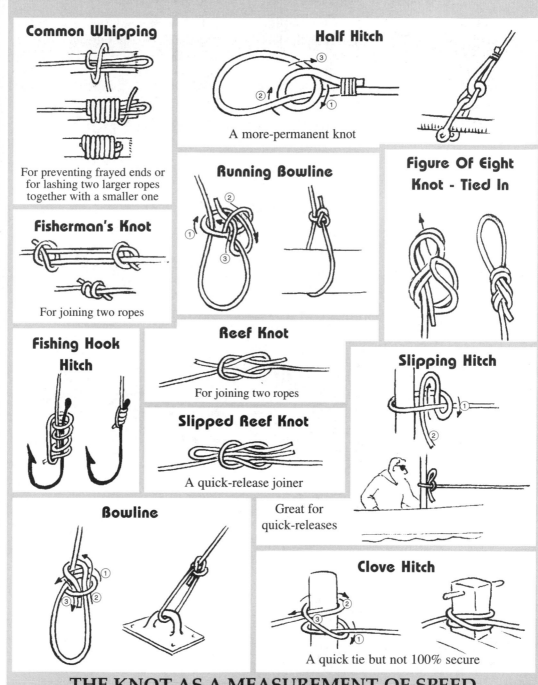

Common Whipping

For preventing frayed ends or for lashing two larger ropes together with a smaller one

Fisherman's Knot

For joining two ropes

Fishing Hook Hitch

Bowline

Half Hitch

A more-permanent knot

Running Bowline

Reef Knot

For joining two ropes

Slipped Reef Knot

A quick-release joiner

Great for quick-releases

Figure Of Eight Knot - Tied In

Slipping Hitch

Clove Hitch

A quick tie but not 100% secure

THE KNOT AS A MEASUREMENT OF SPEED

1 knot = 1 nautical mile per hour = 1.15 miles per hour = 1.852 kilometres per hour
1 kilometre per hour = 0.6213 miles per hour = 0.54 knots
1 mile per hour = 0.8689 knots = 1.6093 kilometres per hour

250 Year Calendar
For the years 1801 through 2050

Match the letter beside the year you require with one of the following 14 Calendars

1801 I	1826 A	1851 G	1876 N	1901 E	1926 K	1951 C	1976 J	2001 C	2026 I
1802 K	1827 C	1852 J	1877 C	1902 G	1927 M	1952 F	1977 M	2002 E	2027 K
1803 M	1828 F	1853 M	1878 E	1903 I	1928 B	1953 I	1978 A	2003 G	2028 N
1804 B	1829 I	1854 A	1879 G	1904 L	1929 E	1954 K	1979 C	2004 J	2029 C
1805 E	1830 K	1855 C	1880 J	1905 A	1930 G	1955 M	1980 F	2005 M	2030 E
1806 G	1831 M	1856 F	1881 M	1906 C	1931 I	1956 B	1981 I	2006 A	2031 G
1807 I	1832 B	1857 I	1882 A	1907 E	1932 L	1957 E	1982 K	2007 C	2032 J
1808 L	1833 E	1858 K	1883 C	1908 H	1933 A	1958 G	1983 M	2008 F	2033 M
1809 A	1834 G	1859 M	1884 F	1909 K	1934 C	1959 I	1984 B	2009 I	2034 A
1810 C	1835 I	1860 B	1885 I	1910 M	1935 E	1960 L	1985 E	2010 K	2035 C
1811 E	1836 L	1861 E	1886 K	1911 A	1936 H	1961 A	1986 G	2011 M	2036 F
1812 H	1837 A	1862 G	1887 M	1912 D	1937 K	1962 G	1987 I	2012 B	2037 I
1813 K	1838 C	1863 I	1888 B	1913 G	1938 M	1963 E	1988 L	2013 E	2038 K
1814 M	1839 E	1864 L	1889 E	1914 I	1939 A	1964 H	1989 A	2014 G	2039 M
1815 A	1840 H	1865 A	1890 G	1915 K	1940 D	1965 K	1990 C	2015 I	2040 B
1816 D	1841 K	1866 C	1891 I	1916 N	1941 G	1966 M	1991 E	2016 L	2041 E
1817 G	1842 M	1867 E	1892 L	1917 C	1942 I	1967 A	1992 H	2017 A	2042 G
1818 I	1843 A	1868 H	1893 A	1918 E	1943 K	1968 D	1993 K	2018 C	2043 I
1819 K	1844 D	1869 K	1894 C	1919 G	1944 N	1969 G	1994 M	2019 E	2044 L
1820 N	1845 G	1870 M	1895 E	1920 J	1945 C	1970 I	1995 A	2020 H	2045 A
1821 C	1846 I	1871 A	1896 H	1921 M	1946 E	1971 K	1996 D	2021 K	2046 C
1822 E	1847 K	1872 D	1897 K	1922 A	1947 G	1972 N	1997 G	2022 M	2047 E
1823 G	1848 N	1873 G	1898 M	1923 C	1948 J	1973 C	1998 I	2023 A	2048 H
1824 J	1849 C	1874 I	1899 A	1924 F	1949 M	1974 E	1999 K	2024 D	2049 K
1825 M	1850 E	1875 K	1900 C	1925 I	1950 A	1975 G	2000 N	2025 G	2050 M

CALENDAR 'A'

JANUARY
```
S  M  T  W  T  F  S
      1  2  3  4  5  6  7
 8  9 10 11 12 13 14
15 16 17 18 19 20 21
22 23 24 25 26 27 28
29 30 31
```

FEBRUARY
```
S  M  T  W  T  F  S
            1  2  3
 5  6  7  8  9 10 11
12 13 14 15 16 17 18
19 20 21 22 23 24 25
26 27 28
```

MARCH
```
S  M  T  W  T  F  S
            1  2  3
 5  6  7  8  9 10 11
12 13 14 15 16 17 18
19 20 21 22 23 24 25
26 27 28 29 30 31
```

APRIL
```
S  M  T  W  T  F  S
                  1
 2  3  4  5  6  7  8
 9 10 11 12 13 14 15
16 17 18 19 20 21 22
23 24 25 26 27 28 29
30
```

MAY
```
S  M  T  W  T  F  S
    1  2  3  4  5  6
 7  8  9 10 11 12 13
14 15 16 17 18 19 20
21 22 23 24 25 26 27
28 29 30 31
```

JUNE
```
S  M  T  W  T  F  S
             1  2  3
 4  5  6  7  8  9 10
11 12 13 14 15 16 17
18 19 20 21 22 23 24
25 26 27 28 29 30
```

JULY
```
S  M  T  W  T  F  S
                  1
 2  3  4  5  6  7  8
 9 10 11 12 13 14 15
16 17 18 19 20 21 22
23 24 25 26 27 28 29
30 31
```

AUGUST
```
S  M  T  W  T  F  S
       1  2  3  4  5
 6  7  8  9 10 11 12
13 14 15 16 17 18 19
20 21 22 23 24 25 26
27 28 29 30 31
```

SEPTEMBER
```
S  M  T  W  T  F  S
                1  2
 3  4  5  6  7  8  9
10 11 12 13 14 15 16
17 18 19 20 21 22 23
24 25 26 27 28 29 30
```

OCTOBER
```
S  M  T  W  T  F  S
 1  2  3  4  5  6  7
 8  9 10 11 12 13 14
15 16 17 18 19 20 21
22 23 24 25 26 27 28
29 30 31
```

NOVEMBER
```
S  M  T  W  T  F  S
          1  2  3  4
 5  6  7  8  9 10 11
12 13 14 15 16 17 18
19 20 21 22 23 24 25
26 27 28 29 30
```

DECEMBER
```
S  M  T  W  T  F  S
                1  2
 3  4  5  6  7  8  9
10 11 12 13 14 15 16
17 18 19 20 21 22 23
24 25 26 27 28 29 30
31
```

CALENDAR 'B' (Leap Year)

JANUARY
```
S  M  T  W  T  F  S
    1  2  3  4  5  6
 7  8  9 10 11 12 13
14 15 16 17 18 19 20
21 22 23 24 25 26 27
28 29 30 31
```

FEBRUARY
```
S  M  T  W  T  F  S
          1  2  3
 5  6  7  8  9 10 11
12 13 14 15 16 17 18
19 20 21 22 23 24 25
26 27 28 29
```

MARCH
```
S  M  T  W  T  F  S
             1  2  3
 4  5  6  7  8  9 10
11 12 13 14 15 16 17
18 19 20 21 22 23 24
25 26 27 28 29 30 31
```

APRIL
```
S  M  T  W  T  F  S
 1  2  3  4  5  6  7
 8  9 10 11 12 13 14
15 16 17 18 19 20 21
22 23 24 25 26 27 28
29 30
```

MAY
```
S  M  T  W  T  F  S
       1  2  3  4  5
 6  7  8  9 10 11 12
13 14 15 16 17 18 19
20 21 22 23 24 25 26
27 28 29 30 31
```

JUNE
```
S  M  T  W  T  F  S
                1  2
 3  4  5  6  7  8  9
10 11 12 13 14 15 16
17 18 19 20 21 22 23
24 25 26 27 28 29 30
```

JULY
```
S  M  T  W  T  F  S
 1  2  3  4  5  6  7
 8  9 10 11 12 13 14
15 16 17 18 19 20 21
22 23 24 25 26 27 28
29 30 31
```

AUGUST
```
S  M  T  W  T  F  S
          1  2  3  4
 5  6  7  8  9 10 11
12 13 14 15 16 17 18
19 20 21 22 23 24 25
26 27 28 29 30 31
```

SEPTEMBER
```
S  M  T  W  T  F  S
                   1
 2  3  4  5  6  7  8
 9 10 11 12 13 14 15
16 17 18 19 20 21 22
23 24 25 26 27 28 29
30
```

OCTOBER
```
S  M  T  W  T  F  S
    1  2  3  4  5  6
 7  8  9 10 11 12 13
14 15 16 17 18 19 20
21 22 23 24 25 26 27
28 29 30 31
```

NOVEMBER
```
S  M  T  W  T  F  S
             1  2  3
 4  5  6  7  8  9 10
11 12 13 14 15 16 17
18 19 20 21 22 23 24
25 26 27 28 29 30
```

DECEMBER
```
S  M  T  W  T  F  S
                   1
 2  3  4  5  6  7  8
 9 10 11 12 13 14 15
16 17 18 19 20 21 22
23 24 25 26 27 28 29
30 31
```

250 Year Calendar

For the years 1801 through 2050
CROSS REFERRENCE INDEX on page 37

250 YEAR CALENDAR

CALENDAR 'C'

JANUARY

S	M	T	W	T	F	S
		1	2	3	4	5	6
7	8	9	10	11	12	13
14	15	16	17	18	19	20
21	22	23	24	25	26	27
28	29	30	31			

FEBRUARY

S	M	T	W	T	F	S
					1	2	3
4	5	6	7	8	9	10
11	12	13	14	15	16	17
18	19	20	21	22	23	24
25	26	27	28			

MARCH

S	M	T	W	T	F	S
					1	2	3
4	5	6	7	8	9	10
11	12	13	14	15	16	17
18	19	20	21	22	23	24
25	26	27	28	29	30	31

APRIL

S	M	T	W	T	F	S
1	2	3	4	5	6	7
8	9	10	11	12	13	14
15	16	17	18	19	20	21
22	23	24	25	26	27	28
29	30					

MAY

S	M	T	W	T	F	S
		1	2	3	4	5
6	7	8	9	10	11	12
13	14	15	16	17	18	19
20	21	22	23	24	25	26
27	28	29	30	31		

JUNE

S	M	T	W	T	F	S
						1	2
3	4	5	6	7	8	9
10	11	12	13	14	15	16
17	18	19	20	21	22	23
24	25	26	27	28	29	30

JULY

S	M	T	W	T	F	S
1	2	3	4	5	6	7
8	9	10	11	12	13	14
15	16	17	18	19	20	21
22	23	24	25	26	27	28
29	30	31				

AUGUST

S	M	T	W	T	F	S
				1	2	3	4
5	6	7	8	9	10	11
12	13	14	15	16	17	18
19	20	21	22	23	24	25
26	27	28	29	30	31	

SEPTEMBER

S	M	T	W	T	F	S
							1
2	3	4	5	6	7	8
9	10	11	12	13	14	15
16	17	18	19	20	21	22
23	24	25	26	27	28	29
30						

OCTOBER

S	M	T	W	T	F	S
		1	2	3	4	5	6
7	8	9	10	11	12	13
14	15	16	17	18	19	20
21	22	23	24	25	26	27
28	29	30	31			

NOVEMBER

S	M	T	W	T	F	S
					1	2	3
4	5	6	7	8	9	10
11	12	13	14	15	16	17
18	19	20	21	22	23	24
25	26	27	28	29	30	

DECEMBER

S	M	T	W	T	F	S
							1
2	3	4	5	6	7	8
9	10	11	12	13	14	15
16	17	18	19	20	21	22
23	24	25	26	27	28	29
30	31					

CALENDAR 'D' (Leap Year)

JANUARY

S	M	T	W	T	F	S
		1	2	3	4	5	6
7	8	9	10	11	12	13
14	15	16	17	18	19	20
21	22	23	24	25	26	27
28	29	30	31			

FEBRUARY

S	M	T	W	T	F	S
					1	2	3
4	5	6	7	8	9	10
11	12	13	14	15	16	17
18	19	20	21	22	23	24
25	26	27	28	29		

MARCH

S	M	T	W	T	F	S
						1	2
3	4	5	6	7	8	9
10	11	12	13	14	15	16
17	18	19	20	21	22	23
24	25	26	27	28	29	30
31						

APRIL

S	M	T	W	T	F	S
	1	2	3	4	5	6
7	8	9	10	11	12	13
14	15	16	17	18	19	20
21	22	23	24	25	26	27
28	29	30				

MAY

S	M	T	W	T	F	S
			1	2	3	4
5	6	7	8	9	10	11
12	13	14	15	16	17	18
19	20	21	22	23	24	25
26	27	28	29	30	31	

JUNE

S	M	T	W	T	F	S
							1
2	3	4	5	6	7	8
9	10	11	12	13	14	15
16	17	18	19	20	21	22
23	24	25	26	27	28	29
30						

JULY

S	M	T	W	T	F	S
	1	2	3	4	5	6
7	8	9	10	11	12	13
14	15	16	17	18	19	20
21	22	23	24	25	26	27
28	29	30	31			

AUGUST

S	M	T	W	T	F	S
				1	2	3
4	5	6	7	8	9	10
11	12	13	14	15	16	17
18	19	20	21	22	23	24
25	26	27	28	29	30	31

SEPTEMBER

S	M	T	W	T	F	S
1	2	3	4	5	6	7
8	9	10	11	12	13	14
15	16	17	18	19	20	21
22	23	24	25	26	27	28
29	30					

OCTOBER

S	M	T	W	T	F	S
		1	2	3	4	5
6	7	8	9	10	11	12
13	14	15	16	17	18	19
20	21	22	23	24	25	26
27	28	29	30	31		

NOVEMBER

S	M	T	W	T	F	S
					1	2
3	4	5	6	7	8	9
10	11	12	13	14	15	16
17	18	19	20	21	22	23
24	25	26	27	28	29	30

DECEMBER

S	M	T	W	T	F	S
1	2	3	4	5	6	7
8	9	10	11	12	13	14
15	16	17	18	19	20	21
22	23	24	25	26	27	28
29	30	31				

CALENDAR 'E'

JANUARY

S	M	T	W	T	F	S
			1	2	3	4	5
6	7	8	9	10	11	12
13	14	15	16	17	18	19
20	21	22	23	24	25	26
27	28	29	30	31		

FEBRUARY

S	M	T	W	T	F	S
						1	2
3	4	5	6	7	8	9
10	11	12	13	14	15	16
17	18	19	20	21	22	23
24	25	26	27	28		

MARCH

S	M	T	W	T	F	S
						1	2
3	4	5	6	7	8	9
10	11	12	13	14	15	16
17	18	19	20	21	22	23
24	25	26	27	28	29	30
31						

APRIL

S	M	T	W	T	F	S
	1	2	3	4	5	6
7	8	9	10	11	12	13
14	15	16	17	18	19	20
21	22	23	24	25	26	27
28	29	30				

MAY

S	M	T	W	T	F	S
			1	2	3	4
5	6	7	8	9	10	11
12	13	14	15	16	17	18
19	20	21	22	23	24	25
26	27	28	29	30	31	

JUNE

S	M	T	W	T	F	S
							1
2	3	4	5	6	7	8
9	10	11	12	13	14	15
16	17	18	19	20	21	22
23	24	25	26	27	28	29
30						

JULY

S	M	T	W	T	F	S
	1	2	3	4	5	6
7	8	9	10	11	12	13
14	15	16	17	18	19	20
21	22	23	24	25	26	27
28	29	30	31			

AUGUST

S	M	T	W	T	F	S
				1	2	3
4	5	6	7	8	9	10
11	12	13	14	15	16	17
18	19	20	21	22	23	24
25	26	27	28	29	30	31

SEPTEMBER

S	M	T	W	T	F	S
1	2	3	4	5	6	7
8	9	10	11	12	13	14
15	16	17	18	19	20	21
22	23	24	25	26	27	28
29	30					

OCTOBER

S	M	T	W	T	F	S
		1	2	3	4	5
6	7	8	9	10	11	12
13	14	15	16	17	18	19
20	21	22	23	24	25	26
27	28	29	30	31		

NOVEMBER

S	M	T	W	T	F	S
					1	2
3	4	5	6	7	8	9
10	11	12	13	14	15	16
17	18	19	20	21	22	23
24	25	26	27	28	29	30

DECEMBER

S	M	T	W	T	F	S
1	2	3	4	5	6	7
8	9	10	11	12	13	14
15	16	17	18	19	20	21
22	23	24	25	26	27	28
29	30	31				

CALENDAR 'F' (Leap Year)

JANUARY

S	M	T	W	T	F	S
			1	2	3	4	5
6	7	8	9	10	11	12
13	14	15	16	17	18	19
20	21	22	23	24	25	26
27	28	29	30	31		

FEBRUARY

S	M	T	W	T	F	S
						1	2
3	4	5	6	7	8	9
10	11	12	13	14	15	16
17	18	19	20	21	22	23
24	25	26	27	28	29	

MARCH

S	M	T	W	T	F	S
							1
2	3	4	5	6	7	8
9	10	11	12	13	14	15
16	17	18	19	20	21	22
23	24	25	26	27	28	29
30	31					

APRIL

S	M	T	W	T	F	S
		1	2	3	4	5
6	7	8	9	10	11	12
13	14	15	16	17	18	19
20	21	22	23	24	25	26
27	28	29	30			

MAY

S	M	T	W	T	F	S
				1	2	3
4	5	6	7	8	9	10
11	12	13	14	15	16	17
18	19	20	21	22	23	24
25	26	27	28	29	30	31

JUNE

S	M	T	W	T	F	S
1	2	3	4	5	6	7
8	9	10	11	12	13	14
15	16	17	18	19	20	21
22	23	24	25	26	27	28
29	30					

JULY

S	M	T	W	T	F	S
		1	2	3	4	5
6	7	8	9	10	11	12
13	14	15	16	17	18	19
20	21	22	23	24	25	26
27	28	29	30	31		

AUGUST

S	M	T	W	T	F	S
					1	2
3	4	5	6	7	8	9
10	11	12	13	14	15	16
17	18	19	20	21	22	23
24	25	26	27	28	29	30
31						

SEPTEMBER

S	M	T	W	T	F	S
	1	2	3	4	5	6
7	8	9	10	11	12	13
14	15	16	17	18	19	20
21	22	23	24	25	26	27
28	29	30				

OCTOBER

S	M	T	W	T	F	S
			1	2	3	4
5	6	7	8	9	10	11
12	13	14	15	16	17	18
19	20	21	22	23	24	25
26	27	28	29	30	31	

NOVEMBER

S	M	T	W	T	F	S
						1
2	3	4	5	6	7	8
9	10	11	12	13	14	15
16	17	18	19	20	21	22
23	24	25	26	27	28	29
30						

DECEMBER

S	M	T	W	T	F	S
	1	2	3	4	5	6
7	8	9	10	11	12	13
14	15	16	17	18	19	20
21	22	23	24	25	26	27
28	29	30	31			

250 Year Calendar

For the years 1801 through 2050

CROSS REFERRENCE INDEX on page 37

CALENDAR 'G'

JANUARY
S	M	T	W	T	F	S
			1	2	3	4
5	6	7	8	9	10	11
12	13	14	15	16	17	18
19	20	21	22	23	24	25
26	27	28	29	30	31	

FEBRUARY
S	M	T	W	T	F	S
						1
2	3	4	5	6	7	8
9	10	11	12	13	14	15
16	17	18	19	20	21	22
23	24	25	26	27	28	

MARCH
S	M	T	W	T	F	S
						1
2	3	4	5	6	7	8
9	10	11	12	13	14	15
16	17	18	19	20	21	22
23	24	25	26	27	28	29
30	31					

APRIL
S	M	T	W	T	F	S
		1	2	3	4	5
6	7	8	9	10	11	12
13	14	15	16	17	18	19
20	21	22	23	24	25	26
27	28	29	30			

MAY
S	M	T	W	T	F	S
				1	2	3
4	5	6	7	8	9	10
11	12	13	14	15	16	17
18	19	20	21	22	23	24
25	26	27	28	29	30	31

JUNE
S	M	T	W	T	F	S
1	2	3	4	5	6	7
8	9	10	11	12	13	14
15	16	17	18	19	20	21
22	23	24	25	26	27	28
29	30					

JULY
S	M	T	W	T	F	S
		1	2	3	4	5
6	7	8	9	10	11	12
13	14	15	16	17	18	19
20	21	22	23	24	25	26
27	28	29	30	31		

AUGUST
S	M	T	W	T	F	S
					1	2
3	4	5	6	7	8	9
10	11	12	13	14	15	16
17	18	19	20	21	22	23
24	25	26	27	28	29	30
31						

SEPTEMBER
S	M	T	W	T	F	S
	1	2	3	4	5	6
7	8	9	10	11	12	13
14	15	16	17	18	19	20
21	22	23	24	25	26	27
28	29	30				

OCTOBER
S	M	T	W	T	F	S
			1	2	3	4
5	6	7	8	9	10	11
12	13	14	15	16	17	18
19	20	21	22	23	24	25
26	27	28	29	30	31	

NOVEMBER
S	M	T	W	T	F	S
						1
2	3	4	5	6	7	8
9	10	11	12	13	14	15
16	17	18	19	20	21	22
23	24	25	26	27	28	29
30						

DECEMBER
S	M	T	W	T	F	S
	1	2	3	4	5	6
7	8	9	10	11	12	13
14	15	16	17	18	19	20
21	22	23	24	25	26	27
28	29	30	31			

CALENDAR 'H' (Leap Year)

JANUARY
S	M	T	W	T	F	S
			1	2	3	4
5	6	7	8	9	10	11
12	13	14	15	16	17	18
19	20	21	22	23	24	25
26	27	28	29	30	31	

FEBRUARY
S	M	T	W	T	F	S
						1
2	3	4	5	6	7	8
9	10	11	12	13	14	15
16	17	18	19	20	21	22
23	24	25	26	27	28	29

MARCH
S	M	T	W	T	F	S
1	2	3	4	5	6	7
8	9	10	11	12	13	14
15	16	17	18	19	20	21
22	23	24	25	26	27	28
29	30	31				

APRIL
S	M	T	W	T	F	S
			1	2	3	4
5	6	7	8	9	10	11
12	13	14	15	16	17	18
19	20	21	22	23	24	25
26	27	28	29	30		

MAY
S	M	T	W	T	F	S
					1	2
3	4	5	6	7	8	9
10	11	12	13	14	15	16
17	18	19	20	21	22	23
24	25	26	27	28	29	30
31						

JUNE
S	M	T	W	T	F	S
	1	2	3	4	5	6
7	8	9	10	11	12	13
14	15	16	17	18	19	20
21	22	23	24	25	26	27
28	29	30				

JULY
S	M	T	W	T	F	S
			1	2	3	4
5	6	7	8	9	10	11
12	13	14	15	16	17	18
19	20	21	22	23	24	25
26	27	28	29	30	31	

AUGUST
S	M	T	W	T	F	S
						1
2	3	4	5	6	7	8
9	10	11	12	13	14	15
16	17	18	19	20	21	22
23	24	25	26	27	28	29
30	31					

SEPTEMBER
S	M	T	W	T	F	S
		1	2	3	4	5
6	7	8	9	10	11	12
13	14	15	16	17	18	19
20	21	22	23	24	25	26
27	28	29	30			

OCTOBER
S	M	T	W	T	F	S
				1	2	3
4	5	6	7	8	9	10
11	12	13	14	15	16	17
18	19	20	21	22	23	24
25	26	27	28	29	30	31

NOVEMBER
S	M	T	W	T	F	S
1	2	3	4	5	6	7
8	9	10	11	12	13	14
15	16	17	18	19	20	21
22	23	24	25	26	27	28
29	30					

DECEMBER
S	M	T	W	T	F	S
		1	2	3	4	5
6	7	8	9	10	11	12
13	14	15	16	17	18	19
20	21	22	23	24	25	26
27	28	29	30	31		

CALENDAR 'I'

JANUARY
S	M	T	W	T	F	S
				1	2	3
4	5	6	7	8	9	10
11	12	13	14	15	16	17
18	19	20	21	22	23	24
25	26	27	28	29	30	31

FEBRUARY
S	M	T	W	T	F	S
1	2	3	4	5	6	7
8	9	10	11	12	13	14
15	16	17	18	19	20	21
22	23	24	25	26	27	28

MARCH
S	M	T	W	T	F	S
1	2	3	4	5	6	7
8	9	10	11	12	13	14
15	16	17	18	19	20	21
22	23	24	25	26	27	28
29	30	31				

APRIL
S	M	T	W	T	F	S
			1	2	3	4
5	6	7	8	9	10	11
12	13	14	15	16	17	18
19	20	21	22	23	24	25
26	27	28	29	30		

MAY
S	M	T	W	T	F	S
					1	2
3	4	5	6	7	8	9
10	11	12	13	14	15	16
17	18	19	20	21	22	23
24	25	26	27	28	29	30
31						

JUNE
S	M	T	W	T	F	S
	1	2	3	4	5	6
7	8	9	10	11	12	13
14	15	16	17	18	19	20
21	22	23	24	25	26	27
28	29	30				

JULY
S	M	T	W	T	F	S
			1	2	3	4
5	6	7	8	9	10	11
12	13	14	15	16	17	18
19	20	21	22	23	24	25
26	27	28	29	30	31	

AUGUST
S	M	T	W	T	F	S
						1
2	3	4	5	6	7	8
9	10	11	12	13	14	15
16	17	18	19	20	21	22
23	24	25	26	27	28	29
30	31					

SEPTEMBER
S	M	T	W	T	F	S
	1	2	3	4	5	6
7	8	9	10	11	12	13
14	15	16	17	18	19	20
21	22	23	24	25	26	27
28	29	30				

OCTOBER
S	M	T	W	T	F	S
				1	2	3
4	5	6	7	8	9	10
11	12	13	14	15	16	17
18	19	20	21	22	23	24
25	26	27	28	29	30	31

NOVEMBER
S	M	T	W	T	F	S
1	2	3	4	5	6	7
8	9	10	11	12	13	14
15	16	17	18	19	20	21
22	23	24	25	26	27	28
29	30					

DECEMBER
S	M	T	W	T	F	S
		1	2	3	4	5
6	7	8	9	10	11	12
13	14	15	16	17	18	19
20	21	22	23	24	25	26
27	28	29	30	31		

CALENDAR 'J' (Leap Year)

JANUARY
S	M	T	W	T	F	S
				1	2	3
4	5	6	7	8	9	10
11	12	13	14	15	16	17
18	19	20	21	22	23	24
25	26	27	28	29	30	31

FEBRUARY
S	M	T	W	T	F	S
1	2	3	4	5	6	7
8	9	10	11	12	13	14
15	16	17	18	19	20	21
22	23	24	25	26	27	28
29						

MARCH
S	M	T	W	T	F	S
	1	2	3	4	5	6
7	8	9	10	11	12	13
14	15	16	17	18	19	20
21	22	23	24	25	26	27
28	29	30	31			

APRIL
S	M	T	W	T	F	S
				1	2	3
4	5	6	7	8	9	10
11	12	13	14	15	16	17
18	19	20	21	22	23	24
25	26	27	28	29	30	

MAY
S	M	T	W	T	F	S
						1
2	3	4	5	6	7	8
9	10	11	12	13	14	15
16	17	18	19	20	21	22
23	24	25	26	27	28	29
30	31					

JUNE
S	M	T	W	T	F	S
		1	2	3	4	5
6	7	8	9	10	11	12
13	14	15	16	17	18	19
20	21	22	23	24	25	26
27	28	29	30			

JULY
S	M	T	W	T	F	S
				1	2	3
4	5	6	7	8	9	10
11	12	13	14	15	16	17
18	19	20	21	22	23	24
25	26	27	28	29	30	31

AUGUST
S	M	T	W	T	F	S
1	2	3	4	5	6	7
8	9	10	11	12	13	14
15	16	17	18	19	20	21
22	23	24	25	26	27	28
29	30	31				

SEPTEMBER
S	M	T	W	T	F	S
			1	2	3	4
5	6	7	8	9	10	11
12	13	14	15	16	17	18
19	20	21	22	23	24	25
26	27	28	29	30		

OCTOBER
S	M	T	W	T	F	S
					1	2
3	4	5	6	7	8	9
10	11	12	13	14	15	16
17	18	19	20	21	22	23
24	25	26	27	28	29	30
31						

NOVEMBER
S	M	T	W	T	F	S
	1	2	3	4	5	6
7	8	9	10	11	12	13
14	15	16	17	18	19	20
21	22	23	24	25	26	27
28	29	30				

DECEMBER
S	M	T	W	T	F	S
			1	2	3	4
5	6	7	8	9	10	11
12	13	14	15	16	17	18
19	20	21	22	23	24	25
26	27	28	29	30	31	

250 Year Calendar

For the years 1801 through 2050
CROSS REFERRENCE INDEX on page 37

CALENDAR 'K'

```
JANUARY                FEBRUARY               MARCH
S  M  T  W  T  F  S     S  M  T  W  T  F  S     S  M  T  W  T  F  S
            1  2                 1  2  3  4  5  6              1  2  3  4  5  6
 3  4  5  6  7  8  9     7  8  9 10 11 12 13     7  8  9 10 11 12 13
10 11 12 13 14 15 16    14 15 16 17 18 19 20    14 15 16 17 18 19 20
17 18 19 20 21 22 23    21 22 23 24 25 26 27    21 22 23 24 25 26 27
24 25 26 27 28 29 30    28                      28 29 30 31
31

APRIL                  MAY                    JUNE
S  M  T  W  T  F  S     S  M  T  W  T  F  S     S  M  T  W  T  F  S
             1  2  3                       1              1  2  3  4  5
 4  5  6  7  8  9 10     2  3  4  5  6  7  8     6  7  8  9 10 11 12
11 12 13 14 15 16 17     9 10 11 12 13 14 15    13 14 15 16 17 18 19
18 19 20 21 22 23 24    16 17 18 19 20 21 22    20 21 22 23 24 25 26
25 26 27 28 29 30       23 24 25 26 27 28 29    27 28 29 30
                        30 31

JULY                   AUGUST                 SEPTEMBER
S  M  T  W  T  F  S     S  M  T  W  T  F  S     S  M  T  W  T  F  S
             1  2  3     1  2  3  4  5  6  7              1  2  3  4
 4  5  6  7  8  9 10     8  9 10 11 12 13 14     5  6  7  8  9 10 11
11 12 13 14 15 16 17    15 16 17 18 19 20 21    12 13 14 15 16 17 18
18 19 20 21 22 23 24    22 23 24 25 26 27 28    19 20 21 22 23 24 25
25 26 27 28 29 30 31    29 30 31                26 27 28 29 30

OCTOBER                NOVEMBER               DECEMBER
S  M  T  W  T  F  S     S  M  T  W  T  F  S     S  M  T  W  T  F  S
                1  2        1  2  3  4  5  6              1  2  3  4
 3  4  5  6  7  8  9     7  8  9 10 11 12 13     5  6  7  8  9 10 11
10 11 12 13 14 15 16    14 15 16 17 18 19 20    12 13 14 15 16 17 18
17 18 19 20 21 22 23    21 22 23 24 25 26 27    19 20 21 22 23 24 25
24 25 26 27 28 29 30    28 29 30                26 27 28 29 30 31
31
```

CALENDAR 'L' (Leap Year)

```
JANUARY                FEBRUARY               MARCH
S  M  T  W  T  F  S     S  M  T  W  T  F  S     S  M  T  W  T  F  S
                1  2           1  2  3  4  5  6           1  2  3  4  5
 3  4  5  6  7  8  9     7  8  9 10 11 12 13     6  7  8  9 10 11 12
10 11 12 13 14 15 16    14 15 16 17 18 19 20    13 14 15 16 17 18 19
17 18 19 20 21 22 23    21 22 23 24 25 26 27    20 21 22 23 24 25 26
24 25 26 27 28 29 30    28 29                   27 28 29 30 31
31

APRIL                  MAY                    JUNE
S  M  T  W  T  F  S     S  M  T  W  T  F  S     S  M  T  W  T  F  S
                1  2     1  2  3  4  5  6  7              1  2  3  4
 3  4  5  6  7  8  9     8  9 10 11 12 13 14     5  6  7  8  9 10 11
10 11 12 13 14 15 16    15 16 17 18 19 20 21    12 13 14 15 16 17 18
17 18 19 20 21 22 23    22 23 24 25 26 27 28    19 20 21 22 23 24 25
24 25 26 27 28 29 30    29 30 31                26 27 28 29 30

JULY                   AUGUST                 SEPTEMBER
S  M  T  W  T  F  S     S  M  T  W  T  F  S     S  M  T  W  T  F  S
                1  2        1  2  3  4  5  6              1  2  3
 3  4  5  6  7  8  9     7  8  9 10 11 12 13     4  5  6  7  8  9 10
10 11 12 13 14 15 16    14 15 16 17 18 19 20    11 12 13 14 15 16 17
17 18 19 20 21 22 23    21 22 23 24 25 26 27    18 19 20 21 22 23 24
24 25 26 27 28 29 30    28 29 30 31             25 26 27 28 29 30
31

OCTOBER                NOVEMBER               DECEMBER
S  M  T  W  T  F  S     S  M  T  W  T  F  S     S  M  T  W  T  F  S
                   1           1  2  3  4  5              1  2  3
 2  3  4  5  6  7  8     6  7  8  9 10 11 12     4  5  6  7  8  9 10
 9 10 11 12 13 14 15    13 14 15 16 17 18 19    11 12 13 14 15 16 17
16 17 18 19 20 21 22    20 21 22 23 24 25 26    18 19 20 21 22 23 24
23 24 25 26 27 28 29    27 28 29 30             25 26 27 28 29 30 31
30 31
```

CALENDAR 'M'

```
JANUARY                FEBRUARY               MARCH
S  M  T  W  T  F  S     S  M  T  W  T  F  S     S  M  T  W  T  F  S
                   1           1  2  3  4  5              1  2  3  4  5
 2  3  4  5  6  7  8     6  7  8  9 10 11 12     6  7  8  9 10 11 12
 9 10 11 12 13 14 15    13 14 15 16 17 18 19    13 14 15 16 17 18 19
16 17 18 19 20 21 22    20 21 22 23 24 25 26    20 21 22 23 24 25 26
23 24 25 26 27 28 29    27 28                   27 28 29 30 31
30 31

APRIL                  MAY                    JUNE
S  M  T  W  T  F  S     S  M  T  W  T  F  S     S  M  T  W  T  F  S
                1  2     1  2  3  4  5  6  7              1  2  3  4
 3  4  5  6  7  8  9     8  9 10 11 12 13 14     5  6  7  8  9 10 11
10 11 12 13 14 15 16    15 16 17 18 19 20 21    12 13 14 15 16 17 18
17 18 19 20 21 22 23    22 23 24 25 26 27 28    19 20 21 22 23 24 25
24 25 26 27 28 29 30    29 30 31                26 27 28 29 30

JULY                   AUGUST                 SEPTEMBER
S  M  T  W  T  F  S     S  M  T  W  T  F  S     S  M  T  W  T  F  S
                1  2        1  2  3  4  5  6              1  2  3
 3  4  5  6  7  8  9     7  8  9 10 11 12 13     4  5  6  7  8  9 10
10 11 12 13 14 15 16    14 15 16 17 18 19 20    11 12 13 14 15 16 17
17 18 19 20 21 22 23    21 22 23 24 25 26 27    18 19 20 21 22 23 24
24 25 26 27 28 29 30    28 29 30 31             25 26 27 28 29 30
31

OCTOBER                NOVEMBER               DECEMBER
S  M  T  W  T  F  S     S  M  T  W  T  F  S     S  M  T  W  T  F  S
                   1           1  2  3  4  5              1  2  3
 2  3  4  5  6  7  8     6  7  8  9 10 11 12     4  5  6  7  8  9 10
 9 10 11 12 13 14 15    13 14 15 16 17 18 19    11 12 13 14 15 16 17
16 17 18 19 20 21 22    20 21 22 23 24 25 26    18 19 20 21 22 23 24
23 24 25 26 27 28 29    27 28 29 30             25 26 27 28 29 30 31
30 31
```

CALENDAR 'N' (Leap Year)

```
JANUARY                FEBRUARY               MARCH
S  M  T  W  T  F  S     S  M  T  W  T  F  S     S  M  T  W  T  F  S
                   1           1  2  3  4  5              1  2  3  4
 2  3  4  5  6  7  8     6  7  8  9 10 11 12     5  6  7  8  9 10 11
 9 10 11 12 13 14 15    13 14 15 16 17 18 19    12 13 14 15 16 17 18
16 17 18 19 20 21 22    20 21 22 23 24 25 26    19 20 21 22 23 24 25
23 24 25 26 27 28 29    27 28 29                26 27 28 29 30 31
30 31

APRIL                  MAY                    JUNE
S  M  T  W  T  F  S     S  M  T  W  T  F  S     S  M  T  W  T  F  S
                1       1  2  3  4  5  6                  1  2  3
 2  3  4  5  6  7  8     7  8  9 10 11 12 13     4  5  6  7  8  9 10
 9 10 11 12 13 14 15    14 15 16 17 18 19 20    11 12 13 14 15 16 17
16 17 18 19 20 21 22    21 22 23 24 25 26 27    18 19 20 21 22 23 24
23 24 25 26 27 28 29    28 29 30 31             25 26 27 28 29 30
30

JULY                   AUGUST                 SEPTEMBER
S  M  T  W  T  F  S     S  M  T  W  T  F  S     S  M  T  W  T  F  S
                   1           1  2  3  4  5              1  2
 2  3  4  5  6  7  8     6  7  8  9 10 11 12     3  4  5  6  7  8  9
 9 10 11 12 13 14 15    13 14 15 16 17 18 19    10 11 12 13 14 15 16
16 17 18 19 20 21 22    20 21 22 23 24 25 26    17 18 19 20 21 22 23
23 24 25 26 27 28 29    27 28 29 30 31          24 25 26 27 28 29 30
30 31

OCTOBER                NOVEMBER               DECEMBER
S  M  T  W  T  F  S     S  M  T  W  T  F  S     S  M  T  W  T  F  S
 1  2  3  4  5  6  7           1  2  3  4                 1  2
 8  9 10 11 12 13 14     5  6  7  8  9 10 11     3  4  5  6  7  8  9
15 16 17 18 19 20 21    12 13 14 15 16 17 18    10 11 12 13 14 15 16
22 23 24 25 26 27 28    19 20 21 22 23 24 25    17 18 19 20 21 22 23
29 30 31                26 27 28 29 30          24 25 26 27 28 29 30
                                                31
```

Tonic For The Soul

Thoughts To Live By

Stories

Poems

Folklore

Humour

Superstitions

& Other Interesting Items

Tonic For The Soul

A KITCHEN PRAYER

In my warm and friendly kitchen
At the close of a busy day
I'm hoping that in all I did
I found the "better" way . . .

Did I work with love and patience
And add a heartfelt wish
For the comfort of my family
To each and every dish?

Did I season with affection . . .
Did I stir with extra care
And offer those I love so well
The first and choisest share?

Well I hope I did a few things well
And that the coming days
Will keep bringing me new chances
To give joy in little ways!

Author unknown

* * *

RECIPE FOR A HAPPY HOME

Preheat home to the both degree: 1 carefully selected woman and 1 carefully selected man.

To the man add the abilities to be a good provider, and give affection. Stir in stability, strength, decisiveness and leadership. Boil until all traces of condescension evaporate.

To the woman, add the abilities to be a good homemaker and give encouragement. Stir in loyalty, tenderness and creativity. Boil until all traces of nagging evaporate.

Grease immediately with maturity, flour with common sense. Add heaping amounts of respect and honesty. Constantly add kindness and understanding. Drain off apartness, but retain individuality.

Whip in sense of humour, grind in patience mixed with insight. Stir in ability to sacrifice. Soften with trust. Cut out all traces of selfishness. For added richness, blend in plans and dreams, and work them out together.

Season with children.

Author unknown

SKIPPER SAYS:

"The main cause of indigestion is trying to fit a square meal into a round stomach!"

* * *

MOTHER'S SECRET

Mother had a secret
And we knew it for a fact
'Cause when we'd ask for apple pie
How funny she would act . . .

She'd let us watch her make the crust
And then she'd chase us out,
And her laugh would make us wonder
What the joke was all about

Then mother told her secret
And believe it if you can
Her 'apples' were really crackers
Boiled in water in a pan!

Now if you've gotten curious
And the whole secret like to know
Mother's secret recipe
Is on this page, below

Elizabeth M. Gerus

MOCK APPLE PIE

Ingredients For Filling:
2 cups water
1 & 1/2 cups white sugar
2 teaspoons cream of tartar
20 Ritz crackers (or similar)

Ingredients For Crumb Crust:
3/4 cup brown flour
1/2 stick soft butter
2 tablespoons flour

Directions:
Boil water, white sugar and cream of tartar for 2 minutes, then pop in crackers. Boil another 2 minutes without stirring. Put filling in a baked pie shell. Blend the crumb crust ingredients with a fork, spread over pie, then serve.
NOTE: The finished product tastes just like apple pie.

* * *

SUPERSTITIONS:
 Eating a mixture of snails dissolved in salt, and inhaling the fumes of cow dung, were once thought to be cures for tuberculosis.

Submitted by Stan Baldwin, Stephenville, Nfld

* * *

THE LITTLE GIRL WHO LAUGHED

by Loreen Haldenby-Adams

The school house which I attended in George's Brook was once a church. The paint had pealed off its weather beaten frame and it was of no describable colour that I can remember, although a little bit of yellowish green sticks in my mind. There was a little entrance porch at the front. This was nearly always filled with wood cut into short lengths to be burned in the pot-bellied stove which sat in the school house.

In the winter time, this pot-bellied stove glowed red with delight as we piled the hearth with our frozen mittens. On the top of the stove a friendly old iron kettle boiled merrily, for we were supplied with cocomalt by the Commission of Government in the 1930s. A teaspoon of cocomalt mixed with boiling water at eleven o'clock every morning supplied us with much needed nourishment.

Two long rows of desks sat on either side of the school house. They were painted a dark brown. A little hollow was carved out in each desk, and here we poured a little water every day for cleaning our slates with a slate rag. We used slate pencils for writing and when our slates were full on both sides, we cleaned them vigorously with the slate rags, using the water and a small bit of borax soap brought from home.

One side of the school house was the boys' side. The boys looked out the tall church windows at the school pond where we skated in winter and at the shabby, decrepit old outhouse divided by a partition to separate the boys from the girls.

We, on the girls' side, looked out the tall church windows too, but we saw the clear waters of Random Sound, blue and untroubled, and filled with dreams.

Sitting against the walls were old church pews, shabby, the varnish peeling, hinting of fallen glory. In winter, they were piled with coats, caps and scarves.

The teacher's desk sat on a low platform. Behind her was the blackboard which covered the whole wall. To her left was a pump organ, to her right, a book-case which contained treasures of books. The Anne books by L.M. Montgomery. Books by Gene Stratton-Porter, Harold Bell Wright, Ralph Connors, Joseph Hocking. Writers that are long forgotten, but all through my childhood, I read them again and again and again.

Our teacher, Miss Lodge, was a brisk, efficient, no-nonsense young lady, but I knew from the very first day I saw her that underneath all that brusqueness lay a heart of pure gold.

Today, she is teaching us a lesson in history. She holds a pointer in her hand and points to our tiny little island on the map of the world.

"See," she says, "we are one of the pink spots. That means we belong to England". "Doesn't that make you proud?" she asks.

"Yes, Miss Lodge," we chorus in unison.

"Not only that," she adds, "we are England's oldest colony. We were a pink spot before India, before Australia." She moves her pointer to the far side of the map.

We look at each other in awe. Imagine that! We are England's oldest colony. We were claimed for England way back in 1497 when John Cabot discovered us.

We knew all about England. We knew where to find it on the map of the world. We knew that across the English Channel lay France and the continent of Europe.

We knew all about the kings of England, the uprising of Oliver Cromwell, the Industrial Revolution, but we knew nothing about the rest of the North American continent. We had heard of Montreal and Halifax, but we had no idea where they were. We said they were up-along. Sometimes, we heard of Boston and Philadelphia. We knew those places were a long distance. We thought they were even further away than up-along.

We were taught a lot about the heathen in in far-away lands. A little white mission box sat on the teacher's desk. We were asked to put any pennies that we could spare into the box to help the missions. Pennies were hard to come by. The box was always almost empty.

Every morning we have devotions. Often we sing about the heathen in far away lands while Miss Lodge plays the organ.

> Once again, dear Lord, we pray
> For Thy children, far away.
> Who have never even heard
> Name of Jesus, sweetest word.

Kathleen, my cousin, stands beside me as we sing. Kathleen, the irrepressible, Kathleen of the dancing black eyes. She, puts her mouth close to my ear and sings words for me alone:

> Once again, dear Lord we pray
> For Miss Lodge to GO AWAY
> If she would come back again
> Wouldn't that be a great big sin?

My face turns brick red. Then, unable to control myself, I burst forth into peals of laughter. Miss Lodge stops playing. The children stop singing. Miss Lodge pivots around on the organ stool. She speaks in a terrible voice.

"Who," she demands, "who dares laugh out loud in the middle of devotions?"

I raise my hand shame-facedly. "That would be me, Miss Lodge," I say almost in a whisper.

"You," she says, her eyes glinting with irritation, "I might have known. To the corner with you and take your slate and arithmetic book with you. Do some borrow-and-pay-back subtraction sums."

I hang my head and walk to the corner beside the book-case.

The singing resumes. I work on my subtraction sums. "Nine from nought, you cannot;' I whisper to myself, but I am trembling with shame. I cannot concentrate. Tears wipe away the numbers on my slate.

Kathleen, in her wild wicked innocence, is always making me laugh and I am in the corner almost every second day.

Kathleen raises her hand to ask permission to leave the room. Miss Lodge is very busy. She has about thirty charges from primer to grade eleven and Kathleen cannot get her attention. She makes loud throat-clearing noises. She puts one of her red soled toe rubbers on her hand. Then she puts both hands in the air with a wildly flapping toe rubber on each one. My laughter peals out, drowning all other sounds. Kathleen finally gets Miss Lodge 's attention, but by this time, the toe rubbers are nowhere to be seen. Kathleen is meekly sitting with one hand upraised and I am the one sent to the corner again.

I never snitched on you Kathleen. Never once. I'm so glad I didn't. You were gone on your fifteenth birthday. Taken away by that terrible plague of tuberculosis that invaded our community in the 30's. You were gone and I was left with memories.

Over fifty years had passed before I again saw Miss Lodge. While visiting my birth-place, I called on a cousin one day, and there, sitting at the kitchen table playing scrabble, was Miss Lodge.

We chatted for awhile, and then before I left, I said, "Miss Lodge, do you remember when I was a little girl? I used to laugh out loud in school and I was always up in the corner."

She smiled a little. "Yes," she said, "I think I do remember that."

I said, "there's something I must tell you. One day I was up in the corner and when you rang the bell for dinner I was sobbing and crying so much I decided to stay up there until all the others had left. You came and took me in your arms and hugged me. I have never forgotten that."

Was that a tear I saw? "Thank you for telling me that," said Miss Lodge.

When I look in the mirror now, my mother's face looks back at me. A face lined with age and wrinkles that no amount of Retinal-A can erase. "Mercy me," I exclaim in dismay, "Oh, mercy, mercy me!" But then in a flash, in a split second, I see the ghost of a little girl. A little girl in the old school in George's Brook who could not keep from laughing.

* * *

The Lighter Side

A young man working in the fruit and vegetable department of a big grocery store was asked by a customer the price of half a head of lettuce. The employee replied that he didn't know and would have to ask the store manager. He left the man, and walking up to the manager, who was some distance away, said, "Some idiot wants to buy a half a head of lettuce!" He then turned and saw that the man had followed him, and had obviously overheard the remark he made, so he quickly added, "and this gentleman would like to buy the other half."

When the customer left, the manager remarked to the employee on how tactful and diplomatic he had been in making the best of a bad situation. "You should be a store manager," he said to the young man, "as a matter of fact, we have a new store opening in Sudbury. I could see to it that you got the position."

"No thanks," replied the store clerk, "I don't want to go to Sudbury. Only whores and hockey players come from Sudbury!"

"My wife comes from Sudbury," said the store manager.

"Is that right," said the clerk, "and which team does she play for?"

* * *

Notable Quotables! by Ron Young

Meanings and origins of well-known expressions

"Rule of thumb"

MEANING: A rough measure.

ORIGIN: One theory for the origin of the expression is that the thumb is used in place of a measuring device sometimes to get a rough measurement. Another popular theory is that it derived from an old English law which made it illegal for a man to beat his wife with anything wider than his thumb.

* * *

FOLK REMEDIES - Boils

Soak 1/2 a slice of bread in boiling water. Scrape off a few flakes of Sunlight soap and mix with bread. Squeeze out excess water and place on a cloth. Put this poultice on the boil and leave overnight to draw out the infection.

Submitted by Trudy S. Simmons, Twillingate, Nfld, (nee Forward, Tizzard's Harbour, Nfld)

BULLETIN BOARD

LOST
Husband and Cat
Reward for Cat

Tamarack Lumber Company
"Come see come saw!"

Tonic For The Soul

SUPERSTITIONS

When leaving the stagehead in the morning, a fisherman would always turn the bow of the boat with the sun, never against it, as this would certainly bring bad luck.

Submitted by John M. Earle, Lewisporte, Nfld

* * *

IS THAT A FACT? *by* Ron Young

Many things have been accepted as facts - not all of them are.

Does more education bring more income?

We have all held the belief that the better our education the better chance we had of earning a higher income. This information has been passed on to children by parents and to everybody by education systems for years.

The fact is (according to a three year study by a Harvard research team) education is only weakly related to earnings of North Americans. Other factors such as: heredity, family and home background, IQ, and quality of schools attended, have a bearing on only 25% of the population. The factors which affect the remaining 75% are personality, natural ability, and luck.

So if you don't have personality or natural ability, spend your education money in a school that develops either or both, and "Good Luck".

You say you think you're a refrigerator - and that doesn't bother you - so why are you here?

Wiff and the Shrink

My wife made me come. I sleep with my mouth open and the light keeps her awake.

SKIPPER SAYS:
"A lot of the titles they got on the front of modern art would make more sense if they were on the back - and said, "This Side Up!"

* * *

ROCK ME TO SLEEP

Backward, turn backward,
    O time in your flight,
Make me a child again
    just for tonight!
Mother come back
        from the echoless shore,
Take me again to your heart as of yore;
Kiss from my forehead the furrows of care,
Smooth the few silver threads out of my hair;
Over my slumbers your loving watch keep; -
Rock me to sleep, mother - rock me to sleep!

Backward, flow backward, O tide of the years!
    I am so weary of toil and of tears, -
Toil without recompense, tears all in vain, -
Take them and give me my childhood again!
I have grown weary of dust and decay, -
Weary of flinging my soul-wealth away;
Weary of sowing for others to reap; -
Rock me to sleep, mother - rock me to sleep!

Tired of the hollow, the base, the untrue,
Mother, O mother, my heart calls for you!
Many a summer the grass has grown green,
Blossomed, and faded our faces between,
Yet with strong yearning and passionate pain
Long I tonight for your presence again.
Come from the silence so long and so deep; -

Tonic For The Soul

Rock me to sleep, mother - rock me to sleep!
Over my heart in the days that are flown,
No love like mother-love ever has shone;
No other worship abides and endures, -
Faithful, unselfish, and patient like yours;
None like a mother can charm away pain
From the sick soul and the world-weary brain.
Slumber's soft calms o'er my heavy lids creep; -
Rock me to sleep, mother - rock me to sleep!

Come, let your brown hair, just lighted with gold,
Fall on your shoulders again as of old;
Let it drop over my forehead tonight,
Shading my faint eyes away from the light;
For with its sunny-edged shadows once more
Haply will throng the sweet visions of yore;
Lovingly, softly, its bright billows sweep; -
Rock me to sleep, mother - rock me to sleep!

Mother, dear mother, the years have been long
Since I last listened your lullaby song:
Sing, then, and unto my soul it shall seem
These years you are gone are only a dream,
Clasped to your heart in a loving embrace,
With your light lashes just sweeping my face,
Never hereafter to wake or to weep; -
Rock me to sleep, mother - rock me to sleep!

Florence Percy

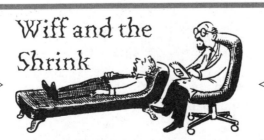

Wiff and the Shrink

I don't know what to do Doctor. I keep thinking I'm a deck of cards.

Could you please wait outside, sir - I'll deal with you later.

SKIPPER SAYS:

"The people who have the biggest problem
understanding how fast light travels are the
ones who think it comes too early in the morning!"

* * *

Notable Quotables! by Ron Young

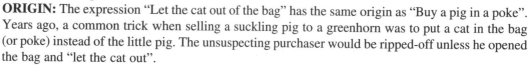

Meanings and origins of well-known expressions

"Let the cat out of the bag"

MEANING: Expose a secret.

ORIGIN: The expression "Let the cat out of the bag" has the same origin as "Buy a pig in a poke". Years ago, a common trick when selling a suckling pig to a greenhorn was to put a cat in the bag (or poke) instead of the little pig. The unsuspecting purchaser would be ripped-off unless he opened the bag and "let the cat out".

* * *

It Never Comes Again

There are gains for all our losses,
There are balms for all our pain,
But when youth, the dream, departs,
It takes something from our hearts,
And will never come again.

We are stronger, and are better,
Under manhood's sterner reign;
Still we feel that something sweet
Followed youth, with flying feet,
And will never come again.

Something beautiful is vanished,
And we sigh for it in vain;
We behold it everywhere,
On the earth, and in the air,
But it never comes again.

Richard Henry Stoddard

* * *

RECIPE RIDDLE

Flour of England. Fruit of Spain - Mixed together in a shower of rain
Put in a bag and tied with a string? - Answer this riddle and I'll give you a ring.

ANS: A Pudding   *Submitted by Gordon LeRoux, Labrador City, Lab*

* * *

Tonic For The Soul

WEATHER LORE

Bright Northern Lights above the hill
A fine day, then a storm foretell

When gulls fly high over sea or land
Stormy weather is close at hand

Mackeral sky and mare's tails
Make the sailor furl his sails

Submitted by Alma Taylor (nee LeDrew, Bell Island), Mount Moriah, Nfld

* * *

The Lighter Side

A lady in a sport car went speeding by the parked police officer, who immediately took chase. The officer had difficulty gaining on the speeding auto, and when he got close enough to activate his lights and siren, the fleeting car turned into a service station and stopped. A woman jumped out and immediately ran into the ladies' washroom as he pulled up.

After about ten minutes she emerged from the facilities, walked briskly up to the impatiently waiting police officer and said, "I bet you thought I wasn't going to make it, didn't you officer?"

* * *

IS THAT A FACT? *by RON YOUNG*

Many things have been accepted as facts - not all of them are.

Is Rome the world's oldest city?

Rome, the eternal city, as everyone knows, is the world's oldest city.

The fact is that Rome is over 2,700 years old, being founded around 753 B.C. A lesser known fact is that Damascus, Syria probably pre-dates Rome as a continually occupied city by a full 20 centuries. It was there before the time of Abraham. Readers of the Bible may verify this by reading Genesis 14:15, 15:2.

Doctor, I have a bad problem. Sometimes I think I'm a tepee and sometimes I think I'm a wigwam.

Wiff and the Shrink

That's your problem - you're two tents!

FOR ALL THOSE BORN BEFORE 1939
We Are Survivors

Consider the changes we have witnessed: We were born before television, before penicillin, before polio shots, frozen foods, Xerox, plastic, contact lenses, frisbies and the PILL.

We were before radar, credit cards, split atoms, laser beams, and ballpoint pens; before panty hose, dishwashers, clothes dryers, electric blankets, air conditioners, drip-dry clothes - and before man walked on the moon.

We got married first and then lived together. How quaint can you be? In our time closets were for clothes, not for "coming out of". Bunnies were small rabbits and rabbits were not Volkswagons. Designer jeans were scheming girls named Jean or Jeanne, and having a meaningful relationship meant getting along with our cousins.

We were before house-husbands, gay rights, computer dating, dual careers and computer marriages. We were before day-care centres, group therapy and nursing homes. We never heard of FM radio, tape decks, electric typewriters, artificial hearts, word processors, yogurt, and guys wearing earrings. For us, time-sharing meant togetherness - not computers or condominiums. A "chip" meant a piece of wood; hardware meant hardware, and software wasn't even a word. In 1940, "Made In Japan" meant junk, and the term "making out" referred to how you did on your exam. Pizzas, MacDonalds and instant coffee were unheard of.

We hit the scene when there were 5 and 10 cent stores where you bought things for five and ten cents. For one nickle you could ride a streetcar, make a phone call, buy a Pepsi or enough stamps to mail one letter and two postcards. You could buy a new Chevy Coupe for $600, but who could afford one? A pity too, because gas was 11¢ a gallon.

In our day, cigarette smoking was fashionable, GRASS was mowed, COKE was a cold drink, and POT was something you cooked in. ROCK MUSIC was grandma's lullaby and AIDS were helpers in the principal's office. We were certainly not before the difference between the sexes was discovered, but we were surely before the sex change; we made do with what we had. And we were the last generation so dumb as to think you needed a husband to have a baby.

No wonder we are so confused and there is such a generation gap today!

BUT WE SURVIVED!!!
WHAT BETTER REASON TO CELEBRATE?

Submitted by Sylvia Ettenson, North York, Ont.

* * *

SKIPPER SAYS:
"If it wasn't for marriage, men and
women would have to fight
with total strangers!"

Lines from Omar Khayyam

by Edward Fitzgerald

The Moving Finger writes; and, having writ,
Moves on: nor all thy Piety nor Wit
Shall lure it back to cancel half a Line,
Nor all thy Tears wash out a Word of it.

* * *

THE RICH MAN

The Rich man has his Jaguar
His country home, his town estate
He smokes a Cuban-rolled cigar
And jeers at fate

He doesn't have to work all day
And penny-pinch to make ends meet
Instead a round of golf he'll play
He finds life sweet

Yet, though my outlook may be dim
Though I must toil for livlihood
Think you that I would trade with him?
You bet I would!

Original version by F. P. Adams

* * *

IS THAT A FACT? *by Ron Young*

Many things have been accepted as facts - not all of them are.

Is fasting good for you?

Fasting is not only good for the soul, but is also healthy and good for the body, many people believe. There is a common belief that doing without food actually purifies and cleanses the body's system.

The fact is going without food and water for a long period of time is quite harmful, even to a very healthy person. Fasting causes a general weakening of the entire body, this in turn makes the body more susceptible to disease which could bring about death long before death by starvation occurs.

Wiff and the Shrink

You say that your problem is that you think you're a goat. How long have you had this problem?

Ever since I was a kid.

SKIPPER SAYS:

"You can stay young if you rest, eat right and exercise, but most people stay young by tellin' lies about their age!"

* * *

The Heart Of The Matter

by Ed Smith

I have solved the cholesterol problem.

For all who suffer from the insidious and chronic problem of high cholesterol, this must be welcome news. It's very immediate news too, because it happened this very day. While other diseases take millions of dollars and years of research to conquer, I have resolved this problem in one fell swoop.

Gee, Smitty, you exclaim, that's wonderful. Would you mind sharing with us exactly how you do it? Certainly not.

I ignore it.

Like all great ideas, of course, this one was not born without having been previously conceived, and gone through a period of gestation. I'm not sure of the exact moment of conception, but it was probably the night I had dinner sitting next to my doctor.

Understand that this is the same physician who diagnosed the condition in the first place, and put me on a strict diet and exercise plan. He even enlisted Other Half's help in keeping me on the straight and narrow.

Some of you will know what's involved in treading that particular straight and narrow. It's considerably worse than trying to stay on the path that leads to everlasting life, I can assure you, although I haven't had much luck with that one, either. In the cholesterol diet, everything that is edible and delicious, Margaret Atwood notwithstanding, is banned.

Actually, that isn't what they said. I could still enjoy my favourite foods, they said, by simply avoiding one or two of the ingredients. Fish and brewis? Sure, but don't add porkfat and scrunchions. Jiggs dinner? Certainly, if you don't eat the salt beef, peas pudding or lumps of fatback. Ever tried eating that stuff that way? It's like trying to kiss a girl with no lips.

Forget eggs, bacon and baloney completely. Confine yourself to skimmed milk. No cream or ice cream and no desserts. And all this, I hasten to add, is just for starters.

But I tried, people. Lord, how I tried. Got my weight down to a slim one hundred and eighty-five, and the cholesterol showed signs that it might at least be thinking about dropping a bit at some future date, if I kept at it. And I did. Suffered like a dog, but I avoided most of the things worth living for and ignored the rest.

Then came this dinner. The occasion doesn't matter, but the menu does. Jiggs dinner, with all the trimmings. This, I thought to myself as I stared longingly at the peas pudding, is what willpower is all about. It didn't help at all that everyone else at the table was tearing into dinner with relish and great abandon while I munched at some dry crackers.

"Good for you," my doctor friend said approvingly through a mouthful of salt beef. "Keep sticking to that diet."

"Easy for you to say," I replied sourly. "You haven't got a cholesterol problem."

"Well," he swallowed a forkful of peas pudding, "actually, I do."

"You do! How come you're eating this stuff?"

"Moderation," he said firmly, reaching for the peaches-and-cream dessert. "Everything in moderation. I watch what I eat most of the time."

Obviously, this wasn't one of those times.

Then the other morning coming back on the ferry from a weekend in Halifax, a whiff of coffee, eggs and bacon awoke me from a cramped sleep in one of those made-in-hell seats. Just ahead of me in the breakfast lineup were two people at least in their eighties, loading their plates with runny eggs, crisp bacon and homefries. It was too much.

What the hell, I said to myself. If they can do it and live that long, so can I. So I piled up my plate with everything fried and greasy in sight, and there, within sight of Channel-Port aux Basques, devoured the works. It had been two years since I'd had a breakfast like that, and it was marvellous. Good for the soul, too. I was by myself, so neither Other Half nor my doctor would ever find out. Sinning can be such fun.

But it was tonight, watching *Here and Now*, that my intention to solve the cholesterol problem by simply ignoring it was fully born. Researchers in Memorial, according to CBC, have recently come up with some amazing facts.

People who eat a hearty breakfast are far less likely to have a heart attack than those who don't eat breakfast at all. That was interesting, but the really great part for me was the discovery that people who eat a breakfast of bacon and eggs do not have significantly higher levels of clotting agents (the culprits in heart attacks) in their blood than those who have the so-called 'healthy' breakfasts of fruits and germs, or whatever it is. Now if that isn't food for thought.

There is no doubt in my mind at all but that those wonderful people at Memorial will soon come up with living proof that scrunchions and peas pudding actually destroy bad cholesterol and are essential aids to a healthy heart. So why lay off Jiggs dinner and hearty breakfasts anymore? Exactly!

Have to go now. Other Half tells me I have to be at the lab early in the morning for a blood test, and she makes it clear she is taking a direct interest in the results.

Ignoring the cholesterol is no problem at all.

Ignoring Other Half is something else again.

* * *

What You Can Buy With The Right Bread

The new 'Missus Power', with her husband did plead
For 'dough' to buy something to wear made of tweed
"Dough," said young Power, "my mom makes with flour!"
Said the wife, "Mister Power, I'll her flour allow her
But the dough that she makes is not something I knead!"

Ron Young

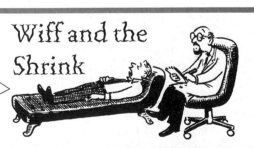

Doctor I told you I like lighting fires, I told you I like looking in people's windows, and I told you I have a compulsion to kill, and you tell me to give up smoking cigarettes before my next visit - What good will that do?

Wiff and the Shrink

It'll save my couch. You've burned three holes in it already!

SKIPPER SAYS:
"The secret to good health is eating onions.
Keeping it a secret is the hard part!"

* * *

FOLK REMEDIES - Sore Eyes
May snow was one time gathered and bottled as a cure for sore eyes.
Submitted by Dolores Lundrigan, Wabush, Lab (nee English, Branch, St. Mary's Bay, Nfld)

* * *

The Value Of A Friend

Oh, the comfort! An inexpressible comfort of feeling safe with a person, having neither to weigh thoughts or measure words, but pouring them all out; just as they are, chaff and grain, certain that a faithful hand will take and sift them, keep what is worth keeping, and with a breath of kindness, blow the rest away!!

* * *

FOLK REMEDIES - Awakening On Time
If you don't own an alarm clock, or don't trust your clock to awaken you in the morning - ask someone who is dead to wake you up and you'll never oversleep again.
Submitted by Addie Holloway, Bloomfield, Nfld

* * *

IS THAT A FACT? *by Ron Young*

Many things have been accepted as facts - not all of them are.
Is eating lobster with milk poisonous?

"Eating lobster and drinking milk at the same time is poisonous to the system and could kill you, as could drinking milk and eating several other kinds of food," is a very popular belief in Canada and the U.S.

The fact is that contrary to this widespread belief, this one falls into the category of 'Old Wives Tales'. Milk and lobster, or milk and anything else combined is not at all harmful. If you can eat two foods separately, you can eat them together. I have washed my lobster down with milk on many occasions and I am still alive, although there are those who will claim this statement is an exaggeration. So if you like cod liver oil on your Brookfield Ice Cream, go ahead. The ice cream may even improve the taste of the cod liver oil, although the cod liver oil won't do much to improve the taste of the ice cream, but it won't kill you. In fact, when you think of it, it's one of the healthiest combinations around today. Healthy or not, I pass.

* * *

Tonic For The Soul

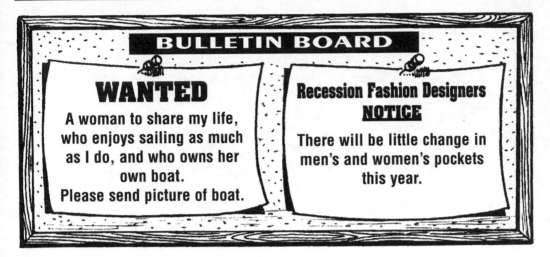

The Lighter Side

A woman bought a little kitten for her young daughter. When she brought the little bundle into the playroom, the girl's eyes lit up in delight. A short time later she heard a scream coming from the playroom and running into the room asked, "What happened?"

"Kitty bit me," replied the little girl, "and it hurt!"

"Oh, poor darling," said the mother, "but kitty is just a baby and she doesn't know that biting hurts."

A short time later the woman heard the shrieking sound of the kitten coming from the playroom.

"What's the matter now?" she shouted as she ran back into the playroom.

The little girl replied, "Now she knows!"

* * *

FOLK REMEDIES - *Cough Drops*
To make cough drops, boil molasses, kerosene oil, Minard's Linament and ginger. Let mixture cool on a plate and cut into candies.
Submitted by Dolores Lundrigan, Wabush, Lab (nee English, Branch, St. Mary's Bay, Nfld)

I know it's crazy Doc, but as much as I try not to, I keep thinking I'm a box of Purity Square Milk Lunch soda biscuits.

Wiff and the Shrink

So we'll just have to do our best to convince you you're not crackers!

Tonic For The Soul

SKIPPER SAYS:

"A man who tries to pull the wool over
his wife's eyes had better choose
the right yarn!"

* * *

Footprints In The Sands Of Time

Rewritten by Ron Young from the original prose 'Footprints'. Author unknown

Across the sky in dream one night
A lone man walked with God
Leaving footprints in the sands of time
Behind them where they trod
Two sets of footprints, clearly left
Behind them in the sand
One set was left behind by God
The other by the man.

Then scenes from his past life
Before the man flashed clear
And at times he only saw
One set of footprints there
And he saw this only happened
When he was hurt and down
When he needed God beside him
Only one set could be found.

"Lord," he said, "you promised
If I would follow thee
That I would never walk alone
That you would walk with me
And I have always followed you
Now I don't understand
When I most needed you there's just
One set of footprints in the sand."

"My precious child," the Lord replied,
"What you now say is true
In life when you had problems
That you could not see through
There is just one set of footprints
Because then, I carried you."

* * *

The Lighter Side

A 72-year-old man met a 21-year-old beauty and after seeing her for some time, proposed marriage to her. Much to the shock of her friends, she accepted.

"Don't you know that these May/December marriages are seldom good for May," one of her friends told the young bride-to-be. "I mean it's O.K. for December, he finds youth and beauty in May, but what does May find in December?"

"Santa Claus," was the girl's reply.

* * *

A REPLY

Sir, I admit your general rule,   That every poet is a fool;
But you yourself may serve to show it,   That every fool is not a poet.

Matthew Prior

* * *

IS THAT A FACT?   *by Ron Young*

Many things have been accepted as facts - not all of them are.

Were the Pilgrims the founding fathers of North America?

Every American knows that the New England States were the original United States of America which were first settled by the Pilgrims in 1620 when they landed at Plymouth, making it the first settlement in North America.

The fact is that in 1607, a hundred and twenty persons established a settlement at the mouth of the Kennebec River in what is now the state of Maine. It didn't last and although certain historians still say it was the first settlement in North America, it wasn't. The community of Renews on the Southern Shore of Newfoundland was settled, probably as early as 1536. It was certainly settled long before 1620 when the Mayflower stopped there for supplies on its way to make history at Plymouth Rock.

Wiff and the Shrink

So, you say you have trouble making up your mind?

Well yes .... and no.

SKIPPER SAYS:

"I used to have trouble remembering names until I took that course that 'What's-His-Name' had out!"

* * *

IS THAT A FACT? *by Ron Young*

Many things have been accepted as facts - not all of them are.

Did a Scotsman invent the bagpipe?

The bagpipe, the instrument most associated with the Scots, was invented by a Scotsman sometime around the time another Scotsman invented golf.

The fact is the bagpipe is a very ancient instrument which pre-dates the birth of Christ by many years. It was probably invented somewhere in the Middle East. The bagpipe was introduced to the British Isles by the conquering Romans. Although the instrument is closely associated with Scotland today, historically speaking it is as much Irish as it is Scottish. Today though, few would refute the fact that the bagpipe is the national instrument of bonnie Scotland.

* * *

Notable Quotables! by Ron Young

Meanings and origins of well known expressions

"Once in a blue moon"

MEANING: Not very often

ORIGIN: According to the Canadian World Almanac, a new moon occurs once every 29 days, 12 hours, 44.05 minutes. Every once in a while there will be two new moons in one month. When this happens the second new moon is called a blue moon. There was a blue moon on January 30, 1995 and again on March 30, 1995. There are no blue moons in the year 1996.

BULLETIN BOARD

NOTICE
Auction this Saturday
Come in and get something for nodding!

Dale's Dating Service
"For the footloose and fiancee free!"

Tonic For The Soul

SPICE OF LIFE

The best cure for love at first sight is to take a second look.

Submitted by Barbara Lucas, Barachois Brook, Nfld

* * *

Go Lovely Rose

Go, lovely rose!
Tell her that wastes her time and me,
That now she knows,
When I resemble her to thee,
How sweet and fair she seems to be.

Tell her that's young,
And shuns to have her graces spied,
That hadst thou sprung
In deserts, where no man abide,
Thou must have uncommended died.

Small is the worth
Of beauty from the light retired;
Bid her come forth,
Suffer herself to be desired,
And not blush so to be admired.

Then die, that she
The common fate of all things rare
May read in thee;
How small a part of time they share,
That are so wondrous, sweet, and fair.

Edmund Waller

* * *

FOLK REMEDIES - Curing Warts

Rub a piece of fresh meat on the wart and bury the meat. As the meat decays, so will the wart.

Submitted by Sharon Bennett, St. George's, Nfld

I keep thinking I'm a set of drapes in the living room, with sun continually shining in, fading the furniture. What can I do Doctor?

Wiff and the Shrink

You'll just have to pull yourself together.

Tonic For The Soul

The Man In The Stands

Author Unknown

One of the football teams at a prominent university in the U.S, had a player named "Fred", who wasn't a particularly good player, but was very devoted to the team and never missed a practice. The coach never allowed Fred to play very often during regular season games, but still Fred never missed. Not only was Fred devoted to the team, but the coach also noticed that he was also very devoted to his father who was many times a spectator when Fred's team was playing. But the coach had never met the father or talked with Fred about him.

One night, a few nights before the most important game of the season, the coach answered a knock at his door to find Fred standing there with sadness written all over his face. "My father just passed away and I wonder if it is all right if I miss practice for the next few days?" he said.

"I'm very sorry to hear about your loss," answered the coach, "and yes you may miss as many practices as you wish. As a matter of fact, you may miss the big game on Saturday if you wish."

Fred thanked the coach, and sadly walked away.

But on Friday night, just hours before the big game, Fred again called on his coach with a request. "Coach, may I please start the game tomorrow?" he asked, "I have never asked before, and I respect your judgement, but I would really like to play in this game."

Realizing how significant this one game was, and how important it was to have the best players in the field, the coach tried to talk Fred out of playing. But the young man insisted, and against his better judgement, the coach conceded to the request.

The coach had trouble sleeping that night. The team they had to play was a tough one to beat, and was favoured by three points over his team. He wondered why he had consented to let the young man play. What if he caught the opening kickoff and fumbled the ball? What if through Fred's ineptness they lost by five or six touchdowns? Obviously he could not let Fred play, even though he had promised. And that was the thought he went to sleep with.

Next day the coach decided to keep his promise. After all, he thought, the ball probably wouldn't go to Fred anyway, and he could later pull him from the game.

Then the opening kickoff, and the almost impossible happened, the ball floated through the air toward Fred.

"Oh no!" moaned the coach, "I blew it!"

But instead of fumbling, as the coach expected, Fred hugged the ball tightly, dodged three onrushing defenders and raced to midfield before he was finally tackled.

Never before had Fred been so agile or played so well. Surprising even himself, the coach had the quarterback call Fred's signal. The quarterback handed off, and Fred responded by breaking tackles for a 20-yard gain. In a few more plays, Fred triumphantly carried the ball over the goal line for a touchdown.

The players on the opposing team were stunned. Who was this kid? He wasn't even in their scouting reports. How could he be? Up to this game Fred had played less than four minutes all year.

The coach left Fred in the game, and he played the entire first half on both offense and defense. Tackling, intercepting and knocking down passes, blocking, running - he did it all.

At halftime the underdogs led by two touchdowns. During the second half Fred repeated his first-half performance, and when the final gun sounded, his team had won.

The winning team could not believe what happened. There was much celebrating going on in the locker room. The coach found Fred sitting quietly in a corner.

"Son, what happened out there?" the coach asked as he put his arm around him. "You've never played that well before. I've never seen you that fast, that agile and that good! What happened?"

"You didn't know it, Coach, but my father was blind," replied Fred, softly, "and this is the first game he ever saw me play."

* * *

Tonic For The Soul

Trading Places

So easy it is to pass judgement on others
So easy it is to see right in ourselves
To see all our failings as faults of our brothers
And when they fail, none to blame but themselves

The brunt of the burden, we believe that we bear
We believe that our brothers, we never can trust
Believe them unworthy this life road to share
That they'd never make it, if it were not for us

If we'd only take time to see things through their eyes
Switch places a while and walk down their road
Their hurdles might seem much higher in size
We may find they carry a heavier load

And while bearing their burdens and walking their way
We may just glance back at what we used to do
Then we may regret things we used to say
And find we're not perfect from their point of view

Ron Young

* * *

A Young Girl Still Dwells

The following poem was found among the possessions of an old lady who died in the ward of Ashludie Hospital near Dundee, Scotland. The staff was so impressed that they distributed copies throughout the hospital.

What do you see, nurse, what do you see?
Are you thinking when you look at me -
A crabbed old woman, not very wise,
Uncertain of habit with faraway eyes?
Who dribbles her food and makes no reply
When you say in a loud voice, "I do wish you'd try!"
Who seems not to notice the things that you do,
And forever is losing a stocking or shoe?
Who resisting or not, lets you do as you will
With bathing and feeding, the long day to fill?
Is that what you're thinking, is that what you see?
Then open your eyes, nurse, you're looking at me.
I'll tell you who I am as I sit here so still.
As I move at your bidding, eat at your will...
I'm a small child of ten with a father and mother,
Brothers and sisters who love one another;
A young girl of sixteen with wings on her feet,

Dreaming that soon a love she'll meet;
A bride at twenty my heart gives a leap,
Remembering the vows that I promised to keep;
At twenty-five now I have young of my own
Who need me to build a secure, happy home;
A woman of thirty, my young now grow fast,
Bound together with ties that should last;
At forty, my young sons have grown up and gone,
But my man's beside me to see I don't mourn;
At fifty, once more babies play 'round my knee,
Again we know children my loved ones and me.
Dark days are upon me; my husband is dead,
I look at the future, I shudder with dread.
For my young are all rearing young of their own,
And I think of the years and the love that I've known.
I'm an old woman now and nature is cruel;
'Tis her jest to make old age look like a fool.
The body it crumbles, grace and vigor depart;
There is a stone where I once had a heart.
But inside this old carcass a young girl still dwells,
And now, again, my embittered heart swells.
I remember the joys, I remember the pain,
And I'm loving and living life over again,
I think of the years, all too few, gone too fast,
And accept the stark fact that nothing can last.
So open your eyes, nurse, open and see
Not a crabbed old woman,
Look closer - see me!

* * *

FOLK REMEDIES - Nose Bleed
To prevent nose bleed tie a green ribbon around the neck.

Submitted by Sharon Bennett, St. George's, Nfld

* * *

SKIPPER SAYS:
"Revenue Canada says, 'To err is human -
to forgive is against government policy!' "

* * *

Tonic For The Soul

Notable Quotables! *by Ron Young*

Meanings and origins of well-known expressions

"Meeting a deadline"

MEANING: Finish something on time.

ORIGIN: During the American Civil war often there were no buildings in which to lock up prisoners of war, so they were often kept on a plot of land with a marked line around it. Prisoners were forbidden to cross the line, and any who did so were shot. The line shortly became known as the deadline.

* * *

The Lighter Side

ASK AND YOU SHALL BE GIVEN!

A United Church minister was surprised to get a phone call from Revenue Canada.

"But we don't pay taxes," said the minister.

"I wasn't calling about your taxes," said the tax collector, "I was calling about one of your parishioners, Sam Parsons. He said he donated $15,000 to your church last year, and I'm checking to see if, in fact, he did.

"We'll I haven't received the cheque yet, but I'm sure I will when I remind him about it," said the Reverend.

* * *

A GOOD COOK

She guessed at the pepper - the soup was too hot
She guessed at the water - it dried in the pot
She guessed at the salt - and what do you think
For the rest of the day we did nothing but drink
She guessed at the sugar - the sauce was too sweet
And by her guessing - she spoiled the meat
What is the moral? It's easy to see
A good cook measures and weighs to the "T"

Submitted by Hazel Warren, Chapel Arm, Newfoundland (nee Cobb, Bell Island)

Wiff and the Shrink

You say you have a short term memory problem - how long have you had this problem?

What problem?

BULLETIN BOARD

Timely Travel Agency

"We have two classes of travel; - First class, and with children."

For Sale
One well, 10 feet deep. Purchaser must remove.

Out Of The Mouths Of Babes

by Lucy Fitzpatrick McFarlane

Children are wonderful, aren't they? They are so refreshingly straight forward, honest and unpretentious. Their minds are like sponges, absorbing everything around them and processing all the information in a way that only children can. And they are such imitators. They'll pick up on little facial expressions, body movements and do the exact same things they see others do. Sometimes, though, you can repeat things you want them to do or say until you're ready to pull out your hair and they'll ignore you. Then, when you least expect it, the little cherubs will blurt out something you've said that wasn't meant for their ears. As parents, I'm sure you've been caught in many embarrassing moments with your children. How many secrets have been inadvertently divulged that have made your cheeks turn red or caused you to apologize or make a hasty exit? Many, I'm sure, and often the things that come out of the mouths of babes are far more genuine and amusing than what any comedian could ever deliver on stage. Kids say the darnest things, don't they?

Before I had children of my own, I never realized just how literally children take things, for they seldom look any farther than the surface. When I was living in Labrador City, I was visiting a neighbour in our apartment building and she was talking about how hard it was to stretch her budget and save money at the same time. Her 6-year-old son's ears perked up and he immediately said he wanted to help her. Patting him on the head, she assured him he was too young to understand what a budget was. Pouting, he said, "I do so know what 'budget' is! That's when sometin' gets stuck and no matter how hard you pulls it, you can't budge it!"

And it was the same little boy who knocked on my door one day to borrow a roll of bathroom tissue because his mom was sick and couldn't go to the store. Knowing that she was in the habit of returning things promptly, I didn't want her to rush to the store to replace such a small item, so I asked him to give her a message. "Tell your mommie there's no need to bring the toilet paper back."

His jaw dropped open in shock. "That's good," he said, "... cause I don't think you'll want it back after I'm done with it!"

Children always say what's on their mind, no matter how personal it is. Take the other day, for instance, when I was in a line-up at the grocery store. Now, because I'm a redhead, I get lots of

freckles in the summer and believe me, all those brown patches can look a little peculiar to some-one who's not used to it. I became aware of a little boy looking me up and down for a long time and then in a loud voice, he said, "Mommie, look ... that lady is getting rusty all over!"

As we all know, tactfulness is not something children concern themselves with. Course they don't mean to be unkind or cruel in what they say. They just speak their minds. I remember repeat-ing something that was better left unsaid when I was a youngster and I got a snock up-side the head for my loose tongue. An elderly lady had dropped in to our house for a cup of tea and while she was there, I heard daddy wishing her a happy birthday. When asked how old she was, she laughed and said she didn't remember. And in all fairness to my innocence, I was only too happy to oblige her with the answer. "I knows that you're really old," I said, feeling very proud of myself, "... cause I heard daddy telling mom just before you came in that you looks older than God's cow."

But that didn't seem nearly as bad as what one of the boys in the Cove said to a man one day when we were hanging around the landwash where the men were splitting fish. One fisherman had an unusually long nose and I suppose it had been mentioned by others in jest on more than one occasion, so quite innocently, one of the boys popped the million dollar question simply because he was so curious. "Me fodder says that your nose is so long dat the dory changes direction when you stands up. Is that really true?"

Oh, yes, I've had more than my share of embarrassing moments with my two sons when they were young, for they were the worse for saying things at the wrong time. You know, the kind that are better left unsaid. Why do I have to blow my nose ... are we having company? How come you got so much hair in your nose? Daddy says you're so boring that the plants fall asleep when you talk to them. You've heard them all, I'm sure. When Tim was about 5 years old, I took him to get a haircut. "How would you like your hair done, Tim?" the hairdresser asked.

Tim focused on an elderly man who was sitting in the next chair getting a trim ... a man with a bald head except for the little bit around his ears and at the back of his head. "I want the top cut out of my head like that man there!" he announced.

I believe my worse moment came when my son, Scott, was about seven. During a children's mass at the church the day before Easter Sunday, the priest was asking informal questions about the meaning of Easter. When he asked who could explain why Easter Sunday was so important, my son raised his hand. Surprised, I leaned forward in the pew to hear what he had to say. "Easter Sunday is the day when Jesus rose from the dead!" he said triumphantly.

The priest's face lit up. "Now there's a young man who knows what he's talking about. Can you tell us more?"

I felt so proud of him that the buttons were bulging on my blouse. But it was short-lived. Scott hesitated for a second as all the other parents listened for his answer. "Uhh ... the angels rolled the stone away from the cave ... " he began, "and then, uhh ... Jesus came out, saw his shadow and went back in for forty days!"

I'm just thankful that he didn't mention the Easter bunny in the same breath as the groundhog. But, it could've been worse, I suppose. Take what happened to my boss when her little nieces and nephews were with her this past Easter. It was Good Friday and as she was driving all the kids to her mother's house, one of the kids wanted to stop at a store to look at toys. Louise explained that the stores were closed because it was a holy day and after lots of questions, she went into the Easter story and ended with Jesus' Resurrection on Easter Sunday. The children were fascinated and when they arrived at her mother's house where all the family had gathered, the youngest lad was burst-ing to tell grandma what his Aunt Louise told them. He told the story in his own words and when he got to the part about why Easter Sunday was so special, he had a lot of difficulty trying to wrap his tongue around the word 'resurrection'. Louise was about to help him out when he suddenly blurted it out. "Don't tell me, I know ... Easter Sunday was the day Jesus got an 'erection'!"

Sometimes we don't realize that children tune in to our conversations even when we're not aware that they are listening. A friend of mine here in Niagara told me about her husband's elderly Uncle Bill and Aunt Maude who came for a week and stayed for a month. Now Maureen is a very accommodating person, so she didn't mind having them around, except she had a slight problem with Uncle Bill. Not only was he nearly deaf and always forgetting where he put things, but he insisted on eating spicy food and as a result, he had the nasty habit of passing gas freely wherever he might be. Now, this annoyed and embarrassed Maureen to no end, when he did it in public and when her 6-year-old daughter questioned her about it, she carefully explained that the man couldn't help it and tactfully referred to the rude noises as 'breaking wind'. Maureen begged her husband to speak to his uncle, but he refused to do so and an argument ensued in which Maureen called Uncle Bill an 'old fart'. She didn't realize that her daughter was in the room until later that evening when Uncle Bill was looking for his jacket that he had mislaid AGAIN. Maureen searched in vain and after inquiring about it to Aunt Maude, she finally asked her daughter, who was sitting in Aunt Maude's lap. "Honey, I don't suppose you'd know where the windbreaker is, do you?"

The little girl answered promptly. "Yeah ... the old fart is sitting out on the front porch with daddy."

You can always trust a child to tell the truth as they see it and they can turn the tables on you at any given time. I heard about an incident back home when all the smuggling liquor and cigarettes from St. Pierre was going on a few years ago. Apparently, when the police were sent by an informant to search one particular home for contraband items, they found nothing. They were about to leave empty-handed and once more an officer asked the man of the house, if they were in possession of cigarettes. He assured the police they had nothing and he would've gotten away scott-free had his young son not turned him in. "Sure you do, daddy! You put a whole bunch of cigarettes under the mattress in my waterbed last night ... remember? Here, officer, I'll show you. ."

So there you have it. Next time when you see an innocent little face with a smile that can light up the whole world, don't forget that behind those bright eyes, a little computer is accumulating everything you say and do. And the joy of it all, is that one day, when you least expect it, that sweet little person will speel forth your secrets and little tidbits of information ... all cherishables that you'll keep locked away for the time when that child becomes an adult. And if you listen carefully, you'll find that some of your most wonderful memories will come from the mouths of babes.

* * *

SKIPPER SAYS:
"With a microwave oven you can be a terrible cook in a lot less time!"

* * *

FOLK REMEDIES - *Sore Throats and Colds (East Africa)*
Boil a 2 inch cinnamon stick that has been broken into pieces, along with a one inch piece of ginger in water until the water turns brown. Add sugar to taste and drink while still hot.

Submitted by Betina Wheeler-Ali, Toronto, Ontario (formerly of St. John's, Nfld)

* * *

Tonic For The Soul

Thᶒ Lightᶒr Sidᶒ

A very exquisitely dressed lady was sitting on a bus when a drunk staggered on. Weaving his way down the aisle he accidently bumped into the lady. With a twisted look on her face the lady said, "You are drunk! You are not only drunk, you are ridiculously drunk! As a matter of fact, you are disgustingly drunk!"

"I know," replied the man, "and you're ugly! You're ridiculously ugly! And on top of that, you're disgustingly ugly! Tomorrow I'll be sober."

* * *

IS THAT A FACT? *by Ron Young*

Many things have been accepted as facts - not all of them are.

Who was Aunt Jemima?

Everybody loves Aunt Jemima pancakes, the delicious pancakes made from instant pancake mix which was concocted by that delightful black cook, Aunt Jemima.

The fact is there was no Aunt Jemima and the instant pancake mix was invented by a man. The story begins in 1889 in St. Joseph, Missouri, when Chris Rutt, a local newspaper man conceived the idea for a reliable self-rising flour. Rutt loved pancakes, but didn't want to wait for them to have to be made from scratch each morning.

Rutt's original mix of flour, salt, phosphate of lime and soda, was originally marketed in a brown paper bag through grocery stores. The product didn't sell very well and Rutt realized he needed a gimmick.

While attending a local vaudeville show he heard "Aunt Jemima", a rhythmic New Orleans-style song performed by a pair of blackface minstrel comedians, Baker and Farrell. The concept of southern hospitality appealed to Rutt and he used the name from the song for his product. Sales increased greatly after that and Rutt sold his interest to the Davis Milling Company. The company decided to display the product at the 1893 Chicago World's Fair, and searched the windy city for a warm and friendly black cook to play the role of Aunt Jemima. They found Nancy Green, who was then employed by a local family. Nancy, playing the role of Aunt Jemima, served the fair's visitors more than a million pancakes. A special detail of policeman had to be brought in to prevent crowds from rushing the concession. Nancy was fifty-nine at the time and she toured the U.S. as Aunt Jemima, helping to establish the pancake as an American tradition until her death thirty years later.

Wiff and the Shrink

You say you like doing bird imitations - I don't see much wrong with that.

That's because you don't have to eat them worms.

Tonic For The Soul

SKIPPER SAYS:

"If your father is a doctor you can be sick for nothing - if he is a minister you can be good for nothing!"

* * *

The Prophecies Of Mother Shipton

Carriages without Horses shall go
And Accidents fill the world with woe
Waters shall yet more wonders do;
How strange, yet shall be true
Iron in the water shall float
As easy as a wooden boat

Around the world thoughts shall fly
In the twinkling of an eye
Under water men shall walk,
Shall ride, shall sleep, shall talk
In the air men shall be seen
In white, in black, and in green

EDITOR'S NOTE: Martha (Mother) Shipton was born in England in 1488 (before America was discovered). She began prophesying at an early age, but not too many people believed her, because not many of her prophecies came to pass by the time she died in 1561. Today though, it is not hard to see that she was probably predicting the coming of automobiles, electricity, iron ships, radio, T.V., the internet, submarines, and airplanes.

* * *

Notable Quotables! by Ron Young

Meanings and origins of well-known expressions

"The coast is clear"

MEANING: There is no likelihood of interference.
ORIGIN: Most likely this expression was first used by smugglers trying to get contraband goods ashore. It would be used when the coast was clear of coast guards.

Tonic For The Soul

DAYS OF OUR CHILDREN

Monday's child is fair of face
Tuesday's child is full of grace
Wednesday's child is full of woe
Thursday's child has far to go
Friday's child is loving and giving
Saturday's child works hard for a living
But the child that is born on the Sabbath Day
Is bonnie, blithe, good and gay.

* * *

The Lighter Side

An elderly lady visited her doctor and asked, "Can you give me a prescription for some of them new birth control pills? I think they will help me sleep better."

"There is nothing in birth control pills that will help you sleep," the doctor informed her, "they are for an entirely different purpose."

The woman insisted and to humour her, the physician wrote her a month's prescription for the pill.

A month later the woman was back in the doctor's office. "Those pills were wonderful," she exclaimed, "I haven't slept so good in a long time."

"I've told you before, and I'll tell you again," reiterated the doctor, "there is nothing in those pills to help you sleep."

"My eighteen-year-old granddaughter has been living with me for some time now," said the senior lady, "and every morning I slip one of those pills into her orange juice. Believe me doctor, I sleep better!"

* * *

FOLK REMEDIES - Constipation
To help with constipation and to start your day off right, take 2 tablespoons of apple cider vinegar and 1 tablespoon of honey in a warm glass of water. Also great on cold mornings.

Submitted by Mrs. Anita Duggan, Sechelt, British Columbia, (nee Shea, Bell Island, Newfoundland)

You say you think you're a horse. I can cure you, but it's going to be costly!

Wiff and the Shrink

Money is no problem Doctor, I just won the Kentucky Derby.

SKIPPER SAYS:

"One way to make sure your car lasts you a lifetime is to drive carelessly!"

* * *

OZYMANDIAS OF EGYPT   *Percey Bysshe Shelley*

I met a traveller from an antique land
Who said: two vast and trunkless legs of stone
Stand in the desert. Near them on the sand
Half sunk, a shattered visage lies, whose frown
And wrinkled lip, and sneer of cold command
Tell that its sculptor well those passions read
Which yet survive, stamp'd on these lifeless things,
The hand that mock'd them and the heart that fed;
And on the pedestal these words appear:
"My name is Ozymandias, king of kings:
Look on my works ye mighty and despair!"
Nothing beside remains. Round the decay
Of that colossal wreck, boundless and bare,
The lone and level sands stretch far away.

EDITOR'S NOTE: In this poem Shelley demonstrates that even the great are merely mortals, and no matter how great their works, time forgets them. Shelley was one of the great poets and thinkers of his time. Today a few know of him, but his works are practically unknown by the general public. Ironically, in their day, Percey's wife Mary, was not considered to be in her husband's calibre of writers and thinkers. Today one of Mary's works is known by virtually everybody. Mary Wollstonecraft Shelley wrote, *Frankenstein.*

* * *

FOLK REMEDIES - *Sprained Wrist*
A rag soaked in a mixture of urine and salt and tied around a sprained wrist was once considered an excellent cure.

Submitted by Stan Baldwin, Stephenville, Nfld

* * *

Notable Quotables! *by Ron Young*

Meanings and origins of well-known expressions
"A flash in the pan"
MEANING: A short-lived success.
ORIGIN: The chamber on a flintlock musket which held the powder was called the 'pan'. When one pulled the trigger, a spark from the flint would ignite the powder. The exploding powder would send the musket ball on its way. Sometimes the flint would "flash in the pan" but would fail to ignite the powder and the gun would misfire. Hence a musket misfire was called a flash in the pan.

Tonic For The Soul

Little Eyes Upon You

Author unknown

There are little eyes upon you
and they're watching night and day.
There are little ears that quickly
take in every word you say.
There are little hands all eager
to do anything you do;
And a little boy who's dreaming
of the day he'll be like you.

You're the little fellow's idol,
you're the wisest of the wise.
In his little mind about you
no suspicions ever rise.

He believes in you devoutly,
holds all you say and do;
He will say and do it your way
when he's grown up, just like you.

There's a wide-eyed little fellow
who believes you're always right;
and his eyes are always opened,
and he watches day and night.
You are setting an example
every day in all you do;
For the little boy who's waiting
to grow up to be like you.

* * *

The Lighter Side

A man walked into a bar with a dog under his arm.

"Sorry buddy," said the bartender, "no dogs allowed!"

"But this dog talks," replied the man, "Is it O.K. if he stays?"

"Come on buddy," laughed the barkeeper, "there's no such thing as a talking dog."

"I'm serious, this dog can talk. I'll prove it to you," and turning to the dog which he had now placed on the bar, he said, "O.K. Ringer, what is the top of a house called?"

"Roof," replied the dog.

"Get outta here!" growled the bartender, "any dog can say that."

"Let me ask one more question," said the customer, "Ringer, what does sand paper feel like?"

"Ruff," answered Ringer.

"Are you nuts?" said the bartender, "There isn't a dog around who can't say 'ruff'."

"Gimme one more chance?" said the man. "Ringer, who was the greatest Yankee outfielder of all time?"

"Ruth," barked Ringer.

"I've had enough of this crap!" shouted the angry bartender, and threw both the man and his dog into the ditch outside.

Ringer looked over to where his master was lying face-down in the dirt and said, "Maybe I should have said, 'DiMaggio'?"

* * *

SKIPPER SAYS:
"Middle age is that time of life when a narrow waist and a broad mind start to change places!"

* * *

Mother Will Never Die

When we are children
we are happy and gay,
And our mother is young
And she laughs as we play.

Then as we grow up
She teaches us truth,
And lays life foundation
In the days of our youth.

And then it is time
For us to leave home,
But her teachings go with us
Wherever we roam.

For all that she taught us
And all that she did,
When we were so often just
A "bad little kid".

We will often remember
And then realize,
Mothers are special
And wonderfully wise.

And as she grows older
We look back with love

Knowing that mothers
Are gifts from above.

And when she goes home
To receive her reward
She will dwell in God's Kingdom
And keep house for the Lord.

Then she'll light up the stars
That shine through the night,
And keep all the moon beams
Sparkling and bright.

And then with the dawn
She'll put darkness away,
As she scours the sun
To new brilliance each day.

So dry tears of sadness
For mothers don't die
They move in with God
And keep house in the sky.

And there in God's Kingdom
Mothers watch from above
To welcome their children
With undying love.

You say you're here because your family thinks you're crazy. Just because you like pies they think you're crazy. What's so crazy about liking pies? I like pies myself!

Wiff and the Shrink

Then you gotta come over to my place Doc, I got eight thousand, two hundred and twelve of them.

IS THAT A FACT? *by Ron Young*

Many things have been accepted as facts - not all of them are.

Sir Walter Raleigh and Tobacco

Many school children, including myself, were taught that the vile habit of smoking was first introduced to Europeans by Sir Walter Raleigh near the end of the Sixteenth Century.

The fact is that tobacco found its way to Spain from Mexico in 1558 by way of a Spanish physician named Francesco Fernandez who was sent to Mexico by King Philip of Spain to investigate products in North America. The new product was supposed to have medicinal healing powers. A year later the French Ambassador to Portugal, Jean Nicot sent some tobacco seeds back to Queen Catherine in France. "Nicotaina", the Latin word for tobacco was derived from the Frenchman's name as well as the now much used word; "nicotine".

There is some evidence that Sir John Hawkins brought tobacco to England in 1565. Walter Raleigh was only thirteen years old at the time.

There is little doubt however that Sir Walter did receive some tobacco from Sir Ralph Lane and Sir Francis Drake when they returned from America in 1586. Raleigh then introduced the tobacco to the Queen's courtiers, and it is believed that the habit of smoking got its start at that time.

* * *

FOLK REMEDIES - Sore Throat

Mix 3 - 4 tablespoons molasses, a pinch of pepper, 1 teaspoon cod oil, 1/2 teaspoon vinegar and a pinch of ginger. Bring to a boil, then let cool. Take one teaspoon as needed.

Submitted by Trudy Simmons, Twillingate, Nfld, (nee Forward, Tizzard's Harbour, Nfld)

* * *

The Lighter Side

A man was seated in the waiting room of a major airport, in a section in which smoking was still allowed. He was puffing contentedly on his pipe when a very expensively dressed woman occupied the seat next to him.

After a few minutes of fanning the smoke with her hand she said, "Sir, if you were a gentleman you wouldn't smoke where others are affected."

"Well why don't you sit in one of those seats across the way where no one is smoking?" asked the man.

"Why should I have to do that?" shouted the now irate lady. "It is my right to sit anywhere I please and not be bothered by the likes of people like you who insist on indulging in filthy habits. Sir, you are a thorn in the side of civilized society, you are an abomination to the modern world, and a despicable person who has no redeeming social value, and if I were married to you I'd give you poison!"

"Madam," replied the man, "if I were married to you, I'd take it!"

* * *

SKIPPER SAYS:
"When a woman lowers her voice it's a sign that she wants something - when she raises it, it's a sign she didn't get it!"

* * *

The Purchase

The local car dealer, who was known to have taken advantage of several people in the community, informed a farmer that he was coming over to purchase a cow.

The farmer priced the cow as follows:

Basic Cow - $499.95
Shipping & Handling - $35.75
Extra Stomach - $79.25
Two-Tone Exterior - $142.10
Produce Storage Compartment - $126.50
Heavy Duty Straw Chopper - $189.60
Four-Spigot-High Output Drain System - $149.20
Automatic Flyswatter - $88.50
Genuine Cowhide Upholstery - $179.90
Deluxe Dual Horns - $59.25
Automatic Fertilizer Attachment - $339.40
4-by-4 Traction Drive Assembly - $884.16
Pre-Delivery Wash and Comb - $69.80
Farmers Suggested List Price - $2,843.36
Additional Dealer Adjustments - $300.00
Total List Price (Including Options) - $3,143.36

Submitted by Edgar Elliott, Toronto, Ontario

* * *

The Lighter Side

Newfoundland's famous train, which was affectionately called the Bullet because it was not noted for its speed, had many stories told in its honour.

One such story is about a passenger who, perturbed because the slow train had made another unscheduled stop, asked the conductor, "Why are we stopping this time?"

"There is a cow grazing on the tracks," replied the railroad employee.

"We stopped ten minutes because of a cow grazing on the tracks," shouted the passenger.

"Yes sir," replied the conductor, "but we've caught up with it again now."

* * *

Notable Quotables! by Ron Young

Meanings and origins of well-known expressions

"Mind your Ps and Qs"

MEANING: Be careful how you behave.

ORIGIN: It is possible that the expression came about as an admonition to children learning the alphabet to be careful to distinguish between the **p** and the **q** which look very similar. There is another belief that the saying originated in British pubs where beer is sold by the **P**int or the **Q**uart. One might be warned to mind how many **P**ints and **Q**uarts (**P**s and **Q**s) were consumed because if you drank too many you may not remember how many when it came time to pay, and therefore may be overcharged.

* * *

His Secret

by Lucy Fitzpatrick McFarlane

The old man sprays cleaner on the window pane
his intense blue eyes resting on the face
of the little boy in the waiting room as he reads
aloud to his mother the story of Peter Rabbit

Deft fingers move swiftly across the glass
ears straining to catch every word spoken by
the child as he reads from the book of Fairy Tales
amazing the old man with his skill

Hands lined with age slow to the rhythm of the
voice
tired eyes stare out the window from atop the
ladder
at the sign on the billboard across the street
flashing out words that he cannot perceive

Alone in a crowded room he shrinks from
probing eyes

confined within these walls of silence he keeps
his deepest secret hidden from the world
sheltered here inside he pushes his mop and
broom

Long after the office grows silent for the night
his heavy footsteps echo through empty halls
the memory of the proud look on the boy's face
a grim reminder of unenlightened years gone past

He opens the pages from the book of Fairy Tales
his fingers trembling as he touches the black
print of the words that the child had read
cursing his own inability to decipher this
unknown code

He stares at the pages where only the pictures
can tell him the stories from the Fairy Tales
craving the miracle of that young boy's gift

Wiff and the Shrink

You say you continually have dreams of beautiful, sexy women? I don't think I'll have much trouble curing you of that problem.

I don't want to be cured, Doctor - I want their phone numbers.

SKIPPER SAYS:

"Men and women have one thing in common - neither of them trust women!"

* * *

I Have Not Time To Be A Saint

Submitted by Marie Whitehorne, Pasadena, Newfoundland (nee Kendall, Ramea, Newfoundland)

Lord of all the pots and pans and things,
Since I have not time to be
A saint by doing lovely things
Or watching late with thee.
Or dreaming in the dawn light,
Or storming heaven's gates;
Make me a Saint by getting meals
And washing up the plates.

Warm all the kitchen with my love
And light it with thy peace;
Forgive me all my worrying
And make my grumbling cease.
Thou who dids't love to give men food,
In room or by the sea,
Accept the service that I do
I do it unto thee.

* * *

The Worth of Seniors

Remember, old folks are worth a fortune, with silver in their hair, gold in their teeth, stones in their kidneys, lead in their feet, and gas in their stomachs.

I have become a little older since I saw you last and a few changes have come into my life since then. Frankly, I have become quite a frivolous (loose and bold) old gal. I am seeing five gentlemen every day.

As soon as I wake up, Will Power helps me get out of bed. Then I go see John. Then Charlie Horse comes along, and when he is here he takes a lot of my time and attention. When he leaves, Arthur Ritis shows up and stays the rest of the day. He doesn't like to stay in one place very long, so he takes me from joint to joint. After such a busy day I'm really tired and glad to go to bed with Ben Gay. What a life!! Oh yes, I'm also flirting with Al Zymer.

P.S. The preacher came to call the other day. He said at my age I should be thinking about the hereafter (dying). I told him, Oh, I do all the time. No matter where I am; in the parlor, upstairs, in the kitchen or down in the basement, I ask myself, "What am I here after?"

Submitted by Vera Curtis, Burlington, Ont.

* * *

The Lighter Side

One Christmas, little six-year-old Cathy was asked at school to draw a picture of the Nativity scene at school. She did an excellent job of drawing the scene complete with the manger, Baby Jesus, Mary, Joseph, all the animals, as well as a rather rotund man in the corner.

"I recognize everyone in the picture except the man in the corner," said the teacher, "Who is he?"

"That's Round John Virgin," answered the little girl.

* * *

IS THAT A FACT? *by Ron Young*

Many things have been accepted as facts - not all of them are.

The mystery of the Bermuda Triangle

Most of us are aware of the 'Bermuda Triangle', also called the 'Devil's Triangle', which has been responsible for mysteriously claiming so many ships and planes over the years, as in the cases of the Mary Celeste in 1872, the USS Cyclops in 1918, and five US Navy trainer planes on a routine flight on December 5, 1945, which just vanished into thin air over the Bermuda Triangle. A sixth plane sent out to find the others also disappeared mysteriously.

The fact is there have probably been more ships vanish mysteriously off the coast of Newfoundland than there have in the Bermuda Triangle, and probably as many planes have vanished near Newfoundland as well.

In the case of the Mary Celeste; the ship which was found abandoned and still under sail on December 4, 1872; that ship was actually found in the north-east Atlantic, nowhere near the Bermuda Triangle.

Some of the people who told the story of the U.S.S. Cyclops claim that the vessel was lost in the Bermuda Triangle in fine weather in March 1918, and although she was one of the few ships at the time equipped with radio, failed to send out a distress signal.

What these people failed to tell was that although the ship was sailing in fine weather on a trip from Barbados to Norfolk, Virginia, a storm with winds of up to 84 MPH roared southward from New York down the Atlantic on the very day that the Cyclops was scheduled to arrive in Norfolk. Such a storm could easily have sunk the Cyclops.

Of the five planes lost in 1945, (about which a movie was made) only one had an experienced pilot. The other four were student flyers. According to Navy reports the leader developed compass trouble and mistakenly flew in the wrong direction out over the Atlantic until he ran out of gas. The four other planes which followed him met the same fate and crashed into the ocean. Although the weather was fine when the planes took off, by the time they went down the wind had picked up considerably and the sea was very rough. When the error was discovered the planes were too far off course to be sent instructions.

A number of rescue planes were sent out but were unable to save the men in the downed planes. It's true that one of the rescue planes did not return, but that plane didn't mysteriously disappear either. It met its fate because of a fuel explosion on board. This was witnessed by a nearby ship.

The other losses in the 'Triangle' can be as easily explained. If all the losses of ships and planes all over the world were looked at one by one, it would be discovered that the area known as the Bermuda Triangle holds no more mystery than any other part of the world's oceans.

All theses visits to my office have finally paid off. You are now completely cured.

Wiff and the Shrink

I don't know if I'm really happy with that doctor. When I first started seeing you I was Napoleon Bonaparte - now I'm a Nobody!

Tonic For The Soul

SKIPPER SAYS:

"Doctors will tell you that if you eat slowly you will eat less, that is especially true if you are a member of a large family!"

* * *

Dad's Special Brew

My mother had an awful cold,
In the winter of fifty-two,
The doctor couldn't come to her,
But my dad knew what to do.

He told my mom, to stay in bed,
He would make her good as new,
He mixed molasses with some rum,
And made his special brew.

Then later on in the night,
I heard my mother crying,
"I feel so hot, and I can't walk,

Oh Bert, I think I'm dying."

I heard dad say, "Don't worry ma,
But I feel just like a skunk,
The special brew I just mixed up,
I think it made you drunk."

But when mom got up next morning,
She was feeling good as new,
I remember her saying to us kids,
"Don't drink your father's brew!"

Rose Oldford Pestrue, daughter of Bert Oldford

* * *

If You Ain't Sure I'm Dead

If when I dies, you ain't certain I'm dead
Just butter some biscuits and new made bread
And spread 'em all over with blueberry jam,
Then step mighty softly to where I am,
An' wave dem vittles above my head -
If my mouf don't open, I'm certainly dead.

Submitted by Alma Taylor, Mt. Moriah, Newfoundland (nee LeDrew, Bell Island, Newfoundland)

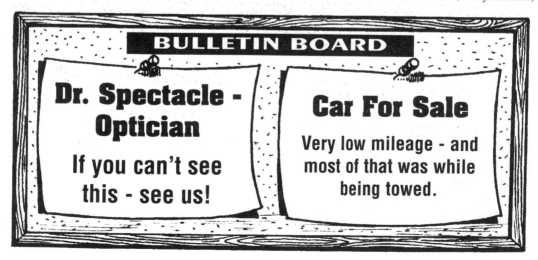

Tonic For The Soul

RAINBOWS

Bad times are naught but gages
So that we can discern
And appreciate the good times
When, as always, they return
There are rainbows all around us
All the time, although
They need the presence of the rain
To make the colours show

* * *

Ron Young

The Lighter Side

Little four-year-old Frankie had a habit of sucking his thumb.

"If you keep sucking your thumb you're going to blow up and bust," his mother told him.

Frankie quit sucking his thumb.

Several weeks later Frankie went to visit his cousin, aunt and uncle, whom he hadn't seen in a year. His aunt was pregnant, and expecting the baby any day.

When Frankie saw her he remarked, "You quit sucking your thumb just in time, didn't you?"

* * *

IS THAT A FACT? *by Ron Young*

Many things have been accepted as facts - not all of them are.

Harem, Scare-um

What red-blooded male wouldn't want to have his own Harem? A Harem is, after all, the place where a flock of wives are kept.

The fact is that a Harem is not necessarily the place where a polygamous man keeps his many wives. The word 'Harem' is an adapted Arabic word which means 'a secluded or forbidden sanctuary'. In the Muslim custom this sanctuary is one set aside for all Muslim women, which include mothers, mothers-in-law, sisters, female servants, sisters-in-law, female relatives, female family friends, or just one wife. This makes a Harem a scary proposition for many males who consider themselves macho.

Wiff and the Shrink

Do you feel as if these visits are helping any, Wiff?

Doctor, you've done wonders for me - last year I wouldn't even answer the doorbell when it rang, and now I answer whether it rings or not.

SKIPPER SAYS:
"If you don't want your children to hear what you are saying pretend you are talking to them!"

* * *

IS THAT A FACT? *by Ron Young*

Many things have been accepted as facts - not all of them are.

Who wrote 'Rudolph The Red-Nosed Reindeer'?

Everybody knows that "Rudolph The Red-Nosed Reindeer" was created in the song of the same name by Gene Autry in 1949.

The fact is that the idea for Rudolph was created by Robert May, an advertising copywriter with the Montgomery Ward department store of Chicago in 1939. The store was looking for something novel for its Santa to distribute to children and parents. May suggested an illustrated poem in a booklet which could be kept year after year and re-read each Christmas. It was also May's idea to have a shiny nosed reindeer as Santa's helper, and he and his artist friend spent many hours at a zoo sketching caribou (reindeer) in many playful positions. The store approved the poem and the sketches and several names for the deer were suggested, including Reginald and Rollo. May's four-year-old daughter liked the name Rudolph and that is the one May went with. Santas in Montgomery Ward stores across the USA handed out 2.4 million Rudolph booklets that Christmas (1939).

In 1947, Johnny Marks, another friend of May's, decided to put the words of the poem to music. A number of singers were asked to record the song but all declined. In 1949 Gene Autry agreed to record the song. The song has since become the second biggest selling song of all time selling over 80 million records. The biggest selling song of all time is another Christmas song, "White Christmas", originally recorded by Bing Crosby.

* * *

FOLK REMEDIES - Headache
Rinse a cloth in vinegar, then place cloth on your head to cure a headache.

Submitted by Trudy Simmons, Twillingate, Nfld

* * *

The Lighter Side

A man went to see a doctor complaining of severe stomach pains. "You know doctor," he said, "I went to see the pharmacist and he gave me three different kinds of pills, but they didn't do me any good."

I know," replied the doctor, "pharmacists often give wrong advice. What else did he tell you?"

"He told me to come and see you!"

* * *

Tonic For The Soul

SKIPPER SAYS:

"Time may heal all wounds, but it sure don't do much for wrinkles!"

* * *

Happiness Cake

Submitted by Gertrude Sweetapple, Glovertown, Nfld

1 cup of good thoughts
1 cup consideration for others
3 cups of forgiveness
1 cup of kind deeds
2 cups of sacrifice
2 cups of well-beaten faults

Mix thoroughly. Add tears of joy, sorrow and sympathy. Flavour with love and kindly service. Fold in 4 cups of prayers and faith. Blend well. Fold into daily life. Bake well with the warmth of human kindness and serve with a smile any time. It will satisfy the hunger of starved souls.

* * *

Notable Quotables! *by Ron Young*

Meanings and origins of well-known expressions

"Charlie Horse"

MEANING: A muscle cramp

ORIGIN: In 1640, Charles I of England expanded the London Police Force. The new recruits were called "Charley's Men" which was quickly shortened to simply "Charleys". There was not enough money to provide horses for all the new recruits, which meant that the policemen without horses, walked. Those who walked were called "Charley's Horses", and since walking caused many leg cramps, leg cramps became known as "Charley's Horses." This was later shortened to "Charley Horse."

* * *

FOLK REMEDIES - *Warts*

Count the warts and write the number of warts in chalk on the back of a stove. As the marks burn off the warts will disappear.

Submitted by Dolores Lundrigan (nee English, Branch, St. Mary's Bay), Wabush, Lab

You say you have a real problem because you can see into the future, that you know everything that's going to happen, and it's awful - when did this problem start?

Wiff and the Shrink

Next Saturday.

A Policeman At Christmas Time

by Ron Young

"What's it really like being a policeman?" That's a question that policemen get asked more than any other, more than; "How can I beat a speeding charge?" and more than; "What can I do about my fifteen year-old who has run away from home?"

The question is seldom answered truthfully by policemen. This is because there is no short answer to this question. And the proper, truthful, long answer conjures up too many unpleasant memories, so a shorter answer that changes the subject is usually given.

"Oh, it's not a bad job," I usually say, and that is true. Sometimes the job is very rewarding. If an old lady gets beaten by an assailant who wants and takes her purse containing her pension money, and if through good investigation, the use of informants, or sheer luck, you arrest the guy, you feel good. Then, if in Court you get a Judge who's mother was just robbed in the same manner, things are really starting to look up. As the criminal is lead away from the court room to spend something more than fifteen days in jail, you feel good, you feel you've accomplished something. There is one less viper on the street to antagonize the people you care about.

The job isn't always like that. Mostly you have to deal with people who don't like you before they've ever met you. They blame you for the bad laws that get worse each year, and don't realize that you hate the bad laws, even more than they do. To them you represent those laws, and you are as close as they'll ever get to the law makers. It's only natural that they take their frustrations out on you, just because you're a policeman.

We all dislike authority figures. We didn't like our parents telling us what to do. We didn't like our teachers for the same reason, and as we grow older this dislike is transferred to the other authority figure, the policeman.

As a police officer you have to deal with the worst problems that people encounter. You have to deal with conflicts between people, and make decisions that make at least one of them unhappy, quite often both of them. Most incidents you encounter are a "damned if you do, and damned if you don't" situation. No matter what you do to help solve problems there is a very good chance that the very people you try to help will go away feeling that you handled it wrong.

You have to deal with the drug dealers and other low-lifes of society, who carry guns and will shoot you if it is to their least advantage. And if you use force to protect yourself (or other citizens, who may be armed or killed by that armed criminal) you have to deal with a society that seems to be just waiting for an opportunity to find fault with your actions. We, as police officers, have to please a society that says: "Go out there and protect us, and solve all our problems, but don't make a mistake, because if you do you're on your own, buddy."

Another factor that eats away at a police officer's soul is the "personal feelings" factor. At police college they teach us to be professional, and not let personal feelings come into play when dealing with situations. That's easy to say, but when you cut the rope that attaches a lifeless body to a chandelier, or see the fear in the eyes of a wife whose face has been battered until it is unrecognizable, or watch the life ebb from the eight year old boy you are holding in your arms, it's a little hard to remain emotionless. To any who watch us in these situations, we appear to be professional and in control, but inside the emotions are running wild, and inside the tears are flowing uncontrolled.

Christmas, the season to be jolly, for the police officer is the worst time of the year. The emotion filled situation encountered on duty seem to be compounded during the festive season. After a Christmas Eve on duty some years ago, I wrote the following poem...

Christmas Eve On The Beat

The afternoon's alive and hopping
Shopper's doing their last minute shopping
The police car finds the curb and stops
Lest someone rob the closing shops
And then the shoppers are all gone
The policeman prowls the streets alone
Christmas lights are everywhere
The sound of church bells fills the air
He enjoys the moment for its worth
And for a while there's peace on earth

Somewhere near a darkened alley
In a house remodelled, trimmed with holly
Well-dressed couples talk and dine
In the alley, Harry drinks his wine
It's been a while since he last ate
He drinks the wine and curses fate
A wasted life with little worth
The bells are chiming "Peace On Earth"

Red for stop and green for go
It's cold but still there is no snow
A streetcar grinds along the rail
Somewhere a siren starts to wail
The radio is quiet no more
The policeman answers back, "Ten-Four"
Let the festivities begin
Peace on earth, Good will to men

A soon-to-be mother left alone
To have the baby on her own
Wonders if Jesus, meek and mild
Cares about her unborn child
The policeman comes, God is not dead
The good nurse tucks her into bed
And sometime before Christmas morn
Unto the world a child is born

No one answers the policeman's knock
So he stands back and kicks the lock
He knew he wouldn't like this call
A cold chill greets him in the hall
He cannot shake the eerie feeling
He turns and looks up at the ceiling
He sees the rope, the eyes that stare
The lifeless form, the toppled chair
He cuts the rope with expedience

And he saves the knot for evidence
But the answer to life that lost all hope
Won't be found in this knot in the rope
One takes his life, one gives birth
Good will to men, Peace on earth

The stars are gone, snow clouds descend
It seems the shift will never end
He goes from one who takes his life
To another who beats his wife
He returns a runaway to one place
Her father cries at her disgrace
An old lady on her own
Sits in her dingy room alone
In one house, son hates mother
Children hungry in another
And in all the things that he goes through
It seems there's nothing he can do
The threat of snow that fills the air
Does little for his deep despair
The radio sends him off again
Peace on Earth, Good will to men

The shift is over, time to go
Already it's begun to snow
As he waits for the traffic light
His thoughts are somewhere in the night
Red for stop, green for go
He drives home slowly through the snow
And pauses just outside the door
Of the haven
that he's waited
for
The snowflakes
slowly slumber
down
In hosts they
ghostly dampen
sound
The Christmas
bells ring out
again
"Peace on
Earth, Good
will to men"

SKIPPER SAYS:
"A friend of mine stopped smoking, drinking, chasing women and over-eating, all at the same time. It was a lovely funeral!"

* * *

IS THAT A FACT? *by Ron Young*

Many things have been accepted as facts - not all of them are.

Was Pope John Paul I murdered?

There are many who think that when Pope John Paul I died on September 29, 1978, after being pope for only thirty-three days, he was actually murdered.

The fact is that Vatican doctors announced that the Pope died of a heart attack without an autopsy ever being performed, and the body was embalmed just fourteen hours after it was found. Officials at the church referred to the Pope's ailing health which backed up the cause of death rendered by the doctors. Relatives of the Pope later said that neither the pope nor any of his close relatives had a history of heart trouble. Indeed the pope had suffered very little ill health prior to his death. In his childhood the pope had pneumonia and later in life had operations for gallstones, adenoids, tonsils, and hemorroids. The pope at one time suffered from a blood clot in his left eye but that cleared up without the need of an operation.

In July of 1978, just two months before his death, the pope had a check-up which included an EKG test. This test showed that there was nothing wrong with the pontiff's heart.

Several others things are worthy of note here; first: the pope favoured an end to the church's ban on birth control, which did not meet with favour from many in the upper echelon of the Roman Catholic Church; and secondly: although the pope's body was found at 4:45 a.m. by Sister Vincenza, it was originally reported that John Paul's body was not found until 5:30 a.m. by the Reverend John MaGee. It was also reported that the pope was holding a copy of *The Imitation of Christ* when found by MaGee, when it later confirmed that the pope had been reading personal papers at the time of his death. These discrepancies in the reporting of events, along with a number of other facts, gave rise to many rumours about the death of the pontiff, and even today many believe that the pope was murdered.

* * *

FOLK REMEDIES - Toothache
Place a raw garlic clove against your gum to ease a toothache.

Submitted by Mary Russell (nee Ash), Brooklyn, Newfoundland

* * *

Indispensable Cooks

We may live without poetry, music and art;
We may live without conscience and live without heart
We may live without friends, we may live without books;
But civilized man cannot live without cooks.

by Lavinia Keeping (nee Coombs), Port aux Basques, Newfoundland

Tonic For The Soul

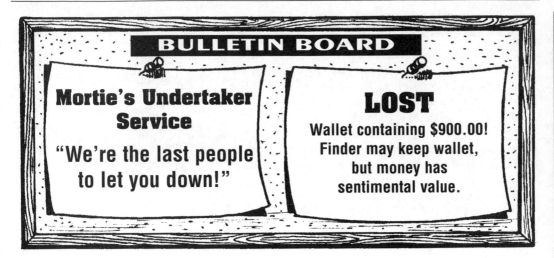

BULLETIN BOARD

Mortie's Undertaker Service

"We're the last people to let you down!"

LOST

Wallet containing $900.00! Finder may keep wallet, but money has sentimental value.

Notable Quotables! by Ron Young

Meanings and origins of well-known expressions

"Kick the bucket"

MEANING: To die

ORIGIN: According to Brewers Dictionary of Phrase and Fable, in Old English "bucket" means "beam" or "yoke". In East Anglia the beam on which a pig is hauled up by the back legs for slaughter is called a bucket. The kicking of the bucket by the pigs before they died probably brought about the expression. A person who stood on an upside-down bucket to commit suicide by hanging may also have been responsible for the expression. His last act before death would have been to kick the bucket out from under him.

* * *

The Lighter Side

A man was broken down on the highway and was under the hood staring helplessly at the engine when to his amazement a cow ambled up. Looking under the hood as well, the cow said, "It's the timing chain, that's the problem. This is going to cost a fortune to fix!"

The shocked man ran down the road and bumped into the cow's owner who was driving several other cows into a field. The farmer listened as the man gaspingly told him what had happened.

"Was she a brown cow with a patch of white between her eyes?" asked the farmer.

"Yes! Yes! That's her," shouted the man.

"I wouldn't take any notice of her if I were you," said the farmer. "That's Betsy, and she don't know a thing about cars."

* * *

Tonic For The Soul

Peril Under The Ice

by Rev. John Ellis Currey

I want to share with you this story of the time that I came the closest to going on to the other world. It is a story involving ice and a pond, and a miraculous escape from death that was possible only by the power of God.

On Sunday, Dec. 4th, 1977, as the United Church Minister to Fogo Island, I was driving from one Church service that I had just conducted at Seldom-Come-By, from 2-3 p.m., to the next service which was to be held at Fogo at 4 p.m. I never got there.

As I topped a little rise about 2 miles north of Seldom at Maul Pond, I saw a ridge of brown slush about a foot high, across the right hand side of the road in front of me - it had obviously fallen off the blade of the grader, and the operator had now shoved it into the ditch. I could not drive around it, as a man was changing a tire on his pickup truck, partly on the narrow shoulder, and partly on the left side of the road. "Not to worry," I thought, "the front right wheel of my car will punch through it." BUT IT WAS FROZEN BROWN ICE! It blocked the front right wheel, and the car instantly spun around in a circle, out of control. On my left was a guardrail, just beyond the pickup truck, and to the left of that, about a 15 foot drop down to the rock wall of the causeway to the edge of the pond, which was covered with ice.

I lunged out of my seat to the right side of the car, to avoid the guardrail, as it appeared that the end of the guardrail might punch into the left door of the car. But the car went over the rock wall just short of the rail. The car turned over as it went down the rock wall, plunged through the ice which was only about 4" thick, and on down to the bottom of the pond, where it came to rest upside down. All I could see was total blackness, because the windows, of course, were under water. The cold water, rising fast on my legs made me think, "I guess this is it!" However, I did PRAY TO GOD that I might be needed for further work for the Lord, because I knew that He could get me out of the situation, IF I was worth the effort.

The water rose up over my chin, and then it stopped rising! I was breathing hard now, as I kept kicking my legs to keep the circulation going. The water was so high that I could not open my mouth fully to take in more air, because when I opened it wider, the water and ice particles entered my mouth! There were large blocks of ice in the car - I know they were large because they moved slowly when I kicked them. I realized after that they had entered the car through the broken windows. I could not turn my head, as it was nipped somehow (it was lodged in the space between the edge of the seat on the passenger's side).

I was actually upright, but the car was upside down. I did not have to move at all, really, except to kick my legs. I heard hammering on the car, so I knew someone was doing whatever they could to get me out. I knew I was by the door handle, but, do as I might, I could not get the door open. I heard the men say after a few minutes, "We'll have to cut through the inner panel of the door, as all we have cut through is the outer panel." I said, "You can't - my head is right there!" After what seemed like a long time, I heard the screech of metal on rocks, and the water began to go down!

It is difficult to describe what a wonderful feeling of thankfulness and gratitude it is to be saved from what would have been certain death in a very few more minutes from hypothermia. The door was yanked open, and I stepped out! I remember what I said - I said, "THANK GOD YOU MEN GOT ME OUT OF THERE!" I would have immediately fallen flat because my legs were like 2 sticks, but one man on each side supported me, and helped me up the rock wall, and into a

Department of Highways truck that the driver of the pickup truck with the flat tire had gone into Seldom and got. In about 9 minutes we covered the 7 miles to Fogo Cottage Hospital. A nurse saw us coming and filled a tub with hot water. I was never so glad to see hot water in my life - I jumped in fully clothed. I was still shaking so much that I could not get my trousers off, so the nurse jumped in fully clothed and hauled them off.

The Doctor - John Verity - an English Doctor, asked me questions, and noted my answers. I stayed in that water until I was completely warm again. He kept me in the hospital overnight for observation, but I didn't even get a cold out of the ordeal. He allowed that my temperature had been down to about 90° Fahrenheit by the time I got out of the car (normal being 98 and three-fifths). He said that a person cannot live below 90°, because hypothermia causes small heart muscles that make up the heart, to beat independently, and the heart then shudders, and stops. I had been in the ice water for 30 minutes.

In looking back, there are several seemingly unimportant details about the whole thing, which, added together, are more than coincidence, and are actually proof that God did see to it that my life was spared.

(1) The name of the man whose truck had the flat tire, was Nehemiah Cobb, and the rock wall of the causeway was not unlike the rock wall of Jerusalem, which Nehemiah walked in days of old. That, of course, would be classified as coincidence.

(2) The next day, when I went out to the pond, down to the edge, and back up the wall, I caught sight of a 'wall-walker' toy, hanging on a rock, which the other Doctor of the hospital had asked me in Gander to purchase for their little boy, as they were in a hurry to catch the Fogo ferryboat a couple of days before - I had put it in the back window of the car until I would be able to give it to him, and it had obviously fallen out when the wrecker had hauled the car out of the pond.

(3) Calvin and Lila (Pope) Rowe and their little boy Kent, who knew me well from Sunday School, were driving from Fogo to Seldom when they saw the crowd on the causeway, and stopped to help. Calvin went down to the pond to help, and Lila, becoming a bit hysterical, said, "Nothing but a dead body will come out of that pond - the Minister's dying!" Little Kent sat there in the car with a calm and smiling face, and said, "Oh, he'll be alright!" "What do you mean?" his mother demanded. The little fellow's reply was, "The Man upstairs will save his life!"

(4) There were 2 men from Barr'd Islands on the shore of the pond - Joyce Primmer and his French-Canadian brother-in-law. The brother-in-law's name was Suave, which means "saved" in English!

The rescue was effected when Joyce or his brother-in-law exclaimed, "Has nobody here got a rope? That man's not going to live much longer", (he could hear me heaving for breath, and I guess he noticed the breathing was slowing down noticeably). Reg and Ross Waterman from Deep Bay got 50 fathom of line out of their truck.

(5) Only the day before, Ross had said, "We might as well take that line out of the truck, because we have now got the knee hauled over the ice from the woods." But Reg replied, "No, we'll leave it in the truck, there might be somebody in TROUBLE on the road!' So then, the next day, they tied the line onto one lower control arm of my car, and all hands got on the line (by this time there were about 30 people gathered on the road), and they HAULED the whole works out of the pond - the car, the water in it, the ice in it, and me! In very few places in this world outside Newfoundland, would it have been possible.

I also want to mention Jim Jacobs of Fogo, who, as the first man to get to the car in the pond, worked tirelessly to get me out, along with Hayward Gill of Fogo. Sad to say, Hayward has since passed away. It was not until after he died in 1980 that I heard about the Carnegie Foundation in Pittsburgh, Pennsylvania, USA, which makes awards for life-saving. I rented a car in Toronto, and drove to Pittsburgh, to endeavour to get some help for Hayward's widow, Marie, who had the dif-

ficult task of raising their fine family of 7 children, but I was told that awards have to be applied for within one year of the occasion.

In regard to the miraculous escape from death that I experienced, it appears obvious that there is undeniable proof that the purposes of God will prevail.

In those years, there was a dire shortage of Ministers. As Jesus said, *"The harvest is plentiful, but the labourers are few. Pray therefore to the Lord of the harvest, to sent out labourers into the harvest." (Luke 10:2).*

* * *

The Lighter Side

A Newfoundlander was driving to Toronto when he was stopped by a police officer for speeding. He was very upset when the officer told him that he would be getting a ticket. He wanted to say something insulting to the officer, but didn't want to say anything that might up the fine. Noticing a fly buzzing around the officer's head he said, "Watch out for that circle fly, officer!"

"What the hell is a circle fly?" asked the policeman.

"Well, we have them back in Newfoundland, and we call them circle flies because they always fly in circles around the horse's ass."

"Are you trying to say that I'm a horse's ass?' shouted the officer.

"No sir, I would never be disrespectful to an officer of the law," replied the man, "but you can't fool them circle flies."

* * *

IS THAT A FACT? *by Ron Young*

Many things have been accepted as facts - not all of them are.

Queen loses her head over a piece of cake?

Marie Antoinette, wife of Louis XVI of France, was beheaded during the French Revolution in 1793. Prior to that time when the peasants were complaining to their monarch because there was no bread to feed themselves and their hungry families, she is reported to have said, "If they have no bread, let them eat cake."

The fact is that it is very likely that the queen never uttered those words. In *Confessions*, the sixth book of Jean-Jacques Rousseau written in 1766, the writer talks of an incident which occurred in 1740, fifteen years before Marie Antoinette was born. In this book, Rousseau writes, "At length I recalled the thoughtless remarks of a great princess, who, when she was told the pheasants had no bread, replied, 'Let them eat cake'."

In 1843 another writer, Alphonse Karr, gives credit for the remark to a Duchess of Tuscany in 1760 or earlier. Karr believes the rumour that Antoinette had said the words were circulated by the revolutionaries who were attempting to overthrow King Louis at the time, in an effort to discredit the queen.

In any case the words played a big part in the eventual revolution which saw the beheading of Louis XVI, Marie Antoinette and thousands of others.

* * *

Tonic For The Soul

SKIPPER SAYS:
"The three stages of a normal sex life are;
Tri-weekly, try weekly and try weakly!"

* * *

Notable Quotables! by Ron Young

Meanings and origins of well-known expressions

"Paying through the nose"

MEANING: Paying a high price.
ORIGIN: When the Danes conquered Ireland in the late 9th century, one of the things they did was impose a heavy tax on the residents. They took a census by counting noses, and those who did not pay sometimes had their noses slit by their conquerors.

* * *

A Recipe For A Day

Submitted by Rita Penney, Salmon Cove, Nfld

Take a dash of cold water,
And a leaven of prayer
A little bit of sunshine gold,
Dissolved in morning air.
Add to your meal some merriment
And a thought of kith and kin

And the prime ingredient,
A plenty of work thrown in.
But spice it all with essence of love
And a little whiff of play,
Let a wise old book and a look above,
Complete a well spent day.

* * *

SUPERSTITIONS:
When a sailor dreams of horses it is a sign that a storm is coming.
Lots of cats about is a sign that a heavy gale is coming.

Submitted by Ernest Tucker, Rexdale, Ont

BULLETIN BOARD

Alf and Bill's Trash Removal
"We're at your disposal!"

Harry's Hot Dogs
Any one of our dogs will feed the hand that bites it!

If

by Rudyard Kipling

If you can keep your head when all about you
Are losing theirs and blaming it on you.
If you can trust yourself when all men doubt you,
But make allowance for their doubting too;
If you can wait and not be tired by waiting
Or being lied about, don't deal in lies,
Or being hated, don't give way to hating
And yet don't look too good, nor talk too wise:

If you can dream - and not make dreams your master
If you can think - and not make thoughts your aim;
If you can meet with Triumph and Disaster
And treat those two imposters just the same;
If you can bear to hear the truth you've spoken
Twisted by knaves to make a trap for fools
Or watch the things you gave your life to, broken,
And stoop and build them up with worn out tools:

If you can make one heap of all your winnings
And risk it on one turn of pitch-and-toss,
And lose, and start again at your beginnings
And never breathe a word about your loss;
If you can force your heart and nerve and sinew
To serve your turn long after they are gone,
And so hold on when their is nothing in you
Except the Will which says to them: "Hold on!"

If you can talk with crowds and keep your virtue,
Or walk with Kings - nor lose the common touch,
If neither foes nor loving friends can hurt you,
If all men count with you, but none too much;
If you can fill the unforgiving minute
With sixty seconds' worth of distance run,
Yours is the Earth and everything that's in it,
And - which is more - you'll be a Man, my son!

* * *

SKIPPER SAYS:
"If we had known the grandchildren would be so much fun we would have had them first!"

* * *

Notable Quotables! *by Ron Young*

Meanings and origins of well-known expressions

"Eating humble pie"

MEANING: To come down from a high position and humble one's self.

ORIGIN: The word "humble" in "humble pie" is a play on the word, "umbles" (from the Latin *lumbulus,* or loin), which came to mean the heart, liver, kidneys, entrails and fatty remains of an animal, especially a wild animal. Thus, a pie made from umbles was called "umbles pie." The lord and his household would dine off venison after a deer was killed, and the huntsmen and household servants would have to eat the humble meal of umbles pie. The expression later changed to humble pie and took on the meaning it has today.

* * *

To My Grown-Up Son

Author unknown

My hands were busy through the day
I didn't have much time to play
The little games you asked me to
I didn't have much time for you...
I'd wash your clothes, I'd sew and cook
But when you'd bring your picture book
And ask me please to share your fun
I'd say: "A little later, son."

I'd tuck you in all safe at night
And hear your prayers, turn out the light
Then tiptoe softly to the door
I wish I'd stayed a minute more...

For life is short, the years must pass
A little boy grows up so fast.
No longer is he at your side
His precious secrets to confide.

The picture books are put away
There are no longer games to play.
No good-night kiss, no prayers to hear
That all belongs to yesteryear...
My hands, once busy, now are still
The days are long, and hard to fill
I wish I could go back and do
The little things you asked me to.

* * *

The Clock Of Life

The clock of life is wound but once
And no man has the power
To tell just when the hand will stop
At late or early hour.
Now is the only time you own
Live, love and toil with a will
Place no faith in tomorrow
For the clock may then be still.

Submitted by Stan Baldwin, Stephenville, Nfld

What I Did On My Summer Vacation

by three-year-old Meaghan Hagerty (as written by her dad, Dave Hagerty)

I had lots of fun on my summer vacation. At first I thought we were going camping, but Daddy said we would be roughing it, just like he used to do in New Fun Land when he was growing up. Mommy says Daddy never did grow up, and the only roughing he did in New Fun Land was helping with the takeover of LaManche Provincial Park every May 24th weekend. And then, it was rougher on the authorities, not to mention Nanny and Poppy Hagerty, than on Daddy.

Oh yeah! Nan and Pop came with us camping. We had so much fun. Even before we left Kamloops, their car was making really funny noises. Poppy and Daddy looked under the hood. They looked like me and my big brother Liam when we're pretending to be something we're not. Mommy said they were two bluffs. I don't know what that means, but I'm pretty sure they were pretending just like I thought. Because by the time we got to Vernon, which isn't very far from Kamloops, that car was running hotter than Daddy himself. The next day when his credit card didn't work at the garage, Daddy blamed it on the credit card company. He says everyone does. He says the people behind the counters and all the customers waiting in line don't ever believe it's the credit card company though. They think you're a deadbeat. Mommy says Daddy's paranoid, whatever that means. Daddy says he's not that para word at all. He says the evil credit card companies are just out to get him. Mommy said she'd make a call and straighten the whole mess out. And that's just what she did.

The next day was REALLY exciting because we got to see a magic trick. A nice man in a real tow truck came to our campsite and unlocked our van door with NO KEYS!!! Daddy says he showed us the magic trick because of Mommy. Mommy says it was Daddy's doing. Whoever did it, me and my brothers were sure happy the man came all the way out in the country to show us ONE magic trick. Actually, Daddy says he did two tricks. Not only did he open our van door while the keys were locked inside, but PRESTO... he made our money disappear too.

Something else that disappeared was my baby brother Sheehan who's not even two yet. I don't know what time it was. I just know it was really dark. So it was a long while after my big brother Liam got car sick and we stopped for what Daddy calls the most horrible lunch ever served to a human bean. And only a short while after Pop, who likes to stay up late and drink coffee, heard a noise in the dark woods, got the creeps and hurried to bed early. (I don't think Pop roughed it much in New Fun Land either!) Anyways, Daddy and Poppy must have been bluffs THAT day too. Because they only pretended to do up the straps that keep us from falling out of the tent trailer when we're sleeping. My baby brother was put on the inside for safety, 'cause he rolls around in his sleep. It didn't seem very safe to me though, when he fell out on the ground. Daddy said he was bear bait in about a second! But I think even bears would be afraid of something screaming like that. He wasn't hurt though. Just scared. I think Mommy and Daddy and Nanny and Poppy were even more scared. I wonder if it gave Pop the creeps.

We gave the camper a rest for a couple (a couple is two) of days and stayed at Nan's and Pop's house in Claresholm, Alberta. Pop and Nan must have had enough of roughing it though, because when we left, they stayed home. We went on to Calgary and Edmonton. We were going to go to Jasper too. But Daddy said he didn't want to freeze his butt off. (Only he didn't say "butt". He said the "a" word that I'm not allowed to say). And besides, Aunt Sharon and Uncle Mike in Calgary had a brand new baby. So we went back to Calgary to see my new cousin Julia Elizabeth Hagerty. She's beautiful! Then we went to Lake Louise in the Rocky Mountains and froze our butts off anyway. As a matter of fact, I heard Daddy tell Mommy it was cold enough to freeze the nuts off a brass bridge. I didn't see any brass bridge. Anyways, Daddy said, "let's get the H-E-two-sticks

Tonic For The Soul

outta here!" I don't know what that means, but we didn't stay another night in the mountains.

It rained in Yard Creek Provincial Park. That's where we stayed after the nuts froze off the brass bridge. Everything got wet but we stayed for two days anyway and Daddy said we'd all have fun if he had to tie us up and tickle our feet with a feather to do it. He didn't have to. I had so much fun. Every chance I got, I'd ask Mommy or Daddy to take me to the really neat bathrooms that had no flushers or water, just a big hole with flies living in it. Mommy and Daddy looked silly breathing through their mouths. Mom said if I fell in, to shout "GOOD-BYE" on the way down because there was no way she was coming in after me. I don't know why she wouldn't, but I'm pretty sure she wasn't joking, so I made sure I didn't fall in. The second day, we woke up from quiet time and Daddy had a fire going. We don't know how he did it since everything was so wet. But for the rest of our vacation, we couldn't find any maps or coloring books or Mom's crossword book or the lantern box or the two decks of cards or the crib board or the big can of camp fuel or the five boxes of matches or even the spare tire for the camper. It was some nice fire though.

Well, except for the time the horrible shower curtain tried to eat me and Mom alive... and the time Daddy burned his hand on a hot fire pit... and the time Daddy tripped on a cold fire pit and really hurt his leg... and the time my big brother Liam nearly poked his eye out with a stick, that's about it. Believe it or not, Mommy and Daddy say our 'roughing-it' vacation was just about perfect and we'll probably do the same thing next year. I don't understand adults!

* * *

You Can

Do all the good you can
By all the means you can
In all the ways you can
In all the places you can
At all the times you can
To all the people you can
As long as ever you can
John Wesley

ONLY

Only as high as I reach
can I grow
Only as far as I seek
can I go
Only as deep as I look
can I see
Only as much as I dream
can I be
Submitted by Stan Baldwin, Stephenville, Nfld

* * *

The Lighter Side

The man drove his car down a city street obeying all the rules of the road, unknowingly being followed by a policeman. Suddenly the man looked in the rearview mirror, and upon seeing the police car, put the accelerator to the mat and sped off. The officer pursued but was unable to get close to the fleeing vehicle. Finally, the car turned down a dead-end street and the officer pulled up behind the trapped vehicle.

Angrily the officer walked up to talk to the driver.

"What's the matter with you?" he shouted at the man! "You were driving fine until you saw me behind you. Why did you take off when you saw me?"

"Well," replied the man, "my wife ran off with one of you police officers about two months ago, and I thought you were bringing her back."

* * *

A Grandma - as seen by a young child

A Grandma is a used mom who is old but still good

This is her head where she keeps all the stories of when I was a little kid

Here are Grandma's glasses so she can read your favourite stories without skipping part 2

Grandma's ears are for hearing prayers

This is Grandma's mouth that she is always kissing with

Grandma's arms are for giving hugs

These are grandma's hands which know how to make really delicious stuff

Grandmas have lots of patience but I don't know where they keep it

Grandma's pocket has lots of tissues for wiping your face (unless you can duck fast)

There is a lap under her apron for sitting on

Grandma's feet for slow walking cuz Grandmas shouldn't run fast or play hard

Grandmas know lots of things like what flowers are called and can answer hard questions like why isn't God married

Everyone should try to have a grandma to love them
* * *

SUPERSTITIONS:

A single sled dog howling alone in the middle of the night was a sure sign of a death in the community.

It was always considered bad luck to start a project on a Friday.

Submitted by John M. Earle, Lewisporte, Nfld

* * *

IS THAT A FACT? *by Ron Young*

Many things have been accepted as facts - not all of them are.

Cure for common cold?

Many people believe that by drinking liquids, chicken soup or taking aspirins, you can get rid of your cold. Others believe you would need none of these cures if you had taken Vitamin C in the first place.

The fact is there is no known cure for the common cold. Some things, when ingested may relieve the discomforts caused by the symptoms of the cold, or may have a positive psychological affect on these symptoms, but to date, no cure has been found.

It is still a controversial issue, whether or not vitamin C will prevent colds. Dr. Linus Pauling believes that massive doses of the vitamin will prevent a cold. Others in the medical profession do not subscribe to his theory. Still others agree with Pauling. Sheila Charleston and Mary Clegg, two researchers at the University of Strathclyde in Scotland, conducted a one-time research in which they used about one hundred subjects. Half of the subjects got daily doses of a pill containing the vitamin, while the other half got a dummy look-alike pill. The results: The subjects given the vitamin pills had nearly 50% fewer colds.

The problem that the medical profession has with the taking of vitamins in large doses, is the possible harmful side effects of these vitamins which may be worse than the common cold.

The Touch of the Master's Hand
Myra Brooks Welch

·Twas battered and scarred, and the auctioneer
Thought it scarcely worth his while
To waste much time on the old violin,
But held it up with a smile,
"What am I bidden, good folks," he cried,
"Who'll start the bidding for me?"
"A dollar, a dollar"; then "Two! Only two?"
Two dollars, and who'll make it three?
Three dollars once; three dollars, twice
Going for three-" but no,
From the room far back, a grey haired man
Came forward and picked up the bow;
Then wiping the dust from the violin,
And tightening up the strings,
He played a melody pure and sweet
As the caroling Angel sings.

The music ceased, and the auctioneer,
With a voice that was quiet and low,
Said: "What am I bid for the old violin
And he held it up with the bow.
"A thousand dollars, and who'll make it two?
Two thousand! And who'll make it three?
Three thousand once; three thousand, twice,
And going, and gone," said he.
The people cheered, but some of them shouted
"We do not quite understand
What changed its worth," swift came the reply:
"The touch of the master's hand."

And many a man with life out of tune,
And battered and scarred with sin
Is auctioned cheap to the thoughtless crowd,
Much like the old violin.
A 'mess of pottage', 'a glass of wine',
'A game', and he travels on.
He is "going" once, and "going" twice,
He is "going" and almost "gone".
But the master comes, and the foolish crowd
Never can quite understand
The worth of a soul, and the change that's wrought
By the touch of the Master's hand.

SKIPPER SAYS:

"You know you're getting old when all the phone numbers in your little black book belong to doctors!"

* * *

Abou Ben Adhem and the Angel

James Henry Leigh Hunt (1784-1859)

Abou Ben Adhem (may his tribe increase)
Awoke one night from a deep dream of peace,
And saw within the moonlight of his room
Making it rich, and like a lily in bloom
An angel writing in a book of gold
Exceeding peace had made Ben Adhem bold
And to the presence in the room he said.
"What writest thou?" - The vision raised its head,
And with a look made of all sweet accord,
Answered, "The names of those who love the Lord."
"And is mine one?" said Abou. "Nay not so,"
Replied the angel. Abou spoke more low,
But cheerily still; and said, "I pray thee then,
Write me as one that loves his fellow men."
The angel wrote and vanished. The next night
It came again with a great awakening light,
And showed the names whom love of God had blessed
And lo! Ben Adhem's name led all the rest.

* * *

Once in a Saintly Passion *by James Thompson (1834-1882)*

Once in a Saintly passion
I cried with desperate grief
"Oh Lord, my soul is black with guile
Of sinners I am chief"

Then stooped my guardian angel
And whispered from behind
"Vanity my little man,
You're nothing of the kind."

* * *

A Wife's Secret

You know what I look like, you know what I say
You know where I go during the day
You know what I spend, you know what I keep
You know when I wake, you know when I sleep
You know what I eat, and you know what I drink
But there's one thing you don't know and that's what I think.

by Hazel Warren, Chapel Arm, Nfld (nee Cobb, Wabanna Mines, Bell Island, Nfld)

* * *

Notable Quotables! *by Ron Young*

Meanings and origins of well-known expressions

"The handwriting is on the wall"

MEANING: Misfortune is imminent

ORIGIN: The expression comes from the Old Testament book of Daniel, chapter 5, verses 5 through 31. The Babylonians, led by King Belshazzer were feasting, drinking, and worshipping idols instead of the God of Daniel, the captive of Judah. A hand appeared and wrote a message on the wall which could not be interpreted, except by Daniel. The writing told King Belshazzer that he had not worshipped the true God, and that he had been "weighed in the balances and found wanting." The writing further said, "God hath numbered thy kingdom and finished it." That night King Belshazzer was slain.

* * *

IS THAT A FACT? *by Ron Young*

Many things have been accepted as facts - not all of them are.

Do Fans Keep The Air Cool?

On those hot summer days it's nice to have a fan or two to keep the room temperature down.

The fact is that fans do not cool the air, but actually bring the temperature up. The heat from the fan motor, the friction caused by the moving parts of the fan, and the friction between the fan blades and the air itself, actually increase the temperature of the air around it. The fan does however have a cooling effect on the body. This is accomplished by increasing the air circulation and thereby allowing moisture on the skin to evaporate into the air more readily.

* * *

Take Time For 10 Things

1. Take time to work - it is the price of success.
2. Take time to think - it is the source of power.
3. Take time to play - it is the secret of youth.
4. Take time to read - it is the foundation of knowledge.
5. Take time to worship - it is the highway of reverence and washes the dust of earth from our eyes.
6. Take time to help and enjoy friends - it is the source of happiness.
7. Take time to love - it is the sacrament of life.
8. Take time to dream - it hitches the soul to the stars.
9. Take time to laugh - it is the singing that helps with life's loads.
10. Take time to plan - it is the secret of being able to have time to take time for the first nine things.

Submitted by Kevin Ryan, Calgary, Alberta

Notable Quotables! by Ron Young

Meanings and origins of well-known expressions

"Happy as a clam"

MEANING: Contented and happy

ORIGIN: The original expression was, "As happy as a clam at high tide". A clam would be happy at high tide because clams are dug at low tide. The saying was later shortened.

* * *

The Lighter Side

A small boy was shopping in a grocery store with his mother when he became very overpoweringly aware of a very large man beside him. So acutely was he aware of the man, who not only towered over him, but seemed to take up the whole aisle, that he blurted out, "Mom, is that man ever fat!"

The red-faced mother raised an up-pointed index finger to her lips and said, "Sssshhh!"

"But Mom, he's so F - A - T," the youngster spelled out in a whisper.

"You wouldn't want anyone talking about you like that, now would you?" chided the mother.

"I suppose not," said the boy and the two went on with their shopping.

At the check-out counter the boy and his mom found themselves in the line-up directly behind the big man, who unbeknownst to the boy was wearing a telephone beeper.

Suddenly a phone call activated the beeper.

A look of fear came over the boys face at the first beep. On the second beep he dove under the counter and shouted, "Look out Mom, he's backing up!"

* * *

IS THAT A FACT? by Ron Young

Many things have been accepted as facts - not all of them are.

Leap year not every fourth year?

Every schoolboy and schoolgirl, and everybody else knows that every fourth year is leap year.

The fact is that every fourth year that can be divided by 4 is a leap year, except years ending in 00 that cannot be divided by 400. The years 1800 and 1900 were not leap years because although they were the fourth year they could not be divided by 400. The year 2000 meets all requirements and will be a leap year. This is because a solar year is actually not exactly 365 1/4 days long but is in fact 365 days, 5 hours, 48 minutes, 46 seconds long, and the hours, minutes and seconds have to be made up.

* * *

LAST DAY IN THE HOME

by Ron Young

The evening's eve has such a feeling
As the sun is sinking low
Thoughts across the years are reeling
Thoughts, no one but me could know

Deep inside my soul is aching
As down this quiet path I go
To watchers there is no mistaking
That their subject's feeling low

Way is doubtful, mood is pensive
Feet not knowing where they go
I feel edgy, apprehensive
But of what, I do not know

Need someone to show some caring
Someone not paid, who doesn't know
Need someone, my soul needs baring
Someone to miss me when I go

My friends were here, and all are free now
Friends that I helped make it, 'tho
I wish that they were here for me now
Wish I didn't have to go

Life with all its hurt and sorrow
Life with all its trials and pain
Is life that I will miss tomorrow
I shall not pass this way again

* * *

SKIPPER SAYS:

"It's a privilege to live in a country
where you can say what you think,
without thinking!"

* * *

Tonic For The Soul

IS THAT A FACT? *by Ron Young*

Many things have been accepted as facts - not all of them are.

Jesse Owens could outrun a racehorse?

Jesse Owens, the great black-American runner who won four gold medals in the 1936 Olympics in Berlin, Germany, thereby upsetting Hitler to the point that he walked out of the stadium rather than congratulate Owens because he was black, could outrun a racehorse, or so it is believed.

The fact is that Jesse could, and did outrun a racehorse in a hundred yard sprint, and he did so on more than one occasion. There was a bit of a trick to it, however. Owens explained how it was done: High-spirited horses were always picked for the race. When the starters pistol was fired the horse would rear back, and as Jesse put it, "I would be off with a tremendous break and by the time he came down I was 50 yards down the track, and at that point even though he would be covering 21 feet for every 7 I covered, it was too late; I would win."

In 200 yards Jesse would not have a chance, but then most of us wouldn't even have a chance in 50 yards.

* * *

The Lighter Side

Some years ago when the T. Eaton Company was still in the mail order business, they got a letter from a lady in Newfoundland that read, "Enclosed please find one dollar to pay for four rolls of toilet paper."

The company sent the lady a letter which read, "We are unable to fill your order at this time as you failed to include your catalogue number. Please look up the number in your catalogue, send it along to us and we will be happy to fill your order promptly."

The reply received by Eatons read, "If I had a catalogue I wouldn't have ordered the toilet paper in the first place."

* * *

Ah, Are You Digging On My Grave? *by Thomas Hardy*

"Ah, are you digging on my grave
My loved one? -planting rue?"
-"No; yesterday he went to wed
One of the brightest wealth has bred.
'It cannot hurt her now,' he said,
'That I should not be true.'"

"Then who is digging on my grave?
My nearest, dearest kin?"
- "Ah, no; they sit and think, 'What use!
What good will planting flowers produce?
No tendance of her mound can loose
Her spirit from Death's gin.'"

"But some one digs upon my grave?
My enemy? -prodding sly?"
- "Nay; when she heard you had passed the Gate
That shuts on all flesh, soon or late,
She thought you no more worth her hate,
And cares not where you lie."

"Then, who is digging on my grave?
Say - since I have not guessed!"
- "O it is I, my mistress dear,
Your little dog, who still lives near,
And much I hope my movements here
Have not disturbed your rest?"

"Ah, yes! *You* dig upon my grave
Why flashed it not on me
That one true heart was left behind!
What feeling do we ever find
To equal among human kind
A dog's fidelity!"

"Mistress, I dug upon your grave
To bury a bone, in case
I should be hungry near this spot
When passing on my daily trot.
I'm sorry but I quite forgot
It was your resting place."

A Recipe to Preserve A Husband

Be careful with your selection, do not choose one too young and take only such varieties as have been raised in a moral atmosphere. When once decided upon and selected, let that part remain forever settled and give your entire time and thought to domestic use. Some insist on keeping them in pickle while others are constantly keeping them in hot water. But even poor varieties may be made sweet and good by garnishing with patience, well-sweetened with smiles, and flavoured with kisses to taste. Then wrap them in a mantle of charity, keep warm with steady flow of devotion, and serve with peaches and cream.

When thus prepared they will keep for years.

Submitted by Pauline Reid, Reidville-Deer Lake, Newfoundland (nee Knee, Corner Brook, Nfld)

* * *

SUPERSTITIONS:

It is bad luck to enter a house through one door and leave through another.

Putting an item of clothing on inside-out will change the weather.

Submitted by Gordon LeRoux, Labrador City, Lab

* * *

IS THAT A FACT? *by Ron Young*

Many things have been accepted as facts - not all of them are.

Who wrote 'Desiderata'?

Many people have read 'Desiderata', the poem that starts "Go placidly amid the noise and haste, and remember what peace there may be in silence" etc, etc. Many have it on a poster on a wall in a special place in their house. At the height of its popularity, when first versions of the poster were sweeping the country, the poster claimed that it was dated in the 1600s and was discovered at Old St. Paul's Church in Baltimore.

The fact is the poem was written by Max Ehrmann and copyrighted by him in 1922. It was re-copyrighted in 1954 by Bertha K. Ehrmann. The poem is still popular today and many posters have credited Mr. Ehrmann with its writing. Others, however, are still signed, "author unknown".

Sweet Sixteen

by Ron Young

It's the age that is most talked about
It's the age that is least understood
When girls trade juvenile joys and toys
For the woes and worries of womanhood.

It's the age that's neither here nor there
It's the stage that's in between
The frivolous Fairy Princess
And the stately, solemn Queen.

It's the age of looking forward child
Without forgetting where you've been
It's the age that poets write about
Sensitive, sweet sixteen.

Be careful at this age, my child
A good name lost is hard regained
For this flirting, fleeting sweet sixteen
Will never come back again.

* * *

BULLETIN BOARD

FOR SALE
Twin Beds -
One hardly used.

Tips For Motorists
When you drive - don't
park, because accidents
cause people!

IS THAT A FACT? *by Ron Young*

Many things have been accepted as facts - not all of them are.

Common cold transmitted more by hand than by sneezing!

My parents always told me to cover my mouth and nose when I had to sneeze or cough because I could pass my cold on to some other person this way. Parents tell their children the same thing today.

The fact is the common cold is more readily spread by hand than it is by sneezing and coughing. Modern research has proven that there is a very low concentration of cold viruses in the saliva of the mouth of people who have a cold. Research has also proven that the air is not a good environment for cold germs, and these nasty little creatures only survive for several minutes in that medium. However, the common cold germ will survive for up to two hours on hands, and for a whopping seventy-two hours on the hard surface of a door knob.

Whether we have a cold or not, we humans seem to be rubbing our mouths, noses and eyes quite often (think about it, but keep your hands away from your face while you do). If we rub our mouth while we have a cold, our germs can easily be transmitted to our hand. If we shake hands with someone, the germs may be transmitted to that person's hand, where they can survive for two hours. Before that time is up, the guy with the germs on his hands is rubbing his eyes or nose, or is wiping his mouth. Then before you know it, he's sneezing and coughing too. If he doesn't shake your hand, or if he is lucky enough to avoid picking up the germ from your hand, but within seventy-two hours, goes through the same door that you used, the germs will probably transfer to his hand. These germs will probably survive until he feels the need to put that hand in the area of his eyes, nose or mouth. Then presto, he's got your cold!

By the way, according to researchers, cold germs can also live for up to an hour on a handkerchief.

So a good way to avoid giving someone else your cold is to use disposable tissues.

To avoid getting a cold you should keep rooms well ventilated. You should also wash your hands regularly, and try to consciously remember to keep them away from your eyes, nose and mouth at all times.

Notable Quotables! *by Ron Young*

Meanings and origins of well-known expressions

"Put up your dukes"

MEANING: Raise your fists in preparedness for a fight.
ORIGIN: Much to the astonishment of upper crust English society in the early 1800s, the Duke of York, Frederick Agustus, took up boxing. The Duke became quite the pugilist and gained the admiration of many in the profession. Before long, boxers and others were referring to their fists as "Dukes of York". This was later shortened to "Dukes".

* * *

The Seekers Of Dreams

by Ron Young

We are the poets of the world
We are the seekers of dreams
We spend hours watching summer unfold
By quiet mind-soothing streams

We wander on desolate beaches
Watching sea gulls frolic with foam
Find delight in derelict homesteads
That only the bats still call home

We linger in weed-ridden church yards
Reading each word on each stone
In our musings re-living the long-ago lives
Of the souls we feel somehow we've known

We revere the pale moon on a harbour
At the end of bewitching fall day
As it looms large over the mountain

It always sends magic our way

And evergreens ever enchant us
When the slow-falling snow sets the mood
Of a dark brooding wood when winter's eve falls
Leaving all in serene solitude

And the patter of rain on a roof top
In the bleak month of March still inspire
The warmest dreams ever shaped from shadows cast
By the flickering flames of a fire

We aren't the only seekers of dreams
There are others who find what we've found
But we are the poets of the world
We have to write them down

* * *

Preserving Choice Children

Take a large grassy field, 1/2 dozen children, 2 or 3 small dogs, a pinch of brooks and some pebbles. Mix children and dogs together well and put them in the field, stirring constantly. Pour the brook over pebbles, sprinkle the fields with flowers, spread over all a deep blue sky and bake in the hot sun. Then thoroughly brown, remove and set away to cool in a bathtub.

Submitted by June Dalley, Bathurst, New Brunswick (nee Howell, Carbonear, Newfoundland)

SKIPPER SAYS:
"Diplomacy is the art of saying, 'Nice Doggie, Nice Doggie,' until you can find a rock!"

* * *

Notable Quotables! by Ron Young

Meanings and origins of well-known expressions

"Steal one's thunder"

MEANING: To use another's achievements for one's self.
ORIGIN: Back in the 1700s, an English dramatist by the name of John Dennis invented a gadget which made a sound like thunder for sound effects in one of his plays. Unfortunately, the play was a flop, and the theatre cancelled it. Later, when Dennis heard that the theatre was using his thunder device in another play, he shouted, "That is my thunder, by God; the villains will play my thunder, but not my play!" From that the expression was born.

* * *

The Man In The Looking Glass

Author unknown

When you've made it in life and you're on the top shelf
And people send praises your way
Just go to the mirror and look at yourself
And see what THAT man has to say

For it isn't your parents, your peers, or your wife
Who, judgement upon you must pass
The person whose verdict counts most in your life
Is the one staring back from the glass

You may be praised and applauded by some
Who will think you a wonderful guy
To the man in the mirror you're only a bum
If you can't look him straight in the eye

The times in your life that you dream and you drift
And your well-planned maneuvers and moves
And your aims and achievements are only good if
The man in the mirror approves

You may fool all the people you meet through the years
And they may all rate you 'first class'
But your final reward will be heartaches and tears
If you've cheated the man in the glass

Notable Quotables! *by Ron Young*

Meanings and origins of well-known expressions

"Take it with a grain of salt"

MEANING: With great limitations or reservations.
ORIGIN: This expression was originally Latin, "cum grano salis" and is applied to any story that is hard to believe, or "hard to swallow." A grain of salt would make the story a bit easier to swallow.

* * *

MOM
by Ron Young

I don't telephone as often as I'd like, Mom
I never say I'm sorry, or I'm wrong
I seldom go to see you for a visit
And when I do I never stay that long

I don't ever do the little things that please
you
Or hug you like I did when just a child
And I forget the worries that I brought you
And the pain I caused when I was young and
wild

I may never say the things I always meant to
say
And I'll never repay the debt that I owe you
But these don'ts don't mean that I don't love
you
So I wrote this poem to let you know I do

* * *

Your Father's Name
Author Unknown

You got it from your father
It was all he had to give,
Now it's yours to carry with you
For as long as you may live.
If you lose the watch he gave you
It can always be replaced,
But a black mark on your name, son
Can never be erased.
It was clean the day you took it
And a worthy name to bear,
When you got it from your father
There was no dishonour there.
So guard it well and wisely
After all is said and done,
You'll be glad the name is spotless
When you give it to your son.

* * *

FOLK REMEDIES - Sprained Arm
Tie a piece of red wool around the wrist. Circle it nine times, and let it stay for nine days. This will cure the sprain.
Submitted by Nora K. Roberts, Woody Point, Nfld

* * *

FOLK REMEDIES - Dieting
In the Victorian era, vinegar was considered good weight-loss medicine.
Submitted by Stan Baldwin, Stephenville, Nfld

Tonic For The Soul

SKIPPER SAYS:
"What most women look for in a man is someone who is tall, dark and has some...!"

* * *

Notable Quotables! by Ron Young

Meanings and origins of well-known expressions

"Toe the line"

MEANING: Obey the rules.

ORIGIN: Many members of the British House of Commons wore swords, and to keep the members from fighting with each other, the government and opposition members were separated by two lines drawn in the carpet which were two sword lengths, plus one foot, apart. Members were required to stay behind their lines and not put so much as a toe outside. To this day members of the House are required to "toe the line".

* * *

Instructions

If you unlock it, lock it up.
If you break it, admit it.
If you can't fix it, call someone who can.
If you borrow it, return it.
If you value it, take care of it.
If you make a mess, clean it up.
If you move it, put it back.
If you don't know how to operate it, leave it alone.
If it will brighten someone's day, say it.

Submitted by Cheryl Keats (nee Dougherty), Hamilton, Ont

* * *

The Lighter Side

A man was passing a cemetary when he heard the anguished sound of a male voice coming from among the headstones, "Why did you die? Oh, why did you die?"

Hoping to be of some solace to the grieving man he approached and asked, "Who was it sir, your wife, sweetheart, sister, brother, son, daughter?"

In an even louder voice the man replied, "Neither, it was my wife's first husband. Why did he die? Why did he die?"

* * *

Fear No More The Heat O' The Sun

by Shakespeare, from "Cymbeline"

Fear no more the heat o' the sun,
Nor the furious winter's rages;
Thou thy worldly task hast done,
Home art gone, and ta'en thy wages:
Golden lads and girls all must,
As chimney-sweepers, come to dust.

Fear no more the frown o' the great
Thou art past the tyrant's stroke;
Care no more to clothe, and eat;

To thee the reed is as the oak:
The sceptre, learning, physic, must
All follow this, and come to dust.

Fear no more the lightening flash
Nor the all-dreaded thunder-stone;
Fear not slander, censure rash;
Thou hast finished joy and moan:
All lovers young, all lovers must,
Consign to thee, and come to dust.

* * *

Notable Quotables! *by Ron Young*

Meanings and origins of well-known expressions

"Stool pigeon"

MEANING: Traitor or informer.
ORIGIN: Hunters would sometimes nail a pigeon to a stool and leave it out in the open. The pigeon's alarming cries would attract other birds into the range of the hunters' guns. Since the birds met their fate after being lured by the "stool pigeon", anyone who attracted another to be captured, or any who informed on another, was called a stool pigeon.

* * *

A HUNDRED YEARS TO COME

Written in the 1800s by an anonymous author

Who'll press for gold this crowded street,
A hundred years to come?
Who'll tread yon church with willing feet
A hundred years to come?
Pale, trembling age and fiery youth
And childhood with his brow of truth,
The rich and poor, on land and sea,
Where will the mighty millions be
A hundred years to come?

We all within our graves shall sleep,
A hundred years to come?
No living soul for us shall weep
A hundred years to come?
But other men our land will till
And others then our streets will fill,
And other words will sing as gay,
And bright the sunshine as today,
A hundred years to come.

* * *

FOLK REMEDIES - Nausea, Headaches, Colds
Ginger tea, made by simmering some fresh peeled ginger root (sliced) is helpful in relieving nausea, even in pregnancy. Add a pinch of cayenne pepper if you have a cold, and for a headache, simmer the ginger with some cardamon pods.

Submitted by Judy Wells, (nee Green) Bonavista Bay, Nfld

FOLK REMEDIES - Earache
For a bad earache put warm olive oil in your ear, using a bit of cotton wadding to keep the oil in.

Submitted by Nora K. Roberts, Woody Point, Nfld

* * *

Tonic For The Soul

A Memorable Meal

by Rex W. Stirling

In the early 50's, before leaving on my first visit to Europe, I asked several friends who had travelled quite extensively what I might expect in England and Scandinavia. They had a number of suggestions, but all agreed that since I was going on a limited budget, I should eat in pubs in England and department store luncheonettes in the Scandinavian countries. "Why?" I asked. "Because," they replied, "the food is good, you can pile up your plate, and it's cheap." That was good enough for me.

While in England, the advice of my friends proved to be sound. As I travelled from London to Hull in the north, I always made it a point to have my meals in a pub. An added bonus to the reasonably priced menu, was the congenial atmosphere I always encountered.

In Sweden, the first stop on my Scandinavian tour, I quickly learned a department store luncheonette was indeed the best place to eat. Each store posts their menu in a window at street level, so people can make their selections in advance. I was staying in a small side street hotel called the Adlon. A few blocks away was a coffee shop where I always stopped for breakfast, which consisted of Cafe en laite (coffee and cream) two, of the three Swedish words I knew. One morning I awoke early with an overwhelming craving for a good, old-fashioned North American breakfast. I decided that this would be the morning, I would forego my usual cup of coffee with cream, and find something more substantial. As I strolled through the streets of downtown Stockholm, I stopped by a large department store and noticed their menu in the window. There, among a group of words was the word agg, which I knew was egg in Swedish. Early morning, a menu in the window, the word agg, obviously a breakfast menu, logical, no?

Taking out my notebook, I carefully copied word for word, the entire menu, I wasn't taking any chances. Going inside, I took the elevator to the seventh floor where the luncheonette was located. I found a small table by a window which overlooked the street. Soon a waitress appeared, smiled and said; "gott morgan mein hier" (good morning sir) after which she proceeded to fill my water glass and offer me a menu which I waved away. I took out my notebook, opened it to the page where I had copied the menu while on the street and showed it to her. She looked at it for a few moments with a puzzled expression, said something in Swedish, all the while looking at me intently. Not wishing to appear unsophisticated, I smiled and nodded. She looked perplexed and repeated what she had said previously. I nodded once more, smiled broadly, and again pointed to the open page of my notebook. She regarded me strangely, then shrugged her shoulders and quickly walked towards the kitchen area.

In anticipation of a hearty breakfast, I gazed out the window at the ever increasing flow of traffic outside, then, looking up, I noticed the luncheonette was quickly filling up with early morning diners. I was glad I arrived early and gotten a nice table. After some time, the kitchen doors swung open, and a busboy, pushing a large wheeled serving trolly headed my way. Once along side my table, he set up a smaller antetable and began transferring a number of dome covered platters from the trolly to it. I was both mystified and startled to see a second busboy, pushing an equally laden trolly approach my table.

By now I had become the center of attraction in the luncheonette, every eye in the room was on me. I silently wished the floor would open and swallow me up. Many of the other diners were openly whispering to each other while some pointed in my direction. Dish after dish was presented to me; eggs in an infinite variety, jams, jellies, a large assortment of cheeses, sweet rolls, poached salmon, sausages, breads and rolls, fresh fruit, thick slices of black forest ham; on and on

it went; my God, what had I ordered? All I wanted was a simple breakfast like I'd get in any restaurant back home in Newfoundland; juice, bacon and eggs, toast and coffee.

In the early 50's, Europe was slowly recovering from the effects of the war. The memories of that horror were still fresh in the minds of many, shortages were still very evident, food not being the least among them, now here was this obviously self-indulgent, greedy individual, ordering a massive meal which he couldn't possibly hope to eat. I was mortified and wished I could disappear. My appetite had vanished; as I looked up into the scornful eyes of the two busboys and the waitress who had now joined them at my table, then around at the other diners who were regarding me with a silent contempt I quickly pushed myself away from the table, and rushed out of there stopping only long enough to pay my rather hefty bill. I learned later I had ordered the banquet breakfast for twelve. I imagine the kitchen staff enjoyed a magnificent meal at my expense that morning.

On the way back to my hotel, I stopped off for a cafe en laite.

* * *

Notable Quotables! by Ron Young

Meanings and origins of well-known expressions

"Son of a gun"

MEANING: A cuss word.

ORIGIN: Woman were taken along on extended sea voyages by British sailors in the Nineteenth Century. Often the inevitable happened and pregnancy occurred and when the time came to give birth the woman was taken to a sectioned-off portion of the gundeck. Since no one was sure who the father was, these babies born near the ship's guns were jokingly called "sons of guns".

* * *

Luck *by Wilfred Gibson*

What bring you, sailor, home from the sea-
Coffers of gold and of ivory?

When first I went to sea as a lad
A new jack-knife was all I had:

And I've sailed for fifty years and three
To the coasts of gold and ivory:

And now at the end of a lucky life,
Well, still I've got my old jack-knife.

* * *

The Lighter Side

Uncle Charlie had been dead for some years before cars arrived in Newfoundland. When John purchased the first one in a certain small community, he took his friend George for his first-ever ride in a motor driven vehicle.

Cruising down the narrow road at the amazing speed of 35 miles per hour, George remarked to John, "I know Uncle Charlie wouldn't get the fright if saw this thing coming down the road now!"

"Not so big a fright as you'd get," replied John, "if you saw Uncle Charlie!"

* * *

BULLETIN BOARD

FOR SALE
Wedding Dress and Wedding Ring
"Used only once - by mistake"

Dachshunds For Sale
"Get a long little doggie"

Notable Quotables! *by Ron Young*

Meanings and origins of well-known expressions

"A cock and bull story"

MEANING: A lie

ORIGIN: The expression probably came from one of the old fables in which the animals talked. Cocks and Bulls were often characters in these old stories. Since no animal, including the cock and the bulls, can talk, any story in which they do is unbelievable. Therefore, a Cock and Bull story is an unbelievable one.

* * *

Mother-In-Law

You are the mother I received
the day I wed your son
And I just want to thank you, Mom
for all the things you've done
You have given me a gracious man
with whom I share my life

You are his lovely mother
and I his lucky wife
You used to pat his little head
and now I hold his hand
You raised in love a little boy
then gave to me a man.

* * *

Weep Not For Me

by Ron Young

Weep not for me, ere now I die
Although you think it due
Our slate is even now, and I
Shall weep no more for you

* * *

The Lighter Side

A census taker was visiting a small Newfoundland settlement when a small girl answered the door.

"How many in your family?" he asked her.

"There's Mom and Dad and me and Jack and Dan and Maryanne, and Isobel and Vic and Peter and George and Sarah and...."

At that point the census taker interrupted her and said, "We're not interested in names, we just need numbers."

"We don't have numbers," replied the girl, "we haven't run out of names yet."

* * *

Little Miss *by Ron Young*

She tried my patience to the core
This little miss
With every fiber I adore
This little miss
When I would rather write, or read
Must discipline the evil deed
Of little miss
From late night shift to bed I creep
The body desperate for sleep
Must rouse myself for morning kiss
From little miss

Life's problems leave but little hope
Sometimes I find it hard to cope
But I still turn the skipping rope
For little miss
When she can't sleep for fear and dread
Must chase the monsters from the bed
Of little miss
Yet, when I must dispel the fright
When I tuck her in at night
I get more than my blessings due
When she says, "Daddy, I love you"
My little miss.

* * *

IS THAT A FACT? *by Ron Young*

Many things have been accepted as facts - not all of them are.

Gold Rush not in Alaska!

Everyone, including every American citizen (and most Canadian citizens, for that matter), knows about the great Bonanza gold rush to the Klondike in Alaska and the bar room tales of sourdoughs in Dawson City, Alaska's best known town.

The fact is that neither the Klondike nor Dawson City are in the American State of Alaska, they are in the Canadian Territory of Yukon. The Klondike is an area around the Klondike River, a tributary of the Yukon River. Dawson is at the junction of the two rivers. The expression 'Bonanza Gold', as used in Johnnie Horton's famous song, "North to Alaska" and in many other stories and songs, refers to the great gold find in 1896 at Bonanza Creek, a smaller tributary of the Klondike River, in the area known as Klondike, Northwest Territories, Canada. Many of the exciting stories of the sourdoughs and trappers are told in rhyme by Canadian (English born) poet, Robert W. Service, including "The Cremation Of Sam McGee", "The Shooting Of Dan McGrew", and my favourite, "The Ballad Of Salvation Bill".

Tonic For The Soul

FOLK REMEDIES

Colds

To break up a cold, boil onions and thicken with flour and milk. Take at bed time.

Submitted by Mary Russell, Brooklyn, Nfld (nee Ash, Come By Chance, Nfld)

Ticklish Cough

Drink 2 tbsp lemon, 1 tbsp honey in 4 oz of water to cure ticklish cough.

Submitted by Barbara Lucas, Barachois Brook, Nfld

Child Hernia

Split a green Witch Hazel tree and pass the child through it to cure hernia.

Submitted by Jody N. Walters, Robinsons, Nfld

Nosebleed

Place on your forehead, a flat rock from the ocean, to cure a nosebleed.

Submitted by Darlene Lane, St. Chad's Nfld

✳ ✳ ✳

Fragrances

"The odor of a fragrant flower doth last,
Long after outward loveliness is gone.
So when a beauteous life seems spent and past
The influence of its goodness liveth on"

Submitted by Ted and Mable Marshall, Boyd's Cove, Nfld

✳ ✳ ✳

SUPERSTITIONS:

Two knives crossed on the table will bring bad luck.

Submitted by Gordon LeRoux, Labrador City, Lab

To throw water out your door on Good Friday was the same thing as throwing it in the Saviours face and was considered to be very bad luck.

Submitted by Stan Baldwin, Stephenville, Nfld

Wiff and the Shrink

So you say you're passionately in love with an octopus - I can only strongly urge you to get rid of this obsession immediately!

O.K. Doctor! I'll be strong! I'll do it! By the way Doctor, do you know anyone who would like to buy eight engagement rings?

Tonic For The Soul

Household Hints

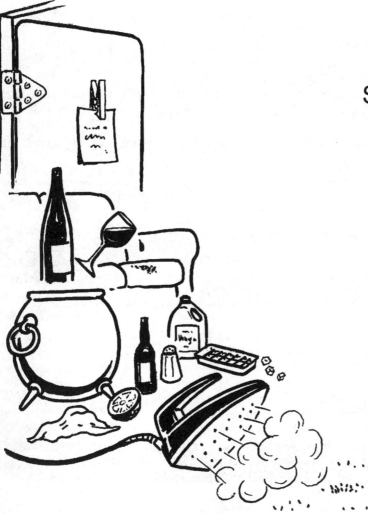

Suggestions

to help

around

the house

COOKING AND BAKING TIPS

Doubling a recipe: When doubling ingredients in a recipe, do not double the seasoning ingredients, add seasoning to taste.

Frozen berries: Don't thaw frozen berries before using them in cobblers, muffins, puddings, etc. They will hold their shape better if left frozen.

Crystallized honey: If your honey has crystallized, place the jar in some hot water and it will soften again.

Garlic bread: Add a teaspoon of garlic powder to your flour when baking bread or biscuits and you'll get a lightly flavoured bread that is delicious, especially if it is served warm or toasted.

Whole wheat bread: Whole wheat bread will rise higher and feel lighter if you mix in a tablespoon of lemon juice to the dough. You won't be able to taste the lemon juice later.

Flaky pie crusts: For flaky pie crusts, use sour cream instead of the usual liquid. Yogurt will also work.

Raisin pie treat: For a raisin pie treat, use leftover morning coffee instead of the liquid in which you cook your raisins. Add 1 teaspoon of vinegar for each pie filling.

Fruit pie tip: When baking fruit pies, sprinkle sugar under the fruit instead of on top to prevent the pie from boiling over.

Tenderizing tough meat: Marinate tough meat in lemon juice in the refrigerator for several hours and it will become tender.

Roasting meat: Whenever possible put your roast in the oven fat side up. This will keep the meat moist and tender.

Double the flavour of roast: Bake a small roast of beef and a small roast of pork together. Each meat picks up flavour from the other and the gravy is out of this world.

Frying bacon: To separate frozen bacon, heat a spatula over the stove, then slide it between the slices, one at a time, to get them apart. To prevent bacon from curling, dip each strip in cold water before frying.

Banana tips: To keep freshly peeled bananas from going dark, put them in lemon juice. Bananas that are on the verge of turning bad may be frozen to preserve them.

Bread tips: Bread will stay fresh longer if you keep a stick of celery inside the bread bag. Bread that has dried out can be freshened by wrapping it in a damp cloth (a towel will do) and placing it in the refrigerator for 24 hours. After removing the cloth, heat the bread in the oven for a few minutes.

Household Hints

Cake tips: To keep your cake moist, place apple portions in the cake box. A slice of fresh bread fastened with toothpicks to the cut edge of a cake will serve the same purpose.

Watery-whipped cream: To keep whipped cream from going watery, add icing sugar instead of granulated sugar.

Testing the cake in the oven: If a toothpick is too short to test a cake to see how well it is done, a piece of uncooked spaghetti will serve as well.

Hot dinner rolls: To keep your dinner rolls hot, place a piece of aluminum foil on them, under the towel.

Measuring baking powder: When measuring baking powder, be exact, too much can be as disastrous as too little.

Corn colouring: To keep sweet corn yellow, add 1 teaspoon lemon juice to the cooking water, a minute or two before you remove it from the stove.

Storing cottage cheese: Cottage cheese will keep twice as long if you store it with the carton upside down.

Crispy crackers: In humid weather crackers wrapped securely and kept in the refrigerator will keep their crispness.

Scaling fish: To scale fish, pour white vinegar over the fish and scale with a dull knife. The scales will come off easily.

Frozen fish: Frozen fish has a better texture if it is cooked without thawing.

Boiling fish: Add a little lemon juice to water while boiling to make fish firm and white.

No fishy taste: Put your frozen fish in a bowl of milk to thaw it and the milk will draw out the frozen taste leaving the flavour of fresh-caught fish. To obtain a sweet, tender taste on your fish, soak your fish in a mixture of vinegar and water before cooking. Also, when frying fish, add a piece of celery to cut down on odors.

Keeping the fish warm: If you are frying fish for a large crowd and want to serve them all at the same time, but can't cook it all at the same time, put some paper towels inside a styrofoam cooler and place the fish on the paper towels. The fish will stay hot until it is all ready.

Crispy fish batter: Use 7UP instead of the usual liquid when you make fish batter for deep frying. The coating will be very crispy.

Deep frying tip: Add 1 tablespoon of vinegar to the fat when deep frying to keep the food from absorbing too much fat. This cuts down on the greasy taste as well.

Household Hints

Sand in mollusks: To get sand out of shellfish, soak them for an hour in cold water with 1/2 cup of oatmeal.

More lemon juice: To get almost twice the amount of juice from your lemon or lime, immerse it in hot water for 20 minutes before squeezing. Lemons stored in a tightly sealed container in the refrigerator will also yield more juice.

Storing celery: Celery will keep longer in the refrigerator if you store it in paper bags instead of plastic ones.

Save celery tops: Save the celery tops and dry them in the oven. Then rub them into powder and store them in a glass jar for flavouring soups, stews and salads.

Preserving onions longer: Onions will last longer if you wrap them individually in foil wrap. Half a left-over onion will keep fresh longer if you cover the cut portion with a layer of butter.

More popcorn popping: You will have fewer "dud" popcorn kernels if you run ice-cold water over the kernels before placing them in the popper.

Frying chicken tips: To get golden brown chicken every time, add a few drops of yellow food colouring to the cooking oil after it has heated. Your flour will stick to the chicken better while frying if you chill the chicken for an hour after applying the flour.

Wet salad greens: If you need to use your wet salad greens right away, put them inside a pillow case and dry in the clothes dryer.

Easy-roll cabbage leaves: To save time and energy preparing leaves for cabbage rolls, remove core from cabbage and place cabbage in a plastic bag and put in the freezer for a day or two. Remove from freezer and thaw. Leaves will then separate very easily from head and are ready to use. Remove heavy spine from leaves for easier rolling.

'Fresh' frozen vegetables: Frozen vegetables will get back their fresh flavour if you pour boiling hot water over them to rinse away all traces of the frozen water. A pinch of sugar added to cooking water will give frozen vegetables a freshly-picked flavour.

Freezing soup: Freeze liquids, such as soups, in coffee cans lined with plastic bags. When the liquid is frozen remove it from the can. It will have its own wrapping and the can may be used again.

Frozen chicken: It is not necessary to thaw frozen chicken before cooking, just cook for 15 to 20 minutes longer than if they were previously thawed.

A great healthy dessert: Open a can of your favourite fruit (preferably unsweetened), and freeze. Later when it's time for dessert, blend the frozen fruit in your food processor or blender, and serve in a tall parfait glass, topped with nuts. It's a taste sensation.

Storing eggs: Never wash eggs before you store them. Washing removes the natural protective

coating which keeps the air and odors from entering the shell. Be sure to store eggs with the large end up.

Whipping egg whites: Egg whites whip better and to a greater volume if they are at room temperature.

Boiling eggs: Add 1/4 teaspoon of cream of tartar to the water when boiling eggs. This eliminates discolouration of the pot, sometimes caused by the eggs.

Baking muffins: Use your ice cream scoop for spooning muffin batter into muffin pans. It's easy and muffins will be uniform in size.

Keeping meringue from falling: A pinch of baking soda in meringue stops it from going down after it has been taken from the oven.

A twist in pie crusts: Roll a bit of grated cheese into the crust dough of your next apple pie for very exciting results.

Unshelling brazil nuts and pecans: Brazil nuts and pecans come out of their shells whole if, just before shelling, put into a 300° oven for 10 minutes.

A smooth and creamy frosting: Add 1 tbsp cake or pastry flour to each cup of confectioner's sugar used in chocolate frosting. This will give it a smooth and creamy texture and it won't crumble when cut.

Keeping cake fresh: To keep cake (or cookies) fresh, place an orange or apple in the cake tin with the cake. This also gives the cake (or cookies) a delicious flavour.

Keeping cheese longer: Cheese will not dry out if it is wrapped in a cloth dampened with vinegar.

Storing lettuce: Store lettuce in a sealed plastic bag in fridge to keep it longer.

Softening butter: To soften butter for spreading, fill a bowl with boiling water, empty it and invert it over the butter dish. Butter will soften without melting.

Golden brown french fries: To get golden brown french fries you must cook them twice. Cut up your fries then par cook them in the deep fryer, until they are soft, but not brown. You will probably require several basketfulls, depending on the number you are feeding. Then let the fat in the fryer heat up a little more. When you throw the par-cooked fries back in they will brown faster.

Keeping pancakes warm: When serving pancakes to a crowd, you can keep a whole batch hot by placing them between folds of a warm towel in a warm oven. Then everyone can enjoy hot pancakes at the same time.

Cooking cauliflower: When cooking cauliflower place it head first in the cooking water and it will stay white.

Pot boiling over: Add a tablespoon of butter to a boiling pot and it won't boil over.

How much water in the soup: When you've added all the ingredients to the pot, bring the water level to 2 inches above the ingredients. Perfect.

Thickening up the gravy: To make that gravy thicker, mix water and flour or cornstarch into a smooth paste. Add gradually, stirring constantly, and bring to a boil. Instant potato mix will also add body to your thin gravy.

Gravy browning substitute: If you're out of gravy browning, soya sauce will serve as well, and will add flavour to the gravy.

Healthier gravy: When serving gravy, use a proper gravy server, one that has a spout and collects the gravy from the bottom, thereby avoiding the grease floating on the top. A teapot will also work. Make sure you throw away the gravy, and refill the server, before it reaches the grease level.

Hurry-up baked potatoes: To have your baked potatoes ready sooner, preheat your oven to 450°F as you boil the potatoes in salted water for about 10 - 15 minutes. Put the potatoes into the hot oven for quick baking. Another way to quick-bake your potatoes is to insert a nail into the centre of the potato.

Hurry-up hamburgers: If you poke holes in the centers of the hamburger patties when shaping, the center will cook quickly. When the holes are gone the hamburgers are done.

Juicy roasts: Let your roast sit in its own juice with the oven turned off for about 15 minutes so it will absorb some of the juice and be more moist when slicing.

Pot liquor: The pot liquor, or vegetable juice left over after you cook vegetables is great for making gravies or sauces. Freeze it in an ice cube tray and the next time you're making gravy or sauce, pop in a few ice cubes for flavour.

No tears onions: You'll shed fewer tears peeling those onions if you: 1) cut the root end of the onion off last, 2) freeze or refrigerate them before chopping, or 3) peel them under cold running water.

Apples and potatoes: Don't store apples near potatoes, because the ethylene gas given off by the apples will spoil the potatoes.

Apples and tomatoes: The same ethylene gas contained in apples, which will spoil potatoes, will help ripen green tomatoes, so store your green tomatoes alongside your apples.

Fat in your soup or stew? Wrap ice cubes in a thin cloth then gently swish the ice cubes around the top of your soup, stew or gravy. The fat on the surface will adhere to the dish cloth and can then be removed. You may also drop the ice cubes loose in the soup and swish them around with a spoon. When the fat adheres to the ice cubes, spoon them out.

Household Hints

Fried foods sticking to the pan: Always heat your pan before adding the butter or oil when frying or sauteeing to prevent your food from sticking to the pan. Even eggs won't stick with this method and you will also get less spattering.

Baked goods sticking to the pan: If your muffins or biscuits are sticking to the tin pan, place the hot pan on a wet towel and they will slide out without sticking.

Dough sticking to the rolling pin: Wash out a pair of old panty hose and cover your rolling pin with one of the legs. Pull the material tight, tie at both ends, then cut the excess away. Dough will never stick to the rolling pin again.

Improving the cake mix: To improve an inexpensive cake mix, add 1 tablespoon of butter to the batter.

Measuring shortening: Before measuring margarine, butter, etc., dip your utensil into hot water and the shortening will slide off easily.

Crunchy coleslaw: For crunchy coleslaw, cut cabbage in half and soak in salted water for an hour. Drain, then proceed with recipe.

Cooking a tough old hen: If you want your stewed old hen to be as tender as chicken, soak it in vinegar for several hours before cooking.

Opening oysters, clams and mussels: Wash your clams, oysters, mussels and mullosks in cold water, place them in a plastic bag and put them in the freezer for about an hour and they will be easy to open.

Boiling rice, spaghetti or noodles: Add a lump of butter or a few teaspoons of cooking oil to the water to prevent your rice, spaghetti or noodles from boiling over. This will also keep them from sticking together.

Measuring honey, molasses and other sticky liquids: Before measuring sticky liquids, oil the cup with cooking oil and rinse in hot water to make the job easier.

Too-hot soup: If the soup is too hot for the children to eat, throw in some frozen peas to cool it down.

Slow-moving catsup: Insert a drinking straw, stir stick, or thin knife into the bottle, push it to the bottom of the bottle, and then remove. Enough air will be admitted to start the catsup flowing.

Removing silk from corn: If you dampen a paper towel and brush downward on the corn cob every strand will come completely off.

Sticky foods to slice or chop: Shake your sticky food in a paper bag containing a little flour to make the chopping easier. To cut or slice sticky food, dip your knife or shears in hot water repeatedly while cutting.

Removing rind from ham? Slit the rind lengthwise and place the ham in the pan with the slit side down. As the ham bakes, the rind will pull away and can be removed easily without lifting the ham.

Eggs stuck to the carton? Soak the carton and the eggs will come out without cracking the shells.

Is that egg fresh? To determine whether an egg is fresh without breaking the shell, immerse the egg in a pan of cool, salted water. If it sinks to the bottom, it is fresh. If it rises to the surface, don't use it.

Separating egg whites from yolks: Hold a small funnel over a bowl and break the egg into the funnel. The white will funnel down into the bowl and the yolk will stay in the funnel.

Keeping egg yolks fresh: Cover egg yolks with cold water and store them in the refrigerator and they will keep for several days.

Baking cakes with eggs: Use medium or large eggs when baking as extra large eggs sometimes cause cakes to fall after baking.

Boiling eggs: Pierce the end of an egg with a pin, and it will not break when placed in boiling water. If an egg is cracked, add vinegar to the water, and it will boil without having the white run out of the shell.

Boiled eggs turning black: Put boiled eggs in cold water immediately and they won't turn black.

Is your egg boiled hard yet? To determine whether an egg is hard-boiled, spin it. If it spins 'round and 'round, it is hard-boiled. If it wobbles and will not spin, it is raw.

Underdone boiled egg: If a boiled egg is underdone after the top is cut off, replace the top and microwave for a few seconds.

Removing shells from boiled eggs: Quickly rinse your boiled egg in cold water and the shell will peel off easily.

Poached eggs: A few drops of vinegar will keep poached eggs from running all over the pan.

Too salty? If you've added too much salt to your soup or stew, just cut up some raw potatoes and add. You can discard the extra potatoes once they have cooked and absorbed the salt. Another way to solve your salty soup and stew problem is to add a teaspoon each of cider vinegar and sugar. Adding just sugar will also help.

Vegetable cooking rule-of-thumb: When cooking something that grows above the ground, start with hot water, when cooking something that grows below the ground, start with cold water.

Keep milk from scorching: To keep milk from scorching, rinse the pot with hot water before using.

Black potatoes: To prevent potatoes from turning black when boiling, add a teaspoon of vinegar to the water.

Too sweet? If your dessert or other dish is too sweet, adding salt will solve the problem. For those oversweetened main courses you can add a teaspoon of cider vinegar to solve the problem.

Sweeter than sweet: To intensify the sweetness of any dish, add a pinch of salt. This works on grapefruit as well.

Lettuce or Celery wilted? Put life back into your lettuce and celery by placing it in a pan of cold water and adding a few raw slices of potato.

Salt Shaker clogging? Keep 6 - 10 grains of rice inside your salt shaker to keep the salt shaking freely.

OTHER KITCHEN HINTS

A ready fire extinguisher: Keep a box of baking soda near your electric stove. Baking soda sprinkled on electrical fires will douse them immediately.

Onion smells on hands: To remove the onion smell from your hands, carefully run your fingers along the flat part of the knife blade while the tap water is pouring over both the knife and your hands. This also works with garlic. Rubbing your hands with dry mustard will also get rid of onion and garlic odors.

Cleaning your food chopper: When putting food through a chopper, finish off with a stale piece of bread. This will partially clean it. To remove grease or stickiness, pour boiling water through it and no further washing is required.

Bleaching the cutting board: To bleach out a discoloured cutting board, rub with the inside of a lemon rind, then wash.

Smelly frying pan: Rub mustard over the frying pan, then wash it to remove fish and onion smells.

Cleaning aluminum pans: Clean aluminum pans with a solution of 1 tsp to 2 tbsp cream of tartar in one quart of water.

Opening a tight jar lid: Loop a medium-size rubber band around a stuck jar lid. It will provide traction, making the jar easier to open. Wearing rubber gloves will also do the trick.

Milk jug drip: Grease the lip of the cream or milk pitcher with butter to prevent it from dripping.

Kitchen hanger-upper: Nail wooden clothespins inside kitchen cabinet doors to serve as clips for your menus, grocery lists, place mats, etc.

Household Hints

Refrigerator deodorizer: Leave half a lemon unwrapped on a refrigerator shelf to help absorb food odors.

Egg yolks on the cutlery: Keep a toothbrush near the kitchen sink for getting egg yolk off fork tines. Rubbing a little salt briskly between thumb and forefinger will also remove egg from cutlery.

Appliances - cleaning and polishing: Rubbing alcohol works as well as commercial waxes in bringing out the lustre of your appliances. Club soda will clean as well as polish on your appliances.

Smelly cutting boards: To get that onion, garlic or fish smell out of your cutting board before you use it again, cut a lime or lemon in two and rub the surface with the cut side of the fruit. A paste made of baking soda and water will also work.

Washing dishes: Adding a little vinegar to your dish detergent (even the cheapest brands) will cut the grease and leave your dishes sparkling clean.

Protecting crystal and china in the sink: A towel in the bottom of your sink will act as a cushion to protect your fine china and crystal while washing them.

Stain removal: A damp cloth dipped in baking soda works wonders in removing tea and coffee stains from fine china. It will also remove cigarette burns.

Refrigerator odors: An open box of baking soda will absorb food odors for at least a month or two. A little vanilla poured on a piece of cotton and placed in the refrigerator will also help get rid of refrigerator odors.

Tea-stain prevention: Place a lump of sugar in the teapot before the tea is made. This will prevent staining if the tea is spilled.

Caked-on food: To quickly remove food that is stuck to a casserole dish, fill with boiling water and add 2 tablespoons of baking soda or salt.

Cleaning electric frying pans: To clean electric fryers and cookers, fill with water, add soap or detergent and heat to boiling. Then drain, rinse and dry.

Clogged drains: Pour a cup of salt and a cup of baking soda into a drain clogged with grease, and follow up with a kettle of boiling water. This will usually dissolve the grease and open the drain. Don't throw coffee grains down the drain. When they mix with the grease and clog the drain they are hard to remove.

Cleaning glassware: Rinse crystal and glassware in 1 part vinegar to 3 parts warm water to clean. Don't use a cup towel, but let them air dry.

Oven cleaning: If you have a spill inside the oven, sprinkle immediately with salt. When the oven cools, brush off burnt food and wipe with a damp sponge. Another way to clean your oven is to set it on warm for about 20 minutes, then it turn off. Place a small dish of full strength ammonia on

the top shelf. Put a large pan of boiling water on the bottom shelf and let it sit overnight. In the morning, open oven and let it air a while before washing off with soap and water. Using this method, even the hard, baked-on grease will wash off easily.

Copper pots: Add 2 - 3 tablespoons of salt to a litre of vinegar. Using an empty spray bottle, apply solution and let sit for a while, then simply rub clean. Ketchup or Worcestershire sauce is also good for cleaning copper pots.

Burnt pots and pans: Baking soda moistened with water makes an excellent solvent for getting that burnt-on food off pots and pans. Just apply the solution to the burnt pan and let it sit for a while.

Washing plastic dishes: Baking soda will help to scour coffee and tea stains from plastic dishes and containers.

Cleaning the sink: Place paper towels across the bottom of your enamel sink, saturate with household bleach and let it sit for an hour and your sink will become sparkling clean. Rust may be removed from stainless steel sinks by rubbing with lighter fluid. Wipe with your regular cleaner after rust is gone. White vinegar will remove stubborn spots from your stainless steel sink.

Tea kettle build-up: To remove lime deposits from your kettle, fill with equal parts of vinegar and water, and bring to a boil. Allow it to stand overnight and it will clean easily in the morning.

Unsticking stuck glasses: When one glass is stuck inside another, do not force them apart. Fill the top glass with cold water and dip the lower one in hot water. They will come apart without breaking.

Cleaning your thermos: A few tablespoons of baking soda added to warm water in your thermos bottle will do the trick.

Cleaning tin pie pans: Scouring your tin pie pans and other tin utensils with a raw potato dipped in cleaning powder will remove rust.

HOUSEHOLD CLEANING

Window washing: If you have trouble telling if the streak on the window is inside or out, shine the inside with vertical strokes and the outside with horizontal streaks. To avoid streaks, wash your windows on a dull day. On sunny days windows dry too fast, which is what causes the streaks.

Cleaning venetian blinds: To clean venetian blinds, lay them flat on the patio. Mix hot soapy water and add a little bleach to water. Use a plastic bristle broom and "sweep the blinds" with the water solution. Rinse with cold water from garden hose.

Cleaning your washing machine: When the hoses, drain and pump of your washing machine starts to get clogged up with soap scum, fill it with clear warm water, add a gallon of vinegar, then run it through a complete cycle once. This will get rid of the soap scum.

Yellow linens: Yellow linens may become white by adding a few drops of turpentine to the rinse water, and then hanging out in the sun to bleach.

Cleaning artificial flowers: Put your dirty artificial flowers in a paper bag, pour in some salt and shake vigorously. Your flowers will be fresh and bright looking.

Cleaning candle holders: To get hardened wax off your silver candle holders, place in the freezer for an hour or so. Once the wax hardens it will easily peel off in a jiffy. NOTE: This method will not harm your silver.

Cleaning chandeliers: A mixture of 1 part alcohol and 3 parts water will clean the droplets on your crystal chandelier. To avoid having to disassemble the chandelier, put the cleaning solution in a drinking glass and raise it up beneath each crystal droplet until the droplet is immersed in the solution. NOTE: Place a dropcloth underneath the chandelier to protect your floor and let the chandelier drip dry.

Cleaning eyeglasses: Vodka and no-name alcohol (which can be purchased in some liquor stores) are great for cleaning eyeglass lenses. Just a drop on each lens will do. Vinegar works well too.

Soot in the fireplace: Throwing salt on logs in your fireplace occasionally will reduce the soot by 60%.

Smoke stains on the fireplace front: Artgum eraser will remove smoke stains from fireplace bricks and stones.

Oil spill on garage floor or driveway: If you've spilled oil on your driveway or garage floor, spread opened newspaper over the spill then saturate the newspaper with water. Press firmly down on the newspapers, then allow the papers to dry completely. When you take up the papers, the oil spill will be gone.

Cleaning inside the steam iron: Fill your steam iron with half and half water and vinegar. Turn it on to steam and let it steam for five minutes. Then disconnect the iron and let it cool for an hour. Empty the contents and the mineral deposits which had built up inside your iron will empty as well. Rinse with clear water.

Cleaning jewellery: Toothpaste on a soft cloth is great for cleaning jewellery.

Cleaning pewter: One of the best ways to clean pewter is to rub it with cabbage leaves.

Cleaning the radiator: To get that dust from inside the ventilators of your hot water radiator, hang a damp cloth behind the radiator, then blow with the blower end of your vacuum cleaner. The dust and dirt will be blown onto the damp cloth.

Bathtub stain remover: Rub your bath tub with a cut lemon to remove slight stains.

Removing bathtub decals: Bathtub decals will be easy to scrape away if you soak them in mineral spirits for a while.

Bathtub brighteners: A solution of salt and turpentine rubbed over a yellowed bathtub will brighten it up and make it sparkle. Turtle wax is great for making old bathtubs look like new. It will also do the same for sinks and toilet bowls. Apply the Turtle wax with a soft cloth and let stand. Before it drys, buff with a soft cloth. An electric buffer will work faster and better than the cloth buffer.

Washing shower curtain: To wash your plastic shower curtain, fill the washing machine with warm water and add 1/2 cup of detergent and 1/2 cup of baking soda. Next, put two large bath towels in the wash water (will not work without the bath towels) with the shower curtain. Run through entire wash cycle but when you get to the rinse cycle, add a cup of vinegar to the rinse water. Do not spin dry or wash the vinegar out. Hang the curtain immediately after rinsing. When the curtains are completely dry the wrinkles will be gone.

FURNITURE

Yellowing wicker furniture: Wash your wicker furniture in a solution of mild salt water to stop it from yellowing.

Sagging wicker furniture: If your wicker furniture is starting to sag, wash it outdoors with hot, sudsy water, rinse with the garden hose and let it dry in the sun. The wicker will bounce back.

Dusting wicker furniture: A paintbrush sprayed with furniture polish makes a great wicker duster.

Cleaning chrome furniture: Club soda is great for cleaning the chrome on your furniture.

Keeping sectional furniture together: A hook and eye, like the one used on screen doors, fastened to the back of your sectional furniture will keep the sections from coming apart. When you want to move it, just unfasten the hook.

Loose casters in furniture: If the hole in the wood in which the caster sits has become worn and is starting to wobble, wrap a rubber band or some string around the caster stem before pushing it back into the hole.

Polish build-up on your furniture: Rub a soft cloth that has been moistened with a solution of half water and half vinegar to remove wax build-up on your polished furniture. Use a dry cloth to wipe off afterward.

Minor cigarette burns on furniture: Mayonnaise rubbed into minor burns on wood furniture will help remove them.

Glue on your furniture: Both peanut butter or salad oil are good for removing cement glue from

wooden furniture.

Glass rings on furniture tops: Cigarette ashes will remove glass rings on furniture. Just rub until spot is gone.

Removing rust on metal furniture: Both turpentine and kerosene rubbed on your metal furniture will remove the rust.

Leather upholstery cracking: To prevent your leather upholstery from cracking, polish it regularly with a cream made of 1 part vinegar and 2 parts linseed oil.

Blood stains on cloth upholstery: Mix cornstarch with cold water to make a paste and rub this paste lightly into the blood stain on your cloth upholstery as soon as possible. Put the item in sunlight and when it drys, brush it off. Repeat until the stain is completely gone.

A different upholstery cleaner: Shaving cream makes a great upholstery cleaner.

FLOORING AND CARPET

Floor tiles lifting: If one of your linoleum floor tiles has come loose or is starting to bulge, place a piece of aluminum foil over the tile and run a hot iron across the top to soften the glue and the tile, then put some heavy books or other objects on the tile to flatten it and keep it in place till the glue and the tile hardens.

Small rugs stiffened: To stiffen small rugs, or mats, apply a coat of white shellac to back of rug and let dry.

A cleaner sweeping broom: Spray the bristles of the broom with some furniture polish and it will collect more dust.

A slippery dustpan: A coat of wax on your dustpan will help dust and dirt slide off more easily.

Better bristles in your broom: Put a hook in the end of your broomstick and hang it in your cleaning closet and the bristles will last longer.

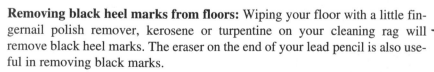

Removing black heel marks from floors: Wiping your floor with a little fingernail polish remover, kerosene or turpentine on your cleaning rag will remove black heel marks. The eraser on the end of your lead pencil is also useful in removing black marks.

Removing crayon marks from floors: Silver polish will remove your child's crayon marks from vinyl tile or linoleum floors.

Getting wax off your floor polisher brushes: Layers of paper towels placed on the brushes of your electric floor polisher will absorb every bit of wax if you place them on the brushes, then

apply a warm iron on the top side.

Cleaning ceramic tile: If you run your shower a while with the hottest tap water available before you start cleaning the walls or tiles, the steam generated will loosen the caked-in dirt and it will come off easier.

Removing stains in your carpet: For fresh stains in your carpet, pour a little plain club soda on the spot and let it set for a few seconds. Then sponge up thoroughly and the spot will be gone. For stains that have been on your carpet for a while, combine 2 tablespoons of detergent, 2 tablespoons of vinegar and 1 litre of warm water. Work this mixture into stain and blot dry. If this doesn't get all the stain the first time, repeat the process.

Repairing burns in the carpet: To hide a burn in your carpet, use some fuzz from another, out-of-sight area of the carpet to repair the burn. You can shave this off the carpet, or use a tweezer to pull it off, then roll the fuzz ball into the shape of the burn. Apply a good cement glue to the backing of the rug and press the fuzz down into the burned spot. Cover the area with a piece of cleansing tissue and place a heavy object (book, brick or flat iron) on top. It will take some time for the glue to dry, so be patient. The results will be worthwhile.

Fluffing flattened carpet: If you decide to move your furniture around and you are left with a flattened area of carpet that shows, the problem can be easily remedied. Get your steam iron steaming and hold it over the flattened spot. Then with a hair brush briskly brush the area. In minutes the flattened area will be fluffed up like the rest of the carpet.

Removing candle wax drippings from carpet: To remove melted candle wax which has now dried into your carpet, place an ink blotter or brown paper bag over the spot and put a hot iron over the blotter. The heat will melt the wax, the paper will absorb the wax, and the problem will be solved.

Brighten up your carpet: Before vacuuming, sprinkle salt (lots of it) on your carpet and let it stand for a while. After vacuuming, your old carpet will look as bright as new.

Removing chewing gum from carpet: Ice cubes held against gum which has stuck to your carpet will make the gum hard and brittle. Then it can be easily broken away and removed. A spot remover will get rid of the traces that remain.

Removing glue from carpet: To remove dried glue from your carpet, saturate the spot with a cloth soaked in vinegar and when the glue dissolves it will remove easily.

Removing ink marks from carpet: To remove ink stains from your carpet, soak the spot with hairspray. When the area dries out, brush lightly with a solution of water and vinegar.

A cleaner sweeping carpet sweeper: Dampen the brushes of your carpet sweeper before using and it will do a much better job of picking up lint from your carpet.

DECORATING

Unstrippable wallpaper: Apply liberal quantities of a mixture of half and half vinegar and hot water, and let it really soak in. Use a paint roller or sponge to apply. If you get the solution right into the old wallpaper to the old glue, the paper should come off in sheets.

Wallpaper patches: If you cut out a patch to cover missing wallpaper with a knife or sissors, the straight edge of the patch will show. Instead tear out the patch to leave an uneven edge (making the patch big enough to match the pattern and still cover the spot). Apply the patch so the pattern matches, and when it dries you won't see the outline.

Crayon marks on wallpaper: A paste of cornstarch and water will remove most crayon marks from wallpaper. Apply, let dry, and when you brush it off the stains will fly.

Quick fix plaster jobs: Make a paste from white wood glue and baking soda, then colour with food colouring to match your ceiling. This will fill up that ugly crack in your ceiling until you get around to doing the complete ceiling.

BEAUTY HINTS

Health spa secret moisturizer: Wash face thoroughly and rub in a tiny amount of petroleum jelly while your face is still wet. Keep wetting your face and rubbing in the jelly until it is spread evenly and no longer appears greasy. Your face will feel soft and smooth. Just remember, the trick is to add the water a little at a time and your face will not stay greasy. Expensive health spas use this method, but they have been keeping it a secret.

Removing dead skin: One of the best ways of removing dead skin is to use Miracle Whip salad dressing. Rub a small amount into skin and let it dry a few minutes. While the skin is still slightly moist, start massaging your face with your fingertips. Rub briskly and the dead skin will roll right off.

Dried up nail polish: If your nail polish has hardened or has started to become gummy, place the bottle in a pan of boiling water. In no time, the polish will be good as new. To prevent your nail polish from getting hard in the first place, store it in the refrigerator. This also works with frosted nail polish.

Tired-looking eyes: Fresh, cold cucumber slices placed on your eyelids will get rid of the redness and puffiness caused by fatigue.

Irritating underarm deodorants: If even the most gentle underarm deodorants irritate your skin, apply a little hand cream before using the antiperspirant.

An oily hair remedy: Three teaspoons of spearmint leaves boiled up in a litre of water makes a great after-shampoo rinse for oily hair.

Hair-spray buildup: If your hair has accumulated a build-up of hair spray you can dissolve it by washing as usual and working a tablespoon of baking soda into the lathered hair.

Cream rinse substitute: A little dab of fabric softener in a glass of warm water is a great cream rinse substitute if you're temporarily out.

Yellowing grey hair: A little bit of laundry bluing added to the final rinse water when you shampoo will prevent grey hair from yellowing.

Fly-away frizzies: A fabric-softener sheet rubbed over your hair is a great cure for the frizzies.

Banishing blemishes: A styptic pencil (the pencil used by men to stop razor nicks from bleeding), applied to a blemish, or pimple, three or four times a day, will dry it up. Dabbing a blemish with lemon juice a few times a day will also do the trick.

CLOTHING AND FOOTWEAR

Yellowing nylon clothing: Pre-soak your nylon clothing in a tubful of warm water to which you've added one-half cup of baking soda. This will prevent it from turning yellow.

Pure white whites: If your white polyester is turning grey, soak it overnight in a solution of water and dishwasher detergent before regular washing and it will come out sparkling white.

Wrinkled permanent-press clothes: To get those wrinkles out of permanent-press clothes, put them in the clothes dryer with a wet towel for about 15 minutes.

Iron in a sweet smell: Add a few drops of your favourite cologne to the water in your steam iron for sweet smelling clothes.

Rejuvenate your corduroy: Press your corduroy face down on another piece of corduroy to get its original look back.

Restoring faded colours: To restore colour to faded clothes, add a little ascetic acid to the rinse water.

No-iron blouses: Remove your blouses from the dryer before they are completely dry and spray them with starch. Then hang them on hangers to dry and you won't have to iron them.

Stuck zippers: Rubbing a cake of soap along a stuck zipper will loosen it.

Mothball smells: To remove mothball odor from clothing, tumble each

item separately in the dryer for ten or fifteen minutes with no heat.

No-slip hangers: Wrap both ends of the hanger with thick rubber bands and your spaghetti-strap dresses will not slip off.

Ink stains on leather: Remove ink from leather by rubbing out the stain with baking soda. This process should be repeated until the ink fades away.

Easy-on cowboy boots: Silicone spray (available at hardware stores) applied to the inside of your tight-fitting cowboy boots will make them easy to slip on and off, as well as get rid of odors.

Tight fitting shoes: If a shoe hurts in a particular spot, saturate a cotton ball with rubbing alcohol and rub the tight spot on the inside of the shoe. Then put both shoes on immediately and walk around. Repeat until the tight shoe feels comfortable.

Quick-drying panty hose: To quick-dry panty hose, hang them over the shower curtain rod and blow-dry them with your hair dryer.

Two-for-one panty hose: If you have a run in one leg of two pairs of panty hose, cut the snagged leg off each pair, you'll then have a good pair of panty hose with a double waist. This is a great remedy for last minute hitches to your last good pair of panty hose.

Ring around the collar: Brush a little hair shampoo into soiled shirt collars before laundering and the shampoo will dissolve the body oils which leave that ring around your shirt collar.

Rough, itchy sweaters: A capful of creme hair rinse in the final rinse water with your sweaters will keep them smooth and fresh looking.

Dainty garments in the washing machine: The washing machine will not harm your dainties if you put them in a pillowcase, tie the end, then wash on a gentle cycle.

Suds overflowing washing machine: If you've put too much detergent in the wash and the suds are overflowing the top, sprinkle with salt and the suds will subside.

Removing a red wine spill: If you spill red wine on a good garment, sprinkle lots of salt on the area at once, then immediately immerse in cold water. The stain will then rub out.

Grease on your good suede: Grease will come out of suede if you apply vinegar to a cloth and sponge it into the stain. After the stain is removed the suede can be restored to its original texture by brushing with a suede brush.

A cure for dirty white socks: When you think your white socks will never look white again, boil some water, add a slice of lemon, then throw in your socks and swish them around with a wooden spoon or paint stir stick.

To dampen clothes for ironing: Place 2 or 3 wet bath towels in your dryer with your overly dry garments, then spin without heat.

Ironing embroidery: Lay the embroidery piece upside down on a thick towel before ironing. All the little spaces between the embroidery will be smooth when you are finished.

Chewing gum on cloth garments: To get gum off your clothing, place the item in a plastic bag and put it in the freezer. When the gum freezes it will scrape off easily.

Fruit stains on cloth garments: Fruit stains can be removed from clothing by stretching the stained area over a bowl or bucket and pouring boiling water through the stain from a height of about 2 to 3 feet.

Ballpoint ink on polyester, rayon, etc: Hairspray applied to a ballpoint stain and rubbed with a clean dry cloth, will remove the ink stain in most cases.

Getting rid of mildew on clothes: Moisten the mildewed area with lemon juice and salt, then let the garment dry in the sun.

Getting rid of mildew on leather: To get rid of mildew on leather, sponge with equal amounts of water and rubbing alcohol.

Scorch cotton or linen: To get a scorch mark out of cotton or linen, dampen a cloth with peroxide, lay it on the scorched area and iron with a warm iron.

Stop losing buttons: A little clear nail polish dabbed on the back and front of all buttons on that new garment will insure you have the buttons for a long time.

Wrinkles away without ironing: Hang your wrinkled garment on the curtain rod in your hotel room bathroom, turn on just the hot water tap in your shower, and close the bathroom door allowing the steam to build up in the bathroom. The steam will remove the wrinkles in short order.

Stains on white suit: If you discover a stain on your white suit just before having to be seen in public, rub in baby powder to cover it up temporarlly.

Shave away fuzz balls from sweaters and shirt collars: A razor will remove fuzz from old shirt collars without harming the fabric.

Creaselines left when lengthening jeans: Blue ink mixed with the right amount of water to match it to the shade of your jeans, then applied to the white hemline left when you let the jeans out will hide the white so it won't be noticeable.

Removing tar from white shoes: Nail polish remover will take tar and grease right off white leather shoes.

Salt on shoes and boots: A solution of half and half vinegar and water will take salt stains off leather footwear.

SEWING

Sharpening scissors: Scissors may be sharpened by cutting through fine sandpaper several times.

Removing buttons: Put a comb between the button and the cloth to avoid cutting into the fabric when cutting off a button with scissors.

Marking a hem by yourself: Having trouble marking that dress you are wearing, so that your new hem will be even? Get out the bathroom plunger and mark the desired length on the handle. The plunger will stand by itself as you move it around your hemline, leaving your hands free for pinning or marking the material.

Sharpening sewing machine needles: The simple way to sharpen sewing machine needles is to stitch through a piece of sandpaper, rough side up.

Sewing heavy material: If you're having trouble getting your sewing machine needle to penetrate heavy material, rub seams with a piece of hard bar soap. The machine needle will then go through the material easily.

Sewing on emblems: If you're having trouble getting that emblem to stay put while you sew it on, glue it into place with a few dabs of any good white glue, let it dry, then sew. The glue will come out when the item is washed.

Sewing plastic: Use dental floss instead of thread when mending plastic items.

Buttonholes in children's clothing: When making children's clothing, sew the buttonholes horizontally to keep them from popping open when the pressures of playtime are applied.

Keeping the drapes together: Velcro fasteners on adjacent panel hems are great for keeping your heavy drapes together.

A dual purpose pin cushion: A cake of soap makes the best pin cushion. It's not only a good place to store needles and pins, it lubricates them so that they will go through stiff fabrics with ease.

Double-balling it: Plastic bags, like the ones potatoes or carrots are purchased in, are handy when knitting, especially if you're using more than one ball of wool. Puncture a small hole in the bag for each ball of yarn you will be using, then thread the different yarns through various holes in the bag. The yarn won't tangle while you knit, and the bags will keep the wool clean.

Household Hints

PLANTS - INDOORS AND OUT

Watering houseplants: You can determine if your plants need watering by sticking your finger about one inch into the soil; if it feels moist, don't water. When your plants do need watering, use water which has been standing inside the house for a day. That way the chlorine will be gone and the water will be at room temperature. Chlorine will turn your green leaves brown, and cold water can kill your plant.

Sick houseplants: If your plant is starting to sag and wilt, cover it with a plastic bag for a few days and it will rejuvenate. Covering your plants with a plastic bag is also a great way to protect them from a change in environment when you're moving from one address to another.

Broken plant stem: A tiny splint made of toothpicks, or wooden matches and tape, will often save the broken stem of a plant.

Plant supports: Plastic drinking straws make great "stakes" to hold plants that need a little extra support.

Transporting plant cuttings: To keep plant cuttings, or cut flowers fresh while transporting them, put them in a large plastic bag. Breathe into the bag and seal.

Glossy plant leaves: A half and half mixture of milk and water will make your plants leaves healthy and shiny.

Greener leaves: Add a few drops of castor oil to the dirt around plants to make the leaves greener.

Fern medicine: Watering your fern with weak tea will rejuvenate it.

Keep cut flowers longer: Hair spray applied to cut flowers will make them last longer without shedding. Turn the flowers upside down and spray in a downward direction to keep them from drooping.

Dried flowers: Bury flowers into a mixture of 3 parts white cornmeal and 1 part borax, and leave them there for 2 weeks. The flowers will dry completely out and keep for years.

Colouring cut flowers: Place your cut flowers in a mixture of food colouring and warm water in a vase and overnight the flowers will change colour.

Killing Poison Ivy: Spray poison ivy with salt water and it will die.

Watering your lawn: If you water your lawn a little each day you will do your lawn more harm than good. Better to give it a good drenching once a week. Grass roots seek out water and when only a little water is present on the surface of your lawn the roots will actually turn up. This will damage your lawn.

Improving on the weather: If you live in a colder climate you can get more out of your sunshine by lining the inside of your fences with aluminum foil, or some other reflective material. This will increase the amount of sunlight and heat getting to your plants.

Weeds in the crevices: If grass and weeds are growing between sections of your cement walkway, apply boiling water to immediately kill them, then sprinkle salt into the crevices to keep them from coming back.

Perpetual green onions: When you use green onions again, just cut up the green stalk and save the white bottom portion. Plant these bulbs in a flower pot and place them in the window to grow. If you water them daily they will grow and you can snip off the green tops as you need them.

Stationary ferns: Ferns don't like to be moved, so to keep them healthy, keep them in one place.

Gelatin a good plant medicine: A mixture of unflavoured gelatin dissolved in hot water and stirred, makes a good medicine for house plants. Instead of the usual watering, use this mixture once a month and you'll see a big improvement in your plants.

HANDYMAN/WOMAN

Damp closets: The charcoal briquets which barbecue your pork chops also absorb moisture. Punch holes in four empty, one-pound plastic margarine containers and fill them with briquets. Put one in each corner of your closet and they will get rid of the dampness.

Postage stamps stuck together: When postage stamps are stuck together, place them in the freezer. They will usually come apart when they freeze, and the glue will still be usable.

Paint surface in can hardening: Tightly fill the lids of paint containers and store upside down to prevent the hard layer from forming.

Paint touch-ups: Instead of using a brush, which you must clean after, for touch-up paint jobs, use throw away Q-tips instead.

Overnight paint brush: If you've finished painting for the day, but must continue the job the next day, wrap your paint brushes in foil wrap (or plastic bag) and put them in the freezer. It will take an hour or so for them to defrost before using them again, but it's much easier than having to clean them.

Easy-clean paint roller pan: If you pull a large plastic bag over your roller pan before putting the paint in, you can just throw the bag away after use, and you won't have to clean the pan.

No paint odor: Two teaspoons of vanilla per quart added to your paint will get rid of paint odors while you are painting.

Household Hints

Strain lumpy paint: An old nylon stocking makes a great paint strainer.

Shopping for things to match your room colour: When you've finished the paint job, put some of the paint to a popsicle stick and let it dry. Then take it with you when you go shopping for furniture, drapes, paintings, etc., for perfect colour matching.

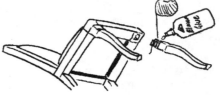

Wooden chair legs wobbly: Wrap cotton thread or string (depending on how big the hole has gotten) around a wobbly chair leg, then re-glue it before re-inserting.

Hole too big for screw: If a wood screw keeps falling out because it is too small for the hole, stick a wooden match or toothpick in the screw hole (or several if the hole is really big) and break it off. Then, put the screw back in.

Difficulty loosening a tight bolt, nut or screw: To loosen a stubborn bolt, nut or screw, nothing works like WD-40.

Dissolving old glue: To loosen age-hardened wood glue, nothing works as well as a liberal application of vinegar.

Finding a wall stud: Studs in walls usually have metal nails. A compass moved across the wall will register some movement when near a nail and will give you the location of hidden studs. NOTE: This will take a little patience and practice, but is better than ruining the wall to find the stud. Keep in mind that once you find one stud you can usually find the next by measuring 16 inches in either direction.
Another way to find wall studs is to turn on your electric razor and run it along the wall and listen to the tone it makes. When it runs across the stud the frequency of the tone will change. This will require a little diligence on your part, but it does work.

Fraying rope: A little shellac applied to the ends of a rope will keep it from getting split ends'.

Fraying nylon rope: Burn the cut end of nylon rope with a cigarette lighter, match, etc., and the individual strands will fuse together and never ravel.

Soft putty: Putty will keep soft and pliable for a full year if completely covered in aluminum foil.

A slipping slot-screwdriver: Rubbing some chalk on the blade of an ordinary slotted screwdriver will help keep it from slipping out of the screw slot while you are getting the screw started.

The hands-off screw: When using screws to fasten wood, the Robinson-square screw will stay on the end of the screwdriver for a one-hand operation in getting the screw started. There are four popular sizes of square holes in Robinson-square screws; number 4, 6, 8 and 10, with each square hole one size bigger according to the number. Each Robinson-square screwdriver handle is colour-coded to indicate the size of screw it will accomodate. The yellow-handled screwdriver fits a num-

ber 4 screw, the green a number 6, the red a number 8, and the black a number 10.

Stop squeaks: Nonstick vegetable spray will lubricate squeaky hinges, sticky locks, sticky door bolts, roller skate wheels, car doors, etc.. The amazing WD-40 also does the job as well, maybe even better.

Frozen water pipes: Frozen water pipes may be thawed out in some instances by using your hair dryer.

Snow sticking to your snowshovel: Spray-wax applied to your metal snow shovel will prevent snow from sticking to it.

A safer ladder: A short, fat, empty can, such as a large tuna-fish can, fastened to the ground with long nails or spikes driven through the bottom of the can, make great safety-cups for the bottom of your ladder.

Removing broken light bulbs: A thick, dry sponge pressed into the jagged bulb base will help get it out of the socket.

Hanging doors: Hanging a door will be a lot easier if you place the proper thickness of newspapers or magazines under the door while you screw the hinges into the frame.

Removing broken window panes: To safely remove a broken windowpane, glue newspaper to both sides of the glass, let it dry, then gently chip away the putty. The pane will come out without scattering glass splinters.

Squeaky floor under the carpet: Floors usually squeak because the builder didn't use enough nails in the plywood floor before the carpet was laid. Two-inch finishing nails driven down completely through the carpet in the area of the squeak will solve the problem.

Clogged kitchen sinks: Clogged kitchen sinks are usually caused by warm liquid grease which has become cold and solid in the trap under your sink. A blow dryer, set on the hottest setting and applied to the outside of the trap will sometimes melt the solid grease and free the drain. Once the drain is free, flush with hot water for a few minutes to rid the trap of any remaining grease. To avoid the problem, always turn on the hot water and let it run while pouring grease down the drain.

Messy paint can rim: Cover the rim of your freshly-opened can of paint before pouring out the paint. Remove the tape after pouring, and the cover will go back on without making a mess.

Paint brush shedding: Before using a brush, comb the loose bristles out with a comb to keep the bristles from getting into the paint.

Sure-stick concrete paint: A coat of vinegar applied to your concrete floor just before painting, will insure that the paint doesn't peel off.

MISCELLANEOUS HOUSEHOLD HINTS

Straight curtain tiebacks: Your window shade makes a great guide for insuring that your tiebacks are straight across from each other.

Inserting drapery hooks: Stick the tips of drapery hooks into a cake of soap and they will push into the fabric much more easily.

Drip-free, long-burning candles: If you want drip-free, long-burning candles, put them in the freezer overnight before burning them.

A non-slip serving tray: A muffin pan makes a great tray for serving drinks with.

Ants in the cupboard: Green sage on each cupboard shelf will keep ants away.

The best roach exterminator: Sprinkle boric acid in cracks, crevices, under sinks and in other places where roaches are seen and after a while your roach problem will be solved. Unlike most pesticides, boric acid does not repel roaches, so they keep going until they pick enough up to kill them. Although other pesticides kill faster than boric acid, if the roach doesn't get a lethal dose the first time, he stays away from the pesticide. Using both products together will also work. Use pesticide first for the quick kill, and boric acid after, to get the ones that the pesticide missed. Cucumbers will repel roaches.

Bees, hornets and wasps in the house: Hairspray works better than insect sprays on most flying insects. It stiffens their wings, immediately immobilizing them.

Insect bites: A poultice of baking soda mixed with vinegar and fresh lemon juice, is an effective remedy for insect bites.

Bee stings: A poultice of baking soda and water is an effective remedy for bee stings.

Fly repellent: A pot of basil on the windowsill deters flies.

A sweet smelling bathroom: A fabric softener sheet in the wastepaper basket will leave your bathroom smelling great. A dab of your favourite perfume on the lightbulb will enhance the aroma of your bathroom whenever the light is on. (The heat from the light will release the aroma)

Unclogging shower heads: If your metal shower head is clogged, take it off and boil it in 1/2 cup vinegar and 1 and 1/2 litres of water for 15 to 20 minutes. Don't boil your plastic shower head, instead, soak it in a hot mixture of equal amounts of vinegar and water.

Household Hints

No corkscrew for the wine bottle: Run hot water on the neck of the bottle and the heat will expand the glass, causing the cork to pop out.

Cigarette smoke: To get rid of cigarette smoke in a room, light up several candles and the smoke will disappear. Vinegar in bowls in a smoking room will also help eliminate the smoke.

Ball point pen clogging: If your ball point pen refill becomes clogged, insert it in the filter portion of a cigarette and give it a few quick turns. Presto, it's ready to use again.

A great room deodorant: A few drops of wintergreen oil (available at drug stores) on cotton balls which are then placed out of sight around your house will leave your house smelling fresh for months.

Shining up the guitar: Toothpaste makes excellent guitar polish. Just rub it on, let it dry, and buff.

Protecting floors from moving furniture: Heavy wool socks slipped over each leg of your heavy furniture will protect your hardwood floor when moving it around.

Wrinkled drapes: Spray your wrinkled drapes with a fine-mist plant sprayer after they are hung and the wrinkles will fall out.

Microwave oven spills: Cover that spot of food on the bottom of your microwave with a damp cloth and turn the oven on high for ten seconds. When the oven cools the spot will wipe right off.

Cleaning gold jewellery: A solution of half-and-half clear household ammonia and warm water does a great job of cleaning gold. Just leave the jewellery in soak for about half an hour, then scrub with a soft brush and rinse with warm water.

Cleaning silver: Dry baking soda applied with a soft cloth will clean your silver. After cleaning, rinse it in water and dry inside a soft towel.

Rings on swollen fingers: If a ring is stuck on a swollen finger, place your hand in a bowl of ice-cold soapy water. This will reduce the swelling and the soap will help slip the ring off.

Fresh smelling house: A solid room deodorizer next to the return vent of your forced-air heating system will circulate through your heating system and make the whole house smell fresh.

Sour smelling humidifier: To get rid of that sour smell coming from your home humidifier, pour three or four tablespoons of bottled lemon juice in the water.

Dusty pleated lampshades: A hand-held hair dryer will gently blow the dust from pleated lamp shades.

Moldy sinks and faucets: An old toothbrush will get that mold

and dirt around the base of the faucets and grooves in your sink.

Lint clogging the drain: An old nylon stocking over your washing machine hose, secured with a thick rubber band, will act as a filter against lint which would otherwise go down the drain and clog it. Nylon window screen placed on the bottom of your laundry sink will serve the same purpose.

Cut down on dust: Fabric-softener sheets which are cut to fit under your floor registers will considerably reduce the dust which circulates through your house.

Drying out a wet book: If you should get a favourite book wet, you can salvage it by drying each page individually with a paper towel between each. A second book, or other weight, on top will help. Usually an overnight drying will do the trick.

Stamps stuck together: Stamps that are stuck to gether will come apart if you run a warm iron over them. Just make sure you get them apart quickly before the glue dries again.

Warped record albums: To make your warped record albums or singles playable again, place it between two sheets of window glass and leave it in the sun for a while. This will usually remove the warp.

Paint odors: A pail of water in a freshly-painted room will help remove the odor.

Yellowing newspaper clippings: To keep newspaper clippings from turning yellow, spray them with hair spray.

Removing super-glue: If you get one of the special glues on your hand, soak it in nail polish remover until the glue goes away.

The last step: Paint lowest step in cellar white so it is easy to know when bottom is reached.

A tightly-tied package: When tying a package, dampen string to prevent it from slipping. As the cord dries it shrinks tight.

BABY AND CHILD CARE

The most important rule for raising children: The most important rule for raising children is being consistent. Decide on the rules you are going to lay down for your child, make sure they are the proper rules, then stick to them. Children understand consistency. Inconsistency breeds doubt in the child's mind. Children have enough to contend with in life. Doubt is something they don't need. Your rules are their protective fence. When they object to your rules, they are merely testing the fence to make sure it is still there. They may try hard to break through the fence, but they will feel let down if they find a weakness and get through. As a parent, you play the most important part in your child's future. Don't let your emotions cause inconsistency in your actions, and thereby rob your child of the future he or she deserves. Parents are required to give their children two basic things; roots

Household Hints

and wings. Make sure that you give your children the proper roots, so that when they are ready to fly, they fly in the right direction.

One way to be consistent: Never do anything with your children that must be corrected later, like standing them on a chair while dressing them, because you will later have to retrain them not to stand on furniture.

Don't say "no" unless you mean it: If your child asks for something, and you don't have time to think about it right away, ask for a little time to think about it. If after thinking about it, there isn't a reason to say, "no" then say "yes". Your child deserves whatever good things life has to offer, within reason. If there is a good reason to say "no", then say "no" and stick to it. Don't ever give in, no matter the pleading, reasoning, threatening, grovelling, or whatever tactic.

Don't say "yes" unless you mean it: Don't promise your child something unless you are absolutely sure you can do it. If you are not sure say, "maybe." Broken promises to children have lead to many a silent broken heart.

Where to draw the line: If there is no distinction between where your driveway ends and the forbidden zone begins, paint a white line across your driveway, and clearly tell your child not to ride his tricycle across it. Make sure the lines are as clear as the white line in your driveway in every rule you lay down for your child.

The last rule in raising children: When, after following all the preceding rules, you get compliments from friends, neighbours and relatives on how well-behaved your child is, loud enough for your child to hear, say, "Thank you, I'm quite proud of him (or her) myself."

Bringing the newborn home: While still at the hospital use your favourite perfume whenever you are around the baby. Once you bring the baby home put a dab of the same perfume on baby's crib sheets or pillow. The smell of mama will give he or she the at-home feeling of being safe and content.

Infant night-time bed wetting: Cover the pad in baby's bassinet with a pillowcase before putting baby down for the night. If baby does have an 'accident' in the middle of the night, you'll be able to quickly turn the pad over to the fresh, clean side.

Pet-proofing baby's bedroom: If your pet has a habit of going into baby's room and you don't want to shut the door for fear of not hearing the baby, install a screen door. This will cost a few dollars, but it may be well worth the effort.

Too-hot baby's bottle: If you've made baby's formula too hot, add a little of the formula you've previously stored in the refrigerator for such an occasion. There's none in the refrigerator? Well, there should have been. Next time make sure there is.

Quick nighttime formula: A thermos bottle filled with boiling water before going to bed will speed up the process of getting baby's late-night formula ready. You forgot to do it? Now to warm it quickly, you'll have to use the microwave. That works too. Just be sure you've taken the cap off before you put it in the microwave.

Sterilizing nipples in the microwave: Put baby's nipples in a jar of water to which you've added a teaspoon of vinegar, and microwave it for a few minutes until the water gets hot. This will kill any germs on the nipples.

Sour baby bottles: Fill those sour baby bottles with warm water, add a teaspoon of baking soda, shake well, and let it sit overnight. This will get rid of the sour smell.

Baby powder substitute: If you find yourself out of baby powder, cornstarch is a great substitute. Just keep it away from baby's face and make sure that he doesn't inhale any. Cornstarch can be harmful if inhaled.

Petroleum jelly substitute: If you find yourself out of petroleum jelly, vegetable shorting will work as well.

Baking soda softener: A half cup of baking soda added to the second washing cycle when you are washing baby's diapers will render them soft and fresh smelling. This is better than using fabric softener which can actually irritate baby's bottom.

The right time to give baby medicine: If baby has to take evil-tasting medicine, put the medicine inside a nipple and give it to him just before his normal feeding time, when he is good and hungry. He may not like the taste but before he realizes it, it will be too late. Then give him his formula to keep him happy and make him forget the medicine.

The right time to give baby liquid vitamins: To avoid having extra baby clothes to launder, give baby his liquid vitamins at bath time.

Read to baby: If taking care of baby doesn't give you time to read your favourite newspaper, magazine or book, read it aloud with baby in your arms (the rocking chair is the best venue for this). He will think you are talking to him and will probably get as much enjoyment out of it as you do.

Cleaning the high chair: High chairs can get really messy. When they do, the best place to clean them in summer time is outside with a garden hose. In the winter, shower them in the bath tub.

Washing cuts and scrapes: If your child gets a cut or scrape, wash the blood away with a red washcloth so it won't show and scare the child.

Applying ointment to cuts and scrapes: Children sometimes become traumatized if you try to apply ointment or liquid antiseptic directly to a cut. Instead put the medication on the bandage before applying it to the affected area.

Locating splinters: If your child picks up a splinter and you can't see it, touch the spot with iodine

and the splinter will darken and be easier to see.

Applying eyedrops to children's eyes: Trying to get eyedrops into your child's eyes can be a chore unless you do it right. The right way is to have your child lie down and close his eyes, then place the eyedrops in the inside corner of each eye. Then, while he is still lying down, have him open his eyes, and the drops will spread gently across the eyes.

Sour smells on baby's shirt: To keep baby smelling fresh everytime he bubbles over onto his shirt after feeding, instead of changing his shirt, moisten a cloth with water, dip it in baking soda and dab on the dribbled shirt. The sour smell will disappear.

Keep the empty crib warm: To keep baby's crib from getting cold while you have him up for night feeding, keep a heating pad beside the crib. Then turn it on to the warm setting and place it between the sheets during feeding. When baby is returned to his crib it will be nice and warm and he will settle down more quickly. (A hot water bottle will work as well as the heating pad) NOTE: Don't leave the heating pad or the hot water bottle in the crib with baby!

Children swallowing pills: If your child has trouble swallowing a pill, place it in a teaspoon of applesauce and it will go down easily.

A tasty tongue depressor: When checking your child for a sore throat, use a sucker (on a stick) instead of a tongue depressor.

Removing splinters: If your child has a splinter in his finger it will come out more easily if you soak it in cooking oil first. Applying an ice cube to the child's finger for several minutes will numb the area and allow the splinter to be removed painlessly.

Removing adhesive tape from children's skin: When removing adhesive tape from your child's skin, just saturate a piece of cotton with baby oil and rub over the tape. The adhesive tape will come right off without hurting the skin.

Bathing baby: To prevent baby from slipping around in the bathtub, before running the water place him in his infant seat after removing the strap and pad. Make sure you have a folded towel behind him for comfort. This will not only prevent baby from slipping, but will allow you to use both hands.

Keeping shampoo out of baby's eyes: Shampoo will not run into baby's eyes if you put petroleum jelly on his eyebrows and eyelids. The soap will run sideways instead of downward. Using a child's diving mask on your child will achieve the same purpose, and it will make shampooing more of a fun experience.

Stopping dropsies: Your childs little hands will be able to hold onto a drinking glass without having it slip from his fingers if you place two tight rubber bands around the glass an inch or so apart.

Removing gum from baby's hair: To get gum out of your child's hair rub ordinary cold cream into the hair. Then using a dry towel, pull down on the affected strands of hair a few times. The

gum should come right off. Also, if you place ice cubes against the gum it will turn brittle and you will be able to break it into pieces and remove it.

PET CARE

Deodorizing your dog: Rub some baking soda into your dog's coat thoroughly after his regular bath and then brush off. The baking soda will clean and deodorize Fido.

Doggy pills: If your dog refuses to swallow his pill, push the tablet into some sweet that he likes, or even into a chunk of his dog food. He will take his medicine without even knowing it.

Furniture-chewing puppy: If puppy likes to chomp on the legs of chairs, chesterfields and tables, apply a little oil of cloves to the wood with a piece of cotton. The oil of cloves, which has a smell and taste offensive to dogs, is available at most drug stores.

Whining puppy: If your new puppy whines it is probably because he misses mommy. A warm, hot water bottle wrapped in a towel, as well as a ticking clock placed in his bed, will simulate mommy and make puppy feel at home.

Cat on the furniture: Cats hate moth balls, so if you stuff a few in the cushions of your sofa or favourite chair pussy will stay away.

Car-proofing your pet: Reflector tape on your dog's or cat's collar will make them more visible to drivers at night.

Puppy-go-potty: If you hang a bell on the doorknob and jingle it every time you put your new puppy outside, when he needs to go he'll ring for service himself.

Softer, shinier puppies: A little baking soda added to your dog's rinse water will make your pet's coat softer and shinier, as well as odor-free.

Blow-drying your dog: A blow dryer, with the temperature set at warm, is great for drying your dog after a bath.

Keeping your dog off the furniture: Sprinkle pepper on the forbidden sofa and this will keep your dog away until he gets the idea.

Preventing fleas: Brewer's yeast rubbed on your dog's coat prevents fleas.

Travelling kitty: If your cat gets sick when travelling by car, keep her in a box so she can't see the fast moving scenery. It will probably make her more secure.

Getting your cat to take medicine: If your cat refuses to take liquid medicine, just spill it on her fur, a little at a time, and she'll lap it down.

Tastes like tuna: Save the liquid from your canned tuna and pour it over kitty's dinner. Kitty will love you for it.

MISCELLANEOUS IDEAS & SUGGESTIONS

A picture is worth thousands of dollars: You should take pictures of your house and grounds during the different seasons. Then, no matter what time of year you sell, you will be able to show your house with a different look. A picture of a flowering crabapple tree, roses in bloom, snow-covered branches, red and gold autumn trees, or a family barbecue will say more about your house to a prospective buyer than you ever could.

Moving day: Put a piece of masking tape on the wall of each room in your new house, and use it to number each room. Then label each box with the proper room number. Make sure the items you'll want first, such as beds, get packed in the moving van last.

Moving fragiles: Sectioned cardboard boxes, like the ones you can get from the liquor store, are great for packing glasses and other breakable items.

Home security tips: 1. Cut a wooden stick, old broom handle, or old hockey stick in the inside track of your sliding door to prevent it from being opened from the outside.
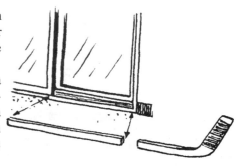
2. Drill a hole, large enough to easily accomodate a four-inch nail in the upper track of your sliding windows, just above the top of the lower window. Keep a nail in place at all times except when you wish to open the window. For extra security put a hole on both sides of the window. Two (nail) heads are better than one.
3. Don't have windows in or near entrance doors. Burglars can break the glass and easily reach in and open the door.
4. A noisy outside burglar alarm is more effective than the silent type which signals a dispatcher at an alarm company. Neighbours can be on the scene much faster than police.
5. Get to know your neighbours, they're better than any security company. Let them know when your away, and leave them a key. Have them pick up your mail and flyers, and tell them to call the police if they're not sure about any visitors.
6. If you are leaving your house after a fresh snowfall, walk in and out your walkway several times to fool potential burglars.

Dogs in the garbage: Spray garbage bags with ammonia to keep dogs away from them.

Get well cards: If you send a get well card to someone in the hospital, use their home address as a return address. That way, he'll get it even if he's been discharged by the time it arrives at the hospital.

Car interior cleaning: Vinyl seats and dashboards will come clean if you use a cloth that's been dampened with self-stripping floor wax cleaner. Small scratches will also disappear with this method.

Non-stick car antenna: Rub your car antenna from time to time with waxed paper and it will not stick.

Car stuck in the snow: One of your hubcaps can be used as a substitute snow shovel if your car should get stuck in the snow. It will also work for gravel, sand or mud.

An emergency funnel: If you run out of gas and after obtaining some, find you have no funnel, use a rolled up magazine or newspaper. Just make sure no one lights up while this is going on.

A use for old keys: Your old keys make great fishing weights.

Boat key fob: The best key fob for your boat key is a cork. If it falls overboard it will float.

The Christmas scent of pine: If you want a Christmas scent in your home at holiday time, soak some real pine cones in water until they are completely wet, then place them in bowls around the room. They will give off a long-lasting pine fragrance.

MY OWN HELPFUL HINTS

MORE OF MY OWN HELPFUL HINTS

Household Hints

Home Remedies & Cures

First aid
suggestions
and suggestions
to help you
stay healthy

NOTE: The advice given here is of a general nature and does not necessarily apply to each individual. Before trying anything you have not tried before, check with your doctor for expert advice.

ACNE - See **SKIN PROBLEMS (Acne)**

ALLERGIES - See **HAY FEVER**

ANGINA - Going on a strict, low-fat, vegetarian diet, which has no animal products except for skim milk, egg whites and nonfat yogurt, will help control angina, sometimes faster than you think. Taking aspirin on a regular basis is also helpful to angina sufferers. Vitamins A, C, and E are helpful in controlling the disease. Sleeping with the top portion of your body raised and the legs lowered will help prevent heart attacks in people with angina, and if you get an angina attack at night, sitting on the edge of the bed with your feet on the floor can have the same effect as taking a nitroglycerine pill. If this does not appear to be working, take the nitroglycerine.

ARTHRITIS - Replacing meat, eggs, dairy products, sugar, and white breads (or other foods which contain gluten) with a vegetarian diet, or a diet which includes cold water fish, is one of the best ways to fight arthritis. A calcium supplement has been used by many as an effective way to ease the pain of arthritis, while others rely on herbal medicines such as alfalfa. The increased humidity and increase in air pressure which occurs when rain is on the way, is an effective, but painful way to predict the weather. Using a humidifier to maintain a constant humidity level in the house is an effective way to decrease or eliminate this pre-rain pain. Don't let the pain of arthritis stop you from doing things; keeping active and fit is still one of the best weapons against the disease.

ASTHMA - Several don'ts for asthma sufferers are: don't eat before going to bed, don't take aspirin, and don't use your inhaler too often. If you find you have to use your inhaler more and more to get the same effect, see your doctor. For pain relief, instead of aspirin, take an acetaminophen such as Tylenol, Aspirin Free Anacin or Panadol. A simple yoga breathing technique, in which you take twice as much time to exhale as you do to inhale, is helpful if done on a consistent basis. Coffee and cola, which contain caffeine, may be harmful to some people, but caffeine is actually good for asthma sufferers and may be used as a substitute for theophyllne in emergency situations. Coffee should not be regularly used as a substitute for, or taken in combination with, your medication.

BAD BREATH - The worst problem with having halitosis (bad breath) is not knowing you have it. If you should find out you have the problem, here are several 'do and don't' remedies: eat oranges, grapefruit or other citrus fruits; use a water pik to flush odour-causing food particles from gums and between teeth, brush with baking soda; don't miss breakfast; drink water after you eat; brush your tongue as well as teeth and gums; don't eat garlic; chew greens such as parsley and wintergreen; and use only mouthwashes that contain zinc. Bad breath will be less of a problem if you brush after meals. If you only brush once a day, make it after breakfast, not before, and brushing before bed at night does nothing to solve your bad breath problem.

BLADDER INFECTIONS - Drink cranberry juice, it has an antibiotic effect. Drink plenty of water to help flush out the bladder. A hot water bottle can help soothe the pain. Women should void their bladder, before and after intercourse, to help flush out any bacteria that may be present.

BLOOD PRESSURE (High) - If you are sure you have high blood pressure, the first thing you should do is see a doctor; if you are NOT sure you have high blood pressure, the first thing you should do is see a doctor. The most serious cause of high blood pressure is a cholesterol build-up inside the blood vessels. Keep your cholesterol intake and your salt intake down. Celery and garlic are two great high blood pressure fighters.

The demon can also be brought on by stress. Aerobic (moving) exercises are highly recommended, isometric exercises (clenching, weight-lifting exercises, etc.) are not. Avoiding stressful situations, such as getting angry, is recommended, and having a good laugh as often as possible is highly prescribed.

BLOOD PRESSURE (Low) - Lack of oxygen to the brain is the cause of all deaths. Although there are many causes for this lack of oxygen getting to the brain, ie: loss of blood, choking, heart failure, hypothermia, etc., the final cause of death is lack of oxygen to the brain. A momentary loss of oxygen to the brain causes dizziness and fainting. When people with low blood pressure get up from a sitting or lying position quickly, it takes their circulatory system a few moments to adapt to the new position, causing the momentary loss of oxygen to the brain, and the dizziness. Standing for long periods of time can have the same effect. Eating a large meal can cause the blood to rush to the digestive area and leave the brain momentarily without oxygen, again causing the same symptoms.

To avoid the problems caused by low blood pressure, drink plenty of non-alcoholic fluids, especially water, don't spare the salt, eat smaller meals more often, and stretch before getting up. If you must stand for a long period of time, don't lock your knees, flex them slightly. Sleeping with the upper body slightly elevated, and walking after meals will also help maintain proper blood pressure levels.

BODY ODOURS - A daily intake of 25 to 50 milligrams of zinc, or eating a certain amount of food with high zinc content, such as oysters, king crab, wheat germ and lean beef, is one way to fight body odour, while taking a bath in warm water into which you've sprinkled generous amounts of baking soda, is another. Avoiding certain spices, such as garlic and curry will help keep B. O. to a minimum, as will shaving excess hair from your armpits.

BOILS - Keeping a warm and wet compress applied to a boil for about 15 minutes is a good treatment. The compress should be kept very warm and very wet and should be applied four or five times daily to be effective. Bread poultice, or poultices made with crushed raw potatoes, are also touted as ways to get rid of boils.

BRUISES - Applying a frozen steak is still a good cure for a black eye. Actually anything cold, such as an ice pack or cold compress is good, as long as it is applied to the injured area within 24 hours of the injury. Taking a vitamin C supplement, or eating foods which contain the vitamin, such as broccoli, cauliflower, citrus fruits, and sweet potatoes is also helpful in preventing bruis-

ing. A light massage to help dissipate the clotted blood in the muscles can help speed up the healing process.

BUNIONS - Bunions are hereditary and are not only caused by wearing improper footwear, however wearing properly fitting footwear is helpful in easing the problems caused by bunions. A bunion is actually a bone overgrowth and wearing running shoes, or wearing no shoes at all, whenever possible, is also helpful for those who suffer with the problem.

BURNS - The quickest first-aid for burns is cool but not-too-cold water. Extreme cold can kill as many skin cells as extreme heat. Soaking a minor burn in milk for 15 minutes is also an excellent remedy. Minor burns are those smaller than a quarter on a child, and smaller than a loonie (dollar coin) on an adult. For anything larger, see your doctor immediately after the initial cool water treatment, keeping up the treatment until you see your doctor. DO NOT put butter or oily paste on the burn.

CHAPPED LIPS - Chapped lips can be caused by the flavouring agents found in candy, chewing gum, and even toothpaste, as well as by dry air. One thing not to do for chapped lips is to lick them. Drinking more water and humidifying your home in winter are two ways of preventing chapped lips. Applying lip balm every two or three hours, or using petroleum jelly (especially one that has a Sun Protection Factor of 15 or more) is good for preventing chapped lips, or for treating them. Making sure your body has plenty of B complex vitamins and iron will also prevent the problem.

CHICKEN POX - The best thing you can do if your child comes down with chicken pox is to keep the child from scratching, and thereby causing further damage. Several baths a day in colloidal oatmeal (raw oatmeal ground to a fine powder and available from drug stores under various trade names) and warm water will prevent itching. Filing the child's fingernails is also a good precaution. You may also want to scrub the child's nails once or twice a day to prevent secondary infection.

COLDS - There is no cure for the common cold, but drinking four or five glasses of orange, grapefruit, pineapple or tomato juice, or taking a vitamin C supplement will help you get rid of it faster. Drinking liquids such as water, and especially chicken soup, is also helpful in combatting a cold. Echinacea can be helpful in fortifying the immune system.

COLD SORES - Cold sores are caused by the herpes simplex 1 virus and have nothing to do with having a cold. Once you have the virus it never goes away, even though you may have the cold sores only once in your life. Applying a sunscreen with an SPF (sunscreen protection factor) of 15 or more to susceptible areas before you go outside can prevent the sores from reoccurring. Limiting your intake of chocolate, cola, peanuts, cereals, cashews, beer, and other arginine-rich foods will also help prevent the problem. A compress of whole milk applied directly to the sore will ease the pain and speed the healing process, as will an over-the-counter product containing zinc. The virus can live for days on your toothbrush, so it is best to throw away your old toothbrush and use a new one once you get the first sore. People who get cold sores often should supplement their diet with daily doses of 2,000 to 3,000 milligrams of lysine. For cold sores or ulcers on the inside of the mouth, rubbing antacids or baking soda on the spot can relieve pain and speed healing.

COLIC - Colic is abdominal pain which possibly originates in a baby's intestines. There is no known cause, so there is no known cure. There are some things you can do to help the problem, including using white sound. White sound is a regular, even sound, such as run-ning a vacuum cleaner near the baby. Placing the baby near your fishtank may be helpful. The sound of the bubbles going through the filters seem to soothe colicky babies. If you don't own a fishtank it might be worthwhile buying one. The sound of air conditioners and washing machines also seem to work. If you place a hot water bottle covered with a towel in the baby's crib and "drape" the baby stomach-down across the bottle, the warmth to the little one's stomach helps a lot.

Gently rubbing the baby's stomach in a circular motion can help relieve pain. Holding the baby, snuggling and giving plenty of TLC is an age-old, but proven recipe, against colic.

CONJUNCTIVITIS - See **EYE PROBLEMS (Pinkeye)**

CONSTIPATION - To regulate bowel movement you should regulate your diet with high fibre meals such as oatmeal, bran, wheat germ, prunes, figs, apricots, apples, nuts, whole wheat bread, berries, raisins, fresh rhubarb in season, and even high fibre cookies to break the monotony. Psyllium, which can be found in health food stores, and Metamucil, which contains psyllium and is sold at drug stores and some supermarkets, is also good for relieving constipation. Drink plenty of liquids but avoid the ones which cause dehydration such as coffee, tea and alcohol. Avoid milk, cheese and other dairy products for a while until you get back on track. Exercising regularly is also helpful in obtaining regular bowel movements.

CORNS ON THE FEET - Corns and calluses are lumps of thickened and hardened dead skin. This condition is mostly caused by walking for long periods of time in improper footwear. Pointed-toe shoes and shoes with elevated heels are the worst offenders. Round-toed shoes with lots of room will prevent corns. Walking barefoot, especially on a beach, whenever possible will also help prevent, as well as help cure, the problem. If you have high arches, an arch sup-port will also be helpful in this area. A paste made of 4 or 5 aspirins (crushed into a powder), 1/2 teaspoon of a mixture of lemon juice and water, and applied directly is helpful in softening the hard skin. Soaking your feet in Epsom salts and warm water twice a day for ten minutes will also help. A certain amount of relief and prevention can be obtained by using proper insoles in your shoes.

CROUP - Croup is an inflammation of the windpipe and voice box which affects children between the ages of 3 months and 5 years, usually at night. A cool-mist vapourizer, which blows directly on the child's face is very helpful in alleviating this problem. Steam created by a boiling kettle is helpful and taking the child to a steamed-up bathroom, (caused by running a hot shower) will also help. Avoid feeding the child phlegm-producing dairy products to help your child to breathe more easily. Keeping your child's head upright will also help, and generous doses of Tender Loving Care is also recommended.

DANDRUFF - See **HAIR CARE (Dandruff)**

DENTURES - Breaking in a new set of dentures is a problem that's only known to those who must survive the ordeal. For those who have had to "gum" their food for a while, the first thing they want to do is to eat some real food, like steak. It's advisable to prolong this urge for a while, until you

get used to the teeth. You will be very self-conscious about your teeth at first and you will feel that you are not pronouncing your words right and that you are not moving your jaws properly. To help you get over this problem read some passages out loud from a book to "sound yourself out". You may also want to videotape yourself so you can see what everyone else is seeing, and make any corrections you feel necessary. New dentures have a tendency to slip at first. This problem should correct itself in a week or two. Don't use denture adhesives, except as a last resort, because these powders and pastes cause an unwanted build-up between gums and dentures. If you must use adhesive, be sure to clean your teeth and gums every night.

Taking frequent sips of water and massaging your gums three or four times a day will help you get used to your new teeth until they finally become a part of you.

DIAPER RASH - Diaper rash is not caused by the diapers themselves, but by the "contents", so to cut down on diaper rash, don't leave the contents near your baby's bottom any longer than necessary. Change the diaper as soon as it has any nasty contents, or better still, just do the first parts of the change. Get the diaper off, get the bottom clean and dry, and leave the new diaper off for a while to allow the baby's skin to air out. After a while you will know how long you can "safely" leave the bottom bare. If you lay your baby on his stomach you can just place the diaper under him for a while without fastening it.

Baby's bottom should be patted dry, not rubbed dry. Using a hair dryer on a low setting for a short period of time (not more than four minutes) is another good way to render a bottom dry.

Adding a 1/4 cup of plain, white vinegar, to your final rinse cycle when washing cloth diapers will change the pH level and help reduce rash. Disposable diapers made with the newer absorbent gelling material, are also good at keeping baby's bottom rash to a minimum.

As a matter of interest, studies show that breast fed babies have less severe rash problems than those fed formulas.

DIARRHEA - Diarrhea is your body's way of getting rid of unwanted material, so having the condition is not necessarily bad, especially if you like to read while sitting. Of course, spending long periods of time in public is definitely out of the question if you have diarrhea. Drinking clear acidity-free liquids is helpful in getting over the condition. That means that you should drink water, tea, flat (non-diet) pop, consomme, bouillon, and apple juice. Citrus juices should be avoided. Excessive consumption of alcoholic beverages causes diarrhea, so drinking when you have diarrhea is a no-no.

High-fibre foods should be avoided by diarrhea sufferers. Translucent food such as jello is good, and so is yogurt. Sugar and sweets are also effective in assisting your body to hold on to the liquids you consume.

Antacids, such as Maalox, Mylanta, and milk of magnesia should be avoided.

DIETING - The most useful diet product you can't get from a store or borrow from a friend, it has to come from you. If willpower wasn't the most necessary ingredient in any diet, we'd all be the proper weight. Eating habits are as important to dieting as what and how much you eat. For instance if you don't eat breakfast you should start. A hard-boiled egg will be plenty. Have a light lunch such as a salad, or an apple. At dinner time eat a full meal. Not only should you not stuff yourself at dinner time, make sure you are still hungry when you stop eating. A few minutes after dinner you will no longer be hungry. Don't eat after 7 PM. Drink lots of water. Avoid in-between

snacks, and no junk food. If you stick to this diet you will lose about 1/2 pound per day. Weigh yourself every day and don't be disappointed if you are not down, or actually appear to have gained weight one day. At the end of the week you will have lost your 3 1/2 pounds to give you your daily 1/2 pound per day average. There are many ways to diet, but like this one, they all require willpower to work.

EAR PROBLEMS (Earache) - The best remedy for an irritating earache is moist heat. This can be achieved by running hot water over a towel, wringing it out, and placing it against your ear. Wet towels wrapped around a hot water bottle, or around a gel pack that's been warmed up in a microwave or in hot water is also useful. A couple drops of warm mineral oil in the ear may also help.

EAR PROBLEMS (Earlobe Allergies to Jewellery) - If you end up with tender, inflamed earlobes after wearing earrings, you are probably allergic to nickel, which is found in most jewellery items. If that is the case, you might as well get rid of the earrings because you won't be able to wear them again. To treat the condition, use gauze or a cotton ball to apply a mixture of equal parts hydrogen peroxide and water to the earlobes. Domeboro powder or hydrocortisone cream may be used to stop the itching. Picking at the affected area with your fingers may cause infection. If the infection is mild, apply an antibiotic ointment such as Neosporin or Polysporin. See your doctor for more serious infections. Using pure gold or pure silver studs are the only guaranteed way to avoid future problems, because many less-than-24-karat gold jewellery items contain a percentage of nickel.

EMPHYSEMA - Emphysema is a condition where the millions of tiny elastic air sacs in the lungs, which supply oxygen to the blood when we breathe, enlarge and rupture. When this happens, we can never fully exhale again and air stays in the lungs. This makes it harder for blood to flow through the lungs and the now-enlarged lungs push down onto the abdomen. Since eating large meals will add pressure and make it more difficult to breathe, emphysema sufferers should eat small meals more often to ensure that the body gets enough nutrients. Exercise, especially walking, is helpful. There is some evidence that fresh fruits and vegetables and food high in vitamin C and beta-carotene content will help fight further lung deterioration. Taking two cod liver oil capsules every day is also recommended. Cigarette smoking is the major cause of the condition, so it goes without saying that people with emphysema should stop smoking immediately.

EYE PROBLEMS (Dark Circles Underneath) - Dark circles under your eyes may be caused by allergies, symptoms of an illness, being overtired, loss of weight, or they may be natural. If they are not natural, applying a washcloth soaked in cold water and wrung out will help. If they are caused by allergies, find out what you're allergic to and remove it. If you're concerned for cosmetic reasons, use cosmetic make-up to cover them up.

EYE PROBLEMS (Night Blindness) - Most people are temporarily blinded when they go from brightness into near darkness. For some people, their eyes never adjust fully and they have trouble seeing in other-than-lighted areas. Taking vitamin A, or beta-carotene can help the problem. If you suffer from night blindness and must drive, do whatever you can to improve the conditions.

Drive on a lighted freeway, and when on country roads make sure your headlights are clean. Drive more slowly and take extra precautions in looking out for pedestrians. Be especially careful if it's raining or foggy and, if at all possible, wait for daylight to make the trip.

EYE PROBLEMS (Pinkeye) - Conjunctivitis, one time called Pinkeye (when the white of your eyes turn pink), is caused by an infection and, is highly contagious. A lesser cause of pinkeye is from allergies. Avoid contact with someone suffering from the problem, and don't use towels, etc., which they have used. If you shake hands with them don't rub your own eyes until you wash your hands. If you get pinkeye wash your hands over and over to prevent further aggravation of the problem. Don't cover your eye with a patch as this raises the temperature of the eye and adds to the problem. Over-the-counter eyedrops will help to soothe the itch, if it is caused by allergies.

EYE PROBLEMS (Strain) - Use proper lighting when reading to prevent fatigue. Wear proper prescription glasses or sunglasses. Take frequent breaks when working with a computer. Look away from the screen every 15 minutes. If performing a lot of close-up work, take a break and stare off in the distance for a few seconds to help relax the eyes.

FEVER - Fever is not a disease, it is a symptom of an infection and a way in which the body fights these infections. A warm bath is probably the best relief for fever. The old remedy of taking a cold bath is not recommended because it causes the body temperature to drop too quickly. Don't do any strenuous exercise if you have a fever. Instead, have a massage and drink plenty of fluids.

FINGERNAIL PROBLEMS (Brittle Nails) - Eating cauliflower, peanuts and legumes (peas, etc.) which contain biotin, or taking a supplement of biotin will cause your fingernails to thicken and become less brittle.

FINGERNAIL PROBLEMS (Nail Biting) - Nail biting is a habit which is often born out of boredom, but it does become a habit, so it must be treated as such to effect a cure. One way to remind you about the habit is to file your nails daily. Since you usually bite the nails without knowing what you are doing, put something on your fingertips and nails to remind you; pepper, tabasco sauce, lemon juice, or any bitter non-toxic substance make great reminders. Wearing gloves whenever you can, especially while out of public view, will also serve as a reminder.

FLU - Flus are almost as inevitable as seasons. Flu shots and taking the proper amount of vitamins and minerals will help with prevention, but if you should come down with the malady there are some things you can do to help the situation. A proper diet is helpful when you have the flu. Vitamin-rich fruit and vegetable juices are excellent ways to wash down your meals. Wash your hands often and get rid of your toothbrush to prevent reintroducing germs into your body. Get plenty of rest and avoid heavy exercises until you get well again. The herb echinacea can help boost the immune system.

FOOD POISONING - As soon as we hear the word poison we think of instant death, but in the case of food poisoning this not always so. Although people do die from food poisoning, this is mostly not the case, and food poisoning is not always caused by food which has spoiled. Sometimes food handled by people with bacteria on their hands can cause the problem. Although not always life-threatening, food poisoning can make you feel miserable until the infection clears up. Drinking water or drinks con-

taining sugar will help. Take the liquid in sips until you can keep it down. If the food poisoning is causing you to vomit, hold off on the liquids until you are able to keep them down.

FOOT PROBLEMS (Bunions) - See **BUNIONS**

FOOT PROBLEMS (Corns) - See **CORNS ON THE FEET**

FROSTBITE - One way to avoid getting frostbitten is to dress warm. Don't just make sure that the extremities, which are first to get frostbitten, are covered, wear a warm coat as well. When the central part of your body gets cold, much-needed heat is kept from reaching the extremities. Drinking fluids, including water, is helpful in preventing frostbite, but avoid drinks that contain caffeine, such as coffee, tea, and colas.

If you do get frostbitten, don't rub snow on the frostbitten area. Although this was thought the thing to do for years, this will only cause you more problems. As a matter of fact, frostbitten areas should not be rubbed with anything. It's best to find a warm place and stay there until the frostbitten area is completely thawed. Thaw yourself out slowly. Avoid high heat which can burn you without your knowledge. A warm bath with the water temperature between 39°C and 43°C (102°F to 110°F) is a good way to thaw out. Don't drink alcohol when you are frostbitten, as it prevents the constriction of blood vessels and don't smoke because this restricts blood flow.

Once you thaw out, protect the frostbitten area for a while by avoiding any activity in which you may bump or further injure the area.

GALLSTONES - The purpose of the gallbladder is to collect the cholesterol-rich bile secreted by the liver. This bile is later used to help break down any fatty food you eat. When there is too much cholesterol or pigment in the bile, it becomes hard. This hard pebble is small at first but as it collects more material it grows bigger and bigger. These gallstones can actually grow as big as eggs. Not all gallstones cause problems but when one gets stuck in a duct it causes problems and pain. If the gallstone passes through the duct the problem is solved. If it falls back into the gallbladder the pain stops, but the relief may be only temporary.

Several ways to avoid gallstones is to lose weight, but don't lose it too fast as this can cause your chances of producing gallstones to increase. Losing about one pound a week is ideal. Eating foods which are low in saturated fats will also help prevent gallstones, but going on a fat-free diet can increase your chances of getting gallstones.

GOUT - Sometimes called 'the rich man's disease' and 'the King's disease', gout is really a form of arthritis which is caused by excessive uric acid. The excessive uric acid crystallizes in the joints causing them to become inflamed, swollen and tender. A gout attack happens suddenly, causes intense pain, then leaves as suddenly as it came. Once you have had an attack of gout you will want to avoid a further encounter. Overweight people generate more uric acid than smaller ones. One way to avoid a second bout is to lose weight, but don't lose the weight all at once because crash diets also increase uric acid levels in the body. Liver and red meats and certain fish, especially certain shell fish, contain high levels of uric acid, as do certain green vegetables such as spinach and turnip greens. Avoiding alcohol and drinking lots of water instead will help, as alcohol produces uric acid and water assists in disposing it through urination. According to a recent study, there is one great way to avoid gout attacks, at least for men. The study showed that men who have sex more often have gout attacks less often. Apparently sexual activity reduces uric acid levels.

HAND CARE (Tip) - Hand lotions are expensive and will never be as effective as pure glycerine

for making your hands look beautiful. For best results, soak your hands in warm water before applying the glycerine as the warm water will open the pores in your skin and allow the healing glycerine to be more readily absorbed.

HANGOVER - Of all the tips for avoiding hangovers, *not drinking* is by far the best, but there are others. Alcohol robs your body of vitamin C, so eating or drinking items that contain this vitamin, including vitamin C pills, before you drink, as you drink, before you go to bed after drinking, or after you wake up with a hangover, is advisable. Since alcohol causes dehydration, drinking water before you retire also helps. Taking aspirin before you start drinking will only increase your problem, but aspirin taken after may help with the headache. However, aspirin may add to your upset stomach problem. Foods which are high in fructose, such as honey, grapes, apples and cherries are recommended to help you get back to normal. Besides orange juice, grapefruit juice and tomato juice, Gatorade, which contains potassium and sodium, is also recommended for hangovers.

HAIR CARE (Dandruff) - Dandruff, for the most part, is nothing but dead cells on your scalp which flake off as new ones are pushed up from the layers of skin below. However, what we sometimes call dandruff is nothing more than residue left over from using hair sprays, styling gels and mousse, especially if we use these products in excess. If the latter is the cause of your particular "dandruff" problem, the remedy is simple; just cut down on the use of such products or change products. One way to solve a "real dandruff" problem is to not simply wash your hair, but wash your head as well. That means doing some rubbing and scrubbing on the scalp when you shampoo. When you do this, your dandruff problem will appear to increase at first, but continue with the scrubbing and your problem should disappear. The problem will not reappear as long as you remember to wash your scalp as well as your hair when you shampoo. Some people have a more serious dandruff problem than others, and for those people, solving their problem is just a matter of shampooing (hair and scalp) for longer periods, or more often, or both.

When using a dandruff shampoo, leave the shampoo on for about five minutes to allow it to do a proper job on your scalp.

People with oily hair should use a tar-based shampoo if other methods fail.

HAIR CARE (Dry Hair and Split Ends) - Dry hair and split ends are sometimes caused by weather conditions, but are often caused by mistreatment. Regular shampooing is helpful in maintaining healthy hair but shampooing too often can cause problems. Some other unnatural causes of split-ends are electric curling irons, electric curlers, and blow dryers. Hair dried without intense heat is much healthier hair. Hair dyes and chlorine found in swimming pools are other culprits that steal the natural look away from your hair.

Using a hair conditioner is helpful in maintaining healthy hair. Two household conditioners are mayonnaise and beer. A dab of mayonnaise worked into your hair once a week and left in for five minutes is good. Beer should be sprayed on from a pump bottle after shampooing and towelling, but before blow-drying or styling.

Wearing a hat when you go outside will help your hair. Without a hat the wind can whip your hair into a frizzied mess, and the hot sun can dry it out in a short period of time.

HAIR CARE (Oily Hair) - Blondes with thin hair have the most problems with oily hair, while

redheads with thick hair have the least. There are a number of causes for oily hair, but whatever the cause the best way to treat it is to use the right shampoo and to shampoo often. Leave the lather on your hair for at least five minutes for better effect. Rinsing your hair in a mixture of water and apple cider vinegar (1 pint water to 1 teaspoon vinegar) or water and lemon juice (1 pint distilled water and the juice of two freshly squeezed lemons) make excellent rinses for controlling oily hair. Talcum powder rubbed into your scalp and hair (one section at a time) will also help control your oily hair problem.

HAY FEVER - Hay fever is an allergy, quite often to pollen. Staying inside in the morning (up to 10:00AM) when pollen counts are the highest will help. Washing your hair after you come in from outside to remove the pollen which may later fall on your pillow as you sleep will also help, as will running your air conditioner.

HEADACHES - See **HEAD PROBLEMS (Neck Tension and Tension Headaches)**

HEAD PROBLEMS (Neck Tension and Tension Headaches) - To help treat neck tension and tension headaches, put two tennis balls in a sock and tie the end of the sock so that the balls are tightly together. Put the balls on your pillow and lay down so that the two muscles at the base of your skull (just above your neck) are resting on the balls with the weight of your head. Stay in that position for a few minutes or until tension releases. Be careful not to push down too hard on the tennis balls.

HEAD PROBLEMS (Migraines) - Although a migraine is a pain in the head it is more than a headache. Most people who claim to suffer from migraines, merely have headaches. A migraine causes severe head pain and often nausea and vomiting. It can cause blind spots, light flashes, dizziness and numbness to one side of your body. Light that is just a little too bright and sound that is just a little too loud, can be almost impossible to bear. Avoid aspartame and NutraSweet (which contains aspartame), as this product is known to cause migraines. Birth control pills have also been known to cause migraines. Try to relax as much as possible, but do it gradually. Don't go from a super-stressful situation immediately into a super-relaxful one. This is probably why most migraines occur on weekends or during vacation. A cold compress or ice pack to the head may help. If you can sleep, this may also get rid of the migraine. Also try the tennis-balls-in-the-sock method mentioned above. The natural product *Feverfew*, can be effective in treating migraines.

HEART PROBLEMS - See **ANGINA**

HEAT RASH - A heat rash is caused when sweat ducts become plugged and the sweat goes into the skin. You can usually solve the problem by staying inside a cool, air-conditioned room for two days. Wearing loose clothing, washing with a mild, anti-bacterial soap, and adding a few tablespoons of baking soda to your bath water will also help.

HEMORROIDS - A hemorroid is a varicose vein in the anal area. This vein can cause itching and burning, can sometimes be quite painful, and sometimes bleed. The straining to have a bowel movement when you are constipated is one cause of the problem, so eating properly will help. Eating high-fibre foods such as rice, barley and oat bran will help. For those with trouble chewing, mashed potatoes, mashed carrots, bean soups and creamy vegetable soups are good. Drinking lots of

HOME REMEDIES & CURES

water will also help fight constipation. To relieve hemorroidal problems, dab on some petroleum jelly or zinc oxide paste after wiping. Wiping should be done with moist, soft paper without zealous rubbing, and using dry toilet paper to pat the area dry afterward. See also **CONSTIPATION** in this book.

HERPES - Herpes Simplex 1 has been around for years, but was, and is, more commonly known as the cold sore. We became aware of Herpes Simplex 2, or Genital Herpes in recent years. One can catch genital herpes by having sex with someone who is carrying the disease. You can't always tell a carrier because some carriers don't know they're carriers. You can't get rid of herpes; once you have it, you have it for life. When it is latent, except for passing it on to someone else, it isn't a problem. It breaks out in the form of burning sores in the genital area. You should see a doctor who will probably prescribe "acyclovir", the only proven herpes fighter. Aspirin will help relieve the pain and fight the inflammation. If drying with a towel after a bath or shower causes problems, use a blow dryer in the affected area. When you are suffering from an outbreak of herpes it is not advisable to have sex because apart from passing the disease on to someone else, you can also cause it to spread on your own body.

HICCUPS - A spoonful of sugar helps calm hiccups. Eating crushed ice or placing an ice pack on the diaphram also works. Drinking water and breathing rapidly into a paper bag works as well. Also massaging the top of the back of the neck can stop a hiccup spasm.

HIVES - Like so many of our little ailments, hives are caused by allergies, so the best way to avoid them is to isolate the allergy and remove it from our presence, or remove our presence from it. Applying a cold compress will relieve the problem as long as you aren't one of the people who actually get hives from ice and cold. Herbal brews such as peppermint, valerian or catnip teas will help make the hives go away. Applying calamine lotion or milk of magnesia directly to the hives will also help dry them up.

INSECT BITES - Mosquito and other insect bites are troublesome. Here are several ways to help avoid them and several ways to treat them if you fail to try the former. Eating food which is high in vitamin B1 (thiamine) will cause your body, when it sweats, to give off an odor which insects find offensive but humans do not. This vitamin can be found in animal livers, hearts and other organs, as well as in whole grains and brewers yeast. Garlic and onions may be offensive to humans, but bugs are bugged by the odours they give off, to the point that they will avoid you if you give off these odours. When buying a repellant in the store read the label to make sure that the product contains DEET (diethyltoluamide), a proven insect repellent.

Some remedies which may be applied to insect bites are calamine lotion; pastes made of meat tenderizers and water; table salt and water; and baking soda and water, all applied with a cloth for 20 minutes; and ice packs applied for 10 minutes. An excellent homeopathic remedy is apis mellifica.

INSOMNIA - Insomnia is caused mostly by an overactive mind. The mind cannot rest until it stops working, so to get to sleep you have to find ways to make it stop working. One way to do that is to cut down on any excitement, including exciting conversation just before bedtime. Try reading a boring book in bed. Don't read an exciting book because your interest in the book may also keep you awake. Certain smells, such as lavender, the salt air found near the seashore, and the smell of baked desserts help some people sleep. Heating pads, which go off with a timer, help some people.

If you're a nightshift worker and get bothered by the daytime sounds of children shouting, cars starting and dogs barking, the sound of an air conditioner (fan only if necessary) can help mask these sounds and help you sleep. White noise machines can have the same effect, day or night. Drinking alcohol, such as a hot toddy, may help you sleep for a while but will cause you more of a sleeping problem in the long run. It may help you get to sleep, but eventually you will have to consume more and more to have the same effect. Alcohol-induced sleep is sometimes only a short sleep and when you wake up, you're awake for the night. Don't eat big meals before retiring because your body will have trouble sleeping when a part of it, your stomach, is still working - digesting the food. A light snack before bed time does help some people sleep.

JET LAG - Drink plenty of clear fluids while on the plane to prevent dehydration. Do not sleep on the plane, wait until bed time after arrival. Moderate exercising after landing helps prevent jet lag. When possible, fly by day to arrive at night. Do not drink alcohol or coffee as they upset your body clock.

KIDNEY STONES - Kidney stones are crystal build-ups of crystals of calcium salts and other minerals, such as oxalate, which were not flushed in your urine. These rough pebbles can cause much pain and can sometimes cause blood in the urine. Most kidney stones are gotten rid of by passing them through ureter. When they are too big to be passed this way, modern technology has now made it possible for the stone to be broken down into smaller pieces using laser treatment, so it may be passed more readily. If neither of these methods work, surgery is required.

To avoid kidney stones, drink plenty of water and avoid calcium-rich dairy products such as milk, butter and cheese. Avoid foods which contain high concentrations of oxalates, such as chocolate, beans, rhubarb, spinach, broccoli, beets, celery, blueberries, grapes and nuts. Protein rich foods such as meats and fish can also cause kidney stones, so it is wise to limit your intake of these foods to an average of 6 ounces per day. Cut down on table salt and avoid foods that are very salt.

If you have had heartburn or suffer from upset stomach caused by acidity, you may be more prone to kidney stones,because many antacids cause kidney stones. See your doctor for advice on this problem. Also ask your doctor for advice on which vitamins to take and which ones to avoid if you have a kidney stone problem. If you have had one kidney stone, you have a problem because in most people they re-occur.

LIPS (Chapped) - See **CHAPPED LIPS**

LOW BLOOD PRESSURE - See **BLOOD PRESSURE (Low)**

MENSTRUAL PAIN - If your menstrual period causes you very severe pains see your doctor to make sure the pain isn't being caused by another problem. Drugs containing ibuprofen, such as Advil, are recommended. Exercise, such as walking and certain yoga exercises, is good. Increase your magnesium and calcium intake by eating whole wheat, buckweat, beans, salmon, shrimp, vegetables, nuts, milk, butter and cheese. A heating pad placed on the stomach, as well as drinking some warm gingerroot tea, will also help ease the pain.

MIGRAINES - See **HEAD PROBLEMS (Migraines)**

MORNING SICKNESS - Weeks 6 to 13 are the pregnancy weeks when morning sickness comes calling. Munching on some dry crackers before the nausea starts may keep it away. Biscuits, bagels and dry toast will also help, and eating small meals more often is better for you during this time than large meals. Especially good are almonds, which are high in protein, fat and B vitamins. Nausea can also be brought on by stress, so try to avoid it as much as possible. Drinking lots of liquids will also help. Your body knows what's best for you, so give into those cravings for food, but try to avoid coffee, sweets, artificial sweeteners, and fried foods, all of which can trigger nausea.

MOTION SICKNESS - See **SEASICKNESS and other MOTION SICKNESS**

MUSCLE PROBLEMS (Aches and Soreness) - Muscle soreness caused by exercising and over-exercising can be remedied in several ways. A hot and cold shower will help. Take a hot shower for several minutes then turn it to cold for 30 seconds. Repeat this five to ten times and the blood vessels will actually open and close, flushing out soreness-causing lactic acid in the process. A bath in a hot tub several hours after exercise will help. Massaging will help relieve sore muscles, as will taking an over-the-counter inflammatory tablet, such as Advil, Anacin 3, Nuprin and Tylenol. Sports drinks such as Gatorade, which are high in carbohydrates, are also very helpful in curing sore muscles.

MUSCLE PROBLEMS (Muscle Spasm) - Muscle spasm is a sudden shortening of the muscles which cause intense pain. Stretching will help the problem, but do it gradually, not suddenly. A hot bath will also help. To avoid the problem, consume more calcium-rich foods such as yogurt, skim milk and ricotta cheese, and foods high in potassium such as bananas, potatoes, dried peaches and prune juice.

NAIL PROBLEMS - See **FINGERNAIL PROBLEMS**

NECK PAINS - Most stiff necks are caused by stress, some are physical, and some are a combination of both. A dry towel, rolled up and wrapped around your neck will help support the neck. A towel dipped in hot water wrung out, rolled up and placed around the neck for 30 minutes, three to four times a day, will be even better. Many neck problems these days are caused by improper seating in front of a computer screen. If you spend a lot of time in front of the screen the problem can be made worse. You should make sure your chair and keyboard are the right height. Your computer screen should be directly in front of you. If you have to look up or down at your screen you may create neck problems. See your chiropractor for advice on proper seating in front of your computer. Don't cradle the telephone receiver between your shoulder and head because this too will cause problems. If you must have your hands free, get a proper headset. Stiff necks are sometimes caused by cold drafts. If this is the case, keep your bedroom window closed while you sleep, and your car window closed when driving.

NECK TENSION - See **NECK PROBLEMS (Neck Tension and Tension Headaches)**

NIGHT BLINDNESS - See **EYE PROBLEMS (Night Blindness)**

NOSEBLEEDING - Nosebleeds are mostly a nuisance, but if they persist, see your doctor. One

remedy when the blood starts to flow is to blow your nose to remove any blood clots which may prevent the blood vessel from sealing. Stand up straight and pinch your nose, this sometimes stops the flow. If you are prone to nosebleeds, use a humidifier, and take C and B complex vitamins to form collagen and free-flowing mucus, which will create a moist, protective lining inside your nose.

PAPER CUTS - One of the best remedies for paper cuts and other minor cuts is to put a dab of crazy glue directly on the cut. It seals the cut immediately and stops the air from getting to the nerve ends, thereby stopping pain instantly. The glue drop will wear off in a day or two.

PINKEYE - See **EYE PROBLEMS (Pinkeye)**

PREMATURE EJACULATION - Premature ejaculation is when a man reaches orgasm too soon. There are a number of remedies for this problem. Don't do physical exercise before sex, as this may be one cause of your problem. Two other ways of solving the problem are having sex more often and changing positions with your partner.

PREMENSTRUAL CRAMPS - Moderate exercise increases blood flow, relaxes muscles, fights fluid retention, and increases body production of endorphins. A hot water bottle over the abdomen can ease cramps. Nutritional supplements of zinc, magnesium, calcium, vitamin B complex, and essential fatty acids can help. Cutting down on the coffee intake will also help.

RASH - See **DIAPER RASH** or **HEAT RASH**

REGULARITY - See **CONSTIPATION**

SEASICKNESS and other MOTION SICKNESS - Motion sickness is caused by dizziness. We get dizzy when two of our senses perceive two different things. Our balance (which is controlled by our inner ear) may perceive one motion, while our eyes see another motion. The confusion causes dizziness and sometimes motion sickness. One way to stop the confusion is to shut your eyes. If it's not too late you may prevent the nausea. Bad odours, such as the smell of fish or engine fumes, may add to the problem so get your nose as far away from these smells as possible. Don't stay confined; if you're in a cabin or down below in a boat, get out on deck. If you're in a car, open a window and smell the fresh air. If you know you have a problem with motion sickness and someone else gets sick, stay away from them or you may be next; and don't just keep your eyes away from them, keep your nose away as well. Eating ginger can help relieve nausea and soothe the stomach. Drinking alcohol, before or during the trip, or even the night before can also bring on the nausea. Smoking a cigarette to keep from getting sick won't help; it will actually add to the problem. Reading a book while you're in motion can also cause motion sickness.

SCARRING - If there is a cut to your body, either an accidental one or one made by planned surgery, there is potential for scarring. There are a number of ways to avoid a scar or at least make the scar less pronounced. Eating foods high in vitamin C, such as citrus fruits, broccoli, and potatoes, will help the wound heal faster and lessen the chances of a scar. Zinc-rich foods such as peanuts, swiss and cheddar cheeses, lean beef, dark turkey meat and Brazil nuts will also speed up

the healing process. Cleaning the wound every day with hydrogen peroxide while it is healing will help, as well as massaging with a moisturizing cream after the wound has healed.

SKIN PROBLEMS (Dry, Itchy Skin) - Dry skin is usually a winter problem. This is because as the artificial heat in our homes is increased, the humidity decreases. Petroleum jelly or mineral oil on the dry skin make great moisturizers. Vegetable oil, hydrogenated cooking oil, Crisco or Mazzola are great. If you have a tendency to break-out, use an oil-free moisturizer, and if you have sensitive skin use a moisturizer that contains no perfumes or lanolin. Warm baths are better for dry-skin sufferers than hot ones, and long baths should be avoided. Put a little bath oil into the tub and use cleansing lotion instead of soap. If you must use soap, use a mild one such as Dove. Don't scrub with a face cloth, use your fingertips, and pat yourself partially dry with a towel afterward. Apply the moisturizer before the skin dries to seal in the water. Wear baggy clothing, made of something other than wool to avoid further irritation of the problem. Men should not shave just before going out into the cold, and don't use aftershaves containing alcohol.

SKIN PROBLEMS (Acne) - Acne is caused by clogged pores of the skin but manifests itself as three different symptoms; blackheads, pimples and whiteheads. Acne is mostly hereditary and is not caused by eating chocolate. An acne attack can be brought on by different factors such as, climate changes, stress, exposure to the sun, the type of make-up you use and even taking birth control pills. Check with your doctor to see if your acne problem is caused by the pill and discuss with him what to do about the problem if it is. There are many who swear that a zinc supplement is the best cure for acne, others attribute vitamin A with clearing up their acne problem. You can squeeze a blackhead but leave the whiteheads alone, as squeezing whiteheads will only add to your problems. Over-the-counter acne remedies such as benzoyl, will help, but use only one remedy at a time. Clean your face thoroughly before applying any medication. You can cover your acne with make-up but be sure you use something that doesn't have an oil base. Stay out of the sun after applying medication or make-up to your face.

SKIN PROBLEMS (Irritation and Cracking) - Cracked skin caused by eczema or psoriasis can be treated by soaking the area each night with warm water. Pat dry after soaking and coat the area in petroleum jelly to seal in the moisture. If the affected areas are on feet and hands, wear cotton socks and gloves to bed.

SKIN PROBLEMS (Oily Skin) - Oily skin seems to be a problem with some people, especially young people. It shouldn't be. Oily skin helps us to maintain younger looking complexions into old age and are a blessing which doesn't disguise us, even when we're young. If you insist on getting rid of the excess oil, a synthetic cleanser rubbed on with your fingertips will help. Clay or mud masks from your beauty shop will also help, as will washing yourself in hot, rather than warm, water.

SLEEPWALKING - About 3 million Canadians are sleepwalkers. Sleepwalking mostly affects children between the ages of 6 and 14, but some carry it on into adulthood. Adults who have the problem should seek the advice of a doctor. Sometimes, in children, the cause of sleepwalking is being overtired, so insure that your children get enough sleep to prevent the sleepwalking.

If someone in your household is a sleepwalker, here are several tips on how to deal with the situation: 1) Don't wake them suddenly because they are not aware of, or responsible for, their actions

at that time and may become momentarily violent. 2) Try to protect the sleepwalker from causing injury to himself. 3) Guide them back into bed talking to them in a soothing voice, and try to get them to lie on their back.

SNORING - When loose tissue in your throat, or your tongue obstructs the airway, the air going past these items sets up a vibration which we know as snoring. One way to avoid snoring is to avoid sleeping on your back. When you sleep on your back, gravity pulls your tongue or the loose tissues in your throat into the air path. If you start out sleeping on your side or stomach and always manage to end up in the snoring position on your back during the night, try wearing pyjamas with a pocket sewn onto the back. Place a couple tennis balls in the pocket, and every time you turn onto your back, the tennis balls will make it too uncomfortable for you to remain in that position and you will turn over. People who drink, or take sleeping pills before going to bed have more of a tendancy to snore than those who don't. Getting more sleep helps prevent snoring, as does sleeping on a firm mattress. There are special pillows available that keep the head and neck in a position that reduces snoring.

SORES - See **COLD SORES**

SOMNAMBULISM - See **SLEEP WALKING**

SPLINTER REMOVAL - Removing a splinter can be painful, especially for the person with the splinter. In the case of children, removing splinters are especially painful, sometimes as much for the adult doing the removal as for the child with the splinter. One painless way to remove splinters is to soak the area in warm water for 10 to 20 minutes. This sometimes causes the wooden splinter to swell, and it may pop out on its own. If this doesn't work, numbing the area with an ice pack before you use the tweezers will help ease the pain. Clean the tweezers with hydrogen peroxide before use, and clean the wound with it after the splinter is removed.

SPRAINS - A sprain is the tearing, or excessive stretching of a ligament. Some sprains can be more painful than breaking a bone. If you have a sprain eat pineapple, which contains bromelain, to speed the healing process. Unfortunately bromelain causes dermatitis in some people so if your skin starts to get itchy, you probably are one of those people. Stop taking the pineapple and consult your doctor. Ice wrapped in a towel and applied directly to the sprained area, will decrease blood flow and reduce swelling. Elevation will also help. An elastic bandage wrapped snugly, but not tightly enough to restrict circulation, will help prevent further injury while the sprain is healing. DO NOT apply heat.

STOMACH ACHES - Stomach aches are caused by what we eat as well as by what we don't eat. Sometimes acidity in the stomach can cause the problem, and sometimes the problem is caused by stress. This is particularly true with children. If you have a bad stomach and you haven't eaten, the problem is acidity. You can solve this problem by eating a light snack or by taking an antacid. If overeating is the problem, take Alka-Seltzer or something similar to bring on that pain-relieving burp.

STOMACH PAIN - See **COLIC**

STUTTERING - Have you ever noticed that people with horrendous stuttering problems can sing without missing a note. There is a reason for that, and anyone reading this, who has a stuttering problem, and who learns that reason, can stop stuttering. The reason singers don't stutter is because the message they have to pass on is laid out for them in a pre-arranged manner. To them, getting the message across is as simple as following the dots in a TV sing-a-long. They know what they have to say word for word. It's just a matter of memorizing the words. Trying to communicate their own message during ordinary conversation is a different matter. In conversation they know the message but are unsure of what words they will use to deliver the message, or how the words will be arranged in that message. They start to speak before the words in the sentence are written down in the proper order on the blackboard of their mind, and the result is stuttering. If people who stutter would slow down and think about exactly what they mean to say, as well as how they mean to say it, they will be well on their way down the road to beating the stuttering problem altogether.

A voice-activated microcassette recorder would be helpful to people with stuttering problems. Conversations should be recorded then played back in private. In hindsight, it is easy to look back and see what we meant to say. When the stutterer listens to what he said, as opposed to what he meant to say, then repeats what he meant to say out loud to himself, it will help in future conversations. This will also build confidence which is very important, because lack of confidence is the biggest enemy of those who stutter.

SUNBURN - Wearing a sunscreen with a sun protection factor of 15 or more will help prevent sunburn, as will not spending too much time under old sol. If you do get a sunburn there are a number of things you can do to relieve the pain. If the sunburn is severe see your doctor. Milk, at slightly less than room temperature on gauze, applied directly to the burn will help. If you boil lettuce for several hours in water, then strain and let water cool in the refrigerator, it too is helpful in relieving the problem. It should be applied with cotton balls. A lukewarm bath with vinegar or a mixture of 1/4 cup of cornstarch and 1/4 cup of baking soda added will also help.

SWELLING - Swelling occurs when fluid travelling through your blood vessels seeps into the surrounding tissue. There are a number of causes for swelling including fractures, sprains, bumping into something, insect bites and stings, allergies (this especially affects eyes), standing or remaining in one position too long, and sometimes for no apparent reason. For swelling caused by allergies, take over-the-counter antihistamine. To reduce the swelling, apply ice or a cold, wet cloth directly to the area. Elevate the swollen area above the level of your heart if possible. A compression bandage wrapped around the swollen area will help, as will rest.

TEETH (False) - See **DENTURES**

TEETHING - When baby starts to teethe he can become very fretful. One way to comfort him is to hold him and sing or hum to him. Massaging the baby's gums with your finger or with a clean cloth will also help. Placing his teething rings and soothers into the fridge to cool before giving them to baby will also help pacify him.

THINNING HAIR - This will not tell you how to grow your lost hair back, but merely give you tips on how to make the most of what you have. Colour your hair to make it look thicker. Colouring actually roughs up the hair for a fuller look. Colour it lighter rather than darker to avoid contrast

with your white scalp. Crack an egg (both white and yolk) over your head and rub it in before shampooing. This will actually thicken your hair. Getting a curly permanent will also make you look like you have more hair. Washing daily with protein shampoos will help with the desired look, and after shampooing, use a conditioner made from a pint of water with a tablespoon of white vinegar added. Massage into hair and rinse out in the shower. This will make your hair more acidic, which will in turn give it a fuller look.

TOOTHACHE - The only real remedy for a toothache is seeing a dentist, but until you can get to see him, here are some remedies which may help. First, rinse the mouth with warm, salt water. Ice wrapped in a towel and applied to the face outside the painful area will also help to relieve pain. Oil of cloves or benzocaine applied directly to the problem area will ease the pain. There is a nerve ending in the fleshy part of your hand between your thumb and forefinger. Massaging this area is said to be good for toothache pain as well as headache pain. Rubbing an ice cube on this area is also said to stop pain.

ULCERS - Ulcers are caused by the caustic effects of stomach acid, and although they don't bother us all the time, they can suddenly flare up at any time causing much pain and distress. These flare-ups are sometimes caused by certain foods. Once you have identified one of those foods, stop eating it. Eating smaller meals more often will keep the flare-ups to a minimum. Avoid aspirin if you have ulcers. For pain relief substitute aspirin with an acetaminophen such as Tylenol. Over-the-counter antacids are helpful in relieving the pain caused by ulcers. NOTE: Smokers develop ulcers twice as often as non-smokers.

VARICOSE VEINS - Two and a half million Canadian men and five million Canadian women have varicose veins. One easy way to get relief from the problem is to take two aspirins every day. Keeping your legs elevated whenever possible will help the problem, as will sleeping with your legs elevated. Raising the foot of your bed by using blocks will do it. Any exercise which will strengthen your legs is also useful in easing the problem.

WARTS - No, you don't need the seventh son of the seventh son to remove warts. You can do it yourself. If the wart is on your finger, wrap adhesive tape around the wart and finger four times. Leave it for 6 1/2 days and remove. If the wart isn't gone let it air out for half a day, then repeat the process. The wart will go away. Another method of removing warts is to apply crushed aspirin to the wart and wrap it in cellophane tape (or any tape that seals out air). When the skin gets soft enough to let the crushed aspirin work on the wart it will disappear. NOTE: If you are allergic to aspirins, do not use this method. Liquid vitamin A applied directly to the wart will also work, as will a paste made from a crushed vitamin C pill mixed with water.

WRINKLES - Wrinkles are as inevitable as old age, but you can do something about wrinkles. Taking your proper vitamins can help keep your complexion smooth. The best ones for your skin are the B complex vitamins, which can be found in eggs, lean beef, chicken, and whole wheat. Also good are vitamins A, C and E, which can be obtained by eating fresh fruit and vegetables, especially green leafy vegetables and carrots. Smoking cigarettes and drinking alcohol cause wrinkles.

Excessive sun and windburn are two other factors which bring on wrinkles.

YEAST INFECTIONS - Yeast infections are not dangerous, but there are times when they can be embarrassing. The symptoms are vaginal itch and a white discharge which resembles cottage cheese in appearance, but smells yeasty, and sometimes fishy. Yeast infections can be triggered by consuming sweets which contain white granulated sugars, mushrooms, bread and beer. Eating potatoes, citrus fruits, and broccoli, which are high in vitamin C, will help solve the problem. Get off that wet bathing suit and get into dry clothing as soon as you are finished swimming and you will eliminate one of the ways in which yeast infections start. Anti-yeast vaginal cream which you can buy over the counter at any drug store works very well in solving the problem. Another way to get rid of the infection is to run six or seven inches of warm water in the bath tub, add 1/2 cup of salt and 1/2 cup of vinegar. Sit in the tub for about 20 to 25 minutes. Do this daily until the infection has cleared up.

Common Herbs and their Medicinal Values

by Dr. Allan Ettenson

The herbs listed here can be either grown in many areas of Canada, or may be purchased in plant or health food stores. All herbs should be used with caution. It is important that you use herbs under the advice and direction of an appropriate health practitioner.

Herbal preparations can be taken by various routes. Some are designed to be taken internally, while others are for external application. Here are a few approaches of how to prepare the herbs for the remedy. For more detailed information consult a herbal text.

Tea: Boil about half a litre of water for one tablespoon of the herb. It should boil about five to ten minutes.

Infusion: It is prepared similar to a tea, but it is steeped for longer periods of time; 10-20 minutes. It can be taken warm or cold.

Decoction: (For herbs which are woody in nature, such as bark, roots or certain fruits.) The herb is placed in a non-aluminum saucepan with water. The preparation is allowed to simmer, just below boiling, for about 30 minutes. The finished mixture can be kept in the refrigerator and used as needed.

Tincture: This is an extraction of the herb using water and alcohol. It is an alternate way of taking the herb avoiding the boiling process of an infusion.

Compress: A clean cloth is soaked in a hot infusion or decoction of herbs. The cloth is applied while hot. When cool it should be replaced.

Poultice: The herb preparation is applied directly onto the skin. It is prepared as a paste and it is applied hot. Body oil should be placed onto the skin first so the poultice will be easier to wash off.

HOME REMEDIES & CURES

Syrup: This is the boiling down of a herbal preparation down to a syrup. The syrup can be taken as needed.

THE HERBS

Aloe: *(Aloe Vera)* It is commonly found in plant stores and can be grown in the home. The jelly-like juice found in the leaves are used for the remedy. The juice is squeezed from the leaves and it is used as a skin cleanser, antiseptic and moisturizer. It is an anti-flammatory for burns, blisters and scrapes of the skin.

Arnica: *(Arnica montana)* Found in the western part of North America. The flowers of the plant are used for the remedy. It is prepared into a salve, oil or liniment. It is an anti-inflammatory and analgesic for sore muscles and joint sprains. Salve may be applied to the skin for closed wounds related to trauma. (Not to be applied on open sores)

Calendula: *(Calendula officinalis)* Plant grows throughout North America and Europe. Flowers are used for the remedy. It can be prepared as a tincture, ointment, infusion or a tea. It is effective as an antiseptic, or antibacterial wash, especially to treat cuts, scrapes and burns.

Catnip: *(Nepeta cataria)* It is found throughout Eurasia and North America. The flowers and leaves are used. It is used as an infusion and it is best used in small quantities, mixed with other herbs such as peppermint and chamomile. In moderation, can be used as a sedative for insomnia, also can be effective for colds, colic, upset stomachs, headaches and fevers.

Cayenne Pepper: *(Capsicum annuum)* It is found in subtropical and tropical zones around the world. The fruit is used. It can be used as an ointment or compress for pain relief from arthritis, trauma and muscle aches.

Chamomile: *(Chanaemelum nobile, Matricaria Recutita)* It grows throughout Europe and North America. The flowers are used. It is prepared as a tea or infusion for headaches and nervousness. As an antispasmodic to treat gastric upsets and menstrual camps. At mealtime it can be taken to increase appetite, at bedtime to calm excitability in insomnia. It is used in diluted quantities to calm colic in babies.

Comfrey: *(Symphytum officinale)* Should be used with caution. It is found throughout the world. The roots and leaves are used. It is employed as an ointment or compress for bruises, sprains, boils and painful breasts during menstruation.

Dandelion: *(Taraxacum officinale)* Found in temperate climates throughout the world. The roots and leaves are used. It may be eaten raw or made into a tea or infusion. Used as a laxative, diuretic for wound healing and for digestive disorders.

Echinacea: *(Euchinacea angustifolia)* It is found in the prairies of North America. The roots are used. Prepared in a tincture or a decoction. Effective treatment for infections and helps to stimulate wound healing including bladder and ear infections, colds and flu. It can be used for internal or external use.

Eucalyptus: *(Eucalyptus globulus)* Found in Australia and other subtropical climates. The leaves are used. It is used as a tincture, lotion and in oil form. It is effective for sore throats, decongestant

for colds and other respiratory illnesses. A classic remedy is inhaling the vapours of the oil in boiling water. For use as a body rub, it should be diluted with water.

Fennel: *(Foeniculum, vulgare)* Found in wooded land in temperate climates. Seeds and roots are used. The remedy is made into a tea or syrup, or eating it raw. The tea is used for bloating and flatulence and the syrup form is used for sore throats, coughs and bad breath.

Feverfew: *(Chrysanthemum panthenium)* It grows in various areas around the world. The leaves are used. It can be eaten raw, in a tea, or tablet form. It is best taken in the tablet form as it is very bitter. Effective treatment for migraines, arthritis or muscle aches.

Garlic: *(Allium satiuum)* It is grown in temperate climates around the world. The root (bulb or clove) is used. It can be taken as a juice, infusion, tablet, salve, or eating the fresh cloves. It has uses as an antibiotic and antiseptic for infections, respiratory problems, sore throats and to deal with atherosclerosis, high blood pressure, and high cholesterol.

Ginger: *(Zingiber officinale)* It is grown in subtropical regions of the world. The roots are used for medicinal purposes. They are taken as a tea, capsules or as a powder. It acts as an antispasmodic for morning sickness, motion sickness and dizziness.

Licorice: *(Glycyrrhiza glabra)* Worldwide distribution. The roots are used in the remedy. It is taken in the form of a syrup, decoction or chewing the raw root. It is used as a laxative for mild constipation and to relieve stomach and intestinal ulcers. Also may be taken for a sore throat.

Passion Flower: *(Passilfora incarnata)* It is found in shaded and wooded areas around the world. The flowers and leaves are used. It is taken in the form of an infusion or tea. It is a common remedy, used as a sedative for insomnia, restlessness and nervous headaches.

Peppermint: *(Mentha pipereta)* Worldwide in distribution. The leaves are used as the remedy. It is used as a tea or an infusion. It is chiefly used as an appetite stimulant and a digestive aid. Peppermint oil in boiling water can be helpful to open up nasal or sinus congestion.

Psyllium: *(Plantago Psyllium)* It has worldwide distribution. The seeds are used as a remedy. It is usually mixed with fruit juice or water and taken as a fibre bulking agent and assists in lowering elevated cholesterol levels.

Rosehips: *(Rosa spp.)* It is worldwide in distribution. The fruit or hip is used. It is taken in the form of an infusion, tincture, or syrup. As a syrup, it is good for sore throats. It is an excellent source of vitamin C and can be helpful for treating colds and flu.

Valerian: *(Valerian officinalis)* It grows in grasslands and meadows. The root is used in the remedy. It is prepared as a tea or infusion and tablet form. It is an effective remedy for insomnia and nervous tension, a "natural tranquilizer". It has a bitter taste, the tablet is the preferred choice of use. Caution should be taken not to use high doses.

Witch hazel: *(Hamamelis Viginiana)* It grows in the woods and along streams. The leaves and bark are used as an infusion, decoction and compress. It is used to control bleeding as in bruises, muscle strains and burns. In a diluted form, it can be used as mouthwash or gargle.

COMMON HERBS

NUTRIENTS AND THEIR USES

by Dr. Allan Ettenson

Beta Carotene (Vitamin A): This vitamin helps us to see better, especially at night. It also helps our skin and membranes to stay healthy.

Calcium: This nutrient helps in the formation and maintenance of bones and teeth. It also helps maintain healthy nerve function and helps with normal blood clotting.

Carbohydrates: Carbohydrates help the body use fats properly and also supplies a source of energy to the body.

Cobalamin (Vitamin B12): Vitamin B12 aids in the formation of red blood cells as well as protecting nerve and gastrointestinal tissue.

Fat: Fats supply energy to the body and assists in the absorption of fat-soluble vitamins. (Should be limited to less than 20% of diet).

Fibre: Fibre is bulk which the body cannot digest. This helps the body in the elimination of waste.

Iron: Together with protein, iron forms hemoglobin, the red blood cell component which transports oxygen and carbon dioxide throughout the body.

Magnesium: Magnesium is important for the formation of healthy bones and teeth. It also has a vital function in the transmission of nerve impulses and the contraction of muscles.

Niacin (Vitamin B3): Important in the function of the nervous system and the conversion of blood sugar into energy. It is shown to be effective in helping to lower blood cholesterol.

Phosphorus: Phosphorus is another nutrient like calcium and magnesium, which helps in the formation and maintenance of bones and teeth.

Protein: Protein is required for repairs to body tissues and builds antibodies.

Pyrodoxine (Vitamin B6): It is essential in protein, fat and carbohydrate metabolism, and in the action of several hormones.

Riboflavin (Vitamin B2): It is important in the body's production of energy. It is also important for the utilization of other B vitamins.

Thiamin (Vitamin B1): Thiamin helps with the body's normal growth and appetite.

Vitamin C: This vitamin helps our body stay healthy, especially the teeth, gums and vessel walls. It is necessary for normal immune system responses to infections and wound healings.

Vitamin D: It is essential for strong bones and teeth. Helps to regulate the balance of calcium in the body.

Vitamin E: Good antioxidant nutrient, protects the cells from pollutants, and can help slow down the aging process of cells.

Zinc: Zinc helps with tissue formation, as well as supplying energy and assisting with metabolism, and the immune response.

NUTRIENTS AND THEIR USES

Popular Alternative
Health Disciplines

Acupuncture

Acupuncture is an ancient Chinese art of healing. Acupuncture treats and prevents disease by affecting key points on the body usually through needle application. It is a means of contacting the electrical centers of the body and influencing the flow of energy (chi) and balance the positive and negative forces (yin/yang). The energy flows through the body by the way of pathways or meridians. It's most effective use is as an anesthetic or for pain relief.

Chiropractic

Chiropractors are primary contact health practitioners who deal with spinal mechanics and the influences of the nervous system on the body. Disturbances of the nervous system can be caused by muscular and skeletal problems. These problems can affect the body's natural defense mechanisms and lead to disease states. Correction of these spinal derangements helps the body's ability to restore health. Chiropractors use spinal manipulation, electrotherapy, exercise and nutrition, in the treatment programs.

Homeopathy

Homeopathy is based on a principle of curing "like with like". It relies on a unique system of diagnosis and treatment to stimulate the immune system to overcome sickness and restore health. The prescribed remedies consist of substances in specially prepared infinitesimal doses. The particular remedies are determined by the total presentation of symptoms by the patient.

Massage

Massage is the act of touch in various pressure contacts. There are several techniques of massage practiced. Through stroking, pressure and kneading, massage relaxes, stimulates, and tones the body. It affects the skin, muscles and can influence the internal organ systems. The contact on the body can be used to increase circulation, stimulate the elimination of waste products through the lymph system, and increase blood supply and nutrition to muscles and other tissues. It can be helpful dealing with mental and emotional stress.

Naturopathy

Naturopathy is a multi-disciplinary approach to illness and health. It involves various systems of diagnosis and treatment. It deals with the body as a whole, rather than dealing with individual symptoms or body sections. Naturopathy treatment strategies deal with balancing body functions and correcting physical obstacles to normal health.

Appetizers

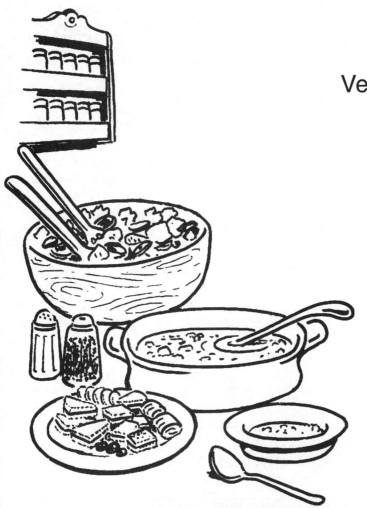

Vegetarian Dishes

Finger Foods

Soups

Salads

Cocktail Meatballs

Ingredients:

1 lb lean ground beef
1 tsp garlic powder
1 - 12oz bottle chili sauce
1 - 10oz jar grape jelly

Directions:

Mix ground beef with garlic powder. Shape into small balls. Pan fry until well cooked; drain. Mix chili sauce and jelly. Add meatballs; heat mixture. Serve warm in chafing dish with toothpicks. Yields 12 servings as cocktail appetizer.

FOOD FOR THOUGHT
When you provide a pig and a boy with everything they want, you'll get a good pig and a terrible boy.

Ham Appetizer

Ingredients:

2 tbsp green pepper, finely chopped
2 tbsp celery, finely chopped
2 tbsp pimiento, finely chopped
1/4 tsp Dijon mustard
2 tsp lemon juice
2 tsp olive oil
dash of salt
dash of pepper
4 slices cooked ham
Stuffed olive or gherkins for garnish

TRIVIA TIDBITS
One six-ounce potato contains about 40% of the vitamin C you need each day. It's also high in fiber, niacin, and potassium, and has just 180 calories - provided you skip the butter and sour cream. Many of the nutrients are found in or near the skin, so eat the skin if possible.

Directions:

Mix green pepper, celery and pimiento together. Mix mustard with lemon juice and olive oil. Add salt and pepper to taste. Pour over vegetables; mix well. Divide equally between ham slices. Fold over; secure with toothpicks. Arrange on serving dish; garnish with stuffed olives or gherkins cut into fan shapes. This can be served as a first course for a dinner party; as a luncheon dish; or each roll can be cut into 4 portions, speared with toothpicks, and served on a canape tray. Makes 4 servings.

Bacon Cheese Appetizers

Charlene Jenkins, Etobicoke, Ontario, (formerly of Springdale, Newfoundland)

Ingredients:

8 slices bacon, cut in half
1/2 lb cheddar cheese, sharp
8 cherry tomatoes, halved
Dash cayenne pepper

FOOD FOR THOUGHT
Happiness can't be saved for future use, but it is possible to create a new supply every day.

In memory of my loving parents **Bennett and Joyce Guy**, Twillingate, Newfoundland, and grandparents **Elizabeth and William Guy**.
Winn Cramm

Directions:
Line a microwave baking dish with double layers of paper toweling. Place bacon slices on dish and cover with a paper towel. Microwave at high power for about 3 minutes. Cut Cheddar cheese in small even cubes and sprinkle with dash of cayenne pepper. Wrap bacon slices around each cheese cube and fasten with wooden picks. Place on a baking sheet or in an ovenproof glass dish. Broil for about 5 minutes, turning over after about 3 minutes or until cheese starts to melt and bacon is cooked to your liking. Garnish with cherry tomatoes. (Serves 4).

Carrot Slaw Sandwiches

Neta Dove, Twillingate, Newfoundland (nee Roberts)

Ingredients:
2 cups finely shredded carrot
1/2 cup chopped celery
1/2 cup raisins
1/4 cup mayonnaise or salad dressing
1/2 tsp salt
1/8 tsp pepper
1/8 tsp nutmeg
4oz cream cheese, softened
8 slices rye bread, buttered

Directions:
Combine all ingredients except cheese and bread. Spread cheese on each bread slice. Spoon on carrot mixture. Makes eight open-faced sandwiches.

> ***TRIVIA TIDBITS***
> Quite often during the Middle Ages, because there was no refrigeration, meat often became rancid. To hide the smell and taste, these meats were often perfumed with musk, violets, roses, primroses and other flowers.

Orange Marinated Vegetables

Neta Dove, Twillingate, Newfoundland (nee Roberts)

Ingredients:
1-16oz pkg frozen mixed vegetables (such as broccoli, onion, mushrooms, red peppers), thawed
1 cup pitted ripe olives
grated peel of 1 small orange
1 bottle Italian salad dressing

Directions:
Drain vegetables, if necessary. In large bowl mix vegetables, olives and grated orange peel. Pour in salad dressing, toss to coat. Cover and chill to marinate at least 2 hours, stirring occasionally. Just before serving, lightly drain. Serve with cocktail picks.

Honey Glazed Carrots

> **FOOD FOR THOUGHT**
> Education teaches us the rules, while experience teaches us the exceptions.

Neta Dove, Twillingate, Newfoundland (nee Roberts)

Ingredients:
4 large carrots, diagonally sliced in pieces
3 tbsp honey
salt and pepper to taste
chopped parsley for garnish
1 cup water

Directions:
In medium saucepan, bring carrots, honey and 1 cup water to a boil. Reduce heat to low, cover with lid slightly open and simmer until water is evaporated and carrots are tender, stirring occasionally. Season with salt and pepper. Garnish with parsley.

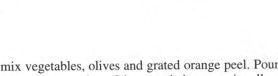

Pineapple Cheese Ball

Ingredients:

2 pkgs (8oz each) cream cheese, softened
1 can (3 1/2oz) crushed pineapple, drained
2 cups chopped pecans, divided
1/4 cup finely chopped green pepper
2 tbsp finely chopped onion
1 tbsp seasoned salt
pineapple, cherries, or parsley for garnish

Directions:

In a medium bowl, beat cream cheese until smooth. Stir in crushed pineapple, 1 cup pecans, green pepper, onion, and salt. Shape cheese mixture into a ball. Roll cheese ball in remaining nuts. Wrap in plastic wrap or foil. Refrigerate at least 6 hours. Garnish with fruit or parsley.

> **TRIVIA TIDBITS**
> Smokers arrive at old age with 20-30% less bone mass than non-smokers. This results in a more fragile skeleton and a greater risk of fractures.

Fruit and Nut Nibble

Ingredients:

1/2 lb raw cashews
1/2 lb pecans
1/2 lb almonds
1 cup chopped dried apples
1 cup flaked coconut
1 cup raisins
1 cup dried apricots, chopped
1 cup carob chips (optional)

Directions:

Mix together all ingredients. Store covered. This nibble is a nutritious, quick-energy snack that is equally appropriate for the lunchbox or the banquet table. Makes about 5 1/2 cups.

> **FOOD FOR THOUGHT**
> The person with dreams and a great imagination is much more powerful than one with all the facts.

Crab Stuffed Mushrooms

Ingredients:

3 dozen large whole fresh mushrooms
1 can (6 & 1/2oz) crab meat, drained and flaked
1/2 cup mayonnaise
1 tbsp chopped fresh parsley
1 tbsp pimiento, chopped
1 tsp chopped olives
1/4 tsp dry mustard

> **SPICE OF LIFE**
> The truth may really be as clear as a bell, but that doesn't mean it is always tolled.

Florence Jean St. Jacques

You mean more to me than I can say, so it's time I think you knew
How much it brightens up my day, to have a mom like you
Love always, your son
John Alan St. Jacques

Directions:
Preheat oven to 375°F. Wash and dry mushrooms. Remove stems for another use. Mix remaining ingredients. Fill each cap with crabmeat mixture. Place stuffed mushrooms on a cookie sheet. Bake 8 to 10 minutes. Makes 36 stuffed mushrooms.

Stuffed Mushrooms

Archie Ridout, Rexdale, Ontario (formerly of Twillingate, Newfoundland)

Ingredients:
20 medium mushrooms
10 tbsp butter or margarine
2 cloves garlic, minced
6 tbsp cheddar cheese, shredded
4 tbsp dry red wine
2 tsp soy sauce
2/3 cup bread crumbs

FOOD FOR THOUGHT
He who slings mud is sure to lose some ground.

Directions:
Remove stems from mushrooms. Melt 3 tablespoons butter; brush mushroom caps. Stir together remaining butter and rest of ingredients until well blended. Place mushrooms cavity side up, on a baking dish. Evenly mound filling in each mushroom, pressing it in lightly. Bake at 450°F until bubbly and lightly browned, 6-10 minutes. (Can be made in advance).

Newfie Pea Soup

Miss Gertrude V. Sweetapple, Glovertown, Newfoundland

Directions:
Soak a piece of salt beef or ham bone overnight. Soak dried peas overnight as well. In the morning cook both together in fresh water. Add chopped carrots, turnip and onion. Boil for 20 minutes. Before serving, put in whole potatoes, if you wish. Serve with dumplings.

Corn and Ham Soup

Ingredients:
2 (13 & 3/4 oz) cans chicken broth
1 (17oz) can whole kernel sweet corn
1 cup diced ham
1/3 cup onion, chopped
1/3 cup green pepper, chopped
1 cup half-and-half cream

SPICE OF LIFE
A sponger is a person who will get and forget as long as others give and forgive.

Directions:
In large saucepan combine all ingredients except half-and-half. Bring to boil; reduce heat. Cover and simmer 15 minutes. Stir in half-and-half; heat through. Serves 6.

Hearty Soup

Ingredients:
2 (13 & 3/4 oz.) cans chicken broth
3 cups tomato juice
1 (17oz) can whole kernel sweet corn
1 (17oz) can green lima beans

SPICE OF LIFE
Often the largest secrets can come from small mouths.

1 cup chicken, diced and cooked
2 medium potatoes, pared & diced
1 medium onion, chopped
1 tbsp Worcestershire sauce
1 tsp basil
1/4 tsp pepper

Directions:

In large saucepan or soup pot combine all ingredients. Bring to boil; reduce heat. Cover and simmer 30 minutes or until potatoes are tender. Ladle into soup bowls. Serves 6.

> **TRIVIA TIDBITS**
> If the water mains in New York City were laid end to end they would reach Russia.

Grandma's Chicken Soup

Charlene Jenkins, Etobicoke, Ontario (formerly of Springdale, Newfoundland)

Ingredients:

1 medium chicken, cut up
10 cups cold water
2 celery stalks with leaves, cut into pieces
1 onion, quartered
5 black peppercorns
6 sprigs parsley
1 cup vermicelli noodles, uncooked
2 eggs
juice of one lemon
salt and pepper to taste
chopped parsley (or carrot slivers) for garnish, optional

SPICE OF LIFE
Perhaps many a person has been saved from losing a lot of money by not having a lot of it.

Directions:

Put cut-up chicken in a heavy pot and cover with water. Add celery, onion, peppercorns and parsley. Bring to a boil. Reduce heat and skim foam which has accumulated on top. Simmer, halfway covered, for 1 & 1/2 hours. Cool slightly. Remove chicken and strain broth. Add salt and pepper to taste. Remove chicken meat from bones and chop. Add 2 cups of chopped chicken to strained broth (reserving the rest for another use). Stir in the vermicelli noodles and simmer for 15 minutes. Beat eggs with the juice of 1 lemon. Add a little of hot soup mixture (so mixture won't curdle). Pour egg mixture into pot. Mix well and heat. Garnish with parsley and/or carrot slivers, if desired. (When reheating this soup, it is important not to bring the soup to a boil because it can curdle. Reheat slowly over medium heat. Serves 4 to 6)

Cream of Cauliflower and Chedder Soup

Violet Noseworthy, Listowell, Ontario (nee Quinlan, Birchy Bay, Newfoundland)

Ingredients:

2 tbsp butter
1/2 cup onion, chopped
3 cups fresh cauliflower, coarsely chopped

> This page is dedicated to our mother, **Bessie Ploughman**,
> living in Trinity, Trinity Bay, Newfoundland.
> Our mother raised a family of ten children after my father was killed
> in a tragic railway accident in 1958, leaving her a widow at age 40.
> *We love you Mom!*

1-10oz can condensed chicken broth
1/4 cup flour
2 & 1/2 cups milk
1 & 1/2 cups cheddar cheese, shredded
buttered croutons
chopped parsley
salt, to taste
pepper, to taste

Directions:
Melt butter in large saucepan and saute onion until tender. Stir in cauliflower and condensed chicken broth. Bring to boil. Cover; reduce heat and simmer 12-15 minutes or until cauliflower is tender. Smoothly combine flour and milk. Add to saucepan. Cook and stir over medium heat until mixture boils and thickens. Add cheese and stir until melted. Add salt and pepper to taste. Ladle into 4 soup bowls and sprinkle with buttered croutons and parsley. Preparation time: 15 minutes. Cooking time: 20 minutes.

> **SPICE OF LIFE**
> A lawyer is always willing to go to court and spend your last cent to prove he is right.

Old Fashioned Corn Chowder

Catherine Irwin, Truro, Nova Scotia

Ingredients:
5 slices lean bacon, fried
1 & 1/2 tbsp bacon drippings
1 & 1/2 cups raw potato, diced
1 cup boiling water
1 tsp salt
1/4 tsp pepper
1 tbsp flour
3 cups milk
1 - 19oz can cream corn

> **FOOD FOR THOUGHT**
> People do not stop doing things because they're growing older; they are more apt to grow older when they stop doing things.

Directions:
Remove fat from the bacon strips. Fry bacon (cut up in small bite size pieces) in the bacon drippings that you got when you fried the fat you already removed. When bacon is done frying (don't burn) remove it. Strain fat. Saute onion in bacon drippings until transparent. Add potatoes, boiling water and seasonings. Cover and simmer until potatoes are 'almost' tender (about 8 minutes). Combine flour with small amount of cooked potatoes - mash. Add to remaining potato mixture. Add milk. Stir and cook until smooth and thick. Crumble bacon and add to mixture along with canned cream-style corn. Heat through. Careful not to scorch. Serves 5-6.

Hangashore Clam Chowder

Ingredients:
1 pt fresh clams
2-3 potatoes, diced
1 onion, chopped
2 tbsp salt pork drippings
1/4 cup (1/2 stick) butter
2 tbsp flour
2 cups milk
1/2 cup light cream
salt & pepper, to taste
1 tbsp finely minced fresh parsley

> **TRIVIA TIDBITS**
> Louis XIV, who ruled France from 1643-1715, had a morbid fear of water. So much so was his fear of H2O that he rarely applied water to any part of his body, other than the tip of his nose.

Directions:
Steam clams, drain, and remove from shells. Cut clams fine with kitchen shears. Cook potatoes until tender. Fry onion in salt pork drippings until tender and yellowed. In the top of a double boiler melt butter over hot water. Stir in flour until smooth. Add milk and cream in a steady stream, stirring to keep smooth. Cook 8 minutes, until hot and thick, stirring occasionally. Add potatoes, onion, salt, pepper, parsley and clams. Cook just long enough to heat through. Serve with common or pilot crackers. Yield: 1 quart.

Eel Soup

Ingredients:
3 or 4 eels
1 tsp vinegar or slice of lemon
milk
salt & pepper

Directions:
Skin the eels and remove backbone. (Nail the eel up by the tail. Cut through the skin around the body just forward of the tail. Peel the skin off over the head. This removes all the fin bones). Cut into 2" pieces and put in a stewpot with water to cover. Add vinegar or a slice of lemon. Cover and boil 20 to 30 minutes or until the flesh starts to leave the bones. Drain; add fresh water and vinegar and stew until tender. Drain again. Add enough milk for stew. (Half cream and half milk improves the flavour.) Season with salt and pepper. Bring to a boil and simmer for a few minutes. Serve on hot, dry toast.

Clam Soup

Ingredients:
1 quart clams
clam liquor
2 quarts water
1 heaping tablespoon butter
1 heaping tablespoon flour
1 quart milk
salt & pepper to taste

Directions:
Strain the liquor from the clams and set aside. Boil clams in water until they are in rags. In another saucepan melt butter, blend in flour. Add milk and bring to a boiling point. Add clams and liquor and boil 3 minutes. Serve with toast.

> **FOOD FOR THOUGHT**
> Luck can best be described as that precise time when preparation and opportunity meet.

> **TRIVIA TIDBITS**
> In 1796, Mary Pitts, a 70-year-old pauper at Wardley Workhouse in Berkshire, England was accused of stealing from another pauper. Mary claimed innocence, and called upon God to strike her down if she were guilty. No sooner were the words out of her mouth when she fell down dead.
>
>

In dedication to our father, Bill Hawco of Chaples Cove, Nfld. He was a great Dad who loved the sea and who taught us the best berths and how to handline. We'll always remember him on the "ledge" catching the cod.

John Hawco, Markham, Ont. & Bill Hawco, Saint John, N.B.

Nova Scotia Scallop Chowder

Ingredients:
2 lbs scallops
butter, size of an egg
6 medium potatoes, cubed
2 small onions, diced
1 & 1/2 quarts milk
salt & pepper to taste

FOOD FOR THOUGHT
No one would have blamed John Cabot if he had turned back, but no one would have remembered him either.

Directions:
Melt butter in skillet and fry scallops on both sides. With a knife, cut scallops into small pieces, making sure they are well browned. Meanwhile, cook potatoes and onions in lightly salted water until tender, but not mushy. Add scallops and milk and season to taste. Bring to just under the boiling point and serve hot with crackers.

Nova Scotia Fish Chowder

Ingredients:
2 lbs haddock fillets
1/2 lb salt pork, diced
1 medium onion, diced
2 cups boiling water
3 cups diced potatoes
4 cups milk
8 small soda crackers, crumbled
2 tbsp butter
2 tsp salt
1/8 tsp pepper
2 tbsp parsley, finely chopped
paprika

SPICE OF LIFE
Everyone who visits makes me happy: some by coming, some by leaving.

Directions:
Cut fillets into 2" cubes. Saute pork until crisp. Add onion and cook until tender but not brown. Add boiling water and potatoes and cook 10 minutes. Add fish and simmer 10 minutes. In another saucepan combine milk, crackers, butter, salt and pepper. Heat just to scalding; do not boil. Combine the two mixtures. Pour into soup tureen or individual bowls. Sprinkle with paprika. Serves 6.

Lobster Chowder

Ingredients:
2 medium potatoes, diced
1 medium onion, chopped
1 cup water
2 tbsp butter
2 cups lobster meat, cut up
1 tsp salt
1/4 tsp pepper
2 cups milk
1 cup light cream
butter, size of an egg

TRIVIA TIDBITS
The following is from a book written in the 1800s entitled, 'Curiosities of Matrimony', and talks about the family relationships which followed the marriage of a 67-year-old man to a 19-year-old relative; *"By the above union the bridegroom has married his sister's granddaughter, which makes the bride a wife to her great uncle, sister to her grandfather and grandmother, aunt to her father and mother, and great-aunt to her brother and sister. She is a stepmother to five children and one great-grandchild."*

Directions:

Cook onion and potato in water until nearly tender. In a frying pan, melt 2 tbsp butter and fry the lobster meat until red. Add to the potatoes. Season with salt and pepper. Add milk, cream, and butter. Heat to boiling point, but do not boil.

Beef and Barley Soup

Ingredients:

2 tbsp vegetable oil
1 lb boneless beef, cut in 1/2-inch cubes
1/2 cup minced onion
1/2 cup pearl barley
1 lb beef bones
1 carrot, cut in 1/2-inch slices
1 stalk celery, cut in 1/2-inch slices
1/2 cup cubed turnip, rutabaga or parsnip
2 tbsp chopped fresh parsley
1 bay leaf
1 tbsp salt
3 quarts water

Directions:

In a large pot, heat oil; saute beef and onion until beef is browned. Add barley. Saute for 5 minutes, stirring constantly. Add remaining ingredients. Cover and simmer for 2 hours. Discard bones before serving. Can be prepared ahead and frozen. Makes 12 servings.

> **TRIVIA TIDBITS**
>
> An English opera singer in the 1700s, by the name of Elizabeth Billington, was world-famous because of her powerful voice. While performing in Naples, Italy in 1704, the volcano Vesuvius decided to erupt during the aria. The scared Italians blamed the eruption on Billington's singing and the lady was lucky to escape with her life.

Cheesy Cream of Potato Soup

Ingredients:

4 peeled medium potatoes
2 bacon slices, diced
1/4 cup minced onion
2 tbsp butter or margarine
1 tbsp chopped fresh parsley
2 tsp salt
1/2 tsp nutmeg
dash cayenne pepper
1/4 tsp dry mustard
1 tsp Worcestershire sauce
3 cups milk
1/2 cup lightly packed shredded Swiss or American cheese

Directions:

In a large saucepan, simmer potatoes in water to cover until tender, about 30 minutes; drain. In a

> **FOOD FOR THOUGHT**
>
> A lot of people boast, but only a few have the right to brag, and they are the people who never do.

In loving memory of **Cecil Ryan** 1931-1993,
formerly of Pouch Cove, Newfoundland. Forever in our hearts,
your loving wife Elaine, children Debbie, Gerry, Winston,
and grandchildren.

skillet, saute bacon and onion over low heat until bacon is brown and onion is tender; drain fat. In a mixing bowl, mash potatoes. Add bacon, onion, butter, parsley, salt, nutmeg, cayenne, mustard, and Worcestershire sauce; blend well. Blend in milk. Stirring constantly over low heat, bring to serving temperature. Sprinkle with cheese. Serve immediately.

Stir-Fried Broccoli and Carrots

Archie Ridout, Rexdale, Ontario (formerly of Twillingate, Newfoundland)

Ingredients:

2 tbsp oil
2 slices ginger, finely chopped
1 & 1/2 cups sm. broccoli flowerets
1 cup carrots, thinly sliced
1 small onion, chopped
3/4 cup chicken broth
1 tsp salt
1 tbsp cornstarch
1 tbsp cold water
1 cup mushrooms, sliced
2 tbsp oyster sauce
1 clove garlic, minced

> **TRIVIA TIDBITS**
> President Woodrow Wilson's First Lady, ran the country instead of the President for 17 months after Woodrow suffered a massive stroke during a speaking tour in Colorado in 1919.

Directions:

Heat oil in a wok or skillet. Add ginger and garlic; stir fry 1 minute. Add broccoli, carrots and onion; stir fry 1 minute. Add chicken broth and salt; cover and cook until carrots are tender, about 3 minutes. Mix cornstarch and water; stir into vegetable mixture. Cook and stir until thickened, about 10 seconds. Add mushrooms and oyster sauce; cook and stir 30 seconds.

Tomato, Macaroni & Cheese

Cathy Gale, Doyles, Newfoundland

Ingredients:

1 can (20 oz) tomatoes
1 cup water
1/2 cup chopped onion
1 & 1/2 tsps ganulated sugar
1/2 tsp salt
1 cup macaroni, uncooked
1 cup cheese spread (or) grated cheddar cheese

> **FOOD FOR THOUGHT**
> Lord make my words sweet and tender today, for I may have to eat them tomorrow.

Directions:

Combine tomatoes, water, onion, sugar and salt in a saucepan. Bring to boiling point. Add macaroni. Cover and cook, stirring occasionally with fork until macaroni is tender, about 15 minutes. Stir in cheese. Top with buttered crumbs and broil until golden.

Deluxe Potatoes

Grace Ryan, Newmans Cove, Bonavista Bay, Newfoundland

Ingredients:

1 pkg frozen hashbrowns
1 cup onion, diced

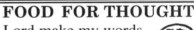

Soups, Salads, Vegetarian Dishes & Finger Foods

Appetizers

1 can cream of chicken soup
1-500g carton sour cream
1/2 cup margarine
1/2 cup grated cheddar cheese
salt & pepper to taste
Corn Fakes, crushed

Directions:

Thaw hashbrowns for 30 minutes. Mix all ingredients except Corn Flakes and pour into a 9x13-inch baking dish. Top with Corn Flake crumbs. Bake at 350°F for 1 hour.

Pretzel Salad

Ina Belcher, Tonawanda, New York (nee Brown, St. John's, Newfoundland)

Ingredients:

2 cups crushed pretzels
1 stick butter, melted
1 pkg (8oz) cream cheese
1 cup sugar
1 (8oz) container cool whip
2 cups boiling water
2 sm pkgs strawberry jello
2 boxes (10oz) frozen strawberries

Directions:

Mix pretzels and melted butter in bottom of glass rectangle dish. Bake at 400°F for 8 minutes. Cool! Beat cream cheese, sugar and cool whip together. Spread over pretzels. Chill about 30 minutes. Add boiling water to jello. Stir to dissolve. Add strawberries and stir until berries are separated. Pour over cream cheese and chill until set.

Easy Summer Salad

Angela Waterman, nee John, Glenwood, Newfoundland

Ingredients:

4 cups diced rhubarb
1 & 1/3 cups water
1/2 cup sugar
2 (3oz) pkgs strawberry jello
1 cup orange juice
1 tsp grated orange rind
1 cup strawberries, sliced

Directions:

Combine rhubarb, water and sugar in saucepan. Cook until tender, about five minutes (if the

This page is dedicated to the memory of my parents
ALFREDA JANE (nee Mullett of Wesleyville, Nfld, Feb. 18, 1893 - May 18, 1985) and **CAPTAIN ARTHUR CARTER** (of Greenspond, Nfld, Feb. 9, 1891 - Dec. 1941). Memories of you both are always with me.
George Blake Carter, Mississauga, Ontario
(formerly of St. John's, Newfoundland)

diced rhubarb mixture is not thick). Pour the rhubarb mixture over the strawberry jello, stirring until the jello powder is dissolved. Add the orange juice and orange rind. Chill until thick and syrupy, then fold in the sliced strawberries. Pour into a lightly-oiled, six-cup mold. Chill until set.

Carrot Salad

Jenny & Josie, Richmond Hill, Ontario (nee Clarke, Port Rexton, Newfoundland)

Ingredients:
3 lg carrots, cooked & sliced
1 green pepper, diced
2 onions, sliced
1 can tomato soup, undiluted
1/4 cup vinegar
1/2 cup salad oil
1 tsp salt
1 tsp prepared mustard
3/4 cup (or less) sugar
dash of worcestershire sauce
dash of pepper

TRIVIA TIDBITS
Over half a million gallons of camouflage paint was used by the British Army during the North Africa campaign of the Second World War. The paint was created from from cement, flour, Worcestershire sauce, and camel dung.

Directions:
In a large bowl, mix all ingredients togther and serve. Keep refirgerated.

Quick and Easy Salad

Jenny & Josie, Richmond Hill, Ontario (nee Clarke, Port Rexton, Newfoundland)

Ingredients:
1 pkg orange jello
1 cup boiling water
1 cup cooked rice
1 cup crushed pineapple
1 cup whipped cream

SPICE OF LIFE
Train your kids in the way you now know you should have taken.

Directions:
Dissolve jello in boiling water. Add cooked rice and crushed pineapple. When beginning to set, fold in whipped cream. Put in refrigerator until set. Ready to serve.

Cottage Cheese Salad

Mrs. Claudine Barnes, Corner Brook, Newfoundland (nee Pye, Cape Charles, Labrador)

Ingredients:
1 sm pkg lime jello
1 sm pkg lemon jello
1 tin crushed pineapple, drain & save liquid
1 tub cottage cheese
1/2 cup milk
1/2 cup mayonnaise

FOOD FOR THOUGHT
The man who says, "It can't be done," is liable to be interrupted by someone doing it.

Directions:
Prepare jello as directed on package. Combine juice from drained pineapple with enough water to make two cups. When jello is partly set, beat and add all other ingredients. Stir well. Let set.

Appetizers

Soups, Salads, Vegetarian Dishes & Finger Foods

Mama's Macaroni Salad

Ingredients:

2 cups uncooked elbow macaroni
1 can sweetened condensed milk
1 cup ReaLemon juice
1 cup vegetable oil
1/4 cup prepared mustard
1 tbsp onion salt
1 tbsp celery seed
2 cups cooked ham, cut in cubes
1 cup green pepper, finely chopped (reserve some to garnish with if desired)

Directions:

Cook macaroni as package directs; drain and set aside. In large bowl, combine sweetened milk, lemon juice, vegetable oil, mustard, onion salt and celery seed. Mix well. Stir in remaining ingredients. If desired, serve on lettuce leaves and garnish with reserved green pepper. Chill for 3 hours to allow all flavours to blend throughout and the macaroni to absorb more sauce.

> **TRIVIA TIDBITS**
> English chemist John Walker invented the match, but because he felt such an important tool should be public property, he never patented it.

Jelly Salad

Mary Holloway, Bloomfield, Newfoundland (nee Ralph, Winter Brook, Newfoundland)

Ingredients:

2 pkgs pineapple jelly
1 cup boiling water
1 apple, chopped
1/2 cup carrots, grated
1/2 cup cheese, grated
1 tin cream
1 can crushed pineapple, drained

Directions:

Mix jelly with 1 cup boiling water, then put in fridge to partly set. Add remaining ingredients. Mix well. Refrigerate.

> **SPICE OF LIFE**
> The surprising thing about young fools is that so many of them have survived to become old fools.

Broccoli Cauliflower Salad

Mary Russell, Brooklyn, Newfoundland, (nee Ash, Come By Chance, Newfoundland)

Ingredients:

1 head cauliflower
1 bunch broccoli
2 tbsp onion, chopped
1/2 green pepper
1 cup sour cream or 1/3 cup milk with 1 tsp lemon juice

> **FOOD FOR THOUGHT**
> If you want the rainbow, you must first put up with the rain.

This page is dedicated to the memory of our grandparents
Jane (nee **Young**); 1891-1981) and
Captain Edward William (Billy) Roberts; 1887-1971.
Forever remembered by Linda Greenham (nee Dove) in Twillingate and Sandra Young (nee Dove) in St. John's.

1 cup salad dressing
1/4 cup white sugar
1 tbsp vinegar
1/8 tsp tabasco sauce
1/8 tsp Worcestershire sauce

Directions:
Cut vegetables into bite size pieces; place in a large bowl. Combine the remaining ingredients; mix well. Pour over the vegetables; toss well. Refrigerate.

> **FOOD FOR THOUGHT**
> A true friend is a person who knows all your faults and is still your friend.

Newfoundland Lobster Salad

Mary Russell, Brooklyn, Newfoundland, (nee Ash, Come By Chance, Newfoundland)

Ingredients:
2 boiled lobsters, shelled
1/2 cup salad dressing
1 onion, minced
2 hard boiled eggs, chopped
1/2 cup sweet relish
1/2 tsp salt
1/8 tsp pepper

> **SPICE OF LIFE**
> Nowadays, young lovers take one another for better or worse ... but rarely for good.

Directions:
Cut lobster into bite size pieces. Mix remaining ingredients together. Toss. Serve on lettuce leaves.

Three Bean Salad

Mrs. Alma Taylor, Mt. Moriah, Bay of Islands, Newfoundland (nee LeDrew, Bell Island, Newfoundland)

Ingredients:
375ml green beans, canned
375ml wax beans, canned
375ml kidney beans
1 onion, cut in thin rounds

Dressing
190ml sugar
125ml vinegar
125ml salad oil
5ml salt
30ml cornstarch

> **SPICE OF LIFE**
> **Skipper's Axioms:**
> When a body is immersed in water - the telephone rings.

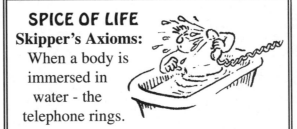

Directions:
Combine sugar, vinegar, salad oil and salt in a saucepan. Thicken with cornstarch. Cool. Poor over strained beans and mix. Let stand for 24 hours before serving.

Frozen Pea Salad

Mrs. Alma Taylor, Mt. Moriah, Bay of Islands, Newfoundland (nee LeDrew, Bell Island, Newfoundland)

Ingredients:
500ml frozen peas
65ml onion, chopped

Appetizers

Soups, Salads, Vegetarian Dishes & Finger Foods

125ml celery, chopped
2ml pepper
6 strips bacon, brown & crisp
125ml sour cream
5 ml salt

Directions:
Crumble bacon. Combine all of the above. Refrigerate 24 hours before serving.

Salmon Salad

Shirley Reader Hicks, Heatherton, Newfoundland, (formerly of Corner Brook, Newfoundland)

Ingredients:
1 cup salmon, cooked & flaked
1 cup celery, diced
1 cup carrot, diced & cooked
1 cup peas, cooked
1 tbsp onion, finely chopped
2 cups macaroni, elbow or shells, cooked
2 tbsp lemon juice
1/2 tbsp sugar
1 cup mayonnaise
lettuce

Directions:
Mix together in bowl salmon, celery, carrot, peas, onion, and macaroni. Combine lemon juice, sugar, mayonnaise. Pour mixture over vegetables, macaroni and salmon. Toss until combined. Serve on crisp lettuce leaves.

TRIVIA TIDBITS
One of the exhibits at the Great Exhibition of 1851 was an alarm bed. At the set time the bed would tilt, sending its occupant(s) onto the floor.

Broccoli Salad

Cindy Cooper, Twillingate, Newfoundland

Ingredients:
1 bunch broccoli flowerets
2 stalks celery, chopped fine
2 or 3 green onions, chopped fine
1 med carrot, grated
1/4 to 1/3 cup cheddar cheese, cubed small
Place all above ingredients in bowl and in separate bowl proceed to **step two**:
1/2 cup sour cream, low fat
1/2 cup salad dressing, low fat
1/4 cup bacon bits
3 tbsp parmesan cheese
1/4 tsp (or more) mustard
1/2 pkg sugar twin (or Equal)

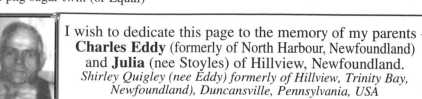

I wish to dedicate this page to the memory of my parents - **Charles Eddy** (formerly of North Harbour, Newfoundland) and **Julia** (nee Stoyles) of Hillview, Newfoundland. *Shirley Quigley (nee Eddy) formerly of Hillview, Trinity Bay, Newfoundland), Duncansville, Pennsylvania, USA*

Appetizers Soups, Salads, Vegetarian Dishes & Finger Foods

dash garlic powder
few dashes paprika
Directions:
Mix above dressing ingredients in separate bowl. When well mixed, add to vegetables. Mix together well. Let set in refrigerator until ready to serve.

Raspberry-Cranberry Wine Salad

Eva F. Canning, Baton Rouge, Los Angeles, USA
Ingredients:
1 - 6oz (or 2 - 3oz) pkg raspberry gelatin, sugar-free
(Add 1/2 pkg plain Knox gelatin softened in a little cold water if firmer salad is desired)
1 - 16oz can (2 cups) whole cranberry sauce
1 - 8 & 3/4 oz (about 1 cup) can crushed pineapple, undrained
1/2 cup Burgundy or Port wine*
1/2 to 3/4 cup chopped walnuts or pecans
1 orange sectioned
1 grapefruit, sectioned
*(If you prefer not to use wine - orange, apple or grape juice can be substituted, or even cranberry juice is fine)
Directions:
Dissolve gelatin in 2 cups boiling water. Stir in plain gelatin if used. Stir in cranberry sauce, undrained pineapple and wine or juice. Chill until partially set. Stir in nuts. Pour into a 6-cup mold. Chill until firm. At serving time, fill centre of mold with orange and grapefruit sections. (Serve with Cheese Fluff Dressing in "Enhancers" section, page 218)

Mom's Hot Cole Slaw

Catherine Irwin, Truro, Nova Scotia
Ingredients:
1/2 large cabbage
celery salt
salt and pepper
pickle juice
cider vinegar
2 onions
1/4 cup Italian Vinaigrette dressing

TRIVIA TIDBITS
As early as 1655, the Dutch used lotteries to raise money for the relief of New York's poor.

Directions:
Slice cabbage, not too thin. Chop up 2 onions. Add shake of celery salt, salt and pepper, some pickle juice, cider vinegar, 1/4 cup Italian dressing. Cook on top of stove until cabbage and onions are limp.

Colorful Garden Salad

Ingredients:
1 bunch leaf lettuce
2 carrots, sliced in rounds
4 radishes, sliced

FOOD FOR THOUGHT
The surest way to knock the chip off a fellow's shoulder is by patting him on the back.

1 small onion, sliced
4 tomatoes, cut into wedges
1 small cucumber, sliced
Yogurt dressing
Directions:
Line a salad bowl with lettuce. In a separate bowl, stir remaining vegetables to mix. Place in lettuce-lined bowl. (Spoon Yogurt Dressing, shown in "Enhancers" section, page 217, over all. Garnish as desired. Makes 4 servings.

Chicken and Rice Salad

Ingredients:
5 cups cooked chicken, cut in chunks
2 tbsp vegetable oil
2 tbsp orange juice
2 tbsp vinegar
1 tsp salt
3 cups cooked long grain rice
1 & 1/2 cups green grapes
1 & 1/2 cups thinly sliced celery
1 can (13 & 1/2oz) pineapple tidbits, drained
1 can (11oz) mandarin oranges, drained
1 cup slivered almonds, toasted
1 & 1/2 cups mayonnaise

TRIVIA TIDBITS

At one time it was against the law in Kentucky to hang male and female underwear on the same washing line.

Directions:
In a mixing bowl, combine chicken, oil, orange juice, vinegar, and salt; toss lightly to mix. Set aside. In a large bowl, combine rice, grapes, celery, pineapple, oranges, and half of the almonds. Stir in mayonnaise. Add chicken mixture; blend well. Sprinkle with remaining almonds. Makes 12 servings.

Three Bean Apple Salad

Ingredients:
2 medium apples, diced
2 cups canned green beans
2 cups canned wax beans
2 cups canned garbanzo beans
1/4 cup chopped green onion
1/4 cup diagonally-sliced celery
1/4 cup Italian dressing
1/2 cup sliced radishes

FOOD FOR THOUGHT
Progress involves risk.
You can't steal second base
and keep your foot on first.
-Frederick Wilcox

Directions:
In a serving bowl, combine all ingredients except radishes; mix well. Refrigerate at least 4 hours to blend flavours. Just before serving, add radishes, toss. Makes 8 servings.

Father
Charles
1908-1967

IN LOVING MEMORY
dedicated by
Harry & Doris Park

Mother
Pearl
1909-1980

Tomato-Accordion Shrimp Salad

Ingredients:
6 firm tomatoes
6 hard-boiled eggs, sliced
lettuce leaves
1 cup boiled shrimp, diced
1/2 cup celery, sliced
fresh parsley
mayonnaise

> **TRIVIA TIDBITS**
> In the late nineteenth and early twentieth centuries, as many as two million American children helped to keep U.S. industry and commerce alive by working in the factories and workshops of the country. Some children worked in chemical vats until late at night, without a stitch of clothes on.

Directions:
Cut thin slice from stem end of each tomato; stand tomatoes upright on cut ends. Cut 5 deep slits in each tomato with sharp knife; fill slits with egg slices. Line large platter with lettuce; arrange tomatoes on lettuce. Toss shrimp with celery; mound in centre of platter. Garnish with parsley; serve with mayonnaise. Makes 6 servings.

Stir-Fried Vegetables

Wanda Greenham, Twillingate, Newfoundland

Ingredients:
1 cup sliced celery
1/4 cup vegetable oil
1 med. onion, thinly sliced
1 cup thinly sliced carrot
1 clove garlic, crushed
1 green pepper, coarsely chopped
1 cup tomato, diced
1 cup thinly sliced zucchini
1 cup thinly sliced mushrooms
1/4 to 1/3 cup soya sauce

> **TRIVIA TIDBITS**
> In 1761 an Oxford pedlar used to sell concentrated beer in cubes, similar to bouillon cubes. Once purchased the cube was dropped in a jug of water to obtain the desired porter. The cubes were advertised as "a tankard of beer on a teaspoon".

Directions:
Heat oil in a large skillet. Add celery, onion, carrot and garlic. Cook and stir over medium-high heat about 2 minutes. Add green pepper, zucchini, tomatoes and mushrooms. Cook and stir 2 to 3 minutes. Stir in soya sauce and serve on cooked rice or pasta. (Makes 6 to 8 servings).

Easy Vegetable Quiche

Ingredients:
1 tbsp butter
1 green pepper, chopped
1 finely chopped onion
1 finely chopped tomato
8oz sliced, fresh mushrooms
1 tsp garlic
1 frozen 9-inch pie shell
5 eggs
1/2 cup milk or cream
1 tsp oregano

> **TRIVIA TIDBITS**
> Queen Victoria always ate her boiled eggs with a solid gold spoon from a solid gold egg-cup.

1/2 tsp paprika
4 oz Monterey Jack cheese, shredded

Directions:
Preheat oven to 350°F. In a large skillet, melt butter. Add green pepper, onion, tomato, mushrooms and garlic. Saute until onion is tender. Arrange vegetables in pie shell. In a mixing bowl, stir together eggs, milk, oregano, and paprika; blend well. Pour over vegetables. Top with cheese. Bake for 45 minutes or until eggs are set in center.

Vegetarian Moussaka

Ingredients:
1 eggplant, (1 to 1 & 1/4lbs)
1/4 cup butter or margarine, melted
2 tbsp vegetable oil
1 medium onion, chopped
1 tbsp flour
1/4 lb mushrooms, sliced
1 cup pitted ripe olives, halved
1 can (8oz) tomato sauce
1/2 cup tomato puree
1 & 1/2 tsp basil
1 & 1/2 tsp oregano
2 tbsp dry bread crumbs
3 medium potatoes, cooked, peeled, and sliced

Directions:
Preheat oven to 400°F. Cut eggplant in 1/4-inch slices and halve each slice. Place eggplant pieces in a shallow baking dish and brush with half the melted butter. Turn and brush other side with remaining butter. Bake 20 minutes or until eggplant is tender. In a large skillet, heat oil. Saute onion until soft. Stir in flour. Add mushrooms, olives, tomato sauce, tomato puree, basil, and oregano. Heat, stirring, until sauce thickens and comes to a boil. Layer half the eggplant in a 2-quart casserole. Sprinkle with half the bread crumbs; add half the olive sauce. Top with potato slices, remaining eggplant, bread crumbs and olive sauce. Top with Cheese Sauce (see below). Bake 40 minutes, or until heated through.

Cheese Sauce for Vegetarian Moussaka

Ingredients:
2 tbsp butter
2 tbsp flour
1 & 1/4 cup milk
3/4 cup grated Cheddar cheese
salt & pepper to taste

This page is dedicated to our parents **Clayton Young**, formerly of Woody Point, Bonne Bay, Newfoundland and **Viola** (nee Crocker), formerly of Trout River, Newfoundland, residing in Curling (Corner Brook), Newfoundland.
- *Loretta Tucker (Young) and Shirley Ciulla (Young), formerly of Curling, Newfoundland.*

Directions:

In a saucepan, melt butter. Blend in flour. Gradually add milk, stirring to blend. Cook, stirring constantly, over medium heat until sauce thickens and just begins to bubble. Stir in cheese, salt and pepper. Heat and stir until sauce is smooth. Pour over Moussaka before baking.

Ruth's Scalloped Potatoes

Ruth Keats, Mississauga, Ontario

Ingredients:

6-7 medium-size potatoes
3 tbsp butter
3 tbsp all purpose flour
1 tsp salt
few grains pepper
2 cups scalded milk
1/4 cup onion, chopped
few grains paprika
grated cheese (optional)

> **TRIVIA TIDBITS**
> The Mayflower was originally scheduled to sail for Virginia, but its destination was changed when word reached the Pilgrims that they would not be welcomed there.

Directions:

Wash and peel potatoes; slice thinly. Spread about 1/3 of the slices in a buttered 1 & 1/2 quart casserole dish. Melt butter in a saucepan; slowly blend in flour, salt and pepper. Gradually add hot milk, stirring constantly. Sprinkle potatoes with half of the onions and 1/3 of the sauce. Cover with another layer of potatoes and remaining onions. Place remaining potatoes on top, then cover with remaining sauce. Sprinkle with paprika and grated cheese, if desired. Bake, uncovered, in a moderate 375°F oven for 1 hour or until done and potatoes are lightly browned on top. Makes 6 servings.

Alma's Baked Beans

Mrs. Alma Taylor, Mt. Moriah, Bay of Islands, Newfoundland (nee LeDrew, Bell Island, Newfoundland)

Ingredients:

2 cups dry white beans
1/4 cup salt pork, diced
3 tbsp brown sugar
1 tsp salt
1 cup molasses
1/2 tsp dry mustard
1 medium onion, chopped
1 tbsp ketchup
dash of Worchestershire sauce
water

> **SPICE OF LIFE**
> **Commentaries on Murphy's Law -**
> 1. If you lose much by having things go wrong, take all possible care. 2. If you have nothing to lose by change, relax. 3. If you have everything to gain by change, relax. 4. If it doesn't matter, it doesn't matter.

Directions:

Wash beans thoroughly. Soak beans in cold water overnight. Place the beans and the water in which they were soaked in a pot and cook for half an hour. Transfer to bean crock. Add the diced salt pork, brown sugar, salt, molasses, dry mustard, chopped onion, ketchup and Worchestershire sauce. Mix well. If there is not enough liquid to cover the beans, add boiling water so the beans will be covered. Cover bean crock and bake in a slow oven, 250°F, for approximately 6 hours. Remove the cover during the last half hour of baking. You may need to add some boiling water

Soups, Salads, Vegetarian Dishes & Finger Foods

Appetizers

to the beans two or three times during the baking in order to keep the beans moist and covered with liquid. Do not add any water during the last half hour of baking.

Copper Carrot Pennies

Charmaine Young, Twillingate, Newfoundland (nee Freake, Joe Batt's Arm, Newfoundland)

Ingredients:
2 pkgs carrots
1 small green pepper, cut in rings
1 med onion, cut in rings
1 can tomato soup
1/4 cup Crisco oil
1/2 cup sugar
3/4 cup vinegar
1 tsp Worchestershire sauce
1 tsp mustard
salt
pepper

SPICE OF LIFE
A bird in the hand is not only worth two in the bush, it is safer than any number overhead.

Directions:
Slice and boil carrots in water till tender. When cooked, alternate layers of carrot, pepper rings and onion rings. Make marinade with remaining ingredients and heat well. Pour marinade over vegetable layers and refrigerate.

Swartz's Potatoes

Brenda Keyes, Durham, Ontario, (nee LeDrew, Pasadena and Corner Brook, Newfoundland)

Ingredients:
1 - 2 lb bag frozen hash browns
1 large can celery soup
1 large sour cream
diced green onions
1 lb cheddar cheese, grated

SPICE OF LIFE
No boss will keep an employee who is right all the time.

Directions:
Mix all together and bake at 300°F for 40 minutes.

Irish Potato Cakes

Ingredients:
2 cups mashed potatoes
1 egg, beaten
2 tbsp butter
1 tsp caraway seeds (optional)

FOOD FOR THOUGHT
It probably is lonely at the top, but it sure beats waiting in the long line at the bottom.

This page is in memory of my brother, **Cory (Bud) Hiscock,** formerly of Grand Falls-Windsor, Newfoundland, who passed away January 29, 1994.
Loving you always - Forgetting you never.
Your sister Terri-Lynn (Hiscock) Wicks, Brampton, Ontario

1 cup all-purpose flour
3 tsp baking powder
1/2 tsp salt
fat for frying

Directions:
Combine potatoes, egg, butter and caraway seeds. Beat until fluffy. Sift the flour, baking powder and salt together and add to potato mixture. Knead lightly until well mixed. Roll on a lightly floured board to 1/4" thickness. Cut in squares or wedges and cook in a greased frying pan over low heat until golden brown. This requires about 5 minutes on each side. Serve at once with plenty of butter. Sprinkle generously with sugar as the Irish do!

Rice Mexicaine

Gerine Collingwood, Rocky Harbour, Newfoundland

Ingredients:
5 cups long grain rice
boiling water
3/4 cup butter
2 medium onions (diced)
2 red peppers (diced)
2 green peppers (diced)
salt & pepper, to taste

Directions:
Cook rice according to package directions. Place rice in steamer and pour in boiling water to separate grains. Set aside in large skillet or heavy saucepan; melt butter over medium heat. Add onions and cook until tender (do not brown). (May be prepared a few hours in advance to this point.) Stir in peppers and cook for 2 minutes. Add rice, season with salt and pepper to taste. (Red and green peppers add a holiday look to this rice dish). Makes 20 servings.

Marie's Baked Beans

Marie Evans, Kitchener, Ontario

Ingredients:
3 slices bacon
1/2 cup chopped onion
2 cans beans in tomato sauce
1/4 cup ketchup
2 tbsp brown sugar
2 tbsp mustard (prepared)
1 tbsp Worcestershire sauce

Directions:
In a skillet cook bacon until crisp. Remove bacon reserving 1 tbsp of drippings. Drain and crumble bacon. Set aside. Cook onion in reserved bacon drippings over medium heat until tender, not brown. Bake in oven in 1 1/2 qt casserole dish. Combine onion, beans, ketchup, brown sugar, mustard, Worcestershire sauce and stir. Top with bacon and bake 350°F for 1 hour. Let stand 5 minutes before serving.

Soups, Salads, Vegetarian Dishes & Finger Foods

Appetizers

(sidebar) **Appetizers** Soups, Salads, Vegetarian Dishes & Finger Foods

Company Rice (Microwave)

Ruth Keats, Mississauga, Ontario

Ingredients:

1 cup uncooked long grain rice
2 tbsp butter
3 tbsp finely chopped celery
3 tbsp finely chopped green onion
1 & 3/4 cups water
2 tbsp soy sauce
2 chicken bouillon cubes
1/3 cup sliced fresh mushrooms
1/2 cup frozen peas

FOOD FOR THOUGHT
Education teaches us how little we actually do know.

Directions:

Combine rice and butter in 1 1/2 quart casserole dish and cook, uncovered, on High power for 3 - 4 minutes or until rice is browned, stirring twice. Stir in celery and green onion and cook an additional minute. Add water, soy sauce, and bouillon cubes and mix well. Cover with casserole lid and cook on High power for 5 minutes, then on Medium-Low power for 14-16 minutes, or until most of the liquid is absorbed. Stir in mushrooms and frozen peas. Let stand, covered, for about 10 minutes. Cook an additional 3 minutes if required. Fluff with fork. Serves 4 to 6.

Cucumbers and Tomatoes in Yogurt (Raita)

Archie Ridout, Rexdale, Ontario (formerly of Twillingate, Newfoundland)

Ingredients:

1 medium cucumber
1 green onion
1/2 tsp salt
2 tomatoes, chopped
2 tbsp parsley
1/2 tsp cumin
1 cup yogurt

> *TRIVIA TIDBITS*
>
> All the body's cells, including those of blood, skin, muscle, etc., are replaced when they die, except for brain cells. When brain cells die they are never replaced.

Directions:

Peel and cut cucumber lengthwise into halves. Scoop out seeds with spoon and chop cucumber. Mix cucumber, green onion and salt. Add tomatoes and remaining ingredients except yogurt. Mix well and refrigerate for 1 hour. Drain and fold in yogurt. Makes 4 servings.

Mango Shrimp Salad

Vidya Bachon, Trinidad, West Indies

Ingredients:

1 small cabbage, shredded
1 lb shrimp, cooked, cut in strips
1 or 2 sweet peppers, cut in strips
2 cups yogurt (plain) preferably, or sour cream
chopped parsley
3 full green mango or half ripe rose mango, peeled, sliced in Julienne strips
dill weed (if available)

> **SPICE OF LIFE**
> An optimist believes we live in the best of all possible worlds. A pessimist fears this is true.

salt & pepper (black pepper and/or hot pepper)
a few drops of lime or lemon juice
Directions:
Combine vegetables, fruit and shrimp together. Add yogurt or sour cream, salt, pepper, dill, parsley and lime juice, blend well with shrimp and vegetables. Serve with sliced ham or roast meat.

Mixed Chinese Vegetables

Hilda Reid, Ignace, Ontario (nee Harnum, Bishop's Falls, Newfoundland)
Ingredients:
5 large dried Chinese mushrooms
1 cup lukewarm water
5oz green cabbage
4oz carrots
4oz cucumbers
5oz canned bamboo shoots
4 tbsp sesame seed oil
2oz frozen peas
1/2 cup hot chicken broth
2 tbsp soy sauce
salt
pinch of sugar
Directions:
Soak mushrooms in water 30 minutes. Shred cabbage. Cut carrot, cucumber, and bamboo shoots into julienne strips. Cube mushrooms. Heat oil in skillet. Add cabbage, cook 2 minutes. Add mushrooms, cucumber, carrots and bamboo shoots, then the peas. Pour in broth. Season with soy sauce, salt and sugar. Simmer over low heat for 15 minutes. Serve immediately.

> **TRIVIA TIDBITS**
> A Canadian cricket team went to England in 1880, to play several British teams, making it one of the first such tours. One of the highlights of one match was that the captain was arrested on the field of play for being a former British army deserter.

Saffron Rice with Spinach (Patchoi)

Vidya Bachon, Trinidad, West Indies
Ingredients:
1 & 1/2 cups long grained rice
1 large onion, sliced
1/4 cup corn oil
3 cups chicken stock (use chicken cubes and hot water)
1/2 tsp saffron powder (soaked in a little hot water)
1 bunch chopped patchoi (or spinach)
salt
hot pepper
a little grated cheese
Directions:
Heat oil in skillet or iron pot, fry sliced onion until clear. Add rice and cook until golden brown. Add saffron, chicken stock, chopped spinach or patchoi, salt and pepper. Cover and bring to a boil. Pour rice into large baking dish with cover and bake at 350°F for 20 - 30 minutes until grains of rice are tender and stock is absorbed. Add extra stock of necessary and, with a fork, stir in a little grated cheese. To this basic recipe, may be added shredded or chopped left-over chicken, ham, beef or any other meat. This recipe may be cooked on top of the stove, but baking makes the rice fluffy and dry.

> **FOOD FOR THOUGHT**
> If you decide to put something on the back burner, make sure the fire does not go out.

Rice with Vegetables and Shrimp

Vidya Bachon, Trinidad, West Indies

Ingredients:

3 tbsp cooking oil
1 onion, chopped
2 chicken bouillon tablets
8ozs shelled shrimps
1 tbsp light soy sauce
1 & 1/2 cup rice
1 & 1/2 pt water (3 cups)
1 tsp curry powder
2 tbsp green peas

TRIVIA TIDBITS
Eric the Red, in an attempt
to encourage his fellow
Norsemen to emigrate
to the cold, inhospitable
land west of Iceland,
called the land
Greenland.

Directions:

Lightly sauté onion in 2 tbsp cooking oil until transparent. Add the rice, chicken bouillon tablets, curry powder, and water. Simmer for 20 - 30 minutes until the rice is dry and tender. In the remaining cooking oil, lightly sauté the shrimps and peas. Add soy sauce and cook for 8 minutes. Garnish the rice with shrimps and peas.

Alma's Salad

Alma Taylor, Mt. Moriah, Bay of Islands, Newfoundland (nee LeDrew, Bell Island, Newfoundland)

Ingredients:

250 ml crushed pineapple
125 ml mayonnaise
250 ml corn kernels

Directions:

Drain crushed pineapple. Mix with corn kernals and mayonnaise. Serve with crisp lettuce cups.

Vegetable Platter (Microwave)

Ruth Keats, Mississauga, Ontario

Ingredients:

Cauliflower, cut into flowerets
Broccoli, cut into flowerets
Zucchini, sliced
Carrots, cut in thin strips

SPICE OF LIFE
Nothing is all wrong. Even a clock that has
stopped running is right twice a day.

Directions:

Arrange vegetables on a platter, placing the thicker parts of the cauliflower and broccoli towards the outside. Insert carrot sticks between pieces of cauliflower and broccoli, arrange zucchini in the centre. Dot with butter. Cover with plastic wrap and cook on High power (about 6 minutes per pound of vegetables). Let stand 5 minutes.

Beer Battered Shark

Vidya Bachon, Trinidad, West Indies

Ingredients:

1 & 1/2 lbs boneless shark
2 eggs

SPICE OF LIFE
One way to save face is to keep
the lower half shut.

1 & 1/2 cups flour
1/2 cup cold beer
1 tsp baking powder
3 cups cooking oil

Directions:

Cut the shark into 1-inch strips. Whip the eggs, 1 cup flour, beer, and baking powder together. Heat the oil to 375°F (190 C). Dust the shark with remaining flour. Dip into the batter, then deep fry in small batches to golden brown, re-serve hot. Once all the shark has been cooked, serve with ketchup or salsa sauce. These are great for sandwiches or to serve on toothpicks.

Candied Carrots

Catherine Irwin, Truro, Nova Scotia

Ingredients:

Carrots (quantity as needed)
1-2 tbsp liquid honey (depending on number of carrots used)
1-2 tbsp butter
juice of 1 or 1 & 1/2 lemons (again, depending on quantity of carrots)

Directions:

Peel and cut carrots diagonally (about 3/4 of an inch). Pour in honey and lemon. Top with butter. Cover and bring to a boil (just to the boil). Reduce to minimum heat and cook for about 15 minutes or until tender. The juice will have turned into a candied syrup.

Calypso Rice

Vidya Bachon, Trinidad, West Indies

Ingredients:

2 cups brown rice
1 tsp salt, or to taste
1 potspoon cooking oil
black pepper
1 clove garlic (crushed)
4 cups boiling water
1 med carrot (grated on coarse side of grater)
1 med sweet pimento pepper (green)

Directions:

Heat oil in heavy bottomed pot. Add garlic, brown garlic and remove from oil. Add carrot, stirring all the time for 2-3 minutes. Add sweet pepper, then rice. Toss 1 min. Add boiling water and salt. Cook until rice is tender and all the water is absorbed. A little butter is added if desired.

Callaloo

Vidya Bachon, Trinidad, West Indies

Ingredients:

About 12 dasheen leaves
1/4 lb salt beef or ham bone
1/4 lb salt pork
2 cups coconut milk

1 tbsp butter
1 green pepper
2 crabs
8 ochroes
2 sprigs thyme
1 onion, 4 chives
1 cup boiling water

Directions:

Strip the stalks and midrib from the dasheen leaves and wash well. Wash and cut up the ochroes and seasonings. Soak and cut up the meat. Scald and clean the crabs. Put all the ingredients except the butter, into a pot with the boiling water and simmer until everything is soft. Swizzle and add the butter. Serve with rice.

Breadfruit Chowder (Soup)

Vidya Bachon, Trinidad, West Indies

Ingredients:

2 strips bacon
1/3 cup sliced onion
2 cups diced raw breadfruit
1 & 1/2 cups milk
2 tsp salt
3 cups boiling water
1 large sweet pepper, diced
1 cup kernel corn
1/2 cup diced raw carrot

Directions:

Chop bacon and fry until light brown; add onion and cook until brown; add vegetables, salt and water. Boil until vegetables are tender, adding sweet pepper and corn towards the end. Add milk, serve hot. Sprinkle the top with chopped parsley or spring onion.

Borscht A La Russe

Archie Ridout, Rexdale, Ontario (formerly of Twillingate, Newfoundland)

Ingredients:

1 & 1/2 lbs beets
1/2 lb cabbage
4ozs carrots
2 stalks celery
4ozs bacon
2ozs tomato puree
8ozs beef, chuck
6 cups beef stock
4ozs leeks
8ozs onions
2ozs butter
fresh dill
1oz vinegar

Directions:

Peel and cut 1 1/4 lbs beets into 2' long by 1/4" thick julienne. Cut beef into 1" julienne. Cut onion, cabbage and leeks into large julienne and the celery on the bias in slices. Cut the bacon into 1/2" pieces. Melt the butter in a pan, add the bacon and sauté. Add onions, beef, leeks, celery and sweat with the lid on for 4 minutes. Add beets, cabbage and continue to sweat. Add the stock and bring to a boil. Skim and set to simmer. Peel and grate the remainder of beets. Place in a bowl with the vinegar, a pinch of salt and enough water to cover the beets. (This will bleed the beets). When the soup is cooked (the beef will be tender) add the strained juice of the grated beets and the chopped dill. Makes 8-10 servings.

Avocado Soup

Vidya Bachon, Trinidad, West Indies

Ingredients:

2 large ripe avocados, cut in pieces
1/4 tsp white pepper
4 cups chicken broth (chicken cubes)
1/2 tsp salt
1 cup evaporated milk
1/3 cup dry sherry or white wine
a few pieces of chopped avocado for garnish

SPICE OF LIFE
Don't marry for money; you can borrow it cheaper.

Directions:

Place in blender, avocado, salt, pepper and 1/2 cup milk and blend until smooth. Add remaining milk and blend just until combined. Heat broth and bring to a boil; stir in the avocado puree. Add sherry and pieces of avocado; adjust seasoning and remove from heat. This soup may be served hot or cold. Makes 4-6 servings.

Garlic-Butter Chips

Sandra Young, St. John's, Newfoundland (nee Dove, Twillingate, Newfoundland)

Ingredients:

3/4 cup butter (or margarine)
2 to 3 cloves garlic, cut into slivers
potato chips

Directions:

Preheat oven to 350°F. Heat butter with garlic for a few minutes; remove garlic. Brush potato chips with garlic butter; place on baking sheets lined with paper towels. Heat 5 minutes; drain on clean paper towels. Yield as desired.

Tuna Puffs

Ingredients:

2 cans (6 & 1/2 or 7 ounces each) tuna, packed in water
1 cup celery, finely chopped
1/2 cup mayonnaise (or salad dressing)
2 tbsp onion, chopped
2 tbsp sweet pickles, chopped
salt to taste

TRIVIA TIDBITS

The word *peninsula* comes from the Latin words *paene*, which means *almost*, and *insula*, which means *island*.

Appetizers

Soups, Salads, Vegetarian Dishes & Finger Foods

Puff shells
Directions:
Drain and flake tuna. Combine all ingredients except puff shells; mix thoroughly. Cut tops from puff shells. Fill each shell with approximately 2 teaspoonfuls tuna mixture. Makes about 55 little appetizers.

Shrimp Balls

Ingredients:
1 medium onion, grated
1 & 1/2 lbs. raw shrimp, shelled, deveined & grated
1 medium raw potato, grated
1 egg, slightly beaten
salt, to taste
pepper, to taste
corn oil, for deep frying
Directions:
Grind or grate onion and shrimp into large bowl. Grind potato; pat dry with paper towels. Stir in egg, salt, and pepper. Potato is the thickening; batter will be thick. Heat fat for deep frying; drop batter in by spoonfuls. Fry until golden brown; remove with slotted spoon. Drain on paper towels. Serve hot. Makes 36 to 48.

TRIVIA TIDBITS
Slinkys were invented by an airplane mechanic. He was playing with an airplane spring when he realized that it might have another use. His income increased drastically because of that one idea.

TRIVIA TIDBITS

When Emperor Valerian declared open season on Christians in the year 258 AD, Saint Lawrence was a treasurer to the pope. For refusing to turn the church's treasures over to the Roman prefect, and instead handing them out to the poor and needy, Lawrence was fried to death on a griddle. Instead of turning away from the heat, which most would instinctively have done, Lawrence lay still and is reported to have said to his tormenters, "Turn me over now. That side is quite done." Although his disciples gained courage from his actions, his foes only mocked him, saying he was too lazy to turn. From this incident, the expression "As lazy as Lawrence" came into being. The expression eventually found its way into the English language and is still in use today.

The griddle on which Lawrence was fried, is to this day, on display for public view at the Church of San Lorenzo, in Rome.

Enhancers

Dressings

Stuffings

Sauces

Spreads

Icings

Oils

Dips

Fresh Strawberry Sauce

Ruby Wellon, Deer Lake, Newfoundland (nee Rideout)

Ingredients:
2 cups sliced strawberries
1 tbsp lemon juice
1/4 cup sugar
1/4 tsp almond extract

Directions:
Combine strawberries, sugar and lemon juice in a saucepan. Simmer about 10 minutes. Add almond extract. Cool.

Fruit Sauce

Ruby Wellon, Deer Lake, Newfoundland (nee Rideout)

Ingredients:
2 tbsp brown sugar
1/2 cup orange juice
2 cups fresh strawberries
1 tbsp cornstarch
1/4 cup water
2 bananas, sliced

FOOD FOR THOUGHT
The only fellow who never steps on anybody else's toes is standing still.
-Franklin P. Jones

Directions:
Combine brown sugar, cornstarch, orange juice and water. Cook and stir until mixture thickens. Cover and refrigerate. At serving time fold in fruit.

Curry Sauce

Betina Wheeler-Ali, Toronto, Ontario (formerly of St. John's, Newfoundland)

Ingredients:
3 tbsp oil
1 lg onion, finely chopped
1 med carrot, finely chopped
1/4 cup unsweetened shredded coconut
1/4 tsp cloves
1/2 tsp ground cardamon
dash of cayenne
dash of salt
dash of pepper
2 tbsp curry powder
1 stalk celery, finely chopped
1 lg apple, finely chopped

TRIVIA TIDBITS
During World War II, a woman was banned from bringing her pet macaw into an air-raid shelter in Vienna because the bird's mimicking of the whine of falling bombs terrified the shelter's occupants.

This page is dedicated to our Mother
Rita Stacey (nee Rodway), **Badger, Newfoundland**
Love, your children - Harold, Baxter, Shirley, Wilson, Roger, Maxine, Rick and Mervin

1 tbsp ginger
1 tbsp honey
1 tbsp tomato paste
1 tbsp lemon juice
1 & 1/2 cups of stock or water

Directions:

Put oil in pan, add curry powder and fry on low heat for a few minutes. Add onion, carrot and celery and saute for 5 minutes. Add ginger and coconut. Cook for a few minutes more. Add everything else and cook on low heat for 15 minutes. Combine with meat, fish, chicken, or seafood and then simmer for 1/2 an hour. Serve over plain, white rice.

Cheddar Cheese Sauce

Ingredients:
2 tbsp butter
2 tbsp flour
1/2 tsp dry mustard
1 cup whole milk
1 & 1/2 cups cheddar cheese, shredded
salt to taste

FOOD FOR THOUGHT
Success is often disguised as hard work.

TRIVIA TIDBITS
The word "parlour", which now means living room or sitting room, originated in the monasteries. Monks were not permitted to speak except in the one room where they could "parler" (speak).

Directions:

Melt butter in saucepan. Blend in flour and dry mustard. Gradually stir in milk. Cook and stir over medium heat until mixture comes to a boil and thickens. Remove from heat. Add cheese and stir until melted. Add salt to taste. Ready to pour over your favourite vegetables. Makes about 1 & 3/4 cups.

Glazed Ham Sauce

Trudy S. Simmons, Twillingate, Newfoundland (nee Forward, Tizzard's Harbour, Newfoundland)

Ingredients:
1/2 tsp cloves
1 cup brown sugar
1 & 1/2 tsp cornstarch
1/2 tsp dry mustard
1 tin pineapple rings, reserve juice

> **FOOD FOR THOUGHT**
> If you are patient in one moment of anger, you will escape a hundred days of sorrow.
> -Chinese Proverb

Directions:

Pour juice from pineapple over already-boiled ham and bake for 1 & 1/2 hours in 350°F oven.

Fish Sauce

Phyllis Labelle, Lynden, Ontario, (nee Hollett, Arnold's Cove, Newfoundland)

Ingredients:
3/4-1 cup sugar
1 cup milk
1 cup vinegar
2 eggs, beaten
1/2 tsp salt

> **SPICE OF LIFE**
> Once my eyes were bigger than my stomach, but my stomach caught up with them.

Enhancers

Dressings, Stuffings, Oils, Spices, Icings, Spreads & Dips

dash of pepper
1 & 1/2 tsp dry mustard
3 tsp flour

Directions:

Combine sugar, milk, vinegar, eggs, salt and pepper and bring to a boil. In a separate bowl, mix dry mustard and flour. Add enough water to make a paste. Stir this into boiling mixture. Let cool. This is delicious served with Perch for those great fish rolls.

Dogberry Sauce

Mrs. Gertie Legge, Heart's Delight, Newfoundland, (nee Fost)

Ingredients:

3 cups dogberries, cleaned & washed
2 cups partridgeberries, cleaned & washed
2 cups apples, peeled & finely cut
5 cups sugar
2 cups water

Directions:

Boil dogberries in water for 20 minutes; put through sieve; use only the juice (about 3 cups). Boil partridgeberries and apple together for 20 minutes. Mash and stir well. Add sugar and juice; stir well and boil hard for 20 minutes. Bottle immediately. This will be like jelly.

> **TRIVIA TIDBITS**
> In 1855, when John D. Rockefeller was only sixteen, he made his first contribution to a philantrophic cause. When he died, eighty-two years later, the multi-millionaire oil magnate had given away $531,326,842.

Crab Meat Spread

Ingredients:

1 can (7oz) King crab meat, drained & flaked
1 tsp prepared horseradish
1/2 tsp seasoned salt
1/4 tsp lemon juice
dash of white pepper
1/2 cup plain yogurt

Directions:

Combine crab meat, horseradish, salt, lemon juice and pepper. Fold in yogurt. Cover and chill. Use to spread on crackers or as a dip. Makes about 1 & 1/4 cup.

> **SPICE OF LIFE**
> People will never lose weight talking about it; they have to keep their mouths shut!
>

Garden Dip

Ingredients:

2/3 cup low-fat cottage cheese
1 tbsp finely grated onion
1 tbsp finely grated carrot
1 tbsp finely chopped green pepper

> **FOOD FOR THOUGHT**
> Better than counting your years is to make your years count.

This page is dedicated to the memory of our parents
MARGARET (nee Hollett, Oct. 18, 1910 - June 2, 1972) and
WILLIAM HYNES, (Oct. 31, 1906 - Oct. 5, 1985) of Arnold's Cove, Newfoundland.
The wonderful memories will live on forever...
Children - Mable Reid (deceased), Shirley Johnston, Pearl Hynes,
Scott, Wilbert and Melvin Hynes.

Enhancers
Dressings, Stuffings, Oils, Spices, Icings, Spreads & Dips

1/2 tsp salt
dash of garlic salt
1 cup plain yogurt
Directions:
In a small bowl mash cottage cheese with fork. Add carrot, onion, pepper, salt and garlic salt. Beat until fairly smooth. Stir in yogurt. Cover and chill for several hours. Serve as a dip with chips or raw vegetables. Makes 1 & 3/4 cups.

Vegetable Dip

Charmaine Young, Twillingate, Newfoundland, (nee Freake, Joe Batt's Arm, Newfoundland)
Ingredients:
1 & 1/2 cups sour cream
2 cups salad dressing
1 & 1/2 tsp lemon juice
2 tbsp parsley flakes
1 small onion, chopped fine (or 1/2 tsp onion powder)
1/2 tsp garlic powder
1 & 1/4 tsp Worchestershire sauce
1/2 tsp pepper
3/4 tsp salt
1/8 tsp curry powder

FOOD FOR THOUGHT
Isn't it strange that each new generation has to learn the stove is hot?

Directions:
Mix all ingredients together and put in dip bowl. Serve with vegetables of your choice.

Crab Dip

Charmaine Young, Twillingate, Newfoundland, (nee Freake, Joe Batt's Arm, Newfoundland)
Ingredients:
1 5oz can crab meat
1 8oz pkg cream cheese
1/2 cup salad dressing
2 tbsp ketchup
3 tbsp French salad dressing
2 tbsp chopped onion (or 1/2 tsp onion powder)

FOOD FOR THOUGHT
Quitters never win.
Winners never quit.

Directions:
Drain crab meat. Beat cheese with salad dressing. Add ketchup, french dressing, onion and crab meat. Chill in fridge for a couple of hours. Great when served on your favourite crackers.

Mayonnaise

Miss Gertrude V. Sweetapple, Glovertown, Newfoundland
Ingredients:
1 small can milk
1/4 cup vinegar
3 tsp prepared mustard
2 tsp sugar
dash of salt

SPICE OF LIFE
Women are people who don't admit their age;
men are people who don't act it.

Enhancers

Dressings, Stuffings, Oils, Spices, Icings, Spreads & Dips

dash of pepper
Directions:
Mix sugar, mustard, pepper and salt with vinegar. Add milk last and beat.

Sour Cream

Grace Ryan, Newmans Cove, Bonavista Bay, Newfoundland
Ingredients:
3/4 cup milk
1/4 cup vinegar (or lemon juice)
Directions:
Stir together and use as a subsitute if you can't buy sour cream.

Mexicali Dip

Brenda Keyes, Durham, Ontario, (nee LeDrew, Pasadena and Corner Brook, Newfoundland)
Ingredients:
1 can Jalopeno bean dip
2 -3 ripe avocados, mashed with 2 tsp lemon juice
1 cup sour cream
1 cup mayonnaise + 1/2 pkg of Taco seasoning mix
1/2 lb Havarti cheese, grated
1/2 lb cheddar cheese, grated
sliced green onions and sliced pitted black olives (garnish the top)
Directions:
Layer each ingredient in the order given. Use a large flat dish (so people will taste all the layers).
Serve with Doritos chips.

Mexican Taco Dip

Helen Hefford, Edmonton, Alberta, (formerly of Buchans, Newfoundland)
Ingredients:
cream cheese
salsa sauce
onions
tomatoes
can shrimp
cheese
Directions:
Spread cream cheese in a Pyrex dish (about 11x8). Cover cream cheese with your favourite Mexican salsa sauce. Add finely chopped onions and tomatoes. Spread on a can of drained shrimp. Spread grated cheese on top. Serve with your favourite taco chips. Delicious.

Barbeque Sauce

Marion Nagle, Kitchener, Ontario, (nee Daniels, Twillingate, Newfoundland)

Ingredients:

1 cup dried onions
1 cup water
2 tbsp Worchestershire sauce
1 cup ketchup
1/4 cup vinegar
1/2 cup brown sugar
2 tsp dry mustard
1 tsp paprika
salt

TRIVIA TIDBITS
The cow is not the only animal used to produce milk, butter and cheese - these products are obtained in many parts of the world from goats, reindeer, lamas and even yaks!

Directions:

Mix together and pour over ribs. Cover & bake at 400°F until done.

Morningside Bar-B-Q Chicken Sauce

Brenda Keyes, Durham, Ontario, (nee LeDrew, Pasadena and Corner Brook, Newfoundland)

Ingredients:

2 cups peanut oil
3 eggs
1/4 cup poultry seasoning
1/4 cup salt
1/8 cup black pepper
4 cups (yes!) of apple cider vinegar

TRIVIA TIDBITS
In the early 1600s, more than 1,000 children were kidnapped in Europe and shipped to America as "indentured" servants.

Directions:

Whip the first two ingredients, then add rest of ingredients, again whipping to a froth. Chicken has to be par-boiled first. Place on a grill on medium heat and slather this stuff on constantly - turning frequently. The complete recipe is enough to do a whole hen house of chickens!! It can be stored for two weeks in the old icebox.

Seafood Sauce

Shirley Yates, Sherwood Park, Alberta, (nee Hefford, Buchans, Newfoundland)

Ingredients:

1/2 cup chili sauce
1/4 cup ketchup
3 tbsp sweet pickle relish
1/2 tsp horseradish
1/2 tsp Worchestershire sauce

FOOD FOR THOUGHT
The years teach much which the days never know.
-Ralph Waldo Emerson

Directions:

Mix all ingredients in a bowl. Chill to serve. Put into a small bowl for dipping. Makes about 1 cup.

Prize Raisin Pudding Sauce

Ingredients:

2 tbsp butter

Dressings, Stuffings, Oils, Spices, Icings, Spreads & Dips

Enhancers

1 cup brown sugar
2 cups boiling water
1/4 tsp salt
1 tsp vanilla

Directions:

Combine all ingredients and pour over top of pudding mixture. Bake in preheated oven at 375°F for 45 minutes. Serve hot or cold upside down with whipped cream.

Steamed Partridgeberry (or Blueberry) Pudding Sauce

Violet Jenkins, Etobicoke, Ontario, (nee Baggs, Twillingate, Newfoundland)

Ingredients:

1 cup brown sugar
1 tbsp flour
1/2 cup water
1 tbsp butter

Directions:

Combine sugar and flour; add water and boil until thickened. Remove from heat and add the butter.

Molasses (Lassy) Duff Sauce

Gordon LeRoux, Labrador City (St. Judes, Deer Lake, Newfoundland)

Ingredients:

1/2 cup water
2 tsp butter
2 tbsp white sugar
1 tsp vanilla
2 tsp cornstarch in 1/4 cup of cold water

FOOD FOR THOUGHT
You can't build a reputation on what you are going to do.
-Henry Ford

Directions:

Bring first four ingredients to a boil. Thicken with cornstarch in water. Makes enough sauce for four servings. (An old family recipe)

White Glaze

Cathy Gale, Doyles, Newfoundland

Ingredients:

1/2 cup icing sugar
2 to 3 tsps milk

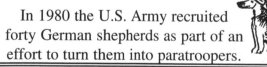

TRIVIA TIDBITS
In 1980 the U.S. Army recruited forty German shepherds as part of an effort to turn them into paratroopers.

Directions:

Add enough milk to icing sugar to make a glaze of good drizzling consistency. Ideal for drizzling over fresh-baked cinnamon rolls.

In loving memory of our father **Aiden Denine** of St. John's, Nfld; (born August 28, 1926 - died December 31, 1990), and our mother **Evelyn** (Collins), formerly of Mint Brook and St. John's, now residing in Weston, Ontario. Remembered by children Dennis, Kitty, Aiden, Carol-Ann, Bernard, Randy, Gary, Jerome, Tina, Flo, Ed, Lucy and Frankie.
Submitted by son Randy

Surprise Spread

June Dalley, Bathurst, New Brunswick, (nee Howell, Carbonear, Newfoundland)

Ingredients:

8oz cream cheese, softened
1/2 cup sour cream
1/4 cup mayonnaise
3-4 cans broken shrimp
1 cup seafood cocktail sauce
2 cups shredded monzarella cheese
1 green pepper, chopped
5 cups onions, chopped
1 tomato, diced

TRIVIA TIDBITS
It was one time illegal in a town in Ohio for a woman to undress in front of a man's

Directions:

Mix first 3 ingredients. Spread over 12 inch plate. Scatter shrimp over cheese mixture, add layers of seafood sauce, monzarella cheese, green peppers, onions and tomato. Cover and chill until ready to serve. Serve with nacho chips. Serves 10-12.

Arlene's Cake Icing

Arlene Gibbons, Stoney Creek, Ontario (nee Sherard, Point Verde, Placentia, Newfoundland)

Ingredients:

1/4 cup butter
2 cups icing sugar
3 tbsp milk
1 tsp vanilla

FOOD FOR THOUGHT
Never complain about getting old because many are denied the privilege.

Directions:

Mix icing sugar and milk together in bowl. Blend well. Add butter and vanilla and mix until it forms a creamy mixture. (Food colouring may also be added, if desired).

Spinach Dip In Bread Bowl

Archie Ridout, Rexdale, Ontario (formerly of Twillingate, Newfoundland)

Ingredients:

2 cups sour cream
1 cup mayonnaise
1 pkg Knorr vegetable soup mix
1 pkg frozen, chopped spinach, thawed and well-drained
1 sm onion, diced
2 lb unsliced Pumpernickle loaf

SPICE OF LIFE
The most important use of the mind seems to be to forget things with.

Directions:

Mix all ingredients except bread and refrigerate until ready to serve. Cut top off loaf and hollow out like a pumpkin. Keep inside of bread in chunks to serve with dip. Just before serving, place dip in hollowed-out bread and serve surrounded by chunks of bread.

Dressings, Stuffings, Oils, Spices, Icings, Spreads & Dips

Enhancers

Bagna Cauda (Hot Anchovy and Garlic Dip)

Archie Ridout, Rexdale, Ontario, (formerly of Twillingate, Newfoundland)

Ingredients:

2 cups whipping cream
1/4 cup butter
8 flat anchovy fillets, drained and minced
3 cloves garlic, minced

Directions:

In a heavy saucepan, bring cream to a boil and cook until reduced to one-half, stirring frequently. In another pan, melt butter; add anchovies and garlic, and cook until garlic is soft but not brown. Stir in cream and bring to a simmer. Do not boil. Pour into small fondue pot or heat-proof earthenware pot and place over a warmer. Stir occasionally. Serve with raw vegetables for dipping.

Cindy's Salad Dressing

Cindy Cooper, Twillingate, Newfoundland

Ingredients:

1/2 cup sour cream (low fat)
1/2 cup salad dressing (low fat)
1/4 cup bacon bits
3 tbsp parmesan cheese
1/4 tsp mustard
1/2 pkg sugar twin
dash garlic
few dashes paprika

Directions:

Mix all ingredients in a bowl. When well mixed, add to salad and refrigerate until ready to serve. (Great with Broccoli Salad, page 188.)

Jenny's Icing

Jenny and Josie, Richmond Hill, Ontario (nee Clarke, Port Rexton, Newfoundland)

Ingredients:

1/2 cup margarine or butter, whipped
1/2 cup white sugar
3 tbsp flour
3 tbsp hot water

Directions:

Whip margarine (or butter), sugar, flour and hot water. Pour over any cake.

This page is dedicated to my father, **Donald Perry**, from Gooseberry Island, Bonavista Bay. Parents - Jacob Henry Perry and Sarah (nee Wells). They left Newfoundland in 1927 and eleven days and nights later arrived in Vancouver, British Columbia. **Don** and **Audrey** celebrated their 60th wedding anniversary June 23, 1995 and live in Greenwood, B. C.
Donalda Brown, Woodville, Ontario, Canada

Enhancers
Dressings, Stuffings, Oils, Spices, Icings, Spreads & Dips

Baked Ham Side Sauce

Charmaine Young, Twillingate, Newfoundland, (nee Freake, Joe Batt's Arm, Newfoundland)

Ingredients:

1 lg can crushed pineapple
2 tbsp butter
1 tbsp lemon juice
sugar (sweeten to taste)
cornstarch

Directions:

Bring to a boil in sauce pan. Thicken with cornstarch.

> **FOOD FOR THOUGHT**
> Fault-finding in friends can find
> faults - and lose friends.

Ron's Special Salad Dressing

Ron Young, St. John's, Newfoundland, (formerly of Twillingate, Newfoundland)

Ingredients:

2 litres vegetable oil
1 litre vinegar
2 eggs, beaten
1 tsp salt substitute
1/2 tsp onion powder
1/2 tsp ground garlic
1/2 tsp oregano
1/2 tsp thyme

> **SPICE OF LIFE**
> A bachelor's little black book is full of near Mrs.

Directions:

Combine all ingredients in large bowl. Mix well before putting into a dispenser. Keep refrigerated and shake everytime before using.

Raisin Gingerbread Frosting (Newfoundland Style)

Miss Gertrude V. Sweetapple, Glovertown, Newfoundland

Ingredients:

1 egg white
dash of salt
1/2 cup honey

Directions:

> **FOOD FOR THOUGHT**
> I had no shoes and I complained
> until I met a man who had no feet.

Beat 1 egg white with a dash of salt until stiff enough to hold up in peak, but not dry. Then pour the cup of honey in a fine stream over the egg white and beat constantly until frosting holds its shape. This will make 2 & 1/4 cups frosting, enough for an average cake and especially good on gingerbread.

Decorator's Frosting (for Little Christmas Cookies)

Ingredients:

2 eggs whites
1 & 1/2 cups confectioner's sugar
1/4 cup light corn syrup
food coloring

> **SPICE OF LIFE**
> Flattery is telling other people exactly
> what they think of themselves.

Enhancers

Dressings, Stuffings, Oils, Spices, Icings, Spreads & Dips

Directions:
Beat egg whites until soft peaks form. Gradually add sugar, beating until sugar is dissolved and frosting stands in stiff peaks. Add corn syrup; beat 1 minute. Divide frosting into several portions. Colour each with food colouring as desired. Add a few drops of water to thin, if necessary. Keep well covered until time to frost.

Asian Stirfry Herb Oil

Winnie Oberderfer, Okanagan Falls, British Columbia, (nee Parsons, Halifax, Nova Scotia)

Ingredients:
6 tbsp fresh coriander
4 tbsp fresh lemon grass
4 tbsp cumin seeds
1/8 tsp whole white pepper
6 peeled garlic
olive oil

> ***TRIVIA TIDBITS***
> Crooked brewers in Victorian Britain used to add sulphate of iron to their brew to give it added head to hide the fact that the beer had been watered down.

Directions:
Wash and dry fresh herbs. Place in a glass bottle, cleared preferred. Cover completely with oil and seal or cover. Stand on a sunny windowsill for 4 weeks. Oil is now ready to use. Remove herbs from oil after 2 months.

Garlic Oil

Winnie Oberderfer, Okanagan Falls, British Columbia, (nee Parsons, Halifax, Nova Scotia)

Ingredients:
14 peeled garlic cloves
1/8 tsp whole black peppers
Olive oil

> **FOOD FOR THOUGHT**
> If you have the 'can do' -
> the 'how to' shows up.

Directions:
Put into a glass jar. Cover completely with olive oil for 4 weeks. Place in a sunny spot. May take garlic and peppers out after 6 weeks.

Herbal Garlic Vinegar

Winnie Oberderfer, Okanagan Falls, British Columbia, (nee Parsons, Halifax, Nova Scotia)

Ingredients:
12 large peeled garlic cloves
white or red wine vinegar
1/2 tsp whole black pepper

Directions:
Put garlic cloves and black pepper in a glass jar and cover for 3 weeks with vinegar before using.

This page is dedicated to our parents,
Elijah and Ivy (nee Beaton) **Price**
Grand Falls-Windsor, Newfoundland.
Children - Geneva, Donna, Ray, Lorne and Kevin

Enhancers
Dressings, Stuffings, Oils, Spices, Icings, Spreads & Dips

Thai Blend Vinegar

Winnie Oberderfer, Okanagan Falls, British Columbia, (nee Parsons, Halifax, Nova Scotia)

Ingredients:

3 small slices ginger, peeled
6 sprigs coriander
8 small dried hot chili peppers
8 cloves peeled garlic
red or white wine vinegar

> **SPICE OF LIFE**
> Show me a family with everything in life, and I'll show you a household about to have a garage sale.

Directions:

Put all ingredients in a glass jar. Cover with vinegar of choice above. Let sit 3 weeks before using. Will keep forever. After 2 months, you may drain, but is not necessary.

Country Blend Spice Mix

Winnie Oberderfer, Okanagan Falls, British Columbia, (nee Parsons, Halifax, Nova Scotia)

Ingredients:

4 tbsp chopped fresh basil
4 tbsp chopped fresh tarragon
4 tbsp chopped fresh chervil
5 tbsp chopped fresh thyme
1/2 tbsp white pepper, ground

> **FOOD FOR THOUGHT**
> Next in importance to having good aim is to recognize when to pull the trigger.
> -Elmer G. Lettermanx

Directions:

Mix altogether and put in a shaker jar.
You may use all ground ingredients instead of fresh, if desired.

Mexican Spice

Winnie Oberderfer, Okanagan Falls, British Columbia, (nee Parsons, formerly of Halifax, Nova Scotia)

Ingredients:

6 tbsp fresh oregano, or ground
6 tbsp fresh coriander, or ground
1 tbsp dried red chili pepper
2 tbsp powdered garlic

> **SPICE OF LIFE**
> Men aren't led into temptation. They find it all by themselves.

Directions:

Mix altogether and put in a shaker jar.
NOTE: Never place spices over stove or near heat as they will lose their strength and aroma. Spices should always be in a cool, dark place.

Fish or Chicken Batter

Arlene Gibbons, Stoney Creek, Ontario (nee Sherard, Point Verde, Placentia, Newfoundland)

Ingredients:

1 cup flour
1 cup milk
1 egg
1/4 tsp salt

> **FOOD FOR THOUGHT**
> A rumor is like a cheque - never endorse it till you're sure it's genuine.
> -Will Henry

Directions:

Mix flour and salt in a medium size bowl. Stir in milk and egg. Mix with fork thoroughly. Dip fish or chicken until completely covered; fry.

Dressings, Stuffings, Oils, Spices, Icings, Spreads & Dips

Enhancers

Cheese Fluff Dressing

Eva F. Canning, Baton Rouge, Los Angeles, USA

Ingredients:

4 cups cool whip
1 - 8oz pkg cream cheese, room temperature
1 & 1/2 to 2 tsp grated orange peel

Directions:

Stir the cream cheese into the cool whip; then fold in grated orange peel. Makes 10 to 12 servings. (Makes a lovely recipe for the Christmas holidays served on lettuce leaves)

> ***TRIVIA TIDBITS***
> Although the civil war was initiated by the North to stop slavery, it was money made from the slave trade by Northern "Yankee" merchants, which was used to build the mills and factories that produced the war materials which enabled the North to defeat the South.

Catherine Irwin's Salad Dressing

Catherine Irwin, Truro, Nova Scotia

Ingredients:

3 cloves minced garlic
1/4 cup cider vinegar
1/8 cup cold water
1/4 cup olive oil
1/4 tsp freshly ground black pepper
1 tsp basil, rubbed with fingers
1/2 tsp oregano, rubbed with fingers
1 tbsp parsley
a shake of cayenne pepper
1 tbsp honey

> ***TRIVIA TIDBITS***
> St. Francis, who founded the Franciscan religious order in 1209, had no theological training. He was born rich, but when he gave away his possessions and embarked on a career of charity and good deeds, his father disowned him.

Directions:

Shake well and serve. If a bit too vinegary, add a wee bit more olive oil. (This salad dressing is well worth making from scratch. Since there are no preservatives it should be consumed within 24 hours. Always refrigerate remaining dressing. The recipe leaves lots of room for creativity and rarely turns out the same way twice).

Grand Finale Salad Dressing

Catherine Irwin, Truro, Nova Scotia

Ingredients:

1 & 1/4 cups mayonnaise
2 tbsp minced parsley
2 tbsp minced chives
1 tbsp tarragon vinegar
1 tbsp fresh lemon juice
1/2 clove garlic, pressed

Directions:

Combine ingredients and refrigerate.

> ***TRIVIA TIDBITS***
> To create the illusion that all Russians were happy and prosperous, the courtiers and noblemen of Catherine the Great created a portable village, complete with actors and actresses to play the parts of villagers for the benefit of the Queen whenever she made a Royal Tour of the country.
> The 'villagers' would wave happily to the Queen as she passed by. Catherine was apparently never aware of this deception.

This page is dedicated to the memory of our grandparents **MARY-ANN** (1894-1944) and **HERBERT DOVE** (1892-1977) of Sansome's Island and Twillingate.
Forever remembered by Linda Greenham (nee Dove) in Twillingate and Sandra Young (nee Dove) in St. John's.

Mom's Old-Fashioned Cooked Salad Dressing

Catherine Irwin, Truro, Nova Scotia

Ingredients:
3/4 (up to 1) cup granulated sugar
3 tbsp all-purpose flour
2 tsp dry mustard
1 tsp salt
1 egg, beaten
1 tbsp butter
1 cup white vinegar
1 cup milk

Directions:
In top of double boiler, stir together sugar, flour, mustard and salt. Blend in egg and beat well. Stir in butter, vinegar and milk (one at a time) until smooth. Place over simmering water and cook, stirring constantly until thick, 10 to 15 minutes. Let cool. Dressing will continue to thicken as it cools. Stir as it cools and store in clean glass jar in refrigerator for up to 1 month. Makes about 2 cups.

TRIVIA TIDBITS

Matrons at St. Bartholomew's hospital in sixteenth century London were allowed to supplement their income by

Yogurt Dressing (for Colorful Garden Salad)

Ingredients:
8oz plain yogurt
1/2 cup mayonnaise
1 tbsp lemon juice
1 tsp chopped onion
dash garlic salt

Directions:
In a small bowl, blend all ingredients. Serve over garden salad. Makes 1 1/2 cups.

FOOD FOR THOUGHT
Tact is the art of building a fire under people without making their blood boil.
-Franklin P. Jones

Mushroom Stuffing

Mrs. Barbara Lucas, Barachois Brook, Newfoundland

Ingredients:
1/4 cup butter
2 cups bread crumbs
2 tsp onion (minced)
1/4 cup chopped celery
1 tbsp lemon juice
1/2 tsp salt
dash of pepper
1 cup mushrooms

FOOD FOR THOUGHT
Diet is something most of us do religiously: We eat what we want and pray we don't gain weight.

Directions:
Melt butter, stir in bread crumbs; add remaining ingredients and mix thoroughly. If dressing seems dry, add a little water to moisten.

Chicken or Turkey Stuffing

June Dalley, Bathurst, New Brunswick, (nee Howell, Carbonear, Newfoundland)

Ingredients:
2 lg onions, finely chopped

Enhancers

Dressings, Stuffings, Oils, Spices, Icings, Spreads & Dips

10-12 potatoes (medium)
4 tbsp margarine
1 & 1/2 tbsp summer savoury
2 cups bread crumbs
Salt to taste

Directions:
Boil potatoes until tender and salt to taste. Once cooked, drain and mash thoroughly. While still hot, add onions and margarine and mix well. Add savoury, mix well again. Sprinkle in bread crumbs, mixing accordingly. In a 9x13" pan, place mixture and pat down until flattened. Coat top with a little bit of margarine, and sprinkle with remaining bread crumbs. Place in oven at 425°F until lightly brown and serve while hot. Serves 8-10 people.

Celery Stuffing

Ingredients:
2 cups toast crumbs
1 cup diced celery
1 sm onion, minced
4 tbsp butter or margarine, melted
1/2 tsp salt
1/8 tsp pepper
1/4 tsp sage

Directions:
Toast bread; crumble into small pieces. Fry celery and onion in butter a few minutes. Add with seasonings, to crumbs. Add a little water. Mix thoroughly.

TRIVIA TIDBITS
Nicholas Breakspear was born in Hertfordshire, England, in the year 1100, but left as a young man and became a beggar. Later, Nicholas found work at a monastery near Avignon, France. His devotion and hard work attracted the attention of Pope Eugene III who appointed him cardinal-bishop of Alba in 1146. In 1154 Breakspear was elected Pope Adrian IV, the only English-born Pope ever.

Onion Stuffing

Ingredients:
6 tbsp butter or margarine
1 & 1/2 to 2 cups hot water
4 cups toasted bread cubes
1/2 tsp salt
1 tbsp sage
1/8 tsp pepper
1/4 cup finely chopped onion
1 tbsp celery, chopped
1 tbsp parsley, chopped

Directions:
Melt 4 tbsp butter in hot water. Mix with remaining ingredients. Use remaining butter to brush on chicken. Makes enough to stuff a 4 lb. chicken.

TRIVIA TIDBITS
A death certificate from a doctor in Edmonton, Alberta, in 1925 gave the reason or contributory cause of death as "Talked to death". The doctor claimed that his patient would probably have made a recovery but for the fact that he had been bothered by relatives anxious about the contents of his will.

This page is dedicated to the late **Lorraine Dwyer** (Cambridge, Ontario 1992) and her two lovely daughters **Jolene** and **Sheri**.

Poultry Stuffing

Ingredients:

1 sm onion
3 tbsp butter or fat
3 cups soft bread crumbs
1 tsp salt
1/8 tsp pepper
1 tsp poultry seasoning

Directions:

Slice onion; saute in butter until delicate brown. Add crumbs, salt, pepper and poultry seasoning. Mix well.

> ### *TRIVIA TIDBITS*
> General George Patton, the World War II American army commander, believed in reincarnation. He believed that he himself, had been on earth on six previous occasions: once as a prehistoric warrior, another as an ancient Greek soldier, then as a soldier in Alexander the Great's army, once as member of Julius Caesar's army, once as an English Knight and at another time one of Napolean's marshals.

Butter Cream Icing

Ruth Keats, Mississauga, Ontario
(Can be used for wedding cake)

Ingredients:

1/2 cup solid Crisco
1/2 cup butter or margarine, (or use another cup of shortening instead of butter)
1 tsp almond extract
4 cups icing sugar (approx. 1 lb)
2 tbsp milk

Directions:

Cream butter and margarine. Add flavouring. Gradually add sugar & beat well. Add milk and beat 'til light and fluffy. Keep covered with a damp cloth until ready to use. For best results, keep icing in bowl in refrigerator when not in use. If refrigerated in tight container, it can be stored 2 weeks. Rewhip before using. Yield 3 cups. Substitute butter with shortening and 1/2 tsp butter extract for pure white icing and stiffer consistency.

> ### SPICE OF LIFE
> The mind is like a television: When it goes blank, it's a good idea to turn off the sound.

Crab Dip

Marie Evans, Kitchener, Ontario

Ingredients:

1 pkg cream cheese (softened)
1 tbsp milk
1 can crab meat
2 tsp green onion or regular onion
1/2 tsp horseradish
1 tsp lemon juice
sprinkle of pepper

Directions:

Blend all ingredients in a dish with grated cheese on top. Bake 350°F for 15 minutes. Serve hot with crackers.

> ### *TRIVIA TIDBITS*
> Pierre and Marie Curie refused to take out a patent on the process of making radium. Radium, they declared, belonged to the world - no one had a right to profit from it.

Crab Pate

Mary Russell, Brooklyn, Newfoundland, (formerly of Come By Chance, Newfoundland)

Ingredients:

1 can mushroom soup, no water
1 & 1/2 envelopes gelatin

> ### SPICE OF LIFE
> Don't use a big word where a diminutive one will suffice.

Enhancers

Dressings, Stuffings, Oils, Spices, Icings, Spreads & Dips

8 oz pkg cream cheese
1 cup miracle whip
2 cups crab meat
Directions:

Add gelatin to 4 teaspoons water. Heat the mushroom soup to boiling, add gelatin. Mix the cream cheese with electric mixer and blend in miracle whip. Fold in crab meat and add to soup and gelatin mixture. Refrigerate. Serve as a chip dip or with your favourite crackers.

Dipping Sauce

Vidya Bachon, Trinidad, West Indies

Ingredients:

2 tbsp mustard
Hot pepper, deseeded and minced
1 cup olive oil
1/4 cup vinegar
2 tsp salt
sprig parsley, chopped
2 red sweet peppers, chopped
bundle of chive, minced
2 or 3 pickles, minced

Directions:

In a blender, combine the vinegar, hot pepper; reduce speed and add oil very slowly. Blend in the remaining ingredients, and process until smooth.

Hot Avocado Sauce

Vidya Bachon, Trinidad, West Indies

Ingredients:

2 ripe avocados, peeled & chopped
2 ripe tomatoes, peeled, seeded and chopped
1 medium onion, finely chopped
2 tbsp parsley, finely chopped
6 pimento, finely chopped
1 large hot pepper, chopped
1 tsp salt

Directions:

Place the avocados and tomatoes in a bowl and mash with the back of a fork. Add all the remaining ingredients and combine well. Serve immediately with chips, tacos or tortillas. If you do not wish to serve immediately, cover tightly with plastic wrap because it darkens when exposed to air. Serve also with meats. Makes 4 servings.

Lemon Licorice Icing

Hilda Reid, Ignace, Ontario, (nee Harnum, Bishop's Falls, Newfoundland)

Ingredients:

1/4 cup butter or margarine

2 tbsp milk
1 tsp grated lemon rind
1 tbsp lemon juice
1/4 tsp anise seed
1/8 tsp salt
2 cup sifted confectioners sugar

Directions:

Cream butter or margarine; add milk, lemon rind, lemon juice, anise seed and salt. Gradually add sugar, creaming until smooth. Frost bars.

Oriental Dressing

Ingredients:

1/3 cup rice vinegar
4 tsp soya sauce
1 tsp Dijon mustard
2 tsp sesame seed oil
1 tsp vegetable oil
2 tsp liquid honey
1/4 tsp minced ginger
1/4 tsp hot sauce

Directions:

Whisk all ingredients together. Can be used over salads or vegetables. Store in refrigerator. Keeps about 1 week.

Salsa (Tomato Sauce)

Trudy S. Simmons, Twillingate, Newfoundland

Ingredients:

1 - 16oz can tomatoes, drained and finely chopped
1 - 4-oz can green chili peppers, chopped
1/2 cup finely chopped onion
1 tbsp vinegar
1 tsp sugar
1/8 tsp salt

Directions:

In mixing bowl, thoroughly combine tomatoes, chili peppers and onion; stir in vinegar and salt. Let mixture stand at least 30 minutes at room temperature. Store in refrigerator. Serve as a relish. Makes about 1 cup.

French Dressing

Vidya Bachon, Trinidad, West Indies

Ingredients:

1/2 cup salad oil
1/2 cup lime juice or vinegar
2 cloves garlic, crushed
1/2 tsp paprika
2 tsp salt

1/2 tsp sugar
1 tsp pepper
Directions:
Cover and shake until thoroughly blended or put all in an electric blender and process for a few seconds. Makes 1 cup. Variations: (1) Add 2 tbsp ketchup and finely chopped chives to the above dressing. (2) Add 1/2 tsp dry or prepared mustard to the above recipe. (3) Add 1/2 tsp curry powder to dressing.

Ron's Special Sauce (Chicken, Ribs etc.)

Ron Young, St. John's, Newfoundland, (formerly of Twillingate, Newfoundland)
Ingredients:
1 - 5 & 1/2oz tin tomato paste
1 - 5 & 1/2oz hot water
1/4 cup barbecue sauce
1 cup sugar
1/8 cup soya sauce
2 tsp salt substitute
1 tsp black pepper
1 tsp onion powder
1 tsp garlic powder
2 tsp Worchestershire sauce
Directions:
Mix all ingredients together.

> ### TRIVIA TIDBITS
> At a meeting of the United Nations, Harold Macmillan, the British Prime Minister, was interrupted by the Soviet leader Nikita Kruschev, who in order to emphasise his disagreement, hammered on his desk with the heel of one of his shoes. Macmillan calmly addressed the intrepreters, saying, "I wonder whether I could have that translated?"

Hot Cheesy-Crab Dip

Ingredients:
1 cup Cheddar cheese, grated
1 cup mayonnaise
1 med onion, chopped
1 can crab meat, drained
Directions:
Mix the ingredients and put in a 1 & 1/2 quart casserole or souffle dish. (The mixture will rise so the dish needs sides). Bake at 350°F for 25 minutes. Serve with crackers or bread sticks.

Fruit Dip

Ingredients:
3oz pkg cream cheese, softened
8oz strawberry or raspberry yogurt
1 tbsp sugar
2 tsp lemon juice
2 cups whipping cream (already whipped)
1/4 tsp almond extract
Directions:
Combine above ingredients and chill before serving with cut fruit.

> ### SPICE OF LIFE
> There are three kinds of people in the world - those who can count, and those who can't.

Great Veggie Dip

Ingredients:

1 - 500g tub sour cream
1/2 cup broccoli tops, chopped
1/2 cup Cheddar cheese (medium)
1 - 45g pkg Vegetable Soup mix

Directions:

In a bowl, mix all ingredients together, one at a time, to make sure it is well mixed. This dip is best if made the night before and allowed to sit out of the refrigerator about 15 minutes before serving. Great with all vegetables.

Taco Salad Dip

Ingredients:

1 lg container sour cream
1 pkg cream cheese
1 pkg Taco seasoning mix
lettuce, chopped or shredded, to taste
1 handful green or red pepper, chopped
1 tomato, diced
1 handful cheddar cheese, grated

Directions:

Mix sour cream, cream cheese and Taco seasoning mix; spread on a circular plate. Top with shredded lettuce; sprinkle diced peppers on top. Spread cheddar cheese on top. Serve with Taco chips.

Cheese Dip

Ingredients:

2/3 of 1lb Velveeta cheese
3/4 cup mayonnaise
6 & 1/2 oz can tuna, drained
8-10 sm green onions, chopped

Directions:

Melt cheese in a double boiler. Add mayonnaise and stir until blended. Add tuna and chopped onion; mix. May be served warm or cold. Ideal for fresh vegetables.

Hot Crab Dip

Ingredients:

8oz cream cheese with onion
1 tin crab meat, rinse and drain
1/4 cup mayonnaise
1 tsp garlic salt
dash of Worcestershire sauce
paprika, for sprinkling

Enhancers

Dressings, Stuffings, Oils, Spices, Icings, Spreads & Dips

Enhancers

Dressings, Stuffings, Oils, Spices, Icings, Spreads & Dips

Directions:
Mix together and heat at 350°F for 10 to 15 minutes. Sprinkle with paprika. Serve with assorted crackers.

Downhome Dip

Ingredients:
1 cup mayonnaise
1 cup sour cream
1/2 pkg onion soup mix
1 tsp soya sauce
1 dill pickle, finely chopped

Directions:
Chop dill pickle very fine. Add remaining ingredients and mix. Use green peppers, carrots, celery, cauliflower or cucumber for dipping. Tastes delicious!

FOOD FOR THOUGHT
Opportunity is often a lot more conspicious going out than coming in.

Lemon Sauce

Ingredients:
3/4 cup sugar
1 & 1/2 tbsp cornstarch
1/4 tsp salt
1 & 3/4 cups water
1 tsp lemon rind
1 tbsp lemon juice
1 tbsp butter

Directions:
Combine the sugar, cornstarch, salt and water; bring to a boil and let bubble gently for about 15 minutes. Just before serving add the lemon rind, lemon juice and butter.

TRIVIA TIDBITS
The petrified forests are actually stone fossils of trees from millions of years ago. The trees were covered with mud and died. As the wood slowly decayed, water carrying minerals seeped in and hardened in the shape of the trees.

Molasses Sauce

Ingredients:
2 cups molasses
1 cup butter
4 tsps vinegar
1 cup water

Directions:
Mix ingredients in a saucepan and cook until mixture boils up. Serve hot or cold.

SPICE OF LIFE
There is no fool like an old fool. If you don't believe this, then ask any young fool.

Dedicated to my mother, **Alma May Hardy (nee Bungay)** and my father, the late **Thomas James Hardy**. Thanks for being my teacher, my chauffeur, my doctor, my banker, my mentor and counsellor, to name just a few. Most of all thanks for all the love, and support, that has helped me become the person I am today.
Maria (Hardy) Young

Casseroles

Chicken

Beef

Fish

Bologna

Turkey

Liver

Wiener

Vegetarian

Vegetable Casserole

Cathy Gale, Doyles, Newfoundland

Ingredients:

1 bunch fresh broccoli (cooked)
2 tins small onions (or fresh grown)
2 tins baby carrots
2 tins cream of mushroom soup (undiluted)
cheddar cheese (old)

Directions:

Combine vegetables in 9 x 12 inch pan. Pour over soup. Grate old cheese on top. Bake at 350°F for 30 minutes.

SPICE OF LIFE
It may be true that men would live longer if they avoided drink, smoke and women. But we'll never know until someone tries it.

Myrtle's Chicken Casserole

Myrte Sturge, Gambo, Newfoundland

Ingredients:

1 chicken
1 chopped onion
3 tbsp butter
2 tbsp flour
1 & 1/4 cup milk
salt
pepper
3/4 cup bread crumbs
1 tsp mixed herbs
tomato pieces

Directions:

TRIVIA TIDBITS
During the 1890's, wealthy "Diamond Jim" Brady of New York, bought his favourite actress, Lillian Russell, a specially built bicycle which was gold-plated and studded all over with diamond chips. The cycle's spokes and hubs were set with diamonds, emeralds, rubies and sapphires, and the handle bars were mother-of-pearl.

Boil chicken till tender. Remove from bones. Fry onion until golden brown in butter. Add flour, pour in milk and stir until sauce thickens. Season with salt and pepper. Put chicken in casserole dish. Stir in sauce. Cover with 3/4 cup breadcrumbs and 1 tsp mixed herbs. Garnish with tomato pieces. Bake 160°C for 15-20 minutes.

Quick Cauliflower Casserole

Jody M. Walters, Robinsons, Newfoundland

Ingredients:

1 bunch fresh cauliflower, trimmed
1 head fresh broccoli, trimmed
1 cup shredded cheddar cheese
2 medium onions, chopped
2 tbsp butter or margarine

FOOD FOR THOUGHT
There's a mighty big difference between good, sound reason and reasons that sound good.
-Burton Hillis

This page is dedicated to our parents
Neta (nee Roberts) and **Douglas Dove**
in Twillingate, Newfoundland.
We love you Mom and Dad!
... *Linda and Sandra*

1 can (28oz) tomatoes, drained
2 tbsp sugar
dash of salt
dash of pepper
2 tbsp parsley, chopped fine
3 tbsp bread crumbs

Directions:

Cook broccoli for 7 minutes and cauliflower for 5 minutes in boiling water. Remove, drain and toss with 3/4 cup cheddar cheese. Saute onions in butter; add remaining ingredients and simmer for 5 minutes. Butter a shallow baking dish and add a layer of sauce, then a layer of vegetables. Top with remaining sauce and cheese. Bake uncovered for 30 minutes at 350°F. Serves 8 to 10 people.

> ### FOOD FOR THOUGHT
> You cannot help men permanently by doing for them what they could and should do for themselves.
> -Abraham Lincoln

Lavina's Chicken Casserole

Lavina Keeping, Port Aux Basques, Newfoundland, (nee Coombs)

Ingredients:

2 - 10oz pkgs broccoli
2 cups cooked sliced chicken (or turkey) (use more meat if desired)
2 cans cream of chicken soup
1 cup mayonnaise
1 tsp lemon juice
1/2 tsp curry powder
1/2 cup grated cheese
1/2 cup buttered bread crumbs

> ### TRIVIA TIDBITS
> On the advice of his doctors, Robert Burns once stood in the Solway Firth up to his armpits. He died shortly thereafter.

Directions:

Cook broccoli as directed and put in bottom of greased baking dish. Cover broccoli with chicken. Mix soup, mayonnaise, lemon juice and curry powder. Pour over chicken. Sprinkle cheese on last and top with bread crumbs. Bake 30 minutes at 350°F. Serves 8-10 people.

Newfoundlander Bologna Casserole

Rosella Rowe, Avondale, Conception Bay, Newfoundland, (nee Moore)

Ingredients:

4oz elbow macaroni
1 onion, chopped
1 green pepper, chopped
1 cup mushrooms, sliced
1 tbsp butter or margarine
1 lb bologna, cubed
1 can Cream of Mushroom soup
1/2 cup cheddar cheese, shredded

> ### SPICE OF LIFE
> It takes a magician to get rabbits out of a hat, but anyone can let the cat out of the bag.

Directions:

Preheat oven to 400°F. Cook macaroni and drain excess water. In a large skillet, saute onion, green pepper and mushrooms in butter until onion is tender. Stir in bologna, macaroni and remaining ingredients. Cover and bake for 30 minutes.

Fish, Beef, Chicken, Bologna, Turkey, Liver & Vegetarian

Casseroles

Casserole of Liver & Onions

Lilly M. Faseruk, Toronto, Ontario, (nee Barnes, Harbour Main, Fortune, Newfoundland)

Ingredients:

1 lb calf's liver

1oz all-purpose flour

1 tsp dry mustard

2 medium cooking apples

2 medium onions

4 rashers bacon

salt to taste

pepper to taste

1 cup water or stock

TRIVIA TIDBITS

J. Edgar Hoover, director of the FBI, hated communism and other left-wing political movements so much that he once ordered his chauffeur to drive all the way from Dallas to Austin without taking any left-turns.

Directions:

Cut liver into bite-size pieces. Mix flour, mustard, salt and pepper together. Coat pieces of liver. Brown liver lightly in frying pan with small amount of oil. Fill a greased casserole dish with alternate layers of liver, sliced cored apples and onions, the top with bacon rashers. Add water or stock (or red wine if feeling generous). Cover casserole and bake in preheated oven 350°F for 1 and 1/2 hours. Remove lid and cook a further 15 to 20 minutes. Serve with creamed potatoes and vegetable of your choice.

Celeste's Corned Beef Casserole

Celeste Gilsdorf, Toledo, Ohio (nee Barbour, Lethbridge, B. Bay, Newfoundland)

Ingredients:

8oz pkg egg noodles

2 tbsp margarine

1 med size onion, chopped

1 stalk of celery, cleaned & chopped

1 can (12oz) corned beef

1 can (10oz) condensed cream of chicken soup

1 can (10oz) condensed cheddar cheese soup

1 pkg (small) slivered almonds

4oz cheddar cheese, shredded

FOOD FOR THOUGHT

To learn something new, take the same path that you took yesterday.

-John Burroughs

Directions:

Cook noodles in water for 8-10 minutes. Drain. Melt margarine in frying pan. Fry chopped onion and celery; then add corned beef. Add soups and drained noodles. Mix. Pour mixture into baking dish. Bake 30-40 minutes at 350°F. Add almonds and shredded cheddar cheese to the top when almost done. Just long enough for cheese to melt.

Dedicated to

Rev. Alex and Mrs. Maisie Smith (nee Penney),

Musgravetown, Newfoundland.

By son Ed, daughter Pat and families, and great-granddaughter, Sami.

Hash Brown Casserole

Jenny & Josie, Richmond Hill, Ontario (nee Clarke, Port Rexton, Newfoundland)

Ingredients:

2lb bag hashbrowns (thawed)
1/2 - 1 cup onion, chopped
2 cups sour cream
2 cans mushroom soup
2 cups cheddar cheese, grated
1/2 cup butter, melted
Parmesan cheese

> **FOOD FOR THOUGHT**
> He who says what he likes, hears what he does not like.
> -Leonard L. Levinson

Directions:

Put in a large, greased, casserole dish. Sprinkle with parmesan cheese on top. Bake 350°F for 1 & 1/2 hours.

Meat and Potato Casserole

Ingredients:

1 & 1/2 - 2 lbs pork shoulder chops or steaks
2 tbsp flour
1 tsp salt
1/4 tsp pepper
1/4 tsp sage or 1/2 tsp. savory
6 to 8 medium potatoes
Hot milk

> **TRIVIA TIDBITS**
> Years ago the island of Cyprus was famous for its copper mines.
> It got its name from "kypros", the Greek word for copper.

Directions:

Trim off the excess fat and melt it in an enamel cast iron casserole. Pound the chops or steaks to flatten them slightly. Roll them in a mixture of the flour, salt, pepper, sage or savory until well-coated, then brown in the melted fat. Peel and halve the potatoes and place them around the meat. Pour enough hot milk on top to cover the potatoes. Bake for 50-60 minutes at 350°F.

Creamed Turkey Noodle Casserole

Ingredients:

6 oz broad noodles
1 & 1/2 cups onion, chopped
2 cups celery, chopped
2 tbsp butter or margarine
4 cups cooked turkey, packed down
10oz condensed cream of mushroom soup
10oz condensed cream of chicken soup
10oz mushrooms, sliced & drained
1 tsp salt
1/4 tsp pepper

> **SPICE OF LIFE**
> You know you've been married too long when it's the dog who brings you the paper and your wife who barks.

Directions:

Cook noodles according to package and drain. Put onion, celery and butter in frying pan. Saute until limp. Add to noodles. Add turkey, mushroom soup, chicken soup, mushrooms, salt and pepper. Stir. Pour into large casserole. Bake uncovered in 350°F (180°C) oven for 35 minutes until bubbly hot. Serves 6-8.

Wiener Casserole

Ingredients:

2-3 potatoes, thinly sliced
1 onion, thinly sliced
2-3 carrots, thinly sliced
1/4 cup long-grain rice, raw
1 cup peas, frozen or fresh
1 lb wieners
1 - 10oz can condensed tomato soup
1 - 10oz can water

Directions:

Arrange layers in order given in 2-quart (2L) casserole. Put wieners on top. Combine soup with water. Pour over top of wieners. Cover. Bake 2 hours in 350°F (180°C) oven until vegetables are tender. Serves 4.

TRIVIA TIDBITS
Louis XII of France had his marriage to Queen Jeanne annulled because "she was excessively ugly".

Cabbage Casserole

Angela Waterman, (nee John) Glenwood, Newfoundland

Ingredients:

1 medium onion, chopped
3 tbsp butter
1/2 lb gound beef
1 tsp salt
1/8 tsp pepper
6 cups cabbage, chopped
1 can tomato soup

Directions:

Saute meat and onion. Place 3 cups cabbage in 2 quart casserole. Cover with meat mixture. Top with remaining cabbage. Pour soup over top. Bake 350°F for 1 hour.

FOOD FOR THOUGHT
A lot of the doing of a thing has to do with the feeling that you can do it.
-Clifton Burke

Steak Casserole

Reta Atkinson, Guelph, Ontario

Ingredients:

1 lb minced steak
1 onion, cut fine
1 cup celery, chopped
1 tin peas and carrots, drained
2 tins mushroom soup
1/2 cup milk
1 sm bag potato chips, crushed

SPICE OF LIFE
A man's hair will be white as long as he lives. A woman's will be black as long as she dyes.

This page is dedicated to the memory of my devoted parents
Edgar and Astella (Best) Hollett of Arnold's Cove, Placentia Bay, Newfoundland. You both will live for generations to come in the memories of your children, grandchildren and their children.
Phyllis Labelle, Lynden, Ontario

Directions:
Cook steak and onions in a little fat until brown and cooked. Mix soup with milk and heat. In a 1 & 1/2 quart casserole, place alternate layers of meat, peas and carrots, and celery until there are two layers of each. Pour soup over top and cover with crushed potato chips. Bake in 350°F oven for 20 minutes. Serve immediately.

Tuna or Shrimp Cashew Casserole

Reta Atkinson, Guelph, Ontario

Ingredients:
1-3oz jar chow mein noodles
1 can condensed cream of mushroom soup, undiluted
1/4 cup water
1 cup chunk style tuna (or see pg. 235 for Shrimp amount)
1/4 lb cashew nuts, salted or unsalted
1 cup celery, finely diced
1/4 cup onions, minced
dash pepper
salt to taste

Directions:
Set aside 1/2 cup of chow mein noodles. In a 1 & 1/2 quart casserole, combine rest of noodles with soup, water, tuna, nuts, celery, onions, and pepper. Taste, and add salt if nuts were unsalted. Sprinkle reserved noodles over top. Bake 40 minutes in 325°F oven. Makes 5 servings.

Tuna Noodle Casserole

Reta Atkinson, Guelph, Ontario

Ingredients:
4 cups cooked noodles
1-7oz tin tuna
1 can cream of mushroom soup, undiluted
1 tsp salt
1 tbsp onion, grated
2 tbsp pimento
1/2 cup milk

TRIVIA TIDBITS
Before the London Metropolitan police started using whistles in 1870, they used to shake wooden rattles to raise the alarm.

Directions:
Combine all ingredients. Mix with a fork until blended. Place in buttered casserole. Bake in 350°F oven for 50-60 minutes. Serves 6 to 8 persons.

Potato Casserole

Ingredients:
2 lb (1 kg) frozen hash browns
1 pt (500 ml) sour cream
1 can cream of mushroom soup
1 cup finely chopped onion
1/4 lb melted butter or margarine
8oz cheddar cheese, shredded

salt
pepper
potato chips (crushed), for topping

Directions:
Make sure hash browns are nearly thawed. Mix together all ingredients, except potato chips. Bake in a 9x13 inch (or larger) pan for 1 hour at 350°F after topping casserole with crushed potato chips. Makes 12 servings.

Veggie Meat Casserole

Ingredients:

1 - 1 & 1/2 lbs hamburger meat
2 cups veg marrow or squash (chopped)
1 lg onion (chopped)
1 med green pepper (chopped)
pinch of garlic
1 can stewed tomatoes
cheese (grated)
1 cup celery (sliced)
salt to taste
pepper to taste

Directions:
Saute in butter - vegetable marrow (or squash), onions, green pepper, celery, garlic, salt and pepper. Fry hamburger meat in separate pan. Drain fat, add tin of stewed tomatoes. Add to first mixture, then add cheese to top. Cook in oven until cheese melts.

Fish Casserole

Ingredients:

2 cups cooked cod or haddock
1 & 1/2 cups white sauce
2 tbsp margarine
4 hard cooked eggs
4 med sized cooked potatoes (sliced)
1/2 cup bread crumbs (day old)

Directions:
Bone and flake fish and place half of it in bottom of a margarine coated casserole dish. Slice eggs and lay over fish. Cover with half of the white sauce. Cover with half of the potatoes (sliced). Repeat these layers again. Melt margarine and add crumbs. Sprinkle over top of casserole. Bake in moderate hot oven at 400°F about 20 minutes. Serves 6-8.

In memory of **Edward G. Keough** 1917-1982, born in St. John's, Newfoundland. Oh! That every child should have such a loving, patient and wonderful father. *"To live in hearts we leave behind is not to die"* (Campbell - Hallowed Ground) *Elizabeth (Bish) Clarke, North Sydney, Nova Scotia*

Macaroni Casserole

Ingredients:
1 can mushrooms (pieces)
1 pkg hamburger meat
1 can tomatoes (whole)
1 onion (diced)
1 can meat sauce
2 cups macaroni

SPICE OF LIFE
Travelling on credit is nothing new - Columbus went on a very long tour on borrowed money.

Directions:
Fry meat and onions; drain off existing fat; add remainder of ingredients and simmer in frying pan for approximately 1 hour. Boil macaroni and add to other ingredients, mixing thoroughly. Place in casserole dish and bake at 350°F for 1 hour.

Green Rice Casserole

Ingredients:
3 cups cooked rice
1/4 cup butter (or margarine) melted
1 tbsp soy sauce
1 tbsp white wine vinegar
1 tsp dry thyme leaves
1 tsp molasses
1-10oz pkg frozen chopped spinach, thawed
1/4 cup chopped green onion, include tops
3 cups (3/4 lbs) shredded cheddar cheese
4 eggs
1 cup milk

TRIVIA TIDBITS
Nottingham General Hospital in Nottingham, England used 12,300 leeches to bleed people in 1929.

FOOD FOR THOUGHT
Don't judge each day by the harvest you reap, but by the seeds you plant. -
Robert Louis Stevenson

Directions:
To cook rice: Bring 2 cups water to a boil in a 3-quart pan on high heat. Stir in 1/2 tsp salt and 1 cup long-grain rice. Bring to a vigorous boil, then reduce heat to lowest setting. Cover pan and let simmer for 25 to 30 minutes until liquid is absorbed and rice is soft. Fluff rice with a fork. Preparation: You can use leftover rice, if desired. To rice add melted butter, soy sauce, vinegar, thyme, molasses and pepper. Squeeze small handfuls of spinach at a time to wring out excess water. Add soinach to rice along with onion, cheese, eggs and milk. Mix well. Spoon mixture into a deep-sided 2-to 2 & 1/2 quart baking dish. Bake at 300°F for 50 to 60 minutes until center no longer appears to be liquid. Garnish with sliced pepper or tomatoes. Serve hot.

Turnip Casserole

Dorothy Troop, Annapolis County, Nova Scotia, (formerly of Bay de Verde, Conception Bay, Newfoundland)

Ingredients:
4 cups cooked turnip
1 tbsp butter
1 & 1/2 cups apple
1/3 cup flour
1/3 cup brown sugar
2 tbsp butter
1/4 cup brown sugar
pinch of cinnamon

TRIVIA TIDBITS
Barbers in Victorian times would also clean customer's teeth as part of their service.

Directions:
Mash cooked turnip with 1 tbsp butter; slice and pare apple. Layer turnip and apple. Top with flour, 1/3 cup brown sugar and 2 tbsp butter. Sprinkle with 1/4 cup brown sugar mixed with pinch of cinnamon.

Casseroles

Fish, Beef, Chicken, Bologna, Turkey, Liver & Vegetarian

Marion's Baked Macaroni & Cheese

Marion Nagle, Kitchener, Ontario, (nee Daniels, Twillingate, Newfoundland)

Ingredients:

3 tbsp butter

3 tbsp flour

1 tsp salt

1/2 tsp pepper

3 cups milk

1 & 1/2 cups (or more) grated cheese

1/2 tsp prepared mustard

2 cups macaroni, cooked

1/3 cup buttered breadcrumbs

1/4 cup grated cheese

Directions:

Melt butter and blend in flour and seasonings. Add milk and cook, stirring constantly until thickened. Remove from heat and add 1 & 1/2 cups cheese, and mustard. Stir until smooth. Cook macaroni; drain. Add sauce and pour into 2-qt baking dish. Sprinkle top with bread crumbs and 1/4 cup cheese mixture. Bake at 400°F about 20 minutes.

Chicken Rice Casserole

Mary Russell, Brooklyn, Newfoundland

Ingredients:

2 & 1/2 cups cubed chicken

3 cups cooked rice

1 cup chopped celery

1 - 10oz can sliced water chestnuts

1 tsp minced onion

2/3 cup mayonnaise

1 can cream of chicken soup

1 cup chicken broth (from soup or cube)

1/2 cup slivered almonds (optional)

2 cups Corn Flakes

Directions:

Mix all ingredients together. Sprinkle crushed corn flakes over top. Bake 45 minutes at 350°F in an ovenproof casserole dish. Makes 8-10 servings.

This page is dedicated to my late husband
George Leonard Penney,
formerly of Salmon Cove, Newfoundland,
who passed away December 4, 1994.
- Rita

Charlene's Rice & Cauliflower Casserole

Charlene Jenkins, Etobicoke, Ontario (formerly of Springdale, Newfoundland)

Ingredients:

1 cup rice (white, brown, long or short-grain)
chicken or beef broth
2 tbsp butter or margarine
2 tbsp vegetable oil
1/2 cup onion, chopped
1/2 carrot, shredded
1/2 cup celery, minced
1 lg clove garlic, minced
1 sm head cauliflower
1 & 1/2 cups Swiss cheese, shredded
freshly ground pepper

SPICE OF LIFE
Another Mother's Day that's authentic but not authorized by law is the day school opens.

Directions:

Cook your favourite rice according to the package directions using chicken or beef broth or a combination. During this time, heat butter and oil in a heavy skillet. Saute the onion, carrot, celery and garlic for a few minutes. Cut cauliflower into bite-size "flowerets". Add to the skillet. Cover. Cook over low heat until cauliflowerets are just tender, about 15 minutes. Stir occasionally. When the rice is cooked, add a little broth so mixture is moist. In a 2-quart shallow baking dish, layer the rice, vegetable mixture and cheese. End with a sprinkling of cheese and pepper. Bake at 350°F for 20 minutes until mixture is heated and cheese melted. Serve hot.

Wanda's Chicken Casserole

Wanda Greenham, Twillingate, Newfoundland

Ingredients:

1 cup diced celery
1/2 cup chopped onion
1/4 cup green pepper
1 cup cooked chicken
1 tin mushroom soup
1 tin chicken soup
1 tin mushroom pieces
1 & 1/4 cup frozen peas and carrots
1 cup Chinese noodles

TRIVIA TIDBITS
It was so cold in the winter of 1925 that Niagara Falls was completely frozen?

Directions:

Saute first three ingredients in frying pan, then add rest of ingredients. Place 1/2 cup chinese noodles in bottom of casserole, then the above mixture and the other 1/2 noodles on top. Bake for 30 minutes at 350°F.

Neta's Corned Beef Casserole

Neta Dove, Twillingate, Newfoundland (nee Roberts)

Ingredients:

1/2 cup chopped onion
1/4 cup chopped green pepper

FOOD FOR THOUGHT
A failure is a man who has blundered but is not able to cash in on the experience.
-E. Hubbard

Casseroles

Fish, Beef, Chicken, Bologna, Turkey, Liver & Vegetarian

2 tbsp shortening

1 can corned beef, cut up

3/4 cup water

1 & 1/2 cups ketchup

1 pkg frozen peas, thawed

1 & 1/2 cups shell macaroni, cooked and drained

Directions:

Saute onion and green pepper in shortening in a skillet. Stir in remaining ingredients and put into a 2-qt casserole. Bake, covered, at 350°F for 30 minutes or until heated through. Makes 6 servings.

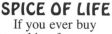

TRIVIA TIDBITS

The German physicist Wilhelm Konrad Roentgen, who discovered X-rays in 1895 refused to apply for any patents in connection with the discovery or to make any financial gain out of it. He won the Nobel Prize for his discovery, but sadly, died poor.

Catherine Irwin's Onion Quiche

Catherine Irwin, Truro, Nova Scotia

Pastry:

Ingredients:

1/3 lb lard

pinch of salt

1 & 1/2 cups flour

5 tbsp milk

Directions:

Heat oven to 450°F. Sift together dry ingredients in a large bowl. Cut in softened lard until mixture is crumbly. Add milk, stirring with fork. Roll out, place in 9 inch pie plate. Prick with fork. Cook for 10 minutes. Reduce heat to 400°F and cook until done. Remove and cool.

SPICE OF LIFE

If you ever buy something for a song, you may have to face the music later.

Filling:

Ingredients:

1 & 1/2 cups medium cheddar cheese, grated

1 rounded tbsp flour

1 large onion, diced

8-10 slices bacon

3 eggs, beaten

3/4 cup water

1/4 cup skim milk powder

1/2 tsp salt

few shakes pepper

FOOD FOR THOUGHT

Remember, no one can make you feel inferior without your consent.

-E. Roosevelt

Directions:

Mix 1 cup of cheese with flour and sprinkle on bottom of pie shell. Fry bacon, reserving bacon fat. Saute onion until transparent in bacon fat. Make a layer of onion followed by a layer of chopped bacon. Combine eggs, water, skim milk powder and seasonings. Pour into pie shell and

This page is dedicated to the memory of my loving parents, **Gordon Dawe** and **May Dawe (nee Heath)**, both formerly of St. John's, Newfoundland, who moved to Stephenville, Newfoundland in 1956, where they lived and worked until they were both called to be with the Lord in 1991.
June (Dawe) Lemieux, formerly of St. John's and Stephenville, Nfld

top with 1/2 cup cheese. Bake at 350°F for 30 minutes or until mixture is set. (If bacon is not the real lean kind, I usually cut off all the fat once it is removed from the pan.) Serve with a tossed salad for lunch or supper. Quiche can be frozen. Makes 4 or 6 small servings.

Babe's Chicken Stew Casserole

Catherine Irwin, Truro, Nova Scotia

Ingredients:

potatoes
onions
carrots
salt & pepper
slab of butter
6 tbsp water
'Shake and Bake' chicken flavour coating for the chicken
chicken breasts for the number you wish to serve

Directions:

Set oven at 400°F. Cut peeled potatoes into large thick slices. Place in bottom of well-greased and floured casserole dish. Now that this layer is complete, make a layer of thickly cut onions, then a layer of carrots that you've peeled and cut 3/4" diagonally (salt and pepper as you go). Repeat this process for as many times as dish will allow and also depending on number of people to be served. Keep in mind you have to leave room for the plump chicken breasts on top. Throw in a slab of butter on top of your last row. Coat chicken breasts with Shake and Bake. Lay breasts on top. Pour in 6 tbsp water. Cover. Place in oven for 1/2 hour at 400°F. Turn back to 350°F for remaining 1/2 hour. This dish steams all the way to the finishing line resulting in the juiciest chicken you've ever eaten!

Cheesy Turkey Casserole

Ingredients:

2 cups frozen green beans
4 tbsp butter or margarine
1/4 cup finely chopped onion
4 tbsp flour
1/2 tsp salt
1 & 1/2 cups milk
2 cups chopped, cooked turkey
2 hard-cooked eggs, chopped
1 cup shredded cheddar cheese
2 tbsp pimiento
1 tbsp chopped fresh parsley
1/2 cup herb croutons

Directions:

Preheat oven to 350°F. Butter a 1 & 1/2-quart casserole. Cook beans according to package directions; drain, reserving 1/2 cup cooking liquid. In a 2-quart saucepan, melt butter; saute onion. Stir in flour and salt until blended. Remove from heat; stir in milk and reserved 1/2 cup liquid. Bring to a boil, stirring constantly. Boil and stir 1 minute. Remove from heat; stir in turkey, eggs, cheese, pimiento, and parsley. Place beans in prepared casserole; cover with sauce. Sprinkle

Casseroles

Fish, Beef, Chicken, Bologna, Turkey, Liver & Vegetarian

croutons over top. Bake for 20 to 25 minutes. Makes 6 to 8 servings.

Heavenly Potatoes

Ina Belcher, Tonawanda, New York, (nee Brown, St. John's, Newfoundland)

Ingredients:

2 lbs frozen hash brown potatoes (thawed)
1 can cream of celery soup
1 can cream of potato soup
2 cups dairy sour cream
1/2 cup milk
1 cup chopped onion
1 cup cooked ham, diced
1 & 1/2 cups grated cheddar cheese
salt & pepper to taste

Directions:

In large bowl combine potatoes, undiluted soups, sour cream, milk and onion. Season with salt and pepper. Pour into rectangle baking dish (sprayed with Pam). Sprinkle with ham and cheese. Bake at 350°F for one hour.

> **TRIVIA TIDBITS**
> The world's first juke box was installed in San Francisco in 1889. It was not much of a success, as it could play only one record.

Easy Morning Wife Saver

June Gates, Woodstock, Ontario

Ingredients:

16 slices white bread, crusts removed
slices back bacon or ham
slices cheddar cheese
6 eggs
1/2 tsp salt
1/2 tsp pepper
1 tsp dry mustard
1/4 cup minced onion
1/4 lb butter
1/4 cup green pepper, finely chopped (optional)
1-2 tsp Worchestershire sauce
3 cups whole milk
Special K or crushed Corn Flakes

> Wyatt Earp, who has been made out to be a hero in the movies, was really a gangster who used his position as Deputy US Marshal to protect his saloon, gambling and other dubious interests.

Directions:

In a 9x13-inch buttered, glass baking dish, put 8 pieces of bread. Add pieces to cover the dish entirely. Cover the bread with slices of back bacon (or ham), cut thin. Lay slices of cheddar cheese on top of bacon, then cover with slices of bread to make it like a sandwich. In a bowl, beat eggs, salt and pepper. To the egg mixture add dry mustard, onion, green pepper,

This page is dedicated to our parents, **Captain Peter Troake** and **Hilda Troake** (nee Primmer), both born in Twillingate, Newfoundland and still living there. Thanks for always being there for us through the years.
- son Jack, daughters Elizabeth and Doreen.

Worcestershire sauce and milk. Pour over sandwiches. Cover and let stand in fridge overnight. In morning melt 1/4 cup butter. Pour over top. Cover with Special K or crushed Corn Flakes. Bake uncovered 1 hour at 350°F. Let sit 10 minutes before serving.

Mexican Cabbage

Margaret & Leonard Parsons, Admirals Beach, St. Mary's Bay, Newfoundland, (formerly of Clattice Harbour, Placentia Bay, Newfoundland)

Ingredients:
2 cups cabbage, chopped
1 tin Chicken with Rice soup
3 medium potatoes
1 onion
1/2 cup uncooked rice
1/2 lb ground beef
paprika
salt to taste
pepper to taste

Directions:
Chop onion and fry with ground beef. Place a layer of cabbage in greased casserole dish, add layer of ground beef and onions, rice and potatoes. Repeat, and pour on chicken with rice soup. Sprinkle top with paprika and bake for one hour in 350°F oven, preheated.

SPICE OF LIFE
A married man who's having an affair not only learns to dress well but quickly.

Betina's Scalloped Potatoes

Betina Wheeler-Ali, Toronto, Ontario (formerly of St. John's, Newfoundland)

Ingredients:
4 cups raw potatoes, thinly sliced
3 tbsp flour
1 & 1/2 cups milk
1 tsp salt
2 lg onions, sliced thin
dash of pepper
3 tbsp margarine

FOOD FOR THOUGHT
Money in the bank is a bit like toothpaste - easy to take out but harder to put back in!

Directions:
Peel potatoes. Cut in thin slices. Cover with boiling water, cover tightly.
Let stand until cool. Combine margarine with flour, salt, and pepper in saucepan. Let bubble for 3 minutes.
Add milk slowly. Cook and stir until thick and smooth.
Remove from heat. Fill an oiled, 2-quart baking dish with alternate layers of sliced potatoes, sliced onions and cream sauce. Bake for 1 hour and 15 minutes. Serves 6.

Casseroles

Fish, Beef, Chicken, Bologna, Turkey, Liver & Vegetarian

Ham and Potato Scallop

Submitted by the children of Joyce Noseworthy

Ingredients:

6 medium potatoes
1 cup diced cooked ham (substitute any other cooked meat)
2 sliced onions
salt
pepper
2 cups thin white sauce (see recipe below)

Directions:

Slice potatoes and cook in boiling salted water 10 minutes. Arrange a layer of potatoes in a greased casserole dish, then layer of ham and a layer of sliced onion. Sprinkle with salt and pepper. Continue to arrange in layers making final layer of potatoes. Pour hot sauce over top. Bake in 325°F oven about 45 minutes.

Thin Sauce for Ham and Potato Scallop

Ingredients:

1 tbsp butter
1 tbsp flour
1 cup milk

Directions:

Blend butter and flour. Scald milk in top of double boiler. Pour milk slowly over mixture and stir until smooth. Season as desired. Stir and cook until thickened.

Cheese Hash Browns

Vernie Warren, Gander, Newfoundland (nee James)

Ingredients:

1 pkg (750g) frozen hash browns
1 - 500g container sour cream
1 lg tin mushroom soup
1 & 1/2 cups grated cheese
1 onion, minced

Directions:

Mix all ingredients together and pour into greased 9x13x2 inch pan. Bake at 350°F for 45 minutes.

Charlene's Cabbage Casserole

Charlene Jenkins, Etobicoke, Ontario (formerly of Springdale, Newfoundland)

Ingredients:

1 lb lean ground beef
1 med onion, chopped

A dedication to **Joyce Noseworthy** (nee Skanes) of Mount Pearl, Newfoundland, a wonderful, caring person; the backbone of this family.
"Life feels empty without you. We all love and miss you. Forever cherished by husband Gerry; children Gerry, Debbie and husband Dan, Rick, Dave and wife Carol; 6 grandchildren; brother Charlie, and everyone whose lives you touched."

Casseroles — Fish, Beef, Chicken, Bologna, Turkey, Liver & Vegetarian

2 tbsp butter or margarine
1 cup finely shredded carrots
3 cups finely shredded cabbage
1 tsp salt
dash black pepper
1 jar (16oz) herb-style spaghetti sauce
1 tbsp Worcestershire sauce
1 tbsp chopped chives
1/2 cup grated cheddar cheese

FOOD FOR THOUGHT
True wisdom consists of knowing how to make a point without making an enemy.

Directions:
In medium skillet, saute onion in butter until soft, but not brown. Add ground beef. Cook, breaking up the meat until meat loses its pink colour. In a 2-qt buttered casserole or baking dish, layer the carrots and half the cabbage. Sprinkle with salt and pepper. Add meat mixture, press down slightly. Add remaining cabbage. To spaghetti sauce, add Worcestershire sauce and chives. Pour sauce over top of casserole. Cover and bake at 350°F for about 1 hour or until cabbage is soft and meat is cooked through. Add cheese on top. Bake uncovered for another 5 to 8 minutes until cheese is melted. Serve immediately.

Corn Beef Quiche

Arlene Gibbons, Stoney Creek, Ontario, (nee Sherard, Point Verde, Placentia Bay, Newfoundland)

Ingredients:
9-inch pie shell
1 can corn beef
1 sm onion
1 cup swiss cheese, shredded
2 tbsp flour
1/4 tsp salt
2 eggs
1 cup milk

TRIVIA TIDBITS
In 1829, when the American sisters, Deborah and Susan Tripp, were only three and five years old, they weighed 124 and 205 pounds, respectively.

Directions:
Prebake pie shell until lightly browned. Crumble corn beef on top of pie shell. Sprinkle onion and cheese on top of beef. Combine remaining ingredients in a bowl and mix well. Pour over top of pie mixture and bake at 350°F for 30-40 minutes until top has settled. Enjoy! Feeds 4-6 people.

Easy Broccoli Quiche

Ingredients:
1 & 1/2 cups Ritz crackers, (any flavour) crushed
1/4 cup butter or margarine, melted
4 eggs, lightly beaten
2/3 cup milk
1 & 1/2 cups cooked broccoli, chopped
1 & 1/2 cups old cheddar cheese, grated
1/2 tsp salt
1/2 tsp pepper
1 tomato, sliced thin

SPICE OF LIFE
The only reason some people are lost in thought is that they're total strangers there.

Casseroles

Fish, Beef, Chicken, Bologna, Turkey, Liver & Vegetarian

Directions:

Heat oven to 350°F. Combine cracker crumbs and melted butter. Press crushed crackers onto bottom and up sides of a 9" pie plate. Bake for 10 minutes. Combine eggs, milk, broccoli, 1 cup of the cheese, salt and pepper. Pour into crust. Place tomato slices on top and sprinkle with remaining cheese. Bake for 30 minutes. Serves 4.

Cabbage Rolls

Mrs. Elsie Fitzgerald, Cambridge, Ontario (nee Clarke, Bell Island, Newfoundland)

Ingredients:

1/2 cup minute rice

1 egg

1/4 cup onion, finely chopped

pepper, sprinkle

garlic, sprinkle

1/2 cup milk

> **FOOD FOR THOUGHT**
> A man has to live by himself, and he should see to it that he always has good company.
> -C.E. Hughes

Directions:

Mix above ingredients and set aside. Cut core from cabbage, boil or steam. Take off leaves, cut back vein and roll.

Sauce for Cabbage Rolls

Ingredients:

1 can tomato soup

1/2 cup water

1 bay leaf

2 tbsp brown sugar

2 tbsp margarine

4 whole cloves

> **TRIVIA TIDBITS**
> In 1632, two gallons of beer were included in the weekly ration for each child in the children's hospital in Norwich, England.

Directions:

Place cabbage rolls in roaster, pour sauce over the rolls. Bake for approximately 2 hours at 325°-350°F heat.

Turnip Puff

Judy Wells, Don Mills, Ontario, (nee Green, Bonavista, Newfoundland)

Ingredients:

6 cups cooked turnip

2 tbsp butter or olive oil

2 eggs, beaten

3 tbsp flour

1 tbsp brown sugar

1 tsp baking powder

3/4 tsp salt

1/8 tsp pepper

pinch of nutmeg

1/2 cup dry bread or cracker crumbs

2 tbsp melted butter (or olive oil)

> **SPICE OF LIFE**
> Some men like a woman who shows style, but most prefer styles that show a woman.

Directions:

Grease 1 & 1/2 quart casserole. Cook turnip, drain and mash. Add 2 tbsp butter (or olive oil) and

eggs; beat well. Combine all other ingredients except last two (bread or cracker crumbs and butter or oil) and stir into turnip. Put in casserole. Mix oil/butter and crumbs and sprinkle over top. May be stored in fridge up to three days or frozen. Bake 25 minutes until puffy and golden brown.

Shipwreck

Ingredients:
1 lb hamburger meat
1 tsp salt
4 potatoes, cut like fries
1 cup chopped celery
1 onion, finely cut
1-10oz can tomato soup
1-19oz can red kidney beans

Directions:
Fry hamburger meat until brown. Saute onion and celery with salt. Butter a 2 quart casserole. Place alternate layers of hamburger, potato and kidney beans. Pour tomato soup over top and dot with butter. Bake at 350°F for 1 hour. Economical and delicious. Make 4 servings.

> **TRIVIA TIDBITS**
> Henry Ford once attended a convention dressed in clothes which had been produced from soya beans to promote their use.

Cabbage Roll Casserole

Ruth Keats, Mississauga, Ontario

Ingredients:
1/4 cup salt pork or bacon, finely diced
1 & 1/2 lb ground chuck (or 1/2 pork & 1/2 beef)
1 & 1/2 cups uncooked rice
2 onions, diced
salt, to taste
pepper, to taste
garlic, to taste
1 med cabbage, coarsely shredded
2 tins tomato soup, mixed with 1 & 1/2 cups water
(or substitute with 2 small bottles Ragu spaghetti sauce)

Directions:
Render salt pork and set aside. Cook rice (according to directions on box). Brown meat and onions - season to taste. Mix together. Grease large casserole dish. Cover bottom with 1/3 cabbage; sprinkle with salt. Add half meat mixture. Pour 1/3 tomato soup over top. Place another layer of cabbage, sprinkle with salt; add rest of meat mixture, then cabbage and rest of tomato soup. Cover with foil and bake at 350°F for about 1 & 1/2 hours.

> **SPICE OF LIFE**
> A diet is when you have to go to some length to change your width.

Macaroni & Cheese Casserole

Ruth Keats, Mississauga, Ontario

Ingredients:
3/4 lb Italian sausage, hot or sweet (or ground beef)
1/4 cup onion, chopped
1/4 cup green pepper, chopped

> **FOOD FOR THOUGHT**
> The time man spend in trying to impress others, they could spend in doing the things by which others would be impressed.
> -Frank Homer

Casseroles

Fish, Beef, Chicken, Bologna, Turkey, Liver & Vegetarian

1 clove garlic, minced
1 can (1 lb) tomatoes, broken up
1/3 cup water
3/4 tsp dried oregano leaves
1/2 tsp dried basil leaves
1/4 tsp salt
1/4 tsp pepper
1/2 cup spaghetti, broken
3/4 cup Mozzarella cheese
1/4 cup Parmesan cheese

Directions:

Remove sausage from casing. Brown meat in a 9- or 10-inch iron skillet (or any oven-safe skillet). Drain all but 1 tablespoon fat. Stir in onion, green pepper and garlic. Saute 5 minutes. Stir in tomatoes, water, oregano, basil, salt, pepper and spaghetti. Stir to combine. Push spaghetti down into liquid. Cover tightly with foil. Bake at 375°F for 30 minutes or until spaghetti is tender. Cover with Mozzarella and Parmesan cheese. Leave uncovered. Bake 5 minutes more until cheese is melted. Serve right from the skillet or transfer to serving dish. Serve hot.

Seven Layer Dinner

Stella Ash, Portland, Newfoundland (nee Ralph, Winter Brook, Newfoundland)

Ingredients:

1 layer sliced raw potatoes
1 layer sliced raw carrots
1 layer hamburger meat
1 layer onion, sliced or chopped
1 layer corn (or green peas)
1 thin layer uncooked dainty rice
1 can tomato soup, undiluted

Directions:

Place layers accordingly in casserole dish. Pour 1 can undiluted tomato soup over top. Cover and bake at 350°F for one hour or until potatoes and carrots are done.

Beef & Rice Casserole

Ingredients:

1/2 lb bacon slices
2 lbs boneless beef chuck
2 onions, peeled & sliced
3/4 cup uncooked rice
1 cup dry red wine
1 & 1/2 cups beef consomme
1 clove garlic, crushed
1 sprig fresh or 1/2 tsp dried thyme
1 tsp parsley, chopped
1/4 tsp saffron
1 cup fresh tomatoes, chopped
1/2 cup grated Parmesan cheeses

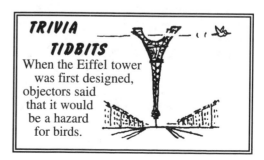

Directions:

Preheat oven to 325°F. Cut bacon into strips; fry in skillet until crisp. Remove to large casserole. Cut meat into cubes; brown in bacon fat. Transfer to casserole, using slotted spoon. Add onions and rice to remaining fat. Stir until rice begins to turn colour; set aside. Put wine, consomme, garlic, thyme, parsley, and saffron into casserole. Cover; cook 1 hour. Remove casserole from oven. Skim off excess fat; stir in rice-and-onion mixture and tomatoes; cover. Return to oven another hour; check occasionally to see if extra liquid is required. Before serving, adjust seasoning and stir in cheese. Makes 4 or 5 servings.

Macaroni, Cheese and Tomato Casserole

Angela Waterman, Glenwood, Newfoundland (nee John)

Ingredients:

1 cup elbow macaroni
1 cup (19oz can) whole tomatoes
1/2 tsp basil (or dilweed)
1/2 tsp prepared mustard
pinch of freshly ground pepper
1 cup skim milk cheese, shredded
2 tbsp Corn Flakes, crushed

SPICE OF LIFE
Marriage is like a bath: Once you've been in it a while, it's not so hot.

Directions:

Cook macaroni in lightly salted boiling water according to package directions; drain. Break up tomatoes in their juice; stir in basil, mustard, pepper, macaroni and cheese. Mix lightly together. Spoon into a 6-cup casserole dish. Sprinkle with cornflake crumbs. Bake in 350°F oven 30 minutes, or until crumbs brown and mixture is bubbly.

Barley Bake

Ruby Matthews, Mississauga, Ontario (nee Coates, Botwood, Newfoundland)

Ingredients:

3 & 1/2 cups boiling water
2 pkg beef bouillon powder
1 cup barley (pearl or pot)
1 cup onion, chopped
2 tsp parsley flakes
1/4 cup green onion, chopped
1/4 tsp pepper
pine nuts or slivered almonds, browned in 350°F oven for about 5 minutes, for garnish

FOOD FOR THOUGHT
Initiative is to success what a lighted match is to a candle.
-C.A. Battista.

Directions:

Stir the bouillon powder into water in a 2-quart casserole dish. Add the next five ingredients. Garnish with nuts. Cover and bake in a 350°F oven for about 1 & 1/2 hours. A nice change from potatoes or rice!

White Bean Casserole

Ingredients:

1 lb dried, white beans
2 tsp salt
1/2 cup salt pork, diced

FOOD FOR THOUGHT
What happens seldom bothers us half as much as what might happen.
-Oscar Wilde

Casseroles

Fish, Beef, Chicken, Bologna, Turkey, Liver & Vegetarian

1 & 1/2 cups cooked ham, diced
2 cups onion, chopped
1 & 1/2 cups carrots, diced
2 cups skinned tomatoes, diced
3 small cloves garlic, pressed
2 bay leaves
2 tbsp parsley, chopped
1/2 tsp oregano
1 freshly ground pepper
4 cups Basic ChickenStock (or 3-10 & 1/2 oz. cans chicken broth
1/2 lb hard salami, slivered
2 cups cooked dark chicken meat, diced
2 cups fine soft bread crumbs

Directions:
Rinse beans thoroughly in cold, running water. Place beans in large saucepan; add enough water to cover. Bring to boil; boil 2 minutes. Remove from heat; let stand 1 hour. Bring to boil again; stir in salt. Reduce heat; simmer 1 & 1/2 hours or until almost tender. Fry pork over low heat until golden. Stir in ham, onions, carrots and tomatoes. Add garlic, bay leaves, parsley, oregano and pepper; blend thoroughly. Stir in stock; bring to a boil. Reduce heat to low; simmer 30 minutes. Drain beans; place in a 4-quart casserole. Add salami and chicken. Pour sauce over all; stir to blend thoroughly. Bake, covered, in preheated oven 350°F oven 30 minutes; stir at 10-minute intervals. Sprinkle bread crumbs evenly over top; pat gently. Reduce oven temperature to 300°F. Bake 30 minutes or until crumbs are browned. Makes 8 to 10 servings.

Easy Weekend Chicken

Ingredients:
6 lg chicken breast, skinned & bone in
1 can cream of mushroom soup
250 ml whipping cream
butter
garlic-salt
paprika

TRIVIA TIDBITS
There's at least 11 million other people on earth that have the same birthday as you.

Directions:
Butter the bottom and sides of an oven-proof casserole dish. Remove skin and excess fat from chicken. Place in casserole dish and sprinkle with garlic salt and paprika. Mix together whipping cream and soup and pour over chicken. Bake uncovered in a 350°F oven for approximately 1 & 1/2 hours. This recipe holds well in a warm oven or can cook for a longer time in a slower oven while you are doing your Saturday shopping.

Breakfast Casserole

Ingredients:
1/2 lb sausage
4 eggs
1/4 cup milk
1 can cream of potato soup (or celery or mushroom)
1/2 pkg hash browns, frozen
salt, to taste
pepper, to taste
onion, to taste

Casseroles

Fish, Beef, Chicken, Bologna, Turkey, Liver & Vegetarian

cheddar cheese, grated
Directions:
Fry sausage, drain and cut into bite size pieces. Mix together eggs, milk and soup. Add this to the
hash browns and mix together. Add dash of salt, pepper and onion to taste. Grate cheddar cheese
over top of other ingredients. Bake at 350°F for 1/2 hour. Makes 4 adult servings.

Home-style Potato Casserole

Ingredients:
2 cups fresh potato, shredded
1 cup onion, finely chopped
1 cup fresh carrot, shredded
2 tbsp butter or margarine
1/2 tsp salt
1/4 tsp white pepper
1 & 1/2 cups whipping cream
chopped fresh basil or parsley, for garnish (optional)

SPICE OF LIFE
Junk is what you keep for years and throw away just days before you need it.

Directions:
In a buttered 1 & 1/2-quart casserole, layer the potatoes alternately with the onion and carrot. Dot
the layers with the butter and sprinkle with salt and pepper. Pour the cream over the final layer.
Smooth the top. Cover. Bake at 350°F for 45 minutes. Remove cover. Continue baking 15 minutes longer until top is just beginning to brown. Sprinkle with the fresh basil or parsley, if
desired. Serve immediately.

Meat Loaf Supreme

Ingredients:
1 & 1/2 lbs ground beef
1 beaten egg
3/4 cup milk
3/4 cup rolled oats
1 tbsp instant onion flakes
1 tsp parsley flakes
1 tsp Worcestershire sauce
1 & 1/2 tsp salt
1/4 tsp pepper
1 cup grated cheddar cheese
4 tbsp ketchup

TRIVIA TIDBITS
In eighteenth century England,
boxing matches sometimes lasted
as long as a hundred rounds.

Directions:
Put all ingredients except cheese and ketchup into a large bowl. Mix together well. Pack half into
loaf pan (9x5x3-inch). Spread grated cheese over meat. Put second half of mixture on top of
cheese and flatten down. Spread ketchup over top and bake in 350°F for 1 & 1/2 hours.
Serves 6 - 8 people.

Pork Casserole

Ingredients:
1 lb ground pork
1/2 cup chopped onion
1 - 14oz can tomatoes

SPICE OF LIFE
Often, father is more pleased to
have his child look like him than
act like him.

1 cup grated cheddar cheese
1 cup bread crumbs
2 cups cooked egg noodles
2 tbsp margarine
Directions:
Fry pork and onions in pan until pork is brown and drain fat. Add tomatoes and cheese and stir. Stir in cooked noodles. Pour into 1 & 1/2-quart casserole. Melt margarine in small saucepan. Add crumbs and stir until well mixed. Bake in uncovered casserole pan for 30 minutes (or until bread crumbs are brown) at 350°F. Serves 4.

Steak and Mushroom Supreme
Ingredients:
1/3 cup all-purpose flour
2 tsp salt
1/4 tsp pepper
1 tbsp dry mustard
2 lbs cubed sirloin steak
4 tbsp cooking oil
2 & 1/2 cups mushrooms, sliced
1 onion, diced
2 tbsp white wine, or apple cider
3 tbsp brown sugar
1 & 1/2 tbsp Worcestershire sauce
1 - 19oz can tomatoes
Directions:
Mix flour, salt, pepper and mustard together. Dampen meat and coat with flour mixture. Heat oil in frying pan and fry steak cubes until brown. Transfer to a 2-litre casserole and bake in 350°F oven for 1 & 1/2 hours until tender.

> **SPICE OF LIFE**
> Skippers Observations: If someone wrote a book on how to fail, and it failed in the bookstores - would it be considered a success?

Chili Con Carne
Ingredients:
2 lbs ground beef
2 onions, chopped
2 tbsp cooking oil
1 - 28oz can kidney beans
1 - 20oz can tomato soup (condensed)
1 tsp chili powder
2 tbsp sugar
2 tsp salt
1/4 tsp pepper
1 tsp Accent
2 cups water
Directions:
Heat the oil in a frying pan and saute onions. Add beef and continue frying until beef is brown. Transfer to large pot. Add beans, soup and water to large pot. Mix together. Sprinkle with chili powder, sugar, salt, pepper and Accent. Stir. Simmer for about 15 minutes, checking seasoning. Can be transferred to casserole to put in oven when needed, at 350°F. Serves 8.

> **FOOD FOR THOUGHT**
> Successful people are people who can think up things to keep the rest of the world busy.

Meats, Poultry & Game

Chicken

Beef

Pork

Bologna

Turkey

Seal

Venison

Wild Fowl

Chinese Pork Chops

Jody M. Walters, Robinsons, Newfoundland

Ingredients:

4 & 3/4-inch thick pork chops (1 & 1/2 lbs)
1 tbsp flour
1 tbsp oil
1/4 cup soya sauce
1/4 cup vinegar
1/2 tsp ginger
1/3 cup sugar
1/4 cup water

Directions:

Flour chops on both sides. Heat casserole dish on high for 5 minutes. Add oil; brown chops on both sides, cook for 5 minutes. Transfer to 9 x 11 glass baking dish. Cover with aluminum foil and cook on medium heat. Combine remaining ingredients and pour over chops. Reduce heat and cook 25 to 30 minutes until chops are tender. Serves 4.

FOOD FOR THOUGHT

Obstacles are those frightful things you see when you take your eyes off the goal.
-Hannah More

Sweet and Sour Spare Ribs

Jody M. Walters, Robinsons, Newfoundland

Ingredients:

3/4 cup chopped onion
1 cup ketchup
1 cup water
1 & 1/2 tsp dry mustard
1/4 cup brown sugar
1/4 cup vinegar

Directions:

Mix together and pour over browned spareribs. Heat for 10 minutes on high, reduce to low and cook for 20 to 25 minutes until ribs are tender. Conventional oven bake at 375°F for 1 hour.

FOOD FOR THOUGHT

It's as hard to admit that your enemy has many virtues as to admit that you have many faults.

The Butts' Chicken a la B-B-Q

Ingredients:

1 onion, chopped
1/2 green pepper, chopped
2 celery stalks, chopped
1/4 cup shortening, or margarine
3/4 cup ketchup
1 cup water
2 tbsp vinegar

SPICE OF LIFE

Skipper's Axioms - People specialize in their area of greatest weakness.

This page is dedicated to the memory of my parents, **Benjamin Butt** of Flatrock, Conception Bay, Newfoundland, and **Nellie P. Butt** (nee Clark) of Victoria, Conception Bay, Newfoundland.
Marie Martin (nee Butt), Madoc, Ontario

Meats, Poultry & Game

Beef, Pork, Chicken, Turkey, Bologna, Venison, Wild Fowl & Seal

2 tbsp sugar
1 tbsp mustard
2 tsp salt
1/4 tsp pepper
1 (4 lb) frying chicken, chopped up
10 potatoes, chopped into quarters

Directions:

Saute onion, green pepper and celery in hot fat until tender, but not browned. Add the next seven ingredients and simmer for 10 minutes. Arrange chicken and potatoes in 1 or 2 shallow bake pans close together in one layer. Drizzle with the sauce. Bake at 400°F for 20 minutes basting once or twice. Lower heat to 375°F and bake 30 to 40 minutes or until the chicken and potatoes are tender. Baste and turn if necessary, adding a little boiling water to prevent sticking. Serves 8.

> **SPICE OF LIFE**
> Skipper's Maxim - Those who are unable to learn from past meetings are condemned to repeat them.

Japanese Moose

Grace Ryan, Newmans Cove, Bonavista Bay, Newfoundland

Ingredients:
1 pkg moose meat
1 egg, beaten
1 cup flour
1 cup butter

Directions:

Cut moose meat into pieces and boil for 1/2 hour. Dip moose into beaten egg, roll in flour and fry in butter. Place moose into baking dish and add sauce.

> **SPICE OF LIFE**
> Skipper's Law - There is no such thing as instant experience.

Sauce for Japanese Moose

Grace Ryan, Newmans Cove, Bonavista Bay, Newfoundland

Ingredients:
3 tsp soya sauce
1/2 cup vinegar
1 cup white sugar
1 & 1/2 cups water
1/2 tsp salt

Directions:

Mix all ingredients together. Bake moose at 350°F for 1 hour, basting frequently.

> **TRIVIA TIDBITS**
> The average adult takes 14 breaths a minute, while infant babies take 33 breaths a minute.

Roast Pork with Garlic

Ina Belcher, Tonawanda, New York (nee Brown, St. John's, Newfoundland)

Ingredients:
1 pork loin
6 cloves garlic, crushed
1 tbsp olive oil
1 tbsp soy sauce
1 tsp dried basil
salt to taste
pepper to taste

> **FOOD FOR THOUGHT**
> Don't let the negative few over-rule the positive many.
> -Dr. Jim Parker

Directions:

In food processor (or small bowl) combine garlic, oil, soy sauce, basil, salt and pepper. With sharp knife, score the pork. Rub with seasoning mixture, all over. Place on a rack in a shallow pan. Roast at 325° about 2 & 1/2 to 3 hours.

Moose Stroganoff

Winnie Marshall, Stephenville, Newfoundland (nee Abbott, Port Au Bras, Placentia Bay, Newfoundland)

Ingredients:

1/4 lb salt pork
1 lg onion
2 celery stalks
1 sm green pepper
1 pt bottle moose meat
1 tin mushrooms and juice
2 cups rice
salt to taste
pepper to taste
Worcestershire sauce, to taste
flour

> ### TRIVIA TIDBITS
> Carolyn Farrell, a nun, of the Sisters of Charity of the Blessed Virgin Mary, ran for mayor in the city of Dubuque, Iowa and won. Carolyn was a feminist with liberal views, as well as an avid golfer, and in spite of papal warnings that Roman Catholic clergy had no place in politics, remained mayor for the full term. She is the only nun ever to be elected mayor of a major U.S. city.

Directions:

Cut pork in strips and fry out. Cut onion into quarters and slice. Cut celery in thin slices. Place onion and celery in pan and fry until tender. (Prepare rice as directed on package). Cut green pepper in quarter slices and place in pan. Put bottle moose in pan with equal amount of water. Add salt, pepper, Worcestershire sauce to taste, and stir in mushrooms with juice. Make flour thickening and add to mixture, stirring constantly. Serve over rice.

Sandra's Lasagna

Ingredients:

1 & 1/2 - 2 lbs lean ground beef
1 can mushroom pieces
1 bottle spaghetti sauce (thick & chunky style)
1 sm container cottage cheese
9 strips lasagna noodles
salt to taste
pepper to taste
1/4 cup onion, chopped (or substitute with onion powder)
sprinkle of parsley
Mozzarella cheese, grated
Parmesan cheese

> ## FOOD FOR THOUGHT
> If wishes were flowers, the world would be one big garden.

This page is dedicated to my sister and I,
and the special friendship we share.
"Although many miles separate us, we will always be close at heart"
Viola Luedee (left) of Codroy Valley, Newfoundland
Irene Luedee (right), formerly of Codroy Valley, Newfoundland

Directions:
Place ground beef in frying pan; add salt, pepper, parsley, and onion (or onion powder); fry until meat is cooked; add mushrooms, frying for a few minutes longer. In a separate pot, add lasagna noodles to water and boil until cooked. Rinse in cold water. In another deep pot or casserole dish, pour in spaghetti sauce, meat and mushroom mixture, and cottage cheese, stirring until well-mixed. In a deep lasagna dish, put a layer of meat mixture on bottom, just enough to cover bottom of dish. Then add 3 strips of lasagna noodles; another layer of meat sauce and spihnkle 3/4 of the Mozzarella cheese over top; add another layer of noodles, then top with remaining meat mixture. Sprinkle remaining Mozzarella cheese over top and then sprinkle with a little of parmesan cheese. Bake in 350°F oven for 20-30 minutes, or until cheese has completely melted and starts to turn brown and crispy around edge. Excellent served with caesar salad and garlic bread.

Polynesian Sausages

Vernie Warren, Gander, Newfoundland (nee James)

Ingredients:

1 lb pork sausages
1/2 medium green pepper, cut in strips
2 stalks celery, thinly sliced
1 sm onion, sliced
14oz can pineapple chunks
1/4 cup vinegar
1 tbsp soya sauce
2 tbsp cornstarch
1/4 cup brown sugar

TRIVIA TIDBITS

During one of his re-election campaigns, President Ford once said: "It's great to be in Texas," which it probably is, but he was in Oklahoma when he said it.

Directions:
In lightly greased pan, fry sausages over moderately low heat for 20-25 minutes or until lightly browned. Remove from pan, drain and keep warm. Drain off all but 2 tbsp fat from pan. Add green pepper, celery and onion. Saute vegetables until lightly brown. Drain pineapple chunks reserving juice. Add pineapple to vegetable mixture. Combine cornstarch and brown sugar. Mix in pineapple juice, vinegar and soya sauce. Slowly add to frying pan and cook, stirring constantly until thickened and clear. Serve over rice.

Garlic Spareribs

Mrs. Denise Brake, Penticton, British Columbia (nee Benoit, Stephenville, Newfoundland)

Ingredients:

1 cup brown sugar
2 tsp dry mustard
1 clove garlic, crushed
1/4 cup soya sauce
2 tbsp water

SPICE OF LIFE
Skipper's Definitions - An old-timer is a person who remembers when you got the landlord to repair something by threatening to move.

Directions:
Boil spareribs in salted water for 1 hour. Drain. Place in casserole dish. In saucepan, mix dry mustard, garlic, soya sauce and water. Boil for 1 minute, stirring constantly. Pour over ribs. Bake in 350°F oven for 1/2 hour, stir ribs and bake 1/2 hour more. Ribs should be covered with lid or foil.

Stir Fried Shredded Beef With Hot Sauce

Archie Ridout, Rexdale, Ontario (formerly of Twillingate, Newfoundland)

Ingredients:

1 lb beef, shredded
2 bamboo shoots, shredded
few dried black mushrooms
2oz green beans, shredded
1 onion, shredded
1/2 lb bean sprouts
4 slices ginger, shredded
4 cloves garlic, chopped
1 green onion, shredded
cooking wine
oil

To marinate beef:

1 tbsp soy sauce
1 tbsp cornstarch
1 tbsp cold water
1 tbsp oil
1 tbsp cooking wine
1/2 tsp sugar

Seasoning sauce:

2 tbsp hot bean paste
1 tbsp bean paste
2 tbsp ketchup
1 tbsp sugar
1 tbsp cornstarch

Directions:

Soak mushrooms in hot water until soft. Heat 1 tablespoon oil in wok; add some garlic, ginger and bean sprouts; stir fry for a few seconds. Heat 3 tbsp oil, add some ginger and garlic, also beef; stir fry for a few minutes, remove. Heat 2 tbsp oil, add rest of ginger and garlic, onion, mushrooms, green beans and cooking wine; stir fry for a few minutes. Add beef, bean sprouts, seasoning sauce; stir well and add green onions. Makes 4 servings.

SPICE OF LIFE
Skipper's Law - No matter what goes wrong, there is always somebody who knew it would.

FOOD FOR THOUGHT
Our opinion of ourselves, like our shadow, makes us either too big or too little.
-Benjamin Franklin

Meatloaf

Ingredients:

2 lbs ground beef
1 egg
1 tsp salt
1/2 tsp pepper

TRIVIA TIDBITS
The wife of Philip the fifth of Spain decided to surprise her husband by having artificial waterfalls and fountains built at his palace. Upon seeing the gift Philip remarked, "It has cost me three million and has amused me three minutes."

This page is dedicated to my grandparents,
Jonas Cooper of Twillingate, Newfoundland, who passed away in 1969
and **Alice Cooper (nee Lambert)**, who passed away on January 20, 1997.
"Thank you for the best summers any boy could have."
Your grandson, Ronnie Young

1/2 tsp Worcestershire sauce
1/2-1 cup onion, diced
2 cups breadcrumbs (or oatmeal)
1 tsp prepared mustard
1 tsp Bell's seasoning
1/2 cup spaghetti sauce with mushrooms
2-3 strips of bacon

Directions:

Mix together all ingredients, except bacon, and put in loaf pan. Place strips of bacon on top and pour spaghetti sauce over top. Bake in 350°F oven for approximately one hour.

> **TRIVIA TIDBITS**
> Franklin Delano Roosevelt's mother was so sure that her son would be a great man that she saved and marked his baby clothes, books and other items for posterity.

Meat Loaf and Potato Favourite

Dolores Lundrigan, Wabush, Labrador, (nee English, Branch, St. Mary's Bay, Newfoundland)

Ingredients:

2 lb ground beef, lean
1/2 cup oatmeal or bread crumbs
1/2 cup ketchup
pepper to taste
8 small potatoes, peeled
1 large bunch green onions, minced

> **FOOD FOR THOUGHT**
> As a man thinks in his heart, so is he.
> -Proverbs 23:7

Directions:

Mix ground beef, oatmeal, ketchup and pepper. Shape into a loaf. Place in a roasting pan with potatoes and green onions all around the loaf.

Sauce for loaf

Ingredients:

4 cups water
4 beef bouillon cubes
2 tbsp brown sugar
1 tbsp mustard
1 tsp garlic powder

> **SPICE OF LIFE**
> Skipper's Axioms - Complex problems have simple, easy-to-understand wrong answers.

Directions:

Mix all ingredients and pour over meatloaf. Bake at 350°F for 1 & 1/2 hours. Baste while cooking. Serve with tossed salad.

Chinese Style Country Spareribs

Mrs. Doreen Halfrey, Framingham, Massachusetts, (nee Young, Black Duck Brook, Newfoundland)

Ingredients:

1/4 cup soy sauce
1/4 cup orange marmalade
2 tbsp ketchup
1 clove garlic, crushed
3 or 4 lbs spareribs

> **FOOD FOR THOUGHT**
> We make a living by what we get; we make a life by what we give.

Directions:

Combine all ingredients. Brush on both side of spareribs. Place in shallow pan. Pour remaining sauce over ribs. Bake at 350°F for 1 hour.

Meats, Poultry & Game

Beef, Pork, Chicken, Turkey, Bologna, Venison, Wild Fowl & Seal

Swiss Meatloaf

Mrs. Doreen Halfrey, Framingham, Massachusetts, (nee Young, Black Duck Brook, Newfoundland)

Ingredients:

2 lb ground beef, lean
1 & 1/2 cups swiss cheese, diced
2 eggs, beaten
1/2 cup onion, chopped
1/2 cup green pepper, chopped
1 & 1/2 tsp salt
1/2 tsp pepper
1 tsp celery salt
1/2 tsp paprika
1 cup bread crumbs
2 & 1/2 cups milk

TRIVIA TIDBITS

In 1990, Swiss designer Rene Jeanneret was stopped by highway police outside Bienne, about a mile from the French border, doing eighty-eight kilometres per hour in an eighty-kilometre-per-hour zone. He was given a speeding ticket, making him the first person to ever receive a speeding ticket while driving a solar-powered automobile.

Directions:

Mix all ingredients in large bowl. Form a loaf in 9x13 inch pan or can be divided to make 2 smaller loaves. Bake, uncovered at 350°F for 1 & 1/2 hours.

Cheesy Meatloaf

Madonna Ash, Portland, Newfoundland, (formerly of Brooklyn, Newfoundland)

Ingredients:

2 lb hamburger meat
1/3 cup grated cheese
2 tbsp onion, finely chopped
1/2 cup bread crumbs
1 tsp salt
1 tsp garlic salt
1 egg

FOOD FOR THOUGHT
Troubles fore-reckoned
are doubly suffered.

-Bovee

Directions:

Combine all ingredients together. Place in a greased loaf dish. Bake 1-1 & 1/2 hours at 350°F.

Baked Swiss Steak

Olive Hickey, Stoneville, Newfoundland

Ingredients:

2 lbs round steak, cut
1 envelope dry onion soup
1 - 10oz can sliced mushrooms, drained
1/4 cup green peppers, chopped
1 - 14oz can tomatoes

TRIVIA TIDBITS
The only English word whose pronunciation remains unchanged when the last four letters are dropped is queue.

This page is dedicated to our father
Patrick Hickey, formerly of Chapels Cove,
Conception Bay, Newfoundland.
Patrick & Pamela Hickey, Stoneville, Newfoundland.

1 tbsp bottled steak sauce
1 tbsp minute tapioca
1 tsp parsley falkes

Directions:
Cut meat in serving size pieces. Arrange in 2-quart casserole dish. Sprinkle dry onion soup over, spread mushrooms over top and sprinkle green peppers over that. In a small bowl, stir tomatoes, steak sauce, tapioca and parsley. Pour over meat. Cover and bake in 350°F for two hours or until meat is tender. Serve with baked potato. Serves 6-8 people.

Porcupine Meatballs

Ingredients:
1 lb ground beef
1 small onion (diced)
2 tbsp baking powder
1/2 cup milk
1/3 cup uncooked Minute Rice
1/2 tsp salt
1/8 tsp pepper
1 can tomato soup
1 can water
1 tsp brown sugar

FOOD FOR THOUGHT
Some people feel the rain. Others just get wet.
-Roger Miller

Directions:
Mix ground beef, onion, baking powder, milk, minute rice, salt, pepper and shape into balls. Combine soup, water, brown sugar and pour over meatballs. Bake uncovered at 400°F for about 35 minutes. Reduce heat to 275°F. Cover and bake another 30 minutes.

Tough-Day Sausage Dinner

Ingredients:
4 or 5 Oktoberfest sausages or smaller spiced sausages
1 med Spanish onion, thinly sliced
1 lg can tomatoes
1 cup long grain rice
1 - 1/2 cups water

Directions:
Brown sausage in large skillet. Drain off any fat. Pour in can of tomatoes and add onion. Cook on medium-high heat until mixture boils. Reduce to medium for approximately 1/2 hour. In the meantime, boil water in small saucepan with a pinch of salt. Add rice and simmer for 20 minutes. Spoon mixture over rice and serve. Makes 2 to 4 servings.

Oriental Beef

Trudy S. Simmons, Twillingate, Newfoundland, (nee Forward, Tizzard's Harbour, Newfoundland)

Ingredients:
1 & 1/2 lbs stewing beef
1 tbsp cooking oil
1/2 cup onion, chopped

1/2 cup dry, white wine
1/4 cup soy sauce
1 clove garlic, minced
2 tsp sugar
1/2 tsp ground ginger
1 - 16oz can tomato wedges
1 - 6oz pkg frozen pea pods
1 - 3oz can mushrooms, pieces & drained
2 tbsp cornstarch

Directions:

Cut meat into 1-inch cubes. In large skillet brown meat in hot oil. Remove from heat; add onion, wine, soy sauce, garlic, sugar, ginger, and 1 cup water. Cover and simmer for 1 & 1/2 hours. Add undrained tomatoes, frozen pea pods and mushrooms. Bring to boil; cook and stir uncovered for 2-3 minutes or until pea pods are crisp or tender. Slowly blend 1/2 cup cold water into cornstarch; stir into hot mixture. Cook and stir until thick and bubbly. Serve over hot cooked rice. Serves 6.

Rita's Jiggs Dinner

Ingredients:

2 - 3 pounds salt beef
1/4 pound junk salt pork
1 pkg split peas (350 grams)
3 - 4 pounds potatoes
1/2 pound carrots
1 turnip (1 pound approx.)
1 cabbage (1 pound approx.)

Directions:

Cover salt beef with cold water and soak overnight. Drain, and add fresh, cold water, salt pork and place peas in a pudding bag. Bring to a boil, reduce heat and cook for about 2 hours. Add potatoes, carrots, turnip and cabbage wedges, about 30 minutes before meat is cooked (serves 4 - 6).

Chili Con Carne For Six

Ingredients:

(In a saucepan cook until evenly browned):
1 lb ground beef
1 cup chopped onion
3/4 cup chopped green pepper
(Stir in):
1 (19oz) can tomatoes
1 (7 & 1/2oz) can tomato sauce
2 (14oz) cans red kidney beans, drained

This page is dedicated in loving memory of my wife
Hilda Laurita (Rita) Bain (nee Cook),
February 21, 1931 - July 1, 1987, Trinity, Trinity Bay, Newfoundland.
Parents; Leander-Port Rexton, Roseann-Isle Aux Morts.
Children - Roxanne, Harry, Hugh and Shelley. Love and happiness to our family.
(Rita was the first Newfoundlander to have a liver transplant.)
Clayton R. Bain

1 tbsp chili powder
1 tsp salt
1 tsp dried parsley flakes
1 bay leaf

Directions:

Bring to a boil, cover, reduce heat and simmer for 1 hour. Remove bay leaf. Serve with hot rolls and a salad. Makes 6 servings.

> **FOOD FOR THOUGHT**
> A good listener is not only popular, but after a while he knows something.

Sweet & Sour Moose

Olive Cheek, Glovertown, Newfoundland, (nee Blackwood)

Ingredients:

1 & 1/2 lbs moose
1/2 cup water
1 - 19oz can pineapple chunks
1/4 cup brown sugar
1/4 cup vinegar
1/2 tsp salt
1 green pepper
1 cup onion, sliced thin
2 tbsp cornstarch
3 tsp soya sauce

> **SPICE OF LIFE**
> Skippers's First Law For Creators - If an experiment works, something has gone wrong.

Directions:

Brown moose in small amount of oil; add water and simmer until tender, about 1 hour. Drain pineapple; reserve syrup. Combine sugar and cornstarch; add pineapple syrup, soya sauce and salt. Add to moose; cook and stir until gravy thickens; add pineapple, green pepper and onions. Cook 2-3 hours. Serve over hot, fluffy rice.

Baked Glazed Ham

Laura Freake, Twillingate, Newfoundland, (nee Brown, Joe Batt's Arm, Newfoundland)

Ingredients:

1 whole ham, (bone-in ham / picnic ham)
1/3 cup apple juice
3 tbsp brown sugar
2 tbsp mustard

> **SPICE OF LIFE**
> Skipper's Theories - If it looks easy, it's tough. If it looks tough, it's damn well impossible.

Directions:

Soak ham overnight. Skew top of ham in squares & triangles. Place in roaster and bake for 1 hour at 275°F. In a bowl, mix brown sugar and mustard. Stir together and add apple juice. Pour 1/3 or 1/4 of mixture over ham. Repeat about 3 or 4 times. Bake for another 3 hours. Baste ham regularly with juice in roaster. If juice starts to evaporate, add more apple juice in roaster and stir.

Charmaine's Sweet & Sour Meatballs

Charmaine Young, Twillingate, Newfoundland, (nee Freake, Joe Batt's Arm, Newfoundland)

Ingredients:

2 pkgs hamburger meat
1/3 cup rolled oats
3 tbsp ketchup
1 egg

> **SPICE OF LIFE**
> Skipper's Law - If you do not understand a particular word in a piece of technical writing, ignore it. The piece will make perfect sense without it.

Meats, Poultry & Game

Beef, Pork, Chicken, Turkey, Bologna, Venison, Wild Fowl & Seal

onion
1 & 1/2 tsp parsley flakes
1 & 1/2 tsp dry mustard
salt, to taste

Directions:

In bowl mix meat and all other ingredients. Form into balls. Place into dish and bake at 350°F until cooked (approximately 20 minutes). Drain excess fat. (Makes 35 meatballs)

Sauce

Ingredients:

1 can tomato sauce
1/2 cup brown sugar
1/2 cup red wine vinegar
1/4 cup onion, chopped
1/4 cup green pepper, chopped
2 tbsp cornstarch
2 tbsp water
1 cup pineapple chunks, drained

Directions:

In saucepan, put first five ingredients. Cook on medium heat for 15 minutes. Thicken with cornstarch. Pour over meatballs. Add pineapple chunks. Cook again for 30 minutes at 350°F.

Seal On A Bun

Mrs. Alma Taylor, Mt. Moriah, Bay of Islands, Newfoundland, (nee LeDrew, Bell Island, Newfoundland)

Ingredients:

250ml cooked seal meat
30ml sweet pickle, chopped
30ml prepared mustard
250ml cheddar cheese, grated
30ml onion, chopped
6 hamburger buns

Directions:

Combine the first five ingredients. Spread mixture on split buns. Wrap each bun in aluminum foil. Bake at 180°C for 20 minutes.

Beef & Broccoli

Ingredients:

3/4 lb boneless beef sirloin steak, sliced across the grain into very thin strips
1 clove garlic, minced
1 tbsp vegetable oil

1 medium onion, wedged
1 (10 & 3/4 oz) can Cream of Broccoli soup
1/4 cup water
1 tbsp soy sauce
2 cups broccoli florets
hot cooked noodles

Directions:

In skillet over medium-high heat, cook beef and garlic in hot oil until beef is browned. Add onion; cook 5 minutes, stirring often. Stir in soup, water and soy sauce. Heat to boiling. Add broccoli. Reduce heat to low. Cover and simmer 5 minutes or until vegetables are tender-crisp. Serve over noodles. Makes 4 servings.

Cheesy Beef Bake

Sandra Young, St. John's, Newfoundland, (nee Dove, Twillingate, Newfoundland)

Ingredients:

1/2 lb ground beef
1/2 cup chopped onion
1 (11 & 1/8 oz) can condensed Italian tomato soup
3/4 cup water
1/8 tsp pepper
2 cups cooked elbow macaroni (1 cup dry)
1 cup cheddar cheese, shredded

Directions:

Heat oven to 400°F. In 10-inch skillet over medium-high heat, cook beef and onion until beef is browned and onion is tender, stirring to separate meat. Spoon off fat. Stir in soup, water, pepper, macaroni and 1/2 cup Cheddar cheese. Spoon mixture into 1 & 1/2-quart casserole. Top with remaining cheese. Bake 25 minutes or until hot and bubbly. Makes 4 servings.

Indoor Barbecued Brisket

Dr. Harold B. Canning, Baton Rouge, Los Angeles, USA

Ingredients:

6 pounds (2.7kg) brisket of beef
1 tbsp (15ml) liquid smoke
2 tsp (10ml) garlic powder or equivalent in fresh minced garlic
2 tsp (10ml) onion salt
2 tsp (10ml) celery salt
2 tsp (10ml) black pepper
2 tsp (10ml) Worcestershire sauce

Sauce

1 cup (250ml) ketchup
1 tsp (5ml) salt
1 tsp (5ml) celery seed
1/4 cup (60ml) brown sugar
1/4 cup (60ml) Worcestershire sauce
2 cups (500ml) water
1 onion, minced

1/4 cup (60ml) vinegar
Directions:
Sprinkle brisket with liquid smoke, garlic powder, onion salt and celery salt. Allow to stand overnight, covered with foil, in refrigerator. The next morning, sprinkle with pepper and Worcestershire sauce. Cover and bake five hours at 275°F (135°C). Drain off grease. Set aside. Mix all ingredients for sauce and boil 15 minutes. Pour sauce over meat; bake uncovered for one hour. Serves 16.

Chop Suey

Marion Nagle, Kitchener, Ontario, (nee Daniels, Twillingate, Newfoundland)
Ingredients:
1 lb hamburger meat
1/4 cup rice
1/4 cup macaroni
1 onion
1 can tomato soup
1 can water
Directions:
Mix all ingredients and cook 1/2 hour at 350°F.

Wanda's Sweet & Sour Meatballs

Wanda Greenham, Twillingate, Newfoundland
Ingredients:
1 egg, beaten
1 lb ground beef
1/2 cup milk
3/4 cup bread crumbs
1 onion
salt & pepper
Worcestershire sauce
Sauce:
3/4 cup brown sugar
1/4 cup vinegar
1 cup ketchup
1 tbsp cornstarch
1/2 cup water
Directions:
Roll and bake first 7 ingredients for 30 minutes at 350°F for. Drain grease. Mix sauce ingredients, pour over meatballs and bake at 325°F for another 30 minutes.

SPICE OF LIFE
Skipper's Basic Baggage Principle - No matter which carousel you stand by, your baggage will come in on another one.

In loving memory of our mom **FRANCES DRISCOLL** (nee Geiou) - August 7, 1920-Lamaline-December 5, 1989 and our dad **SIMEON DRISCOLL** - August 2, 1915-New Melbourne-April 10, 1996
Love from all your children - Dave, Frank, Rob, Clyde, Don, Ralph, Eugene, Marjorie, Pamela, Daphne, Madonna, Violet
God Bless - Rest in Peace. ... *I love you* - Dave

(Sidebar, vertical text): **Meats, Poultry & Game** — Beef, Pork, Chicken, Turkey, Bologna, Venison, Wild Fowl & Seal

Louisiana Roast Beef

Mary Doreen Halfrey, Framingham, Massachusettes, (nee Young, Black Buck Brook, Newfoundland)

Ingredients:

1/4 cup finely chopped onion
1/4 cup finely chopped celery
1/4 cup finely chopped green pepper
1/2 tsp cayenne pepper
1/2 tsp dry mustard
2 tbsp butter
1 tsp salt
1 tsp pepper
3/4 tsp garlic, minced
1 - 3 & 1/2 to 4 lb roast beef
1 sm onion, chopped
1 can beef broth

TRIVIA TIDBITS

The single-humped camel, or dromedary, is the only one you'll find on the deserts of Arabia and North Africa, and all are domesticated. The Bactrians, or double-hump camel is limited to Mongolia, and found mostly in the Gobi Desert. Most Bactrians live in the wild in packs of five and six.

Directions:

In a medium bowl, combine all ingredients. Place roast in pan fat side up. With a large knife make 4 or 5 deep slits in the meat to form pockets. Do not cut all the way. Fill pockets with vegetable mixture. Save 1 tablespoon to rub all over the roast. Add 1 small chopped onion and 1 can beef broth to pan. Bake, uncovered, at 300°F about 3 hours.

Meat Cakes

Marion Nagle, Kitchener, Ontario (nee Daniels, Twillingate, Newfoundland)

Ingredients:

1 tin can-corned-beef
2 grated potatoes
1 onion
1 egg
1 tsp dry mustard
pepper
oregano

SPICE OF LIFE
Skipper's Proclamation-
Murphy was an optimist.

Directions:

Mix all intredients and form into cakes. Roll in flour & fry in frying pan.

Pickled Kolbassa

Winnie Oberderfer, Okanagan Falls, British Columbia, (nee Parsons, Halifax, Nova Scotia)

Ingredients:

2 lbs smoked kobassa, sliced
2 onions
2 red peppers
2 bay leaves
2 tbsp whole black pepper corns
2-4 minced or crushed garlic cloves
white vinegar

FOOD FOR THOUGHT
You never get a second chance to
make a first impression.

Directions:

Slice kolbassa and put in a glass jar. Slice onions, red peppers and add to jar. Add bay leaves and

Meats, Poultry & Game

Beef, Pork, Chicken, Turkey, Bologna, Venison, Wild Fowl & Seal

black pepper corns. Add garlic cloves, (depending on desired taste). Cover completely with white vinegar. Keep in fridge and let set for at least 3 weeks before eating. Will keep forever.

Make Your Own Corned Beef

Ingredients:
5-6 lbs brisket or rump
8 cups water
1 cup salt
3 tbsp sugar
1 bay leaf
6 peppercorns
1 garlic clove, minced
2 tsp mixed pickling spice

> **SPICE OF LIFE**
> Skipper's Observations - If people listened to themselves more often, they would talk less.

Directions:

In a crock, combine and stir well the water, salt, sugar and seasonings. Add the brisket or rump. Cover with a plate and place a heavy weight on it. Leave in the brine at least 2 days; longer is preferable. Remove from brine and start cooking in cold water, in which additional peppercorns and clove of garlic may be added if desired. Bring to a boil, reduce heat and remove build-up. Cover and simmer until tender, about one hour per pound.

Saucy Baked Pork Chops

Neta Dove, Twillingate, Newfoundland, (nee Roberts)

Ingredients:
1 onion, chopped
3/4 cup water
3 tsp vinegar
3 tsp Worchestershire sauce
1 tsp salt
1/4 tsp cinnamon
1 tbsp sugar
1/4 cup ketchup

> ***TRIVIA TIDBITS***
> In 1930, to help raise funds for the starving poor of Berlin, Albert Einstein sold auto-graphed photographs of himself for $5 each.

Directions:

Trim fat from chops and season with salt and pepper. Combine all ingredients in saucepan and heat to boiling point. Pour over chops and bake for 1 hour at 350°F or until ready.

Sweet & Sour Pork Chops

> **FOOD FOR THOUGHT**
> A man convinced against his will is of the same opinion still.
> -Dale Carnegie

Wanda Greenham, Twillingate, Newfoundland

Ingredients:
4 pork chops
1 onion, chopped

This page is dedicated to my parents
Gordon H. and **Gladys C**. (Primmer) **Harnum**
Heart's Delight and Twillingate, Newfoundland
Louise Hrymewick, Acton, Massachusetts

2 Oxo beef cubes, crumbled
1 cup water, boiling
3 tbsp lemon juice
2 tbsp brown sugar
1/2 tsp cinnamon
1 cup crushed pineapple
1 tbsp cornstarch
1/2 cup cold water

Directions:

Brown pork chops and place in casserole. Top with onion. In saucepan add beef cubes to boiling water. Stir until dissolved. Add lemon juice, brown sugar, cinnamon and crushed pineapple. Bring to a boil. Stir cornstarch into cold water. Mix into sauce and cook until thickened. Pour sauce over chops and bake 1 & 1/2 hours at 325°F.

Nan's Special Meat Loaf

Marion Nagle, Kitchener, Ontario, (nee Daniels, Twillingate, Newfoundland)

Ingredients:

1 & 1/2 lbs ground beef
1 & 1/2 cups rolled oats
1 grated carrot
1 green pepper
Worchestershire sauce
ketchup
1 tin tomato soup
2 onions
1 cup milk
salt & pepper

Directions:

Mix all ingredients and form into a loaf; bake at 350°F for 1 & 1/2 hours.

Creamy Golden Pork Chop Delight

Catherine Irwin, Truro, Nova Scotia

Ingredients:

6 pork chops (1 & 1/2 lbs)
1 - 10oz can Campbells Golden Mushroom Soup
1/4 cup water
1 cup carrots, peeled, thinly sliced diagonally
1/2 cup chopped onion (medium sized pieces)
generous dash sage
1 small green pepper, cut in strips

Directions:

In electric frying pan, brown chops (in shortening). Pour off fat. Stir in soup, water, carrots, onions, and sage. Cover and cook over low heat 15 minutes. Add green pepper. Cook another 15 minutes until done. Stir occasionally. Serve along with mashed potatoes. Serves about 4.

Japanese Chicken

Claudine Barnes, Corner Brook, Newfoundland

Ingredients:

3 lbs chicken pieces

1 egg, beaten

1 cup flour

Dip chicken in beaten egg. Roll in flour and fry in oil until brown on both sides. Put in casserole dish. Make following *sauce*:

3 tbsp soya sauce

3 tbsp water

3/4 cup sugar

1/2 cup vinegar

1 tsp salt

Directions:

Bring to a boil. Pour over chicken. Bake at 350°F for about 1 & 1/2 hours.

Baked Herb Chicken

Anne B. Penney, St. John's, Newfoundland

Ingredients:

1 tsp lemon rind

2 tbsp lemon juice

1/4 tsp salt

1/4 tsp basil

1/4 tsp oregano

1 can cream of mushroom soup

1 medium chicken

Mozzarella cheese (if desired)

Directions:

Combine rind, juice, salt, herbs and soup. Cut chicken into pieces and place in baking dish. Bake uncovered at 325°F until browned and drain off the fat. Add the soup mix and continue baking for at least another hour. Sprinkle with grated mozzarella cheese for the last 10 minutes, if desired. Delicious with rice and vegetables.

Peachy Chicken

Grace Ryan, Newmans Cove, Bonavista Bay, Newfoundland

Ingredients:

4 lbs chicken, cut up

1 cup ketchup

1/2 cup chopped celery

This page is dedicated to our parents
Harold and **Carrie** (nee Gillard) **Roberts**
in Twillingate, Newfoundland
Love - Bruce, Wallace, Lloyd, Thelma and Dianne

1/2 cup chopped onion
1 tsp Worchestershire sauce
1 cup canned peaches, chopped
1/4 cup peach juice
1/4 cup brown sugar
1/2 cup white vinegar
1 & 1/2 tsp soya sauce

Directions:
Pat chicken dry with paper towel, dip lightly in flour. Brown in oil, drain. Arrange chicken in roaster. Combine all ingredients. Pour over chicken and cover. Bake at 350°F for 30 minutes.

Chicken Supreme

Ina Belcher, Tonawanda, New York, (nee Brown, St. John's, Newfoundland)

Ingredients:
6 whole chicken breasts (halved & skinned)
1/2 cup flour
salt & pepper to taste
1 tsp paprika
1/4 cup vegetable oil
3 tsp cornstarch
1 & 1/2 cups milk
1 lemon
1 cup sliced mushrooms
1 cup grated swiss cheese

Directions:
Combine flour, salt, pepper and paprika. Coat chicken with this mixture. Heat cooking oil. Add the
chicken and brown. Add 1/2 cup water, cover and simmer for 30 minutes. Arrange in Pam-sprayed
baking dish. Brown mushrooms and sprinkle over chicken. Add cornstarch to 1/2 cup milk.
Combine remaining milk, juice from lemon, and grated lemon rind, to pan. Add cornstarch/milk
and cook until thickened. Pour over chicken. Bake at 350°F for 20 minutes. Top with swiss cheese
and return to oven for about 10-15 minutes. Serve with rice pilaf.

Chicken in Chili Sauce

Ingredients:
1 box (or pkg) chicken wings
1 onion, chopped
salt
1/2 cup chili sauce
1/2 cup water
4 tbsp vinegar
3 tbsp brown sugar

Directions:
Place chicken wings (with small amount of water to keep from sticking) in small roaster. Add
onion. Add salt to taste. Cook this for 1/2 hour. To prepare sauce, in a medium size bowl put chili
sauce, water, vinegar and brown sugar. Stir until sugar is dissolved. After cooking chicken for 1/2
hour, pour sauce mixture over top and cook for another hour. Great served with mashed potatoes
and vegetable of your choice.

Honey-Glazed Chicken Breasts

Ingredients:

1/4 cup almonds, sliced
1 med onion, sliced
1 stalk celery, sliced
1 carrot, sliced
1 sprig parsley
1 tsp salt
1/2 tsp pepper
1 tsp dried rosemary leaves
1 small bay leaf
1 can (10 & 3/4oz) condensed chicken broth, undiluted
1 cup water
4 (12oz) whole chicken breasts, halved
1/3 cup honey
green grapes, optional
watercress, optional

Directions:

The day ahead: arrange sliced almonds in a single layer in a shallow baking pan. Broil one minute or until almonds are golden brown. Watch carefully: almonds burn very quickly; you may have to stir them several times. Cool; transfer to a covered container for use the next day. In a 6-quart pot, combine onion, celery, carrot, parsley, salt, pepper, rosemary, bay leaf, undiluted chicken broth and water. Bring mixture to a boil; add the chicken breasts and cover. Simmer 30 minutes or until chicken is tender. Remove pot from heat; place immediately in the refrigerator and chill chicken mixture overnight. Next day: remove pot from the refrigerator and place over low heat. Cook until chicken is heated through (about 10 minutes). Remove the chicken from the broth; place skin side up in a large, shallow baking pan. Spoon 1 cup chicken broth into the pan. Strain remaining broth; discard vegetables and save broth for use in other recipes for soups or stews. Using a pastry brush, brush chicken with half of the honey. Broil, 4 inches from heat source, for 2 minutes. Brush again with honey and broil 1 to 2 minutes longer. Brush with more honey and broil until chicken is glazed and golden brown. Remove chicken from broiler and arrange the honey-glazed breasts on a heated platter. Sprinkle with sliced almonds and garnish, if desired, with green grapes and crisp watercress. Serve immediately. Makes 8 servings.

Turkey Loaf

Dolores Lundrigan, Wabush, Labrador, (nee English, Branch, St. Mary's Bay, Newfoundland)

Ingredients:

2 & 1/2 cups ground cooked turkey
1/2 cup celery, chopped
1 & 1/4 cups milk

1 tsp salt
2 eggs, beaten
1 cup rolled oats
1/2 cup onions, chopped
2 tbsp parsley
1/2 tsp pepper

Directions:
Combine all ingredients. Grease loaf pan and bake at 350°F for one hour.

> **FOOD FOR THOUGHT**
> Some houses will be built to last,
> while others may be built to sell.

Chicken Amaretto

Ingredients:
4 whole chicken breasts, skinned, boned & halved
3 tbsp flour
1 tsp salt
1 tsp ground pepper
2 tsp paprika
1 & 1/2 tsp garlic salt
1 tbsp oil
3 tbsp butter
1 & 1/2 tbsp Dijon mustard
1 - 6oz can frozen orange juice (thawed)
1 cup Amaretto

> **TRIVIA TIDBITS**
> Loreta Janeta Velasquez joined the
> Confederate Army as Harry T. Burford.
> She served with distinction in many
> important battles, and was highly praised
> by General Stonewall Jackson,
> who never
> found out she
> was a woman.

Directions:
Combine flour, salt, pepper, paprika and garlic salt. Coat chicken with this mixture. Heat oil and butter in skillet and saute chicken until brown. Remove to casserole. In same skillet, add mustard, orange juice, 1/2 can of water and Amaretto. Bring to a boil and cook, stirring until thickened. Pour over chicken and bake, covered at 350°F for 45 minutes. Makes 6 to 8 servings.

Chicken Breast Rolls

Phyllis Labelle, Lynden, Ontario, (nee Hollett, Arnold's Cove, Newfoundland)

Ingredients:
6 single chicken breasts
1 & 1/2 cups soft white bread crumbs (put 7 slices of bread in blender)
1/2 cup grated parmesan cheese
1 tsp salt
3/4 cup butter, melted
1/4 tsp garlic powder
1/2 tsp dry mustard
3/4 tsp Worcestershire sauce
1/4 tsp parsley flakes

> **SPICE OF LIFE**
> Skipper's Suppliment To Murphy's Law
> - In precise mathematical terms, 1+1=2,
> where "=" is a symbol of meaning
> "seldom, if ever".

Directions:
Mix together cheese, parsley, salt and bread crumbs. Melt butter and garlic. Add mustard and Worcestershire sauce (set aside - don't let congeal). Debone chicken breasts, grease Pyrex dish. Dip chicken in butter mixture and coat with bread crumbs. Roll chicken and place open side down in butter dish. Pour remaining crumbs over chicken. Bake at 325°F for 1 & 1/4 hours.

Meats, Poultry & Game
Beef, Pork, Chicken, Turkey, Bologna, Venison, Wild Fowl & Seal

Hungarian Paprika Chicken

Madge Witzing, London, Ontario, (nee Bailey, Baie Verte, Newfoundland)

Ingredients:
1 roasting chicken
3/4 cup onion, chopped
4 tbsp butter
1 tbsp paprika
salt to taste
sprinkle of pepper
1/2 cup tomatoes, chopped
2 tbsp flour
1 & 1/4 cups sour cream
2/3 cup water
1 green pepper

FOOD FOR THOUGHT
One of the most difficult mountains for people to climb is the one they make out of a molehill.
-Homer Phillips

Directions:
In a large Dutch skillet, brown the onion in butter until transparent. Add paprika and stir until reddish brown. Cut the chicken into pieces and fry until brown all over. Add the salt, pepper, chopped green pepper and tomatoes. Add 2/3 cup water, stir well and cover with tight fitting lid. Cook over very low heat for 1 & 1/2 hours. Mix sour cream with flour and a little water to form a smooth paste. Remove the chicken and add mixture to pan drippings. Pour sauce over chicken. May be served with rice or noodles.

Hawaiian Wings

Davis Hull, Mississauga, Ontario, (formerly of Springdale, Newfoundland)

Ingredients:
1 box chicken wings
1 - 19oz can crushed pineapple
1/4 cup soya sauce
1/2 cup white sugar
1/2 cup ketchup
3 tbsp brown sugar

TRIVIA TIDBITS
Louis XI of France brought a large number of deeply religious men and women to Paris to pray for him so that he wouldn't die. It didn't work.

Directions:
Place chicken wings in casserole dish. Add all other ingredients. Mix together and bake for 1 & 1/2 hours at 350°F.

Chicken & Broccoli Supreme

Charmaine Young, Twillingate, Newfoundland, (nee Freake, Joe Batt's Arm, Newfoundland)

Ingredients:
2 tbsp margarine or butter
4 (1 lb) chicken breasts, skinless & boneless

2 cups broccoli
1 & 1/2 cups mushrooms, sliced
10oz can condensed cream of chicken & broccoli soup
1/4 cup milk
1 tbsp Dijon mustard
4 cups noodles, hot cooked (my choice is egg noodles)

Directions:
In large skillet over medium-high heat, melt half of the margarine. Brown chicken 5 minutes on each side. Remove from skillet. Set aside. In same skillet over medium high heat, melt remaining margarine. Stir fry broccoli and mushrooms until tender. Add soup, milk and mustard. Bring to a boil. Return chicken to skillet. Reduce heat to low. Cover and simmer for 5 minutes or until chicken is no longer pink, stirring occasionally. Serve with noodles.

FOOD FOR THOUGHT
One way people can renew their appreciation for life is by sharing their blessings.

Buffalo-Style Chicken Wings

Ingredients:
12 chicken wings (about 2 lbs)
1 envelope onion soup mix
1/4 cup butter or margarine, melted
1 tbsp white vinegar
1 clove garlic
1 & 1/2 tsp ground red pepper
1/2 tsp ground cumin
2 tbsp water
1 cup chunky blue cheese dressing
celery sticks

TRIVIA TIDBITS
Verona, Italy, the city in which Shakespeare's most famous lovers, Romeo and Juliette lived, receives about 1,000 letters addressed to Juliette every Valentine's Day.

Directions:
Heat broiler. Cut tips off chicken wings. Halve the remaining wings at joint. In food processor or blender process soup mix, butter, vinegar, garlic, red pepper, cumin and water until blended; set aside. Broil chicken 5 minutes. Turn wings over; broil 5 more minutes. Brush with half the soup mixture, then broil 2 minutes or until crisp. Turn wings again and brush with remaining soup mixture. Broil 2 more minutes or until crisp. Serve with blue cheese dressing for dipping and chilled celery sticks. Serves 4.

Golden Chicken Nuggets

Ingredients:
1 envelope onion soup mix
3/4 cup dry bread crumbs
1 & 1/2 lbs boneless chicken breasts, cut into 1-inch pieces
1/4 cup butter or margarine, melted

TRIVIA TIDBITS
China has more foreign borders than any other country on earth.

Directions:
Heat oven to 400°F. Combine onion soup mix with bread crumbs. Dip chicken into bread crumb mixture, coating well. Place in lightly greased, large shallow baking pan and drizzle with butter. Bake, turning once, 10 to 15 minutes or until chicken is tender. Makes about 2 dozen.

Meats, Poultry & Game
Beef, Pork, Chicken, Turkey, Bologna, Venison, Wild Fowl & Seal

Meats, Poultry & Game
Beef, Pork, Chicken, Turkey, Bologna, Venison, Wild Fowl & Seal

Barbequed Chicken

Wanda Greenham, Twillingate, Newfoundland

Ingredients:

4 skinless, boneless chicken breasts, halved

Sauce:

1/4 cup reduced-sodium ketchup

3 tbsp cider vinegar

1 tbsp ready-made white horseradish

2 tsp firmly packed dark brown sugar

1 clove garlic, minced

1/8 tsp dried thyme

1/4 tsp black pepper

Directions:

Preheat broiler, heat a charcoal grill until coals form white ash, or preheat a gas grill to medium. To prepare sauce, in a small saucepan, combine all ingredients except pepper. Mix well. Bring to a boil over medium-low heat. Cook, stirring frequently, until thickened, about 5 minutes. Remove from heat; stir in pepper. Brush tops of chicken pieces lightly with sauce. Place chicken, sauce side down on a foil-lined broiler pan or grill rack. Brush other side lightly with sauce. Broil or grill 3 inches from heat, basting with remaining sauce and turning until no longer pink in center, about 5 to 7 minutes per side. Let chicken stand for 5 minutes before serving.

TRIVIA TIDBITS

Ex-school teacher, Anna Edson Taylor, on October 24, 1901, her forty-third birthday, squeezed into a 3 foot by 4 and 1/2 foot wooden barrel and at 4:23 pm on that day, the barrel, still containing Anna, went over Niagara Falls. She was knocked unconscious but survived, making her the only woman in history to do so.

Hawaiian Chicken

Neta Dove, Twillingate, Newfoundland, (nee Roberts)

Ingredients:

1 whole chicken, cut in pieces

Sauce:

1 tbsp Worchestershire sauce

1/2 cup ketchup

1 small can crushed pineapple, drained

2/3 cup brown sugar

2 tbsp barbecue sauce

Directions:

Brown chicken in oil and butter. Combine sauce ingredients. Pour sauce over chicken, cover and bake at 300°F for 1 hour. Uncover and bake for 1 hour more. (Freezes well).

FOOD FOR THOUGHT

I've usually felt very assured and confident right before falling flat on my face.

Wanda's Chicken Breasts

Wanda Greenham, Twillingate, Newfoundland

Ingredients:

4 lg skinless, boneless chicken breast halves (or 8 small)

1/2 tsp salt

1/4 to 1/2 tsp black pepper

2 tbsp olive or salad oil

FOOD FOR THOUGHT

Temper gets most of us into trouble. Pride is what keeps us there.

This page is dedicated to my late grandmother, **Jessie French** and her youngest daughter, **Jessie Jean (Carr)**, my mother.
Both formerly of French's Cove, Newfoundland
- moved to British Columbia in 1931.
submitted by Harry M. Wagner, Delta, British Columbia

2 tbsp butter or margarine
3 tbsp chopped fresh chives or green onions
juice of 1/2 lime or lemon
2 tbsp chopped parsley
2 tsp Dijon mustard
1/4 cup chicken broth

Directions:

Place chicken breast halves between sheets of waxed paper or plastic wrap. Pound slightly with mallet and sprinkle with salt and black pepper. Heat 1 tbsp each of oil and butter in large skillet. Cook chicken over high heat, 4 minutes on each side. Do not cook longer or they will be over-cooked and dry. Transfer to warm serving platter. Add chives or green onion, lime juice and brandy (if desired) parsley and mustard, to pan. Cook 15 seconds, whisking constantly. Whisk in broth. Stir until sauce is smooth. Whisk in remaining butter and oil. Pour sauce over chicken. Serve immediately.

Russian Chicken

Neta Dove, Twillingate, Newfoundland, (nee Roberts)

Ingredients:

2 lbs chicken pieces, skin removed
1 bottle Russian dressing
1 envelope onion soup mix
1 small bottle apricot jam

Directions:

Mix sauce ingredients and pour over chicken. Bake until ready. Serve with rice or mashed potatoes.

Celebrity Chicken

Sadie Keeping, Ramea, Newfoundland, (nee Priddle, Francois, Newfoundland)

Ingredients:

1 broiler chicken
1 pkg onion soup mix
1/2 cup ketchup
1/4 cup brown sugar
1/4 cup water

Directions:

Cut broiler chicken into pieces and arrange in a casserole dish or roaster. Mix rest of ingredients together and pour over chicken. Cover and cook at 370°F for 1 hour.

Winnie's Hot Wings

Winnie Oberderfer, Okanagan Falls, British Columbia, (nee Parsons, Halifax, Nova Scotia)

Ingredients:

2-2 & 1/2 lbs chicken wings
1/3 cup soya sauce
1/4 cup chili garlic sauce
1/4 tsp dried oregano

Meats, Poultry & Game
Beef, Pork, Chicken, Turkey, Bologna, Venison, Wild Fowl & Seal

1/8 tsp ground ginger
2 tsp garlic powder
2 tbsp melted butter
1/4 cup honey

Directions:

Mix all ingredients, except chicken, together in a bowl. Pour over chicken wings. Bake in preheated oven at 350°F for 20 minutes and at 400°F for 10 minutes.

Maritime Country Chicken

Catherine Irwin, Truro, Nova Scotia

Ingredients:

3 & 1/2 lbs chicken, cut up and remove some excess bones
1/4 cup flour
2 tsp salt
1/4 tsp pepper
1/2 cup Mazola oil
1 onion, chopped (not too fine)
2 cloves garlic, peeled and whole
1 green pepper, coarsely chopped
1/2 cup celery, chopped
1 tsp curry powder
2 cups canned tomatoes
parsley
1 cup chicken stock (boil bones, neck and old bits of chicken that are not used in main dish. Sometimes add a chicken bouillon cube for more flavour. Taste for salt. These cubes are usually quite salty.)

Directions:

Combine flour, salt and pepper and place in a paper bag. Shake pieces in the bag until well coated. Put Mazola oil in a fairly deep frying pan and heat. Add onion and garlic. Saute until lightly browned or transparent. Then remove the onions and garlic for later. In hot oil fry chicken until lightly browned, turning often. Then add the green pepper, celery and cook just a little while until the celery and green pepper turn colour. Now add the curry powder and the canned tomatoes, the chicken stock and the onions and garlic cloves. Cover and simmer for 45 minutes or until chicken is tender. Remove the garlic cloves from the sauce before serving. Garnish as desired with parsley.

Chicken San Jose

Catherine Irwin, Truro, Nova Scotia

Ingredients:

1 & 1/2 tsp garlic salt
1 & 1/2 tsp celery salt

Meats, Poultry & Game
Beef, Pork, Chicken, Turkey, Bologna, Venison, Wild Fowl & Seal

This page is dedicated to the memory of our dad
TED CLARKE, who passed away November 28, 1980;
and to our mom **MABEL** (nee Butler) **CLARKE**,
who resides in Port Rexton, Newfoundland.
Love children ~ Jenny, Josie, Mildred, Linda and Maisie

1 & 1/2 tsp paprika
1/8 tsp cayenne pepper
2 to 2 & 1/2 lbs choice chicken pieces
1 & 1/4 cup uncooked brown rice
1/2 cup onion (chopped, but not fine)
1/2 cup celery (sliced, not fine)
2 cups well-drained canned tomatoes, quartered
1 & 1/2 cups boiling chicken broth
3 tbsp chopped parsley
1/4 cup sliced pitted ripe olives

> **FOOD FOR THOUGHT**
> Gratification in life is obtained by doing something nice each day for somebody else.

Directions:
Blend seasonings and sprinkle on each side of the chicken (shake everything in a plastic bag). Arrange in a lightly greased shallow 2 & 1/2 quart casserole dish, skin side up. Brown in a 450°F oven for 30 minutes. Remove from oven, push chicken to one side. Add rice, onions, celery, tomatoes, and broth. Stir well. Arrange chicken over the rice. Cover and continue baking for 25 minutes or until rice and chicken are tender and the liquid is absorbed. Garnish with parsley and olives. Serves 6.

Marinated and Braised Deer, Moose, Caribou, Rabbit

Brenda Keyes, Durham, Ontario, (nee LeDrew, Pasadena and Corner Brook, Newfoundland)

Ingredients:
2 & 1/2 lbs of cubed deer meat (or other meat)
1/4 cup vegetable oil
1/4 cup flour
1 tbsp tomato paste
1 & 1/4 cups beef broth
12 cooked and glazed onions
2 cups mushrooms, cooked and sliced
chopped fresh parsley

Marinade Ingredients:
1/2 bay leaf
2 cloves garlic
2 tbsp juniper berries
1 tbsp crushed peppercorns
pinch of marjoram
pinch of thyme
1 med onion, cut up
1 small carrot, cut up
1/2 celery stalk, cut up
1 large unpeeled garlic clove
1 & 1/2 cups red wine (which means one can drink the rest of the bottle)

> **TRIVIA TIDBITS**
> In 1982 at the Expo in New York City, Roberto Monsivais displayed his patented, 'Life Detector', a device for people who fear they may be inadvertently embalmed or buried alive. Should a doctor declare someone dead because of lack of vital signs, and the person later recover, the device triggers an alarm and an emergency oxygen supply is activated until rescuers can open the coffin.

Directions:
Place spices for marinade in cheese cloth and tie. Place other ingredients, including spices for marinade, in glass or crockery bowl. Add meat and turn to coat well. Place plate on meat with weight on top to keep meat submerged. Cover and keep in refrigerator for 48 hours. Drain meat in strainer 1 hour; reserve liquid and spice bag. Remove meat, reserve vegetables and pat dry. In a skillet, saute meat in oil over high heat; sprinkle with salt and flour. Stir to completely coat meat; place in

stewing pot. Brown reserved vegetables in skillet and add to meat along with tomato paste. Deglaze skillet with marinade and add to meat. Add reserved liquid and spice bag. Cook over low heat until meat is tender, 2 to 2 & 1/2 hours. Strain sauce and reduce if necessary; add meat but discard vegetables and spice bag. Add cooked onions and mushrooms. Reheat and serve. Garnish with parsley.

Partridge With Cabbage

Ingredients:

2 partridges
1 large apple, cored, peeled and diced
3 stalks celery, diced
2 slices bacon or salt pork
1 large onion, quartered
1 head cabbage, quartered and cored

SPICE OF LIFE
Skipper's Rule of Gossip - If you don't say it, they can't repeat it.

Directions:

Pluck, clean and wash partridges, rinsing the inside cavity well with cold water. Season with salt and pepper inside and out and fill with dressing made of apple and celery. Tie bacon or salt pork over the breast and place in a deep roasting pan with onion pieces. Butter the outside of the birds and bake in a moderate oven about 3/4 of an hour, or until partially cooked. While birds are browning in the oven, place the prepared cabbage in boiling water. When half cooked, drain. Place the cabbage around the partridges and continue cooking another 3/4 of an hour, or until the birds are well cooked. Remove partridges and cabbage to a platter and make gravy with the pan drippings, adding additional water and a flour paste to thicken. The gravy should be dark and rich.

Rabbit Stew with Dumplings

Ingredients:

2 rabbits
1/2 lb salt pork
2 large onions, cut up
1 medium turnip, sliced
6 carrots, quartered
6 potatoes, quartered
salt & pepper

SPICE OF LIFE
The probability of someone watching you at any given time is directly proportional to the stupidity of your action at that time.

Directions:

Soak rabbits overnight in cold water. Next morning, dry well and cut into serving pieces. Dredge in flour, sprinkled with salt and pepper. In the meantime, cube pork and fry out in a skillet. When pork is nicely browned, remove pieces to the stewpot, leaving fat in the skillet. Put the pieces of rabbit in the hot fat until browned on both sides. Remove to the stewpot with enough water to just cover. Simmer for 1 & 1/2 hours, or until nearly tender. Add vegetables and simmer until done. Fifteen minutes before vegetables are tender, drop in the dumplings and cover tightly. *(See recipe for Dumplings in "Doughy Delights" section).*

In loving memory of my parents,
Rita Flynn (nee Walsh) of Marystown, Newfoundland
and **Fergus Flynn** of Petite Forte, Newfoundland
Your son, Jimmy Flynn

Meats, Poultry & Game
Beef, Pork, Chicken, Turkey, Bologna, Venison, Wild Fowl & Seal

Moose Roast

Directions:
This is a good method for cooking the less tender cuts such as the shoulder, rump or neck. Roll meat in seasoned flour and brown on all sides in a heavy pan. Add 1/2 cup water and cover tightly. Simmer over low heat until meat is tender, about 2 & 1/2 to 3 hours. Half an hour before meat is done add any desired vegetables, such as carrots, turnip and onions. Remove the meat and vegetables when done, and make a nice gravy.

Rabbit Fricassee

Ingredients:
2 young rabbits
1 small onion, chopped
1/4 tsp pepper
2 cups stock (vegetable, chicken or beef)
1 cup cream or milk
2 eggs, well beaten
1 tbsp butter
flour to thicken
juice of 1 lemon
a little nutmeg
pinch of mace
herbs to taste

SPICE OF LIFE
Skipper's Law of Driving - There is no traffic until you need to make a left turn.

Directions:
Prepare the rabbits, cut in sections and soak in salt and water for at least an hour. Drain, and cover with fresh water. Add onion, herbs, spices and pepper. Cover and simmer until tender, about an hour. Remove from pot and place in oven to keep warm. Using 2 cups of the stock in which the rabbits were cooked, add the cream, stir in beaten eggs a little at a time, and add butter. Thicken with flour mixed in a little milk. Bring to a boil and remove from heat. Stir in the lemon juice, and pour over the rabbits. Serve hot.

Turr Omelette

Ingredients:
6 eggs
1/2 cup butter
salt & pepper
breast of turr (or remains of any cold game)
a little minced onion
chopped parsley

TRIVIA TIDBITS
During Elizabethan times, potatoes were sometimes served in a sweet caramel sauce.

Directions:
Break eggs into a frying pan; add butter, salt and pepper. Fry quickly as for an ordinary omelette. In a separate saucepan combine minced game, onion and parsley, and heat. When omelette is ready spread the game mixture over the top; fold quickly and serve. It must be taken to the table piping hot or it will be leathery.

Meats, Poultry & Game
Beef, Pork, Chicken, Turkey, Bologna, Venison, Wild Fowl & Seal

Cornish Game Hens with Orange Sherry Glaze

Ingredients:

4 cornish game hens
1/4 cup butter
1/2 cup chopped onion
1/2 cup chopped green pepper
2 tbsp chopped fresh parsley
1/2 tsp thyme
salt & pepper to taste
3 cups cooked white or brown rice

FOOD FOR THOUGHT
If you don't check
it out, the flashlight in your
glove compartment may
only be a handy item for
carrying dead batteries.

Directions:

Clean hens inside and out; pat dry. In a skillet, melt butter. Saute onion and green pepper until onion is golden. Stir sauteed vegetables, parsley, thyme, salt and pepper into rice. Stuff birds with rice mixture; truss. Place birds breast side up in a roasting pan. Roast, uncovered, 30 minutes. Brush with Orange Sherry Glaze. Bake an additional 30 minutes, basting frequently. Makes 4 servings.

Orange Sherry Glaze

Ingredients:

1/3 cup sugar
1 tbsp cornstarch
1/4 tsp orange peel
1/4 tsp lemon peel
1 cup orange juice
1/4 cup sherry

TRIVIA TIDBITS
Water is hotter before boiling
than when it has actually boiled.

Directions:

In a saucepan, stir together all ingredients. Bring to a boil over medium heat, stirring constantly. Reduce heat; simmer 2 minutes or until glaze thickens.

Pheasant in Cream

Ingredients:

1 pheasant (2 & 1/2 to 3 lbs) quartered
1 can (10 & 1/2oz) condensed cream of mushroom soup
1/2 cup sour cream
1 can (4oz) sliced mushrooms, drained
1/4 cup grated Parmesan cheese
1/4 cup chopped onion

SPICE OF LIFE
If you must borrow, borrow from a
pessimist - he doesn't expect it back!

Directions:

Preheat oven to 350°F. Place pheasant, skin side up, on a rack in a 9x13-inch baking pan. In a medium bowl, stir together soup, sour cream, mushrooms, cheese and onion; pour over pheasant. Bake 1 & 1/2 to 2 hours or until pheasant is tender. Baste occasionally with sauce. Makes 4 servings.

**John
William
1880-1950**

PARK FAMILY REUNION
1994
Family is Solidarity
dedicated by Harry and Doris Park

**Ida
May
1882-1978**

Meats, Poultry & Game
Beef, Pork, Chicken, Turkey, Bologna, Venison, Wild Fowl & Seal

Wild Duck with Apple Stuffing

Ingredients:

6 cups croutons
1 cup cubed, unpeeled apple
1/2 cup raisins
3/4 cup butter or margarine, melted
2 tsp salt
1/2 tsp pepper
1/4 tsp cinnamon
1/8 tsp ground ginger
3 ducks

Directions:

Preheat oven to 450°F. In a mixing bowl, stir together all ingredients, except ducks. Stuff the ducks; truss. Place ducks breast side up on a rack in a roasting pan. Roast, uncovered, for 15 minutes. Reduce heat to 325°F. Lightly cover ducks with foil. Roast, allowing about 20 minutes per pound to reach an internal temperature of 190°F. Makes 6 servings.

> **SPICE OF LIFE**
> Medical research has really made great strides - what used to be an itch is now an allergy.

> **TRIVIA TIDBITS**
> Tomatoes were considered poisonous and used as unusual garden plants a few hundred years ago.

Bologna Stew

Miss Gertrude V. Sweetapple, Glovertown, Newfoundland

Ingredients:

1 lb bologna, thickly sliced and cut in quarters
salt to taste
1 med onion, sliced
carrot, diced
turnip, diced
potatoes, cut in cubes
water
2-3 tbsp ketchup (if desired)

Directions:

Thickly slice one pound of bologna, cut in quarters, and fry until slightly brown. Put in saucepan, add salt, onion, carrots, turnip and potato. Add enough water to barely cover. Let boil slowly until vegetables are tender. Then add 2 or 3 tbsp of ketchup for flavour (if desired).

> **FOOD FOR THOUGHT**
> Some men believe in law and order as long as they can lay down the law and give the orders.

Sweet 'N' Sour Beef Stew

Ingredients:

1 tbsp shortening (or corn oil)
2 lbs lean stewing beef, cubed
1/2 tsp salt
2 cups canned tomatoes
1/3 cup brown sugar
1/3 cup vinegar
1/2 cup onion, finely chopped
1/2 bay leaf
1 green pepper, cut into thin strips

> **TRIVIA TIDBITS**
> Among the recipes in a certain cook book from the 1500s, was one for a "Tart to Provoke Courage Either in Man or Woman".

Directions:

Melt shortening in large skillet. Brown beef on all sides. Add salt, tomatoes, brown sugar, vinegar, onion and bay leaf. Cover skillet. Lower heat. Let simmer about 2 hours, until beef is tender. Add pepper strips to beef; cook 10 minutes to blend all flavours. Serve with hot rice, noodles or baked potatoes. Makes 6 servings.

Creamed Vegetable Stew

Ingredients:

1 cup carrots, diced
1 cup potatoes, cubed
1/2 cup green pepper, diced
1/2 cup green onions, sliced
1 cup celery, diced
salt to taste
1/2 lb salt pork
1/2 cup all-purpose flour
4 cups milk

TRIVIA TIDBITS
In ancient Egypt it was believed that toothache was caused by a demon that took the form of a worm and invaded teeth.

Directions:

Place carrots, potatoes, pepper, onions and celery in large saucepan. Add 2 teaspoons salt and enough water to cover vegetables; bring to a boil. Reduce heat; simmer until vegetables are tender. Drain; set aside. Wash salt pork; remove rind. Cut into cubes; place in large saucepan. Cook over medium heat until brown; stir frequently. Add flour; mix well. Stir in milk; bring just to a boil, stirring constantly. Reduce heat; simmer until thickened. Season with salt to taste. Add vegetables; heat through. Makes 8 servings.

Pork Vegetable Stew

Ingredients:

1 lb boneless pork shoulder
1 med size onion, sliced
3 med size carrots, sliced
2 & 1/2 cups water
1 tsp salt
1 cup uncooked macaroni
2 cups cooked or canned green beans, undrained

FOOD FOR THOUGHT
Anxiety does not empty tomorrow of its sorrows, but only empties today of its strength.
-Charles Spurgeon

Directions:

Cut meat into small pieces; brown in large greased pan. Add onion and carrots to meat. Stir in water and salt; bring to boil. Lower heat; cover. Boil slowly about 45 minutes, until meat and carrots are tender. Stir in macaroni and beans; cover. Boil gently about 10 minutes, until macaroni is tender. Stir once in awhile to keep from sticking. Add water during cooking if mixture seems dry. Makes 6 servings.

In memory of **Joseph Whiffen**,
Bonavista, Newfoundland
A wonderful Dad.
Betty Andrews, Naples, Florida

Newfoundland Bologna Stew

Elisabeth Dillon, St. Mary's, St. Mary's Bay, Newfoundland

Ingredients:

2 cups bologna, cubed

1/2 cup celery, chopped

1/2 cup onion, chopped

1 tsp butter or margarine

1 cup carrots, diced

1 cup turnips, diced

salt to taste

pepper to taste

3 cups water

4 cups potatoes, diced

2 cups beef bouillon

1/4 cup ketchup

2 tbsp flour

1/4 cold water

Directions:

Saute celery and onion in butter until onion is transparent. Add carrot, turnip, salt, pepper and 3 cups water. Cover and bring to a boil. Reduce to medium/low heat and cook for 10 minutes. Add potatoes and continue to cook another 10 minutes. Add bouillon cubes and bologna cubes. Cover and cook until vegetables are tender. Add ketchup. Mix flour with 1/4 cup water. Stir into stew to thicken. Let simmer for 10 minutes.

Crock Pot Beef Stew

Ingredients:

2 lbs stewing beef (cubed)

1/2 cup flour

1 & 1/2 tsp salt

1/2 tsp pepper

1 & 1/2 cups beef broth

1 tsp Worcestershire sauce

1 clove garlic

1 bay leaf

1 tsp paprika

4 carrots (sliced)

3 potatoes (diced)

2 onions (chopped)

1 stalk celery (sliced)

Directions:

Place meat in crock pot. Mix flour, salt and pepper. Pour over meat, stir to coat meat. Add remaining ingredients and stir to mix well. Cover and cook on low for 10 to 12 hours or on high for 4-6 hours. Stir stew thoroughly before serving.

Meats, Poultry & Game

Beef, Pork, Chicken, Turkey, Bologna, Venison, Wild Fowl & Seal

Lob Scouce

C. Milley Johnson, Port Union, Newfoundland, (nee Edgecombe, Little Catalina, Newfoundland)

Ingredients:

1 lb salt meat, cubed

1 med onion

2 tbsp rice

1 cup carrot, diced

1 cup turnip, diced

1 cup potatoes, diced

1 parsnip, diced

1 cup cabbage, chopped

Directions:

Soak meat overnight to remove the salt. Drain. Add 6 or 7 cups of cold water and boil for 1 hour. Then add the vegetables and rice. Cook until vegetables are tender. (Spare ribs may be used instead of salt beef, if desired).

> **FOOD FOR THOUGHT**
> Perhaps the world little notes nor long remembers individual acts of kindness - but people do.
> -H. Albright

Chunky Beef Stew

Davis Hull, Mississauga, Ontario, (formerly of Springdale, Newfoundland)

Ingredients:

1 & 1/2 lbs beef, cut in 2 inch cubes

3 tbsp flour

2 tbsp oil

3 cups beef bouillon

1 tbsp soya sauce

1 tbsp Worchestershire sauce

4 potatoes, halved

6 sm onions, quartered

4 lg carrots, cut in 2 inch pieces

1 sm turnip, cut in 2 inch pieces

pepper to taste

garlic to taste

1 bay leaf

1/4 tsp ginger

1/4 tsp thyme

1/4 tsp salt

> **SPICE OF LIFE**
> Some folks carefully study the odds at the racetrack so they can become better bettors.

> **FOOD FOR THOUGHT**
> People who never do more than they are paid to do are never paid for any more than they do.
> -Elbert Hubbard

Directions:

Coat meat with flour and heat in oil until brown. Pour off fat. Sprinkle meat with remaining flour. Add remaining ingredients, except vegetables, and bring to a boil. Cover and simmer for 1 hour. Add vegetables and cook until vegetables are done.

In loving memory of our dear mother, **Lucy Cullen Parsons** (nee Lane 1902-1992).
She is sadly missed every day, our dear mother who has passed away...
When the joys are still remembered, but the sorrow has quietly gone
There will always be a special place in the heart, where love lives on.
Her loving children - David, Mildred, Ann & Lucy, Bell Island, Newfoundland.

India Meatless Stew

Catherine Irwin, Truro, Nova Scotia

Ingredients:

2 large onions

1 large clove garlic

4 slices ginger root (peeled first)

5 shakes tumeric

4 shakes cayenne pepper

2 large tomatoes

2 tsp Gramasala (Health Food Store, or East Indian Specialty Store)

1/4 cup water

1/2 tsp salt

3 large potatoes, cubed

Directions:

Saute onion in butter. Add rest of ingredients, cover and cook. (I prefer to add a few more ingredients to the above dish.) My favourite 'extra' ingredients are: 2 carrots, cut in thin, diagonal 1 & 1/2-inch pieces, 2 cabbage slices, cut in 1-inch pieces and quarter each slice. Celery is nice too, cut in 1 & 1/2-inch diagonal pieces. At the very end of cooking time, you can also add 1/2 cup of frozen peas. This recipe can be served with or without meat. Serves about 2 or 3.

Mama's Barbecue Stew

Catherine Irwin, Truro, Nova Scotia

Ingredients:

3 lbs beef, cut in 1 inch pieces

1 & 1/2 cups water

1 tsp salt

8 small whole potatoes

1 cup barbecue sauce

8 carrots, peeled, cut in 1 & 1/2-inch pieces

2 celery sticks, cut in 1-inch pieces

4-6 medium sized onions

1/3 cup cold water

3 tbsp flour

Directions:

Marinate beef in barbecue sauce in refrigerator for 6 hours. Place the beef and marinade, in huge pot. Add water and salt. Bring to a boil; cover and simmer 15 minutes. Add carrots; cover, continuing to cook about another 10-15 minutes. Now add potatoes, onions and celery and continue to cook at medium setting, until tender. To cold water, add flour. When creamy, add to hot pot slowly. Within 2 minutes turn off stew. This dish is completed.

Shepherd's Pie with Rice Topping

Ingredients:

2 tsp vegetable oil

2 carrots, diced

1 onion, chopped

1 lb lean ground beef

2/3 cup beef stock
1 tbsp tomato paste
1 tbsp Worcestershire sauce
salt
pepper
3/4 cup green peas, fresh or frozen
3 cups rice, cooked
1 egg, beaten
1 cup cheddar cheese, shredded
1/2 cup sour cream

Directions:

In ovenproof 10-inch (25cm) skillet, heat oil over medium heat. Cook carrots and onion for 3 minutes. Add beef, and cook for about 5 minutes or until browned. Drain off fat. Stir in stock, tomato paste, worcestershire sauce and salt and pepper to taste. Cook for 5 minutes, uncovered, stirring occasionally. Add peas, cook for 1 more minute. Spread evenly in pan. Stir together cooked rice, egg, cheese and sour cream. Spread evenly over meat. Broil for 7 minutes or until rice is heated through.

Macaroni Chili

Ingredients:

2 cups macaroni
3 tbsp olive oil
1 qt tomato juice
3 cloves garlic
2 tbsp chili powder
1/2 tsp oregano
1/2 tsp cumin
1 bay leaf
1 cup chopped sweet mixed pickles
2 lbs hamburger meat
1 - 28oz can tomatoes
2 cups chopped onion
4 tsp salt
1/2 tsp tabasco sauce
1 - 19oz can red kidney beans, drained

Directions:

Brown hamburger meat in oil. Add tomatoes, juice, onions, garlic, salt and seasonings. Simmer, covered for 1 hour. Stir in kidney beans and pickles. Cook 1/2 hour longer. Remove bay leaf. Cook and drain macaroni. Stir into chili. Serve in bowls. Makes 4 to 6 servings.

Three Bean Chili

Ingredients:

1/2 lb spicy sausage, chopped
1 onion, chopped
2 cloves garlic, crushed
1 (14 & 1/2 oz) can chili style chunky tomatoes

FOOD FOR THOUGHT
Time is not your enemy
until you try to kill it.

SPICE OF LIFE
Skipper's Highway Observations - If there's a hole in the road, your tire will find it.

TRIVIA TIDBITS
Australian aborigines were treating wounds with moulds growing on trees thousands of years before penicillin was produced from moulds.

1 (15oz) can barbecue-style beans
1 (15oz) can black or pinto beans, drained
1 (8 & 3/4oz) can kidney beans, drained
sour cream
green onion, sliced

Directions:
In large saucepan cook sausage, onion and garlic until tender; drain. Add tomatoes and beans. Cover and simmer 15 minutes or until heated through, stirring occasionally. Garnish with sour cream and sliced green onion, if desired.

Country-Style Pork with Beans

Ingredients:
2 slices bacon, diced
3 boneless pork chops (3/4 lb) sliced, 1/4-inch thick with fat trimmed off
1 medium onion, chopped
1 clove garlic, minced
1 tsp thyme, crushed
1 (17oz) can green lima beans, drained
1 (14oz) can original style stewed tomatoes, chopped
1 (8oz) can kidney beans, drained
salt to taste
pepper to taste

Directions:
In large skillet, over low heat, cook bacon until just crisp. Raise heat to medium; stir in meat, onion, garlic and thyme. Stir fry for 5 minutes; drain off excess fat. Add remaining ingredients; bring to boil. Reduce heat and simmer, uncovered, 10 minutes. Season to taste with salt and pepper. Makes 4 servings.

Enchiladas

Gerine Collingwood, Rocky Harbour, Newfoundland

Tortillas

Ingredients:
1 egg
1 2/3 cup water
1 cup Tea-Bisk
2/3 cup cornmeal

Directions:
Beat egg and water together. Beat in tea-bisk and corn meal until smooth. Preheat a 7-inch frying pan or crepe pan and brush with butter. Pour 2 tbsp batter into pan. When edges become dry, turn and cook the other side. Repeat until all batter is used. Tortillas may be made several days ahead, wrapped and stored in refrigerator or freezer. Makes 20 7-inch tortillas.

Chicken Filling Ingredients:
2 cups chopped cooked chicken
1/2 cup chopped green pepper
1/2 cup cubed cheddar cheese
2 tomatoes, peeled and chopped

1 tsp salt
1/8 tsp pepper
1/4 cup tomato sauce
Directions:

Combine filling ingredients in a bowl. Spoon about 2 tbsp of filling down centre of 12 tortillas. Roll up tightly (ends open) and place in 13x9 inch baking dish.

Tomato Sauce Ingredients:

1 (14oz) can tomatoes
2 tbsp chili peppers, finely chopped
1/2 tsp salt
Directions:

Combine ingredients in a blender and blend until smooth. Use 1/4 cup sauce for chicken filling. Pour remaining sauce over enchiladas. Bake at 350°F for 15-20 minutes. Sprinkle with 1/2 cup grated cheese and return to oven until cheese melts. (Sprinkle with chopped green onion. Serve with sour cream and shredded lettuce if desired.) Makes 6 servings.

Beef Filling

Ingredients:

2 tbsp butter
1 onion, finely chopped
1/4 cup chopped green pepper
2 tbsp chopped red pepper
1/2 lb lean ground beef
1 cup crushed tomatoes
1/4 tsp oregano
1/4 tsp chili powder
salt to taste
pepper to taste
Directions:

Melt butter in saucepan. Saute onion and peppers until tender. Add beef and cook until meat loses its redness. Stir in tomatoes and seasonings. Cook over medium heat for 30 minutes until sauce thickens. Spoon about 3 tbsp filling in each enchilada. Fold edges over filling and place in 13x9 inch baking dish. Continue as for chicken enchiladas.

Ruth's Meatloaf

Ruth Keats, Mississauga, Ontario
Ingredients:

1 egg, slightly beaten
1 tbsp sweet relish
1 tbsp ketchup or chili sauce
1/2 onion, grated
1 tsp salt
1/4 tsp pepper
1 tsp parsley
1/2 tsp onion flakes
2 & 1/2 lbs ground beef
1/2 cup Oglivie Quick Oats (or other brand)

Directions:

Combine slightly beaten egg with relish, ketchup, onion and seasonings. Add ground beef and quick oats; mix thoroughly. Pack into a 9"x5"x3" loaf pan. Bake in a moderate oven at 350°F for 1 hour.

Chicken Wings in Soup Vinegar Sauce

Ruth Keats, Mississauga, Ontario

Ingredients:

3 lbs chicken wings (or more)

1 tbsp soy sauce

1 tbsp cooking oil

1/4 cup brown sugar

1/2 tsp salt

1 tin tomato soup

1 tsp chili powder

1 tsp celery seed

1/4 cup vinegar

Directions:

Pat wings dry with towel and arrange in layers on large shallow baking pan. Mix together oil and soy sauce and brush over all the wings. Mix together sugar, salt, chili powder, and celery seed. Sprinkle over top. Place 5 inches below preheated broiler and brown for about 10 minutes. Remove from oven; add soup and vinegar mixture over wings. Bake at 350°F for 1 & 1/4 hours or until tender and sauce reduces to a rich mahogany.

Chicken Wings

Ruth Keats, Mississauga, Ontario

Ingredients:

1/2 cup honey

1/4 cup lemon juice

1/2 cup water

3 tbsp ketchup

2 cloves garlic, crushed

1 tsp salt

1 tsp ground ginger

3 lbs chicken wings

1/4 cup butter

TRIVIA TIDBITS
During WWII people could purchace 'mock banana', which was actually made from parsnips.

Directions:

Marinate chicken in first 7 ingredients for several hours (the longer the better). Melt butter in glass 9x13-inch pan; place and turn wings so there is butter on both sides. Bake for 25 minutes at 400°F then turn over the wings and bake for another 20 minutes. (Total baking time is 45 minutes).

Mom's Meatloaf

submitted by Dave Parsons, Whitby, Ontario in memory of his mother, Lucy Cullen Parsons (nee Lane)

Ingredients:

2 lbs hamburger meat

1 tsp salt

1 med onion

1 cup milk

1 tsp Worcestershire sauce

2 eggs, beaten

1 tsp pepper

1 cup bread crumbs

1/3 cup ketchup

Directions:

Mix all ingredients together and shape into a loaf. Place in a loaf pan and bake at 375°F for 1 hour.

SPICE OF LIFE
Skipper's Observations - why is "abbreviation" such a long word?

Trinidad Stewed Chicken

Vidya Bachon, Trinidad, West Indies

Ingredients:

1 chicken (3 & 1/2 to 4 lb) cut up

1 tbsp seasoning

2 cloves garlic, minced

2 tbsp sugar

1 tbsp cooking oil

1 onion, chopped or sliced

salt to taste

pepper to taste

Directions:

Cut up chicken, rinse quickly, do not soak in water. Add seasonings, garlic, onion, salt and black pepper and leave to marinate for 1/2 hour. Heat oil in a heavy pot, add sugar and allow to brown. Add chicken and allow to brown all over, cook until water dries out. Add 1 cup water and cover pot; cook until chicken is tender. Potatoes may be cut up and added towards the end with carrots and sweet peppers. Serve hot with rice or potatoes, salad and vegetables. Dumplings can also be added during the last 10 minutes of cooking.

FOOD FOR THOUGHT
Let him who would enjoy a good future waste none of his present.
-Roger Babson

Curry Chicken

Vidya Bachon, Trinidad, West Indies

Ingredients:

3 tsp curry

2 cloves garlic

1 slice hot yellow pepper

2 tomatoes

4 tbsp cooking oil

1 sprig thyme

1 whole chicken, cut in peices

1 sprig chives

TRIVIA TIDBITS
King Louis XIV bathed in a mixture of wine and cream two or three times a week.

---

1 onion
1 tsp Angostura bitters
Directions:
Cut chicken in small pieces. Cut up or mince seasonings and add to chicken. Let stand for 30 minutes. Heat oil in an iron pot. Mix curry powder with 1/2 cup cold water until smooth. Add to hot oil and cook 2-3 minutes. Add chicken and stir to coat in curry. Allow all water to dry out; stir well. Then add hot water and allow to cook until tender; add Angostura bitters and season to taste.

Barbecue-Style Meat Loaf

Catherine Irwin, Truro, Nova Scotia
Ingredients:
1 & 1/2 lb ground (medium) beef
1/2 cup fresh whole wheat bread crumbs
1 onion, chopped
1 egg, beaten
1 & 1/2 tsp salt
1/4 tsp pepper
2 cans tomato sauce
1/2 cup water
3 tbsp vinegar
3 tbsp brown sugar
2 tbsp prepared mustard
2 tsp Worcestershire sauce

> **SPICE OF LIFE**
> Skipper's Definitions:
> A shin is a device
> for finding furniture
> in the dark.

Directions:
Mix ground beef, bread crumbs, chopped onion, egg, seasonings, and 1/2 can tomato sauce. Form into a loaf or fill a narrow, greased loaf pan. Combine remaining tomato sauce with water, vinegar, brown sugar, mustard and Worcestershire sauce. Pour over the loaf. Bake at 350°F for 1 hour. Serves about 6. (This is an oldie, but goodie I've been serving for many years. The romance of this recipe is its high flavour. It is inexpensive and easy to make. I serve this dish with baked or mashed potatoes, frozen peas and my special 'candied carrots'. Very colourful plate).

Creole Rice

Vidya Bachon, Trinidad, West Indies
Ingredients:
1 lb lean beef, cubed
1 cup rice, uncooked
1 green sweet pepper, cut in strips
1/4 cup tomato paste
1/4 lb bacon, cut up
1 red sweet pepper, cut in strips
1 lg onion, chopped
1 tsp salt
2 & 1/2 cups water
1 tbsp peanut butter

TRIVIA TID-BITS
In Burma, around 5,000 people die from poisonous snake bites each year.

Directions:
Cook beef and onion in deep saucepan. Add bacon and cook for 5 minutes. Add other ingredients and cover. Simmer until rice is cooked and meat is tender. Garnish with parsley and serve with a salad.

Beef and Yogurt Curry

Archie Ridout, Rexdale, Ontario, (formerly of Twillingate, Newfoundland)

Ingredients:

1 lb tender boneless beef

3 lg onions, diced

2 - 1-inch pieces ginger, crushed

2 cloves garlic, crushed

1/4 tsp ground cardamom

1 tsp ground coriander

4 whole cloves

1/4 tsp cinnamon

1 & 1/2 cups yogurt

salt to taste

1 tsp chili powder

1/2 tsp turmeric

3 tbsp oil

2 bay leaves

SPICE OF LIFE
A smile increases your face value.

Directions:

Cut the meat into 1-inch pieces. Mix the onions, ginger and spices (except bay leaves) with the yogurt. Place meat into yogurt mixture and marinate for at least 1 hour up to 24. Heat the oil in a skillet. Lightly fry the bay leaf, then add the marinated meat. Stir and heat thorough, then reduce heat, cover the pan and cook for 1 - 1 & 1/2 hours or until the meat is tender. Makes 4 servings.

Fried Rice with Ham and Bean Sprouts

Vidya Bachon, Trinidad, West Indies

Ingredients:

2 tbsp oil

2 onions, finely chopped

1 clove garlic, crushed

6 cups cooked rice

1 cup cooked ham, diced

2 tbsp soy sauce

2 eggs, beaten

salt, if desired

black pepper, if desired

hot pepper, if desired

1 cup bean sprouts

TRIVIA TIDBITS

There were no banks in the thirteen colonies prior to the American Revolution.

Directions:

Heat the oil in a heavy pot (iron) and fry the onions and garlic for 2 minutes over medium heat. Add the rice. Mix well and heat through. Mix the ham with the soy sauce. Add it to the rice mixture and mix well. Season the beaten egg with salt and pepper and pour into the rice in a thin stream, stirring until the eggs are cooked. Stir in the bean sprouts and heat through. Serve immediately.

Meats, Poultry & Game

Beef, Pork, Chicken, Turkey, Bologna, Venison, Wild Fowl & Seal

Biryani

Archie Ridout, Rexdale, Ontario, (formerly of Twillingate, Newfoundland)

<u>Ingredients:</u>

3 chicken breasts

1 tsp ginger

2 garlic cloves, minced

1 & 1/2 tsp salt

1 tomato, peeled and chopped

1 cup buttermilk

Mix all the above ingredients and leave to marinate for at least 1 hour; then add the following:

1 cup onion, chopped

1 tsp red pepper

1/2 tsp nutmeg

1/2 tsp cloves

3 tsp coriander

1/2 tsp cinnamon

1/2 tsp cardamon

<u>Directions:</u>

Cook slowly until tender. Remove chicken from bone, reserve liquid. Add enough water to the cooking liquid to make 3 cups. Cook 2 cups of rice in this liquid until done. Add rice to the chicken and mix well. Decorate with raisins, cashews and eggs. Makes 6-8 servings.

> **TRIVIA TIDBITS**
> The word avocado derives from ahuacatl - the Nahuatl world for "testicle."

> **FOOD FOR THOUGHT**
> Joys shared are doubled
> - sorrows shared are halved.

Chili Con Carne (Hot Chili with Meat)

Trudy S. Simmons, Twillingate, Newfoundland, (nee Forward, Tizzard's Harbour, Newfoundland)

<u>Ingredients</u>:

5 slices bacon

8 oz Italian sausage links, sliced

1 & 1/2 lb stewing beef, diced

1 sm green bell pepper, chopped

1 clove garlic, minced

2 pickled jalopeno peppers, seeded & chopped

1 - 1 & 1/2 tbsp chili powder

1/2 tsp crushed red pepper

1/2 tsp salt

1/4 tsp dried oregano, crushed

2 & 1/2 cups water

1 - 12oz can tomato paste

1 - 15 & 1/2oz can pinto beans, drained

> **TRIVIA TIDBITS**
> The rainbow trout makes its nest from pebbles which it carries in its mouth.

<u>Directions:</u>

In large saucepan or dutch oven, cook bacon until crisp; drain and crumble. Discard drippings; set bacon aside. Brown sausage in same pan. Drain sausage reserving 2 tbsp drippings; set sausage aside. In reserved drippings, brown diced beef, onions, green pepper and garlic. Add the cooked bacon, sausage, jalepeno peppers, chili powder, crushed red pepper, salt and oregano. Stir in water and tomato paste. Bring to boiling; simmer uncovered for 1 & 1/2 hours, stirring occasionally. Stir in beans; simmer covered for 30 minutes more. Makes 8 servings.

Meats, Poultry & Game

Beef, Pork, Chicken, Turkey, Bologna, Venison, Wild Fowl & Seal

Chicken Sukiyaki

Hilda Reid, Ignace, Ontario (nee Harnum, Bishop's Falls, Newfoundland)

Ingredients:

2 & 1/2 - 3 lbs chicken
3 tbsp shortening
1 lg onion, sliced
1 can bamboo shoots, sliced
1/2 cup sugar
3/4 cup soya sauce
3/4 cup hot water and mushroom liquid
1 can mushrooms, drained
1/2 - 1 lb bean sprouts
5 green onions, cut up
1 tofu - soybean curd

Directions:

Cut chicken from bones and fry in hot shortening. Add onions and bamboo shoots. Add 3 tbsp sugar, 1/4 cup soya sauce and 1/2 cup liquid. Boil gently for 5 minutes. Add mushrooms, bean sprouts and green onions. Continue to cook adding remaining sugar, soya sauce and liquid, a little at a time. Add tofu and allow to cook for a few minutes. Makes 6 servings.

> ### *TRIVIA TIDBITS*
> The world famous Parisian restaurant, Maxim's, now stands on the site of a former ice-cream shop. The ice-cream shop may have been there today except for the fact that its owner, an Italian, foolishly decorated the front of his business with German flags on Bastille Day back in 1890. He was quickly forced out of business.

Pork Chow Mein

Hilda Reid, Ignace, Ontario (nee Harnum, Bishop's Falls, Newfoundland)

Ingredients:

1 lb pork
1 med stalk celery
1 lb bean sprouts
3 med onions
1 can (10oz) mushrooms
1/2 lb fried noodles
2 cloves garlic
2 tsp sugar
2 & 1/2 tsp salt
1 & 1/2 tsp accent
2 eggs

Directions:

Wash vegetables and drain. Cut celery into thin lengths, half onions and slice thin. Dice garlic very small. Slice the mushrooms. Cut meat into thin strips. Heat large skillet. Fry meat with garlic; add 1/2 tsp salt, celery, onion, bean sprouts and mushrooms. Mix well and add 2 tsp salt, sugar and accent. When vegetables begin to cook, add noodles. Turn heat low and cook a few minutes while mixing constantly. Beat and fry egg; garnish with egg and green onions. Let cool and slice in thin lengths.

SPICE OF LIFE
Skipper's Sober Advice - Never sleep with anyone crazier than yourself.

Samosas

Archie Ridout, Rexdale, Ontario, (formerly of Twillingate, Newfoundland)

Ingredients (for Pastry):

1 & 1/2 cups flour

> **SPICE OF LIFE**
> If folks need to be liked, they shouldn't think out loud.

1/4 tsp salt
4 tbsp clarified butter
6 tbsp warm water
Ingredients (for Filling):
4 tbsp oil
1 med onion, peeled and minced
3/4 piece of ginger, peeled and minced
6 cloves garlic, minced
1 lb ground beef
1/2 tsp ground tumeric
1 tsp salt
1 tsp garam masala
2 tbsp parsley, minced

FOOD FOR THOUGHT
If you are going to kill time
why not work it to death?

SPICE OF LIFE
An outside elevator will drive some
people up a wall.

Directions (for pastry):
Place flour and salt in a bowl. Rub in the butter with your fingertips so that the flour resembles fine bread crumbs. Add warm water, a tablespoon at a time, and begin to gather the flour into a ball. Knead well. Wrap dough in plastic wrap and leave in refrigerator until ready to use.

Directions (for Filling):
Heat the oil in a skillet over medium heat. Add onions and fry until golden. Add ginger and garlic and fry another minute. Add the beef, tumeric and salt, and fry for 4-5 minutes. Stir in 1/4 cup of water; bring to a boil, cover and reduce heat and simmer gently for 30 minutes. Add garam masala and parsley. Stir and dry off any liquid. Make a paste with 2 tbsp of flour and 2 & 1/2 tbsp luke-warm water. Set aside. Roll pastry out on a floured surface as thin as possible. Cut into rounds. Fill each round with 1 tbsp of filling. Fold over the edges and use the flour paste to seal. Heat 2" of oil in a pan on medium heat and fry the Samosas about 1-2 minutes on each side. Drain on paper towels and keep warm in a 200°F oven until ready to serve. Makes 6-8 servings.

Golden Coin Beef

Charlene Jenkins, Etobicoke, Ontario (formerly of Springdale, Newfoundland)

Ingredients:
1 & 1/2 lb round steak
1/2 tsp baking soda
1 tbsp cornstarch
1 tsp sugar
1 tbsp soy sauce
2 tbsp cooking oil
1/2 tsp pepper
2 tbsp water
Sauce:
2 tbsp tomato sauce
1 tsp Worcestershire sauce
1 & 1/2 tbsp soy sauce
1 tsp Accent
2 tbsp sugar
1 tsp salt

FOOD FOR THOUGHT
Things may come to those who wait, but only the
things left by those who hustle.
                                    -Abraham Lincoln

Directions:
Pound round steak on both sides and cut away fat. Soak with all the ingredients for 3 hours or

longer. Saute steak until done. Cook sauce separately and add water to thin it. Cook a bit longer. Pour sauce over meat and serve hot. Serves 6.

Little Loaves

Denise Hibbs, Springdale, Newfoundland, (nee Jenkins)

Ingredients:

1 lb lean ground beef
1/4 cup finely chopped onions
1/4 cup bread crumbs, fine dry
1 (7 & 1/2 oz) can tomato sauce
1 egg
1 tsp salt
pepper, to taste
1 green pepper, cut in strips
1/4 cup marmalade

TRIVIA TIDBITS
In late Victorian England it was possible to buy shoes with revolving heels.

Directions:

Combine beef, onion, bread crumbs, egg, 1/2 can tomato sauce, salt and pepper. Shape into 4 small loaves. Top each loaf with green pepper strips. Bake at 450°F for 15 minutes. Remove and brush with marmalade. Pour on remaining tomato sauce and bake for 20 minutes more. NOTE: Bran can be substituted for bread crumbs.

Seafood

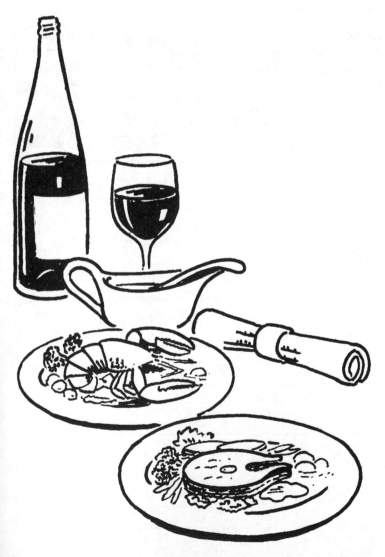

Swimmers

Crawlers

&

Creepers

Fisherman's Brewis

Ruby Wellon, Deer Lake, Newfoundland, (nee Rideout)

Ingredients:

2 & 1/2 - 3 lbs fresh cod

5-6 cakes hard bread

1 tsp salt

Directions:

Soak bread in cold water until soft (for several hours or overnight). Boil fish in salted water for approximately 1/2 hour. (Fish may be cut in smaller pieces if desired) Remove fins, skin and bones from fish. Flake fish into large bowl. During last five minutes, break hard bread into a very small pieces (a potato masher is ideal to use). Add flaked fish, mix together well and serve hot. Makes eight servings.

> **SPICE OF LIFE**
> If ignorance is bliss, why aren't more people happy?

Spiced Newfoundland Herring

Miss Gertrude V. Sweetapple, Glovertown, Newfoundland

Ingredients:

4 fresh herring, filleted

2 tsp salt

2 tbsp vinegar

2 tbsp water

1 & 1/2 tbsp sugar

1/4 tsp pepper

pinch of ground cloves

2 tbsp browned bread crumbs

Directions:

> **TRIVIA TIDBITS**
> The wife of Philip the fifth of Spain decided to surprise her husband by having artificial waterfalls and fountains built at his palace. Upon seeing the gift, Philip remarked, "It has cost me three million and has amused me three minutes."

Rub the filleted herring with salt and place them in a flat baking dish so that they overlap slightly. Mix together vinegar, water, sugar, pepper and cloves. Pour over the herring. Sprinkle with bread crumbs if you wish. Bake at 350°F for 25-30 minutes.

Baked Cod Tongues

Anita Wilson, Renews, Newfoundland, (nee Coombs, Portugal Cove South, Trepassey, Newfoundland)

Ingredients:

24 cod tongues

2 tbsp salt

1 cup milk

1 cup bread crumbs

Directions:

> **FOOD FOR THOUGHT**
> Use the stumbling blocks of life as stepping stones to success.

Wipe tongues with damp cloth. Soak in milk in which salt is dissolved for about 10 minutes. Drain and roll in crumbs. Place on greased sheet and bake 450°F oven for 10 minutes. Serve with lemon slices.

> In loving memory of my mother, **E. Mae Isaacs**, born June 16, 1903, Bulls Cove, Burin, Newfoundland, died January 5, 1990 at Guelph, Ontario.
> My father, **Wm. H. Croft**, born August 6, 1899, Square Islands, Labrador, died October 14, 1961 at Guelph, Ontario.
> Forever in our hearts.
> *Reta Atkinson (nee Croft)*

Seafood — Swimmers, Crawlers & Creepers

Newfoundland Fish & Brewis

Marie Maher, St. John's, Newfoundland (nee Whitty, Torbay, Newfoundland)

Ingredients:

1/2 lb salt codfish, skinned

2 cakes hard bread

2 medium size carrots, cut in slim circles

1 green pepper, cut on the round

1 lg onion, cut in circles

Directions:

Soak fish in cold water overnight. Change water before boiling next day. Boil for 10 minutes, drain. Soak hard bread in another saucepan, covering with water. Next day just bring hard bread to a boil and drain. Cut carrots in slim circles. Cut green pepper on the round, slim as possible. Cut onion in circles. In iron frying pan or wok, melt 1 tbsp of margarine and stir fry vegetables until crisp or to taste. Use pepper and salt as desired. After fish and brewis are drained, break up in small pieces. Use a little pepper if desired and sprinkle 2 tsp of melted shortening over the whole thing mixed together. In a casserole dish put half of the fish and brewis, then lay on the carrots, green pepper, and onion. Then place on the remainder of fish and brewis. Sprinkle on a couple of tablespoons of grated mozzarella or cheddar cheese. Put under broiler for a few minutes until heated through. Use margarine and cheese to your taste. This is a very nice meal with a green salad.

Fried Squid with Rice

Rosalee Bungay, Seal Cove, White Bay, Newfoundland

Ingredients:

(Depends on how many people you are serving)

2 squid (per person)

1/2 cup minute rice (per person)

1 lg onion, chopped

butter

salt to taste

pepper to taste

Directions:

Cut squid into rings. Fry in butter until golden brown and tender. Add onion, salt and pepper; cook 1-2 minutes. Add equal parts water to rice. Remove from heat and let stand 5 minutes. Stir and serve.

Angela's Salmon Pie

Angela Waterman, Glenwood, Newfoundland, (nee John)

Ingredients:

1 can salmon

3 tbsp flour

potatoes

1 egg, unbeaten

1 & 1/2 cups potato water

1/4 cup butter

1/4 cup warm milk

2 onions
Directions:
Cook onions in butter, then remove pan from stove and mix in flour using fork to stir. Add water, slowly stirring all the time. Add salmon and return to stove to thicken. Mash potatoes well while hot with 1/4 cup warm milk and butter. Add one egg unbeaten and mash well. Spread potato mixture over the salmon and bake in hot oven until golden brown. Serve with green peas or carrots.

Salmon Burgers

Margaret & Leonard Parsons, Admirals Beach, St. Mary's Bay, Nfld (formerly of Clattice Harbour, Placentia Bay, Newfoundland)

Ingredients:
1 can salmon
1/2 cup chopped onion
1/2 cup butter
1/3 cup salmon liquid
1/3 cup bread crumbs
2 eggs
1/4 cup parsley, chopped
1 tsp mustard
1/2 tsp salt
6 buttered hamburger buns

FOOD FOR THOUGHT
The people to get even with are the ones who have helped you.

Directions:
Drain and flake salmon. Reserve liquid. Beat eggs. Cook onion in butter. Add salmon liquid, bread crumbs, eggs, parsley, mustard, salt and salmon. Mix well. Shape into cakes; roll in breadcrumbs. Fry in pan until golden brown on both sides. Place in buttered buns.

Claudine's Cod Au Gratin

Mrs. Claudine Barnes, Corner Brook, Newfoundland (nee Pye, Cape Charles, Labrador)

Ingredients:
4 cups cooked codfish (boiled fresh cod)
3 tbsp melted butter
4 tbsp flour
1/2 tsp salt
1/8 tsp pepper
2 cups milk (1 canned, 1 fresh)
1 & 1/2 cups grated cheese
1 onion

SPICE OF LIFE
Divorce comes from having popped the question before questioning the pop.

Directions:
Flake fish. Make white sauce with next five ingredients. Boil till thickened. Arrange flaked fish and onion in casserole dish, cover with white sauce. Top with grated cheese. Bake at 350°F for about 45 minutes.

This page is dedicated to my parents, **Garfield Marsden** of Francois, Newfoundland, and **Elizabeth** (nee Pink of Cape La Hune), now living in Burgeo, Newfoundland. Garfield fished out of Lunenburg, Nova Scotia in the 1940's. In the 1950's and 60's he was lightkeeper at Western Point Francois.
Jim G. Marsden, Burgeo, Newfoundland

Seafood
Swimmers, Crawlers & Creepers

Scallops Louisiana

Rex Sterling, Pasadena, Newfoundland

Ingredients:

1/2 cup onions, chopped

1 clove garlic

1/4 cup green pepper, chopped

4 tbsp margarine

2 tbsp flour

1 can whole tomatoes

1 & 1/2 tsp salt

dash of pepper

dash of cayenne

1 tsp chili powder

1/2 tsp sugar

1/4 cup grated Parmesan cheese

1 lb scallops, fresh or frozen

3 cups hot, cooked rice

Directions:

Saute onion, garlic and green pepper in margarine 5 minutes or until delicately browned. Add flour and blend well. Add tomatoes, salt, pepper, cayenne, chili powder, sugar and cheese. Add scallops. Spread hot rice in a shallow casserole and pour sauce with scallops over it. Heat in a 325°F oven for 15 minutes, just until the edges of the scallops curl. Time 55-60 minutes. Serve with salad, chilled grapefruit segments, and hot biscuits.

FOOD FOR THOUGHT

Even if you are on the right track, you'll get run over if you just sit there.
-Oliver Wendell Holmes

TRIVIA TIDBITS

London, Ontario, has more thunder and lightening storms than any other part of Canada. It averages approximately 36 days of thunderstorm activity per year.

Shrimp Quichelettes

Archie Ridout, Rexdale, Ontario (formerly of Twillingate, Newfoundland)

Ingredients:

pastry for 24 tartlets

eggwash

Filling:

2 eggs

1 cup light cream

pinch pepper

pinch nutmeg

1/4 tsp salt

1/2 lb cooked shrimp

1/2 cup Swiss cheese, grated

SPICE OF LIFE

Marriage is a three-ring circus: engagement ring, wedding ring, and suffering.

Directions:

Prepare tartlets in tartlet tins or use purchased tartlets. Brush with eggwash and prick bottoms with fork. Bake at 400°F for 7-9 minutes. Cool. Beat eggs, cream and seasonings. Distribute shrimp among tartlet crusts. Add some of the egg mixture. Sprinkle some of the grated cheese on each tartlet. Bake in middle of oven at 375°F for 12-15 minutes. Serve warm.

Seafood

Swimmers, Crawlers & Creepers

Seafood
Swimmers, Crawlers & Creepers

Crab-Stuffed Flounder (or Sole)

Reta Atkinson, Guelph, Ontario

Ingredients:
1/4 cup onion, chopped
1/4 cup celery, chopped
1/4 cup sweet red pepper, chopped
4 tbsp butter or margarine
1/4 lb crabmeat, picked over and flaked
1/2 cup soft bread crumbs
3 tsp lemon juice
1/2 tsp salt
1/8 tsp pepper
few drops liquid red pepper seasoning
4 small flounder fillets, about 4 ounces each
paprika

SPICE OF LIFE
When our daughter married, we lost her but gained a telephone number.

Directions:
Preheat oven to moderate (350°F). Butter small shallow baking dish. Saute onion, celery and red pepper in 2 tbsp butter in saucepan until soft, about 2 minutes. Mix in crabmeat, bread crumbs, 1 tsp lemon juice, salt, pepper and red pepper seasoning. Place fillets skin-side up. Mound crab mixture in centre of fillets. Overlap ends of fillets over top of stuffing. Fasten with wooden picks. Place in prepared dish. Melt remaining 2 tbsp butter in small saucepan; stir in lemon juice. Pour over fish; sprinkle with paprika. Bake in prepared moderate oven at 350°F for 18 to 20 minutes or until fish flakes when pierced with fork. Garnish with lemon wedges and parsley and serve with herb-seasoned rice, if you wish. Makes 4 servings.

Baked Almond Shrimp

Reta Atkinson, Guelph, Ontario

Ingredients:
4 tbsp butter
3/4 cup green onion, chopped
2 lbs shrimp, cooked, cleand & diced
3 cups cooked rice
1 & 1/2 tsp salt
1/8 tsp tabasco
1/8 tsp nutmeg
1/4 cup pimiento-stuffed olives, chopped
1 cup tomatoes, peeled & chopped
1-8oz can green peas, drained
1 cup heavy cream
1/4 cup dry sherry

TRIVIA TIDBITS
The President's residence became known as the 'Whitehouse' during the Anglo-American War of 1812. When a British force captured Washington, one of the many buildings they set on fire was the President's mansion. Not much damage was done to the building and a coat of whitewash was sufficient to cover the smoke-stain; hence, the name.

This page is dedicated to my parents -
the late **Martin and Mary (Best) Melvin**,
La Manch, Southern Shore, Newfoundland.
My dad Martin Melvin 1891-1949; my mom Mary (Best) Melvin 1899-1966.
R.I.P. my love - Frank Melvin, Manitouwadge, Ontario

1/2 cup blanched sliced almonds
1/4 cup blanched ground almonds
Directions:
Melt the butter in a skillet; saute the green onions 5 minutes. Mix together the sauteed onions, shrimp, rice, salt, Tabasco, nutmeg, olives, tomatoes, peas, cream, sherry, and sliced almonds. Turn into a 2-quart buttered baking dish. Sprinkle with the ground almonds. Bake in a 350°F oven 30 minutes or until delicately browned. Serves 6-8.

Cod Fillet Dish

Mary Russell, Brooklyn, Newfoundland, (nee Ash, Come By Chance, Newfoundland)

Ingredients:
1 lb cod fillets
1/2 tsp salt
1 cup milk
2 tbsp butter
2 tbsp flour
1/2 tsp dry mustard powder
1 cup cheese, grated
1 cup bread crumbs

> ### *TRIVIA TIDBITS*
> California was named by Spanish explorers, possibly after an island in a popular Spanish story. It was a province of Spanish-speaking Mexico until it was captured by U.S. troops in the Mexican war of 1846 to 1848. It became the 31st state of the Union in 1850. Many expatriate Mexicans now live in California, some of whom entered a land which was once theirs, illegally.

Directions:
Cut fish into serving size pieces and place in a greased baking dish. Make cheese sauce and pour over the fish. Top with bread crumbs and bake 35 minutes at 350°F. CHEESE SAUCE: Melt butter and blend in flour, mustard powder and salt. Gradually add the milk, stirring constantly until sauce is thickened. Add grated cheese until melted.

Tuna Burgers

Angela Waterman, Glenwood, Newfoundland, (nee John)

Ingredients:
1 tin tuna
1 tin mushroom soup
1 tbsp vinegar
1 cup celery, chopped
1/4 cup onion, chopped
hamburger buns

> ### FOOD FOR THOUGHT
> We, whoever we are, must have a daily goal in our lives, no matter how small or great, to make that day mean something.
> *-Maxwell Maltz*

Directions:
Mix first five ingredients together and spread on hamburger buns. Top with cheese slices. Broil at 350°F for 20 minutes or until cheese melts.

Squid Rings

Mrs. Alma Taylor, Mt. Moriah, Bay of Islands, Newfoundland, (nee LeDrew, Bell Island, Newfoundland)

Ingredients:
2 squid, cleaned and skinned
250ml flour
2ml sugar
2ml salt

> ### SPICE OF LIFE
> Contentment sometimes depends on a person's position; other times, on his disposition.

Seafood
Swimmers, Crawlers & Creepers

1 egg, beaten
250ml milk
30ml oil
Directions:
Wash and clean squid. Remove skin. Prepare batter, beating until smooth. Cut squid in rings. Dip in batter and deep fry until golden brown. Batter may be used for shrimp, scallops or onion rings.

Salmon or Tuna Loaf

Mrs. Alma Taylor, Mt. Moriah, Bay of Islands, Newfoundland, (nee LeDrew, Bell Island, Newfoundland)
Ingredients:
1 lg can salmon or tuna
125ml salad dressing
1 egg
125ml green pepper, chopped
15ml lemon juice
1 can cream of mushroom soup
125ml celery, chopped
250ml bread crumbs
125ml onion, chopped
Directions:
Combine all ingredients. Press into a greased loaf pan. Bake at 180°C for 1 hour.

> **TRIVIA TIDBITS**
> It takes approximately 55 hours and to drive from Toronto to Vancouver.

Lobster Newburg

Mrs. Alma Taylor, Mt. Moriah, Bay of Islands, Newfoundland, (nee LeDrew, Bell Island, Newfoundland)
Ingredients:
250ml cooked lobster meat
2ml salt
65ml flour
64ml white wine
375ml milk
65ml butter
1ml pepper
Directions:
Cut the lobster into bite-size pieces.
Melt butter in a saucepan. Add flour and stir, add milk gradually, stirring until thick.
Season with salt and pepper.
Add lobster and wine.
Heat through and serve.

FOOD FOR THOUGHT
Life does not consist in holding good cards, but in playing a poor hand as well.
-*Thomas Fuller*

Seafood
Swimmers, Crawlers & Creepers

Marinated Herring

Mrs. Alma Taylor, Mt. Moriah, Bay of Islands, Newfoundland, (nee LeDrew, Bell Island, Newfoundland)

Ingredients:
125ml vinegar
125ml salad oil
1 bottle red wine
2ml thyme
5 ml salt
2 carrots, sliced
2 onions, sliced
2ml black pepper
2ml whole cloves
1 bay leaf

SPICE OF LIFE
A credit card is a way to increase your yearning capacity.

Directions:
Mix ingredients and pour over fish. Make sure marinade covers the fish. Refrigerate, turning fish over frequently, for 12-24 hours. Pour off marinade. Cook fish in 230°C oven for 20 minutes.

Cod Fish Balls

Mrs. Alma Taylor, Mt. Moriah, Bay of Islands, Newfoundland, (nee LeDrew, Bell Island, Newfoundland)

Ingredients:
250ml salt cod fish
1 egg, beaten
1ml pepper
750ml raw potato, diced
30ml butter

TRIVIA TIDBITS
Canadian males spend an average of 11.7 days in hospital, while Canadian women spend an average of 11.3 days.

Directions:
Soak cod fish overnight in cold water. Drain. Cut fish into small pieces. Cook potato and fish in boiling water until tender. Drain. Mash with egg, butter and seasonings. Drop by spoonfuls into hot fat or roll in balls and drop. Fry until golden brown, about 2-3 minutes.

Simple Scallop Splendor

Rachel Hollett, Cambridge, Ontario, (nee Lomond, Grand Bay, Port aux Basques, Newfoundland)

Ingredients:
1 to 1 & 1/2 lbs fresh scallops
1/4 cup whipping cream
1/4 cup homogenized milk
1/4 cup + 2 tbsp butter
1 cup graham wafer crumbs
1/2 tsp salt
1/4 tsp pepper

FOOD FOR THOUGHT
More statues have been erected for those who have been criticized than for those who have criticized.
-Jim Deyoe

Directions:
Grease an 8x8 inch pan. Pat each scallop with paper towel to dry. Place in single layer in pan. Mix cream and milk together. Melt butter; add crumbs, salt and pepper to the melted butter. Pour half of cream mixture over scallops. Sprinkle with crumb mixture. Pour rest of liquid over all. Bake at 375°F for 20-30 minutes.

Seafood
Swimmers, Crawlers & Creepers

Fisherman's Lasagna

Goldie White, Twillingate, Newfoundland

Ingredients:

1 & 1/2 lbs cod fillets (3 fillets)
1/4 cup onion, chopped
1/3 cup green pepper, chopped
2 tbsp butter
5 & 1/2oz can tomato paste
1 - 19oz can tomatoes
1/2 tsp salt
dash pepper
1/2 tsp basil
6 lasagna noodles
12oz sliced Mozzarella cheese
1/4 cup Parmesan cheese

Directions:

Cut fish into one-inch pieces. Saute vegetables until onion is translucent. Stir in tomato paste, tomatoes and seasoning. Simmer for 5 minutes. Add fish and simmer another 5 minutes. Layer half noodles in shallow baking dish; cover with half fish sauce and half cheese. Repeat and sprinkle with parmesan cheese. Bake at 375°F for 30 minutes or until bubbly and light brown.

FOOD FOR THOUGHT
Success comes in cans;
failure comes in can'ts.

TRIVIA TIDBITS
The great crowds which attended regular public executions in London, England often had their pockets picked by professional pick pockets, even though some of those being executed were paying the price for being pick pockets themselves.

Stuffed Flounder Rolls

Ingredients:

3 large flounder fillets (about 1 & 1/4 lbs)
freshly ground pepper to taste
2 tbsp olive oil
1 & 1/2 cups mushrooms, sliced
1/4 cup minced onion
1/2 cup diced carrots, cooked tender-crisp
1 tbsp minced parsley
1/2 cup Italian salad dressing

Directions:

Heat oven to 400°F. Cut fillets in half lengthwise. Sprinkle with pepper. Roll up each fillet lengthwise and place in greased muffin tins, leaving a cavity in the centre. In skillet over medium-low heat saute mushrooms and onion in oil until soft. Do not brown. Stir in carrots and parsley. Stuff mixture into fish cavities. Spoon dressing over fillets. Bake 15 minutes. Remove from tins and spoon juices over each fillet.

Serves 4 to 6.

TRIVIA TIDBITS
The fastest creature on four legs is the cheetah which has been known to travel at speeds over 70 mph.

This page is dedicated to our parents, **Martin and Mary Ryan** on their 50th Wedding Anniversary in 1997. Martin formerly of Petit Forte and Mary (nee Griffiths) formerly of Ship Harbour, both in Placentia Bay, now residing in Stephenville, Nfld.
Love, your children...
Donna, Sheila, Mary, Ann, Joe, Martin, Kevin, Gerard, Jack and Ross.

Seafood Florentine Bake

Ingredients:

2 lbs fish fillets (flounder, haddock, etc)

1 tsp salt

1/2 tsp onion powder

1/2 tsp pepper

1 (10 & 3/4oz to 11oz) can condensed cream of shrimp or cheddar cheese soup mix

1 (10oz) pkg frozen chopped spinach, thawed & well-drained

2 cups Bisquick baking mix

1/3 cup grated parmesan cheese

1 cup milk

2 eggs

Directions:

Heat oven to 350°F. Arrange fish fillets in a greased 13 x 9 x 2-inch baking dish; sprinkle with salt, onion powder and pepper. Spoon soup over fillets; top with spinach. Beat remaining ingredients with wire whisk or hand beater about 1 minute or until almost smooth; pour over spinach. Bake uncovered about 40 minutes or until top is golden brown. Let stand 10 minutes before serving. Makes 8 servings.

Eva's Shrimp Creole

Eva F. Canning, Baton Rouge, Los Angeles, USA

Ingredients:

1/2 cup cooking oil

1 lg green pepper, chopped

1 lg onion, chopped

2-3 ribs of celery, chopped

1 - 2 cans whole tomatoes

1 can tomato sauce

2 lg cloves of garlic, minced

1/2 tsp tobasco sauce

1 tbsp Worcestershire sauce

1 tbsp fresh parsley, (dried is ok, but only use half the amount)

2 tbsp cornstarch

salt to taste

pepper to taste

1 lb shrimp, cooked, cleaned and deveined

green onion tops for garnish

Directions:

Saute onions, green pepper and celery in cooking oil until limp but not brown. Add tomatoes, which have been slightly crushed, and the tomato sauce. Bring to boiling point; add seasonings. Dissolve cornstarch in a little cold water and add to the mixture. Boil up again. Add shrimp. Simmer until heated through. Add water for desired consistency, if too thick. Serve over hot cooked rice. Garnish with green onion tops. Serves 4.

NOTE: You can microwave celery for a few seconds to soften as this takes a bit longer than the onions and pepper. This much sauce can take another 1/2 pound of shrimp.

Shrimp Victoria

Eva F. Canning, Baton Rouge, Los Angeles, USA

Ingredients:

1 lb raw shrimp, peeled and cleaned
1 small onion, finely chopped
1/4 cup butter or margarine
1 can (6oz) mushrooms
1 can mushroom soup
1 can cream of shrimp soup
1/4 tsp salt
dash of cayenne pepper
1 cup sour cream
1 & 1/2 cups cooked rice

Directions:

Saute shrimp and onion in butter for 10 minutes or until shrimp are tender. Add mushrooms, mushroom soup and cream of shrimp soup and cook for 5 minutes more. Sprinkle in salt and pepper. Stir in sour cream and cook gently for 10 minutes, not allowing mixture to boil. Serve over rice. Makes 4 to 6 servings.

TRIVIA TIDBITS
The driest city in Canada is Medicine Hat, Alberta. It averages 271 days per year without measurable precipitation.

Eva's Shrimp and Crabmeat Fettucine

Eva F. Canning, Baton Rouge, Los Angeles, USA

Ingredients:

2 tbsp butter or oleo
10 green onions with tops, chopped
1 tbsp Worcestershire sauce
1 tsp basil
1 tsp garlic puree or 2 cloves, minced
salt to taste
pepper to taste
4 - 4 & 1/4oz cans medium shrimp with juice
4 - 6 & 1/2oz cans of lump crabmeat with juice
1 - 8oz carton of sour cream
1 - 8oz pkg cream cheese
1 pkg Alfredo Pasta mix
8oz dry Fettucine pasta (noodles)
Coffee cream or half-n-half as needed
Parmesan cheese

TRIVIA TIDBITS
In the early 1800s, potatoes were the only food of about a third of the population of Irland, and was a crucial part of the diet of a large percentage of the rest. A fungal disease known as late blight', hit the country's potato crop during the years 1845 to 1850, causing the crop to fail. The result of that was what became known as the potato famine. More than 12% of the residents died of starvation and another 1.5 million emigrated to North America during that time.

Directions:

Melt butter in large skillet. Saute onions until soft but not brown. Add Worcestershire sauce, basil, salt and pepper. Add garlic and mix in. Add shrimp and crabmeat with juices. Stir in sour cream

In loving memory of **John and Lottie Fitzpatrick** of Lord's Cove, Newfoundland.
"Your love always shone through"
Marceline, Fred, Raphael, Kate, Harve, Louis, Helena, Leona and Lucy

and heat thoroughly, but do not boil. Prepare Alfredo sauce as per package directions and add to other mixture. Cook noodles in boiling water about 10 minutes or until tender. Drain well. Combine with seafood mixture. Garnish with Parmesan cheese and chopped parsley, if desired. NOTE: •If using fresh shrimp you will need about 1 & 1/2 pounds of peeled shrimp. Saute in butter until pink and add to sauce. •This can be frozen. •This will serve 8-10 people, depending on what else is served with it. A green salad goes nicely with it, topped with a very smooth, light vinaigrette.

Lobster Nova Scotia Style

Phyllis Munroe, Bridgewater, Nova Scotia, (nee Bowering, St. John's, Newfoundland)

Ingredients:
2 tbsp butter
2 cups freshly cooked & shelled lobster meat
2 tsp cider vinegar
1 cup whipping cream or light cream
salt & pepper to taste

> **SPICE OF LIFE**
> A gossip's greatest fear is having no friends to speak of.

Directions:
Melt butter in a skillet. Add lobster and saute a few minutes. Stir in vinegar, then cream, salt and pepper. Heat through gently over medium-low heat. Serve with rice or mashed potatoes. Makes 4 servings (1/2 cup lobster meat each).

New Orleans Fish Fillets

Charlene Jenkins, Etobicoke, Ontario, (formerly of Springdale, Newfoundland)

Ingredients:
4 boneless fish fillets (6 ounces each)
1/2 cup all-purpose flour
1 tbsp paprika
1/2 tsp red pepper
1/4 tsp garlic powder
1/2 tsp white pepper
1/2 tsp salt
dash black pepper
2 tbsp vegetable oil

> **SPICE OF LIFE**
> Surely table manners were invented by somebody who was never hungry.

Directions:
Rinse and dry each fillet. Combine all dry ingredients. Flour each fillet with this mixture, being sure to pat off any excess. Heat oil in large frying pan. Brown the fillets for about 1 minute on each side. Place fillets in oven-proof dish. Bake at 350°F for about 10 minutes or until fish flakes easily. **NOTE:** Do not over-cook fish or it will dry out.

Codfish Casserole

Daphne D. Richard, Rexton, New Brunswick

Ingredients:
3-4 medium potatoes
bread crumbs
savoury
onions

> **SPICE OF LIFE**
> A bed is where people who are run down wind up.

1/4 cup butter
salt & pepper
Directions:
Preheat oven to 400°F. Cook potatoes and mash while hot. Add to bread crumbs, savoury, onions (sauteed in butter), salt and pepper. Place dressing in bottom of a greased casserole dish. Arrange pieces of cod (haddock or halibut) on top of dressing. Prepare **Basic White Sauce** (below). Pour over fish and bake at 400°F for 20-25 minutes. Grated cheese may be sprinkled over top during last 5 minutes of baking.

Basic White Sauce
Ingredients:
2 tbsp butter or margarine
2 tbsp flour
1/2 tsp salt
few grains pepper
1 cup milk

Directions:

In a saucepan, melt butter or margarine, blend in flour, salt, & pepper. Gradually stir in milk. Cook, stirring constantly, until thickened. Makes 1 cup. For this casserole, recipe may be doubled or tripled.

> **SPICE OF LIFE**
> Don't ever ask folks how they feel unless you already know.

Salmon Loaf

Marion Nagle, Kitchener, Ontario, (nee Daniels, Twillingate, Newfoundland)
Ingredients:
1 can salmon, drained & flaked
1 cup celery soup
1/2 cup chopped onion
1 tbsp lemon juice
1/2 cup mayonnaise
1 egg, beaten
1 cup dry bread crumbs
1 tsp salt
1/4 cup chopped green pepper

Directions:
Combine in greased loaf pan. Bake for one hour at 350°F.

> **FOOD FOR THOUGHT**
> The best heart exercise is reaching down and helping someone up.

Solomon Gundy

Ingredients:
1/2 doz salt herring
2 medium onions
2 cups vinegar
2 tbsp pickling spice

> **FOOD FOR THOUGHT**
> To handle yourself, use your head; to handle others, use your heart.

This page is dedicated to **Pamela Lee Richards** (the good Lord's most beautiful creation), formerly a west coast Newfie who now resides in the K/W area of Ontario.
I'll always love you Pam.
M.M.N., formerly of Central, Newfoundland

(side tab) **Seafood** Swimmers, Crawlers & Creepers

1/2 cup sugar
Directions:
Remove tails and heads from herring. Clean inside and remove the skin. Cut in pieces about 1" thick and fillet the pieces. Soak in cold water about 24 hours. Squeeze the water from herring. Place in a bottle with slices of onion, in alternate layers. In a saucepan, heat the vinegar and add pickling spice and sugar. Let cool; then pour over the herring in the bottles.

Baked Stuffed Fish

Ingredients:
2 lbs fillets or 1 whole codfish
2 cups soft, fine bread crumbs
1 tsp sage or summer savoury
1 tsp salt
1 tsp pepper
1 tsp onion juice
2 tbsp melted butter or fat
milk to mix dressing (about 1/2 cup)

> **_TRIVIA TIDBITS_**
> There are an average of 2,979 hours of clear skies each year in Estevan, Manitoba.

> **FOOD FOR THOUGHT**
> Take good care of your future because that's where you're going to spend the rest of your life.
> *-J.K. Kettering*

Directions:
Clean the fish, or wipe the fillets with a damp cloth. Mix the other ingredients to form a dressing and stuff the whole fish. If fillets are used, place a fillet on a greased pan with the dressing on top, and another fillet over the dressing.

Sauce
Ingredients:
3 tbsp butter or melted fat
3 tbsp flour, sifted and blended into butter
2 cups milk
1 tsp salt

> **SPICE OF LIFE**
> Computers are not really smarter than humans - they just think they are.

Directions:
Cook until thick in top of double boiler, stirring constantly to keep smooth. Pour over fish and bake in a 400°F oven, allowing 10 minutes for each inch of thickness of fish. Serves 6-7 people.

Garlic Grilled Scallops

Charlene Jenkins, Etobicoke, Ontario, (formerly of Springdale, Newfoundland)

Ingredients:
1 lb scallops
1/2 cup butter or margarine
3 lg cloves garlic, minced or pressed
1/4 cup finely chopped shallots
1/4 cup minced parsley
1/4 tsp nutmeg
1/8 tsp celery salt
12 cherry tomatoes
1 green pepper, cut into 12 squares

> **_TRIVIA TIDBITS_**
> Lord Byron, when he was a student at Cambridge, was told that he could not keep a pet dog in his room. He obeyed the rules, but went out and got a pet bear which he kept in his room.

Directions:
Thaw scallops compeltely, if frozen. Dry on paper towelling. In frying pan, combine first six ingredients and saute at low heat for 5 minutes, stirring occasionally. Meanwhile, string scallops on 4 wooden skewers alternately with the cherry tomatoes and green peppers. Start charcoal. When

coals are coated with an even layer os grey ash, place skewers on the grill. Grill, brushing with the butter mixture and turning often, for 6 to 7 minutes or until scallops are cooked through.

Scalloped Oysters

Ingredients:
1 pint oysters
4 tbsp oyster liquor
2 tbsp cream
1 cup cracker crumbs
1/2 cup bread crumbs
1/2 cup melted butter
salt (if needed)
pepper

SPICE OF LIFE
The real penalty for bigamy is having two mothers-in-law.

Directions:
Drain oysters. Mix cracker and bread crumbs and add melted butter. Put a thin layer of crumbs in a buttered dish; add half the oysters, sprinkle with pepper, and salt if needed. Add half each of oyster liquor and cream; repeat and cover with crumbs. Never have more than two layers of oysters. Bake from 20 to 30 minutes in hot oven.

Baked Scallops

Ingredients:
1 lb scallops
1/2 cup butter
1 cup bread crumbs
milk
salt & pepper

TRIVIA TIDBITS
Calgary had a dry period back in 1985. Starting on August 31, that year, the city went 71 consecutive days without precipitation.

Directions:
Grease a baking dish and cover with half of the bread crumbs. Place the scallops evenly over the crumbs and season with salt and pepper. Add enough milk to come to the top level of the fish, but not enough to cover. Dot generously with butter. Melt 1/2 cup butter and add the other half cup of bread crumbs. Arrange the buttered crumbs on top of scallops and bake in a 350°F oven for about 40 to 45 minutes.

Fried Smelts

Ingredients:
4 to 6 smelts per serving
1 egg, slightly beaten
whole wheat flour

FOOD FOR THOUGHT
Do unto others as you would have them do unto you.
-Luke 6:31

Directions:
Dip each fish in beaten egg and run it through flour, preferably whole wheat. Lay the fish in a row in a frying pan and fry until golden brown in butter or olive oil. Turn them over once.

This page is dedicated to my grandparents -
Bernard and Betty Stacey of Dunville, Newfoundland
and **Sadie Mooney** of Kilbride, Newfoundland.
My grandparents have always been a great inspiration to me in how they have lived their lives. I love them very much.
- Paula Mooney Hender, formerly of Kilbride, Newfoundland, now living in New Orleans, Louisiana

Seafood
Swimmers, Crawlers & Creepers

Fried Eels
Ingredients:
3/4 lb eels per person
Directions:
Skin and clean eels. Cut into desired lengths and place in a pan with salted water to cover. Parboil 8 to 10 minutes. Drain and wipe dry. Roll lightly in seasoned flour and fry in a small amount of pork fat to a nice brown.

SPICE OF LIFE
Diets are for people who are thick and tired of it.

Herring and Potatoes
Directions:
Soak herring overnight. Next day, clean thoroughly. Scrub unpeeled potatoes, taking a slice off both ends to prevent skins from splitting. Place in a pot and boil. About 20 minutes before potatoes are done, lay herring on top and cook until tender.

Scallops in Shells
Ingredients:
scallops
salt & pepper
parsley
cracker crumbs, rolled very fine
1 tbsp butter
1 tsp cream

FOOD FOR THOUGHT
Keep away from people who belittle your ambitions. Small people do that, but the really great make you feel that you, too, can become great.
-Mark Twain

Directions:
Wash scallops and dry well. Cut each scallop in half. Place 4 sections on a scallop shell. Add salt, pepper and a sprinkling of parsley. Cover with cracker crumbs. Add butter and cream to each shell. Bake in a hot oven, 400°F, until well browned.

Oysters on the Half Shell
Directions:
Never allow oysters to stand in water before opening for they would absorb the water. Wash the shells and then scrub them vigorously with a stiff brush. To open oysters, insert a knife under the back end of the right valve, and push forward until the mussel is cut. Open the oysters carefully so as not to lose any of the juice. For each serving, arrange 6 chilled oysters in their half shells, on a deep plate of crushed ice. A small glass of cocktail sauce my be placed in the centre of the plate.

Boiled Salmon with Egg Sauce
Directions:
Wipe a piece of salmon with a damp cloth. Wrap in 2 folds of cheesecloth, drawn into a bag and tied with a string. Boil gently without a cover, in salted water, allowing 15 minutes to each inch of thickness. Add two chopped hard-cooked eggs to 1 cup medium white sauce.
White Sauce
Ingredients:
1 tbsp butter
1 tbsp flour
1 cup milk
salt & pepper

TRIVIA TIDBITS
In the 1500s, the Royal Navy beer ration was a gallon a day for each sailor.

Seafood
Swimmers, Crawlers & Creepers

Directions:

These ingredients make a thin sauce. To make a medium sauce increase butter and flour to 2 table-spoons each. To make a thick white sauce, increase butter to 3 tablespoons and flour to 3-4 table-spoons.

Planked Salmon

Directions:

For this old-fashioned barbecue you will need a hardwood plank about 3 inches thick, 14 to 16 inches wide and 2 & 1/2 to 3 feet long. A lumber dealer can cut this for you, and it should be kept only for the purpose of planking fish. Salmon is as successfully "planked" in front of the fireplace as it is outdoors in front of a good fire. The salmon can weigh from 3 to 7 pounds. Don't be afraid of leftovers - there seldom is anything left, but if there is, it can be used in a salad or a casserole. Clean the salmon and run a sharp knife along both sides of the backbone, making it easy to remove. Remove head, tail and all fins. Small bones inside can be removed with the aid of a pair of pliers. Sprinkle the inside generously with salt and close for a couple of hours, while the fire is being pre-pared. Arrange two bricks, a couple of feet apart, in front of the fireplace and stand the plank on its edge to heat. When plank is hot, place the salmon thereon, skin side down. To hold the salmon in place, green saplings can be criss-crossed over the fish and nailed at the ends with shingle nails. Sprinkle salmon with flour and stand on edge in front of the hot fire until brown. Allow about 10 minutes for each inch of thickness of fish. Serve with hot butter brushed over the top.

Crumb Topped Fish Fillets

Ingredients:

6 green onions, chopped
1/3 cup mushrooms, sliced
2 lbs fish fillets
1 tsp salt
1/2 tsp pepper
1 tsp marjoram
2 tbsp dry white wine
2 tsp lemon juice
1/4 cup Monterey Jack cheese, grated (or other brand)
1/4 cup bread crumbs
1/2 cup butter, melted

> ### *TRIVIA TIDBITS*
> Before being used to ferry the Pilgrim Fathers to America, the Mayflower was used to transport sherry from Spain to England.

Directions:

Preheat oven to 400°F. Butter a baking dish large enough to hold the fillets in one layer with slight overlapping. Sprinkle the green onions and mushrooms over bottom of the dish. Arrange fillets over the vegetables, covering the thin part of each fillet with the thick part of another to prevent overcooking. Sprinkle fillets with seasonings, wine, and lemon juice. Top with cheese and bread crumbs. Pour butter over all. Wrinkle a piece of waxed paper, wet it, and place lightly over fish. Bake 7 minutes. Remove waxed paper; bake 5 minutes longer. Makes 4 to 6 servings.

Imperial Crab

Ingredients:

1/4 cup butter
1 cup half-and-half

> ## FOOD FOR THOUGHT
> When a happy man comes into a room, it is as if another candle had been lit.
> *-R.W. Emerson*

1 egg, lightly beaten
1 tsp lemon juice
1 tsp dry mustard
2 tsp Worchestershire sauce
salt & pepper to taste
1 lb crab meat
cracker crumbs

TRIVIA TIDBITS
Falcons are the longest-living members of the bird world, some are believed to have a life span of 150 years.

Directions:
Preheat oven to 400°F. In top of a double boiler, melt butter. Stir in half-and-half, egg, mustard, lemon juice, Worchestershire sauce, salt, and pepper. Stir in crab meat. Spoon into individual casseroles. Sprinkle with cracker crumbs over tops. Bake 30 minutes. Makes 4 servings.

Mussel Stew

Wash mussels thoroughly, rinsing two or three times to make sure they are free of sand. Put them in a stewpot, cover and let simmer until the shells are opened. Remove from shells. Strain the liquid through a sieve and, using 1 cup of liquor to 1 quart of mussels, put them back in the stewpot. Add 2 tbsp butter rolled in flour and a little mace. Simmer until done. Serve on toast.

Cape Breton Lobster Stew

Ingredients:
1 quart milk
2 cups boiled lobster meat, cut up
1 cup rolled cream sodas
2 tbsp butter
1 tsp salt

SPICE OF LIFE
Be nice to your kids.
They'll choose your nursing home.

Directions:
Scald the milk in the top of a double boiler, or over low heat to prevent scorching. Add the rest of the ingredients and simmer slowly for 10 to 15 minutes, stirring often. Do not boil. Serve hot.

Marie's Cod au Gratin

Marie Evans, Kitchener, Ontario

Ingredients:
4 cups cod fillets, cooked
3 tbsp butter
4 tbsp flour
1/2 tsp salt
1/8 tsp pepper
2 cups milk
1 cup cheese, grated

FOOD FOR THOUGHT
Just because the bird of trouble flies over our head, we don't have to let him build a nest in our hair.
-Chinese proverb

Directions:
Flake fish; make white sauce with flour, salt, pepper and milk, stirring until thick. Arrange fish in dish; cover with sauce, top with grated cheese. Bake at 300°F for 25 minutes.

Seafood
Swimmers, Crawlers & Creepers

Seafood
Swimmers, Crawlers & Creepers

Quick and Easy Fish Cakes

Danny Bath, Durrell, Twillingate, Newfoundland

Ingredients:

1 can tuna (undrained)

1 & 1/2 cups cornflakes, crushed

1/4 cup dried bread crumbs

1 egg

salt to taste

pepper to taste

Directions:

In a bowl, mash corn flakes until fine. Add bread crumbs and egg; add tuna, salt and pepper to taste. Roll in balls and pat down in frying pan. Fry until brown.

Shirley's Fish Cakes

Shirley Reader Hicks, Heatherton, Newfoundland (formerly of Corner Brook, Newfoundland)

Ingredients:

1 cup cooked salt codfish

1 small onion, chopped fine

3 cups mashed potatoe

1 egg, well beaten

1 tbsp butter

1/2 tsp pepper

Directions:

Combine ingredients and make into patties; fry in fat until golden brown. Delicious served with Partridgeberry Jam.

Fish and Stoffle

Hilda Reid, Ignace, Ontario (nee Harnum, Bishop's Falls, Newfoundland)

Ingredients:

2 lbs cod fillets, fresh or thawed

4 cups dry bread cubes

1 onion, finely chopped

1/2 cup milk

1 egg, beaten

1 tsp prepared mustard

1 tsp salt

1/4 tsp pepper

1/2 tsp poultry seasoning

2 tsp grated lemon rind

1 tbsp butter, melted

1 tsp lemon juice

salt to taste

pepper to taste

paprika

4 strips bacon, diced

> **TRIVIA TIDBITS**
> Each year St. John's, Newfoundland, averages 121 days of fog.

> **SPICE OF LIFE**
> A marriage license is the only license that never expires.

> **TRIVIA TIDBITS**
> The average time Canadians spend abroad travelling is 9 nights.

Directions:

Combine bread cubes, onion, milk, egg, mustard, salt, pepper, poultry seasoning, and lemon rind. Toss until milk is absorbed. Arrange mixture in a greased baking dish. Lay fillets over stuffing to completely cover. Brush fillets with combined melted butter and lemon juice. Sprinkle with salt, pepper and paprika. Scatter bacon over fish. Bake 450°F, 15-20 minutes or until fish flakes easily.

Fish Casserole

Ingredients:

2 cups cooked cod or haddock
1 & 1/2 cups white sauce
2 tbsp margarine
4 hard cooked eggs
4 med sized cooked potatoes (sliced)
1/2 cup bread crumbs (day old)

SPICE OF LIFE

A marriage licence is a hunting license for one dear only.

Directions:

Bone and flake fish and place half of it in bottom of a margarine-coated casserole dish. Slice eggs and lay over fish. Cover with half of the white sauce. Cover with half of the potatoes (sliced). Repeat these layers again. Melt margarine and add crumbs. Sprinkle over top of casserole. Bake in moderate hot oven at 400°F about 20 minutes. Serves 6-8.

Seafood Mousse

Ingredients:

2 envelopes unflavoured gelatin
1/2 cup dry, white wine
1 can (15 & 1/2oz) salmon, drained & flaked
1 can (5oz) lobster meat, drained & chopped
1 can (4oz) baby shrimp, drained
1/2 cup sour cream
1/3 cup chili sauce
1/4 cup celery, finely chopped
1/4 cup green pepper, finely chopped
2 tbsp sweet pickle relish
1/2 tsp salt (optional)
Ritz crackers (or your choice)

> **TRIVIA TIDBITS**
> The yard was introduced as a unit of measurement by Henry I. It was to be the distance between his nose and his outstretched thumb.

Directions:

Sprinkle gelatin over wine in small saucepan. Dissolve over low heat. Combine remaining ingredients, except crackers, in bowl. Stir in gelatin. Spoon into 4 cup (1 litre) mould. Cover and chill until set, about 3 hours. Unmould onto serving plate and serve surrounded by crackers.

Old-Fashioned Lobster Roll

Ingredients:

1 cup cooked lobster (or 1 - 14g/5oz can)
1 tsp lemon juice
1 cup grated cheddar cheese
1/4 cup celery, diced
1 tbsp onion, finely chopped

> **FOOD FOR THOUGHT**
> Sometimes, sharp words are the only sort some people get in edgewise.

Seafood

Swimmers, Crawlers & Creepers

1 tbsp salad dressing

6 rolls

Directions:

Cut lobster in bite-size pieces and combine with cheese, celery and onion. Blend salad dressing and lemon juice together. Add to lobster mixture. Butter rolls and fill with the lobster mixture. Serves 6.

Gary's Lobster Stew

TRIVIA TIDBITS
A person dies in Canada every 2.7 minutes on the average.

Ingredients:

1-2 cups lobster meat, cooked

1/4 cup butter

4 cups scalded milk or half-and-half,

(or 3 & 1/2 cups light cream, warmed and 1/2 cup clam juce)

salt to taste

pepper to taste

dash cayenne

sprinkle paprika

Directions:

First: (with scalded milk) Saute lobster in butter over a low heat until the butter is pinkish; stirring constantly. Remove from heat and allow to cool a little, then slowly add scalded milk, salt, pepper and cayenne. This stew is best if refrigerated for a few hours, then reheated. Sprinkle with paprika to serve. *Second:* (with cream/clam juice) Saute lobster in butter until very hot, then stir in mixed cream and clam juice. Season with salt, pepper, cayenne and paprika and let steep off the heat for a few minutes before serving. Can be reheated, if necessary. Serves 2-4. **NOTE:** Cooked lobster can be replaced with canned or frozen, thawed and drained.

Lobster Corn Chowder

Ingredients:

1 lobster (approx 1 & 1/2 lb)

2 med potatoes

1 med onion

4 ears of fresh corn (or 2 cups frozen corn kernels)

1 quart half & half

4 tbsp butter

1/8 tsp cayenne pepper

1/4 tsp salt

1/4 tsp ground black pepper

4 qt water

SPICE OF LIFE
A disc jockey is someone who works for the love of mike.

Directions:

Bring 4 qt (4 litres) of water to a boil in a 6-8 quart soup pot. Add lobster, cover, and boil about 10 minutes. Remove lobster and drain, retaining liquid. Remove meat and reserve shells and carcass, for stock. Cut lobster meat into large chunks. Peel and cut potatoes into 1/2-inch dice. Mince onion (1 cup). Remove corn kernels from cobs (or drain and set aside thawing corn). Put reserved lobster shells and carcass in a large saucepan with half and half. Bring half and half to a boil, lower heat, and simmer for 4 minutes. Remove from heat and set aside. Melt butter in a pot. Add potatoes, onion and corn kernels and saute over medium-low heat until onion is translucent; about 5 minutes. Strain the lobster cream over the vegetables, bring to a simmer, and then simmer slowly until

Seafood
Swimmers, Crawlers & Creepers

potatoes are tender, 6-8 minutes. Stir in lobster meat, cayenne pepper, 1/4 tsp salt and 1/4 tsp pepper. Simmer just until lobster meat is hot; about 5 minutes. Ladle into bowls and serve hot. Serves four.

Mussels & Pasta-Seashells Casserole

Ingredients:
1 & 1/2 cups mussels
1 tbsp butter (or margarine)
2 cloves garlic, minced
dash pepper
dash marjoram
1/4 cup parsley, chopped
1 - 10oz cream of mushroom soup
1/2 cup milk
1/4 cup mussel broth, strained
5 cups cooked pasta sea shells, small
bread (or cracker) crumbs

Directions:
Saute garlic, pepper, marjoram and parsley. Gradually add soup, milk and mussel broth. Cook, stirring gradually until thick and well-blended. Mix seashells and mussel meat into prepared sauce. Pour all ingredients into a 1 & 1/2 quart casserole dish. Sprinkle top with crumbs. Bake at 400°F for 10-15 minutes. Serves 6.

Crab Chops

Ingredients:
1 lb blue-crab meat, fresh, frozen or pasteurized
1/2 cup butter or margarine
3/4 cup all-purpose flour
1/2 tsp salt
1/4 tsp cayenne pepper
1 cup milk
1/4 cup parsley, chopped
1/4 cup green onion, chopped
2 eggs, beaten
2 cups soft bread crumbs
1/4 cup cooking oil
lemon wedges
tartar sauce

Tartar Sauce:
1 & 2/3 cup mayonnaise
3 tbsp sweet pickle, chopped
3 tbsp stuffed olives, chopped
1 tbsp capers, chopped
1 tbsp onion, minced
1 tbsp parsley, minced
1 tsp vinegar
1 tsp lemon juice

Directions for Tartar Sauce:
Combine all ingredients; taste for seasoning. A little extra vinegar or lemon juice and a pinch of

salt may be required, depending on kind of mayonnaise used. Can be served with any fish or seafood. Makes about 2 cups.

Directions for Crab Chops:

Thaw crab meat if frozen; remove shell or cartilage. Melt 1/4 cup margarine in small saucepan; blend in 1/4 cup flour, salt and cayenne. Gradually stir in milk; cook and stir until thickened. Mix in crab meat, parsley, and onion; cover. Refrigerate for 2 hours. Divide into 6 equal portions; pat and shape each portion into "chop" about 5-inches long and 1/2 inch thick. Place each chop in flour mixture; turn to coat both sides. Dip each chop into egg, then in bread crumbs to coat evenly. Refrigerate at least 30 minutes to firm coating. In heavy 12-inch frying pan, heat 1/4 cup butter and oil until hot, but not smoking. Fry chops over moderate heat until delicately browned on both sides, about 10 minutes. Serve with lemon wedges and Tartar Sauce. Makes 6 servings.

Beer-Battered Fried Shrimp

Ingredients:

2 lbs shrimp, shelled, deveined
1 (12oz) can beer
1 cup flour
1 tbsp salt
1 tbsp paprika
dash of red pepper, to taste
fat for deep-frying

Directions:

Shell and devein raw shrimp. Pour beer into large bowl. Blend dry ingredients into beer to make pancake-like batter. While using batter, stir from time to time. Thoroughly coat each shrimp with batter just before frying. Fry shrimp, a few at a time, in hot, deep fat until golden brown and crusty. Drain shrimp on paper towel; transfer to hot platter. Makes 6 servings.

TRIVIA TIDBITS
King Alfonzo of Spain was so tone deaf that he couldn't even recoginze the National Anthem of his own country, so he hired someone to tell him when it was being played so he could stand to attention.

Salt Cod Casserole

Ingredients:

2 cups (or 1 lb) cooked cod
1 & 1/2 cups cooked rice
2 tbsp onions, chopped
2 tbsp green pepper, diced
1 & 1/2 cups thin white sauce
1/4 cup fresh tomatoes, chopped (or substitute with can tomatoes)
1 cup soft bread crumbs, buttered

FOOD FOR THOUGHT
Do something every day to make others happy - even if it is just leaving them alone.

Directions:

Flake cod and place 3/4 cup of rice in bottom of greased 1 & 1/2 quart casserole, and cover with cod. Sprinkle with onions and pepper (if used). Add 3/4 cup of white sauce and remainder of rice, pour remainder of sauce over rice and sprinkle with tomatoes. Top with buttered crumbs and brown in moderate oven 20 to 30 minutes or until bubbling hot and crumbs are brown. Serves 6. NOTE: Salt halibut may be used in place of cod.

Doughy Delights

Breads

Muffins

Buns

Biscuits

Puddings

Doughnuts

Pancakes

Etc.

Beer Muffins

Cathy Gale, Doyles, Newfoundland

Ingredients:

3 cups flour
5 tsp baking powder
1/2 tsp salt
3 tbsp white sugar
1 bottle of beer

SPICE OF LIFE

Here I sit under a romantic moon
Abandoned and left by my man
Repeatedly singing out of tune
"I'll never eat garlic again!"

Directions:

Measure dry ingredients into bowl and pour beer over, stirring to blend. Spoon into greased muffin cups and brush tops with butter. Bake at 350°F for 15-20 minutes. Serve hot. A little grated cheddar cheese sprinkled on top of these before baking makes them even better. (Great served with cabbage rolls).

Oatmeal Muffins

Cathy Gale, Doyles, Newfoundland

Ingredients:

1 cup oats
1 cup sour milk
1 cup flour
1/2 tsp baking soda
1 tsp baking powder
1/2 tsp salt
1 cup brown sugar
1 egg, beaten
4 tbsp melted shortening

TRIVIA TIDBITS

Contrary to popular belief, *Chop Suey* is not a Chinese food, as it was invented in the United States. It was first served around the end of the Nineteenth Century. There are several different versions of who actually created the dish; one is that it was created by a dish-washer in San Francisco, the other is that it was created by Chinese restaurant owners in Brooklyn, N.Y.. *Chop* is an English word, *Suey* comes from the Chinese word *sui*, meaning 'bits'.

Directions:

Mix oats and milk together and set aside. Measure flour in a bowl, add sugar, baking powder, baking soda, and salt. Stir to blend. Add oats mixture to egg and melted shortening. Pour over dry ingredients all at once. Stir until dampened. Fill muffin tin 2/3 full. Bake in 400°F oven for 20 minutes. Remove from tin immediately.

Muffins That Taste Like Doughnuts

Vera E. Coburn, Labrador City

Ingredients:

1 & 3/4 cups flour
1 & 1/2 tsp baking powder
1/2 tsp salt
1/2 tsp nutmeg
1/4 tsp cinnamon

FOOD FOR THOUGHT
Your real friends are the ones who are unafraid to tell you the truth.

This page is dedicated to our parents **Claude and Margaret** (nee Green) **Hender** of Gander, Newfoundland (L), and **Leonard and Betty** (nee Stacey) **Mooney** of Kilbride, Newfoundland. We love and miss you very much. We are always thinking of our families.
- Derek Hender and Paula Mooney-Hender,
now living in New Orleans, Louisiana

1/3 cup oil
3/4 cup white sugar
1 egg
3/4 cup milk
Topping:
1/2 cup melted butter
3/4 cup sugar
1 tsp cinnamon
(Mix sugar and cinnamon together)
Directions:
In a bowl, combine dry ingredients. In another bowl thoroughly combine oil, sugar, egg and milk. Add liquid ingredients to dry and stir only to combine. Bake at 350°F for 20 to 25 minutes. Take muffins out immediately and while hot, dip in melted butter, then sugar and cinnamon. For a delicious variation, fill muffin tins half full of batter, put a tsp of jam on top and then top with more batter.

> ### FOOD FOR THOUGHT
> Fear is the sand in the machinery of life.
> E Stanley Jones

Mincemeat Muffins

Vera E. Coburn, Labrador City
Ingredients:
Cream together
2 eggs
1 cup white sugar
3/4 cup vegetable oil
Add:
2 cups milk
1 cup all-bran
2 cups flour
2 tsps soda
2 tsp baking powder
1 tsp salt
1 cup mincemeat
Directions:
Bake at 375°F for 15 to 20 minutes, or according to your oven.

> ### TRIVIA TIDBITS
> While visiting Mahon, a city on the island of Minorca, Duc de Richelieu discovered a food product which was used by the residents, and which he brought back to France. French chef's loved it and called it 'Mahonaisse'. In America, it was called 'mayonaise' and was used for only the most elegant of meals for over 100 years. In 1912, a German immigrant by the name of Richard Hellman began packing the product in jars and selling it from his delicatessen in New York. From there, the product was made available for the masses, and the rest is history.

Mainland Muffins

June Gates, Woodstock, Ontario
Ingredients:
4 eggs
2 cups white sugar
1 & 1/2 cups oil
1 - 14oz can (or 2 cups) pumpkin
3 cups flour
1 tsp cinnamon
2 tsp baking soda
2 tsp baking powder
1 tsp salt

> ### TRIVIA TIDBITS
> Water is one substance that abounds in all three forms, solid, liquid and gaseous. We have the polar caps, miles deep, from which come glaciers and icebergs; we have oceans, lakes of rivers of liquid water; and we have water vapour in the air in the form of fog, clouds and steam, to the degree that if it were condensed all at the same time it would cover North America to a height of about 11 feet.

Breads, Muffins, Buns, Biscuits, Puddings, Doughnuts, Pancakes, Etc.

Doughy Delights

2 cups raisins
1 cup chocolate chips
Directions:
Beat eggs slightly. Add sugar, oil and pumpkin and mix thoroughly. Add baking soda and stir well. Add flour, cinnamon, baking powder and salt. Stir and fold in raisins and chocolate chips. Bake at 375°F for 15 minutes.

Banana Muffins

June Gates, Woodstock, Ontario
Ingredients:
1 cup mashed bananas
1 cup miracle whip
1/2 cup white sugar
1 & 1/2 cups flour
3/4 cup oatmeal
2 tsp baking soda
1/2 tsp salt

SPICE OF LIFE
A good salesperson is one who makes a living going door to door selling signs that read, "No Salespeople Allowed".

Directions:
Beat together bananas, miracle whip and sugar. Stir in rest of ingredients. Bake at 350°F for approximately 20 minutes.

Corn Meal Muffins

Ingredients:
1 cup corn meal
1 cup flour
1/3 cup sugar
1/2 tsp salt
4 tsp baking powder
1 egg
1/4 cup shortening (room temperature)
1 & 1/4 cups milk

TRIVIA TIDBITS
A recent edition of *Bartlett's Familiar Quotations* quotes 2,200 persons, of which only 164 are women. The original version, published in 1855, quoted only four women.

Directions:
Sift together dry ingredients into medium size bowl. Add milk, egg and shortening. Beat with a rotary egg beater until smooth (one minute - do not over-beat). Fill muffin cups 3/4 full and bake in preheated oven at 425°F for about 20 minutes.

Apple Cheddar Muffins

Ingredients:
1/2 cup margarine
1/2 cup sugar

FOOD FOR THOUGHT
They that mistake life's accessories for life itself are like them that go too fast in a maze: Their very haste confuses them.
                                                                    Seneca

---

Dedicated to **Eileen McFarlan**e of Stayner, Ontario
A wonderful, loving grandmother to
Scott and Tim McFarlane of Niagara Falls, Ontario

Sidebar (vertical text): **Doughy Delights** — Breads, Muffins, Buns, Biscuits, Puddings, Doughnuts, Pancakes, Etc.

2 eggs
1 & 1/2 cups all-purpose flour
1 tsp baking soda
1/2 tsp allspice
1/2 tsp salt
1 cup applesauce
3/4 cup rolled oats
1 cup old cheddar cheese, shredded
1/2 cup chopped nuts
1/4 cup milk

Directions:
Cream margarine and sugar until light. Blend in eggs. Add combined flour, soda, allspice and salt. Mix well. Stir in applesauce, oats, 3/4 cup of cheese and nuts. Add milk and stir to blend. Spoon into 12 greased muffin pan cups, filling almost to the top. Top each one with remaining cheese. Bake at 400°F for 20-22 minutes.

Diet Bran Muffins

Marion Nagle, Kitchener, Ontario, (nee Daniels, Twillingate, Newfoundland)

Ingredients:
2 cups bran flakes
1 cup milk
1 egg
1 cup flour
1/4 cup oil
1/4 cup molasses
1 tsp salt
1 tsp baking soda
1 tsp cinnamon
raisins

Directions:
Mix all ingredients together. Bake at 350°F for 20 minutes.

Corn Muffins

Elizabeth Clarke, North Sydney, Nova Scotia, (nee Keough)

Ingredients:
1 egg
1 cup milk
1 cup creamed corn
1/2 tsp salt
1 & 1/2 cups flour
3 tsp baking powder
slices of bacon

Directions:
Beat egg. Add milk and creamed corn. Mix dry ingredients gradually into corn mixture to make a smooth batter. Line muffin pan with bacon and fill each to 2/3 full. Bake at 425°F for 25 to 30 minutes. Makes 12 muffins.

Breads, Muffins, Buns, Biscuits, Puddings, Doughnuts, Pancakes, Etc.

Doughy Delights

Blueberry Oat Muffins

Dolores Lundrigan, Wabush, Labrador, (nee English, Branch, St. Mary's Bay, Newfoundland)

Ingredients:
1 cup rolled oats
1 cup buttermilk or sour milk
1 cup flour
1 tsp baking powder
1/2 tsp baking soda
1/2 tsp salt
3/4 cup brown sugar
1 egg, beaten
1/4 cup melted butter
1 cup blueberries

SPICE OF LIFE
Men have a much better time of it than women. For one thing they marry later. For another thing, they die earlier.
W. H. Auden

Directions:
Combine oats and buttermilk in small bowl. Let stand. Combine flour, baking powder, soda, salt and brown sugar in mixing bowl. Stir well to blend. Add egg and melted butter to oat mixture (mix well). Add oat mixture all at once to dry ingredients. Stir until moistened. Gently fold in blueberries. Fill greased muffin cups 3/4 full and bake at 350°F for 15-20 minutes.

Old Fashioned Pork Buns

Roy Perry, Pickering, Ontario (in memory of parents Harriett & Harry Perry)

Ingredients:
1/4 lb salt pork
3 tsp baking powder
1/2 cup warm water
1 & 1/4 cups seedless raisins
3 cups flour
1 cup sugar

FOOD FOR THOUGHT
True friendship comes when silence between two people is comfortable.

Directions:
Cut salt pork in 1/4-inch squares. Place in frying pan and fry until golden brown. Combine dry ingredients in bowl. Mix fat and warm water together. Mix well into dry ingredients. Roll into buns and place in pan. Bake at 400°F until golden brown.

Best Ever Banana Muffins

Marion Nagle, Kitchener, Ontario, (nee Daniels, Twillingate, Newfoundland)

Ingredients:
3 lg bananas
3/4 cup white sugar
1 egg
1 tsp baking soda

FOOD FOR THOUGHT
Cold feet might be the end result of burnt fingers.

This page is dedicated to the memory of our parents
HARRY PERRY, formerly of Gooseberry Islands, Newfoundland
and **HARRIETT** (nee Butt), formerly of Cowards, Flat Island, Newfoundland.
Lovingly remembered by children Alica, Harry and Alfred in Glovertown, Newfoundland, and Roy, in Pickering, Ontario.

1 tsp baking powder
1/2 tsp salt
1 & 1/2 cups all-purpose flour
1/3 cup melted butter

Directions:
Mash bananas. Add sugar and slightly beaten egg. Add the melted butter. Add the dry ingredients and bake at 375°F for 20 minutes.

Blueberry/Partridgeberry Muffins

Beulah Cooper, Gander, Newfoundland, (nee Collins, Corner Brook, Newfoundland)

Ingredients:
1 cup rolled oats
1 cup sour milk
1 cup flour
1 tsp baking powder
1/2 tsp soda
1/2 tsp salt
1 cup brown sugar
1 egg
4 tsp margarine, melted
1 cup berries

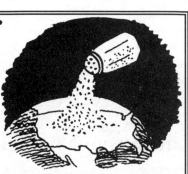

TRIVIA TIDBITS
Ten per cent of all the salt that's produced in the world anually is used on roads in the United States for de-icing. That ten per cent equals over 9 million tons and costs $200 million.

Directions:
Put rolled oats in bowl, add milk and let soak. Measure flour, sugar, baking powder, soda and salt. Add egg and melted margarine to oat mixture. Combine all ingredients, add berries. Bake in muffin pan for 20 minutes at 400°F.

Rhubarb Pecan Muffins

Josephine Hynes, Etobicoke, Ontario, (nee Elliott, Twillingate, Newfoundland)

Ingredients:
Dry Mixture:
2 cups (500ml) all-purpose flour
3/4 cup (175ml) sugar
1 & 1/2 tsps (7ml) baking powder
1/2 tsp (2ml) baking soda
1 tsp (5ml) salt
3/4 cup (175ml) pecans, chopped
Moist Mixture:
1 lg egg
1/4 cup (50ml) vegetable oil
2 tsps (10ml) orange peel, grated
3/4 cup (175ml) orange juice
1 & 1/4 cups (300ml) fresh rhubarb

TRIVIA TIDBITS
Yeast is a fungal organism which breaks down or ferments sugar into CO_2 and alcohol. When dough is kneaded it traps the CO_2 which the yeast and sugar created. This causes small bubbles in the bread which makes the bread rise. Most of the alcohol created by the process dissipates as the bread bakes.

Directions:
Preheat oven to 350°F (180°C) and prepare 12 muffin cups. Combine dry mixture in a large bowl. Finely chop the fresh rhubarb. In a medium bowl beat egg lightly and combine moist mixture. Add moist mixture to dry mixture all at once and stir until batter is moist but still lumpy. Fill 12 prepared muffin cups 2/3 full. Bake 25-30 minutes.

Breads, Muffins, Buns, Biscuits, Puddings, Doughnuts, Pancakes, Etc.

Doughy Delights

Breads, Muffins, Buns, Biscuits, Puddings, Doughnuts, Pancakes, Etc.

Doughy Delights

Bran Muffins

Carol Thornhill, Bobcaygeon, Ontario

Ingredients:

3 eggs

2 cups brown sugar

1 & 1/2 cups corn oil

4 cups health bran

4 cups flour

4 tsp baking powder

4 tsp baking soda

4 tsp salt

4 cups milk

raisins or grated carrot, optional

Directions:

Beat eggs and brown sugar well. Add rest of ingredients. Bake at 400°F for 20 minutes. Batter may be stored in refrigerator for 3-4 weeks in bowl with lid. Very moist muffins.

TRIVIA TIDBITS
One of every three American families reports alcohol abuse by a family member. More than half of all alcoholics have an alcoholic parent, and in about 90% of child abuse cases, alcohol is a significant factor.
National Association for Children of Alcoholics

Pineapple Muffins

Josephine Hynes, Etobicoke, Ontario, (nee Elliott, Twillingate, Newfoundland)

Ingredients:

Dry Mixture:

2 cups (500 ml) all-purpose flour

3 tsp (15 ml) baking powder

1/2 tsp (2 ml) salt

Moist Mixture:

1 lg egg

1/4 cup (50 ml) vegetable oil

1/2 cup (125 ml) sugar

1 cup (250 ml) milk

3/4 cup (175 ml) crushed pineapple, drained

FOOD FOR THOUGHT
You can get by on charm and good looks for a short while, but after that, you had better know something.

Directions:

Preheat oven to 400°F (200°C) and prepare 18 muffin cups. Combine the dry mixture in a large bowl. In a medium bowl, beat egg lightly and mix in the rest of the moist mixture. Add moist mixture to dry mixture all at once and stir until batter is mixed but still lumpy. Fill 18 prepared muffin cups 3/4 full. Bake 20-25 minutes. NOTE: Be sure the crushed pineapple is well drained before measuring or your batter will be too moist.

This page is dedicated to the memory of my mother **Mrs. Rachael Purchase**, who died in December 1994, age 96 & 1/2 years. Widowed twice - took on the role of father and mother with a large family during the 30's and early 40's because father was away working most of the time.
Happy memories mother, love son George

Chocolate Chip Banana Muffins

Josephine Hynes, Etobicoke, Ontario, (nee Elliott, Twillingate, Newfoundland)

Ingredients:
Dry Mixture:
2 cups (500ml) all-purpose flour
1 tsp (5ml) baking soda
1 tsp (5ml) salt
1 cup (250ml) semi-sweet chocolate chips
Moist Mixture:
1/2 cup (125ml) butter
3/4 cup (175ml) sugar
2 lg eggs
1 tsp (5ml) vanilla extract
1 cup (250ml) ripe bananas, (approx. 2-3 bananas)

SPICE OF LIFE
Automatic teller machines have convinced kids that money doesn't grow on trees - now they think it comes out of a wall!

Directions:
Preheat oven to 350°F (180°C) and prepare 12 muffin cups. In a large bowl, mix together the first 3 ingredients of the dry mixture. Stir in chocolate chips. Cream together butter and sugar with an electric mixer. Beat in eggs one at a time. Mash the bananas and add bananas and vanilla to the moist mixture. Add the moist mixture to the dry mixture all at once. Stir until batter is moist but still lumpy. Fill 12 muffin cups 3/4 full of batter. Bake 25 minutes.

Partridgeberry Muffins

Josephine Jenkins, Springdale, Newfoundland, (nee Young, Twillingate, Newfoundland)

Ingredients:
1 & 3/4 cups flour
2/3 cup sugar
2 & 1/2 tsp baking powder
1 cup partridgeberries
1/4 cup melted butter
1 cup milk
1 tsp vanilla (optional)
1 egg, beaten

FOOD FOR THOUGHT
A wise woman is one who puts a grain of sugar into everything she says, and takes everything she hears with a grain of salt.

Directions:
Blend together flour, baking powder and sugar. Add berries. Combine egg, milk, vanilla and butter. Add to dry ingredients. Stir until well blended. Fill pans 2/3 full. Bake at 350°F for 20-25 minutes, or until done. Cool for 1/2 hour before taking out of pans. Makes 12 medium muffins or 6 large.

Banana Oatmeal Muffins

Charlene Jenkins, Etobicoke, Ontario, (formerly of Springdale, Newfoundland)

Ingredients:
1/4 cup butter or margarine (softened)
3/4 cup brown sugar, packed
1 egg, beaten
1 cup buttermilk

Breads, Muffins, Buns, Biscuits, Puddings, Doughnuts, Pancakes, Etc.

Doughy Delights

1 cup rolled oats
1 cup all-purpose flour
1 tbsp baking powder
1/2 tsp salt
1/2 tsp allspice
2 medium bananas, chopped

Directions:

Cream together butter and brown sugar. Mix in egg and buttermilk. Mix together oats, flour, baking powder, salt and allspice. Add to creamed mixture. Stir in bananas. Spoon into greased or paper-lined muffin pan, filling almost full. Bake at 400°F to 425°F for 20 to 25 minutes until golden brown.

> **FOOD FOR THOUGHT**
> It's better to ask twice than to lose your way once.

Newfoundland Pork Buns

Miss Gertrude V. Sweetapple, Glovertown, Newfoundland

Ingredients:

3 cups of all-purpose flour
5 tsp baking powder
1/2 lb salt pork, cut small
1/2 cup shortening
1 cup cold water
1 & 1/2 cups raisins

> **SPICE OF LIFE**
> Skipper's Observations;
> Money must be tainted - 'taint yours and taint mine.

Directions:

Mix in order given. Roll out and cut with biscuit cutter and place on cookie sheet. Bake at 375°F for 20-30 minutes.

Anita's Molasses Buns

Anita Wilson, Renews, Newfoundland, (nee Coombs, Portugal Cove South, Trepassey, Newfoundland)

Ingredients:

1 cup molasses
1/2 cup salt pork, fried
1/2 tsp baking soda
1 cup boiling water
1/2 tsp cinnamon
1 & 1/2 cups flour

> **FOOD FOR THOUGHT**
> Every person's success is pure luck!
> Ask any failure.

Directions:

First, cut up pork in small pieces. Fry out and let cool. Pour boiling water in bowl; add baking soda and cool. Sift flour and cinnamon. Combine all ingredients together. Roll out on floured board and cut out. Bake 350°F for 15 to 20 minutes.

Brother
Richard
1930-1991

IN LOVING MEMORY
dedicated by
Harry & Doris Park

Sister
Rowena
1928-1995

Marie's Molasses Buns

Mrs. Marie Whitehorne, Pasadena, Newfoundland, (nee Kendall, Ramea, Newfoundland)

Ingredients:

1 cup molasses
1 cup butter
1 cup sugar
1 cup warm water
4 tsp baking soda
5 cups flour
1 tsp cinnamon
1 tsp ginger
1 tsp allspice
1/2 tsp cloves
1/8 tsp salt

FOOD FOR THOUGHT
Too many people belive that the way up the ladder of success is to kiss the feet of those above them and step on anyone below them!

Directions:

Mix well. Roll to 1/2-inch thickness and cut to shape. Bake on cookie sheet at 400°F for 15 to 20 minutes.

Pineapple Tea Buns

Josephine Hynes, Etobicoke, Ontario, (nee Elliott, Twillingate, Newfoundland)

Ingredients:

1/2 lb butter
1 cup sugar
1 sm can crushed pineapple
5 cups flour
5 tsp baking powder
2 eggs

FOOD FOR THOUGHT
There's nothing licking and sealing an envelope for inspiring a fresh thought.

Directions:

Cream butter, sugar and eggs together; add pineapple. Mix together. Add flour and baking powder. Bake at 350°F for 15-20 minutes.

Prune & Orange Tea Buns

Ingredients:

3 cups (750ml) flour
1/2 cup (125ml) sugar
4 tsp (20ml) baking powder
1/2 tsp (2ml) salt
1/2 cup (125ml) margarine or butter
1 egg
1 cup (250ml) buttermilk
1 cup (250ml) chopped, pitted prunes
2 tsp (10ml) orange peel, grated
egg wash: 1 egg beaten with 1 tbsp (15ml) cream or milk

SPICE OF LIFE
It's the woman with the face lift, wearing the padded bra who always asks where all the real men are!

Directions:

In a large bowl, mix flour, sugar, baking powder and salt. Using pastry blender or two knives, cut in margarine (or butter) until mixture resembles course meal. In small bowl beat egg with butter-

Breads, Muffins, Buns, Biscuits, Puddings, Doughnuts, Pancakes, Etc.

Doughy Delights

milk; add to flour mixture with prunes and orange peel. Mix well. Turn dough onto floured surface; lightly knead 5 or 6 times, adding more flour as needed to keep dough from sticking. Divide dough into 18 equal portions. Shape each portion into a ball; flatten into discs 1/2-inch (1.25 cm) thick. Place apart on ungreased baking sheet; brush lightly with egg wash. Bake in 375°F (190°C) oven for 20 minutes or until golden brown. Serve warm or at room temperature. Tea buns can be tightly wrapped and frozen up to one month. Makes 18 tea buns.

Raisin Tea Buns

Violet Jenkins, Etobicoke, Ontario, (nee Baggs, Twillingate, Newfoundland)

Ingredients:

1/4 lb butter

1 cup sugar

1 egg

3 cups flour

7 tsp baking powder

1 cup milk

1 cup raisins

Directions:

Cream together butter, sugar and egg; sift together flour and baking powder; mix with milk and add raisins. Cut to desired size and bake at 375°F approximately 30 minutes.

> **SPICE OF LIFE**
> A restaurant is the only place where people are happy when they are fed up!!

Cheddar Cheese Buns

Sandra Young, St. John's, Newfoundland, (nee Dove, Twillingate, Newfoundland)

Ingredients:

1 egg

1/2 cup sugar

1/2 cup butter

3 cups flour

2-3 tsps baking powder

1 cup cheddar cheese, grated

milk

> **TRIVIA TIDBITS**
> Our taste blends are derived from four primary tastes: sweet and salt (at the tip of the tongue); sour (at the sides of the tongue); and bitter (at the back of the tongue).

Directions:

Mix sugar, flour and baking powder together;

beat egg and add to dry mixture. Add cheese.

Mix with enough milk to make mixture hold together.

Press out on wax paper and cut to preferred size.

Place on cookie sheet (grease well if not Teflon style) and bake for 15-20 minutes.

This page is dedicated to our parents, **John** (Jack) and **Josephine Jenkins** (nee Young), both formerly of Twillingate, Newfoundland, now residing in Springdale, Newfoundland.
Love, Denise (Hibbs), Springdale, Newfoundland and Charlene Jenkins, Etobicoke, Ontario
"Thank you for everything!"

Doughy Delights

Breads, Muffins, Buns, Biscuits, Puddings, Doughnuts, Pancakes, Etc.

Black Bun

Catherine Milley, St. John's, Newfoundland, (nee McPherson)

Pastry

Ingredients:

1 lb flour
1 tsp baking powder
pinch of salt
6 oz margarine and baking fat mixed
1 egg
water to mix

Directions:

First sift flour with baking powder and salt for the pastry, rub in fat finely and mix with beaten egg and water to give a good short crust. Roll out thinly and line the bottom and sides of a large cake tin. Make sure all edges overlap well and allow enough at the top to double over. Roll out a round to fit the top.

Filling

Ingredients:

1/2 oz flour
1/2 tsp baking soda
1/2 tsp cream of tartar
1/2 tsp ground ginger
1/2 tsp ground cinnamon
1/2 tsp allspice
6 oz brown sugar
1 lb currants
1 lb stoneless raisins
6 oz blanced almonds
4 oz chopped peel
1 egg
1 or 2 tbsp brandy or sherry
milk

Directions:

For the filling, sift the flour with the dry ingredients and add the sugar. Prepare all the fruit - chopping almonds, etc. - and stir in. Beat the egg and add the brandy or sherry and milk to a stiff consistency. Pack into the pastry case, making the top flat. It must not come to the top of the tin. Dampen the pastry edges very well, fold over and press on the pastry top firmly, allowing room for expansion. Prick the top all over with a fork and run a skewer right through the mixture in four places. Brush lightly with beaten egg. Bake in a slow oven that has been well heated for 3 to 3 & 1/2 hours, lowering the heat if necessary when half cooked. Keep for about two weeks before cutting, storing when cold in an air-tight tin. Oven heat - 350°F.

Ginger Buns

Ingredients:

3/4 cup butter or margarine
1 cup white sugar
1 egg, well beaten

Breads, Muffins, Buns, Biscuits, Puddings, Doughnuts, Pancakes, Etc.

Doughy Delights

1 cup molasses
1 tsp baking soda
4 cups flour
1 tsp cinnamon
2 tsp powdered ginger
1 tsp salt
3/4 cup hot water

> **FOOD FOR THOUGHT**
> It is useless for the good sheep to pass resolutions in favour of vegetarianism while the wolf remains of a different opinion.

Directions:
Cream butter, sugar and well-beaten egg until light and fluffy. Add molasses and hot water. Beat again. Add dry ingredients to creamed mixture. Drop from teaspoon on greased cookie sheet giving dough lots of room. Bake in moderate oven 350°F for 8 - 10 minutes.

Buttermilk Tea Biscuits

Josephine Hynes, Etobicoke, Ontario, (nee Elliott, Twillingate, Newfoundland)

Ingredients:
2 cups all-purpose flour
1 tsp salt
1 tsp baking powder
1/2 tsp soda
4 tbsp pure lard
3/4 cup buttermilk or sour milk

> **SPICE OF LIFE**
> The handwriting on the wall is often Greek to most of us.

Directions:
Sift together dry ingredients, then cut in lard until you have a mealy mixture. Add enough buttermilk or sour milk to mix into a rather soft dough. Turn onto a floured board and knead gently 5-6 turns - never knead too much. Roll out gently to about a 3/4-inch thickness. Cut into rounds and place on a greased baking sheet. Bake at 425°F for 15-18 minutes or until golden brown.

Fluffy Biscuits

June Dalley, Bathurst, New Brunswick, (nee Howell, Carbonear, Newfoundland)

Ingredients:
2 cups all-purpose flour
4 tsp baking powder
1 tsp salt
1/2 cup shortening
3/4 cup 7-Up
(I usually add 1-2 tsp white sugar)

> **FOOD FOR THOUGHT**
> You don't grow old.
> When you cease to grow, you are old.

Directions:
Mix flour, baking powder and salt into a bowl. Combine shortening until it resembles coarse meal. Add 7-Up all at once. Stir briskly with a fork, only until evenly moistened. Turn onto floured surface. Knead 8-10 times. Roll to 3/4 inch thickness. Allow dough to rest a few minutes. Cut and place on sheet. Brush with butter. Bake at 450°F for 10-12 minutes. (Very light & fluffy)

Cloud Biscuits

Catherine Irwin, Truro, Nova Scotia

TRIVIA TIDBITS
Even in the 1500s, con artists made a fortune selling "water to make women beautiful forever"!

Ingredients:

2 cups flour
4 tsp baking powder
1 tbsp sugar
1/2 tsp salt
2/3 cup milk
1 egg, beaten
1/2 cup Crisco or shortening

Directions:

Sift flour, baking powder, sugar and salt. Cut in shortening until coarse crumbs appear. Combine milk and egg. Add to flour all at once. Stir until dough follows flour around the bowl. Turn out on lightly floured board. Knead gently with heel of hand 20 times. Roll out 3/4-inch thickness. Dip 2-inch cutter in flour. Cut straight down. Do not twist cutter. Place on ungreased pan. Bake at 450°F 10-14 minutes. Can be put in refrigerator and baked later, if desired. Makes about 6-8 medium-sized biscuits.

Tea Biscuits

Arlene Gibbons, Stoney Creek, Ontario (nee Sherard, Point Verde, Placentia, Newfoundland)

Ingredients:

2 cups flour
2 tbsp sugar
1 tsp salt
4 tsp baking powder
1/2 tsp cream of tartar
1/2 cup butter (or margarine)
1 cup milk

SPICE OF LIFE
Golf was once considered a rich man's game but it has many poor players today.

Directions:

Combine flour, sugar, salt, baking powder and cream of tartar in bowl. Cut in butter until crumbly. Pour in milk. Knead dough and roll out until 1/2 to 3/4-inch thickness. Cut into shape (a glass can be used). Bake at 450°F for 12-15 minutes. Brush with milk before baking.

Potato Pork Buns

Ingredients:

6 - 8 potatoes
2 cups flour
1/2 lb salt pork, minced
5 tsp baking powder
2 -3 tbsp butter

TRIVIA TIDBITS
The original Siamese twins, Chang and Eng Bunker, not only lived for 63 years, but both also married and had children.

Directions:

Boil potatoes, drain, then add butter and minced pork. Mash well. Add the sifted flour and baking powder to make a soft dough. Cut out and bake in hot oven for 15 - 20 minutes. Great served with hot, boiled salt fish.

Breads, Muffins, Buns, Biscuits, Puddings, Doughnuts, Pancakes, Etc.

Doughy Delights

Doughy Delights

Breads, Muffins, Buns, Biscuits, Puddings, Doughnuts, Pancakes, Etc.

Lassy Bread

Sharon Bennett, St. George's, Newfoundland

Ingredients:

1 tsp sugar
1/2 cup lukewarm water
1 pkg active dry yeast
2 & 1/2 cups milk or water
1/4 cup butter
1 tbsp salt
1/2 cup molasses
7 cups flour, all-purpose
2 tsp cinnamon
1 tsp spice
1 tsp cloves
3 cups raisins

TRIVIA TIDBITS
Eureka, in the Northwest Territories, received 621 hours of sunlight back in May 1973. That was a Canadian record for sunshine in one month.

Directions:

Dissolve yeast in lukewarm water to which sugar has been added; leave for 10 minutes. In saucepan heat milk, butter and salt until butter melts. Let cool to lukewarm. In a large mixing bowl combine molasses, yeast mixture, and 3 cups flour, spices and raisins; mix with wooden spoon for 2-3 minutes. Continue adding flour until moist, soft dough is formed. Knead dough for about 10 minutes until it becomes smooth and elastic (add more flour if dough sticks to surface). Place in a lightly oiled bowl in a warm place until doubled in bulk (1 & 1/2 to 2 hours). Divide dough and shape into loaves, place in greased loaf pans and let rise until doubled (1-2 hours). Loosely cover with damp cloth. Bake at 375°F (in preheated oven) until loaves are brown and gives a hollow sound when tapped on bottom (about 50 minutes). Brush tops with butter while hot.

Raisin Gingerbread - Newfoundland Style

Miss Gertrude V. Sweetapple, Glovertown, Newfoundland

Ingredients:

1 cup raisins
1/2 cup shortening
1/4 cup sugar
6 tbsp dark molasses
2 eggs, beaten
2 & 1/2 cups flour
1/2 tsp salt
2 tsp ginger
2 tsp cinnamon
3/4 cup buttermilk
1 tsp soda

FOOD FOR THOUGHT
Trust yourself; you'll find you may know more than you think you do.

This page is dedicated to the memory of **Cy Parsons** - the one who taught us the importance of making memories.
With love... his family.

Directions:
Rinse raisins in hot water, drain and dry on a towel. Cream shortening and sugar. Stir in molasses. Add beaten eggs and beat well. Add flour, sifted with salt and spices, alternately with the buttermilk, in which soda has been dissolved. Beat well. Stir in raisins. Pour into a greased 8x12-inch baking pan. Bake at 350°F for 40 minutes. Serve hot with butter or with frosting shown in "Enhancers" section.

Brown Sugar Raisin Bread

Winnie Marshall, Stephenville, Newfoundland, (nee Abbott, Port Au Bras, Placentia Bay, Newfoundland)

Ingredients:
2 pkg yeast
1/2 cup warm water
2 tsp white sugar
3 cups raisins
2 & 1/2 cups brown sugar
5 tsp salt
1/2 cup butter
2 cups boiling water
2 cups milk, undiluted
2 eggs
1 tsp baking soda
12 cups flour

SPICE OF LIFE
A wedding is a funeral where you can smell your own flowers...

Directions:
Soak yeast in 1/2 cup warm water, to which is added 2 tbsp white sugar. Pour enough boiling water over raisins to cover. Let stand for 5 minutes. Pour off water and dredge with flour. Combine brown sugar, salt and butter. Add the 2 cups of boiling water and stir until butter is melted. Add milk. Let stand until lukewarm. Add beaten eggs. Mix soda with flour and combine all together. Knead until smooth. Cover until it rises double in bulk. Knead down and let rise again. Place in pans and let rise until double in bulk. Bake for 1 hour at 300°F. *This bread is delicious. I always make it for Christmas.*

Rhubarb Bread

Ingredients:
1 & 1/2 cups firmly packed brown sugar
2/3 cup vegetable oil
1 cup buttermilk
1 egg
1 tsp vanilla
2 & 1/2 cups all-purpose flour
1 tsp salt
1 tsp baking soda
1 & 1/2 cups finely chopped rhubarb
1/2 cup chopped nuts
2 tbsp sugar

TRIVIA TIDBITS
Rudolph Valentino, of Castellaneta, Italy, was idolized as "the Great Lover" of the 1920s in the United States. He died suddenly of a ruptured ulcer on August 23, 1926 at the age of 31, causing worldwide hysteria, suicides, and rioting in the area where he lay in state, where a crowd that stretched for 11 blocks had gathered. For many years after his death a mysterious "Woman in Black" was seen at his tomb on the anniversary of his death.

Directions:
Beat brown sugar, oil, buttermilk, egg and vanilla in a mixing bowl. Mix flour, salt and baking soda. Add to brown sugar mixture and stir until blended. Stir in rhubarb and nuts. Turn into 2 greased 8x4x2-inch loaf pans. Sprinkle 1 tbsp sugar over each. Bake at 325° F for 1 hour, or until done.

Breads, Muffins, Buns, Biscuits, Puddings, Doughnuts, Pancakes, Etc.

Doughy Delights

Doughy Delights

Breads, Muffins, Buns, Biscuits, Puddings, Doughnuts, Pancakes, Etc.

Pumpkin Apple Bread

Ingredients:
1/4 cup oil
1/4 cup melted butter or margarine
3/4 cup sugar
1 cup canned pumpkin
1 cup grated, unpeeled apple
2 cups flour
1 tsp baking soda
1/2 tsp baking powder
1/4 tsp salt
1/2 tsp cinnamon
1/4 cup chopped nuts
1 egg
1/2 cup raisins
Topping:
2 tbsp butter or margarine
2 tbsp sugar
2 tbsp flour
1/2 tsp cinnamon
Directions:
Combine oil, butter, egg, pumpkin and apple. Mix dry ingredients and add to oil mixture, mixing well. Add raisins and nuts. Spoon into greased 8x4x3-inch loaf pan. Mix topping ingredients until crumbly and sprinkle over top. Bake at 350°F for 1 hour.

> **SPICE OF LIFE**
> Skipper's Observations: When most people put in their two cent's worth, they aren't overcharging.

> **SPICE OF LIFE**
> Some women don't care for a man's company - unless he owns it.

Ginger Bread

Phyllis Labelle, Lynden, Ontario, (nee Hollett, Arnold's Cove, Newfoundland)
Ingredients:
1/2 cup butter or lard
1/2 cup sugar
1 egg, beaten
1 cup molasses
2 & 1/2 cups flour, sifted
1 & 1/2 tsp baking soda
1/2 tsp cloves
1/2 tsp salt
1 tsp cinnamon
1 tsp ginger
1 cup hot water

> ***TRIVIA TIDBITS***
> John Sedgwick was a general during the American Civil War. He is known because of his famous last words. His last words were: "They couldn't hit an elephant at this dist..."

Directions:
Cream butter (or lard) with sugar, add egg and molasses. Blend in other ingredients and add hot water. Bake at 350°F for approximately 45 minutes.

This page is dedicated to our wonderful parents,
Shirley Hickey (nee Breen) and **Bill Hickey**,
native Newfoundlanders, who raised a large family in St. John's,
some of whom have moved away.
Your children, Michael, Paul, Sharon, Frank, Janet, Colleen and Billy.
Though we aren't always together, we're never far apart.

Partridgeberry Bread

Grace Perry, Brigus, Newfoundland

Ingredients:

1/2 cup margarine

1 cup sugar

2 eggs

1/4 tsp salt

1 tsp vanilla

2 & 1/2 cups flour

2 tsp baking powder

1/2 cup orange juice

1 cup partridgeberries

Directions:

Cream together margarine, sugar and eggs until fluffy. Add vanilla. Combine dry ingredients and fold into creamy mixture. Alternately, with orange juice, fold in partridgeberries. Pour into a greased loaf pan and bake at 350°F for 1 hour.

Tennessee Pumpkin Bread

Gertrude Sweetapple, Glovertown, Newfoundland

Ingredients:

1 & 2/3 cups all-purpose flour

1/4 tsp baking powder

1 tsp baking soda

3/4 tsp salt

1/2 tsp cinnamon

1/2 tsp nutmeg

1/3 cup shortening

1 & 1/4 cups sugar

1/2 tsp vanilla

2 eggs

1 cup canned mashed pumpkin

1/4 cup water

1/2 cups nuts, chopped

Directions:

Grease a regular loaf pan (9x5x3) or use a nonstick coated one and do not grease. On waxed paper, sift together the flour, baking powder, baking soda, salt, cinnamon and nutmeg. In a medium mixing bowl, cream shortening, sugar and vanilla. Add eggs one at a time, beating thoroughly after each addition. Stir in pumpkin. Stir in dry ingredients alternately with water until smooth. Fold in nuts. Turn batter into prepared pan. Bake at 350°F about 45 to 55 minutes.

Banana & Apple Bread

Elvie Genge, Glovertown, Newfoundland

Ingredients:

2 eggs (medium)

2 & 1/2 cups white flour

1/2 cup dark brown sugar

1/3 cup vegetable oil

3 medium bananas, mashed
2 medium apples, raw & mashed
1 & 1/4 cup dark raisins
1/2 cup red or green cherries, cut in small pieces
1/2 cup walnuts, crushed
1 tsp baking soda
2 heaping tsps baking powder
1 tsp (or less) salt
1 tsp allspice
2 tsp cinnamon
cold water

TRIVIA TIDBITS
Elizabeth Barry, an actress in the 1600s, deliberately stabbed a rival actress on stage during the performance of a play entitled, "The Rival Queens".

Directions:
Mix together all ingredients, adding cold water as necessary; pour into well-greased loaf pans and bake in moderate oven until done.

Figgy Duff

Marion Nagle, Kitchener, Ontario, (nee Daniels, Twillingate, Newfoundland)

Ingredients:
1/2 cup butter
1 egg
2 tsp baking powder
1 cup raisins
2 cups flour
3/4 cup sugar
1/2 cup milk or water
pinch of salt

FOOD FOR THOUGHT
A well adjusted, secure person is one who can play golf or cards as if they were games.

Directions:
Combine dry ingredients and add milk and eggs. Place in cloth bag for 1 hour in pot of boiling water. This can also be steamed in pudding mold.

White Bread

Ingredients:
2 cups 2% milk
1/4 tsp sugar, divided
4 tsp salt
1/4 cup shortening
2 cups lukewarm water, (105-115F), divided
1 - 16g pkg Fleischmann's Traditional Yeast
9 & 1/2 cups all-purpose flour

SPICE OF LIFE
The best way to break a habit is to drop it.
-Leo Aikman

This page is dedicated with love to my mother **Lillian Rowsell Pittman** (nee Matthews) of Bonne Bay, Newfoundland, and in loving memory of my father **Norman Rowsell** (1919 - 1981) of Musgravetown, Bonavista Bay, Newfoundland.
-- Keith Rowsell, Pickering, Ontario

Directions:
Scald milk and pour into large bowl. Add 1/4 tsp sugar, salt, shortening and 1 cup of water. Stir until shortening melts and cool to lukewarm. Meanwhile, dissolve 2 tsp sugar in remaining 1 cup of lukewarm water. Over this, sprinkle yeast. Let stand for 10 minutes, then stir briskly with fork. Add softened yeast mixture to lukewarm milk mixture. Stir till blended. Stir in 5 cups flour. Gradually stir in enough remaining flour to make a soft dough which is easy to handle. Turn dough onto a lightly floured surface and knead with palms of hands until smooth and elastic, about 10 minutes. Shape into a ball and place in a greased bowl, turning dough to grease top. Cover with damp cloth and allow to rise in warm, draft-free place until double in size (about 1 & 1/2 hours). Punch down dough. Divide dough into 4 equal pieces. Shape each piece into a loaf. Place each loaf into a well-greased 8 & 1/2 by 4 & 1/2 inch (22x11 cm) loaf pan. Grease tops, cover with damp cloth and allow to rise until double in size again (about 1 & 1/2 hours). Bake in a preheated 400°F oven for 30-35 minutes. Remove from pan to wire rack. Makes 4 great loaves.

Brown Bread

Ingredients:
1 cup rolled oats
2 cups boiling water
1 & 1/3 tbsp sugar, divided
1/2 cup lukewarm water (105-115F)
1 - 16g pkg Fleischmann's Traditional Yeast
1/2 cup molasses
1 tbsp shortening, melted
2 tsp salt
5 cups all-purpose flour

TRIVIA TIDBITS
The only recorded example of a war fought over a soccer match was in 1969. Fighting broke out at a match between El Salvador and Honduras. Feelings in both countries ran so strongly that they became involved in a war which cost over 2000 lives before the two countries were brought to the peace table.

Directions:
In a large bowl, combine rolled oats and boiling water. Cover and let stand 1 hour. Dissolve 1 tsp sugar in lukewarm water. Over this sprinkle yeast. Let stand for 10 minutes, then stir briskly with a fork. Add softened yeast mixture, molasses, shortening, salt and remaining 1 tbsp sugar to cooked rolled oats. Stir well to combine. Stir in enough flour until dough is easy to handle. Turn dough onto a lightly floured surface and knead with palms of hands until smooth and elastic, about 5 minutes. Shape into a ball and place in a greased bowl, turning dough to grease top. Cover with damp cloth and allow to rise in warm, draft-free place until double in size (about 2 hours). Punch down dough. Divide dough into 3 equal pieces. Shape each piece into a loaf. Place each loaf into a well-greased 8 & 1/2 by 4 & 1/2 inch (21x11 cm) loaf pan. Cover with a damp cloth and allow to rise until double in size again (about 45 minutes). Bake in a preheated 350°F oven for 45-50 minutes. Remove from pan to wire rack. Makes 3 great loaves.

Sweet Molasses Raisin Bread

Ingredients:
2 cups raisins
3/4 cup brown sugar
1/2 cup molasses
1/4 cup shortening
1 tbsp salt
2 tsp ground cinnamon

SPICE OF LIFE
Folks who are stuck on themselves just never have any cause for jealousy.

Breads, Muffins, Buns, Biscuits, Puddings, Doughnuts, Pancakes, Etc.

Doughy Delights

Doughy Delights

Breads, Muffins, Buns, Biscuits, Puddings, Doughnuts, Pancakes, Etc.

1 tsp cloves
2 cups boiling water
1 tsp sugar
3/4 cup lukewarm water (105-115°F)
2 - 16g pkgs Fleischmann's Traditional Yeast
6 & 1/2 cups all-purpose flour
1 tbsp margarine

Directions:

In a large bowl combine raisins, brown sugar, molasses, shortening, salt, ground cinnamon and cloves. Pour boiling water over raisin mixture and let stand till lukewarm (105-115F). Meanwhile, dissolve sugar in lukewarm water. Over this sprinkle yeast. Let stand for 10 minutes, then stir briskly with a fork. Add softened yeast mixture to raisin mixture. Stir. Gradually beat in enough flour to make dough easy to handle. Turn dough onto a lightly floured surface and knead with palms of hands until smooth and elastic, about 5 minutes. Shape into a ball and place in a greased bowl, turning dough to grease top. Cover with damp cloth and allow to rise in warm, draft-free place until double in size (about 1 & 1/2 hours). Punch down dough. Divide dough into 3 equal pieces. Shape each piece into a loaf. Place each loaf into a well-greased 8 & 1/2 by 4 & 1/2 inch (21x11 cm) loaf pan. Cover with a damp cloth and allow to rise until double in size again (about 1 & 1/2 hours). Bake in a preheated 350°F oven for 50-60 minutes. Remove from pan to wire rack. Brush tops with margarine to keep soft. Makes 3 great loaves.

Gingerbread

Gerine Collingwood, Rocky Harbour, Newfoundland

Ingredients:

1 cup butter
1 & 1/2 cups flour
2 tbsp yellow ginger
5 eggs
1 & 1/2 cups powdered sugar
1 tsp baking powder

Directions:

Cream butter, add flour (mixed with ginger) gradually. Beat yolks of eggs until thick and lemon coloured, add sugar gradually. Beat egg whites until stiff, add baking powder. Add this to mixture and beat thoroughly.
Turn into buttered deep cake pan. Bake for 3/4 hour at 325°F.

Dedicated in appreciation of my mother-in-law
Delilah M. Smith of Hodges Cove, Newfoundland.
This lady, born in 1906, is very special to her family.
Submitted by Kathleen Smith, Hillview, Newfoundland

Onion Rye Bread

Ingredients:

3 cups all-purpose flour
2 & 1/2 cups rye flour
1/4 cup brown sugar
2 pkgs active dry yeast
2 tsp salt
1 envelope onion soup mix
1 & 1/4 cups water
1 cup milk
2 tbsp butter or margarine
1/2 tsp caraway seed
melted butter or margarine

SPICE OF LIFE
A facelift is something that takes care of a multitude of skins.

Directions:

In a medium bowl, stir together all purpose flour and rye flour. In a large bowl, stir together 1 & 1/2 cups mixed flour, brown sugar, yeast and salt. In a saucepan, combine onion soup mix, water, milk, 2 tablespoons butter, and caraway seeds. Heat, stirring constantly, until lukewarm. Gradually beat liquid mixture into yeast mixture until blended. Gradually stir in enough additional flour (2 to 3 cups) to make a soft dough. Cover and let rise in a warm place until doubled, 40 to 50 minutes. Preheat oven to 350°F. Butter a 2-quart casserole. Stir dough down. Place in buttered casserole. Brush top with melted butter. Let rise until doubled, 20 to 30 minutes. Bake 50 to 60 minutes. Remove from casserole; brush crust with melted butter. Cool on wire rack. Makes 1 large round loaf.

Toutons

Ingredients:

1 tbsp + 1 tsp sugar
1/2 cup lukewarm water
1 - 16g pkg Fleischmann's Traditional Yeast
1 cup 2% milk
2 tbsp shortening
1/2 cup cold water
1/2 tbsp salt
5-6 cups all-purpose flour
1/8 - 1/4 pound salt pork, diced

> **SPICE OF LIFE**
> We should always remember that a tightly closed mouth will gather few feet.

Directions:

Dissolve 1 tsp sugar in lukewarm water. Over this sprinkle yeast. Let stand for 10 minutes, then stir briskly with a fork. Scald milk; add shortening and stir until melted, then add cold water, salt and 1 tbsp sugar. Cool to lukewarm. Add softened yeast mixture to lukewarm milk mixture. Stir until blended. Add 2 cups flour to liquid mixture and beat with a wooden spoon until smooth. Gradually add enough flour to make a moist dough which no longer sticks to the bowl. Turn dough onto a lightly floured surface and knead with palms of hands until smooth and elastic, about 10 minutes. Shape into a ball and place in a greased bowl, turning dough to grease top. Cover with damp cloth and allow to rise in warm, draft-free place until double in size (about 1 1/2 hours). Punch down dough and cut off small portions (about 1/3 cup). With palms of hands flatten dough into equal circular or triangular pieces; each 1/2-inch thick. Fry salt pork until brown and crisp.

Breads, Muffins, Buns, Biscuits, Puddings, Doughnuts, Pancakes, Etc.

Doughy Delights

Remove any pork scraps. Fry flattened bread dough in pork fat until brown on both sides. Serve with warm molasses, butter, applesauce, maple syrup or marmalade. Makes about 25 toutons.

Zucchini Loaf

Violet Noseworthy, Listowell, Ontario, (nee Quinlan, Birchy Bay, Newfoundland)

Ingredients:

3 eggs
1 & 1/2 cups sugar
2 tsp vanilla
2 cups all-purpose flour, sifted
3 tsp ground cinnamon
1 tsp salt
1 cup vegetable oil
2 cups zucchini (ground fine and drained well)
1 tsp baking powder
3/4 tsp baking soda
1 cup raisins
1 cup walnuts

Directions:

Beat eggs lightly in a large bowl. Stir in oil, sugar, zucchini and vanilla. Sift flour, baking powder, baking soda, cinnamon and salt unto wax paper. Stir in raisins and nuts. Spoon batter into well-greased loaf pans. Bake in moderate oven 370°F for 1 hour depending on oven or until centre springs back when lightly pressed. Cool in pans on wire rack for 10 minutes. Remove from pans and cool and store or freeze.

TRIVIA TIDBITS
One hundred and eighteen centimetres of snow fell in 24 hours in Lakelse Lake, British Columbia on January 17, 1974.

FOOD FOR THOUGHT
The art of conversation depends upon an equal amount of listening.

Chatelaine Banana Bread

Catherine Irwin, Truro, Nova Scotia

Ingredients:

1 & 3/4 cup sifted flour
2 tsp baking powder
1/4 tsp baking soda
1/2 tsp salt
1/3 cup shortening
2/3 cup sugar
2 eggs + 1/2 tsp vanilla
1 & 2/3 cups mashed bananas

Directions:

Preheat oven to 350°F. Sift flour, baking powder, soda and salt together. In separate bowl, cream shortening, add sugar gradually. Beat eggs into cream mixture. Beat well. Stir in dry ingredients and bananas alternately. Pour into well-greased loaf pan (10x5). Slightly lumpy looking. Bake 70 minutes. Test after 55 minutes.

SPICE OF LIFE
The difference between a wife and a mistress is night and day.

Dedicated to the memory of **Allen and Sarah** (Greening) **Stares** who left Port Blandford to live in Sault Ste. Marie, Ontario, and who remembered Newfoundland with love.
Mickey & Ray Stares.

Mom's Lemon Loaf

Catherine Irwin, Truro, Nova Scotia

Ingredients:

1/2 cup (or less) lard
1 cup white sugar
2 eggs, beaten
1 & 1/2 cups flour
1 tsp baking powder
1 tsp salt
1/2 cup milk

Directions:

Mix together. Bake for approximately 1 hour at 350°F. Mix up 1/2 cup sugar and juice of one lemon. Pour over cake while still in pan.

FOOD FOR THOUGHT
Intelligent people know everything;
shrewd people know everyone.

Dark Pineapple Date Loaf

Ingredients:

2 cups flour
1/4 cup light brown sugar, firmly packed
1 tbsp baking powder
1 tsp salt
1 can (8oz) crushed pineapple
1 & 1/4 cups chopped, pitted dates
1 cup chopped pecans
2 eggs
2/3 cup milk
1/4 cup vegetable oil

TRIVIA TIDBITS
The following notice was actually seen in the window of a Chicago invisible mending firm during the 1920's: "Bullet holes rewoven perfectly in damaged clothes, low prices".

Directions:

Preheat oven to 350°F. Butter an 8x4-inch loaf pan. Line pan with waxed paper; grease paper. In a mixing bowl, stir together flour, sugar, baking powder and salt. Set aside. In a small saucepan, combine pineapple, pineapple liquid, and dates. Cook over low heat, stirring, until liquid is absorbed and mixture is dark and thick. Stir in nuts. Remove from heat; cool 10 minutes. In a mixing bowl, combine eggs, milk, and oil. Add date mixture; stir until smooth. Add to flour mixture, stirring only until flour is moistened. Pour batter into prepared pan. Bake 60 minutes or until bread tests done. Cover the bread lightly with foil during the last 15 minutes of baking time to prevent excess browning. Cool in the pan on a wire rack. Makes 1 loaf.

Apricot Pecan Loaf

Dolores Lundrigan, Wabush, Labrador, (nee English, Branch, St. Mary's Bay, Newfoundland)

Ingredients:

2 cups flour
2 tsp baking powder
1/2 tsp salt
1/2 tsp cinnamon
1/2 cup granulated sugar
1/2 cup dried apricot, finely chopped
3/4 cup pecans, finely chopped

SPICE OF LIFE
That a black cat brings bad luck
depends on whether you are a man
or a mouse.

Breads, Muffins, Buns, Biscuits, Puddings, Doughnuts, Pancakes, Etc.

Doughy Delights

1 egg, slightly beaten
1 cup milk
1/4 cup vegetable oil

Directions:

Sift together flour, baking powder, salt, cinnamon and sugar. Stir in chopped apricots and pecans. Beat together egg, milk and vegetable oil. Add liquid to dry ingredients and beat for about one minute. Turn into greased 8x4 loaf pan. Bake in preheated 350°F oven for 55 to 60 minutes or until a toothpick inserted in center comes out clean.

Molasses Pudding

Claudine Barnes, Corner Brook, Newfoundland

Ingredients:

1 cup molasses
1/2 cup sugar
1 tsp cinnamon
1 tsp cloves
1 tsp allspice
1 tsp baking soda
1/4 cup hot water
1 egg
1/2 cup melted butter
3 cups flour
1 tsp baking powder
1/2 tsp salt
1 cup blueberries or partridgeberries

Directions:

Mix molasses, sugar and spices. Dissolve baking soda in hot water and add to molasses mixture. Add egg, mix well. Add melted butter, then add flour, baking powder and salt. Stir in berries. Put in greased mold and steam for 2 hours. Serve with jigs dinner or with sauce of your choice.

Lizzie's Savoury Pudding

Addie Holloway, Bloomfield, Newfoundland

Ingredients:

4 slices homemade bread
4 potatoes (boiled & chopped fine)
1 onion, chopped fine
Newfoundland savoury

Directions:

Soak bread in cold water for one minute, drain and cut up fine. Add potatoes, onion and savoury. Bake in loaf pan for 1/2 hour. Sprinkle a few tablespoons of the drippings from your roast or chicken. Bake for 1 hour more or until brown. Serve with gravy, meat and vegetables.

To my wife **Grace**,
who has been there for me through good times and bad.
A wonderful wife, mother, and human being.
dedicated by her husband, Rex Stirling

Molasses (Lassy) Duff

Gordon LeRoux, Labrador City, (formerly of St. Judes, Deer Lake, Newfoundland)

Ingredients:

4 cups flour
1/2 lb butter
1/2 lb shortening
1/2 tsp salt
1/2 tsp ginger
1/2 tsp mixed spice or allspice
1 tsp cinnamon
1/4 tsp nutmeg
1-2 lb raisins
1 & 1/2 cups molasses
2 tsp baking soda
1/2 cup boiling water

TRIVIA TIDBITS
It gets below the freezing temperature for an average of only 15 days per year in Vancouver.

Directions:

Beat butter and shortening together. Add molasses and water with baking soda, and mix together. Add mixed ingredients and enough water to make hard batter. Spoon batter into pudding bag. Tie top of bag securely. Leave about an inch of space between top of batter and where you tie the bag. Shape the dough from the outside of the tied bag - until it sticks all around the inside. All the space inside the bag should be filled out with the batter to prevent water from getting in. Bring water to a boil in deep pot. Put the pudding in, put cover on pot, and keep boiling for about 3 hours. Occasionally add water to keep it up to level of the top of the pudding. Pudding may be served with cooked dinner or as a dessert. Good warm or cold. Makes 8 servings. (Serve with sauce shown in "Enhancers" section, page 210).

Old-Fashioned Figgy Duff

Margaret & Leonard Parsons, Admirals Beach, St. Mary's Bay, Newfoundland (formerly of Clattice Harbour, Placentia Bay, Newfoundland)

Ingredients:

3 cups bread crumbs
1 cup raisins
1/2 cup brown sugar
1 tsp ginger
1 tsp allspice
1 tsp cinnamon
1/4 cup butter, melted
3 tbsp molasses
1 tbsp baking soda
1 tbsp hot water
1/2 cup flour

FOOD FOR THOUGHT
Success is getting what you want;
happiness is wanting what you get.
-Dave Gardner

Directions:

Soak bread in water for a few minutes. Squeeze out water. Mix all above ingredients with bread crumbs. Add flour. Mix well. Pour into dampened pudding bag. Tie top tightly. Boil for 1 & 1/2 hours. Serve with boiled vegetables and salt beef.

Breads, Muffins, Buns, Biscuits, Puddings, Doughnuts, Pancakes, Etc.

Doughy Delights

Doughy Delights

Breads, Muffins, Buns, Biscuits, Puddings, Doughnuts, Pancakes, Etc.

Steamed Molasses Pudding

Muriel Harvey, Fort McMurray, Alberta (nee Butt, Hickman's Harbour, Newfoundland)

Ingredients:

1 cup raisins
3 tbsp shortening
1 cup boiling water
1/2 cup fancy molasses
1 & 1/2 cups sifted flour
1/2 cup sugar
1 tsp salt
1 egg, beaten
1 tsp soda

Directions:

Place raisins and shortening in a bowl. Add boiling water. Blend in sugar and molasses. Add beaten egg and sifted dry ingredients. Pour into greased 1-quart mold. Steam 2 hours. Serve hot with desired sauce.

FOOD FOR THOUGHT
The bitterness of poor quality lingers on long after the sweetness of cheap price is forgotten.

Hard Bread Pudding

Juanita Ings, Hillgrade, Newfoundland

Ingredients:

4 cakes hard bread
1 tsp pepper
1 onion
1/4 lb salt pork

Directions:

Soak hard bread overnight. Strain and mash. Chop onion fine and add to mashed bread; and add pepper. Put in pudding bag and tie tightly. Boil with jigs dinner for 2 hours. Serve with molasses, or corn syrup if used for dessert.

SPICE OF LIFE
Why is it that night falls, but it's day that breaks?

Hard Times Pudding

Juanita Ings, Hillgrade, Newfoundland

Ingredients:

1 & 1/2 cups flour
1 tsp mixed spice
1 tbsp butter, melted
1 tsp cream of tartar
2 cups currants
1/2 pint molasses
1 tsp baking soda

TRIVIA TIDBITS
During the London Blitz, a London borough council complained to the Anti-Aircraft Command that the vibration of their guns was cracking the lavatory pans in council houses and public conveniences. The council suggested that the offending guns - there to protect the borough from German air raids - should be sent elsewhere.

1/2 tsp salt
1 cup raisins
1/2 pint cold water

Directions:
Sift together flour, cream of tartar, salt and spice. Add fruit and mix well. Add soda to molasses, then melted butter and cold water. Add this to the first mixture. Beat into a smooth batter and steam for 2 hours.

> **TRIVIA TIDBITS**
> The average life-expectancy for Canadian males is 74 years, for females it is 80.6 years.

Spiced Bread Pudding

Violet Jenkins, Etobicoke, Ontario, (nee Baggs, Twillingate, Newfoundland)

Ingredients:
1 cup toasted bread crumbs
1 cup brown sugar
1 tsp soda
1/2 tsp cloves
1/2 tsp nutmeg
1 tsp cinnamon
1 cup sour milk
1 cup raisins

> **SPICE OF LIFE**
> Our standard of living has become so high that only a few of us can afford it.

Directions:
Combine crumbs, sugar and spices. Add milk and raisins. Mix well. Put into a greased baking dish and bake at 325°F for 1 hour. Serves 4-6.

Steamed Partridgeberry Pudding (or Blueberry)

Violet Jenkins, Etobicoke, Ontario, (nee Baggs, Twillingate, Newfoundland)

Ingredients:
1 & 1/2 cups sifted flour
3 tsp baking powder
1/4 tsp salt
1/4 cup sugar
1/4 cup margarine
1 egg, beaten
1 & 1/4 cups fresh berries
1/2 cup milk

> **SPICE OF LIFE**
> Skipper's Observations: Marriage is when you go from swearing to love to loving to swear.

Directions:
Sift dry ingredients into a bowl; rub in the margarine. Add the berries, then the milk and egg. Stir lightly to make a batter. Pour into a greased onequart mold. Place over boiling water and steam for 1 hour. (Serve with sauce shown in Enhancers" section, page 210).

Half-Hour Pudding

Sandra Young, St. John's, Newfoundland, (nee Dove, Twillingate, Newfoundland)

Ingredients:
1/3 cup brown sugar
1 cup all-purpose flour
2 tsp baking powder
1/4 tsp salt

> **FOOD FOR THOUGHT**
> We find the secrets of success will not work unless we do.

Breads, Muffins, Buns, Biscuits, Puddings, Doughnuts, Pancakes, Etc.

Doughy Delights

1/2 cup raisins

3/4 cup milk

2 cups boiling water

1 tbsp butter

3/4 cup brown sugar

1/4 tsp nutmeg

Directions:

In a medium mixing bowl, combine the 1/3 cup brown sugar, flour, baking powder, salt and raisins. Beat in milk. Put batter in greased pudding dish or square cake pan. Combine boiling water, brown sugar, butter and nutmeg. Pour over batter in cake pan and bake in preheated 350°F oven for 30 minutes, or until batter has set and a toothpick inserted in middle comes out clean. Serve warm. Great topped with unsweetened whipped cream or vanilla ice cream.

Prize Raisin Pudding

Ingredients:

1 cup raisins

1/2 cup nuts

1 tbsp shortening

1/2 cup sugar

1 tsp baking powder

1 tsp soda

1/2 tsp cinnamon

1 tsp vanilla

1/4 tsp salt

1/2 cup milk

1 cup flour

Directions:

Combine all ingredients and pour into greased pan. Set aside.

TRIVIA TIDBITS

Ivan IV, of Russia became known as 'Ivan the Terrible' for many reasons. One of them had to do with petticoats. In Russia at the time of the Tsar, a respectable woman was required to wear at least three petticoats. One evening Ivan noticed that his daughter-in-law was wearing only two, and started to beat her, even though she was pregnant. Ivan's son intervened on behalf of his wife and Ivan clubbed his son to death.

Dumplings

Arlene Gibbons, Stoney Creek, Ontario (nee Sherard, Point Verde, Placentia, Newfoundland)

Ingredients:

1 cup flour

1 tsp baking powder

1 tsp sugar

1/2 tsp salt

1/2 cup milk

1 tbsp butter or margarine

FOOD FOR THOUGHT

Opportunity is sometimes hard to recognize if you are only looking for a lucky break.

This page is dedicated to our late grandparents
Thomas and Susan Woolridge of Howley, Newfoundland.
Phyllis Richmond - Peterborough, Ontario
Geraldine McMahon - Fredericton, New Brunswick

Directions:
In a bowl, mix flour, sugar, salt and baking powder. Cut in butter and stir until crumbly. Add milk to make soft dough. Drop by spoonfuls into boiling stew or soup. Cover and simmer for 15 minutes without lifting lid. Ready to serve.

Palacsinta (Pal-a-chinta) Hungarian style **Paper Thin Pancakes**

Matilda Bara, Vancouver, British Columbia
Ingredients:
2 eggs
oil
1 cup flour
1 cup milk

SPICE OF LIFE
Not everyone repeats gossip
- some improve it.

Directions:
Combine eggs, flour and milk with whisk, blender or mixer and mix until smooth - will be very thin in texture. Heat a medium-size frying pan on medium heat and add 1/4 tsp or less of oil. Rotate around pan. Add 2 tbsp batter so that it flows over entire surface of pan. Cook until surface is drying and edge is lightly browned. Turn with a spatula and let bottom brown lightly. Turn pancake out on to a dinner plate (almost same size). Fill with filling of your choice - my choice is 2 scoops vanilla ice-cream and fold pancake over it (in middle). Cover with hot apple pie filling (cinnamon added) and sliced almonds.

Mandarin Pancakes

Archie Ridout, Rexdale, Ontario (formerly of Twillingate, Newfoundland)
Ingredients:
2 cups flour
3/4 cup boiling water
1/4 tsp salt
vegetable oil

TRIVIA TIDBITS
Visitors to Canada from other countries
spend an average of 5.4 nights.

Directions:
Mix flour, water and salt until dough holds together. Knead on a lightly floured board until smooth, about 8 minutes. Cut into 18 pieces. (Cover pieces of dough with plastic wrap to prevent drying). Shape each piece of dough into a ball; flatten slightly. Roll each ball into a 3-inch circle. Brush top of one circle with oil and top with another circle. Roll each double circle into a 6-inch circle. Repeat. Cover circles to keep from drying out. Heat skillet over medium heat. Cook each circle in the ungreased skillet, turning frequently, until pancake is blistered by air pockets and turns slightly translucent, about 2 minutes. (Do not brown or overcook or pancakes will become brittle) Carefully separate into 2 pancakes. Fold each pancake into fourths.

Plain Doughnuts

Vera E. Coburn, Labrador City
Ingredients:
3 & 1/2 cups all-purpose flour
1 tsp soda
1/2 tsp salt
1/4 tsp cinnamon

FOOD FOR THOUGHT
The man who would control others
must be able to control himself.
-B.C. Forbes

Breads, Muffins, Buns, Biscuits, Puddings, Doughnuts, Pancakes, Etc.

Doughy Delights

1/2 tsp nutmeg
2 eggs
1 cup sugar
2 tbsp melted shortening
1 tsp vanilla
1 cup thick sour cream (to replace sour cream, use 1 cup undiluted milk and 1 tbsp vinegar and only half the soda)

Directions:

Sift together soda, salt, cinnamon, nutmeg and flour. Beat the eggs until very light; add the sugar and melted shortening. Add flour mixture alternately with the sour cream. If necessary, add a little more flour so that the mixture will handle, but keep it as soft as possible. Roll to 1/2 inch thickness. Cut out with doughnut cutter and fry in hot fat (lard or oil desired) using a deep fryer. Drain on paper towels. Sprinkle with plain sugar, or cinnamon and sugar. Makes 3 & 1/2 dozen.

Chocolate Doughnuts

Vera E. Coburn, Labrador City

Ingredients:

1 cup sugar
2 eggs
3 tbsp vanilla
1 cup sour milk with 1 tsp soda
3 & 1/2 cups flour
3/4 cups cocoa
1 tsp baking powder
1 tsp salt
1/4 tsp ginger

Directions:

Beat eggs and sugar together until light. Add cream and vanilla, then add sour milk and soda. Sift cocoa, baking powder, salt and ginger with flour. Roll out and fry in hot fat. Sprinkle with sugar while warm.

Marion's Tea Biscuits

Marion Nagle, Kitchener, Ontario, (nee Daniels, Twillingate, Newfoundland)

Ingredients:

3 cups flour
1/3 cup sugar (or 2 tbsp sugar twin)
3 tsp baking powder, heaping
1/2 cup margarine

In loving memory of our parents **James Traverse and Bridget (Keating) Traverse**; our sisters **Mae Philpott, Alice Traverse, Kathleen Hurley, Anna Traverse** and **Margaret Traverse**; our brothers **Art Traverse** and **Bill Traverse**. May their souls rest in peace. The four of us remaining are grateful to be able to say we were born at Coachman's Cove, White Bay, Newfoundland. Thank you Mom and Pop!
Signed Clara, Jack, Leslie and Raymond

1 tbsp lard
1 egg, slightly beaten
1 cup water
raisins, optional

Directions:
Sift together dry ingredients. Cut or rub in margarine. Mix egg and water. Do not over-mix. Roll out and cut in rounds. Bake in preheated 450°F oven for 20 minutes.

Pancakes

Beulah Cooper, Gander, Newfoundland, (nee Collins, Corner Brook, Newfoundland)

Ingredients:
1 & 1/2 cups flour
3 tsp baking powder
1/2 tsp salt
3 tbsp sugar
1 egg
3 tbsp butter (melted)
1/4 tsp vanilla
1 & 1/4 cups milk

Directions:
Mix dry ingredients. Beat egg, add milk. Make a well in centre of dry ingredients. Add egg and milk mixture. Add melted butter and vanilla. Mix only enough to make mixture smooth. Fry on hot grill.

Catherine's Old English Cheese Scones

Catherine Irwin, Truro, Nova Scotia

Ingredients:
1 cup plain flour
1/4 to 1/2 tsp salt
1 tsp bicarbonate of soda
2 tsp cream of tartar
4 oz butter
milk to mix
6 oz sharp "old" cheddar cheese, shredded coarsely
1/4 to 1/2 tsp cayenne pepper

Directions:
Mix all dry ingredients in bowl. Add cheese and cayenne pepper. Add fat and rub in to breadcrumb consistency. Add enough water to make a soft dough. Turn onto a floured surface. Lightly "pat out" to about 1-inch thickness. Cut into rounds with a large mouthed drinking glass. Place on a floured baking sheet. Bake near top of a hot oven 450°F for about 10 minutes. These freeze well.

Buckwheat Pancakes

Ingredients:
2 tsp dry yeast
1 tsp sugar
1/4 cup lukewarm water

2 cups buckwheat flour

1 cup all purpose flour

1 1/4 cups lukewarm water

2 tbsp molasses

2 tbsp melted bacon fat

1/2 tsp salt

3/4 tsp baking soda

1 tbsp boiling water

1/2 cup sour cream, buttermilk or sour milk

Directions:

Dissolve the yeast and sugar in 1/4 cup lukewarm water. Combine the buckwheat and all-purpose flours and add 1 & 1/4 cups of lukewarm water. Add the sugar and yeast mixture and set aside to raise. When ready to cook, add the molasses, bacon fat, salt, soda (which has been dissolved in the boiling water), and the milk. If too thick for frying, add a little boiling water. Spoon out on a hot greased griddle. To keep hot and prevent sogginess, place each pancake between the folds of a napkin or tea towel.

FOOD FOR THOUGHT

Give me the benefit of your convictions, if you have any, but keep your doubts to yourself, for I have enough of my own.

Goethe

Bread Pancakes

Ingredients:

2 cups milk

2 cups bread crumbs

2 eggs, beaten

2 cups flour

1 tsp cream of tartar

1/2 tsp baking soda

a little salt

Directions:

Soak the bread crumbs in milk for at least a couple of hours. If serving the pancakes for breakfast, soak the bread crumbs overnight. Add the beaten eggs, then the flour, cream of tartar, soda and salt, which have been sifted together. Fry in a little shortening in a hot frying pan.

TRIVIA TIDBITS

Billy the Kid, the infamous American gunfighter-outlaw, was left-handed, weighed only 98 pounds and had buck teeth.

Old-Fashioned Griddle Cakes

Ingredients:

2 eggs, beaten

2 & 1/4 cups milk

1/3 cup melted butter

2 cups flour

4 tsp baking powder

2 tbsp sugar

1 tsp salt

Directions:

SPICE OF LIFE

Some old-timers can recall when the tanning parlors in town were the woodsheds.

Combine in a large bowl the beaten eggs, milk and melted butter. Add the dry ingredients which have been sifted together. Beat with an egg beater until smooth. Spoon the batter on a hot, greased griddle, or pour from a pitcher. Makes about 16 griddle cakes.

Blueberry Griddle Cakes

Ingredients:

2 cups flour

2 tsp baking powder

1/2 tsp baking soda

1/2 tsp salt

3 tbsp sugar

1 & 1/2 cups sour milk or buttermilk

1 egg

3 tbsp melted butter

1 cup blueberries

TRIVIA TIDBITS
The British Stock Exchange actually began in a London Coffee House.

Directions:

Mix and sift together the flour, baking powder, soda, salt and sugar. Beat together the milk and egg and gradually add to the dry ingredients, mixing thoroughly. Add the butter and blueberries. Drop by spoonfuls on a hot, greased griddle and brown on both sides.

Maui Muffins

Charlene Jenkins, Etobicoke, Ontario, (formerly of Springdale, Newfoundland)

Ingredients:

1 cup rolled oats, regular or quick

1 cup buttermilk

1 cup all-purpose flour

1/4 tsp salt

1/2 tsp baking soda

1 & 1/2 tsp baking powder

1/2 cup melted butter, or margarine

1/2 cup brown sugar, not packed

1 egg

3/4 cup shredded coconut

1/4 cup crushed pineapple, drained

1/3 cup chopped macadamia nuts, or slivered/sliced almonds

Brown Sugar Topping

1/4 cup all-purpose flour

2 tbsp rolled oats

1/4 cup brown sugar

3 tbsp butter or margarine

1/4 tsp cinnamon, optional

FOOD FOR THOUGHT
Genius is one percent inspiration and ninety-nine percent perspiration.
-Thomas Edison

SPICE OF LIFE
Love is a word consisting of two vowels, two consonants, and two fools.

Directions:

Mix rolled oats and buttermilk. In separate bowl, combine next 5 ingredients. Use a metal whisk to blend easily. Stir together melted butter, brown sugar, egg, coconut, pineapple, and nuts. Stir into oat mixture, then add dry ingredients and stir only until moistened. Spoon into greased muffin cups. For variation, combine brown sugar topping until crumbly and sprinkle over muffins before baking. Bake at 400°F for 20 minutes. Let sit for a few minutes and remove to a rack. Serve warm.

Breads, Muffins, Buns, Biscuits, Puddings, Doughnuts, Pancakes, Etc.

Doughy Delights

Doughy Delights — Breads, Muffins, Buns, Biscuits, Puddings, Doughnuts, Pancakes, Etc.

Orangy Peanut Butter Muffins

Ingredients:
1 & 3/4 cups unsifted all-purpose flour
1/2 cup sugar
2 tsps baking powder
1/2 tsp salt
1 cup peanut butter flavoured chips
1/2 cup golden raisins
2 tsps grated orange peel
1 egg, beaten
3/4 cup milk
1/4 cup melted butter (or margarine)

TRIVIA TIDBITS
John Knox, the famous Scottish man of God, was a very strict disciplinarian. One morning when one of his daughters was a little late for breakfast, John, the devine, greeted her by saying, "Child of the devil," to which she replied, "Good morning, Father!"

Directions:
Combine flour, sugar, baking powder and salt in mixing bowl. Stir in peanut butter chips, raisins and orange peel. Combine egg, milk and melted butter in a bowl. Add to other ingredients, blending just enough to moisten. Spoon into greased muffin cups. Bake in a 400°F degree oven for 15 to 20 minutes or until golden brown.

Pork Bang Belly

Juanita Ings, Hillgrade, Newfoundland

Ingredients:
2 cups molasses
1 tsp baking soda
1 lb salt pork
1 tsp allspice
4 cups flour
1 tsp nutmeg

FOOD FOR THOUGHT
Strong minds suffer without complaining; weak minds complain without suffering.

Directions:
Heat molasses on stove. Cut pork in small cubes and fry. Add to molasses while hot. Dissolve soda in 1/2 cup boiling water. Add spices to flour and mix all together. Grease pan, lay rind of pork in bottom, and bake for 1 hour in moderate oven in shallow pan. Eat while warm.

Stuffed French Toast

Ruby Matthews, Mississauga, Ontario, (nee Coates, Botwood, Newfoundland)

Ingredients:
1 8oz package cream cheese, softened
1 tsp vanilla
1/2 cup chopped walnuts
1 - 16oz loaf French bread
4 eggs
1 cup whipping cream
1/2 tsp vanilla
1/2 tsp ground nutmeg
1 - 12oz jar (1 & 1/2 cups) apricot preserves
1/2 cup orange juice

TRIVIA TIDBITS
The birthday of Scottish poet, Robert Burns is celebrated in Scotland, and other parts of the world, every year on the night of January 25. A dinner, which includes a sheep sausage called *Haggis* is served, in honour of Burn's poem, *Ode To Haggis..*

Directions:

Beat together the cream cheese and 1 tsp vanilla until fluffy. Stir in nuts; set aside. Cut bread into ten to twelve 1 & 1/2-inch slices; cut a pocket in the top of each. Fill each with 1 & 1/2 tablespoons of the cheese mixture. Beat together eggs, whipping cream, the remaining 1/2 teaspoon vanilla and the nutmeg. Using tongs, dip the filled bread slices in egg mixture, being careful not to squeeze out the filling. Cook on a lightly greased griddle till both sides are golden brown. To keep cooked slices hot for serving, place them on a baking sheet in a warm oven. Meanwhile, heat together the preserves and juice. To serve, drizzle the apricot mixture over hot French toast.

Sparkling Cranberry Muffins

Hilda Reid, Ignace, Ontario, (nee Harnum, Bishop's Falls, Newfoundland)

Ingredients:

1 cup fresh cranberries

2 tbsp sugar

2 cups flour

1/3 cup sugar

2 tsp baking powder

1/2 tsp salt

1/2 cup butter

3/4 cup orange juice

1 egg, slightly beaten

1/4 cup butter

1/4 cup sugar

> **FOOD FOR THOUGHT**
> Be kind. Remember, everyone you
> meet is fighting a hard battle.
> *-T.H. Thompson*

Directions:

Heat oven to 400°F. In a small, bowl combine cranberries and 2 tbsp sugar. Set aside. In large bowl, stir together flour, 1/3 cup sugar, baking powder and salt. Cut in 1/2 cup butter until mixture is crumbly. Stir in orange juice and egg just until moistened. Fold in cranberry/sugar mixture. Spoon batter into greased 12-cup muffin pan. Bake 20-25 minutes or until golden brown. Cool 5 minutes - remove from pan. Dip top of each muffin in 1/4 cup melted butter, then in 1/4 cup sugar. Serve warm.

Tea Buns

Marie Evans, Kitchener, Ontario

Ingredients:

2 cups flour

4 tsp baking powder

1/4 cup sugar

1/2 cup butter

2 eggs

milk

salt (pinch)

raisins

> **TRIVIA TIDBITS**
> So convinced was the Queen of Spain that the Spanish siege of Gibraltar in 1779 would be shortly successful, that she sat on a hill facing the conflict and vowed not to move until Gibraltar was taken. As days passed without victory for the Spanish, the British commander took pity on her and gallantly waved the Spanish flag for a couple of minutes so that the Queen could move without losing face. The seige lasted until 1783, without success by the Spanish.

Directions:

Mix dry ingredients with butter; add eggs. Add enough milk to make soft dough. Press dough on board, cut out with cutter. Brush top of buns with egg. Bake 400°F for 15 minutes.

Breads, Muffins, Buns, Biscuits, Puddings, Doughnuts, Pancakes, Etc.

Doughy Delights

Doughy Delights

Breads, Muffins, Buns, Biscuits, Puddings, Doughnuts, Pancakes, Etc.

Homemade White Bread

Ruth Keats, Mississauga, Ontario

Ingredients:

10 cups flour

1 quart warm water

1/4 cup melted butter

1 & 1/2 tbsp salt

1 tbsp sugar

1 pkg yeast

Directions:

Let yeast rise according to package directions. Mix other ingredients together. Add yeast and mix well. Let rise in mixing pan 2-3 hours. Knead and let rise again in greased bread pans. Bake at 350°F for 3/4-1 hour. Makes 3 loaves.

FOOD FOR THOUGHT

If you can't have the best of everything, make the best of everything you have.

Best Banana Muffins

Daphne Holloway, Portland, Newfoundland (formerly of Come By Chance, Newfoundland)

Ingredients:

1/2 cup sugar

6 tbsp vegetable oil

1 cup ripe mashed bananas

1 egg (slightly beaten)

1 & 1/4 tsp vanilla

1/2 cup all-bran cereal

1 cup flour

1 tsp baking powder

1 tsp baking soda

TRIVIA TIDBITS

It rained for 157 consecutive hours in Spring Island, B.C., starting on January 25, 1971.

Directions:

Combine sugar, oil, banana, egg, vanilla and all-bran cereal. Let stand 5 minutes. Sift flour, baking powder and baking soda. Then add to bran mixture. Stir just until moistened. Bake 20-25 minutes in 350°F oven.

Plain Buns

Nora K. Roberts, Woody Point, Newfoundland

Ingredients:

2 cups flour

4 tsp baking powder

1/2 tsp salt

3 to 5 tbsp lard

2/3 cup milk

Directions:

Mix all ingredients together and cut into buns.

Bake until golden brown at 400°F.

TRIVIA TIDBITS Mexico once had three different Presidents in one day.

Pineapple Loaf

Angela Waterman, Glenwood, Newfoundland

Ingredients:

1/4 cup butter

1 cup sugar

2 eggs

3 cups flour

3 tsp baking powder

1/4 tsp soda

1/2 tsp salt

1 tin crushed pineapple, undrained

1/2 cup nuts

1/2 cup cherries

Directions:

Cream butter and sugar. Add eggs and beat thoroughly. Combine remaining ingredients and add to butter, sugar and eggs. Bake in two loaf pans for about 1 & 1/2 hours at 300°F.

TRIVIA TIDBITS

A Scottish law passed in 1288 made it an offence for a man to refuse a woman's offer of marriage during a leap year. Any who refused were fined £1.

Partridgeberry Loaf

Nellie Russell, Brooklyn, Newfoundland, (nee Pike, Portland, Newfoundland)

Ingredients:

1/2 cup margarine

1 cup sugar

2 eggs

1/4 tsp salt

1 tsp vanilla

2 & 1/2 cups flour

2 tsp baking powder

1/2 cup orange juice

1 cup partridgeberries

FOOD FOR THOUGHT
Motorists with patience today are not patients tomorrow.

Directions:

Cream together margarine, sugar and eggs until fluffy. Add vanilla. Combine dry ingredients and fold into creamed mixture alternately with orange juice. Fold in partridgeberries. Pour into greased loaf pan and bake at 350°F oven for 1 hour.

Mou Shu Pork with Mandarin Pancakes

Archie Ridout, Rexdale, Ontario, (formerly of Twillingate, Newfoundland)

Ingredients:

1 lb boneless pork loin

2 tsp soy sauce

1 tsp cornstarch

6 large dried mushrooms

1 tbsp oil

2 eggs, slightly beaten

1/4 tsp salt

2 tbsp oil

1 - 8oz can bamboo shoots, drained and cut into 1/4-inch strips

FOOD FOR THOUGHT
A true friend walks in when everyone else is walking out!

Breads, Muffins, Buns, Biscuits, Puddings, Doughnuts, Pancakes, Etc.

Doughy Delights

1/4 cup water
3 tbsp soy sauce
1 clove garlic, minced
1 tsp sugar
1 tbsp cold water
1 tsp cornstarch
2 green onions, cut diagonally in 1/4-inch pieces

TRIVIA TIDBITS
When Coco-Cola was first sold in 1886, it was advertised as a "brain tonic".

Pancakes

Directions:

Cut pork into thin strips. Mix with 2 tsp soy sauce and 1 tsp cornstarch. Cover and refrigerate 30 minutes. Soak mushrooms in warm water until soft, about 30 minutes. Drain, discard stems; cut caps into thin slices. Heat 1 tbsp oil in a skillet or wok. Mix eggs and salt. Cook eggs until firm, turning once. Remove eggs and cut into thin strips. Heat 2 tbsp oil in skillet or wok. Cook and stir pork until no longer pink. Add mushrooms, bamboo shoots, 1/4 cup water, 3 tbsp soy sauce, garlic and sugar. Heat to boiling. Mix 1 tbsp water and 1 tbsp cornstarch; stir into pork mixture. Cook and stir until thickened, about 1 minute. Add egg strips and green onions; cook and stir 30 seconds. Pour pork filling into serving bowl; arrange hot pancakes on platter. To serve, unfold pancake and spoon some filling down the centre. Roll up; fold one end over to contain filling.

Japanese Snow Pudding

Hilda Reid, Ignace, Ontario, (nee Harnum, Bishop's Falls, Newfoundland)

Ingredients:

2 envelopes unflavoured gelatin
1/2 cup cold water
2/3 cup sugar
2 cups boiling water
2 tsp lemon rind, grated
1/4 cup lemon juice
3 egg whites
1/4 cup light corn syrup

FOOD FOR THOUGHT
Happiness is not a station you arrive at, but a manner of travelling.
-M. Runbeck

Directions:

Sprinkle gelatin over cold water, let soften 5 minutes. Combine sugar and boiling water, stir until sugar and gelatin are completely dissolved. Stir in lemon rind and juice. Chill until slightly thickened (about 1 hour). Beat egg whites until foamy. Gradually add sugar beating until stiff peaks form when beater is raised. Fold in gelatin mixture. If mixture layers, chill 5 - 10 minutes and fold again. Repeat if necessary until well blended. Pour into 9-inch square pan. Chill until set and cut in oblong shapes. Garnish as desired.

Lily's Biscuits

Catherine Irwin, Truro, Nova Scotia

Ingredients:

2 cups flour
1/4 tsp salt, or less
4 tsp baking powder (heaping)
1/4 cup white sugar or 1 heaping tbsp
1/2 cup margarine
1 egg, beaten in 3/4 cup milk

TRIVIA TIDBITS
During World War II, a circus clown was hired by the British government to demonstrate to agents, who were to be dropped into France, how to fall properly.

Directions:

Mix dry ingredients. Cut in soft margarine or butter until mixture resembles loose crumbs. Then combine beaten egg with milk. Add wet with dry ingredients. Mix until all flour is absorbed. Make into ball, flatten top with fingers. No rolling pin here. Cut out and bake in 450°F oven about 12-15 minutes.

Jiffy Pudding

Hilda Reid, Ignace, Ontario, (nee Harnum, Bishop's Falls, Newfoundland)

Ingredients:

2 cups cooked long grain rice

1 - 3 & 1/4oz pkg vanilla instant pudding

1/4 cup raisins

1 - 10oz can mandarin oranges, drained

Directions:

In a large bowl, prepare the instant pudding according to directions on the package. Add the other ingredients and combine thoroughly. Serve warm or cold.

Kentucky Biscuits

Charlene Jenkins, Etobicoke, Ontario, (formerly of Springdale, Newfoundland)

Ingredients:

2 cups all-purpose flour

2 & 1/2 tsp baking powder

1/2 tsp baking soda

dash salt

1 tbsp granulated sugar

1/2 cup butter, margarine or shortening

3/4 cup buttermilk

1 tbsp melted butter

> **SPICE OF LIFE**
> There's nothing that takes the starch out of folks like a reducing diet.

Directions:

Mix flour, baking powder, baking soda, salt and sugar in a mixing bowl. Cut in butter or shortening with pastry blender until mixture resembles coarse crumbs. Add buttermilk. Mix quickly to make a soft dough. Turn out onto lightly floured surface. Knead a few times to make a soft dough, don't overknead or the biscuits will turn hard and dry. Roll out to a 6-by-6-inch square. Place on ungreased baking sheet. With knife, cut dough into 12 even portions. Do not separate. Bake at 400°F until golden, about 15 minutes. Dust with flour, if desired, when biscuits come out of the oven. Serve piping hot with butter, jam and/or honey

Dough Boys

Alma Taylor, Mt. Moriah, Bay of Islands, Newfoundland, (nee LeDrew, Bell Island, Newfoundland)

Ingredients:

375ml flour

65ml butter

5ml salt

15ml baking powder

125-180ml water or milk

> **TRIVIA TIDBITS**
> The Roman emperor, Constantine decreed Sunday an official holiday in the year 321AD. The decree forbade all trade on this day and disallowed any kind of work with the exception of necessary agricultural labour. Public entertainment was prohibited by later emperors.

Breads, Muffins, Buns, Biscuits, Puddings, Doughnuts, Pancakes, Etc.

Doughy Delights

Directions:
Cut butter into small pieces in the flour, baking powder and salt. Add liquid to make a soft dough. Drop by teaspoonfuls into soup. Cover pot tightly and simmer for 20 minutes.

Carrot Pudding

Ruby Matthews, Mississauga, Ontario, (nee Coates, Botwood, Newfoundland)

Ingredients:
1 cup raisins
1/2 cup currants
1 tbsp brandy
1 cup ground suet
1 cup dark brown sugar
1 cup grated carrot
1 cup grated potato
1 cup flour
1 tsp baking soda
1/2 tsp salt
1 tsp cinnamon
1/2 tsp nutmeg
1/4 tsp cloves

FOOD FOR THOUGHT
When you teach your children, you teach your children's children.

Directions:
Combine raisins and currants in micro-safe bowl; sprinkle with brandy; and micro on High for 30 seconds. Combine suet, sugar, carrot, potatoes, raisins and currants. Combine flour, baking soda and seasonings. Stir into carrot mixture until moist. Put into greased mold, cover with plastic wrap leaving a small vent. Micro at 50% Medium - 8 minutes; and High for 2-3 minutes. Let stand 10-15 minutes covered, then invert onto a plate and let cool.

Bread Pudding

Lenora Batstone, Clarenville, Newfoundland

Ingredients:
bread
1 cup milk
2 eggs, separated
1/2 cup sugar, halved
1 tsp butter

SPICE OF LIFE
There are those who say very few words and say them too often.

Directions:
Break bread into small pieces. Place in a bowl about 2 cups. Throw milk, egg yolks, 1/4 cup sugar, and butter over bread. Soak for 1/2 hour. Mix up egg whites with remaining 1/4 cup sugar. Place on top of mixture. Bake at 250°F until brown - about 20 minutes.

TRIVIA TIDBITS

Frank Mars, a Chicago candy-maker, had a dispute with his son Forrest in 1930, and told him to leave the country. With only a few thousand dollars, Forrest set up shop in England selling a version of his father's 'Milky Way' chocolate bars. While in England, the younger Mars discovered 'Smarties', a candy-coated chocolate, popular in that country. He bought the rights to produce the candies in America and went into partnership with a man named Murrie. They called the product M & Ms, after Mars and Murrie. M & Ms became a big hit in the US. In 1964 after many family disputes, the British and American Mars' companies merged.

Sweets & Treats

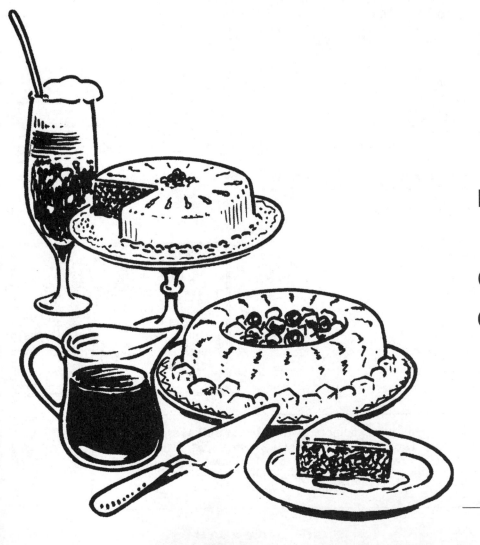

Pies

Pastries

Cakes

Cookies

Candies

Etc.

Captain Blueberry Cake

Myrtle Sturge, Gambo, Newfoundland

Ingredients:
3/4 cup butter (white)
3/4 cup sugar
1 egg
1 tub sour cream
1 tsp vanilla
2 cups flour
1 tsp baking powder
1 tsp baking soda
1/4 tsp salt
2 cups blueberries

Directions:
Cream butter, sugar, eggs, sour cream and vanilla. Add dry ingredients. Pour 1/2 cup batter in spring form pan; then add blueberries. Pour other half of batter on top. Spread with topping before baking. Bake 350°F for 40-50 minutes.

Topping

Ingredients:
2 tbsp butter
1/2 cup brown sugar
1 & 1/2 tsp cinnamon
1 tbsp flour

Directions:
Melt butter. Mix all ingredients together and spread on top of batter (before baking cake).

TRIVIA TIDBITS
John Wesley, who founded Methodism, which later became the United Church, had a very strict mother. She was also a firm believer in not sparing the rod to her children. She once said, "the most odious noise of the crying of children is rarely heard in the house."

Never Fail Chocolate Cake

Vera E. Coburn, Labrador City

Ingredients:
1 cup sugar
1/2 cup cocoa
1/2 cup shortening
1/2 cup milk
1 tsp vanilla
1 egg
1/2 tsp salt
Mix all together ... *add*
1 & 1/2 cups flour
1 tsp soda

FOOD FOR THOUGHT
Facts are stubborn and stand firm; statistics are much more pliable.

In loving memory of **Elizabeth (Bet) Westcott,** (nee Thompson) and **Douglas Westcott**, St. John's, Nfld. From Ann, Florence, Sherry, Dawn, Doug Jr., Shelly, Joyce and Lilly.
Submitted by daughter Ann

Mix well. Batter will be stiff. Add 1/2 cup hot water. Mix well. Bake in 8x8x2 inch pan (or make cup cakes) or 2 round pans in a 350°F oven. Ice as desired.

Nutmeg Loaf Cake

Vera E. Coburn, Labrador City

Ingredients:

1 cup white sugar
1/2 cup margarine
1 egg
1/2 tsp salt
1 cup sour milk
1 tsp soda
1 & 1/2 tsp nutmeg
2 cups flour
1 tsp vanilla (optional)

Directions:

Cream margarine and sugar. Add egg. Mix well together. Add sour milk, then dry ingredients and vanilla. Mix until smooth. Put in a greased and floured loaf pan. Bake about 1 hour, or until done, in a 350°F oven.

> **TRIVIA TIDBITS**
> The worst thing that could happen to a Viking Chief was that he should die peacefully in bed.

Banana Split Cake

Grace Ryan, Newmans Cove, Bonavista Bay, Newfoundland

Ingredients:

2 cups graham wafer crumbs
1/4 lb margarine
Crumble together, spread in bottom of 9x11-inch pan.

First layer:
2 cups icing sugar (I use less)
1/4 lb margarine
Mix with electric mixer for 15 minutes

Second layer:
5 bananas, sliced

Third layer:
1 can crushed pineapple, drained

Fourth layer:
1 container of cool whip or pkg. of dream whip
Follow directions as above and put chopped pecan and cherry halves on top.

> **TRIVIA TIDBITS**
> British explorer and naval captain James Cook, who explored the seaways and coasts of Newfoundland and and eastern Canada and conducted three expeditions to the Pacific Ocean, unlike other seafarers of his time, never had a sailor die of scurvy. This is because Captain Cook made sure that his sailors paid close attention to diet and had proper ventilation aboard ship.

Chocolate Cinnamon Snaps

Charlene Jenkins, Etobicoke, Ontario (formerly of Springdale, Newfoundland)

Ingredients:

2 cups all-purpose flour
1/2 tsp baking soda
dash salt
1/3 cup unsweetened cocoa powder

> **SPICE OF LIFE**
> English is a language in which double negatives are a no-no...

2 tsp cinnamon
3/4 tsp cloves
1/2 cup softened butter or margarine
1/2 cup granulated sugar
1/4 cup molasses
1 egg
cinnamon-sugar

Directions:
Combine flour, baking soda, salt, cocoa powder, cinnamon and cloves. In another bowl, cream butter until soft. Gradually add sugar, beating until fluffy. Beat in the molasses and egg. Add flour mixture. Blend until a stiff dough forms. Roll dough (half or a quarter of dough is easier to work with) on a lightly floured board to a 1/8- to 1/4-inch thickness. Cut into favourite shapes. Place on a lightly greased cookie sheet. Sprinkle with cinnamon-sugar. Bake at 350°F for 10 to 12 minutes depending on thickness. Cool a minute on sheet before removing to a rack. Store in a tin when complete cooled. NOTE: The cookies can be sprinkled with chocolate sprinkles or holiday coloured sugar.

Boiled Raisin Cake

Grace Ryan, Newmans Cove, Bonavista Bay, Newfoundland

Ingredients:
1 pkg raisins
3 cups cold water
2 cups sugar
5-6 tbsp cocoa
1/2 lb butter
1 tsp cinnamon
1 tsp cloves
1 tsp baking soda
1/2 cup cold water
4 cups flour
1 tsp salt
1 tsp baking powder

Directions:
Boil first 7 ingredients for 20 minutes and cool. Mix baking soda in 1/2 cup cold water and add to cooled mixture. Then add flour, salt and baking powder. Bake in 300°F oven for about 1 & 1/2 hours.

Apple Cake

Grace Ryan, Newmans Cove, Bonavista Bay, Newfoundland

Ingredients:
1 tin apple pie filling
1 cup white sugar

This page is dedicated to the memory of our parents
Daisy Elliott (nee Dove; 1919-1981) and
Peter Elliott (1916-1995), of Twillingate, Newfoundland.
Forever remembered by your children -
Harry, David, Bruce, Ross, Margaret, Phyllis, Josephine and Bonnie

(side tab) **Sweets & Treats** — Pies, Pastries, Cakes, Cookies, Candies, Etc.

2 eggs
2 tsp baking powder
2 cups flour
1/2 cup oil
2 tsp cinnamon
1 tsp salt

Directions:

Mix all ingredients together with a spoon. Bake at 350°F for 45-60 minutes.

Icing (for Apple Cake)

Ingredients:

1 cup butter
1/2 cup white sugar
2 tsp flour
3 tsp milk
3 tsp hot water
1 tsp vanilla

Directions:

Cream together butter and sugar;
add rest of ingredients and mix well.

FOOD FOR THOUGHT
Don't be so busy making a living that
you forget to make a life.
-Clifton Burke

TRIVIA TIDBITS
In Cumberland, England, in 1832, a farmer by
the name
of Joseph
Thomson sold his
wife in Carlisle
market for
twenty shillings
and a
Newfoundland
dog.

Dump Cake

Grace Ryan, Newmans Cove, Bonavista Bay, Newfoundland

Ingredients:

1 can (20oz) crushed pineapple, undrained
1 can (21oz) cherry pie filling
1 deluxe yellow cake mix (any brand)
1 cup pecans (or walnuts), chopped
1/2 cup butter (or margarine) cut in thin slices

Directions:

Preheat oven to 350°F. Grease a 13x9x2-inch pan. Spoon undrained pineapple in pan. Spread evenly. Add pie filling and spread in even layer. Sprinkle cake mix onto cherry layer, evenly. Sprinkle pecans (or walnuts) over cake mix. Place butter over top. Bake at 350°F for 48-53 minutes. Served warm or cooled, it is very good. 12-16 servings.

Earthquake Cake

Ina Belcher, Tonawanda, New York, (nee Brown, St. John's, Newfoundland)

Ingredients:

1 pkg chocolate cake mix
1 & 1/2 cups flaked coconut
1 cup chopped nuts
1 pkg (8oz) cream cheese
1/2 cup butter, melted
1 lb confectioner's sugar

SPICE OF LIFE
The road to success is under
constant construction.

Directions:

Grease and flour 9x13x2-inch pan. Sprinkle coconut, then nuts, evenly in bottom of pan. Prepare the cake mix as directed on box. Pour over coconut and nuts. Combine butter, cream cheese and

confectioner's sugar and beat until smooth. Spread over the cake batter (or drop by spoonfuls). Bake at 350°F for 50 minutes or until toothpick inserted halfway comes out clean. Cool completely. To serve, cut into serving pieces and turn upside down on plate.

Chocolate Eclair Cake

Ina Belcher, Tonawanda, New York, (nee Brown, St. John's, Newfoundland)

Ingredients:
1 box graham crackers
2 sm pkgs Instant French vanilla pudding
3 cups milk
1 sm container cool whip
1 can milk chocolate flavour frosting
2 tbsp hot water

> **FOOD FOR THOUGHT**
> The truth is most people aren't troubled by improper thoughts; they enjoy them.

Directions:
Layer 9x13-inch pan with graham crackers. Mix pudding and milk. Fold in cool whip. Pour over graham crackers. Mix frosting with hot water. Frost top layer of graham crackers. Chill overnight.

Rum Cake

Ina Belcher, Tonawanda, New York, (nee Brown, St. John's, Newfoundland)

Ingredients:
1 yellow cake mix
1 sm pkg vanilla instant pudding mix
4 eggs
1/2 cup cooking oil
1/2 cup Rum
1/2 cup water
1 cup chopped nuts

> **TRIVIA TIDBITS**
> In the early 1900s the parishioners of Tharomindah in Queensland, Australia built a church out of straw and hessian. One morning, the villagers awakened to find that goats had eaten the entire church.

Directions:
Mix those ingredients well. Fold nuts in last. Well grease a bundt bake pan. Lightly flour. Sprinkle with additional chopped nuts. Bake at 350°F for 1 hour or until inserted toothpick comes out clean. During last 10-15 minutes - in saucepan, combine and cook for five minutes the following:
1/4 cup water
1 cup sugar
1 stick butter

After boiling for five minutes - remove from heat and add 1/2 cup rum. Prick hot cake all over with a toothpick. Pour hot sauce over hot cake - slowly so it seeps into cake. Cool in pan before removing.

"A salute to our parents, **Frank and Floss LeDrew** of Pasadena, who are the 'glue' that kept this large family clan together and forever wanting . . . to be home for Sunday dinner.
Shirley, Dave, Stewart (Butch), Bren-da, Deborah (Deb) and Terry LeDrew

Black Beauty Cake

Ina Belcher, Tonawanda, New York, (nee Brown, St. John's, Newfoundland)

<u>Ingredients:</u>

6 oz chocolate chips
1/4 cup evaporated milk
1/4 cup hot water
Blend in blender or on stove to melt chocolate chips. Pour into 9x13-inch cake pan. Add:
1 cup mini marshmallows
1 cup chopped nuts

<u>Directions:</u>

Mix one small cake mix as directed on package. Pour over mixture. Bake at 350°F for 30 minutes. Serve warm with ice cream.

Mrs. Smallwood's Fruit Cake

June Dalley, Bathurst, New Brunswick, (nee Howell, Carbonear, Newfoundland)

<u>First Ingredients:</u>

1 lb raisins
1 lb currants
1 lb dates
1/4 lb mixed peel
1 cup cherries
1 cup chopped nuts
1/2 cup brown sugar

<u>Second Ingredients:</u>

3 eggs
1 lb butter
1 tsp vanilla
1 tsp soda
2 tsp maple flavouring
2 tsp almond flavouring
2 tsp lemon flavouring
2 & 1/2 cups flour
1 tsp mace
1 tsp nutmeg
1 tsp cinnamon
1/4 tsp cloves
1/4 tsp ginger
1/2 cup warm water

> **FOOD FOR THOUGHT**
> A hero is no braver than an ordinary man, but is brave five minutes longer.
> -R.W. Emerson

> **TRIVIA TIDBITS**
> Frank James, brother of outlaw Jesse James, and onetime member of his gang, eventually gave up a life of crime and joined other family members in the selling of "Genuine Jesse James Souvenirs", including items of his dead brother's clothing and even pebbles from Jesse's grave.

<u>Directions:</u>

Mix first ingredients together and set aside.
Cream butter and sugar, add eggs and cream well.
Then add flavourings. Stir flour and spices together.
Sprinkle one cup flour and spices mixture over the first mixture and coat well.
Add the fruits to butter mixture, add remainder of flour.
Add soda (dissolved in 1/2 cup warm water), and if desired,
add one cup of strawberry jam and 1/2 cup rum. Bake in 275°F oven for 3 & 1/2 hours.

Rhubarb Cake

June Gates, Woodstock, Ontario

Ingredients:

1 & 1/2 cup raw rhubarb, cut fine

1 cup brown sugar

1/2 cup white sugar

1 egg

1/2 cup margarine

1 cup buttermilk or sour milk

1/2 tsp salt

1 tsp soda

1 tsp vanilla

2 cups flour

Directions:

Cream sugar and margarine. Add egg and salt. Stir in milk, soda, vanilla and flour. Add rhubarb. Pour in pan 9x13x2-inch. Sprinkle with 1/4 cup sugar and 1 tsp cinnamon. Bake at 375°F for 35 minutes.

SPICE OF LIFE
A taxi is a public automobile that will disappear completely when it rains hardest.

FOOD FOR THOUGHT
Hospitality doesn't depend on size or supply. If the heart is big enough, so is the table and so is the house.

War Cake

Gordon LeRoux, Labrador City (formerly of St. Judes, Deer Lake, Newfoundland)

Ingredients:

2 cups water

1 tsp salt

1 tsp allspice

2 cups brown sugar

1 tsp cinnamon

1 pkg raisins

4 tbsp shortening

1/2 tsp cloves

2 tsp baking soda

1/2 tsp vanilla

1/2 tsp lemon

2 & 1/2 cups flour

Directions:

Mix first eight ingredients and boil for five minutes.

Next, when cool, add baking soda, vanilla, lemon and flour.

Mix well together and bake for 1 hour at 350°F.

TRIVIA TIDBITS
When they were first introduced in Britain, some people claimed that the potato was the forbidden fruit referred to in the Bible.

This page is lovingly dedicated to our parents,
Cecil and Violet (nee Froude) Young in Twillingate.
Your children, Gary, Josephine and Ronnie

Sweets & Treats
Pies, Pastries, Cakes, Cookies, Candies, Etc.

Election Cake

Mrs. Queen Maloney, Bay Bulls, Newfoundland

Ingredients:

1 & 1/2 cups butter

2 cups white sugar

3 eggs

2 cups raisins

1 cup currants

1 lb mixed peel

1/2 lb nuts

1 cup milk

3 tsp baking powder

1 & 1/2 tsp vanilla

Directions:

Cream butter well, gradually add sugar, creaming until light and fluffy. Beat eggs well and add to mixture. Add flavouring. Sift together flour and baking powder. Add alternately to the mixture, beginning and ending with flour. Lastly, stir in fruit. Bake in a large pot which has been lined with greased brown paper. Bake in moderate oven for 2 & 1/2 hours.

Mum's Scotch Cake

Ruby Collins, Hare Bay, Newfoundland

Ingredients:

1 lb butter

2/3 cup white sugar

2 egg yolks

4 cups flour

2 tsp salt

1/2 tsp soda

1 tsp cream of tartar

2 tsp vanilla

nuts or cherries (your choice)

Directions:

Cream together butter, sugar and egg yolks. Sift together flour, salt, and soda. Add cream of tarter and vanilla to creamed mixture. Add dry ingredients to cream mixture. This recipe should be kneaded a lot. Roll out and cut with favourite cookie cutter. Bake at 325°F-350°F until lightly brown. Do not over bake. When cool, frost tops with a butter frosting and top with nuts or cherries.

Peach Fruit Cake

Ruby Hancock, Labrador, Newfoundland (nee Pelley, Southside, Carbonear, Newfoundland)

Ingredients:

1 cup butter

1 & 1/2 cups sugar

3 eggs, well beaten

1 - 20oz tin peaches, drained & crushed (reserve liquid)

3 cups raisins

1 & 1/2 cups cherries, cut up
1 cup coconut
3 cups flour
1 tsp baking powder
1/2 tsp salt
2 tsp vanilla

> **FOOD FOR THOUGHT**
> The difference between being nearsighted and shortsighted is that the former can be corrected.

Directions:

Cream butter and sugar. Add well-beaten eggs. Blend in the crushed peaches, raisins, cherries and coconut. Stir in dry ingredients. Add vanilla. (A little peach juice may be added if the batter seems dry). Put into a large round or square pan which has been well-greased. Bake at 275°F for about 3 hours.

Gladys Keepings' Coconut Pudding with Vanilla Sauce

Ingredients:

Cream together:
3/4 cup sugar
1 tsp vanilla
1/4 cup butter
1 egg

Sift together:
1 tsp salt
1 cup flour
2 tsp baking powder

> **TRIVIA TIDBITS**
> Frank Gusenberg was a gangster who was one of the victims of the St. Valentine's Day Massacre. As he lay dying with fourteen bullets in his body, a policeman asked him who shot him. He replied, "Nobody shot me!"

Directions:

Add sifted ingredients to creamed mixture and stir; then add 1/4 cup lukewarm water. Stir to moisten.

In a square dish put:
2 tbsp butter
3 tsp sugar
1 cup hot water

Stir to melt butter; add pudding mixture; spread evenly in dish. Sprinkle with 1/2 cup coconut and bake at 350°F for 30 minutes or until golden brown;

To make extra sauce, boil together:
1/2 cup sugar
1/2 tsp vanilla
1 & 1/2 cups water
1 tbsp butter

Directions:

Mix 1 & 1/2 tsp cornstarch with 1/4 cup water - add to boiling mixture; Stir until thicken; serve warm with pudding - Enjoy!

This page is dedicated to the memory of our parents
John and Gladys Keeping of Grand Bank, Newfoundland.
Always remembered - Forever loved.
-daughters Phoebie, Amy, Grace, Mary, Sarah, Jane, Carolann and Peggy -sons Bill, Morgan, Freeman, Bruce and Jack.

Tomato Soup Cake

Betina Wheeler-Ali, Toronto, Ontario (formerly of St. John's, Newfoundland)

Ingredients:

3/4 cup shortening
1 tsp baking soda
1 & 1/2 tsp cinnamon
1 tsp cloves
3 cups all-purpose flour
3/4 cup water
1 & 1/2 cups chopped nuts
1 & 1/2 cups sugar
3/4 tsp salt
3 tsp baking powder
1 & 1/2 cups raisins
1 can tomato soup

Directions:

Measure shortening and sugar into bowl, blend combined soup, water and soda. Add shortening mixture alternately with all sifted, dry ingredients. Stir in raisins and nuts. Bake in a large loaf pan for one hour at 325°F.

Frost with cream cheese icing:

3oz cream cheese
2 tbsp butter
1/2 tsp vanilla
1 & 3/4 cups icing sugar

TRIVIA TIDBITS
In 1875 the director of the U.S. patent office resigned his job because he felt there was "nothing left to invent".

SPICE OF LIFE
Most people don't act stupid; it's the real thing.

Apple Raisin Cake

Betina Wheeler-Ali, Toronto, Ontario (formerly of St. John's, Newfoundland)

Ingredients:

2 & 1/2 cups all-purpose flour
1 tsp cinnamon
1 beaten egg
1/2 cup raisins
1 tsp baking soda
1/2 cup margarine
1 cup molasses
1 - 8 & 1/2oz can of applesauce

SPICE OF LIFE
The fellow who tries to do something and fails is definitely better than the fellow who tries to do nothing and succeeds.

Directions:

In a bowl, combine flour, soda, cinnamon, and 1/2 tsp salt. Cut in margarine to resemble coarse crumbs. In another bowl, stir together egg, molasses and applesauce. Blend into flour mixture until moist. Add raisins. Bake at 350°F for 40-45 minutes. Cool in pan for 15 minutes.
*Glaze with butter icing that has had a tsp of lemon juice added to it.

Pies, Pastries, Cakes, Cookies, Candies, Etc.

Sweets & Treats

Sweets & Treats
Pies, Pastries, Cakes, Cookies, Candies, Etc.

Newfoundland Cake

Rosella Rowe, Avondale, Conception Bay, Newfoundland, (nee Moore)

Ingredients:

1/2 lb butter or margarine
2 cups white sugar
3 large eggs
3 cups flour
3 tbsp baking powder
1 cup warm milk
1 tsp vanilla
1 cup raisins

Directions:

Mix butter, sugar and eggs together. Add flour, baking powder, milk and vanilla. Dust raisins with flour and add to mixture. Bake in 325°F oven for 2 hours.

> **FOOD FOR THOUGHT**
> Making the household budget will make you worry before you spend instead of afterward.

Cut Glass Squares

Submitted by Joanne Wellon, in memory of parents Violet and Reginald Wellon.
"This recipe was one of my mom's favourites"

Ingredients:

3 pkgs Jello (lemon, lime & strawberry)
1 & 1/2 cups hot water for each pkg of Jello
2 envelopes plain gelatin
1 cup hot pineapple juice
1/4 cup cold water
2 cups heavy cream, whipped
1/2 cup sugar
1 tsp vanilla

Crust:

2 dozen crushed graham wafers
1/2 cup melted butter
1/2 cup sugar

TRIVIA TIDBITS
In 1922, a 24-year-old woman pleaded guilty in England to 61 bigamous marriages, all in the space of five years.

Directions:

Dissolve each package of Jello with 1 & 1/2 cups of hot water in separate pans. Chill until firm. Cut in half-inch cubes. Soften gelatin in cold water, then add to hot pineapple juice. Cool; fold into whipped cream mixture, into which you have beaten sugar and vanilla. Blend jelly cubes into whipped cream mixture. Spread unto the crust which was pressed into a square pan. Chill for 6 to 12 hours. Cut in squares.

In memory of my parents **Violet** (nee **Ball**)
who passed away March 5, 1980 and **Reginald C. Wellon**, who passed
away November 1, 1995, of Millertown, Newfoundland.
God has you in his keeping, I have you in my heart,
So my memories are my keepsake, with which I'll never part.
Dearly missed and lovingly remembered today and every day...
your daughter Joanne, Andy and grand-daughters Terri and Brandi... xx

Carrot Cake

Lilly M. Faseruk, Toronto, Ontario (nee Barnes, Harbour Main, Fortune, Newfoundland)

Ingredients:

2 cups grated carrot

3 eggs

1 cup granulated sugar

3/4 cup oil

1 & 1/2 cups sifted all-purpose flour

1 & 1/4 tsp baking powder

1 & 1/4 tsp baking soda

1 & 1/2 tsp cinnamon

1/2 tsp salt

1/2 cup walnuts

3/4 cup raisins

Directions:

Grate carrots. Set aside. Beat eggs well until thick and leamon coloured.
Add sugar gradually and continue to beat. Add oil and beat well. Sift together flour, baking powder, baking soda, cinnamon and salt. Add chopped nuts and raisins to flour mixture. Add flour mixture and carrots alternately to egg mixture. Mix only until blended. Pour batter into greased and floured 6-cup bundt pan. Gently bang on counter to release bubbles. Bake in preheated 300°F oven for 1 hour.

> **TRIVIA TIDBITS**
> During World War I, sauerkraut was renamed "liberty cabbage" by anti-German Americans.

Magic Fast 'N' Fabulous Fruit Cake

Ingredients:

2 & 1/2 cups all-purpose flour

1 tsp baking soda

2 eggs, slightly beaten

3 cups (1-28oz can) mincemeat

1 can sweetened condensed milk

1 & 1/2 cups mixed candied fruit

1/2 cup red & green glace cherries, halved (optional)

1 cup walnuts, coarsely chopped

> **SPICE OF LIFE**
> Infants don't have nearly as much fun in infancy as adults have in adultery.

Directions:

Preheat oven to 300°F. Grease a 9 inch tube pan; line with waxed paper and grease again (or use generously greased and floured 10 inch bundt pan). Sift together flour and baking soda; set aside. In large bowl, combine eggs, mincemeat, condensed milk, fruit and nuts. Add dry ingredients. Blend well. Pour into prepared pan. Bake for 1 hour and 50 minutes or until toothpick inserted near centre comes out clean. Cool 15 minutes. Turn out of pan; remove waxed paper. If desired, garnish with glace cherries or walnuts. Tip: To store cake, cool thoroughly; wrap well in aluminum foil and refrigerate or freeze.

Pineapple Light Cake

Ingredients:

3 eggs

1/2 lb butter

2 tbsp baking powder

> **FOOD FOR THOUGHT**
> God gives every bird its food, but He does not throw it into the nest.

Sweets & Treats

Pies, Pastries, Cakes, Cookies, Candies, Etc.

1 cup crushed pineapple
1/4 lb cherries
1 lb raisins
1 & 1/2 cups sugar
2 & 3/4 cups flour
2 tsp vanilla extract
1/2 cup pineapple juice
1 cup coconut

Directions:

Cream butter and sugar; add eggs, one at a time. Add crushed pineapple to butter. Add flour, baking powder, pineapple juice, coconut and other fruit. Add vanilla. Mix well. Bake in moderate oven for 2 hours.

FOOD FOR THOUGHT
Most people who moan that they don't get what they deserve, should be grateful.

Tomato Soup Loaf

Gertrude Finn, Mississauga, Ontario (nee Tucker, St. John's, Newfoundland)

Ingredients:

1 egg
1/2 cup crisco
1 cup white sugar
1 & 3/4 cups flour
1 tsp soda
1 tsp cinnamon
1 tsp nutmeg
1 can tomato soup
1 cup raisins

TRIVIA TIDBITS
Working class parents in class-conscious Victorian England often attempted to help get their off-springs a better start in life by giving them a title as a first name. Some of the popular first names at the time were; Abbott, Admiral, Alderman, Count, Duke, Earl, Squire and Viscount.

Directions:

Cream shortening, sugar and eggs. Add dry ingredients, soup and raisins. Turn in loaf pan. Bake at 350°F for 45 to 60 minutes.

Date & Nut Loaf

Gertrude Finn, Mississauga, Ontario (nee Tucker, St. John's, Newfoundland)

Ingredients:

1/2 lb butter
1 cup walnuts
1 cup sugar
1 lb dates
2 eggs
2 cups flour
1 tsp soda

SPICE OF LIFE
A cheese cake is something that turns to pound cake when you eat it.

Elizabeth Burke
Daughter of Cyril and Agnes Burke, born Tilting, Fogo District, February 18, 1940 and lived in Norris Arm from 1950-1957. Graduated from St. John's General Hospital School of Nursing in 1960 and worked in the cottage Hospitals of Botwood, Burgeo and Grand Bank, in Gander Hospital (coordinated some of the activities of the opening of the James Paton Memorial Hospital) and spent a year Nursing in Weston, Ontario. She graduated from Dalhousie University with a Bachelor of Nursing degree on May 17, 1967 and died June 12, 1967 from cancer diagnosed in her final year of University.
A short life, many accomplishments, still missed. *Matilda Bara*

1 cup cold water
Directions:
Dissolve dates in water and soda, let stand overnight. Beat butter, sugar and eggs. Add dates and nuts. Mix well. Bake about 1 & 1/2 hours in moderate oven. Will keep for one month when put in cellophane bag. Makes a big loaf.

Cherry Cake

Gertrude Finn, Mississauga, Ontario (nee Tucker, St. John's, Newfoundland)

Ingredients:
1/2 cup butter
1/4 tsp salt
3/4 cup sugar
3 tsp baking powder
3 cups sifted flour
1 lb cherries
5 eggs, beaten
1 tsp lemon juice

TRIVIA TIDBITS
In 1740, in France, a cow was found guilty of sorcery. The sentence, "Death by Hanging" was carried out shortly thereafter.

Directions:
Let the cherries stand for one hour in the flour. Then mix all ingredients together and bake at 325°F for 1 & 1/2 hours.

Chocolate Cake

Angela Waterman, Glenwood, Newfoundland, (nee John)

Ingredients:
1 cup hot water
1/2 cup oil
2 squares unsweetened chocolate
2 cups all purpose flour, sifted
2/3 tsp salt
1 & 1/3 tsp soda
2 eggs, beaten
1 & 1/2 cups sugar
2/3 cup sour cream
1 tsp vanilla

FOOD FOR THOUGHT
No one ceased scaling the ladder of success for lack of another rung.

FOOD FOR THOUGHT
Life can give you what you want if you want it for long enough - however, not necessarily at the time you want it most.

Directions:
Put water, oil and chocolate in top of double boiler. Melt chocolate mixture; set aside. Sift flour with salt and soda. Beat eggs; add sugar, sour cream and vanilla. Add flour mixture to egg mixture alternately with chocolate mixture. Mix only until flour is blended. Bake at 350°F for 30 to 35 minutes using a 9-inch greased pan.

Gum Drop Cake

Susan Rowsell, (nee Snooks, Corner Brook and York Harbour, Newfoundland)
Ingredients:
1 cup butter
1 & 1/2 cups sugar

4 eggs
1 - 8oz pkg cream cheese
1 tsp vanilla extract
2 & 1/4 cups flour
1 & 1/2 tsp baking powder
2 cups gum drops, cut in half with scissors

FOOD FOR THOUGHT
Children are imps who cause parents to feel old and grandparents to feel young.

Directions:
Cream butter and sugar; add cream cheese; beat until fluffy; add eggs, one at a time. Sift in dry ingredients and gum drops. Mix well. Spray tube pan with Pam to keep from sticking. Bake in 275°F oven for 2 hours. Cool cake in pan for 2 hours.

Hilda Luedee's Boiled Raisin Cake

Ingredients:
3 cups sifted flour
2 tbsp baking soda
2 cups sugar
1/2 cup butter
1 lb raisins
1/2 tsp salt
1 tsp cinnamon
1 tsp allspice
1/2 tsp ginger and cloves
2 cups boiling water

TRIVIA TIDBITS
Charles Mackintosh who invented a new water-proof cloth, (which was later made into raincoats called Mackintoshes), was so careful to protect the secret of its production, that he hired Highland workers who only spoke Gaelic to work in his Glasgow factory.

Directions:
Mix all ingredients together and let boil for 5-10 minutes, stirring intermittently. Let cool completely. Mix in 3 cups sifted flour and 2 tbsp baking soda. Bake at low heat (250°-275°F) for about 2 to 2 & 1/2 hours.

Dark Fruit Cake

Agnes Thiesen, Orlando, Florida, (nee Flynn, Lake View, Harbour Main, Conception Bay, Newfoundland)
Ingredients:
1 cup molasses
1 tbsp cinnamon
1 tbsp allspice
1 tbsp cloves
1 cup butter
1 cup granulated sugar
5 eggs, well beaten
3 & 1/2 cups flour, sifted

FOOD FOR THOUGHT
Treasure this day; it is a gift from time set in the ring of years.

Sweets & Treats
Pies, Pastries, Cakes, Cookies, Candies, Etc.

1/2 tsp salt
3 cups currants
3 cups raisins
2 cups citron peel
2 cups lemon peel
1 & 1/4 cups dates (if desired)
1 tsp soda
2 tbsp hot water

Directions:
Steep spices in molasses over a low heat. (Do not let boil, but the longer it is allowed to steep, the darker your cake will be). Cream butter and sugar, then add the well-beaten eggs and cooled molasses mixture. Dust fruit with 1/4 cup of the flour. Add remaining flour and the salt to the butter mixture and blend well. Stir in floured fruit. Last of all, mix soda which has been dissolved in hot water. Bake in a large cast iron pot, lined with three layers of brown paper. Pot should be at least 10 inches wide and 3 inches deep. Bake at 275°F for 3 to 3 & 1/2 hours.
A glass of whisky or rum brushed on top of the cake before icing adds a great flavour.
**My mom used white icing, a recipe which can be obtained from the powdered sugar box.*

Raisin Apple Coffee Cake

Dolores Lundrigan, Wabush, Labrador, (nee English, Branch, St. Mary's Bay, Newfoundland)

Ingredients:
2 cups flour
1 cup sugar
3 tsp baking powder
1 tsp salt
1/3 cup soft butter
1 cup milk
1 egg
1 cup apples, finely grated and peeled
1/2 cup raisins
1/2 cup sugar
1/2 tsp cinnamon

Directions:
Sift flour, 1 cup sugar, baking powder and salt together in mixing bowl. Add butter, beat egg and milk together lightly with a fork and add to flour mixture. Beat hard for 2 minutes. Stir in apples and raisins. Spoon into greased 9-inch square pan. Spread evenly. Combine: 1/2 cup sugar and cinnamon and sprinkle over top of batter. Bake at 350°F for 35 minutes. Serve warm.

Diet Fruit Cake

Myrtle Ash, Portland, Newfoundland

Ingredients:
1 tsp nutmeg or mace
2 tsp cinnamon
2 cups raisins
1/2 cup oil
salt

1/2 cup unsweetened orange juice
2 & 1/2 cups water
2 cups whole wheat flour
1/2 tsp vanilla
2 tsp baking soda
1 tsp baking powder
1/2 cup dates and cherries (optional)

Directions:

Boil water, orange juice, raisins, spices and (dates & cherries) for 5 minutes. Let cool. Add oil and vanilla. Mix dry ingredients together and add to cool mixture. Bake for 1 hour at 350°F.

Lemon Cake

Ingredients:

1 angel food cake
2 pkg Jello lemon pie filling
1/2 lb cream cheese
1/2 lemon, grated and squeezed
1 & 1/2 cups icing sugar
butter, if desired

Directions

Break angel food cake into small pieces. Layer cake and pie filling alternately in tube pan, ending with pie filling. Refrigerate 2-3 hours. Whip cream cheese, juice, rind and sugar until smooth. Invert cake and remove from pan. Ice top and sides. Refrigerate a few hours.

TRIVIA TIDBITS
In the 1700's, many English hospitals had breweries on the premises to supply doctors, nurses and patients with beer.

Banoffi Pie

Recipe given to Marilyn MacDonald by Penelope Aspery

Ingredients:

12oz pie pastry shell (pre-cooked or crumb bottom with no cooking required)
13oz tin sweetened condensed milk
1 pound bananas (ripe-ready to eat)
3/4 pint double cream
1/4 tsp powderd coffee
1 tsp sugar
little fresh, ground coffee (optional)

Directions:

Immerse unopened can of condensed milk into pot of boiling water. Cover and boil for 1 & 1/2 to 2 hours making sure can is always covered with water. Remove can, wait few minutes and then pour soft toffee (condensed milk has now carmelized) into baked pastry shell. Peel and half length ways bananas and place on top of toffee. Spoon or pipe on the whipped cream/coffee/sugar/ mixture, cover bananas/toffee completely. Lightly sprinkle top with ground coffee (optional). Optional: slivered nuts can be added to top of pie.

Memories of our "Jolly Girls Outing"
Havana-Miami, January, 1995.
(L-R) **Roseann Mason**, Southport, U.K.
Penelope Aspery, St. Annes On Sea, U.K.,
and **Marilyn MacDonald**, Havana
formerly of Deer Lake, Newfoundland.

Sweets & Treats
Pies, Pastries, Cakes, Cookies, Candies, Etc.

Blueberry Cake

Ingredients:

1 cup sugar

1/3 cup butter

1 cup blueberries

1 & 1/2 cups flour

1/2 cup milk

2 tsp baking powder

2 eggs

1 tsp lemon flavouring

Few grains salt

Directions:

Cream butter thoroughly and add the sugar gradually. Cream together well. Add well beaten eggs. Sift flour 3 times, baking powder and salt. Add flour alternately with milk. Add flavouring. Add berries and mix lightly. Pour into a greased loaf pan and bake in a moderate oven about 45 minutes.

> ### *TRIVIA TIDBITS*
> Jimmy Hoffa, the well known labour leader, with suspected underworld connections, reportedly went to meet with a New Jersey Teamster official and a mobster from Detroit at a restaurant in Bloomfield Hills, Michigan on July 30, 1975. He was never seen again. The Teamster and the mobster both denied such a meeting. Hoffa was officially declared "presumed dead" in 1982.

Igloo Cake

Pauline Reid, Deer Lake, Newfoundland, (nee Knee, Corner Brook, Newfoundland)

Ingredients:

1 sponge cake

2 envelopes gelatin

19oz can crushed pineapple

1 cup pineapple juice

1 cup white sugar

3 tbsp lemon juice

1/2 tsp salt

3 envelopes dream whip (or Nutri-Whip)

1 cup boiling water

4 tbsp cold water

coconut (if desired)

> ## FOOD FOR THOUGHT
> Hard work never killed anyone,
> but why take a chance?
> *(Edgar Bergen, 1903-1978)*

Directions:

Dissolve gelatin in 4 tbsp cold water. Add 1 cup boiling water, pineapple juice, pineapple, sugar, salt and lemon juice. Mix well. Refrigerate until partially set. Add 2 envelopes of dream whip (prepared as directed on package), to refrigerated mixture. Break cake into small pieces; fold together with mixture and put in tube pan. Refrigerate overnight. Turn out of tube pan and frost with last envelope of dream whip. Cake can then be sprinkled with coconut, if desired.

Blueberry Cake

Grace Perry, Brigus, Newfoundland

Ingredients:

1/4 lb butter

1 cup brown sugar

1 egg

1 tsp vanilla

> ### *TRIVIA TIDBITS*
> Taking a bath in sea water was one time considered a cure for anyone who had been bitten by a mad dog.

1 cup flour
2 cups blueberries
1 tsp baking powder

Directions:

Cream butter, egg and vanilla. Add flour and baking powder together. Add blueberries last. Mix well. Bake at 350°F for 35 minutes.

Old Fashioned Pork Cake

Mrs. Alma Taylor, Mt. Moriah, Bay of Islands, Newfoundland, (nee LeDrew, Bell Island, Newfoundland)

Ingredients:

250ml diced salt pork
250ml boiling water
12ml baking soda
250ml molasses
250ml sugar
500ml raisins
500ml currants
2000ml flour
5ml allspice
5ml cloves
5ml mace
5ml cinnamon

Directions:

Mix baking soda with boiling water; pour over pork scraps. Add sugar and molasses. Sprinkle fruit with flour and add to mixture. Add rest of flour and spices. Mix well. Grease a 2-litre pan and spread in the batter. Bake at 150°C for 2 hours.

Cocoa Apple Cake

Submitted by Patricia Ullom, Muncie, Indianna, USA, (nee Foley, Grand Falls-Windsor, Newfoundland)

Directions:

3 eggs
2 cups sugar
1/2 cup water
1 cup margarine or butter (2 sticks)
2 & 1/2 cups flour
2 tbsp cocoa
1 tsp soda
1 tsp allspice
1 tsp cinnamon

This page is dedicated to my wonderful family -
Patrick (Paddy) & Elizabeth (Bessie) Foley; sis Nina, brothers Austin & Clem (deceased) and George, living in Grand Falls-Windsor.
This picture of me Patricia (Patsy), George and our cat Tom, was taken in our potato patch in Grand Falls, Newfoundland. "Those were the days!"
Patricia (Foley) Ullom, Muncie, Indianna, USA

1 cup finely chopped nuts
1/2 cup semi-sweet chocolate chips
2 cups apples, chopped
1 tsp vanilla

Directions:
Beat eggs, sugar, water and margarine until fluffy. Sift together dry ingredients. Blend until well mixed (by hand). Fold remaining ingredients until evenly distributed. Spoon into greased and floured 10-inch tube pan. "This is a prize winner". Bet you can't eat just one piece!

Mississippi Mud Pie

Charlene Jenkins, Etobicoke, Ontario, (formerly of Springdale, Newfoundland)

Ingredients:
20 chocolate wafer cookies
1/4 cup butter, melted
1 to 1 & 1/2 pints vanilla ice cream, softened
1 to 1 & 1/2 pints chocolate ice cream, softened
chocolate fudge sauce
marshmallow creme
chopped nuts

Directions:
In a food processor or blender, process cookies until crumbly. Mix in melted butter. Pat mixture into bottom and sides of a 9-inch deep dish pie plate. Spread softened vanilla ice cream over crust. Pour a generous amount of fudge sauce and marshmallow creme over ice cream. Sprinkle with chopped nuts. Repeat layer with chocolate ice cream, fudge sauce, marshmallow and nuts. Chill for at least 3 hours. Remove from freezer for 10 minutes before serving for best results.

Lazy Daisy Cake

Carol Thornhill, Bobcaygeon, Ontario

Ingredients:
1/3 cup milk
1 tbsp butter
1 cup flour
1/2 tsp salt
1 & 1/4 tsp baking powder
2 eggs
1 cup white sugar
1 tsp vanilla

SPICE OF LIFE

Palimony is when a woman doesn't take a broken relationship to heart, but to court.

Directions:
Scald milk, add butter and cool. Slightly mix all ingredients. Bake at 350°F for 25 minutes. Cool.

Topping for Lazy Daisy Cake

Ingredients:
1 tbsp butter
1/2 cup coconut
1/2 tsp vanilla
2 tbsp milk
1/2 cup brown sugar

Directions:
Mix ingredients together, pour over baked cake and broil until brown.

Sweets & Treats

Pies, Pastries, Cakes, Cookies, Candies, Etc.

Banana Cake

Marion Nagle, Kitchener, Ontario, (nee Daniels, Twillingate, Newfoundland)

Ingredients:

1 cup mashed bananas
1/4 cup corn oil
3/4 cup sugar
1/2 tsp vanilla
1/4 tsp salt
1/2 tsp baking soda
2 tsp baking powder
1 & 1/4 cups flour

Directions:

Blend bananas, oil, sugar and vanilla in large bowl.
Add dry ingredients. Pour into greased 8-inch square pan.
Bake 370°F for 25 minutes.

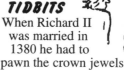

TRIVIA TIDBITS
When Richard II was married in 1380 he had to pawn the crown jewels to pay for the wedding.

Pizza Cake

Beulah Cooper, Gander, Newfoundland, (nee Collins, Corner Brook, Newfoundland)

Ingredients:

1 pkg yellow cake mix
1 pkg vanilla instant pudding
1/2 cup oil
1 cup water
3 eggs
1 tin mandarin oranges, drained

Directions:

Mix together and pour into 13x9-inch pan and bake at 350°F for 35-40 minutes.

Topping for pizza cake

Ingredients:

1 tin crushed pineapple, drained
1 pkg vanilla instant pudding
1 large container cool whip

Directions:

Mix together and spread on top of cake.

FOOD FOR THOUGHT
He who agrees with all that you say will also lie to others.

SPICE OF LIFE
Things come to he who waits - if he can wait for them to come.

Jo's Simple Fruit Crisp

Josephine Hynes, Etobicoke, Ontario (nee Elliott, Twillingate, Newfoundland)

Ingredients:

1 (21oz) can fruit pie filling (of your choice)
1 cup all-purpose flour

Jim - After the years and times that you went through to find your brothers, Fred, John and Frank and found us, it was the most wonderful times of our life. But so short. Thank you for the time we had together.
Never forgotton. Always remembered with special love.
Fred Boland

1/2 cup firmly packed brown sugar
1/2 tsp cinnamon, if desired
1/2 tsp nutmeg, if desired
1/3 cup butter or margarine, softened

Directions:

Heat oven to 375°F. Spread pie filling in ungreased 8-inch square (1 & 1/2 quart) baking dish. In medium bowl, combine all remaining ingredients until crumbly; sprinkle over filling. Bake at 375°F for 25 to 30 minutes or until golden brown. If desired, serve warm with ice cream.

Cucumber Loaf

Adam Young, Twillingate, Newfoundland

Ingredients:

3 eggs
1 & 1/2 cups sugar
2 tsp vanilla
2 cups all-purpose flour, sifted
3 tsp ground cinnamon
1 tsp salt
1 cup vegetable oil
2 cups cucumber (ground fine and drained well)
1 tsp baking powder
3/4 tsp baking soda
1 cup raisins
1 cup walnuts

Directions:

Beat eggs lightly in a large bowl. Stir in oil, sugar, cucumber and vanilla. Sift flour, baking powder, baking soda, cinnamon and salt unto wax paper. Stir in raisins and nuts. Spoon batter into well greased loaf pans. Bake in moderate oven 370°F for 1 hour depending on oven or until centre springs back when lightly pressed. Cool in pans on wire rack for 10 minutes. Remove from pans and cool and store or freeze.

Grapefruit Loaf

Ingredients:

1/2 cup (or less) lard
1 cup white sugar
2 eggs, beaten
1 & 1/2 cups flour
1 tsp baking powder
1 tsp salt
1/2 cup milk

Directions:

Mix together. Bake for approximately 1 hour at 350°F.
Mix up 1/2 cup sugar and juice of one grapefrui.
Pour over cake while still in pan.

Brenda's Black Forest Cake

Catherine Irwin, Truro, Nova Scotia

Ingredients:
Duncan Hines Chocolate, Dutch chocolate, or Devil's Chocolate Cake mix
500ml Nutri Whip
8 red cherries, halved and towel-dried
1/2 square semi-sweet chocolate
1 can cherry pie filling

Directions:
Grease and flour 2 round cake tins. Follow original recipe on box. Have 4 cake racks ready. Cool 2 cakes. Slice each cake in half. Lay out each on one of 4 racks. Grate 1/2 square semi-sweet chocolate (wax paper underneath). Set aside. Half the 8 bottled cherrie; dry, set aside. Whip up Nutri Whip per package instructions. Set aside a little better than 1/3 for outer surface covering of cake. Into the remaining 2/3, add can of cherry pie filling. Mix well. Distribute evenly between each cake layer. Cover outer sides, top with plain Nutri Whip. Sprinkle grated chocolate all over outside of cake. Place 8 cherries atop! This can be made a day ahead, covered and refrigerated. The mess is gone. Feeds 8 - 10 easily. Not rich. A real winner.

Chocolate Bars

Jenny & Josie, Richmond Hill, Ontario (nee Clarke, Port Rexton, Newfoundland)

Ingredients:
1/2 cup butter
1 cup sugar
2 eggs
1 tsp vanilla
1 cup flour
4 tbsp cocoa
1 cup nuts

Directions:
Cream butter, sugar and eggs, then add vanilla. Mix together flour, cocoa and nuts. Put into 8x8-inch greased pan and bake 350°F for 30 minutes or until done.

No-Bake Peanut Butter Balls

Jenny & Josie, Richmond Hill, Ontario (nee Clarke, Port Rexton, Newfoundland)

Ingredients:
1/2 cup white sugar
1/2 cup corn syrup
2 cups Rice Krispies
1 cup peanut butter

 Dedicated to my father, **Rosario Paulo Souza-Couth**, and my mother, **Maria Julia Souza-Couth** of the Village of Saligao, Goa, India.
Mel D'Souza

Directions:
Bring to a boil the sugar and corn syrup. Remove from stove and stir in rice krispies and peanut butter. Roll in balls.

Coconut Feather Squares

Myrtle Sturge, Gambo, Newfoundland
Ingredients:
4 tbsp butter
3 eggs
1/2 cup white sugar
3 tsp milk
1 tsp baking powder
1 tbsp corn starch
1/2 tsp salt
1 cup flour
1 tsp vanilla extract

> **FOOD FOR THOUGHT**
> Why is it that we seem to get angrier when we are wrong?

Directions:
Cream butter, sugar and egg yolks together. Add sifted ingredients. Mix well and spread in square pan. Bake 20 minutes. Take from oven and spread with jam. Beat 3 egg whites stiff with 1/2 cup sugar. Spread on top of jam and cover with 1/2 cup coconut. Bake until brown.

Cranberry Squares

Jody M. Walters, Robinsons, Newfoundland
Ingredients:
2 cups rolled oats
1 cup brown sugar
1 cup flour
1 tsp baking powder
3/4 cup melted butter
2 & 1/2 cups cranberry jam or sweetened cranberries

> **SPICE OF LIFE**
> A little honey is good for a man's health, unless his wife finds out.

Directions:
Combine rolled oats, sugar, flour, baking powder and melted butter and mix. Press half of mixture in greased 8x12-inch pan. Spread with cranberry jam or cranberries; add remaining rolled oats mixture. Bake at 350°F for 30 minutes.

Raspberry Cup Cakes

Vera E. Coburn, Labrador City
Ingredients:
1/3 cup shortening
1/2 cup sugar
1 egg
1 & 1/2 cups flour (scant)
1 & 1/2 tsp baking powder
1/2 tsp salt
1/4 tsp nutmeg
1/2 cup milk

> **TRIVIA TIDBITS**
> During a critical stage of the American Civil War, President Abraham Lincoln was so perturbed by the apparent lack of action by General George McLellan and his army, that he wrote McLellan a note which read: "My dear McLellan, if you don't want to use the army, I should like to borrow it for a while."

Sweets & Treats
Pies, Pastries, Cakes, Cookies, Candies, Etc.

coconut
Directions:
Cream sugar, shortening and egg. Sift together flour, baking powder, salt and nutmeg. Stir in alternately with milk. Fill muffin tins (or baking cups) 2/3 full. Bake 20-25 minutes until golden brown. When cool spread with raspberry jam and dip in fine coconut.

Mud Balls

Anne B. Penney, St. John's, Newfoundland
Ingredients:
large, coloured marshmallows
Mix together:
1/2 cup margarine (melted)
2 tbsp cocoa
1 tsp vanilla
1 can sweetened condensed milk
Stir in:
1 cup rolled oats
1 cup graham wafer crumbs
1 & 1/2 cups coconut
Directions:
Using large, coloured marshmallows, roll the mixture around each one. Then roll them in coconut. Chill and slice. These cookies are very colourful and are great for parties.

> **SPICE OF LIFE**
> For most people, the worst kind of blood test is putting up with relatives.

Fudge Balls

Mrs. Barbara Lucas, Barachois Brook, Newfoundland
Ingredients:
1/2 cup butter
1/2 cup milk
1 cup sugar
1 cup coconut
1/2 cup cocoa
1 tsp vanilla
2 & 1/2 cups rolled oats
Directions:
Combine butter, milk, sugar and vanilla in saucepan. Bring to a boil and cook for 2 minutes. Remove from heat and add cocoa, rolled oats and coconut. Let cool. Roll in balls and then roll in more coconut. Store in refrigerator until set.

TRIVIA TIDBITS
In 1626, Manhattan Island was bought from the local Indians for 24 dollars worth of trinkets.

Dedicated to the memory of my grandfather, **Pearce Young**, who built me a wheelbarrow. Grandfather, who was a fisherman, is buried beside his wife, Florence, in an unmarked grave in a cemetary at Platter's Head, Twillingate, "lost in time among the tuckamores."
Ron Young

(sidebar) **Sweets & Treats** — Pies, Pastries, Cakes, Cookies, Candies, Etc.

Grace's Five Star Cookies

Grace Ryan, Newmans Cove, Bonavista Bay, Newfoundland

Ingredients:

2 cups coconut

1 & 1/2 cups graham wafer crumbs

1/2 cup butter, melted

1 can sweetened condensed milk

4 Aero bars

Directions:

Mix together the top four ingredients and bake in a 7x11-inch baking dish for 5-7 minutes at 350°F. Melt bars and spread on top. Keep in refrigerator.

> **FOOD FOR THOUGHT**
> An ounce of apology is worth a pound of loneliness.
> -Joseph Jobert

Eat-Most Bars

Grace Ryan, Newmans Cove, Bonavista Bay, Newfoundland

Ingredients:

1 cup Karo syrup

1 cup peanut butter

1 cup chocolate chips

1 cup peanuts

3 & 1/2 cups Rice Krispies

1 tsp vanilla

Directions:

Place Karo, peanut butter and chocolate chips in saucepan and bring to a boil. Add peanuts, Rice Krispies and vanilla. Mix together and put in 13x9-inch pan. Makes 4 dozen bars.

> **SPICE OF LIFE**
> You know a man is henpecked when the champagne bottles in his home all go "mom".

Crispy Bar Dessert

Grace Ryan, Newmans Cove, Bonavista Bay, Newfoundland

Ingredients:

1 cake mix, white

1 pkg vanilla instant pudding mix

2 crispy crunch bars

1 pkg dream whip

Directions:

Bake cake mix following directions on package and let cool. Mix pudding according to directions on package, then mix in 1 & 1/2 of the bars. Let set and top with dream whip. Use remaining half of bar for top.

> **FOOD FOR THOUGHT**
> Your reputation is your most valuable asset.

Breakfast Cookies

Miss Gertrude V. Sweetapple, Glovertown, Newfoundland

Ingredients:

1 cup raisins

1 cup water

1 cup applesauce

1 cup dates

> **TRIVIA TIDBITS**
> King Henry III of France was so concerned about his appearance that he went to bed wearing a facial mask of flour and the whites of eggs.

Pies, Pastries, Cakes, Cookies, Candies, Etc.

Sweets & Treats

2 lg bananas
3 cups rolled oats
1 & 1/2 cups whole wheat flour
1/2 cup coconut (optional)
1 tsp salt
1 tsp cinnamon
1/3 cup oil
1 tsp vanilla
1/2 cup raisin liquid
1/2 cup walnuts or pecans
1/2 cup bran (optional)

SPICE OF LIFE
Beauty is in the eye of the beer holder.

Directions:

Simmer raisins in water until plump. Drain raisin liquid into cup and add water to make 1/2 cup liquid. Blend applesauce, dates and bananas. Pour into mixing bowl. Sift together oats and flour, salt and cinnamon. Add to ingredients in bowl. Add remaining ingredients. Drop by heaping spoonfuls on cookie sheet and bake 20 minutes at 350°F. Brown under broiler.

Cry Baby Cookies

June Gates, Woodstock, Ontario

Ingredients:

1 cup shortening
1 cup sugar
1/2 cup molasses
1 tbsp vinegar
1 cup hot, strong coffee
2 tsp baking soda
2 cups raisins
4 cups flour
2 tsp cinnamon
1 tsp ginger
1/2 tsp salt

> **TRIVIA TIDBITS**
> Nikita Krushchev, who later became the Russian leader, in a speech made in 1936, spoke of Joseph Stalin as: "One whose name millions of toilers pronounce every hour, with pride and boundless love; our dear friend; our wise leader; everything that is best in the possessions of humanity; the greatest of all men; Stalin is hope; he is expectation; Stalin is our banner; Stalin is our will; Stalin is our victory; our friend and father; the greatest man of our epoch, the greatest genius of humanity." Twenty years later, in another speech in 1956, Krushchev denounced Stalin as a tyrant.

Directions:

Pour hot coffee over raisins and soda and let stand.
Beat shortening and sugar until light. Add eggs. Beat in vinegar and molasses.
Add raisins, coffee and soda. Then add flour, salt and spices.
Spoon by rounded teaspoonful onto buttered cookie sheet.
Bake at 375°F for 7-9 minutes. Cool on cake racks.

In loving memory of our son and brother, **Seamus Flynn**, who passed away on August 2, 1996.
"Thank you Seamus, for leaving us a legacy of love."
Forever remembered by
Father-Jimmy, Mother-Sylvia, Brother-Luke, Sister-Angelina

Gumdrop Balls

Angela Waterman, Glenwood, Newfoundland, (nee John)

Ingredients:
1 can sweetened condensed milk
1/4 tsp salt
1/2 cup nuts
3 cups Corn Flakes
1 cup (heaping) gumdrops, cut
1 tsp vanilla (or any flavouring)
coconut

TRIVIA TIDBITS
The man who was reputed to have the world's longest beard tripped over that same beard and fell down a flight of steps to his death in Vienna, Austria in 1567.

Directions:
Pour milk in top of double boiler. Add salt, cook until thickened. Add 3 cups corn flakes, finely crushed. Measure before crushing. Add gumdrops, nuts and flavouring. Take out by teaspoonfuls and roll in coconut. Let stand on waxed paper until firm.

Lucretia's Molasses Cookies

Ruby Collins, Hare Bay, Newfoundland

Ingredients:
1 cup shortening
1 cup white sugar
1 cup molasses
1 cup flour
2 eggs, beaten
1 tsp salt
2 tsp cinnamon
2 tsp ginger
1 & 1/4 tsp soda
1/4 cup warm water
4 - 6 cups flour

TRIVIA TIDBITS
An American company once claimed that rattlesnake oil cured deafness.

Directions:
Melt shortening, sugar and molasses together and bring to a bubbling simmer. Remove from stove and immediately add flour, stirring well with a wire whip. Let cool. Then add eggs, salt, cinnamon, and ginger. Melt soda in warm water and add to batter. Mix enough flour (approx. 4-6 cups) into batter so that a ball forms and it can be rolled out. Roll out to 1/2 inch thickness. Cut out and bake at 325°F for 15 minutes.

Popcorn Squares

Mrs. Marie Whitehorne, Pasadena, Newfoundland, (nee Kendall, Ramea, Newfoundland)

Ingredients:
4 cups popped popcorn
1 pkg marshmallows
1/2 cup unsalted crushed peanuts
1/4 cup butter
1 pkg gumdrops, chopped

SPICE OF LIFE
A diet is a weigh of life.

Directions:

Melt marshmallows and butter. Stir in popcorn, gumdrops and peanuts in a square greased pan. When cool cut into squares. Kids will love them.

Black and White Squares

Betina Wheeler-Ali, Toronto, Ontario (formerly of St. John's, Newfoundland)

Ingredients:

Rub together and pat into the bottom of a 9x9-inch pan:

1/2 cup butter

1/2 cup brown sugar

1 cup flour

Mix together:

1 cup brown sugar

2 tsp flour

1/2 tsp salt

1/2 tsp baking powder

2 eggs

1 cup chopped nuts

3 lg tsp cocoa

TRIVIA TIDBITS
An old English cure for whooping-cough called for chopped hairs from a donkey's back to be eaten on bread and butter.

HEE HAW

Directions:

Pour over bottom and bake at 350°F for 25-30 minutes. Make a butter icing and add 2 tsp strong coffee, then ice squares.

Chocolate Chip Coconut Brownies

Betina Wheeler-Ali, Toronto, Ontario (formerly of St. John's, Newfoundland)

Ingredients:

1 cup margarine

3 eggs

1/4 tsp salt

1 cup chocolate chips

2 cups brown sugar

1 tsp vanilla

2 cups flour

1 cup shredded coconut (unsweetened)

> **FOOD FOR THOUGHT**
> The only person who gets anything from running other people down is the elevator man.

Directions:

Mix margarine and sugar.

Add eggs, then flour, salt and remaining ingredients. Put in greased 13x9x2-inch pan.

Bake at 325°F for 20-30 minutes. Let cool before cutting into squares.

This page is dedicated to the loving memory of my grandmother **FAY ROSCO**, who took the role of a father and mother, as a new Canadian in the 1930s, raising my mother. She passed away on July 24, 1994, but remains an inspiration to all the lives she touched.
Allan Ettenson, D.C.

(sidebar) **Sweets & Treats** — Pies, Pastries, Cakes, Cookies, Candies, Etc.

Chocolate Chippers

Robert Hann, Toronto, Ontario (formerly of Petites, Newfoundland)

Ingredients:

1 cup butter or margarine, softened
1 & 1/2 cups brown sugar, packed
2 eggs
1 tsp vanilla
2 cups all-purpose flour
1/4 cup cornstarch
3/4 tsp salt
1 tsp baking soda
2 cups chocolate chips, semi-sweet
1 cup walnuts, chopped & optional

Directions:

Cream butter and sugar together. Beat in eggs, one at a time. Add vanilla. Stir flour, cornstarch, salt and baking soda together and add to first mixture. Stir in chocolate chips and nuts. Drop by spoonfuls onto greased baking sheet. Bake in 350°F oven for 10 to 15 minutes. Makes about 5 dozen.

Pumpkin Cookies

Robert Hann, Toronto, Ontario (formerly of Petites, Newfoundland)

Ingredients:

1/2 cup margarine or shortening
1 & 1/4 cups brown sugar, packed
2 eggs
1 tsp vanilla
1 cup pumpkin, canned
2 cups all-purpose flour
4 tsp baking powder
1/2 tsp salt
1/2 tsp cinnamon
1/2 tsp nutmeg
1/4 tsp cloves
1/4 tsp ginger
1 cup raisins
1 cup nuts, chopped

Directions:

Cream butter and sugar together well. Beat in eggs, add vanilla and pumpkin. Stir remaining ingredients together and add to above. Mix well. Drop by teaspoonfuls onto a greased pan. Bake in a 375°F oven (190C) for about 15 minutes, until lightly browned. Makes 5 dozen.

Nanaimo Bars

Archie Ridout, Rexdale, Ontario (formerly of Twillingate, Newfoundland)

Ingredients:

1/2 cup butter
1/4 cup granulated sugar

Sweets & Treats
Pies, Pastries, Cakes, Cookies, Candies, Etc.

5 tbsp cocoa
1 egg, lightly beaten
1 tsp vanilla
1 & 1/2 to 2 cups graham wafer crumbs
1 cup desiccated coconut
1/2 cup chopped walnuts
1/4 cup softened butter
3 tbsp milk
2 tbsp vanilla custard powder
2 cups sifted icing sugar
4oz semi-sweet chocolate

Directions:

Lightly grease a 9-inch square baking dish. Melt butter in a heavy-bottomed saucepan. Stir in sugar and cocoa. Remove from heat and whisk in the egg and vanilla. Stir in graham wafer crumbs. Stir in coconut and walnuts. Press into the bottom of prepared pan. In a small bowl, cream the butter, milk, custard powder and icing sugar together. Spread over wafer base. Place in freezer to cool slightly. Melt the chocolate and spread in a thin, even layer, over top of cooled base. Refrigerate until the chocolate is firm.

> ### *TRIVIA TIDBITS*
> Apache chief Geronimo, after hostilities against the American authorities ceased, went to live on a reservation in Oklahoma.
> While living on the reservation he became a member of the Dutch Reformed Church, but was later expelled from the church for gambling.

Archie's Rum Balls

Archie Ridout, Rexdale, Ontario (formerly of Twillingate, Newfoundland)

Ingredients:
1 & 1/2 cups vanilla wafer crumbs
1/4 cup dark rum
1/4 cup honey
2 cups ground walnuts
confectioner's sugar

Directions:
Combine all ingredients, except sugar. Blend thoroughly. Shape into small balls about 1 inch in diameter. Roll in sugar. Store in tightly covered containers. Makes about 2 & 1/2 dozen.

> ### FOOD FOR THOUGHT
> A ship in harbour is safe, but that is not what ships are built for.

Almond Cookies

Archie Ridout, Rexdale, Ontario (formerly of Twillingate, Newfoundland)

Ingredients:
2/3 cup lard or shortening
1 & 2/3 cup sugar
1 egg
1/2 tsp almond extract
3-3 & 1/4 cups flour
2 tsp baking powder

> ### FOOD FOR THOUGHT
> The most important thing to wear out is your smile.

This page is dedicated to two loving parents, and grandparents,
Janice (nee Roberts) and **Eric Hibbs**
of Springdale, Newfoundland.
*Your son, Jeff, daughter-in-law, Denise
and granddaughters, Kaitlyn and Chelsea*

1 tsp soda
36 almonds
Directions:
Cream lard and sugar; add egg and almond extract. Blend in flour, baking powder and soda.
Knead dough until very smooth. Form into 3 dozen small balls. Press an almond into the top of
each cookie. Bake in 400°F oven for 15 minutes. Serve with a fruit salad that has 1 can litchis
added to it.

Texas Ranger Cookies

Hazel Warren, Chapel Arm, Trinity Bay, Newfoundland, (nee Cobb, Wabana Mines, Bell Island, Newfoundland)

Ingredients:

1 cup brown sugar
1 cup white sugar
1 cup shortening
1 & 1/2 tsp baking powder
salt
2 cups flour
2 eggs
2 cups oatmeal
1 cup Rice Krispies
1 cup Corn Flakes
1 cup coconut
nuts

TRIVIA TIDBITS
The man responsible for the
construction of the famous Tower of
London was Bishop Flambard,
who was the King's chief minister
at the time. Ironically, he was the
first prisoner to be incarcerated in
the Tower in 1108. The good
Bishop was also the first prisoner
to escape from the Tower a
short time later.

Directions:
Combine all ingredients together until well blended. Drop onto baking sheet and bake at 350°F
for 12 minutes.

Scandinavian Drops

Hazel Warren, Chapel Arm, Trinity Bay, Newfoundland, (nee Cobb, Wabana Mines, Bell Island, Newfoundland)

Ingredients:
1/2 cup butter
1/4 cup brown sugar
1 egg, separated
1 cup flour
3/4 cup nuts, chopped
tart jelly

FOOD FOR THOUGHT
History is ninety-nine percent the
achievements of normal, ordinary
people who never made history.

Directions:
Cream butter; blend in sugar. Add egg yolk. Blend in flour and roll into small balls. Beat egg
white. Dip each ball into egg white, roll in chopped nuts. Place on greased baking sheet and bake
at 300°F for 30-35 minutes.

Simple Simon Danish Squares

Hazel Warren, Chapel Arm, Trinity Bay, Newfoundland, (nee Cobb, Wabana Mines, Bell Island, Newfoundland)

Ingredients:
1 cup butter or margarine

SPICE OF LIFE
A cow is an animal that owes all it has to udders.

Sweets & Treats
Pies, Pastries, Cakes, Cookies, Candies, Etc.

2 tbsp water
3 eggs
2 cups flour
1 tsp almond flavouring
1 cup water
chopped nuts

Directions:

Cut 1/2 cup butter into one cup of flour. Add 2 tbsp water. Mix well. Press into 9x13-inch pan. Boil 1/2 cup butter with 1 cup water. Remove from heat. Add flavouring. Stir in one cup flour while mixture is hot. Add eggs. Spread over unbaked dough. Bake at 350°F for 1 hour. Make a butter icing glaze and drizzle over cake, sprinkle with nuts and cut in squares.

> **FOOD FOR THOUGHT**
> Any person who is his own boss will definitely be working for a demanding employer.

Cherry Squares

Ingredients:

2 cups graham wafer crumbs
1/2 cup butter
2 cups miniature marshmallows
1/2 pint whipped cream
1 tin cherry pie filling

Directions:

Mix together graham wafer crumbs and butter. In a separate bowl, mix together marshmallows, whipped cream. Grease 8-inch pan. Arrange in layers beginning with half of the crumb mixture; then half of marshmallow mixture; then whole can of cherry pie filling; then remaining marshmallow mixture; ending with remaining crumb mixture. Chill in refrigerator overnight. Cut in squares to serve.

> **FOOD FOR THOUGHT**
> A spendthrift is someone who treats his friends lavishly with money he owes someone else.

Pineapple Cubes

Linda Greenham, Twillingate, Newfoundland (nee Dove)

Ingredients:

1/2 cup butter
1 cup icing sugar
2 cups coconut
1 tsp vanilla extract
graham wafer crumbs
1 can pineapple cubes, drained

Directions:

Cream butter and sugar until smooth.
Add coconut and vanilla. Roll around pineapple cubes.
Roll in graham wafer crumbs.

> **TRIVIA TIDBITS**
> The inhabitants of Belize, in Central America, eat more fruit than anyone on earth, about 540 pounds per person per year. This is more than twice the American average.

This page is dedicated to the memory of my mother,
Doris (Dot) Lambert (nee Blake), of Twillingate, Newfoundland, who passed away in 1975.
Your daughter, Patsy

Parowax Balls

Sandra Young, St. John's, Newfoundland, (nee Dove, Twillingate, Newfoundland)

Ingredients:

1 pkg chocolate chips
1 pkg (or block) parowax
3/4 cup peanut butter
1 cup dates
1 cup walnuts, chopped
1 cup icing sugar
1 tsp vanilla

> **TRIVIA TIDBITS**
> Bourbon whisky was actually invented by an American Baptist Minister.

Directions:

Melt together in small saucepan chocolate chips and parowax. In a medium size bowl, combine the remaining ingredients. Roll mixture in balls and dip with toothpick into the hot parowax mixture. Place each one on wax paper to set.

Molasses Oatmeal Cookies

Ingredients:

2 & 1/2 cups rolled oats (old-fashioned type, not instant)
1 cup all-purpose flour
1/2 cup brown (or white) sugar
2 tsp baking powder
1/2 tsp soda
1/2 tsp salt
1/2 tsp nutmeg
1 tsp cinnamon
1/4 tsp cloves
1/3 cup raisins (optional)
2/3 cup melted margarine (or bacon fat)
3/4 cup molasses
1 tbsp milk
1 egg, beaten

> **TRIVIA TIDBITS**
> In the early part of the 20th century, Emperor Menelek of Abyssinia imported an electric chair from the United States, so that criminals in his country could be put to death more humanely. There was a slight problem however, Abyssinia did not have any electricity at the time. To save face Menelek had the chair converted into a throne.

Directions:

Measure the rolled oats into a bowl and sift over them the next 8 ingredients. Add raisins and stir well. Melt fat and remove from heat. To it, add remaining ingredients and mix well. Add to dry ingredients, blend and drop by spoonfuls on to greased pans. Bake 15 minutes at 350°F.

Simple Macaroons

Debbie Hynes, St. John's, Newfoundland, (formerly of Brampton, Ontario)

Ingredients:

1 can sweetened condensed milk
coconut (use own judgement)
cherries, cut

Directions:

Pour condensed milk in bowl and add enough coconut to roll mixture in balls. Place on baking sheet and flatten slightly with fork. Put piece of cherry on top and bake in 300-350°F oven until light brown (or done).

Pies, Pastries, Cakes, Cookies, Candies, Etc.

Sweets & Treats

Chocolate Chip Macaroons

Ingredients:

2/3 cup sweetened condensed milk

2 cups coconut

1 pkg chocolate chips

1/2 cup walnuts

1/2 cup cherries

1 tsp vanilla

Directions:

Mix together all ingredients. Drop by teaspoonful onto well-greased baking sheet. Bake 10-12 minutes at 350°F.

SPICE OF LIFE

If you don't have a leg to stand on, it's best not to kick.

Apricot & Coconut Balls

Gertrude Finn, Mississauga, Ontario (nee Tucker, St. John's, Newfoundland)

Ingredients:

2/3 can sweetened condensed milk

1 & 1/2 cups dried minced apricot

2 cups angle flake coconut

Directions:

Mix all of these together and press into balls. Leave to dry on a tray at room temperature. Dust with icing sugar before serving if desired. Store in a covered tin.

SPICE OF LIFE

Divorce is the result of a marriage that went from tense to past tense.

Partridgeberry Crumbles

Dolores Lundrigan, Wabush, Labrador, (nee English, Branch, St. Mary's Bay, Newfoundland)

Ingredients:

1 cup flour

1 cup brown sugar

1 cup rolled oats

1/2 cup butter or margarine

1 & 1/2 cups partridgeberry jam

Directions:

Cut 1/2 cup butter into flour, brown sugar and rolled oats until crumbly.

Press half of crumb mixture into greased pan. Spread with partridgeberry jam.

Cover with remaining crumbs and pat smooth.

Bake in preheated oven at 350°F for 35 minutes or until light golden brown.

Cool and cut into squares.

FOOD FOR THOUGHT

The happiest people could be those who are too busy to notice whether they are.

Sweets & Treats

Pies, Pastries, Cakes, Cookies, Candies, Etc.

Chocolate Crunchies

Lisa Ash, Portland, Newfoundland, (formerly of St. John's, Newfoundland)

Ingredients:

1 cup chocolate chips
1 pkg regular marshmallows
2 tbsp milk
1 tbsp vanilla extract
3 cups Rice Krispies
1/2 cup coconut
1/2 cup nuts, chopped

> **SPICE OF LIFE**
> The most discouraging thing about my telling a good story is that it can remind some fool of a better one.

Directions:

Melt chocolate chips over low heat, stirring until melted. Stir marshmallows, milk and vanilla. Continue stirring over low heat until melted. Add Rice Krispies, coconut and nuts. Mix lightly, cool slightly, form into balls. Roll in coconut or nuts. Chill until firm. Makes 3 & 1/2 dozen.

Sweet Mary-Anne Bars

Ingredients:

1/2 cup brown sugar
1/2 cup peanut butter
1/2 cup corn syrup
1 tbsp butter
2 cups Rice Krispies
1 cup peanuts
1 cup (at least) chocolate chips

> **TRIVIA TIDBITS**
> In 106 A.D. the Irish King of Leinster paid his tax to Rome with 150 slave girls, 150 pigs and 150 cows.

Directions:

Heat the first 4 ingredients together. Combine well, but do not boil. Add Rice Krispies and peanuts. Mix. Press into an 8x8-inch buttered pan. Sprinkle chocolate chips on top. Melt in oven until they spread easily. Chill and then cut into squares.

Sour Cream Rhubarb Squares

Ingredients:

1 & 1/2 cups sugar
1/2 cup shortening
1 egg
2 cups flour
1 tsp baking soda
1/2 tsp salt
1 cup sour cream
1 & 1/2 cups rhubarb (cut in small pieces)

Topping:

1/2 cup sugar
1/2 tsp cinnamon
1/2 cup flour

> **TRIVIA TIDBITS**
> During the 1800s in England, divorce was possible only by an act of Parliament. A story comes from that era about a Town Clerk who was very unhappily married. While the clerk was drafting a Waterworks Bill for his town, he inserted in a clause concerned with technical details, the following phrase; "and the town Clerk's marriage is hereby dissolved". Everybody was so bored with the reading by the time it got to that part that nobody ever noticed the phrase. The bill got passed in Parliament, and the clerk gained his freedom.

1/4 cup butter

Directions:

Cream sugar and shortening together. Mix all ingredients and cover with topping before baking. Bake in 9x13-inch pan at 350°F degrees for 45 minutes. Cut in squares when cool.

Nut Loaf Bars

Claudine Barnes, Corner Brook, Newfoundland

Ingredients:

Melt together -
1 cup chocolate chips
2 cups chocolate wafers
3/4 cup peanut butter
1/2 cup butter

Directions:

Remove from heat and stir in -
1 cup walnut pieces
1 sm pkg small white marshmallows
Put in 8x8-inch square pan immediately. Let cool and cut into squares.

FOOD FOR THOUGHT

The man who wins may have been counted out several times, but he didn't hear the referee.

-H.E. Jansen

Butterscotch Squares

Neta Dove, Twillingate, Newfoundland, (nee Roberts)

Ingredients:

2 - 6oz pkgs butterscotch chips
1/2 cup margarine
1 cup peanut butter
2 cups miniature coloured marshmallows

Directions:

In saucepan, melt butterscotch chips, margarine and peanut butter. Add marshmallows. Mix together. Put into greased pan and place in fridge. Let cool and cut into squares.

SPICE OF LIFE

A sweater is a garment worn by a child when its mother feels cold.

Frying Pan Cookies

Ethel Keeping, Burnt Islands, Newfoundland

Ingredients:

2 eggs
1 & 1/2 cup dates
3 cups Rice Krispies
1 cup sugar
1 tsp vanilla extract
dash of salt
coconut

FOOD FOR THOUGHT

People who tell everything that they know aren't so bad, providing that's where they stop.

Jessie Chippett (Zen) - Jul. 29, 1902 - Oct. 4, 1995

Dedicated to the memory of our 'Nan'. As mother, grandmother, great grandmother, great-great grandmother, and great-great-great grandmother, she taught us all the true meaning of 'forever young'

Directions:
Put eggs, sugar and dates in frying pan and stir slowly until thick. Remove from heat and add salt, vanilla, and Rice Krispies. When mixture is cool, form into balls and roll in coconut.

Oatmeal Chocolate Chip Cookies

Ruth Keats, Mississauga, Ontario

Ingredients:
2 cups butter
2 cups white sugar
2 cups brown sugar, light or dark
4 eggs
2 tsp vanilla
4 cups flour
5 cups oatmeal
1 tsp salt
2 tsp baking powder
2 tsp baking soda
1 - 24oz bag chocolate chips
1 - 8oz Hershey bar, grated
3 cups nuts, chopped

TRIVIA TIDBITS
To prove how silly the superstition about bad-luck Fridays was, the British government had a ship built called 'Friday'. The construction of the ship began on a Friday, and she was launched on a Friday. Friday sank on her first voyage. It is unknown whether or not she sank on a Friday.

Directions:
Cream together butter, white sugar and brown sugar; add eggs and vanilla. In a separate bowl mix together flour, oatmeal (put small amounts of oatmeal into blender until it turns to powder - measure then blend), salt, baking powder and baking soda. Mix the dry ingredients with the creamed mixture and add chocolate chips, Hershey bar and nuts. Make golf ball size cookies, place inches apart on ungreased cookie sheet. Bake at 375°F for 6 minutes. To make flatter cookies, flatten with a spatula after 5 minutes in the oven, then bake an additional 3 to 5 minutes depending on your oven. Makes 100-115 cookies.

Pecan Pie Squares

Eva F. Canning, Baton Rouge, Los Angeles, USA

Ingredients:
1 box yellow cake mix (reserve 2/3 cup of dry mix for use in filling)
1 egg
1 stick butter or oleo, melted

Directions:
Remove 2/3 cup dry cake mix. Add egg and melted butter to remaining cake mix and mix thoroughly. Pat into 9x13-inch pan sprayed with Pam. Bake at 350°F for 10 minutes. Let cool.

Filling

Ingredients:
1 & 1/4 cups light corn syrup
1/3 cup brown sugar
3 eggs
1 tsp vanilla
2/3 cup dry cake mix
1 & 1/2 to 2 cups chopped pecans

FOOD FOR THOUGHT
You'll find retirement is the time when you don't always stop working after eight hours.

Sweets & Treats

Pies, Pastries, Cakes, Cookies, Candies, Etc.

Directions:

Mix ingredients and pour over crust. Place in oven and cook at 350°F for 45 minutes or until mixture has crusty top. Be careful not to over-bake. Cool thoroughly and cut into bite-size squares.

Date Squares

Marion Nagle, Kitchener, Ontario, (nee Daniels, Twillingate, Newfoundland)

Ingredients:

1 & 1/2 cups rolled oats

1 cup soft butter

1 & 1/2 cups flour

1/8 tsp salt

3/4 cup brown sugar, well-packed

1 tsp baking soda

Filling:

2 cups dates

1 cup hot water

1 cup brown sugar

1 tbsp lemon juice

TRIVIA TIDBITS
One Indian Maharajah had a bed which had bedposts that dispensed rum, whisky and dry martinis.

Directions:

To make filling, cook the four ingredients until dates are soft, then mash. Mix other ingredients until crumbly. Press half the mixture into greased 9-inch square pan. Spread on filling. Pat on remaining crumbs. Bake at 350°F for 20-25 minutes. Cut in squares.

Lemon Crumbles

Marion Nagle, Kitchener, Ontario, (nee Daniels, Twillingate, Newfoundland)

Ingredients:

2 cups flour

3/4 cup sugar

1 cup butter

1/2 tsp salt

2 cups coconut (sweetened, flaked)

1 pkg lemon pie filling

FOOD FOR THOUGHT
There's nothing wrong with drinking like a fish, provided you drink what a fish drinks.

Directions:

Mix dry ingredients together by hand, rubbing in butter. Place half of mixture into large pan and press. Spread pie filling on bottom mixture and add remaining mixture over top. Bake at 350°F for 25 minutes.

Dedicated to our parents, **Hubert and Carrie Bennett (nee Barnes)** of Horwood, Newfoundland.
Love, Susie, Beulah, Linda, Francis, Randolph, Austin, Ford, Rowena, Lorne, Stanley, Eldred and Barry.

Blueberry Squares

Beulah Cooper, Gander, Newfoundland, (nee Collins, Corner Brook, Newfoundland)

Ingredients:

2 cups blueberries
3 tbsp lemon juice
3 tbsp sugar
1 pk vanilla pudding
2 cups skim milk
1 envelope dream whip
graham wafers

Directions:

Beat blueberries, lemon juice and sugar until thick. Beat vanilla pudding with milk. Beat dream whip and then beat both together. Line 9-inch square pan with graham wafers and pour 3/4 pudding mixture on top, then another layer of graham wafers and layer of blueberry mixture and another layer of graham wafers, then remaining pudding mix.

Tops & Bottoms

Sadie Keeping, Ramea, Newfoundland, (nee Priddle, Francois, Newfoundland)

Ingredients:

Bottom:

1/2 cup brown sugar
1/2 cup butter
4 tbsp cocoa
1 cup flour

Top:

2 eggs
1 cup brown sugar
1 cup coconut
1/2 cup cherries
2 tbsp flour
1 tsp vanilla
1/2 tsp baking powder
1/2 cup nuts

Directions:

Mix together bottom ingredients and press into a 9" square pan. Bake at 350° for 15 minutes. For the top, beat 2 eggs and brown sugar together. Add rest of ingredients and bake at 350° for 20-25 minutes. Cool. Then ice with chocolate icing.

Sadie's Five Star Cookies

Sadie Keeping, Ramea, Newfoundland, (nee Priddle, Francois, Newfoundland)

Ingredients:

1/2 cup butter, melted
2 cups graham wafers
2 cups coconut
1 can sweetened condensed milk

1 tsp vanilla
4 Aero bars
1/4 cup oil
Directions:

Mix above ingredients together. Pour into a 9x13-inch greased pan. Bake at 350°F for 5 to 8 minutes. Melt the Aero bars in oil and pour over cookies; chill.

Fresh Fruit Tart

Charlene Jenkins, Etobicoke, Ontario, (formerly of Springdale, Newfoundland)

Ingredients:

Cookie Crust:

1/2 cup butter, softened
1/2 cup granulated sugar
1/8 tsp salt
1 egg yolk
1 tbsp half and half
1 tsp vanilla extract
1/2 tsp lemon zest
1 & 1/2 cups all-purpose flour

Cream Filling:

1 - 8oz pkg cream cheese, softened
1/3 cup granulated sugar
1/2 tsp vanilla extract
1/2 tsp lemon juice
1/4 tsp lemon zest
1 basket strawberries

Glaze:

In small pot, whisk 1/4 cup currant jelly and 1 tbsp water over medium heat until melted. Boil 30 seconds. Brush mixture over fruit. Chill tart.

Directions:

Cream together butter, sugar and salt. Beat in yolk, vanilla, lemon zest and half and half. Blend in flour. Line a cookie sheet with parchment paper. Pat dough onto paper into a 10-inch diameter circle. Pinch dough along edges to make a slightly raised rim. With fork prick dough every 1/2 inch. Bake at 375°F for 10 minutes. Dough will be slightly soft but will firm up as it cools. To make filling, beat together cream cheese and sugar until well combined. Beat in vanilla, lemon juice, and lemon zest. Spread mixture on cooled cookie crust. Arrange fruit over filling. Glaze tart as directed above.

TRIVIA TIDBITS
The first time Bretons saw a Judo demonstration was as part of a music hall act in 1899.

SPICE OF LIFE
Saving your money is a good idea.
Some day it may be worth something again.

Mr. Reginald and Mrs. Edith O'Brien
"To mom and dad - living in beautiful Newfoundland
You must be shaped by the land and the sea
I wish and wonder that I could be
So wonderful and full of sunshine as ye"
Love, your son, Bob

Napoleans

Catherine Irwin, Truro, Nova Scotia

Ingredients:

1 pkg graham wafer crumbs

2 & 1/2 pt whip cream

1 large (or 2 small) Jello Vanilla Pie Pudding (kind you cook)

1 square chocolate

3 tsp vanilla

2 cups icing sugar

3 cups whole milk

Directions:

Line 12x12-inch (or longer) pan with graham wafers. Make up pie pudding according to box instructions. Let cool (not cold). Spread over wafers. Melt chocolate and keep warm. Whip cream with 2 tsp vanilla + tbsp sugar. Spread cream over pudding. Place graham wafers on top. Make a glaze by beating 2 cups sifted icing sugar, 3 tbsp hot milk and 1 tsp vanilla. Pour over top of wafers. Dip knife or tiny spoon in melted chocolate and weave (draw) criss-cross lines approximately 1-inch apart on glaced surface. Create the "feathered" look. I use a small "pie fork" for my artistic job. Chill 3 - 4 hours. Keeps 24 hours in fridge. Very rich and great for festive occasions.

Pictou County Oat Cakes

June Chaulker, St. Thomas, Ontario

Ingredients:

2 cups oatmeal

1 cup flour

1 cup brown sugar

1 tsp salt

3/4 cup shortening

1/4 tsp baking soda

1/4 cup boiling water

Directions:

Combine dry ingredients in a large bowl and cut in shortening. Dissolve baking soda in the boiling water and add to dry ingredients. Mix well. Mold with hands and shape into a long roll. Cut in 1/2 inch slices and bake in a 400°F degree oven for 10 minutes.

Lassie Cookies

Gerine Collingwood, Rocky Harbour, Newfoundland

Ingredients:

1 cup sugar

1/2 cup molasses

1 cup butter

1/4 cup shortening

3 - 4 cups flour

1/2 tsp salt

2 tsp baking soda (dissolve in 2 tbsp milk)

Sweets & Treats

Pies, Pastries, Cakes, Cookies, Candies, Etc.

1 egg
Directions:
Cream butter and sugar. Add egg, molasses, salt and baking soda. Harden with flour. Make into rolls 1 & 1/2-inches in diameter. Refrigerate for 5 - 6 hours. Slice thin and put two together with a small bit of jam, press edges with a fork. Bake at 375°F until browned.

Laura's Oatmeal Raisin Cookies

Catherine Irwin, Truro, Nova Scotia
Ingredients:
3/4 cup margarine
1 cup white sugar
1 egg
1 & 1/2 cups flour
1/4 cup molasses
1 tsp soda
1/4 tsp salt
1 tsp cinnamon
1 tsp ginger
1 cup quick oats
2/3 cup raisins (I use 1 full cup and I plunk them in hot water and drain before adding them to mixture)
Directions:
Pat out onto no-stick cookie sheet. (I make mine as big and round as an orange and fairly thick - 1/4-inch at least!. They spread out to width of grapefruit slice.) Place on 2nd or 3rd shelf down from the top and bake at 325°F for 10 - 15 minutes.

> ### SPICE OF LIFE
> When you see the handwriting on the wall, you know a two-year old is around.

Apricot Creams

Charlene Jenkins, Etobicoke, Ontario, (formerly of Springdale, Newfoundland)
Ingredients:
3/4 cup butter or margarine
3/4 cup granulated sugar
4oz cream cheese, softened
1 egg
1 tbsp lemon juice
1 tsp lemon rind
1/2 tsp vanilla
6oz dried apricots, chopped
2 cups + 2 tbsp all-purpose flour
3/4 tsp baking powder
apricot preserves

FOOD FOR THOUGHT
There's nothing more difficult than knowing when to get down off your high horse gracefully.

This page is dedicated to the memory of our dear parents
Elias and Stella O'Quinn (Aucoin) of Kippens, Nfld.
Forever remembered by your children;
Ralph, Clarence, Lillian, Reggie, Kevin and Rebecca.

Directions:
Cream the butter and sugar together. Blend in the cream cheese. Combine well. Beat in the egg, lemon juice, lemon rind, vanilla and dried apricot pieces. In a bowl, combine the flour and baking powder. Add to the cream cheese mixture. Mix well. Chill dough in refrigerator or freezer for about 30 minutes. Shape dough into 1-inch balls. Place on ungreased cookie sheets. Make a thumb print in each cookie. Fill each with about 1/2 teaspoon preserves. Bake at 350°F for 15 minutes.

Ginger Snaps

Ingredients:

1/2 cup white sugar

1 cup molasses

1/2 cup hot, melted shortening

1/2 cup clear, hot tea

1 tsp baking soda

3 & 1/2 - 4 cups all-purpose flour

1 tsp salt

2 tsp ginger

1/2 tsp cloves

TRIVIA TIDBITS
Indian ink does not come from India, but from China.

Directions:
Put sugar and molasses into a mixing bowl. Dissolve the baking soda in the hot tea and add, together with the shortening, to sugar mixture. Let stand until lukewarm, then add the dry ingredients. Chill dough overnight, or at least 2 hours, before rolling out. This chilling improves the flavour and makes the dough easier to handle. The dough should be rolled thin (about 1/8-inch) and more flour may be added, if necessary for easier handling. Bake in a 400°F oven for 8 to 10 minutes.

French Apple Pie

Grace Ryan, Newmans Cove, Bonavista Bay, Newfoundland

Ingredients:

5-6 large apples, peeled and sliced thin

3/4 cup sugar

1 tsp cinnamon

FOOD FOR THOUGHT
The universe is full of great things patiently waiting for our wits to grow sharper.

Directions:
Combine sugar and cinnamon. Sprinkle over sliced apples and mix lightly. Place in prepared pastry lined pan and cover with topping (below).

Topping for French Apple Pie

Ingredients:

1 cup flour

1/2 cup butter

3/4 cup brown sugar

SPICE OF LIFE
Some people get carried away with the sound of their own voice, but not far enough.

Directions:
Mix flour and brown sugar, cut in butter until mixture resembles coarse crumbs. Sprinkle over apples in pie pan. Bake at 400°F for 40-45 minutes. Good served with ice-cream.

Pies, Pastries, Cakes, Cookies, Candies, Etc.

Sweets & Treats

Sweets & Treats
Pies, Pastries, Cakes, Cookies, Candies, Etc.

Violet's Cranberry Pie

Mrs. Violet Crowley, Western Bay, Newfoundland, (nee Johnson, Job's Cove, Conception Bay, Newfoundland)

Ingredients:

2 cups cranberries (or partridgeberries)
1 & 1/2 cups sugar
1/2 cup chopped nuts
3 eggs
1 tsp vanilla (add to eggs)
1 cup flour
1/2 cup melted butter
1/4 cup vegetable oil

Directions:

Butter well, 10-inch pie plate. Spread berries on plate and sprinkle with 1/2 cup sugar and nuts. Beat eggs thoroughly. Add 1 cup sugar and beat well. Add flour, melted butter and oil to egg mixture. Beat well. Pour over top of berries. Bake in slow oven 325°F for 1 hour. Cool. Serve fruit side up. Top with ice-cream.

> ***TRIVIA TIDBITS***
> The first US President to be assassinated was Abraham Lincoln.

Sour Cream Rhubarb Pie

Betina Wheeler-Ali, Toronto, Ontario (formerly of St. John's, Newfoundland)

Ingredients:

4 cups rhubarb, cubed
1/3 cup all-purpose flour
1 & 1/2 cups white sugar
1 cup sour cream
1/4 cup soft butter
1/2 cup all-purpose flour
1/2 cup brown sugar
10-inch unbaked pie shell

Directions:

> ***TRIVIA TIDBITS***
> The flowers for Queen Victoria's funeral cost £80,000.

Put rhubarb in pie shell. Mix white sugar, sour cream and 1/3 cup of flour and pour over rhubarb. Combine remaining ingredients until crumbly and sprinkle over top. Bake at 450°F for 15 minutes, then 350°F for 30 minutes until fruit is tender. The filling should be set and the crumbs golden brown.

Streusel-Topped Pear Pie

Mrs. Anita Duggan, Sechelt, British Columbia (nee Shea, Bell Island, Newfoundland)

Ingredients:

2 & 1/4 cups all-purpose flour
salt
1 cup butter or margarine
2 & 1/2 to 3 tbsp cold water

> **FOOD FOR THOUGHT**
> Each dawning day is a personal gift.
> Perhaps that is why it is called the present.

This page is dedicated to our mother, **Hazel Day**, residing in Campbellton, Nfld. "Mom, your strength and love is the tie that binds our family together - wherever - forever! We love you!"
Loretta, Harold and Dulcie (In memory - Hank and Junior)

5 medium pears
1/2 cup sugar
2 tbsp lemon juice
1/2 cup packed light brown sugar
1 tsp ground cinnamon
1/4 tsp ground nutmeg
1/4 tsp ground cloves
1/2 cup cheddar cheese, shredded

Directions:

In medium bowl with fork, stir 2 cups flour and 1 tsp salt. With pastry blender, or 2 knives used scissor-fashion, cut in 3/4 cup butter until mixture resembles coarse crumbs. Measure 1 cup mixture into medium bowl; reserve. To remaining flour mixture, add cold water, 1 tbsp at a time, mixing lightly with a fork after each addition until moist enough to hold together. With hands, shape pastry into a ball. On lightly floured surface with lightly floured rolling pin, roll pastry into an 11-inch circle; use to line 9-inch pie plate. Trim pastry edges, leaving 1-inch overhang. Fold overhang under; bring up over pie-plate rim; pinch to form a high edge; make a fluted edge. Peel, core and cut pears into thick slices to measure about 4 & 1/2 cups. In a large bowl, toss pears with sugar, lemon juice, 1/4 cup flour and 1/4 tsp salt; put in crust. Preheat oven to 425°F. In medium bowl, combine reserved flour mixture, brown sugar and next 3 ingredients. With pastry blender, cut in cheese and 1/4 cup butter until mixture resembles coarse crumbs and ingredients are well blended. Sprinkle over pears. Bake 40 minutes; cover with foil and bake 20 minutes more. Serve warm or refrigerate to serve cold. **NOTE:** I use green pears and the juice from a whole lemon. I don't know how ripe pears taste in this pie. The pie tastes better cold and even better the next day.

> **FOOD FOR THOUGHT**
> I receive lots of advice from folks who want me to do what they haven't done.

Rhubarb Custard Pie

Ingredients:
3 cups frozen unsweetened cut rhubarb
3/4 cup granulated sugar
2 tbsp all-purpose flour
2 eggs
1/4 cup milk
1 tbsp butter, melted
9-inch frozen pie shell

> **TRIVIA TIDBITS**
> Although Christopher Columbus was from Genoa, Italy, he wrote only in Spanish. One theory for this is that Christopher came from a Spanish-Jewish family and could not read or write before he left home. He moved to Spain and there he learned the spoken and written language of his new associates.

Directions:

Preheat oven to 425°F. Place frozen rhubarb in a bowl. Cover with boiling water while preparing rest of ingredients. Measure sugar and flour into a large bowl. Stir with a fork until blended. Add eggs, milk and butter. Whisk until well mixed. Drain rhubarb well and pat dry with paper towels. Cut into even-sized pieces, about 1/2 inch wide. It should now measure about 2 & 1/2 cups. Stir into egg mixture. Turn into frozen pie shell placed on a baking sheet. Bake on bottom shelf of preheated oven for 10 minutes, until crust starts to brown. Then reduce heat to 350°F and bake until centre seems set, about 20 minutes more. Makes 8 servings.

Apple Pie with Cider Crust

Charlene Jenkins, Etobicoke, Ontario, (formerly of Springdale, Newfoundland)

Ingredients:
8 cups peeled, sliced apples
1 can (12oz) frozen apple juice concentrate
1 tsp cinnamon

Pies, Pastries, Cakes, Cookies, Candies, Etc.

Sweets & Treats

Apple Cider Crust:
1 & 3/4 cups all-purpose flour
1/4 cup whole wheat flour
1/4 tsp salt
1/4 cup apple juice concentrate
12 tbsp unsalted butter or margarine

Directions:
Combine apple slices, apple juice and cinnamon in a 3-quart saucepan. Leave uncovered. Simmer over low heat until most of liquid has cooked into the apples. Stir occasionally. After about 30 minutes the apples will be ready. Cool slightly. In a bowl, combine the white and whole wheat flour and the salt. Combine 1/3 of mixture with 1/4 cup of apple juice concentrate. Mix into a paste. Cut butter into remaining flour mixture until mixture resembles coarse meal. Stir in the paste. Form a soft dough. Do not knead! Roll out half of dough. Fit into pie plate. Fill with cooked apples. Top with upper crust. Trim and press edges together with a fork. Prick a few vents in top crust. Bake at 425°F for 10 minutes. Lower heat to 375°F. Bake 15 to 20 minutes until golden brown. Serve warm, at room temperature, or cold. Excellent with sharp New England Cheddar cheese.

Eva's Favourite Deluxe Strawberry Pie

Eva F. Canning, Baton Rouge, Los Angeles, USA

Ingredients:
4 cups fresh strawberries, washed and capped (reserve some for garnish)
3 tbsp cornstarch
1 cup granulated sugar
1/2 tsp baking powder
3 drops red food colouring
9-inch baked pie shell
whipped cream or sour cream

Directions:
Spread 2 cups of berries over bottom of cooled baked pie shell.
Mash or break remaining berries.
Add sugar, cornstarch, baking powder and mix well together.
Place over low heat, bring to a boil gradually; reduce heat and cool, stirring constantly about 10 minutes.
Add red food colouring to deepen red mixture.
Cool. Pour into baked pie shell and refrigerate, chilling thoroughly.
Garnish with whipped cream or sour cream and decorate with whole berries, reserved earlier from the ones put into baked pie shell.

TRIVIA TIDBITS
For over a hundred years, from the 1300s until the 1500s, it was illegal for an Englishman to eat three meals a day.

This page is dedicated in loving memory of my parents
SUSIE (nee Chatman, 1919-1991)
and **STEWART SKEFFINGTON**, (1915-1981),
both of Canning's Cove, Bonavista Bay, Newfoundland.
-- Beth Rowsell (nee Skeffington), Pickering, Ontario

Eva's Pecan Pie

Eva F. Canning, Baton Rouge, Los Angeles, USA

Ingredients:

3 eggs, slightly beaten
1 cup Karo syrup
1/8 tsp salt
1 cup granulated sugar
1 & 1/2 tsp vanilla extract
1 & 1/4 to 1 & 1/2 cups pecan halves (depending on size)

Directions:

Mix together all ingredients, adding nuts last. Pour into a 9-inch pie plate lined with a rich pie crust. Bake in a hot oven 450°F for 10 minutes. Reduce heat to 350°F and continue baking until a silver knife comes out clean when inserted into mixture.

> **SPICE OF LIFE**
> Have you ever noticed that immediately after you buy an item, you find a coupon for it?

Florida Key Lime Pie

Elizabeth Andrews, Naples, Florida

Ingredients:

4 eggs
1 can condensed milk
3/4 cup fresh lime juice (key lime)
7 tbsp sugar

Directions:

Beat egg yolks, milk and lime juice until thick. Fold in sugar. Pour into baked pie shell. Top with meringue and brown in 350°F oven.

> **FOOD FOR THOUGHT**
> Parents who put their foot down will find their kids reluctant to step on their toes.

Rhubarb Pie

Marion Nagle, Kitchener, Ontario, (nee Daniels, Twillingate, Newfoundland)

Mix together:

1 egg, beaten
1/2 cup maple syrup
1/2 cup brown sugar
2 tbsp flour

Stir In:

2 cups diced rhubarb and pour into unbaked pie shell.

Mix:

3/4 cup flour
1/2 cup brown sugar
1/3 cup margarine
Cover rhubarb and bake for 30 minutes at 350°F.

> **SPICE OF LIFE**
> Teenagers are people who stop asking where they came from and won't tell you where they're going...

Cranberry Pie Supreme

Ingredients:

pastry for a 9-inch pie shell
1 can (8oz) pineapple chunks, drained; reserve juice

> **SPICE OF LIFE**
> It's not the minutes spent at the table that put on weight, it's the seconds.

Sweets & Treats

Pies, Pastries, Cakes, Cookies, Candies, Etc.

Sweets & Treats
Pies, Pastries, Cakes, Cookies, Candies, Etc.

1 lb fresh cranberries
2 cups sugar
2 tbsp unflavoured gelatin
1 tsp grated orange peel
1/4 tsp nutmeg
juice of 1 lemon
whipped cream
chopped nuts

Directions:
Prepare pie shell. Roll out any remaining pastry; cut out with cookie cutters. Bake pie shell and pastry cutouts; set aside. Add water to reserved pineapple juice to equal 1 cup. In a large saucepan, combine cranberries, sugar, pineapple, pineapple juice, gelatin, orange peel, nutmeg, and lemon juice; bring to a boil. Boil 10 minutes, stirring occasionally. Cool to room temperature. Pour into pie shell. Chill pie until set. Top with pastry cutouts. Store in refrigerator until serving time.

Pumpkin Cheese Pie

Ingredients:
8oz cream cheese, softened
3/4 cup sugar
2 & 1/2 tsp pumpkin pie spice
1/2 tsp salt
3 eggs
1 can (16oz) pumpkin
1 tsp vanilla
9-inch pie shell, unbaked

Directions:
Preheat oven to 350°F. In a mixing bowl, beat cream cheese until fluffy. Gradually beat in sugar, spice and salt. Add eggs, one at a time, beating well after each addition. Beat in pumpkin and vanilla. Pour into pie shell. Bake for 40 minutes or until a knife inserted near the center comes out clean. Chill before serving.

Molasses Tarts

Ruby Wellon, Deer Lake, Newfoundland, (nee Rideout)
Ingredients:
4 cups flour
2 & 1/2 tsp cloves
2 & 1/2 tsp cinnamon
1 tsp ginger
1 cup margarine

This page is dedicated to the memory of my sister-in-law, **Anna MacKenzie,** who was born in 1939 and who died in 1978. "Days of sadness still come over us and tears fall in silence. Your memory will always be near us and no one can ever take your place."
June Chaulker

3/4 cup molasses
2 tsp baking soda
1/2 cup tea
partridgeberry (or marshberry) jam

Directions:
Preheat oven to 425°F. Sift together flour, cloves, cinnamon and ginger. Cream margarine and beat in molasses. Mix together to dissolve and blend in baking soda and tea. Stir in dry ingredients. Turn onto a lightly floured surface and roll to 1/8-inch thickness, cut into rounds and line 5 dozen (1 & 1/2 inch) tart pans. Fill with your choice of jam.

Drumsticks

Brenda Dalley, Churchill Falls, Labrador

Ingredients:
1/2 cup graham wafer crumbs
1/2 cup crushed peanuts
1/4 melted butter
8oz pkg cream cheese
1 & 1/2 cups white sugar
2 tbsp peanut butter
4 eggs
2 tbsp vanilla extract

Directions:
Mix first three ingredients together and press into greased pan. Beat rest of ingredients until fluffy Add 1 large or 2 small tubs of cool whip. Fold into mixture; pour over bottom layer. Drizzle brown cow over top. Cover with 1/4 cup crushed peanuts. Keep in freezer. Chill 4-5 hours before serving.

Jam Cushions

Ruby Wellon, Deer Lake, Newfoundland, (nee Rideout)

Ingredients:
8oz pkg cream cheese
2 cups flour
1 cup jam (Apricot, Strawberry or Raspberry)
1 cup butter
1 cup finely chopped nuts

Directions:
Blend cream cheese and butter and stir in flour to make a dough. Chill 3 hours. Prepare filling by combining the nuts and jam. When dough has chilled, divide into 4 pieces and work with one piece at a time. Roll out thin and cut in 2-inch circles. Top centre of circle with scant 1 tsp. of nut and jam mixture. Cover with another circle and seal edges by pressing with a fork. Bake at 400°F for 12 to 15 minutes.

Chocolate Dessert

Ina Belcher, Tonawanda, New York, (nee Brown, St. John's, Newfoundland)

Ingredients:
1 cup flour
1 stick butter
1/2 cup chopped nuts

1 pkg (8oz) cream cheese
1 cup confectioner's sugar
1/2 cup cool whip (thawed)
2 sm pkgs Instant chocolate pudding
3 cups cold milk
Additional cool whip and chopped nuts
Few chocolate sprinkles, optional

Directions:
Mix flour, butter and 1/2 cup nuts together. Pat into 13x9-inch pan. Bake at 350°F for 15 minutes. Cool. Mix together, cream cheese, sugar and 1 & 1/2 cups cool whip. Spread on cooled crust. Mix pudding and milk and pour over cream cheese mixture. Refrigerate at least 6 hours. Spread with more cool whip and chopped nuts.

Yummy Dessert

June Gates, Woodstock, Ontario

Ingredients:
2 lg containers Cool Whip
saltine crackers (unsalted)
2 vanilla instant puddings
raspberry or blueberry pie filling (I use thickened partridgeberries)

Directions:
First, get a 9x13-inch pan. First layer-cool whip on bottom; second layer-crackers; third layer-pudding; fourth layer-cool whip; fifth layer-crackers; sixth layer-pudding. Put pie filling on when ready to eat.

Raisin Bars

Angela Waterman, Glenwood, Newfoundland, (nee John)

Ingredients:
(Filling)
1/2 lb seedless raisins
2 cups water
1/2 cup sugar
2 & 1/2 tbsp flour
(Batter)
1 cup brown sugar
1 cup granulated sugar
1 cup Crisco
3 eggs
1 tsp soda

This page is dedicated to my Grandparents,
Catherine Clemens and the late **William (Billy) Clemens**
of Open Hall, Bonavista Bay, Newfoundland.
Samuel Clemens Jr.

4 cups flour
1 tbsp vanilla
Directions:
Boil filling ingredients together for 10 minutes. Cool. Cream well sugar and Crisco. Add remaining ingredients and mix thoroughly. Spread half the batter in ungreased 10x14-inch pan. Flour hands and work batter around pan, pressing firmly. Spread filling over batter. Drop remaining batter by spoonfuls over filling. Bake at 350°F for 30 minutes.

Blueberry Grunt

Mrs. Marie Whitehorne, Pasadena, Newfoundland, (nee Kendall, Ramea, Newfoundland)

Ingredients:

1 cup butter
3 eggs
2 & 1/2 cups flour
3 tbsp baking powder
1 tsp vanilla
1 cup sugar
blueberries

Directions:

Cream butter, add sugar gradually. Add eggs one at a time. Add vanilla and dry ingredients. Bake in hot oven.

> **FOOD FOR THOUGHT**
> Friendship is like money ...
> easier made than kept.
> *(Samuel Butler, English Novelist, Essayist - 1835-1902)*

Banana Boats

Ingredients:

1/4 cup salted peanuts
4 large bananas
1 ctn (4oz) frozen whipped topping (thawed)
4 maraschino cherries

Directions:

Chop 1/4 cup peanuts on cutting board. Gently wash 4 bananas. Carefully slit top of each banana and peel lengthwise, leaving about 1 inch uncut at each end. Cut away about 1/2 inch of the peel on each side of the slit with scissors. Empty the whipped topping into a bowl. Scoop out each banana in small pieces with teaspoon into the bowl. Save the banana peel shells. Fold the banana pieces into the topping with rubber scraper. Fill each banana peel shell with 1/4 of the banana topping mixture. Sprinkle with 1/4 of the chopped peanuts and top with one cherry. Serve right away or refrigerate as long as one hour.

> **SPICE OF LIFE**
> Some women are blonde on
> their mother's side, some on
> their father's side, but most
> on peroxide.

Summer Dessert

Ingredients:

1 pkg lemon supreme cake mix
1 pkg lime Jello (4 serving size)
1 envelope whipped topping mix (2-2 & 1/2 cups)
1 pkg lemon instant pudding mix (4 serving size)
1 & 1/2 cups cold milk
Directions:

TRIVIA TIDBITS
As a boy, the man who was knighted for his services to the British Empire and became known as, 'Clive of India', led a gang that extorted money from local shopkeepers.

Sweets & Treats
Pies, Pastries, Cakes, Cookies, Candies, Etc.

Dissolve gelatin in 3/4 cup boiling water. Add 1/2 cup cold water. Set aside. Mix and bake cake as directed in a 9x13x2-inch pan. Cool 20-25 minutes. Poke holes about 1 inch apart in cake (still in pan), with a meat fork or a straw. Pour Jello mixture into holes. Refrigerate cake while preparing topping.

Topping:

In chilled bowl, blend and whip topping mix, instant pudding and milk until stiff (3-8 minutes). Frost cake at once and store in refrigerator. Serve chilled. Can be frozen. Makes 16 servings.

Apple Crumble

Ingredients:

1 egg
2 tbsp flour
1/8 tsp salt
1/2 tsp vanilla
1 tsp baking powder
1/2 tsp almond extract
1/4 cup walnuts
2/3 cup sugar
1 cup coarsely grated peeled apples
Ice cream (or custard sauce)

TRIVIA TIDBITS
In 1762, the Venetian Monk, Abbe Grioni, lost all his clothes gambling. The gambling Monk returned to his monastery completely naked.

Directions:

Heat oven to 350°F. Grease an 8-inch round layer cake pan. Beat egg and sugar together. Stir in flour, baking powder, salt, vanilla and almond extract. Fold in nuts and apples. Spoon into prepared pan and spread evenly. Bake 35 minutes. Spoon into individual serving dishes or sherbert glasses while warm and serve topped with your favourite ice cream. Serves 4-6.

Pineapple Cheesecake

Sandra Young, St. John's, Newfoundland, (nee Dove, Twillingate, Newfoundland)

Ingredients:

1 graham wafer pie shell (or make your own)
1 lg & 1 sm pkg cream cheese
1/4 can sweetened condensed milk
2 tsps ReaLemon juice
1 lg can crushed pineapple (drained)
1 tsp vanilla extract

SPICE OF LIFE
Often the mother who remembers her first kiss has a daughter who can't remember her first husband.

Directions:

Combine in bowl, Realemon juice, cream cheese and sweetened condensed milk, mixing with spoon until fairly smooth. Pour into pie shell and let stand in fridge until base is completely set. Spread crushed pineapple over top and refrigerate.

Cherry Cheesecake

Susan Rowsell, (nee Snooks, Corner Brook and York Harbour, Newfoundland)

Ingredients:

1 & 1/4 cups graham wafer crumbs
1/4 cup melted butter
8oz pkg cream cheese

FOOD FOR THOUGHT
Aim for the stars, but make sure you keep both feet planted firmly on the ground.

Sweets & Treats — Pies, Pastries, Cakes, Cookies, Candies, Etc.

1 cup icing sugar
1 pkg Dream Whip
1 can cherry pie filling

Directions:
Bottom: mix graham wafer crumbs and melted butter together. Press into 9x12-inch pie pan and put into refrigerator. Do not bake. *Top:* To cream cheese, add sugar, and beat until creamy. Prepare Dream Whip as directed on package and add to mixture. Beat until light and fluffy. Pour over bottom mixture. Top with cherry pie filling. Chill and serve.

Rocky Road Cheesecake

Dorothy Troop, Annapolis County, Nova Scotia, Bay de Verde, Conception Bay, Newfoundland)

Ingredients:
2 cups angleflake coconut
2 tbsp melted butter
3 - 250g pkgs cream cheese
3 eggs
1 cup sugar
1 - 250g pkg semi-sweet chocolate, melted

Directions:
Mix coconut and butter. Press into 9-inch spring form pan and bake at 350°F for 12 minutes. Beat cream cheese, eggs and sugar. Add semi-sweet chocolate which has been melted and cooled. Pour over coconut crust and bake for 10 minutes at 425°F and then 30 minutes at 250°F. Cover with mini marshmallows and put under broiler until lightly browned. Cover with cherries and melted caramel or toffee chips.

Baked Rice Pudding

Juanita Ings, Hillgrade, Newfoundland

Ingredients:
1/2 cup cooked rice
1 & 1/2 cups skim milk powder
1/2 cup sugar
6 cups water
1 tsp salt
1/4 cup raisins

Directions:
Wash rice. Put in large baking dish. Add all ingredients, except raisins. Bake in oven at 325°F for 1 & 1/2 hours. Take out of oven and stir in raisins and bake another 1/2 hour.

Rice Pudding

Marion Nagle, Kitchener, Ontario, (nee Daniels, Twillingate, Newfoundland)

Ingredients:
1/4 cup rice
6 eggs
1 tin milk
1 tin water
1/2 cup sugar
vanilla

Directions:
Boil rice. Beat together other five ingredients. Add rice to egg mixture. Dot with butter. Bake for 1 hour at 350°F. Place dish in pan of water.

Raspberry Ribbon

Lillian Butler, Bay St. George, Newfoundland (nee Berry, Sandy Point, Newfoundland)
Ingredients:
6oz pkg raspberry jello
1/4 cup white sugar
2 & 1/4 cups boiling water
15oz pkg frozen raspberries
1 tbsp lemon juice
6oz pkg cream cheese
1/3 cup icing sugar
1 tsp vanilla
1/2 pint whipping cream

TRIVIA TIDBITS
A tribal chief
in the Belgian Congo
was once found
to be using a stolen
flush toilet
as a throne.

Directions:
Dissolve jello and sugar in boiling water. Add frozen raspberries and lemon juice. Stir until berries thaw. Chill until partly set. Cream together: cream cheese, icing sugar, and vanilla. Whip the whipping cream and fold into cheese mixture. Layer alternately in bowl. Chill till set.

Baked Pineapple Toast

Angela Waterman, Glenwood, Newfoundland, (nee John)
Ingredients:
1/4 cup butter or margarine, melted
1/2 cup brown sugar, firmly packed
8oz can crushed pineapple, drained
6 bread slices, white
2 eggs
1 & 1/2 cups milk
1/2 tsp salt

SPICE OF LIFE
Alimony is an arrangement in
which two people make a mistake,
but only one pays for it.

Directions:
Combine butter, sugar and pineapple. Spread on bottom of 13x9-inch baking dish. Top with bread. Beat eggs, milk and salt together. Pour over bread. Bake uncovered at 375°F for 25 minutes or until golden brown. Cool slightly. Transfer to heated serving platter.

Molasses Fudge

Ingredients:
1 cup brown sugar
1 cup white sugar
1/4 cup butter
1/2 cup molasses
1/2 cup cream
2 squares unsweetened chocolate
1/2 tsp vanilla

TRIVIA TIDBITS
In case the Germans should attack America,
a practice air raid took place in New York
City during the Second World War. The
event was ineffective as no one could hear
the sirens because of the noise and din
created by the city. It was not tried again,
and luckily the real thing was not necessary.

1/2 cup chopped nuts
Directions:
Combine white and brown sugars, cream, molasses and butter. Bring to a boil for 2 minutes. Add chocolate which has been grated and boil 5 minutes longer, stirring until well blended, and then only occasionally to prevent burning. Remove from heat and add vanilla. Stir until creamy. Pour into well-buttered pan and cut in squares.

Molasses Candy

Ingredients:
3 tbsp butter
2/3 cup white sugar
2 cups molasses

SPICE OF LIFE
You have to buy the drugstore's vitamins so you can get the strength to open their medicine bottles.

Directions:
Melt the butter in a saucepan. Tip the pan to grease the sides. Add molasses and sugar and stir until sugar is well dissolved. Bring mixture to a boil, stirring slowly all the while. Cook and test by dropping a bit of the mixture into cold water. When it becomes brittle (265°) the candy is done. Pour into a well-buttered platter to cool until it can be handled. Grease the hands and pull the taffy from hand to hand until it becomes firm and turns a golden color. Draw into a smooth band or twist into a rope. Cut into short lengths, using the kitchen scissors. Wrap pieces in waxed paper.

Triple Layer Fudge Cake

Charlene Jenkins, Etobicoke, Ontario, (formerly of Springdale, Newfoundland)

Ingredients:
3 cups sifted cake flour
2 tsp baking soda
1 tsp salt
1 cup butter, softened
1 cup granulated sugar
1 cup brown sugar
3 eggs
4oz unsweetened chocolate, melted
2 tsp vanilla extract
2 cups buttermilk
Chocolate Frosting:
3/4 cup butter, softened
5oz unsweetened chocolate, melted
3 tsp vanilla extract
5 tbsp milk
6 cups powdered sugar, sifted
sliced almonds, for garnish (optional)

TRIVIA TIDBITS
George Washington once had a set of false teeth made of wood. He later tried a set made from ivory but these had such a bad odor that he had to soak them in port wine every night to improve the smell and taste.

Directions:
Sift flour with baking soda and salt. Set aside. Cream butter with sugars until light and fluffy. Add eggs, melted chocolate and vanilla, beating well. Mix in the buttermilk and flour mixture, alternating until mixture is light and fluffy. Grease and flour three 9-inch pans. Pour batter evenly among pans. Bake at 350°F for 30 to 35 minutes, or until cake tester comes out clean. Cool for

Sweets & Treats

Pies, Pastries, Cakes, Cookies, Candies, Etc.

10 minutes. Remove from pans. Cool completely before frosting. Cream butter for frosting with melted chocolate and vanilla. Add milk and powdered sugar alternately, beating until frosting is creamy. Frost between layers and top and sides of cake, smoothing surface. Sprinkle sliced almonds over top rim of cake, if desired.

Country Shortcake

Charlene Jenkins, Etobicoke, Ontario, (formerly of Springdale, Newfoundland)

Ingredients:
2 cups all-purpose flour
1/3 cup granulated sugar
4 tsp baking powder
1/4 tsp salt
1/2 cup butter or margarine
2 eggs
1/2 cup milk
blueberries (or raspberries)
whipped cream

TRIVIA TIDBITS
At one time in Hollywood, Western sets were made on a smaller-than-life scale (seven-eighths of actual size) to make the heroes seem larger-than-life.

Directions:
Combine the flour, sugar, baking powder and salt. Cut in the butter until the mixture resembles cornmeal. Combine the egg yolks and milk. Stir into the flour mixture. Form to a soft dough. Pat into 4 or 6 rounds, about 1-inch thick. Brush the tops with egg white. Sprinkle with a little sugar. Bake on a greased cookie sheet at 425°F for 12 minutes or until just turning golden. Cool slightly on a rack. Serve warm or at room temperature. For serving, split and top with blueberries or raspberries. Top with whipping cream.

Almond Toffee

Ingredients:
1 cup butter
1 cup sugar
3 tbsp water
1/2 cup chopped almonds, divided
12oz semi-sweet chocolate chips, divided

SPICE OF LIFE
Without doubt, free speech is an important right; too bad so much of it isn't worth listening to.

Directions:
In a medium saucepan, combine butter, sugar, and water. Cook over medium heat until the mixture turns a caramel colour and reaches 300°F on a candy thermometer. Remove syrup from heat. Stir in 1/4 cup nuts. Pour into a buttered 9x13-inch baking pan. Sprinkle 1/2 of the chocolate chips over the nuts; let stand a few minutes until chips melt. Smooth melted chips over the nuts; cover with waxed paper. Invert pan to remove candy. Spread with remaining chocolate chips; top with remaining nuts. Let cool until candy is hard. To serve, break into pieces. Makes 1 1/2 pounds.

Egg Yolk Cookie Paint

June Chaulker, St. Thomas, Ontario

Ingredients:
2 egg yolks
2 tsp milk
food colourings

FOOD FOR THOUGHT
There is no one so smart as the one who says nothing at the right time.

Sweets & Treats
Pies, Pastries, Cakes, Cookies, Candies, Etc.

Directions:
Mix egg yolk and milk. Divide mixture into as many portions as needed. Tint with food colourings. Use clean brush for each colour to paint on cookies before baking.

Never Fail Pie Crust

Ruth Keats, Mississauga, Ontario

SPICE OF LIFE
It's sure a small world, but not to the man who chases his hat on a windy day.

Ingredients:
1 lb lard
5 cups flour
2 tsp salt
1 egg
3 tbsp brown sugar
3 tbsp vinegar
2/3 cup water

Directions:
Blend first three ingredients together. Whip egg, brown sugar, vinegar, and water. Add to first mixture. This pie dough can be stored in the refrigerator in tin foil for three months.

Butter Tarts

Ruth Keats, Mississauga, Ontario

Ingredients:
3 eggs, slightly beaten
1 cup brown sugar, firmly packed
1/2 cup corn syrup
1/4 cup butter, softened
1/2 tsp salt
1 tsp vanilla
1 cup raisins soaked in water for 15 minutes

FOOD FOR THOUGHT
The fool is not so stingy with folly as the wise man is with his wisdom.

Directions:
Gather "Never Fail Pie Crust" pastry into ball and divide in half. Roll out each half on lightly floured surface. Cut into circles, with large cookie cutter and fit into tart pans. Combine first six ingredients of filling. Beat until mixture is smooth. Stir in raisins. Spoon into tart shells, filling each 2/3 full. Bake at 375°F oven for 20 minutes. Makes 20-24 medium tarts.

Chocolate Chip Squares

Marie Evans, Kitchener, Ontario

Ingredients:
3/4 cup brown sugar
1/2 cup butter
1/2 cup peanut butter
1/2 tsp salt
1/2 tsp baking soda
1 cup flour
1/2 cup rolled oats
1 egg

FOOD FOR THOUGHT
Education is the thing that remains once your memory has forgotten all the names, dates, and facts.

Pies, Pastries, Cakes, Cookies, Candies, Etc.

Sweets & Treats

1/2 cup cold water
Directions:
Spread 1/2 mixture in pan. Cover with chocolate chips. Spread remaining mixture over chips.
Bake at 350°F for 25-30 minutes. Ice with chocolate icing.

Key Lime Pie

Brenda Keyes, Durham, Ontario, (nee LeDrew, Pasadena and Corner Brook, Newfoundland)

Ingredients:
1 can condensed milk
4 egg yolks
1/2 cup lime juice
Directions:

> **SPICE OF LIFE**
> It's always going to take a person longer to
> tell you what he thinks than what he knows.

Beat 1 egg white stiff. Fold into above mixture. Beat 3 egg whites and gradually add 6 tbsp sugar
and 1/2 tsp cream of tartar. Put into baked pie shell and bake until egg whites are golden brown
(350°F).

Graham Cracker Cake

Charlene Jenkins, Etobicoke, Ontario, (formerly of Springdale, Newfoundland)

Ingredients:
2 cups graham cracker crumbs
1/2 cup butter or margarine
1 cup light brown sugar, packed
3 eggs, separated
3/4 cup half-and-half
1 tsp vanilla extract
1 tbsp baking powder
Topping:
1 pkg (12oz) frozen raspberries, thawed
3 tbsp granulated sugar
1 tbsp cornstarch
Directions:

> ***TRIVIA TIDBITS***
> The famous novel Moby Dick, by
> Herman Mellville, was actually based on
> the exploits of a real whale named
> Mocha Dick. The real whale actually
> sank three ships and over a dozen whale
> boats, taking the lives of thirty whalers.

Preheat oven to 375°F. Grease and flour 9-inch fluted or plain 8 & 1/2-inch tube pan. Cream butter and sugar. Add egg yolks. Gradually add half-and-half, stirring constantly. Mixture will look
curdled. Fold in crumbs and vanilla. Sprinkle with baking powder. Stir to blend well. Beat egg
whites until stiff. Fold into batter. Pour batter into cake pan. Bake at 375°F 35 to 45 minutes for
Bundt, 50 minutes for tube, until center is firm. For topping, stir in raspberries and juice in
saucepan. Combine with sugar and cornstarch. Cook and stir until the mixture thickens, about 5
minutes. Set aside to cool slightly. Remove cake from oven when done. Cool 5 minutes. Slice
pieces from pan. Serve topped with raspberries. Serve with sour cream, scoops of whipped cream
or vanilla ice cream.

Peanut Butter Cream Pie

Ruby Matthews, Mississauga, Ontario, (nee Coates, Botwood, Newfoundland)

Ingredients:
4oz cream cheese
1 cup confectioners sugar

1/3 cup smooth peanut butter
8oz cool whip (thawed)
9-inch chocolate crumb pie crust
chopped peanuts

Directions:
Whip cheese until soft and fluffy. Beat in sugar and peanut butter. Fold in cool whip. Pour into pie shell. Sprinkle with chopped peanuts. Chill until firm.

One-Bowl Chocolate Cake

Joan Jenkins, Wild Cove, Twillingate, Newfoundland, (nee Roberts)

Ingredients:
1 & 1/2 cups sugar
1 & 3/4 cups flour
1/2 cup butter
2 eggs
1/2 cup cocoa
1 tsp vanilla
1 tsp baking soda
1 & 1/2 tsp baking powder
1 & 1/4 cup milk

Directions:
Mix all ingredients together. Bake at 350°F for 35-40 minutes.

Newfie Rum Balls

Rose Shannon, Downsview, Ontario, (nee Carberry, Burgoyne's Cove, Newfoundland)

Ingredients:
3 cups vanilla wafer crumbs
1 cup icing sugar
1 & 1/2 tbsp cocoa
1 & 1/2 cups finely chopped walnuts
3 tbsp corn syrup
1/2 cup Newfie Screech
fruit sugar

Directions:
Stir crumbs, icing sugar and cocoa. Combine thoroughly, sifted mixture with walnuts, syrup and Screech. Roll into small balls, approximately 1-inch in diameter. Roll in fruit sugar. Store in tightly-covered container.

Dark Cake

Trudy S. Simmons, Twillingate, Newfoundland, (nee Forward, Tizzard's Harbour, Newfoundland)

Ingredients:
3/4 lb butter
1 & 1/2 cups brown sugar
3 cups flour
2 tsp vanilla

Pies, Pastries, Cakes, Cookies, Candies, Etc.

Sweets & Treats

Sweets & Treats
Pies, Pastries, Cakes, Cookies, Candies, Etc.

1 cup strong coffee

1 cup apple sauce

3 eggs (unbeaten)

2 tsp soda

2 tsp cocoa

1/4 cup molasses

1 lb raisins

1 lb currants

1/2 lb cherries

1/2 lb mixed fruit

1/2 lb dates

1/2 lb nuts

1 tsp cloves

2 tsp cinnamon

1 tsp spice

Directions:

Cream butter, sugar and molasses together. Beat in eggs one at a time. Stir in apple sauce, stir in fruit, use cocoa & coffee. Stir in soda mixed in flour, and remaining ingredients. Put into two greased tube pans. Bake until tester comes out clean in 350°F oven.

Fudge

Nora Roberts, Woody Point, Newfoundland

Ingredients:

2 cups white sugar

1/2 cup butter

1/2 cup milk

3 tbsp cocoa

1 cup flour

1/2 cup coconut

1 tsp vanilla

few ground-up nuts

Directions:

Boil first four ingredients on stove in a large saucepan until everything melts. Then boil rapidly for 3 minutes. Take off and add flour, coconut, vanilla and ground-up nuts, if desired.

Coffee Cake

Ruby Matthews, Mississauga, Ontario, (nee Coates, Botwood, Newfoundland)

Ingredients:

1 box yellow cake mix

1 box instant Vanilla Pudding (dry, unprepared)

8oz sour cream

1 cup cooking oil

4 eggs

1 cup white sugar

6 tsp cinnamon

FOOD FOR THOUGHT
Better to teach children the roots of labor than to hand them the fruits of your own.

FOOD FOR THOUGHT
The humblest friendship is a treasure more dear than all the great triumphs of a genius.

SPICE OF LIFE
Self-doubt can turn a man's hair gray overnight, and a woman's hair any color in an hour.

Directions:
Mix very well for at least 4 minutes. Mix 1 cup white sugar with 6 tsp cinnamon. Grease bundt pan, sprinkle sugar and cinnamon mixture around pan generously. Layer cake batter, and sugar/cinnamon mixture three times. Bake 1 hour at 325°F. It's delicious.

Caramel Bananas with Rum

Archie Ridout, Rexdale, Ontario, (formerly of Twillingate, Newfoundland)

Ingredients:
3 bananas, sliced
1/4 cup brown sugar
1/4 cup butter
1 lemon
1/4 cup rum

SPICE OF LIFE
Thanksgiving is a day when the turkey gets stuffed in the morning and the family in the afternoon.

Directions:
Place sugar and butter in a pan and cook over a low heat to form caramel. Add the rest and juice of the lemon and stir. Add bananas and coat well with sauce. Add rum and light. Stir until well-mixed. Serve. Makes 4 servings.

Whipped Shortbread

Trudy S. Simmons, Twillingate, Newfoundland

Ingredients:
1 lb soft butter
1 cup icing sugar
1/2 cup cornstarch
3 cups flour
1 tsp vanilla

TRIVIA TIDBITS
During the reign of Emperor Tiberius of Rome, twelve elephants were clothed like men and women and trained to perform a dance.

Directions:
Beat all ingredients together until creamed. Drop from spoon unto cookie sheet. Bake 12-15 minutes in 350°F oven.

Sex-In-A-Pan

Phyllis Labelle, Lynden, Ontario, (nee Hollett, Arnold's Cove, Newfoundland)

Ingredients:
1 cup chopped pecans
1/4 cup icing sugar
1 cup flour
1/2 cup melted margarine
Mix above ingredients together and press into 9x9-inch dish. Bake at 350°F for 15 minutes. Let cool.

Filling:
8oz Philadelphia cream cheese
1 cup sugar
1 cup cool whip
Spread on bottom layer

Topping:
1 large pkg Instant Chocolate Pudding

FOOD FOR THOUGHT
Doing a thing from mere sense of duty is like eating when you are not hungry.

Sweets & Treats
Pies, Pastries, Cakes, Cookies, Candies, Etc.

1 large pkg Instant Vanilla Pudding
Shaved chocolate
Mix and add 3 cups of milk. Beat and spread on filling. Let set overnight.

Rhubarb Squares

Phyllis Labelle, Lynden, Ontario, (nee Hollett, Arnold's Cove, Newfoundland)
Ingredients:
Base:
1 cup flour
1/2 cup butter
1 tbsp sugar
Filling:
2 & 1/2 cups rhubarb
1 & 1/4 cups sugar
2 tbsp flour
3 egg yolks
dash of salt

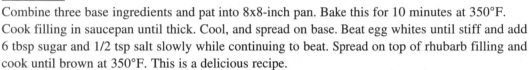

TRIVIA TIDBITS
A medieval monk was once expelled from an English monastery for deliberately giving pilgrims the wrong directions.

Directions:
Combine three base ingredients and pat into 8x8-inch pan. Bake this for 10 minutes at 350°F. Cook filling in saucepan until thick. Cool, and spread on base. Beat egg whites until stiff and add 6 tbsp sugar and 1/2 tsp salt slowly while continuing to beat. Spread on top of rhubarb filling and cook until brown at 350°F. This is a delicious recipe.

Pina Colada Cake

Hilda Reid, Ignace, Ontario, (nee Harnum, Bishop's Falls, Newfoundland)
Ingredients:
1 white cake mix
1 pkg instant vanilla pudding
4 eggs
1 cup flaked coconut
3/4 cup water
1/3 cup dark rum
1/4 cup oil

TRIVIA TIDBITS
The famous American gunslinger Bat Masterson, is buried in the "Primrose" section of Woodlawn Cemetery in the Bronx.

Directions:
Beat 4 minutes, pour into 2 (9-inch square) pans. Bake 350°F for 25-30 minutes.
Frosting:
1 can crushed pineapple and juice
1 pkg instant coconut cream pudding
1/3 cup dark rum
2 (9oz) cool whip

SPICE OF LIFE
If you think old soldiers fade away, you should watch one trying to get into an old uniform.

Directions:
Combine pineapple, juice, rum and pudding mix and mix well. Whip cool whip and mix with these ingredients. Ice cake.

Eggnog Tarts

Hilda Reid, Ignace, Ontario, (nee Harnum, Bishop's Falls, Newfoundland)

Ingredients:

1 - 4-serving size pkg vanilla pudding
1 envelope unflavoured gelatin
dash ground nutmeg
3 cups eggnog
1/4 cup light rum
1/2 cup whipping cream-whipped
12 baked tart shells

> **SPICE OF LIFE**
> We all better endeavour to put our best foot forward when we haven't a leg to stand on.

Directions:

In saucepan combine pudding mix, gelatin and nutmeg. Add eggnog. Cook according to package directions. Remove from heat, stir in rum. Chill until partially set. Turn into large mixer bowl; beat with electric mixer until fluffy. Fold in whipped cream. Chill until mixture mounds. Pile into tart shells.

Sherry Pie

Elizabeth (Bish) Clarke, North Sydney, Nova Scotia, (nee Keough)

Ingredients:

1/4 cup brown sugar
1 cup flour
1/2 cup butter
1/2 cup pecans (crushed)

> **FOOD FOR THOUGHT**
> You'll never have a better tomorrow as long as you are worrying about yesterday all the time.

Directions:

Mix together and bake in 375°F oven, stirring twice during baking time. Remove from oven, shape crust in a 9-inch pie plate. Reserve 1/4 cup of the pecans for the top of the pie. Let cool. In double boiler put 1/2 cup sherry and 1/2 lb marshmallows. Cook until marshmallows are completely melted. Remove from stove, cool. In a separate bowl, add 1/2 pint of whipping cream. Whip until firm. Add the sherry to the mixture. Mix well, pour into pie crust. Add the remaining pecan crumbs to top of pie. Let cool for 6-8 hours before serving.

5 Minute Fudge

Alma Taylor, Mt. Moriah, Bay of Islands, Newfoundland, (nee LeDrew, Bell Island, Newfoundland)

Ingredients:

1 & 2/3 cups sugar
2/3 cup undiluted Carnation Milk
2 tbsp butter
1/2 tsp salt
2 cups Kraft miniature marshmallows
1 & 1/2 cups semi-sweet chocolate chips
1/2 cup chopped walnuts
1 tsp vanilla

> **TRIVIA TIDBITS**
> The famous biblical city Jericho, lies about five miles from the Dead Sea. Today, the site of the ancient city is covered in mud. Archaeologists have discovered that underneath Jericho, which at one time was surrounded by a 20-feet-high stone wall, are other buried cities. The oldest of these is believed to date back to 7,000 BC, making it one of the oldest cities on earth.

Directions:

In medium sized, heavy saucepan, combine sugar, milk, butter and salt. Cook, stirring over medium heat, until mixture comes to a boil. Boil 4 to 5 minutes, stirring constantly; remove from

Sweets & Treats

Pies, Pastries, Cakes, Cookies, Candies, Etc.

heat. Stir vigorously until marshmallows melt and blend. Pour into foil-lined 8-inch square cake pan. Chill, cut into squares. Store in refrigerator.

Butter Tart Squares

Ruth Keats, Mississauga, Ontario

Ingredients:

2 tbsp sugar

1 & 1/2 cups flour

1/4 cup margarine

2 eggs

1 & 1/2 cups brown sugar

1 tbsp vinegar

1/4 cup margarine

1 cup raisins

1 tsp flour

TRIVIA TIDBITS

Spain got its name from the Carthaginians in the sixth century. They called it Sapnia, which in their language meant, 'land of rabbits'.

Directions:

In a medium bowl, combine sugar and flour. Cut in 1/4 cup margarine. Press into 9-inch square pan. Bake at 350°F for 10 minutes. Combine remaining ingredients. Pour over baked base. Return to oven. Bake 25-30 minutes. Cool and cut into squares. Makes 9-16 squares. (252 calories per square)

Fresh Raspberry Pie

Charlene Jenkins, Etobicoke, Ontario, (formerly of Springdale, Newfoundland)

Ingredients:

Crust:

2 cups all-purpose flour

1 tsp salt

2/3 cup shortening

2 tbsp butter or margarine

4 tbsp water

Filling:

4 heaping cups fresh raspberries

2/3 cup granulated sugar

1/4 cup all-purpose flour

2 tbsp butter, cut into small pieces

TRIVIA TIDBITS

In 1803 an Australian husband traded his wife for six bushels of wheat and a large pig.

Directions:

Sift together flour and salt. Cut in shortening and butter until small granules form. Add water. Mix gently until mixture forms a ball. Chill for 15 minutes. Roll out half of the pie dough to fit a 9-inch pie dish. Line plate and crimp edges. Refrigerate while making filling. Rinse raspberries quickly and dry gently. Mix the berries with the sugar and flour. Spoon into pie crust. Top with butter. Refrigerate while making the lattice crust. Roll out remaining pie dough. Cut into 1/2-inch strips. Weave the strips over the pie. Press into crimped edges. Bake pie at 400°F for about 40 minutes. Let cool on rack.

Country Squares

Rachel Hallett, Cambridge, Nova Scotia

SPICE OF LIFE
The fastest method of getting folks to start talking about their kids is to begin talking about yours.

Ingredients:

1 cup cocoa

1 cup hot water

3/4 cup butter or margarine

2 eggs (beaten)

2 cups white sugar

2 & 1/2 cups flour

1 tsp vanilla

1/2 cup milk

1 tsp baking soda

1/2 tsp salt

1 cup chopped pecans

1 cup peanut butter

1 pkg miniature marshmallows

12oz pkg chocolate chips

3 cups Rice Krispies

TRIVIA TIDBITS
Rhubarb was introduced to Europe from China by Marco Polo.

Directions:

Mix together cocoa, hot water, and butter (cool). Sift together dry ingredients and add alternately to above mixture with eggs and milk. Fold in nuts. Spread on greased cookie sheet. Bake 375°F for 20 minutes. Next, spread marshmallows over top of baked cake. Return to oven until melted, then cool. Melt peanut butter and chips together in double boiler. Stir in Rice Krispies and spread over cake. Cool and cut in squares.

What-Is-It-Holiday Bars

Hilda Reid, Ignace, Ontario, (nee Harnum, Bishop's Falls, Newfoundland)

Ingredients:

1/2 cup butter or margarine, softened

5 tbsp sugar

1 egg (well beaten)

1 tsp vanilla

2 & 1/2 cups graham wafer crumbs

1 cup dessicated coconut

1 cup chopped walnuts

1/2 cup cut-up maraschino cherries

TRIVIA TIDBITS
An Australian once bought a wife for £5 cash and a gallon of rum.

Directions:

Combine butter or margarine, sugar, egg and vanilla in bowl. Set over warm water. Stir until custard-like consistency. Mix wafer crumbs, nuts, coconut and cherries and add to mixture. Pack into ungreased 9-inch pan. Chill until set, then ice with lemon-licorice icing *(shown in "Enhancers" section, page 220)*. When icing is firm, cut into squares. A different flavoured bar!

Sweets & Treats

Pies, Pastries, Cakes, Cookies, Candies, Etc.

Sweets & Treats
Pies, Pastries, Cakes, Cookies, Candies, Etc.

Ambrosia Dessert Squares

Hilda Reid, Ignace, Ontario, (nee Harnum, Bishop's Falls, Newfoundland)

Ingredients:

1 & 1/2 cups graham wafer crumbs
1/2 cup butter or margarine, melted
1 pkg (6-serving size) jello vanilla pudding (pie filling mix, not instant)
1 pkg (250g) cream cheese, softened
2 medium bananas
1 can (10oz) mandarin oranges, drained
2 envelopes Dream Whip

Directions:

Heat oven to 350°F. Mix graham crumbs and butter. Press firmly into bottom 13x9-inch pan. Bake for 5 minutes, cool. Prepare pudding & pie filling mix according to package directions. Beat cream cheese into hot filling. Cover with plastic wrap and chill 40 minutes. Slice the bananas over crumb crust. Stir pudding and fold in oranges, then spoon over bananas. Spread whipped topping over filling. Chill 3 hours. Cut in squares.

"Death by Chocolate" Truffle Cake

Brenda Keyes, Durham, Ontario, (nee LeDrew, Pasadena and Corner Brook, Newfoundland)

Ingredients:

4 eggs
1 lb semi-sweet chocolate
1 tsp flour
1/2 tsp sugar
line spring form pan
1/2 cup unsalted butter

TRIVIA TIDBITS
In Puritan, England, it was illegal, even for married couples, to kiss on Sunday.

Directions:

Melt chocolate. Melt butter. Blend the two together. Beat eggs (room temp) and fold eggs into cooled mixture of chocolate and butter. Add the small amounts of flour and sugar and mix. Bake in pre-heated 400 degree oven for only 15 minutes. Cool immediately in fridge overnight. Serve the small, very rich, slices with cream: Fresh (sour cream and whipped cream) or with my favourite, a serving of thawed and mashed raspberries (unsweetened).

Strawberry Rhubarb Cobbler

Ruby Matthews, Mississauga, Ontario, (nee Coates, Botwood, Newfoundland)

Ingredients:

Filling:
3/4 cup granulated sugar
2 & 1/2 tbsp cornstarch
1/8 tsp cinnamon
1/3 cup cranberry juice cocktail
1/8 tsp finely grated lemon rind
2 & 2/3 cups diced rhubarb
1 & 1/2 cups halved fresh strawberries

SPICE OF LIFE
It is against the law to send threatening letters through the mail unless it's Revenue Canada doing it.

1/2 tsp butter
Topping:
1 & 1/3 cup all-purpose flour
1 & 1/2 tbsp granulated sugar
1/2 tsp baking powder
1/4 tsp salt
2 tbsp butter (cut into small pieces)
1 tbsp canola oil
5 or 6 tbsp skim milk
2 tsp fresh lemon juice

FOOD FOR THOUGHT
If we saw ourselves as other folks see us, perhaps we might never speak to them again.

Directions:
Filling: In a 2-quart saucepan, stir together sugar, cornstarch and cinnamon. Slowly stir in cranberry juice and lemon rind. Add rhubarb, strawberries and butter. Heat 3 minutes or until liquid is bubbly and clear. Pour into 2-quart casserole. *Dough:* In a medium-size bowl, blend flour, sugar, baking powder and salt. Add butter and oil. Cut butter into mixture until it resembles coarse meal. Stir together milk and lemon juice. Add to flour mixture, mixing just until blended. Form into a ball, place between two sheets of waxed paper and press into a round, large enough to cover filling. Peel off one sheet of paper. Place dough waxed paper side up on filling. Lift off top sheet. Make a few slashes or vents on surface of dough. Bake in a 375°F oven 35 to 45 minutes or until top is nicely browned. Spoon into bowls, garnish with ice cream. Makes 6 servings. Cobbler may also be refrigerated for up to 3 days and reheated in a 300°F oven just before serving.

Boiled Fruit Cake

Mary Russell, Brooklyn, Newfoundland, (nee Ash, Come By Chance, Newfoundland)

Ingredients:
1 cup raisins
1 cup cherries, chopped in half
1 & 1/2 cups date, chopped
1 cup walnuts, chopped
2 & 1/4 cups brown sugar
2 tsp cinnamon
1 tsp cloves
1 tsp allspice
2 & 1/4 cups water
1 cup butter

SPICE OF LIFE
Most men who go out drinking leave fit as a fiddle, but come home tight as a drum.

Place above ingredients in sauce pan and boil for 5 minutes. Let cool.

Then add:
3 & 1/3 cups flour
2 tsp baking powder
2 tsp baking soda
3/4 tsp salt

FOOD FOR THOUGHT
It is a special person who can be thrifty without being stingy, and generous without being wasteful.

Directions:
Sift dry ingredients together and add to the cooled boiled mixture.
Put into a well-greased pan 2/3 full and bake 1 & 3/4 hours in 300°F oven.

Sweets & Treats

Pies, Pastries, Cakes, Cookies, Candies, Etc.

Sweets & Treats
Pies, Pastries, Cakes, Cookies, Candies, Etc.

Rum-Soaked Cake

Archie Ridout, Rexdale, Ontario, (formerly of Twillingate, Newfoundland)

Ingredients:

1 pkg active dry yeast
1/2 cup warm water (105° to 115°)
3/4 cup margarine
4 eggs, beaten
2 tbsp sugar
1/2 tsp salt
2 cups flour

Rum syrup:

1 cup water
1 cup sugar
1/2 lemon
1/4 tsp vanilla
1/4 cup rum

Directions:

In a bowl, dissolve the yeast in warm water. Stir in the margarine, eggs, sugar, salt and 1 cup flour. Beat until smooth. Stir in remaining flour and beat for 1 minute. Spread the batter into a well-greased 8-cup metal mold or greased muffin tins. Cover and let rise in a warm place for 50 to 60 minutes. Bake in a 375° oven for 25 to 30 minutes. Cool, drizzle with syrup until all syrup is absorbed. For syrup, heat all ingredients except rum to boiling then simmer for 2 minutes. Cool, stir in rum.

FOOD FOR THOUGHT
When you really want the last word in an argument, try saying, "I guess you are right."

SPICE OF LIFE
It's not hard to meet expenses - they're everywhere.

English Trifle

Ruth Keats, Mississauga, Ontario

Ingredients:

pound cake, broken in chunks
sherry
can of fruit, drained (your choice, reserve juice
jello, your choice of flavour
custard, prepare as directed on package
whipped cream
nuts
coconut
cherries

Directions:

Using a deep glass bowl,
place pound cake chunks,
that have been soaked in sherry, in the bottom of this dish. Place a layer of canned, drained fruit, keeping the juice for the jello. Make jello, replacing cold water with juice. Pour over mixture in the bowl before set. Mix up custard fairly thick. Cool a little and lift the skin off. Pour over the mixture and let set in fridge. Add whipped cream and refrigerate. Decorate with nuts, coconut, cherries, etc.

TRIVIA TIDBITS
Gerard de Nerval, a nineteenth century French poet, often walked the streets of Paris with a pet lobster attached to a leash.

Lemon Moments

Hilda Reid, Ignace, Ontario, (nee Harnum, Bishop's Falls, Newfoundland)

Ingredients:

1/2 cup butter
1/2 cup white sugar
1 egg
1/2 cup flour
1/4 tsp baking powder
1 can condensed milk
juice of 2 lemons
2 egg whites
1/2 cup white sugar
1/2 tsp lemon juice
1/2 cup coconut

TRIVIA TIDBITS
Pepper was so valuable in medieval Europe that there are known cases where men traded their wives for it.

Directions:

Base: Cream butter & sugar. Add egg, flour and baking powder. Spread in 8x8-inch pan. Bake for 25 minutes at 350°F. **Filling:** Blend condensed milk and juice of 2 lemons with mixer for 5 minutes and spread on base. **Topping:** Beat 2 egg whites until stiff, add sugar. Fold in coconut and lemon juice. Spread on filling and bake 10 minutes at 400°F.

Lazy Day Cake

Charlene Jenkins, Etobicoke, Ontario, (formerly of Springdale, Newfoundland)

Ingredients:

3 eggs
1 & 1/2 cups granulated sugar
1 & 1/2 tsp vanilla extract
1 & 1/2 cups all-purpose flour
1/4 tsp salt
1 & 1/2 tsp baking powder
3/4 cup milk
1 & 1/2 tbsp butter

Sauce:

1 pkg (6oz) frozen strawberries
3/4 cup water
2 tbsp granulated sugar
2 tsp cornstarch

SPICE OF LIFE
A toupee is a top secret.

Directions:

In your electric mixer, beat the eggs until light. Beat in the sugar until light and thick. Add the vanilla. Combine the salt and baking powder and mix with the flour. Heat the milk and butter just until it starts to boil. Add the dry ingredients to the egg mixture alternately with the hot milk. Stir just to mix. Turn into a greased 9-inch square baking pan. Bake at 350°F for 30 minutes or until the cake springs back, when pressed lightly in the center. For the sauce, bring the water and the sugar to a boil in a small sauce pan. Add the strawberries. Dissolve cornstarch in a little water. Add to the sauce. Bring to a boil. Boil for 1 minute. Remove from heat. Serve a piece of warm cake covered with the strawberry sauce.

Peach and Cream Cheese Pie

Charlene Jenkins, Etobicoke, Ontario, (formerly of Springdale, Newfoundland)

Ingredients:
1 & 1/3 cups graham cracker crumbs (7-8 whole crackers, crushed)
1 tsp ground cinnamon
1/4 cup brown sugar, packed
1/4 cup butter, or margarine
1 can (29oz) cling-free peach halves
1 pkg (8oz) cream cheese
1/2 cup granulated sugar
1/2 tsp vanilla
1/2 cup sliced blanched almonds
peach slices, optional

> ### TRIVIA TIDBITS
> Windsor Castle, the official home of the Queen of England, is more than a third of a mile long and is 540 feet wide, making it the largest inhabited castle in the world. It is situated on 23 acres of land.

Directions:
In a small bowl, stir together cracker crumbs, cinnamon and brown sugar. Melt butter and add to crumbs. Mix. Pour crumb mixture into a 9-inch pie plate. Press firmly to pack in an even layer over bottom and up sides of pans. Bake at 350°F for 15 minutes. Cool. Lift peach halves from juices (reserve juices). Drain. Arrange, cut sides down, in pie crust. In a small bowl, beat together until fluffy the cream cheese, sugar, vanilla, and 1/4 cup of the peach juices. Spoon evenly over peach halves. Sprinkle almonds over top. Bake at 350°F for 35 to 40 minutes. Let cool at least 30 minutes or refrigerate to serve chilled. Garnish with extra peach slices, if desired. Cut in wedges to serve.

> ### TRIVIA TIDBITS
> Dr. Matthew Parker, who was Chaplain to King Henry VIII at the time of his marriage to Anne Boleyn, was so inquisitive and pried so much into the affairs of the couple, that he earned himself the unofficial title of, 'Nosey Parker'. The title stands to this day.

Dedicated to the memory of Fred Cooper, of Twillingate, Newfoundland, our dear husband, father, and grandfather, who passed away on September 29, 1996, age 61.
Wife - Hilda; Daughters - Violet, Linda and Michelle;
Grandchildren - Crystal, Paige, Brock, Carly and Joshua.

Sweets & Treats
Pies, Pastries, Cakes, Cookies, Candies. Etc.

Beverages

Alcoholic

&

Non-Alcoholic

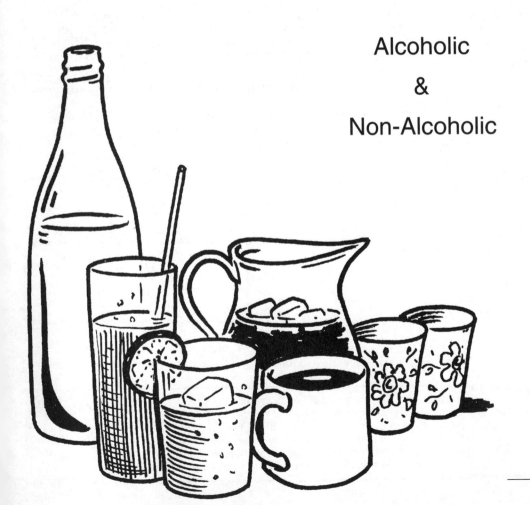

Slush Plus

Barbara Parsons, Sudbury, Ontario (nee O'Quinn, New Waterford, Nova Scotia)

Ingredients:

1 - 48oz can pineapple juice
1 - 16oz frozen orange juice
1 - 16oz frozen lemonade
1 - 26oz Vodka (or Rum)
2 cups strong tea (or coffee)
7-Up, Sprite or Coke

TRIVIA TIDBITS
Hollywood voted Rin Tin Tin,
'The Most Popular Film Performer
of the Year for 1926'.

Directions:

Combine pineapple juice, orange juice, lemonade, tea and Vodka together. Place in deep freezer. When ready to serve, put 2 scoops in glass and fill with your choice of 7-Up, Sprite or Coke.

Dogberry Wine

Julie Irene Pierog, Edson, Alberta, (formerly of Burin, Newfoundland)

Ingredients:

4 cups dogberries
16 cups boiling water
8 cups sugar
2 lemons
2 oranges
1 pkg yeast

SPICE OF LIFE
The problem with so many
marriages is that what starts
out as puppy love often goes
to the dogs.

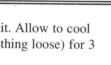

Directions:

Put berries in a large container, add boiling water, then sugar and sliced fruit. Allow to cool before adding yeast. Stir thoroughly. Let sit uncovered (or cover with something loose) for 3 weeks. May need to strain several times before bottling.

Slush

Barbara Parsons, Sudbury, Ontario (nee O'Quinn, New Waterford, Nova Scotia)

Ingredients:

1 - 10oz can frozen orange juice
1 - 10oz can frozen lemonade
2 cups Vodka
2 cups water
1 tbsp brown sugar
7-Up, Sprite or Coke

FOOD FOR THOUGHT
If you have not figured out where
you're going, you will be lost even
before you start.

Directions:

Combine orange juice, lemonade, Vodka, water and brown sugar and stir well. Put in freezer. When ready to serve, put 2 scoops in glass and top with your choice of 7-Up, Sprite or Coke.

This page is dedicated to my dear grandmother
Jessie Irene Brushett (Nan), who passed away on April 7, 1995.
She lived in Burin, Newfoundland all her life. Nan was more special
to me than words can ever say and I am thankful that I have
thirty years of treasured memories to remember her by.
Julie Irene Pierog, Edson Alberta, formerly of Burin, Newfoundland

Beverages
Alcoholic and Non-Alcoholic

Newfoundland Blueberry Wine

Mrs. Marie Whitehorne, Pasadena, Newfoundland, (nee Kendall, Ramea, Newfoundland)

Ingredients:

2 quarts blueberries

4 quarts boiling water

6 cups sugar

3 cups prunes

cheese cloth

bottles

corks

crock or jar

TRIVIA TIDBITS
Anne Boleyn, one of Henry VIII's wives, had six fingers (including her thumb) on her right hand.

Directions:

To 2 quarts of blueberries add 4 quarts of boiling water. Let simmer until it begins to boil. Strain and add 6 cups sugar to each gallon of juice. Boil 5 minutes. When cool add 3 cups prunes. Put in a crock or jar. Cover with cheese cloth and let stand 2 months. Strain, bottle and cork. (The wine is strong and will keep from year to year.)

Irish Cream Liqueur #1

Betina Wheeler-Ali, Toronto, Ontario (formerly of St. John's, Newfoundland)

Ingredients:

13oz whisky

4 eggs

10 & 1/2oz sweetened condensed milk

coconut flavouring (or 1 tsp finely shredded coconut)

3 tbsp liquid chocolate (i.e. milkmate)

1 sm container whipping cream

FOOD FOR THOUGHT
Beware of the person who knows too much, especially if he or she happens to be yourself.

Directions:

Blend eggs and sweetened condensed milk in a blender for 2 minutes. Add the remaining ingredients and blend for another 2 minutes.

Irish Cream Liqueur #2

Jenny & Josie, Richmond Hill, Ontario (nee Clarke, Port Rexton, Newfoundland)

Ingredients:

1 can sweetened condensed milk

1 - 1 & 1/2 cups Irish Whisky or Rye

1 cup table cream

3 eggs

1 tbsp milk-mate chocolate syrup

1/4 tsp coconut extract

SPICE OF LIFE
The best exercise for losing weight is pushing yourself away from the table.

Directions:

Mix all ingredients together in a blender until smooth. Keep refrigerated and shake before pouring. Store in refrigerator up to one month.

Beverages
Alcoholic and Non-Alcoholic

JJ's Cream De Menthe

Jenny & Josie, Richmond Hill, Ontario (nee Clarke, Port Rexton, Newfoundland)

Ingredients:

simmer 8 cups water

6 cups white sugar

Add 1 pint (2 cups) of Vodka

3 tbsp peppermint extract

green food colouring

Combine all ingredients and store in refrigerator.

> **TRIVIA TIDBITS**
> Cleopatra of Egypt, had the floors of her royal apartments covered in an eighteen-inch layer of red rose petals for her first meeting with Mark Anthony.

Dutch Liqueur

Jenny & Josie, Richmond Hill, Ontario (nee Clarke, Port Rexton, Newfoundland)

Ingredients:

3 & 1/2 cups water

1 & 1/2 cups sugar

1 & 1/2 cups brown sugar

1 - 26oz Vodka

1oz almond extract

> **SPICE OF LIFE**
> Perfume manufacturers are people who stick their business in other people's noses.

Directions:

Put water and both sugars in a pot and simmer on low for 20 minutes. Cool and add Vodka and almond extract. Mix well and bottle.

Coffee-Chocolate Liqueur

Jenny & Josie, Richmond Hill, Ontario (nee Clarke, Port Rexton, Newfoundland)

Ingredients:

10 & 1/2 cups water

4 cups sugar

2oz vanilla (or vanilla bean)

3 tbsp instant coffee

26oz Vodka

> **SPICE OF LIFE**
> A child is someone who knows all the questions at age eight, and all the answers at age eighteen.

Directions:

Boil water, sugar and vanilla for 30 minutes. Dissolve instant coffee in a 1/2 cup of boiling water and add to the pot. Cool and add Vodka.

Passion Punch

Jenny & Josie, Richmond Hill, Ontario (nee Clarke, Port Rexton, Newfoundland)

Ingredients:

1-2 bottles Ginger Ale

1-2 bottles Hawaiian Punch

1 pkg frozen strawberries or raspberries

1 sherbert (any flavour)

Vodka or Rum

> **FOOD FOR THOUGHT**
> Crime should not be cured in the electric chair. It should be cured in the high chair.

Directions:

Mix all ingredients together and bottle.

Beverages
Alcoholic and Non-Alcoholic

Chocolate Mint Liqueur

Ingredients:
1 (300ml) can sweetened condensed milk
1 cup (250ml) milk
1/2 cup (125ml) creme de cacao
1/2 cup (125ml) creme de menthe
1/2 cup (125ml) alcohol
1/4 cup (50ml) chocolate syrup
1 tsp (5ml) vanilla
2 tsp (10ml) peppermint flavouring

Directions:
Mix all ingredients together in a blender until smooth. Keep refrigerated and shake before pouring. Store refrigerated for up to one week. Makes approximately 4 cups (1L).

SPICE OF LIFE

You know old age is catching up with you when your knees buckle but your belt doesn't!

Winnie's Slush

Winnie Oberderfer, Okanagan Falls, British Columbia, (nee Parsons, Halifax, Nova Scotia)

Ingredients:
26oz vodka
1 large can unsweetened pineapple juice
1 can frozen orange juice
4oz lemon juice
3 cups sugar
8 cups water
gingerale or 7up (diet or regular)

FOOD FOR THOUGHT
Parents who always give their children nothing but the best can actually end up having nothing but the worst.

Directions:
Add all ingredients together, mixing well. Put all ingredients in a 4-litre plastic ice cream container. Place container in freezer and stir every 8 hours for 2 days. Spoon 2-4 tbsp into a tall glass and top with your choice of soft drink. **NOTE:** Leave in freezer; spoon out desired amount. Will keep indefinitely.

Rum Cream Liqueur

Ingredients:
1 can (300ml) sweetened condensed milk
1 & 1/2 cups (375ml) rum
1 cup (250ml) table cream
2 eggs
2 tbsp (25ml) chocolate syrup
2 tsp (10ml) vanilla

TRIVIA TIDBITS
When King George II's horse bolted during the early stages of the battle of Deltingen, Bavaria, in 1743, the King fought the remainder of the battle on foot at the head of his troops. He was the last British king known to fight a battle on foot.

Directions:
Mix all ingredients together in a blender until smooth. Keep refrigerated and shake before pouring. Store refrigerated for up to one week. Makes approximately 4 cups (1L).

Beverages
Alcoholic and Non-Alcoholic

Coffee Liqueur #1

Charley Alford, Toronto, Ontario

Ingredients:

3 cups white sugar
2 cups water
2 tbsp vanilla
6 tbsp instant coffee
26oz bottle Vodka
9 tbsp glycerine

Directions:

Boil sugar and water exactly 3 & 1/2 minutes.
Remove and let cool. In a measuring cup, mix vanilla and instant coffee. When sugar and water mixture is cooled, add vanilla and coffee mixture, then add LCBO alcohol. Add glycerine to thicken. Stir well and bottle. Makes 58 ounces.

TRIVIA TIDBITS
The Great Wall of China is the only man-made structure which can be seen from outer space (through a telescope, of course) The wall was built in 221 BC by a Chinese Emperor to keep his enemies out. It didn't work.

Coffee Liqueur #2

Charley Alford, Toronto, Ontario

Ingredients:

2 & 1/2 cups white sugar
2 tsp instant coffee
1 tsp vanilla
1 & 1/2 cups cold water
26oz bottle Vodka
9 tbsp glycerine

Directions:

Boil and simmer water, sugar, coffee and vanilla for five minutes. Cool completely. Add alcohol; add glycerine to thicken. Ready to bottle.

SPICE OF LIFE
Perhaps the very best way for folks to save face is to keep the lower half of it shut.

Prairie Dream

Ingredients:

2oz rye
2oz ginger ale
2oz Whisky Sour Mix, or 1 individual envelope Whisky Sour mix dissolved in 2oz water.

Directions:

Pour ingredients over ice. Stir. Garnish with lemon wedge.

FOOD FOR THOUGHT
Being an intelligent and fair politician wins the votes of thinking people. Unfortunately, election requires a majority.

Stage Coach

Ingredients:

1oz rye
1oz coffee liqueur

Directions:

Pour rye over ice in a "rocks" glass. Add coffee liqueur. Stir.

SPICE OF LIFE
We might as well laugh at ourselves time and again - others do.

Beverages
Alcoholic and Non-Alcoholic

Pilgrim's Delight

Ingredients:
2oz rye
3oz cranberry juice
3oz ginger ale
Directions:
Add ingredients over ice in a tall glass. Garnish with a lemon slice.

> **FOOD FOR THOUGHT**
> Many great ideas are lost along the way because those who had them couldn't handle being laughed at.

Nine Yards

Ingredients:
2oz rye
1oz lemon juice
1 tsp sugar
Directions:
Add ingredients over ice in a cocktail shaker. Shake well. Pour into a glass. Garnish with maraschino cherry and orange slice.

> **TRIVIA TIDBITS**
> Haj Ahmel, who was once King of Algeria, had 385 wives. To avoid household problems, the King made sure that each of these wives came from different parts of the world so that they could not communicate with each other.

Hot Cow

Ingredients:
1oz rye
6oz hot coffee
4 tsp chopped milk chocolate, or 1 tsp chocolate drink syrup
Directions:
Pour rye into coffee mug. Add coffee and chocolate. Stir until dissolved. Garnish with whipped cream and grated chocolate.

> **FOOD FOR THOUGHT**
> Apple seeds can be counted, but not the apples in a seed.

Horse's Mane

Ingredients:
2oz rye
grapefruit juice
Directions:
Pour rye over ice. Top with grapefruit juice. Stir. Garnish with orange slice or twist.

> **TRIVIA TIDBITS**
> There have only been three left-handed monarchs on the English throne, James I, Queen Victoria and George VI.

Coffee Nog

Ingredients:
2 quarts eggnog, chilled
1/4 cup firmly packed brown sugar
2 tbsp instant coffee powder
1/4 tsp cinnamon
1/2 cup coffee liqueur, optional
1/2 cup bourbon or brandy, optional
1 cup whipping cream
1/4 cup confectioners' sugar
1 tsp vanilla

> **SPICE OF LIFE**
> Many a wicked man flee when no one pursueth, but he makes better time
> ?! when the cops are after him.

Beverages
Alcoholic and Non-Alcoholic

Beverages
Alcoholic and Non-Alcoholic

nutmeg
cinnamon sticks
Directions:
In a large bowl, combine eggnog, brown sugar, instant coffee, and cinnamon. Beat until sugar and coffee are dissolved. Stir in liqueur and bourbon, if desired. Chill. In a small bowl, combine cream, confectioners' sugar, and vanilla. Beat until stiff. Pour eggnog mixture into a punch bowl. Top with whipped cream. Sprinkle with nutmeg; serve with cinnamon sticks. Makes 10 servings.

Bay Robert's Root Beer

Ron Young, St. John's, Newfoundland, (formerly of Twillingate, Newfoundland)
Ingredients:
1oz Vodka
1/2oz Tia Maria
1/2oz Galiano
4oz Coke, Pepsi or Diet
Directions:
Add Vodka, Tia Maria and Galiano to 8 ounce glass containing ice cubes. Add Coke last and stir. (**NOTE:** finished product tastes like Root Beer)

> **SPICE OF LIFE**
> The fundamental reason for middle names is so you will be able to tell when you are in real trouble.

Ginger Beer

Vidya Bachon, Trinidad, West Indies
Ingredients:
3 lbs freshly dug ginger
3 litres boiled water, cooled
2 lbs sugar (or to taste)
Directions:
Clean the ginger and cut into small chunks. Grate the ginger. Or use a food processor to mince, using a little of the water. Put grated ginger and water into large glass jar and cover loosely. Store in a cool place for at least 24 (to 48) hours. Strain carefully and sweeten. Brown sugar gives it a dark colour. White sugar will give you a lighter coloured "beer". Bottle and refrigerate. If there is further sedimentation, pour off the ginger beer carefully. Serve over crushed ice.

> **TRIVIA TIDBITS**
> In some parts of Australia there are earthworms that measure 6 feet in length.

Pina Colada

Vidya Bachon, Trinidad, West Indies
Ingredients:
1 cup rum
1 & 1/2 cups coconut milk
1 & 1/2 cups pineapple juice
6 cups crushed ice
1/2 cup pineapple chunks
3oz heavy cream or evaporated milk
Directions:
Combine rum, coconut milk, cream, pineapple juice and chunks in a blender and blend. Add ice and process until ice is crushed. Serve in tall glasses with crushed ice and garnish.

> **FOOD FOR THOUGHT**
> Can modern youth be expected to be strong, courageous, and prepared to pay more taxes than their parents?

Calypso Drink

Vidya Bachon, Trinidad, West Indies

Ingredients:

1 tin grapefruit juice or 5 fresh, large grapefruits

1 pkg strawberry flavoured kool aid

1 tin calypso punch

1 cup sugar

ice for cooling

3-4 cups water

Directions:

Mix all ingredients, taste, then add ice. Serves 6 persons. Serve as cold as possible.

Slush #2

Mary Russell, Brooklyn, Newfoundland (nee Ash, Come By Chance, Newfoundland)

Ingredients:

2 cups sugar

8 cups water

48oz tin unsweetened pineapple juice

1/4 cup lemon juice

1 tin frozen orange juice

2 well-mashed bananas

Directions:

Boil water and sugar together for 15 minutes. Let cool. Add the remaining ingredients and mix well. Put in freezer. To serve - put two scoops of slush in a glass and add ginger ale, maraschino cherries and a straw.

Spruce Beer

Rose Shannon, Downsview, Ontario, (nee Carberry, Burgoyne's Cove, Newfoundland)

Ingredients:

Black spruce boughs from young trees

water

5 lbs sugar

1 qt molasses

1/4 tsp yeast

Directions:

Break up spruce boughs and fill a 5 gallon pot (20-litre). Cover with water and boil for 1 hour or until rind peels easily - pour water into a 15 gallon container (60-litre). Do not strain bits of needles, etc. Add lukewarm water to total 10-12 gallons (pour first couple of gallons over boughs to get all substance); add sugar and molasses, stirring until dissolved. Sprinkle yeast on top; do not stir. Let stand in warm place for about 3 hours, skimming off foam if desired. Strain through gauze cloth, bottle and cap. Let stand in a warm place for 1 day, then store in fridge or cooler.
NOTE: Keep bottled beer cold or they could explode.

Beverages
Alcoholic and Non-Alcoholic

Rickey

Ingredients:
1 & 1/2oz mild Whisky
1 & 1/2oz Lime juice
club soda

Directions:
Combine the whisky and the lime juice; add ice; fill the glass with soda and stir. Touch it up with a twist of lime.

> **FOOD FOR THOUGHT**
> Proof that I am supposed to listen more than talk is one mouth and a pair of ears.

Super Summertime Slush

Stephanie Crummey, Western Bay, Newfoundland

Ingredients:
8 cups water
3 & 1/2 cups sugar
Boil these two ingredients; let cool. Add -
2 bananas, mashed
4 bottles lemonade (or 40oz lemonmade from frozen concentrate)
48oz can pineapple juice
26oz bottle vodka

Directions:
Mix all together. Store in freezer. For a super summertime drink, fill a tall glass 1/3 full of slush mixture; add gingerale or seven-up. Garnish with slices of orange or lemon.

> ***TRIVIA TIDBITS***
> An estimated one million, four hundred thousand people were killed due to earthquakes in China in the year 1976. The shock waves from one of the quakes were felt 3,500 miles away in Alaska.

Horse's Neck

Ingredients:
2 & 1/2oz mild whisky
1 lemon
ginger ale

Directions:
Carefully peel the lemon so that the peel turns out one long spiral strip. Pour out the mild whisky; drop in the spiral peel. Add ice and ginger ale. Squeeze in a few drops of the lemon's juice and gently stir.

> **FOOD FOR THOUGHT**
> The problem with most parents today is that they give their kids a free hand... but not in the right place.

Irish Cream Liqueur #3

Charlie Alford, Toronto, Ontario

Ingredients:
1 or 1 & 1/2 cups of rye
1 cup table cream
1 can sweetened condensed milk
3 eggs
1 tbsp chocolate syrup

Directions:
Mix all ingredients vigorously... *mix like hell!*

> **SPICE OF LIFE**
> While it's true that some women can attract men with their minds, more attract men with what they don't mind.

Eggnog

Charlie Alford, Toronto, Ontario

Ingredients

13oz "Paarl" brandy
1 - 26oz Vodka
36 egg yolks
1 lg can carnation milk
2 tsp vanilla extract
4 cups sugar

Directions:

Separate eggs. Beat yolks slightly (till broken and mixed). Add brandy slowly, still beating yolks; add alcohol very slowly, still stirring. Add remaining ingredients and mix well. Beat slowly for 1-2 minutes. Strain and bottle. Keep refrigerated. (Gets better with age!). Makes 2 - 40oz. bottles plus 6-8 ounces.

Charlie's Creme De Menthe

Charlie Alford, Toronto, Ontario

Ingredients:

1 sm bottle peppermint extract
2 & 1/2 cups white sugar
1 & 1/2 cups cold water
1 - 26oz bottle Vodka
green food colouring

Directions:

Boil and simmer for 5 minutes; cool completely. Add Vodka. Bottle 1/2 of batch for white creme de menthe. Add lots of green food colouring to the remaining for (green creme) de menthe.

Old-Fashioned

Rose Shannon, Downsview, Ontario (nee Carberry, Burgoyne's Cove, Newfoundland)

Ingredients:

1 & 1/4oz Newfoundland Screech
soda, cola, gingerale, or water
slice of lemon

Directions:

Pour Screech in glass; top off with soda, cola, ginger ale or water. Add a slice of lemon.

Newfie Nightcap

Rose Shannon, Downsview, Ontario (nee Carberry, Burgoyne's Cove, Newfoundland)

Ingredients:

1 & 1/4oz Newfoundland Screech
1-2 tsp brown sugar
coffee
whipped cream

Directions:

Pour Screech in glass; add brown sugar and coffee; stir. Top with whipped cream (stir into drink, if desired.

Beverages
Alcoholic and Non-Alcoholic

Muffled Screech

Rose Shannon, Downsview, Ontario (nee Carberry, Burgoyne's Cove, Trinity Bay, Newfoundland)

Ingredients:
1oz Newfoundland Screech
1/4oz Triple Sec
2oz cream or milk

> **FOOD FOR THOUGHT**
> It's better to sleep on something before doing it, than to do it wrong and stay awake worrying.

Newfie Bullet

Rose Shannon, Downsview, Ontario (nee Carberry, Burgoyne's Cove, Trinity Bay, Newfoundland)

Ingredients:
1oz Newfoundland Screech
1oz coffee liqueur
Directions:
Serve over ice chips.

> **SPICE OF LIFE**
> A good pickpocket can remove your wallet with the skill of a surgeon... though he won't make as much money.

French Connections

Rose Shannon, Downsview, Ontario (nee Carberry, Burgoyne's Cove, Trinity Bay, Newfoundland)

Ingredients:
1oz Newfoundland Screech
1oz Dubonnet
Directions:
Stir on ice; garnish with slice of lemon.

> **FOOD FOR THOUGHT**
> People can be eggheads, good eggs, bad eggs, or rotten eggs; and occasionally they can be pretty hard-boiled.

Come By Chance

Rose Shannon, Downsview, Ontario (nee Carberry, Burgoyne's Cove, Trinity Bay, Newfoundland)

Ingredients:
1oz Newfoundland Screech
1/4oz triple sec
4-6oz orange juice
Directions:
Garnish with a slice of orange or a cherry.

> **TRIVIA TIDBITS**
> A common sign outside eighteenth century gin shops would read; "Drunk for a penny, dead drunk for two pence".

Screech Parfait

Rose Shannon, Downsview, Ontario (nee Carberry, Burgoyne's Cove, Trinity Bay, Newfoundland)

Ingredients:
Vanilla Ice Cream
1/2oz Newfoundland Screech
Crushed walnuts
Directions:

> **FOOD FOR THOUGHT**
> Growing old is mandatory growing up is always optional.

Place two scoops of vanilla ice cream in individual serving dish. Pour 1/2 ounce of Screech over ice cream. Sprinkle with crushed walnuts.

Beverages *Alcoholic and Non-Alcoholic*

Ron's Coffee Liqueur

Ron Young, St. John's, Newfoundland (formerly of Twillingate, Newfoundland)

Ingredients:

3 cups sugar
4 tbsp instant coffee
1 tbsp chocolate syrup
4 tsp vanilla
4 cups water
25oz Vodka

SPICE OF LIFE
One guidance applies to fat and thin people alike: If you're thin, don't eat fast. If you're fat, don't eat ... fast.

Directions:

Mix water, sugar and coffee together and bring to a boil. Add chocolate syrup and simmer for 2 & 1/2 hours. Let cool and add alcohol. Age two weeks for best results.

Irish Cream Liqueur #4

Ron Young, St. John's, Newfoundland (formerly of Twillingate, Newfoundland)

Ingredients:

8 eggs
2 & 1/2 cups table cream
3 tbsap chocolate syrup
2 cups sugar
4 cups powdered skim milk
1/4 cup butter or margarine
1 cup water
25oz Vodka

TRIVIA TIDBITS
When it was announced in 1851, that a bathroom was to be installed in the White House in Washington, the announcement was met with vocal opposition. The protesting taxpayers of the day regarded it a needless expense.

Directions:

Add 1 cup boiled water to sugar, butter and powdered skim milk and beat until smooth. Add the other ingredients and beat again. Refrigerate and serve.

Banana-Pineapple Liqueur

Ron Young, St. John's, Newfoundland (formerly of Twillingate, Newfoundland)

Ingredients:

1 tsp pineapple extract
1 tsp anise extract
1 & 1/2 tsps banana extract
2 tsp vanilla extract
1 cup water
2 cups sugar
2 tsp yellow food colouring
25oz Vodka

TRIVIA TIDBITS
Napoleon Bonaparte, the fearless Emperor of France who came near to conquering the whole of Europe, was afraid of cats.

Directions:

Stir sugar into boiling water until dissolved. Let cool and add other ingredients. Let sit for two weeks for best results.

Beverages
Alcoholic and Non-Alcoholic

Summer Ale

Charlene Jenkins, Etobicoke, Ontario, (formerly of Springdale, Newfoundland)

Ingredients:
1 banana
1 cup orange juice
1 cup pineapple juice
1oz red syrup
1/2 cup ice cream
cherries, for garnish

FOOD FOR THOUGHT
You won't strike a spark of flame in another person's heart until it's a forest fire in your own.

Directions:
Blend all ingredients in blender for 30 seconds. Garnish with cherries.

Fruit Juice Punch

Charlene Jenkins, Etobicoke, Ontario, (formerly of Springdale, Newfoundland)

Ingredients:
2 bottles maraschino cherries & juice
2 qts unsweetened pineapple juice
2 qts unsweetened orange juice
6 oranges (washed & cut in whole & half slices)
6 cans gingerale

SPICE OF LIFE
A chauvinist is a man who believes he can marry any girl he pleases. Trouble is, he doesn't please any of them.

Directions:
Mix above ingredients (except gingerale) and let sit overnight in covered bucket. About half an hour before serving, add gingerale and ice cubes. Can also add a little grenadine for extra pink colour. NOTE: For larger crowd, double recipe.

Catherine Irwin's Blender Breakfast

Catherine Irwin, Truro, Nova Scotia

Ingredients:
1 ripe banana, peach or peeled/seeded orange
1/2 cup whole milk (or low fat plain yogurt)
1 tsp honey, sugar or maple syrup
1 tbsp natural bran

FOOD FOR THOUGHT
One individual with conviction can always do more than multitudes who only have interest.

Directions:
Combine banana, milk, honey and bran in blender or food processor. Whirl until smooth. Pour into tall glass. (Nutrient value per serving: 217 calories, 3g fat, 179 RE vitamin A, 11.5 mg vitamin C). *Breakfast... "Break the fast!" Why not have this meal in a glass! Only minutes to make and it is packed with nutrients. Makes 1 serving.*

This page is dedicated to my parents, Ford Tucker, formerly of Mansfield Point, Newfoundland and Madeline (nee MacDonald) formerly of Wood's Island, Newfoundland, who now live in North York, Ontario.
Roy Tucker, formerly of Maple Valley, Newfoundland

Beverages
Alcoholic and Non-Alcoholic

Christmas

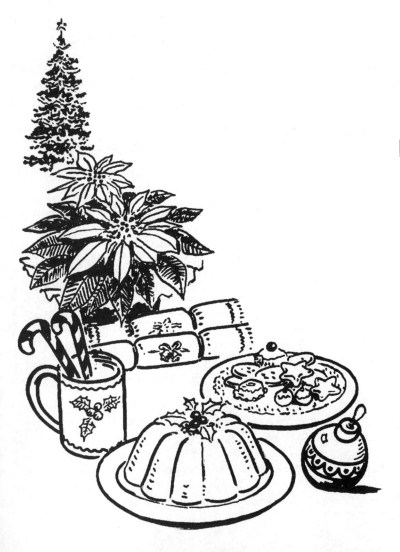

Recipes

that

suit the

season

Boiled Dark Fruit Cake

Winnie Marshall, Stephenville, Newfoundland (nee Abbott, Port Au Bras, Placentia Bay, Newfoundland)

Ingredients:

1 pkg raisins
1 pkg currants
1/2 lb dates
1/2 lb cherries
1/2 cup walnuts
1/2 cup mixed fruit
2 cups water
2 cups brown sugar
1 cup margarine
1 tsp cinnamon
1 tsp cloves
1 tsp allspice
1 tsp vanilla
3 cups flour
2 tsp baking soda

> ***TRIVIA TIDBITS***
> When a worker at a paper mill in Buckinghamshire, England, in the 1800s, forgot to add sizing materials to a vat of pulp which was being made into paper, it was discovered that the imperfect paper produced by that error readily absorbed ink, and ink-blotting paper was thus invented.

Directions:

Prepare and cut up fruit. Add all ingredients and place in a large pot. Simmer on top of stove for 10-15 minutes. Let cool. Add flour and baking soda. Mix well. Bake for 2 & 1/2 to 3 hours at 275°F.

Miniature Christmas Fruit Cake

Barbara Parsons, Sudbury, Ontario (nee O'Quinn, New Waterford, Nova Scotia)

Ingredients:

1/2 cup light molasses
1/4 cup water
1 tsp vanilla
1 - 15oz box raisins
1 lb candied fruit, chopped
1/2 cup butter or margarine
2/3 cup sugar
3 eggs
1 cup plus 2 tbsp all-purpose flour
1/4 tsp baking soda
1 tsp ground cinnamon
1 tsp ground nutmeg
1/4 tsp ground allspice
1/4 tsp ground cloves
1/4 cup milk
1 cup nuts

SPICE OF LIFE
Marriage may be compared to a cage; the birds are outside trying to get in and those inside are trying to get out.

Directions:

Use small paper cups (tiny). In saucepan combine molasses, water and vanilla. Add raisins and bring to a boil. Reduce heat and simmer for 5 minutes. Remove from heat and stir in fruit. Let cool. Meanwhile, in a mixing bowl cream butter and sugar. Add eggs one at a time, beating well

Christmas
Recipes that suit the season

after each addition. Stir together dry ingredients in another bowl. Add to cream mixture alternately with milk. Stir in fruit mixture from saucepan. Mix well and fold in nuts. Spoon into muffin tins lined with tiny paper cups. Bake 325°F for 25 minutes. Store in tight containers.

Christmas Jelly Delight

Ingredients:

1 cherry or strawberry Jello
1 lime Jello
1 pkg Dream Whip
1 banana
1 - 20oz can pineapple tidbits

Directions:

Red layer:

Dissolve 1 cherry Jello in 1 cup hot water. Add 3/4 cup of cold water. Chill until slightly thickened. Pour into 6-cup ring mold. Slice a banana and stand slices in thickened Jello. Chill until firm.

White layer:

Dissolve lime Jello in 1 cup hot water. Add 3/4 cup pineapple syrup. Chill 1/2 cup lime Jello. Prepare 1 packet Dream Whip. Fold Dream Whip into 1/2 cup chilled lime Jello. Pour over cherry Jello in mould. Chill.

Green layer:

Chill remaining lime Jello. Fold in one 20 ounce can drained pineapple tidbits. Pour over white layer. Chill until firm. Unmould. Centre of mould can be filled with other fruit.

> **FOOD FOR THOUGHT**
> Everyone is an unwitting fool for at least five minutes every day; wisdom consists of not exceeding the limit.

Christmas Refrigerator Cookies

Joan Simpson, Lindsay, Ontario, (nee Snow, Bell Island, Newfoundland)

Ingredients:

2 & 1/4 cups sifted flour
1 tsp baking powder
1/4 tsp salt
1/3 cup almonds or walnuts
1/2 cup red & green cherries
1/2 cup soft butter
1/2 cup soft shortening
1/2 tsp lemon extract
1/2 tsp vanilla
1/2 cup brown sugar
1/2 cup white sugar
2 eggs, well beaten

Directions:

Sift dry ingredients; add nuts and cherries; mix well. Cream butter and shortening until fluffy. Add flavourings. Gradually add sugar; mix until creamy. Add beaten eggs; add dry ingredients. Shape dough into rolls (chill if too soft to make rolls), 2 inches in diameter. Wrap in wax paper. Chill 8 hours in refrigerator. Slice and bake in moderate oven 8-10 minutes at 350°F or until light brown in colour.

> **TRIVIA TIDBITS**
> An early book on motoring in England suggested that women drivers should always carry a hand mirror in the tool chest for "repairing" their make-up after a drive.

Christmas
Recipes that suit the season

Christmas — Recipes that suit the season

Christmas Wreath Pie

Ingredients:

1/3 cup candied mixed peel
3 tbsp rum or sherry
1 pkg JELL-O vanilla pudding and pie filling (6-serving size)
1 cup whipping cream, whipped stiff
1 & 1/2 cups Kraft miniature marshmellows
9-inch baked pie shell, cooled
toasted sliced almonds
maraschino cherries with stems

Directions:

Combine candied peel and liqueur in small bowl; let stand. Prepare pudding mix as directed on package for pie, reducing milk to 2 & 1/2 cups. Drain liqueur from candied peel into pudding and stir. Reserve softened peel. Cover surface of pudding with plastic wrap. Chill 40 minutes, stirring occasionally. Stir cooled pudding well. Fold in 1 cup of the whipped cream and marshmallows. Spread into pie shell. Chill 3 hours. To create a Christmas wreath, decorate edge of pie with ring of remaining whipped cream. Sprinkle cream with reserved peel and toasted almonds. Place maraschino cherries in ring of cream. A wonderful ending to a Christmas dinner.

Fast 'N' Fabulous Fruitcake

Ingredients:

2 & 1/2 cups all-purpose flour
1 tsp baking soda
2 eggs, slightly beaten
1 jar mincemeat
1 can sweetened condensed milk
2 cups chopped mixed candied fruit
2 cups chopped red and green candied cherries
1 cup coarsely-chopped walnuts
whole candied cherries

Directions:

Preheat oven to 300°F. Grease two 9x5x3-inch loaf pans. Stir together flour and baking soda; set aside. In large bowl, combine eggs, mincemeat, sweetened condensed milk, chopped candied fruit and nuts. Add dry ingredients; mix well. Divide batter between prepared pans. Bake 1 hour and 20 to 25 minutes or until done. Cool 15 minutes. Turn out of pans ; cool completely. Garnish with candied cherries. Wrap well in foil. Store in refrigerator or freezer. Makes two loaves. (You may also use a 10-inch tube pan or bundt pan, baking 1 hour and 50 minutes or until done.).

Dedicated to our parents, **Vincent John Rodgers** and
Emily Phyllis (nee Legge) of Paradise, Newfoundand.
"Thank you for all your support over the years!"
Your sons, Gary, Bob and Wayne Rodgers

Raspberry Almond Christmas Wreaths

Ingredients:
1 pkg shortbread mix
1 cup ground almonds
1/2 cup butter or margarine, softened
1 tsp almond extract
3/4 cup raspberry jam
icing sugar
green and red icing to decorate, optional

Directions:
Combine first four ingredients. Mix according to package directions until well-blended. Roll out on lightly floured board 1/8-inch thick. Cut in 2-inch rounds and cut centres from half the cookies with a 1-inch round cutter. Place on baking sheets. Bake at 325°F for 8-12 minutes, or until very lightly golden around edge. Cool. Spread top of solid cookies with thin layer of jam. Place a cookie ring on top. Sift icing sugar lightly over cookies. Fill centres with more jam. Decorate with green holly leaves and red berries, if desired. These cookies add colour to your cookie tray!

Little Christmas Cookies

Ingredients:
1 cup butter
1/2 cup confectioners' sugar
1 tsp vanilla
1/8 tsp salt
1 cup cornstarch
1 cup sifted flour
decorator's frosting

Directions:
Preheat oven to 375°F. Grease cookie sheets. In a mixing bowl, cream butter; gradually blend in sugar. Blend in remaining ingredients. Chill several hours. On a floured surface, roll out dough to 1/2 inch thickness. Cut out with miniature cookie cutters or cut into small squares, rounds, bars and triangles. Place on cookie sheets. Bake 6-10 minutes. Small cookies will bake more quickly than larger ones. *(Frost with Decorator's Frosting shown in "Enhancer" section, page 213.)*

Spotted Cake - A Mummer's Delight!

Mrs. Audrey Janes, Hant's Harbour, Newfoundland -- submitted by Garry Cranford, St. John's, Newfoundland)

Ingredients:
1 cup butter
1 lb currants
1 lb raisins
1/2 lb mixed peel
2 cups sugar
2 cups water
1 cup walnuts
1/2 pkg cherries
1/2 pkg dates

Christmas
Recipes that suit the season

1 tsp cloves
1 tsp allspice
1 tsp cinnamon
1 tsp mace
1 tsp nutmeg
1 tsp baking powder
1 tsp baking soda
3 cups flour
3 eggs (if desired)

FOOD FOR THOUGHT
If your foot slips you may recover your balance, but if your tongue slips, you cannot recover your words.

Directions:

Boil the first 14 ingredients together, slowly, for 15 minutes. Cool. (Mrs. Janes does this in the evening to allow it to cool overnight, ready for the next day's baking). Add the baking powder, baking soda, flour and eggs. Bake for 2 hours in a slow oven 300-325°F.

Dark Fruit Cake

Joan Simpson, Lindsay, Ontario, (nee Snow, Bell Island, Newfoundland)

Ingredients:

2 3/4 cups raisins
1 & 1/2 cups water
1 & 1/2 cups brown sugar
1/4 cup margarine
1 tsp baking soda
2 eggs
Dry ingredients:
2 & 1/2 cups flour
1/2 tsp salt
1/2 tsp cloves
1/2 tsp allspice
1 cup cherries
1 tsp baking powder
1/2 tsp cinnamon
1 cup walnuts (optional)

TRIVIA TIDBITS
When the wife of the famous poet, Dante Rossetti died in 1862, the poet was so grieved by the loss of his love, that he decided to bury with her the only copy of one of his unpublished manuscripts of love sonnets. Later on, he had a change of heart and had her coffin dug up. He retrieved the sonnets and had them published.

Directions:

Wash, drain and boil raisins, water, brown sugar and margarine. Boil for 10 minutes. Chill, add soda and eggs and mix. Add dry ingredients and mix well. Bake at 275°F for 2 & 1/2 hours.

Christmas
Recipes that suit the season

Bottles & Jars

Jams

Jellies

&

Preserves

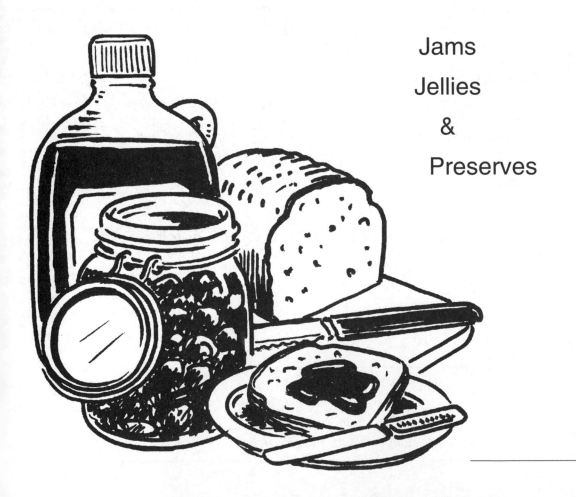

Gooseberry Jam

Mrs. Alma Taylor, Mt. Moriah, Bay of Islands, (nee LeDrew, Bell Island, Newfoundland)

Ingredients:
500ml gooseberries
1 pkg certo crystals
25ml water
2L sugar

FOOD FOR THOUGHT
A man who knows how will always find a place in life, but the man who knows why will always be his boss.

Directions:
Wash berries and remove tops and tails. Add water and certo crystals. Bring to a full rolling boil. Boil hard for 1 minute. Add sugar; bring to a full rolling boil again. Boil 1 minute. Remove from heat, stir and skim for 5 minutes. Pour into clean sterile jars and seal with hot wax.

Raspberry Jam

Mrs. Alma Taylor, Mt. Moriah, Bay of Islands, (nee LeDrew, Bell Island, Newfoundland)

Ingredients:
2L raspberries
250ml water
500ml sugar

FOOD FOR THOUGHT
A brat is a kid whose training didn't begin at the bottom...

Directions:
Combine berries and water and crush in a large pot. Add sugar and cook to jelly stage. Seal in clean sterile jars. Seal with hot paraffin wax.

Bakeapple Jam

Mrs. Alma Taylor, Mt. Moriah, Bay of Islands, (nee LeDrew, Bell Island, Newfoundland)

Ingredients:
500ml bakeapples
440ml sugar

Directions:
Wash and measure berries. Let sugar stand on berries overnight. Bring to a boil and cook slowly for 20 minutes. Seal in hot jars.

Anne's Mustard Pickles

Anne B. Penney, St. John's, Newfoundland

Ingredients:
2 lbs onions
3 large cucumbers
1/4 cup salt
2 & 1/2 cups white sugar

SPICE OF LIFE
Ever notice that the people who give you a piece of their minds are usually the ones who can least afford to?

This page is dedicated to our mother **Catherine Cleary** (nee Power), of Little Bay, Notre Dame Bay, Nfld.
From your children -
Phil, Clarence, Maggie (Hewlett), Mike and Mary (Dawe)

Bottles & Jars
Jams, Jellies & Preserves

2 tbsp dry mustard
1/2 cup water
1 large cauliflower
1 red pepper
1 quart white vinegar
1/2 cup cornstarch
2 tbsp tumeric powder

Directions:
Peel onions and cut in small pieces, separate cauliflower and cut into pieces (not too small), cut
unpeeled cucumber and red pepper. Place in a large pot and cover with cold water to which the
1/4 cup of salt has been added. Let stand overnight. The next day, boil the vegetables for 8 to 10
minutes in the same water they were soaked in, then drain. Heat vinegar and sugar in a medium
saucepan. Make a smooth paste with the cornstarch, mustard and tumeric powder. Add this to the
vinegar and sugar and boil until thick. Pour over the hot vegetables and stir together well. Pour
into bottles while still hot. Yield: 12 or more bottles. **NOTE:** These pickles are very similar to
the old-fashioned cabbage pickles.

Denise's Mustard Pickles

Mrs. Denise Brake, Penticton, British Columbia (nee Benoit, Stephenville, Newfoundland)

Ingredients:
2 lbs cabbage
2 lbs onions
1/3 cup salt
2 & 1/2 cups water
2 cups vinegar
1/2 cup flour (mix with water for thickening)
2 & 1/2 cups sugar
1 & 1/2 tbsp tumeric spice
6 tbsp dry mustard

SPICE OF LIFE
A sure sign of age
is when you admire
the dish your food
came in at the
restaurant, instead
of the dish who
brought it.

Directions:
Cut onion and cabbage in small cubes. Mix remaining ingredients in large bowl and pour over
vegetables. Pour mixture into large pot and boil for 20-25 minutes, stirring constantly. Remove
from heat and bottle in appropriate mason jars.

Pumpkin Pickles

Trudy S. Simmons, Twillingate, Newfoundland, (nee Forward, Tizzard's Harbour, Newfoundland)

Ingredients:
16 cups pumpkin
8 cups onion
2 cucumbers
1/2 cup salt, coarse
4 cups white vinegar
4-5 cups sugar
1 tsp celery seed
2 tsp mustard seed
1 & 1/2 tsp tumeric powder

2 tsp pickling spice
1/2 red pepper
1 head cauliflower

Directions:

Cover pumpkin, onions and salt with water and soak overnight. Drain and add vinegar, sugar, celery seed, tumeric powder and pickling spice. Bring to a boil. Add red pepper and cauliflower and cook until tender.

Uncooked Tomato Relish

Ruth Keats, Mississauga, Ontario

Ingredients:

6-quart basket of ripe tomatoes
7 onions
2 bunches of celery
3/4 cup pickling salt, coarse
5 cups white sugar
2 cups white vinegar
2 sweet red peppers, cut up
1 green pepper, cut up
3oz mustard seed
12 - 8oz jars
1 cheese cloth bag

SPICE OF LIFE
Love is something that evolves over the years: It goes from her sinking into his arms with joy to her arms in a sink with Joy.

Directions:

Peel tomatoes. Cut up and cover with salt. Hang in cheese cloth bag overnight. Throw away juice. Add sugar, vinegar, red peppers, green pepper and mustard seed. Let stand a day before putting in jars. Seal jars. Makes 12, 8oz jars.

Cucumber Pickles

Ingredients:

3 cucumbers
2 lb onions
2 lb cabbage
1/2 cup salt
4 cups sugar
1 cup flour
4 cups vinegar
6 tbsp dry mustard
1 tbsp tumeric

Directions:

Cut up cucumber, onions and cabbage. Add salt and cover with water. Bring to boil and boil for

(Sidebar, left margin:) **Bottles & Jars** — Jams, Jellies & Preserves

a few minutes. Drain. In a separate bowl mix sugar, flour, dry mustard and turmeric. Add vinegar and mix. Add this mixture to first ingredients and let simmer until tender. Put in jars.

Apple Relish

Davis Hull, Mississauga, Ontario, (formerly of Springdale, Newfoundland)

Ingredients:

1 lg can tomatoes
6 lg apples, sliced
6 lg onions, chopped
2 cups white sugar
2 tsp salt
1 tsp pepper
1 & 1/2 cups vinegar
2 tsp allspice

TRIVIA TIDBITS
Gangster Al Capone's business card described him as a "Second Hand Furniture Dealer".

Directions:

Mix all ingredients together and boil for about 3/4 to 1 hour. Ready for jars.

Tomato Pickles

Davis Hull, Mississauga, Ontario, (formerly of Springdale, Newfoundland)

Ingredients:

19oz can tomatoes
1 lb onions
2 lg apples
1 cup sugar
1 cup vinegar
1 tsp allspice
1 tsp salt

SPICE OF LIFE
A bore is a fellow talker who can change the subject to his topic of conversation faster than you can change it back to yours.

Directions:

Mix all ingredients together and boil until onions and apples are cooked. Ready for jars.

Pickled Mushrooms

Davis Hull, Mississauga, Ontario, (formerly of Springdale, Newfoundland)

Ingredients:

12oz cans whole mushrooms, reserve broth
1 cup cider vinegar
1 cup brown sugar
1 tbsp pickling spice

FOOD FOR THOUGHT
We can learn more from a wise man when he is wrong, than from a fool when he is right.

Directions:

Drain mushrooms; reserve broth. Combine vinegar, brown sugar and pickling spice. Bring to a boil; add mushroom broth and simmer for five minutes. Pour over mushrooms. Cover and refrigerate for 24 hours.

Bottles & Jars
Jams, Jellies & Preserves

Red Tomato Chow

Davis Hull, Mississauga, Ontario, (formerly of Springdale, Newfoundland)

Ingredients:

1 qt onions, diced
1 qt cucumbers, diced
salt
water
1 qt red tomatoes
3 cups sugar
2 cups vinegar
1 tbsp salt
1 tsp tumeric
1 red pepper
1 green pepper
1 tsp celery seed
1 tbsp dry mustard
1/2 cup flour

Directions:

Sprinkle salt over onions and cucumber; cover with water and let stand overnight. Drain and add tomatoes, sugar, vinegar, salt, tumeric, red and green peppers and celery seed. Boil until tender, approximately 1/2 hour. Thicken with dry mustard and flour. Place in jars and seal.

Ripe Tomato Relish

Neta Dove, Twillingate, Newfoundland, (nee Roberts)

Ingredients:

20 large, ripe tomatoes
4 onions
4 apples
2 red peppers
2 green peppers
1 head of celery
3 cups sugar
1 pt vinegar

Directions:

Chop fruit and vegetables fine. Mix in sugar and vinegar. Boil slowly for 1 hour. Bottle while hot.

> **TRIVIA TIDBITS**
> Lenin, the first communist dictator of Russia, although opposed to capitalism, owned a Rolls-Royce automobile that he had specially made to his specifications.

> **FOOD FOR THOUGHT**
> Many a person who believes the world owes him a living will find it's a mighty hard debt to collect.

To the **Schuetz Family**
(Gary Martin, Christine, Eric Robert, Kathy & Gerd)
Where all that is served is seasoned with love
With loving thoughts always...Helga

Bottles & Jars
Jams, Jellies & Preserves

Pickled Beets

Beulah Cooper, Gander, Newfoundland, (nee Collins, Corner Brook, Newfoundland)

Ingredients:
For each quart of beets, allow
1 & 1/2 cups brown sugar
1 tsp salt
3/4 cup vinegar
3/4 cup water in which beets were boiled

Directions:
Wash beets and cut top and bottom off. Boil until tender and peel them. Heat beets in above mixture until it boils. Fill hot sterilized jars.

> **FOOD FOR THOUGHT**
> Being a big success at the office will not be worth it if it means being a failure at home.

Green Tomato Pickles

Beulah Cooper, Gander, Newfoundland, (nee Collins, Corner Brook, Newfoundland)

Ingredients:
10 lb green tomatoes
3 medium cucumbers
3 green peppers
3 red peppers
1 cauliflower
5 lb onions
1 cabbage heart
1 cup salt
4 lb sugar
2 tbsp dry mustard
2 tbsp tumeric
4 cups vinegar
1 cup flour

Directions:
Cut vegetables in small pieces and soak overnight in salt. Drain off liquid and add 3 cups of the vinegar and the 4 lbs sugar. Boil for 30 minutes. Make a paste of flour, tumeric, dry mustard and remaining cup of vinegar and add to boiled mixture. Cool & bottle.

> **SPICE OF LIFE**
> A mother-in-law is someone who thinks the man who wasn't good enough to marry her daughter has fathered the brightest grandchild on earth.

Newfoundland Fruit Chutney

Elvie Genge, Glovertown, Newfoundland, (nee Feltham, Deer Island, Bonavista Bay, Newfoundland)

Ingredients:
2 large tins pineapple tidbits (unsweetened)
2 tins mandarin oranges
4 large apples, peeled and chopped
3 large oranges, peeled and chopped
4 clementines, peeled
1 large red pepper, chopped
1 medium green pepper, chopped
1 medium yellow pepper, chopped
2 lb onions, cut in small pieces

> **TRIVIA TIDBITS**
> The Chinese calendar is based on the movements of the moon, not the sun which causes the Chinese New Year to fall on a different day each year. The Chinese new year usually falls between January 21st and February 19th.

Bottles & Jars
Jams, Jellies & Preserves

3 cups white sugar (or to taste)
3 cups white vinegar (more or less)
Directions:
Boil all ingredients together over medium heat until done (about 1 hour), stirring often to prevent it from burning. Pour into hot, sterilized bottles and seal immediately. Best for eating after 2 weeks.

Rose Hip Jam

Ingredients:
2 lbs fresh rose hips
1 & 1/4 cups water
1 cup sugar (or more)
Directions:
Remove stems, seeds and blossom ends from rose hips. Wash quickly. Bring to a boil and simmer, covered, for about 1/2 hour or less, until tender. Strain through a sieve and weigh the pulp. Add 1 cup of sugar for every pound of pulp. Bring to a boil, stirring continuously, and boil for 10 minutes. Pour into hot jars, cool and seal.

TRIVIA TIDBITS
Indoor rocking horse racing was very much a craze in the 1930's.

Pickled Eggs

Ingredients:
12 hard-cooked eggs
3 cups white wine vinegar
2 tbsp sugar
1 tsp salt
1/2 tsp mustard seed
4-8 whole cloves
4 bay leaves
1 or 2 chili peppers
Directions:
Bring vinegar to a boil with other ingredients. Shell eggs, being careful not to break them. Put eggs in a glass jar and cover with vinegar mixture which has been allowed to cool slightly. Seal and put in refrigerator. These should stand a week to ten days before using.

SPICE OF LIFE
You know you have a drinking problem when you keep asking people for the time, and can't understand why you keep getting different answers.

Peach Orange Marmalade

Ingredients:
12 to 15 peaches, peeled and cut in small pieces
1 whole orange, ground
1 cup maraschino cherries, ground
sugar

FOOD FOR THOUGHT
A real genius could be described as someone who will shoot at something no one else can see, and hit it.

This page is dedicated in loving memory of my parents, **Peter Mulrooney**, formerly of Red Island, Placentia Bay, Newfoundland and **Hannah** (nee Hynes), formerly of Davis Cove, Newfoundland. *Marian Schlagel, Macomb Twp. MI, USA, formerly of Placentia, Newfoundland*

Bottles & Jars
Jams, Jellies & Preserves

Directions:
In a large pot, combine fruits. For every cup of fruit, add one cup sugar. Mix well. Simmer uncovered, stirring often, for about 1 hour. Ladle into half-pint jars to within 1/4 inch of the top. Seal with 2-piece vacuum lids according to manufacturer's directions. Process in a boiling water bath for 5 minutes. Makes 9 half-pints.

Rhubarb Relish

Violet Jenkins, Etobicoke, Ontario, (nee Baggs, Twillingate, Newfoundland)

Ingredients:
1 qt rhubarb
1 qt onions
1 pt vinegar
1 & 1/2 lb sugar
1 tsp salt
1 tsp allspice
1 tsp cinnamon
1 tsp cloves
1 tsp pepper

TRIVIA TIDBITS
Many ships taking emigrants to America in the nineteenth century were so unseaworthy and overcrowded that they were known as "coffin ships".

Directions:
Soak rhubarb, onions and vinegar overnight. Boil until tender. Add sugar and salt and boil for 10-15 minutes. Add allspice, cinnamon, cloves and pepper. Boil for 10 minutes. Stir frequently. Put in sterilized jars.

Carrot Jam

Violet Jenkins, Etobicoke, Ontario, (nee Baggs, Twillingate, Newfoundland)

Ingredients:
1 lb carrot pulp
1 lb white sugar
strained juice of 2 lemons
grated rind of 1 lemon
6 bitter almonds (chopped)

FOOD FOR THOUGHT
The boy who got a wristwatch when he graduated from high school, now has a son who wears one to kindergarten.

Directions:
Wash and scrape carrots. Cut into very small pieces. Place in saucepan. Cover with water and simmer until tender. Drain well. Press through a sieve. Weigh pulp and replace in saucepan. Add sugar, lemon juice and rind. Bring to boiling point and boil for 5 minutes, stirring and skimming frequently. Then add almonds. Seal in sterilized jars. (Good with or without almonds).

Cranberry Orange Relish

Violet Jenkins, Etobicoke, Ontario, (nee Baggs, Twillingate, Newfoundland)

Ingredients:
4 cups fresh cranberries
2 cups sugar
2 oranges

SPICE OF LIFE
Don't worry about being middle-aged; you'll outgrow it.

Directions:
Put through a food chopper the cranberries and oranges which have been quartered and seeded. Add sugar. Mix well and chill in refrigerator several hours before serving. Makes one quart. Serve with turkey.

Bread & Butter Pickles

Violet Jenkins, Etobicoke, Ontario, (nee Baggs, Twillingate, Newfoundland)

Ingredients:
7 cucumbers, sliced
5 onions, sliced
1 green pepper, chopped
1 sm red pepper, chopped
1/4 cup salt
cracked ice

Pickling Solution:
2 & 1/2 cups white vinegar
2 & 1/2 cups sugar
1 tbsp mustard seed
1 tsp celery seed
1/4 tsp powdered cloves
3/4 tsp tumeric

Directions:
Prepare vegetables; mix in salt and cracked ice. Put in a cool place and let stand for at least 3 hours. Drain. Mix pickling solution. Add to drained vegetables in pot. Bring mixture to boiling point; remove vegetables to jars immediately and pour hot liquid over; seal. Makes about 6 pints. CAUTION: If pot is allowed to boil, pickles will become soft. Make sure mixture is only brought to a boil.

> **TRIVIA TIDBITS**
> A Mrs. Fitzherbert died in hysterics in 1782, in London, as a result of laughing so much at a performance of *The Beggar's Opera* at the Drury Lane Theatre.
>
> RIP

Cabbage Pickles

Violet Jenkins, Etobicoke, Ontario, (nee Baggs, Twillingate, Newfoundland)

Ingredients:
1 qt cabbage, chopped fine
1 qt onions, chopped fine
Add 1 qt vinegar and boil for 10 minutes.
Add:
1 cup sugar
1 tsp salt
Mix:
1 tbsp curry powder (optional)
1 tbsp tumeric powder
1 tbsp dry mustard
1/2 cup flour
Add:
1/2 cup water (to make a paste)

Directions:
Stir in boiling pickles and boil for 20 minutes. Bottle while hot.

> **SPICE OF LIFE**
> No two children are alike - especially when one is yours and the other isn't.

Dried Apple Pickles

Violet Jenkins, Etobicoke, Ontario, (nee Baggs, Twillingate, Newfoundland)

Ingredients:

1 lb dried apples

water (enough to make soft)

1 & 1/2 lb onions, finely chopped

3 cups sugar (brown/white)

1 tsp cinnamon

1 tsp allspice

1 tsp salt

1 tsp pepper

1 cup vinegar

Directions:

Boil dried apples and water until like jam. Add the finely chopped onions and boil for a few minutes. Then add the sugar and spices. Simmer for about 30 minutes. Remove from heat and stir in vinegar. Bottle in sterilized jars.

SPICE OF LIFE
Use some common sense while you're eating or your will have to weigh the consequences.

Rhubarb Jam

Ingredients:

4 cups fresh rhubarb, with small amount water

2 cups sugar

1 (3oz) pkg strawberry or raspberry jello

Directions:

Stir rhubarb and sugar and let sit for 2 hours. Put in pot and boil until rhubarb tender. Add Jello and stir. While hot pour into sterilized jars leaving 2 inches head space. Refrigerate or freeze.

NOTE: If you use frozen rhubarb, omit water.

TRIVIA TIDBITS
Before being adopted as a symbol of naziism, the swastika was a symbol of prosperity and good fortune and was used on coins in ancient Mesopotamia. The symbol was also used by the Mayas in Central America and the Navajos in north America.

Sugarless Strawberry Jam

Ingredients:

1 envelope unflavoured gelatin

2 cups crushed strawberries

1 tbsp fresh lemon juice

1 & 1/2 to 2 tbsp liquid artificial sweetener

Directions:

In custard cup, soak gelatin (1 tbsp) in 1/2 cup crushed strawberries for 5 minutes. Place cup in gently boiling water for 5 minutes to dissolve gelatin. Stir into remaining strawberries and lemon juice. Add sweetener. Pour into jars, seal and refrigerate. Keeps for up to 6 weeks. Makes 2 cups of jam, about 8 caloriesper tablespoon. **NOTE:** Unsweetened, frozen, thawed berries can also be used.

Bottles & Jars
Jams, Jellies & Preserves

Plum Jam

Ingredients:

6 cups purple plums, quartered & stones removed
1 cup water
4 cups sugar
1 tbsp lemon juice

Directions:

Combine plums and water in heavy enamel or stainless-steel pan; bring to a boil. Reduce heat to low; cook until fruit is tender. Meanwhile, measure sugar into bowl; place near pilot light to warm, or place in electric oven and set temperature on warm. Leave element on 3 minutes, turn off. Leave sugar in oven until ready for use. When fruit is tender, add sugar and lemon juice; stir until sugar is dissolved. Increase heat; boil 30 minutes, stirring to prevent burning, or until mixture jells when tested on cold saucer. Pour into hot sterilized jars; seal. Makes 6 cups.

My Favourite Recipes

My Favourite Recipes

MY FAVOURITE RECIPES

My Favourite Recipes

My Favourite Recipes

HOUSEHOLD HINTS

HOME REMEDIES & CURES

RECIPES

RECIPES

RECIPES

RECIPES

RECIPES

RECIPES

RECIPES

* * *

MY FAVOURITE THINGS IN THIS BOOK ARE:	ON PAGE:

Important Notes

A short pencil is better than a long memory - write it down!

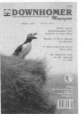
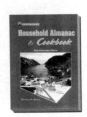

**This is the First Dedication Edition of
Downhomer Household Almanac & Cookbook.**

If you missed getting a dedication to your friend relative, or loved one in this edition, and would like to dedicate a page in the 2nd edition,

please send a cheque or money order for $45.00 (all taxes included),
to:
Downhome Publishing,
303 Water Street,
St. John's, NF,
A1C 1B9

P.S. "Don't forget to include the dedication and photos"

Any size photograph will do, and your subject can be copied from group photographs as well. Make sure you indicate which person(s) in the group is/are the one(s) you wish copied. Photographs will be returned.

NOTE: Dedications will be accepted on a first come, first served basis.

Phone: 709-726-5113
Fax: 709-726-2135
Email: downhome@nfld.com
Home Page: www.netfx-inc.com/downhomer